1b

McDOUGAL LITTELL

¡En español!

Teacher's Edition

AUTHORS

Estella Gahala

Patricia Hamilton Carlin

Audrey L. Heining-Boynton

Ricardo Otheguy

Barbara J. Rupert

CULTURE CONSULTANT

Jorge A. Capetillo-Ponce

McDougal Littell

A HOUGHTON MIFFLIN COMPANY

Evanston, Illinois • Boston • Dallas

Cover Photography

Center: Large image taken in Otavalo, Ecuador, by Martha Granger/EDGE Productions.

Bottom, from left to right: Keel-billed toucan *(Ramphastos sulfuratus: Ramphastidaej),*
Range: Mexico to Venezuela, Tom Boyden; Hand-painted oxcart in Sarchí, Costa Rica, Brent
Winebrenner/International Stock Photo (also on back cover); Woven baskets in Oaxaca, Mexico,
Martha Granger/EDGE Productions; Detail of Parc Güell by Gaudí in Barcelona, Spain,
Martha Granger/EDGE Productions.

Photography

T4 RMIP/Richard Haynes (tl, br); Norman Rothschild/International Stock Photo (bc); Robert Frerck/Odyssey
Productions/Chicago (tr); Martha Cooper/Peter Arnold, Inc. (cr); T5 Chuck Szymanski/International Stock Photo (tl);
Robert Frerck/Odyssey Productions/Chicago (bl); RMIP/Richard Haynes (tr); T6 RMIP/Richard Haynes; T12 RMIP/
Richard Haynes; T19 School Division/Houghton Mifflin (l, r); E.R. Degginger/Photo Researchers, Inc. (c); T23 Degas-
Parra/Ask Images/Viesti Associates, Inc. (l); Suzanne Murphy-Larronde/FPG International (c); Fernando Botero,
Los Musicos, 1979. Courtesy Marlborough Gallery, New York (r); T48 Joe Viesti/Viesti Associates, Inc. (tl); Martha
Cooper/Peter Arnold, Inc. (tc); Chuck Szymanski/International Stock Photo (tr); Otis Imboden/National Geographic
Image Collection (b); T49 Mirielle Vautier/Woodfin Camp & Associates (tl); Kimball Morrison/South American
Pictures (tcl); RMIP/Richard Haynes (tcr); Robert Frerck/Odyssey Productions/Chicago (tr); Sharon Smith/Photonica
(b); 1A UPI/Corbis-Bettmann (tr); 1B Robert Frerck/Odyssey Productions/Chicago (l); Sygma (tr); Farrell Grehan/
Photo Researchers, Inc. (cr); 81A School Division, Houghton Mifflin Company (tr); 81B Patricia A. Eynon (cl); School
Division, Houghton Mifflin Company (cr); 249A School Division, Houghton Mifflin Company (tr); Inga Spence/DDB
Stock Photo (br).

All other photography: Martha Granger/EDGE Productions

ISBN: 0-395-91080-3   1 2 3 4 5 6 7 8 9 - VMI - 05 04 03 02 01 00 99

Internet: www.mcdougallittell.com

CONTENTS

About the Authors

Estella Gahala holds a Ph.D. in Educational Administration and Curriculum from Northwestern University. A career teacher of Spanish and French, she has worked with a wide range of students at the secondary level. She has also served as foreign language department chair and district director of curriculum and instruction.

Patricia Hamilton Carlin completed her M.A. in Spanish at the University of California, Davis and a Master of Secondary Education with specialization in foreign languages at the University of Arkansas. She currently teaches Spanish and methodology at the University of Central Arkansas.

Audrey L. Heining-Boynton received her Ph.D. in Curriculum and Instruction from Michigan State University. She is a Professor of Education and Romance Languages at The University of North Carolina at Chapel Hill, where she is a second language teacher educator and Professor of Spanish. She has also taught Spanish, French, and ESL at the K–12 level.

Ricardo Otheguy received his Ph.D. in Linguistics from the City University of New York, where he is currently Professor of Linguistics at the Graduate School and University Center. He has written extensively on topics related to Spanish grammar as well as on bilingual education, and the Spanish of the United States.

Barbara J. Rupert has taught Level 1 through A.P. Spanish during her many years of high school teaching. She is a graduate of Western Washington University, and serves as the World Languages Department Chair, District Trainer and Chair of her school's Site Council.

Jorge A. Capetillo-Ponce
Culture Consultant is presently a Ph.D. candidate in Sociology at the New School for Social Research, where he is also Special Consultant to the Dean of The Graduate Faculty. His graduate studies at the New School and El Colegio de México include international relations, socio-political analysis, cultural theory, and sociology.

For further information about the authors see page xxii.

Middle School Reviewers

Mary Jo Aronica
Springman School
Glenview, IL

Laura Bertrand
Explorer Middle School
Phoenix, AZ

María Corcoran
Sacred Heart Model School
Louisville, KY

Diane Drear
Brown Middle School
Hillsboro, OR

Beverly Fessenden
Carwise Middle School
Palm Harbor, FL

Alma Hernández
Alamo Junior High School
Midland, TX

Robert Hughes
Martha Brown Middle School
Fairport, NY

Nancy Lawrence
Cross Cultural Education Unit
Albuquerque, NM

Lucille Madrid
Taylor Junior High School
Mesa, AZ

Sally Nickerson
Broadview Middle School
Burlington City, NC

Lynn Perdue
Fuller Junior High School
Little Rock, AR

Leela Scanlon
West Middle School
Andover, MA

Kathleen Solórzano
Homestead High School
Mequon, WI

Michael Veraldo
Mason Middle School
Mason, OH

Jaya Vijayasekar
Griswold Middle School
Rocky Hill, CT

Colleen Yarbrough
Canon Mcmillan Middle School
Canonsburg, PA

Consulting Authors

Dan Battisti

Dr. Teresa Carrera-Hanley

Bill Lionetti

Patty Murguía Bohannan

Lorena Richins Layser

¡En español!

Welcome back!

WHERE: ¡En español!

A new kind of Middle School Spanish program

WHAT: *A program that...*

- *Boosts student confidence and retention and motivates language learning.*

- *Balances teaching for communication and accuracy, offering a balance of proficiency and grammar.*

- *Adapts to the varied learning styles and ability levels of today's students.*

- *Integrates technology to immerse students in authentic language and culture.*

¡En español!

Building Confidence for Communication

● Balances proficiency and grammar

- Activity sequences lead students through controlled, transitional, and open-ended activities to assure development of communication skills.

- Grammar is presented with multiple examples, graphics, and visuals to illustrate concepts clearly.

Boosts student confidence and retention

- Strategies for developing listening, speaking, reading, and writing skills as well as for comparing cultures are included in each *etapa* of the pupil edition.

- Special student study hints are included in each unit. These hints help students learn how to approach learning a language more effectively.

● Adapts to varied learning styles and abilities

- Middle School Classroom Community notes in the Teacher's Edition provide guidance for managing pair and group work right at point–of–use.

- Teaching Middle School Students notes in the Teacher's Edition offer extra help and more challenging activities, activities suited to the various intelligences as well as material for the native speaker.

Integrates technology to immerse students in authentic language and culture

- Fully–integrated video provides input for presenting vocabulary and grammar in their cultural context.

- CD-ROM provides levelled practice and review of core vocabulary and grammar in a motivating game format.

- Electronic Teacher Tools with Test Generator offers the flexibility of having all ancillaries on CD-ROM.

- ClassZone, a dynamic Internet connection, is available to all users of ¡En español!

Middle School Program Resources

Extensive resources tailored to the needs of today's students!

TEACHER'S EDITIONS

PUPIL'S EDITIONS

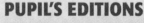

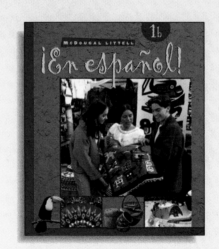

STUDENT WORKBOOKS

- *Más práctica (cuaderno)* **PE**
- *Cuaderno para hispanohablantes* **PE**

TEACHER'S RESOURCE PACKAGE

- **Unit Resource Books**

Includes resources for each unit:
  Más práctica (cuaderno) TE
  Cuaderno para hispanohablantes TE
  Information Gap Activities
  Family Involvement
  Video Activities
  Videoscript
  Audioscript

Assessment Program
  Cooperative Quizzes
  Etapa Exams, Forms A & B
  Exámenes para hispanohablantes
  Unit Comprehensive Tests
  Pruebas comprensivas para hispanohablantes
  Multiple Choice Test Questions
  Portfolio Assessment

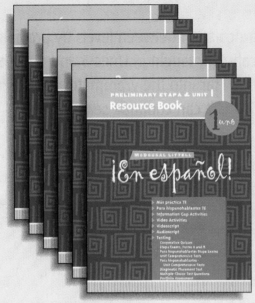

- **Block Scheduling Copymasters**

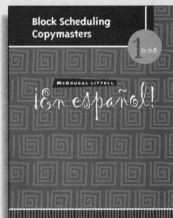

- **Electronic Teacher Tools/Test Generator CD-ROM**

ADDITIONAL RESOURCES

- **Middle School Bridging Packet**

  Activity and Assessment Copymasters
  Audiocassette/Audio CD
  Overhead Transparencies

- **Overhead Transparencies**

TECHNOLOGY

Audio Program
- Completely integrated with the text and ancillaries.
- Available on cassette and audio CD.

Canciones
- Audiocassette or audio CD

Video Program
- Completely integrated video program provides comprehensible input and cultural information
- Available on videocassette and videodisc

Intrigas y aventuras CD-ROM
- For levels 1 and 2

INTERNET RESOURCES

Visit the World Languages curriculum area at **www.mcdougallittell.com** for a wide range of resources.

Easy Articulation

¡En español! addresses the challenges of articulation between levels by providing a unique instructional overlap. All the grammar and vocabulary taught in Units 5 and 6 are covered again in the following level, so teachers can choose how far into the grammatical and functional sequence they wish to go. Students' study of Spanish can continue seamlessly!

GRAMMAR ACROSS LEVELS

LEVEL 1B

Bridge Unit

Etapa 1
- Greetings (p.6)
- Subject pronouns and *ser* (p. 7)
- *Ser* + *de* (p. 8)
- *Gustar* + infinitive (p. 9)
- Definite articles (p. 14)
- Indefinite articles (p. 16)
- Noun-adjective agreement: gender (p. 17)
- Noun-adjective agreement: number (p. 18)
- *Tener* (p. 22)
- Possession using *de* (p. 23)
- Possessive adjectives (p. 24)
- Giving dates (p. 25)

Etapa 2
- Regular *-ar* verbs (p. 32)
- Adverbs of frequency (p. 34)
- *Tener que, hay que* (p. 35)
- *Ir* (p. 40)
- Telling time (p. 41)
- *Estar* + location (p. 43)
- Interrogative words (p. 44)
- *Ir a* + infinitive (p. 48)
- Present tense regular *-er* and *-ir* verbs (p. 49)
- Irregular *yo* forms (p. 51)
- *Oír* (p. 52)

Etapa 3
- *Estar* + adjectives (p. 58)
- *Acabar de* + infinitive (p. 59)
- *Venir* (p. 60)
- *Gustar* + infinitive (p. 61)
- *Jugar* (p. 66)
- Stem-changing *e → ie* verbs (p. 67)
- *Saber* (p. 68)
- Comparatives (p. 69)
- Weather expressions (p. 74)
- Direct object pronouns (p. 75)
- *Tener* idioms (p. 76)
- Present progressive (p. 78)

Unit 4

Etapa 1
- *Decir* (p. 92)
- Prepositions of location (p. 95)
- Regular affirmative *tú* commands (p. 97)

Etapa 2
- Stem-changing verbs: *o → ue* (p. 118)
- Indirect object pronouns (p. 121)
- Indirect object pronoun placement (p. 124)

Etapa 3
- *Gustar* + nouns (p. 144)
- Affirmative and negative words (p. 147)
- Stem-changing verbs: *e → i* (p. 150)

LEVEL 1A

Unit 1

Etapa 1
- Greetings (p.34)
- Subject pronouns and *ser* (p. 36)
- *Ser* + *de* (p. 39)
- *Gustar* + infinitive (p. 41)

Etapa 2
- Definite articles (p. 60)
- Indefinite articles (p. 62.)
- Noun-adjective agreement: gender (p. 63)
- Noun-adjective agreement: number (p. 65)

Etapa 3
- *Tener* (p. 86)
- Possession using *de* (p. 88)
- Possessive adjectives (p. 90)
- Giving dates (p. 92)

Unit 2

Etapa 1
- Regular *-ar* verbs (p. 118)
- Adverbs of frequency (p. 121)
- *Tener que, hay que* (p. 123)

Etapa 2
- *Ir* (p.143)
- Telling time (p. 147)
- *Estar* + location (p. 149)
- Interrogative words (p. 150)

Etapa 3
- *Ir a* + infinitive (p. 170)
- Present tense regular *-er* and *-ir* verbs (p. 173)
- Irregular *yo* forms (p. 175)
- *Oír* (p. 177)

Unit 3

Etapa 1
- *Estar* + adjectives (p. 202)
- *Acabar de* + infinitive (p. 205)
- *Venir* (p. 206)
- *Gustar* + infinitive (p. 209)

Etapa 2
- *Jugar* (p. 228)
- Stem-changing *e → ie* verbs (p. 230)
- *Saber* (p. 233)
- Comparatives (p. 234)

Etapa 3
- Weather expressions (p. 254)
- Direct object pronouns (p. 259)
- *Tener* idioms (p. 258)
- Present progressive (p. 262)

LEVEL 2

Unit 1

Etapa 1
- Regular preterite verbs (p. 36)
- Preterite with -*car,* -*gar,* and -*zar* spelling changes (p. 38)
- Preterite of *ir, ser, hacer, dar, ver* (p. 40)

Etapa 2
- Irregular preterite verbs (p. 61)

Etapa 3
- Demonstrative adjectives and pronouns (p. 82)
- Stem-changing preterite verbs (p. 84)
- Preterite verbs with *i* to *y* spelling change (p. 85)

Unit 2

Etapa 1
- Reflexive pronouns and verbs (p. 110)

Etapa 2
- Progressive tenses (p. 130)
- Ordinal number agreement (p. 132)

Unit 3

Etapa 1
- Pronoun placement (p. 180)

Etapa 2
- Affirmative *tú* commands, regular and irregular (p. 202)
- Negative *tú* commands (p. 204)
- Adverbs ending in -*mente* (p. 206)

Unit 5

Etapa 1
- Reflexive verbs (p. 175)
- Irregular affirmative *tú* commands (p. 177)
- Negative *tú* commands (p. 180)
- Pronoun placement with commands (p. 182)

Etapa 2
- Pronoun placement with the present progressive tense (p. 202)
- *Deber* (p. 206)
- Adverbs with -*mente* (p. 209)

Etapa 3
- Superlatives (p. 228)
- Regular -*ar* preterite verbs (p. 230)
- -*car,* -*gar,* -*zar* preterite verbs (p. 233)

Unit 6

Etapa 1
- Regular -*er,* -*ir* preterite verbs (p. 260)
- Preterite verbs with *i* to *y* spelling change (p. 262)
- Preterite forms of *ir, hacer, ser* (p. 264)

Etapa 2
- Adverbs of location (p. 286)
- Demonstrative adjectives and pronouns (p. 289)
- Ordinals (p. 291)
- Irregular preterite verbs (p. 293)

Etapa 3
- All review

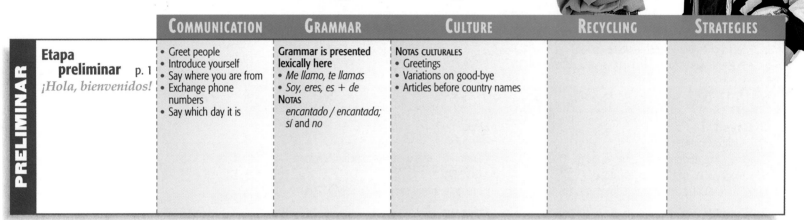

¡En español!

Level 1A Scope & Sequence

		COMMUNICATION	GRAMMAR	CULTURE	RECYCLING	STRATEGIES
PRELIMINAR	**Etapa preliminar** p. 1 *¡Hola, bienvenidos!*	• Greet people • Introduce yourself • Say where you are from • Exchange phone numbers • Say which day it is	**Grammar is presented lexically here** • *Me llamo, te llamas* • *Soy, eres, es + de* **NOTAS** *encantado / encantada; sí* and *no*	**NOTAS CULTURALES** • Greetings • Variations on good-bye • Articles before country names		
UNIDAD 1 Mi mundo • Estados Unidos	**Etapa 1 Miami** p. 24 *¡Bienvenido a Miami!* **UNIT OPENER CULTURE NOTES** • *Fajitas* • Murals • The Alamo • *Cascarones* • *Sándwich cubano* • Jon Secada	• Greet others • Introduce others • Say where people are from • Express likes	• Familiar and formal greetings • Subject pronouns and *ser* • *Ser + de* • *Gustar* + infinitive: *me, te, le* **NOTAS** *le presento a / te presento a; vivo en*	**EN VOCES** *Una estudiante de Nicaragua* **CONEXIONES** • *Los estudios sociales: Festival de Calle Ocho* • *Los estudios sociales/La geografía:* Latinos in the United States • *Los estudios sociales: compare communities* **NOTAS CULTURALES** • Miami: international city • Architectural influences	Vocabulary from *Etapa preliminar*	**LISTENING** Listen to intonation **SPEAKING** Practice; Understand, then speak **READING** Look for cognates
	Etapa 2 San Antonio p. 50 *Mis buenos amigos*	• Describe others • Give others' likes and dislikes • Describe clothing	• Definite articles • Indefinite articles • Noun–adjective agreement: gender • Noun–adjective agreement: number **NOTAS** *llevo; como + ser; tiene; ¿Qué lleva?;* shortened forms of adjectives	**EN COLORES** *El conjunto tejano* (video) **CONEXIONES** • *La historia:* Spanish place names • *La música:* music styles **NOTAS CULTURALES** • informal dress • *la charreada*	**Activity 3** *gustar* + infinitive	**LISTENING** Listen to stress **SPEAKING** Trust your first impulse; Think, plan, then speak **CULTURE** Recognize regional music
	Etapa 3 Los Ángeles p. 76 *Te presento a mi familia*	• Describe family • Ask and tell ages • Talk about birthdays • Give dates • Express possession	• *Tener* • Possession using *de* • Possessive adjectives • Giving dates **NOTAS** *hay; ¿De quién es…?, Es de…; ¿Quién es?, ¿Quiénes son?*	**EN VOCES:** Los Ángeles: *Una carta del pasado* **EN COLORES:** *La quinceañera* **EN LA COMUNIDAD** **CONEXIONES:** *El arte:* Fernando Botero; murals • *La historia/La geografía:* Independence days; Spanish explorers **NOTAS CULTURALES** • Extended family • The oldest house in L.A. • Writing the date • The suffix *-ito/-ita*	**Activity 5** personal characteristics **Activity 9** adjectives **Activity 13** *ser,* clothing vocabulary **Activity 20** clothing vocabulary	**LISTENING** Visualize; Get the main idea **SPEAKING** Rehearse; Practice speaking smoothly **READING** Picture clues **CULTURE** Compare rites of passage

		COMMUNICATION	GRAMMAR	CULTURE	RECYCLING	STRATEGIES
UNIDAD 2 Una semana típica • Ciudad de México	**Etapa 1** p. 108 *Un día de clases* UNIT OPENER CULTURE NOTES • *Tortillas* • Diego Rivera • *El Palacio de Bellas Artes* • *El Ballet Folklórico* • *El metro* • Lázaro Cárdenas	• Describe classes and classroom objects • Say how often you do something • Discuss obligations	• Present tense of regular *-ar* verbs • Adverbs of frequency • *Tener que, hay que* NOTA Use of articles with titles	EN VOCES *Una leyenda azteca: El origen de la Ciudad de México* CONEXIONES • *La historia/Las ciencias: La Piedra del Sol; La Plaza de las Tres Culturas* • *Las matemáticas:* take a survey NOTAS CULTURALES • The grading system • The origin of *pluma*	**Activity 3** *hay,* colors **Activity 4** *hay,* numbers	LISTENING Listen for feelings SPEAKING Develop more than one way of expressing an idea; Expand the conversation READING Look for context clues
	Etapa 2 p. 134 *¡Un horario difícil!*	• Talk about schedules • Ask and tell time • Ask questions • Say where you are going • Request food	• *Ir* • Telling time • *Estar* + location • Interrogative words NOTAS *¿Quieres comer...?* and *¿Quieres beber...?;* "on" + days of the week; *al*	EN COLORES: *¿Quieres comer una merienda mexicana?* CONEXIONES • *Las matemáticas:* telling time with the 24-hour system • *La salud/La historia:* American contribution to European diet; nutrition NOTAS CULTURALES • Mealtimes • Mexican high school schedules • Arrival times for social gatherings • *torta, bocadillo, pastel*	**Activity 6** days of the week	LISTENING Listen for the main idea SPEAKING Take risks; Help your partner CULTURE Compare snack foods
	Etapa 3 p. 160 *Mis actividades*	• Discuss plans • Sequence events • Talk about places and people you know	• *Ir a* + infinitive • Present tense: regular *-er* and *-ir* verbs • Irregular *yo* forms: *hacer, conocer;* personal *a* • *Oír* NOTA *tener sed, tener hambre*	EN VOCES: *Una leyenda mexicana: La Casa de los Azulejos* EN COLORES *El Zócalo: centro de México* (video) CONEXIONES: *El arte:* Carmen Lomas Garza • *Las ciencias: el Bosque de Chapultepec* • *La historia: El Metro* • *La salud:* natural medicine EN LA COMUNIDAD NOTAS CULTURALES • *Museo Nacional de Antropología* • *Bosque de Chapultepec*	**Activity 6:** food and drinks **Activity 8:** telling time **Activity 10:** activities **Activity 13:** adverbs of frequency **Activity 18:** people **Activity 21:** places	LISTENING Listen and observe SPEAKING Use all you know; Ask for clarification READING Follow plot CULTURE Compare places
UNIDAD 3 El fin de semana • San Juan, Puerto Rico	**Etapa 1** p. 192 *¡Me gusta el tiempo libre!* UNIT OPENER CULTURE NOTES • Gigi Fernández • *Pasta de guayaba* • El Morro • Luis Muñoz Marín • *Taínos* • *El loro puertorriqueño*	• Extend invitations • Talk on the phone • Express feelings • Say where you are coming from • Say what just happened	• *Estar* + adjectives • *Acabar de* + infinitive • *Venir* • *Gustar* + infinitive: *nos, os, les* NOTAS *cuando; del; conmigo, contigo*	EN VOCES: *El bohique y los niños* CONEXIONES • *La historia/La música: la bomba and la plena* • *La música:* music with Spanish influences NOTAS CULTURALES • Dating practices • The name *Puerto Rico*	**Activity 3–5:** activities **Activity 12:** verbs **Activity 16:** place names **Activity 20** activities, *gustar* **Activity 22:** interrogatives	LISTENING Listen for a purpose SPEAKING Personalize; Use your tone to convey meaning READING Use context
	Etapa 2 p. 218 *¡Deportes para todos!*	• Talk about sports • Express preferences • Say what you know • Make comparisons	• *Jugar* • Stem-changing verbs: *e →ie* • *Saber* • Comparatives	EN COLORES *Béisbol: El pasatiempo nacional* CONEXIONES: *Los estudios sociales:* Puerto Rico and the U.S. • *Los estudios sociales: La Copa Mundial* EN LA COMUNIDAD NOTAS CULTURALES: Surfing in Puerto Rico • Spanish baseball vocabulary borrowed from English • Roberto Clemente	**Activity 4:** *gustar* **Activity 13** sports vocabulary **Activity 21** stem-changing verbs, sports vocabulary	LISTENING Listen for "turn-taking" tactics SPEAKING Monitor yourself; Give reasons for your preferences CULTURE Reflect on sports traditions
	Etapa 3 p. 244 *El tiempo en El Yunque*	• Describe the weather • Discuss clothing and accessories • State an opinion • Describe how you feel • Say what is happening	• Weather expressions • *Tener* expressions • Direct object pronouns • Present progressive NOTAS *llevar; creer*	EN VOCES: *Una leyenda taína* EN COLORES *Una excursión por la isla* (video) CONEXIONES: *Las ciencias:* seasons; Celsius; rain forests • *La geografía:* altitude and latitude • *La historia:* civilizations in the Caribbean NOTAS CULTURALES • *El Yunque* • National Puerto Rican Day Parade	**Activity 3:** *hay* **Activity 8:** *gustar* **Activity 10:** *ir a,* clothing vocabulary **Activity 12:** *tener* **Activity 16** sports vocabulary **Activity 21:** *estar*	LISTENING Sort and categorize details SPEAKING Say how often; Get specific information READING Skim CULTURE Define travel and tourism

¡En español!

Level 1B Scope & Sequence

BRIDGE UNIT

	COMMUNICATION		GRAMMAR		
Etapa 1 p. 2 **Estados Unidos** *Mi mundo*	• Greet and introduce others • Express likes and dislikes • Describe people	• Talk about dates and ages • Express possession	• Familiar and formal greetings • Subject pronouns and *ser* • *Ser + de*	• *Gustar* + infinitive • Noun-adjective agreement: gender/number • Definite/Indefinite articles	• *Tener* • Possession using *de* • Possessive adjectives • Giving dates
Etapa 2 p. 28 **Ciudad de México** *Una semana típica*	• Talk about school • Discuss obligations and plans • Request food	• Talk about schedules and time • Sequence events	• Regular *-ar* verbs • Adverbs of frequency • *Tener que, hay que* • *Ir*	• Telling time • *Estar* + location • Interrogative words • *Ir a* + infinitive	• Present tense regular *-er* and *-ir* verbs • Irregular *yo* forms • *Oír*
Etapa 3 p. 54 **San Juan, Puerto Rico** *El fin de semana*	• Extend invitations • Say what just happened and what is happening • Express feelings and preferences	• Talk on the telephone • Discuss sports • Make comparisons • Describe weather and clothing	• *Estar* + adjectives • *Acabar de* + infinitive • *Venir* • *Gustar* + infinitive	• *Jugar* • Stem-changing *e→ie* verbs • *Saber* • Comparatives	• Weather expressions • Direct object pronouns • *Tener* idioms • Present progressive

UNIDAD 4 ¡De visita! • Oaxaca, México

	COMMUNICATION	GRAMMAR	CULTURE	RECYCLING	STRATEGIES
Etapa 1 p. 80 *¡A visitar a mi prima!* **UNIT OPENER CULTURE NOTES** • *Animalitos* • *Pesos* • *Mole negro* • Rufino Tamayo • Benito Juárez • *Monte Albán*	• Identify places • Give addresses • Choose transportation • Request directions • Give instructions	• *Decir* • Prepositions of location • Regular affirmative *tú* commands **NOTAS** *por; salir;* numbers in addresses	EN VOCES: *Benito Juárez, un oaxaqueño por excelencia* CONEXIONES: *La salud:* farmacias • *Los estudios sociales:* international road signs • *La educación física:* Mexican folk dances **NOTAS CULTURALES** • Neighborhood shops • Travel by bus • The name *Oaxaca*	**Activity 4** seasons **Activity 5** *hay* **Activity 14** activities **Activity 16** sequencing **Activity 17** direct object pronouns	**LISTENING** Listen and follow directions **SPEAKING** Recognize and use set phrases; Use variety to give directions **READING** Recognize sequence
Etapa 2 p. 108 *En el mercado*	• Talk about shopping • Make purchases • Talk about giving gifts • Bargain	• Stem-changing verbs: *o→ue* • Indirect object pronouns • Indirect object pronoun placement **NOTAS** *para; cuesta(n); dar*	EN COLORES • *El Mercado Benito Juárez* CONEXIONES • *La historia/La artesanía:* Oaxaca • *Los estudios sociales:* market days • *Las matemáticas:* un mercado NOTAS CULTURALES: • Oaxacan crafts • Advertisements • Benito Juárez	**Activity 5** numbers **Activity 7** places **Activity 8** time **Activity 9** places, transportation	**LISTENING** Observe as you listen **SPEAKING** Express emotion; Disagree politely **CULTURE** Compare bargaining customs
Etapa 3 p. 134 *¿Qué hacer en Oaxaca?*	• Order food • Request the check • Talk about food • Express extremes • Say where you went	• *Gustar* + nouns • Affirmative and negative words • Stem-changing verbs: *e→i* **NOTAS** *fui/fuiste; poner; ningunos (as);* superlatives; *desayunar; traer*	EN VOCES: *Una leyenda oaxaqueña: El fuego y el tlacuache* EN COLORES: *Monte Albán* CONEXIONES: *La salud:* fruit • *La historia:* ancient civilizations of Oaxaca • *Las matemáticas:* currencies EN LA COMUNIDAD NOTAS CULTURALES • Oaxaca's cuisine • Nahuatl • Zapotec livelihood	**Activity 6** stores **Activity 7** prepositions of location **Activity 9** clothing **Activity 19** direct object pronouns	**LISTENING** Integrate your skills **SPEAKING** Vary ways to express preferences; Borrow useful expressions **READING** Make a story map **CULTURE** Analyze and recommend

		COMMUNICATION	GRAMMAR	CULTURE	RECYCLING	STRATEGIES
UNIDAD 5 Preparaciones especiales • Barcelona, España	**Etapa 1** p. 166 *¿Cómo es tu rutina?* **UNIT OPENER CULTURE NOTES** • *Las Ramblas* • *Joan Miró* • *Cristóbal Colón* • *Aceitunas* • *Cervantes* • *La Sagrada Familia*	• Describe daily routine • Talk about grooming • Tell others to do something • Discuss daily chores	• Reflexive verbs • Irregular affirmative *tú* commands • Negative *tú* commands • Pronoun placement with commands	**EN VOCES:** *La Tomatina: Una rara tradición española* **CONEXIONES** • *Los estudios sociales:* languages • *El arte:* Pablo Picasso • *El arte:* style of painting **NOTAS CULTURALES** • *Las Ramblas* • *Rock con raíces*	**Activity 3** Telling time **Activity 17** Direct object pronouns	**LISTENING** Listen for a mood or a feeling **SPEAKING** Sequence events; Use gestures **READING** Predict
	Etapa 2 p. 192 *¿Qué debo hacer?*	• Say what people are doing • Persuade others • Describe a house • Negotiate responsibilities	• Pronoun placement with present progressive • *Deber* • Adverbs with *-mente* **NOTAS** *si; reflexive pronouns*	**EN COLORES:** *Las tapas: Una experiencia muy española* **EN LA COMUNIDAD** **CONEXIONES** • *El arte:* sculpture and architecture in Barcelona • *Los estudios sociales:* abbreviations **NOTAS CULTURALES** • *La planta baja* • *paella* and *tortilla española*	**Activity 5** daily chores **Activity 10** reflexive verbs **Activity 14** affirmative *tú* commands **Activity 20** interrogative words	**LISTENING** Note and compare **SPEAKING** Negotiate; Detect misunderstandings **CULTURE** Predict reactions about restaurants
	Etapa 3 p. 218 *¡Qué buena celebración!*	• Plan a party • Describe past activities • Express extremes • Purchase food	• Superlatives • Regular *-ar* preterite verbs • *-car, -gar, -zar* preterite **NOTAS** *¿A cuánto está(n)...?*	**EN VOCES:** *Correo electrónico desde Barcelona* **EN COLORES:** *Barcelona: Joya de arquitectura* (video) **CONEXIONES** • *Las matemáticas:* la peseta; metric measurements • *La salud:* favorite foods • *La historia:* Moorish influence in Spain • *Las ciencias:* astronomy **NOTAS CULTURALES** • *tortilla española* • *Parque Güell* • Gothic Quarter	**Activity 4** adverbs of frequency, direct object pronouns **Activity 7** grooming vocabulary **Activity 10** reflexive verbs **Activity 12** daily chores	**LISTENING** Listen and take notes **SPEAKING** Say what is the best and worst; Maintain conversational flow **READING** Note details **CULTURE** Make a historical time line
UNIDAD 6 La ciudad y el campo • Quito, Ecuador	**Etapa 1** p. 384 *La vida de la ciudad* **UNIT OPENER CULTURE NOTES** • *La casa de Sucre* • *Papas* • *La Mitad del Mundo* • *Atahualpa* • *Tapices* • *Rondador*	• Tell what happened • Make suggestions to a group • Describe city buildings • Talk about professions	• Regular *-er, -ir* preterites • Preterite verbs with *i → y* spelling change • Preterite of *ir, hacer, ser* **NOTAS** *estar de acuerdo; ver; vamos a + infinitive*	**EN VOCES:** *Un cuento ecuatoriano: El tigre y el conejo* **EN LA COMUNIDAD** **CONEXIONES** • *La geografía:* Ecuadoran volcanoes • *Las ciencias:* Soroche **NOTAS CULTURALES:** Quito • *Plaza de la Independencia* • Sucre	**Activity 7** superlatives **Activity 17** places	**LISTENING** Distinguish what is said and not said **SPEAKING** Exaggerate and react to exaggerations; Relate details **READING** Follow the sequences
	Etapa 2 p. 406 *A conocer el campo*	• Point out specific people and things • Tell where things are located • Talk about the past	• Location words • Demonstrative adjectives and pronouns • Ordinals • Irregular preterite **NOTAS** *darle(s) de comer*	**EN COLORES** *Los Otavaleños* **CONEXIONES** • *Las ciencias:* animales • *Los estudios sociales:* los andenes • *Las ciencias:* animales **NOTAS CULTURALES** *Quichua*	**Activity 5** professions **Activity 7** places **Activity 9** school items **Activity 13** comparatives	**LISTENING** Listen for implied statements **SPEAKING** Recall what you know; Use words that direct others' attention **CULTURE** Research cultural groups
	Etapa 3 p. 428 *¡A ganar el concurso!*	• Talk about the present and future • Give instructions to someone • Discuss the past	• Review: present progressive, *ir a...* • Review: affirmative *tú* commands • Review: regular preterite • Review: irregular preterite	**EN VOCES:** *El murciélago cobarde* **EN COLORES:** *Cómo las américas cambiaron la comida europea* **CONEXIONES** • *La geografía:* Pan-American Highway • *La música:* percussion • *El arte:* Hugo Licta • *La salud:* New World foods • *Los estudios sociales:* geographic regions of Ecuador • *La historia:* Inca civilization **NOTAS CULTURALES:** Ecuadoran habitats	**Activity 3** text vocabulary **Activity 4** clothing vocabulary **Activity 5** activities **Activity 6** family, daily routine, preferences	**LISTENING** Listen and take notes **SPEAKING** Use storytelling techniques; Rely on the basics **READING** Use pictures **CULTURE** Identify international foods

¡En español!

Level 2 • Scope & Sequence

		COMMUNICATION	GRAMMAR	CULTURE	RECYCLING	STRATEGIES
PRELIMINAR	**Etapa preliminar** p. 1 **Northeastern U.S.** *Día a día*	• Exchange greetings • Discuss likes and dislikes • Describe people and places • Ask for and give information • Talk about school life • Talk about the new school year	**NOTA** *Gustar* and indirect object pronouns	**NOTAS CULTURALES** • *En Nueva York y New Jersey* • *La población latina* • *De Connecticut* • «*City Year*»	• Use adjectives to describe • The verb *tener* • *ser* vs. *estar* • Interrogative words • Tell time • Regular present tense verbs • The verb *ir* • Stem changes: *e→ie, o→ue* • Irregular *yo* verbs	**SPEAKING:** Give and get personal information
UNIDAD 1 ¿Qué pasa? • Estados Unidos	**Etapa 1** p. 28 **Los Ángeles** *Pasatiempos* **UNIT OPENER** **CULTURE NOTES** • *La misión San Fernando Rey de España* • *Hispaños en Hollywood* • *Tostones* • *Artistas y la comunidad* • *Televisión* • *Gloria Estefan* • *Jorge Ramos y María Elena Salinas*	• Talk about where you went and what you did • Discuss leisure time • Comment on airplane travel	**NOTA** expressions of frequency	**EN VOCES** *¿Cuánto sabes?* **TÚ EN LA COMUNIDAD** **NOTAS CULTURALES** • *La calle Olvera* • *Los murales*	• Regular preterite • Preterite with *-car, -gar,* and *-zar* spelling changes • Irregular preterite: *ir, ser, hacer, dar, ver* **Ya sabes:** Preterite with *-car, -gar,* and *-zar*	**LISTENING:** Identify key words **SPEAKING:** Encourage others; get more information **READING:** Read, don't translate; use visuals and titles to predict the general idea; scan for cognates
	Etapa 2 p. 50 **Chicago** *¿Qué prefieres?*	• Comment on food • Talk about the past • Express activity preferences • Discuss fine art	• Irregular preterite verbs	**EN COLORES:** *El arte latino de Chicago:* murals (video) **CONEXIONES** *El arte:* artists' inspirations **NOTAS CULTURALES** • *El Centro Museo de Bellas Artes de Chicago* • *La cena*	• Stem-changing verbs: *e→i, u→ue* **Activity 3:** *¡A viajar!* (travel) **Activity 14:** *¿Cuántas veces?* (expressions of frequency)	**LISTENING:** Identify the main idea **SPEAKING:** Use all you know; give reasons why **CULTURE:** Learn about other cultures; describe the nature of murals
	Etapa 3 p. 72 **Miami** *¿Viste las noticias?*	• Discuss ways to communicate • React to news • Ask for and give information • Talk about things and people you know	• Demonstrative adjectives and pronouns • Stem-changing preterite **NOTAS** *estar bien informado;* adjectives of nationality; *saber* vs. *conocer; hubo; i→y* with preterite	**EN VOCES** *¿Leíste el periódico hoy?* **EN COLORES** *Miami: Puerta de las Américas* **CONEXIONES** *Las matemáticas:* calculate percentages of television viewing **NOTAS CULTURALES** • *A la fiesta* • *Periódicos por computadora*	**Activity 3:** *¡Qué reunión!* (irregular preterite) **Ya sabes:** stem-changing verbs	**LISTENING:** Listen with a purpose **SPEAKING:** Present findings; provide additional information **READING:** Skim for the general idea; scan for specific information **WRITING:** Bring your event to life **CULTURE:** Identify characteristics of neighborhoods

UNIDAD 2 · Ayer y hoy · Ciudad de México

	COMMUNICATION	GRAMMAR	CULTURE	RECYCLING	STRATEGIES
Etapa 1 p. 100 *De pequeño* UNIT OPENER CULTURE NOTES • *Los tamales* • *La piñata* • *Hoy no circula* • *El Popocatépetl* • Christian Castro • Frida Kahlo • *Padre Miguel Hidalgo y Costilla*	• Describe childhood experiences • Express personal reactions • Discuss family relationships	• Possessive adjectives and pronouns • Imperfect tense NOTAS *dentro y fuera;* uses of *tener (tener hambre, tener sed,* etc.); *había*	EN VOCES *El monte de nuestro alimento:* legend CONEXIONES *Los estudios sociales:* Aztec calendar NOTAS CULTURALES • *Las marionetas* • *El Bosque de Chapultepec*	• Reflexive pronouns and verbs **Activity 3:** *¡Los conozco!* (nationalities)	LISTENING: Listen for related details SPEAKING: Tell when you were always or never (im)perfect; add variety to your conversation READING: Analyze folkloric traditions
Etapa 2 p. 122 *Había una vez...*	• Narrate in the past • Discuss family celebrations • Talk about activities in progress	• Progressive tenses • Preterite vs. imperfect	EN COLORES *¡Temblor!:* the earthquake of 1985 CONEXIONES: *El arte: El muralista Diego Rivera* NOTAS CULTURALES • *La piñata* • *El Museo Nacional de Antropología*	**Activity 4:** *Una reunión escolar* (imperfect) **Activity 5:** *Reacciones* (reflexives)	LISTENING: Listen for a series of events SPEAKING: Brainstorm to get ideas; interact by expressing approval, disapproval, or astonishment CULTURE: Observe and generalize
Etapa 3 p. 144 *Hoy en la ciudad*	• Order in a restaurant • Ask for and pay a restaurant bill • Talk about things to do in the city	• Double object pronouns NOTAS i.o. pronoun with verbs like *gustar; dar una vuelta*	EN VOCES: *Teotihuacán: Ciudad misteriosa* (video) EN COLORES *¡Buen provecho! La comida Mexicana* TÚ EN LA COMUNIDAD NOTAS CULTURALES • *El baile folklórico* • *El Palacio de Bellas Artes* • *Las telenovelas*	• Direct object pronouns • Indirect object pronouns **Activity 3:** *¡A divertirse en la ciudad!* (preterite vs. imperfect)	LISTENING: Listen for useful expressions SPEAKING: Personalize responses; resolve misconceptions READING: Identify gaps in knowledge WRITING: Develop your story CULTURE: Compare meals and mealtimes

UNIDAD 3 · Sol y sombra · Puerto Rico

	COMMUNICATION	GRAMMAR	CULTURE	RECYCLING	STRATEGIES
Etapa 1 p. 172 *¿Estás en forma?* UNIT OPENER CULTURE NOTES • *El observatorio de Arecibo* • *Los pasteles* • *Piratas* • *La ceiba de Ponce* • *El Yunque* • Marc Anthony	• Discuss ways to stay fit and healthy • Make suggestions • Talk about daily routine and personal care	• Commands using *usted/ustedes* • Formal *usted/ustedes* commands and pronoun placement	EN VOCES *Puerto Rico: Lugar maravilloso* CONEXIONES *La ciencia:* phosphorescence NOTAS CULTURALES • *El béisbol* • *El Viejo San Juan*	• Pronoun placement **Activity 4:** *¿Siempre o nunca?* (expressions of frequency, double object pronouns) **Ya sabes:** *las preparaciones*	LISTENING: Listen and sort details SPEAKING: Use gestures to convey meaning; react to daily routines READING: Observe organization of ideas
Etapa 2 p. 194 *Preparaciones*	• Discuss beach activities • Tell someone what to do • Talk about chores • Say if something has already been done	• Negative *tú* commands NOTA *acabar de* + infinitive	EN COLORES *El Yunque Bosque Nacional* (video) TÚ EN LA COMUNIDAD NOTAS CULTURALES • *Después de las clases* • *El manatí*	• Affirmative *tú* commands • Adverbs ending in *-mente* **Activity 3:** *Por la mañana* (daily routine) **Ya sabes:** *los quehaceres*	LISTENING: Listen and categorize information SPEAKING: Improvise; encourage or discourage certain behaviors CULTURE: Recognize unique natural wonders
Etapa 3 p. 216 *¿Cómo te sientes?*	• Describe time periods • Talk about health and illness • Give advice	• *Hacer* with expressions of time • Subjunctive with impersonal expressions NOTA *doler* with i.o. pronouns; subjunctive after impersonal expressions	EN VOCES *El estatus político de Puerto Rico* EN COLORES *Una voz de la tierra* CONEXIONES *La historia:* pirates NOTAS CULTURALES • *Los huracanes* • *La celebración de Carnaval* • *La cultura de los jíbaros*	**Activity 3:** *Los quehaceres en tu casa* (chores)	LISTENING: Listen sympathetically SPEAKING: Give feedback; use language for problem-solving READING: Activate associated knowledge WRITING: Compare and contrast to make strong descriptions CULTURE: Discover many cultures inside one country

		COMMUNICATION	GRAMMAR	CULTURE	RECYCLING	STRATEGIES
UNIDAD 4 Un viaje • Madrid, España	**Etapa 1** p. 244 *En la pensión* **UNIT OPENER** **CULTURE NOTES** • *El Prado* • *La guitarra* • *Paella* • *El rey y la reina de España* • Antonio Banderas • El Greco	• Talk about travel plans • Persuade others • Describe rooms, furniture, and appliances	• Subjunctive to express hopes and wishes • Irregular subjunctive forms	**EN VOCES** *Felices sueños:* hotel descriptions **CONEXIONES** *El arte:* Spanish artists **NOTAS CULTURALES** • *La Plaza de la Cibeles* • *Alojamiento*	**Activity 4:** *Es mejor que…* (subjunctive) **Activity 15:** *El metro de Madrid* (giving directions) **Ya sabes:** expressing hopes and wishes	**LISTENING:** Listen and check details **SPEAKING:** Persuade; make and express decisions **READING:** Compare related details
	Etapa 2 p. 266 *Conoce la ciudad*	• Describe your city or town • Make suggestions • Ask for and give directions	• Subjunctive stem-changes: *-ar, -er* verbs • Stem-changing *-ir* verbs in the subjunctive • Subjunctive vs. infinitive **NOTAS:** *ni;* question words such as *cuando* and *donde* as bridges mid-sentence	**EN COLORES** *Vamos a bailar:* Gipsy Kings **CONEXIONES:** *La tecnología:* creating a webpage **NOTAS CULTURALES** • *La Plaza Mayor* • *El paseo* • *Los gitanos y flamenco*	**Activity 3:** *Una lección* (giving advice using the subjunctive)	**LISTENING:** Listen and distinguish **SPEAKING:** Ask for and give directions; work cooperatively **CULTURE:** Identify characteristics of successful musical groups
	Etapa 3 p. 288 *Vamos de compras*	• Talk about shopping for clothes • Ask for and give opinions • Make comparisons • Discuss ways to save and spend money	• Subjunctive with expressions of doubt • Subjunctive with expressions of emotion	**EN VOCES** *Nos vemos en Madrid:* highlights of the city (video) **EN COLORES:** *¿En qué te puedo atender?:* shopping **TÚ EN LA COMUNIDAD** **NOTAS CULTURALES** • *Miguel de Cervantes* • *¿Qué talla usas?*	• Comparisons and superlatives **Activity 4:** *¿Qué me sugieres?* (making suggestions using the subjunctive) **Ya sabes:** equal/unequal comparisons, expressions of doubt, expressions of emotion	**LISTENING:** Listen and infer **SPEAKING:** Interpret the feelings or values of others; observe courtesies and exchange information **READING:** Categorize details **WRITING:** Persuade your reader **CULTURE:** Draw conclusions about shopping as a cultural activity
UNIDAD 5 La naturaleza • Costa Rica	**Etapa 1** p. 316 *En el bosque tropical* **UNIT OPENER** **CULTURE NOTES** • José Figueres • *Gallo pinto* • Francisco Zúñiga • *El quetzal* • *La cerámica de nicoya* • *El fútbol*	• Describe geographic characteristics • Make future plans • Talk about nature and the environment	• Future tense • *Por* • *Nosotros* commands	**EN VOCES** *El Parque Nacional de Volcán Poás* **CONEXIONES** *La geografía:* tropical forest locations **NOTAS CULTURALES** • *El 8 de septiembre de 1502* • *Los saludos*	**Activity 3:** *Predicciones* (making predictions)	**LISTENING:** Organize and summarize environmental information **SPEAKING:** Share personal plans and feelings; anticipate future plans **READING:** Confirm or deny hearsay with reliable information
	Etapa 2 p. 338 *Nuestro medio ambiente*	• Discuss outdoor activities • Describe the weather • Make predictions • Talk about ecology	• Irregular future • Expressions with *para*	**EN COLORES** *Costa Rica, ¡la pura vida!* (video) **TÚ EN LA COMUNIDAD** **NOTAS CULTURALES** • *Los parques nacionales* • *Navegar los rápidos*	• Weather expressions with *hacer* **Activity 5:** *¿Qué vas a hacer este verano?* (future tense)	**LISTENING:** Observe relationships between actions and motives **SPEAKING:** Describe it; make recommendations **CULTURE:** Predict appeal to ecotourists
	Etapa 3 p. 360 *¿Cómo será el futuro?*	• Comment on conservation and the environment • Talk about how you would solve problems	• *Por* or *para* • Conditional tense **NOTA** *Si estuviera… o Si pudieres…*	**EN VOCES:** *La cascada de la novia:* legends **EN COLORES:** *Cumbre ecológica centroamericana: Se reúnen jóvenes en San José* **CONEXIONES:** *Los estudios sociales:* advertising about the environment **NOTAS CULTURALES** • *Los campamentos* • *Las leyendas* • *La economía*	**Activity 5:** *¿Cómo será?* (future tense) **Activity 6:** *¿Por o para?* (por vs. para)	**LISTENING:** Propose solutions **SPEAKING:** Identify problems and your commitment to solving them; hypothesize about the future **READING:** Recognize characteristics of legends **WRITING:** Present a thorough and balanced review **CULTURE:** Prioritize

		COMMUNICATION	GRAMMAR	CULTURE	RECYCLING	STRATEGIES
UNIDAD 6 El mundo del trabajo • Quito, Ecuador	**Etapa 1** p. 388 *Se busca trabajo* UNIT OPENER CULTURE NOTES • *Llapingachos* • *Las Islas Galápagos* • *La música Andina* • *Andar en bicicleta de montaña* • *La toquilla* • Antonio José de Sucre	• Discuss jobs and professions • Describe people, places, and things • Complete an application	• Impersonal *se* • Past participles used as adjectives	EN VOCES *Bienvenidos a la isla Santa Cruz:* Galapagos Islands (video) CONEXIONES *La geografía:* equatorial regions NOTAS CULTURALES • *Quito* • *La ocarina*	• Present and present progressive **Activity 5:** *Una cápsula de tiempo* (conditional)	LISTENING: Evaluate a plan SPEAKING: Participate in an interview; check comprehension READING: Use context to find meaning
	Etapa 2 p. 410 *La entrevista*	• Prepare for an interview • Interview for a job • Evaluate situations and people	• Present perfect • Irregular present perfect	EN COLORES *Ciberespacio en Quito* CONEXIONES *La música:* pan flute NOTAS CULTURALES • *Los grupos indígenas* • *Las empresas del mundo hispano*	• Preterite and imperfect **Activity 3:** *¿Qué está dibujado?* (past participle)	LISTENING: Evaluate behavior SPEAKING: Give advice; refine interview skills CULTURE: Assess use of e-mail
	Etapa 3 p. 432 *¡A trabajar!*	• Talk on the telephone • Report on past, present, and future events • Describe duties, people, and surroundings	• Reported speech	EN VOCES Jorge Carrera Andrade— *Pasajero del planeta* EN COLORES *Música de las montañas:* Andean music TÚ EN LA COMUNIDAD NOTAS CULTURALES • *Guayaquil* • *Los festivales*	• Future tense • Conditional tense **Activity 3:** *¿Nunca?* (frequency, present perfect) **Activity 4:** *¿Quién lo ha hecho?* (present perfect) **Activity 15:** *Una cartita de agradecimiento* (recycles everything learned in the year)	LISTENING: Report what others said SPEAKING: Persuade or convince others; report on events READING: Observe characteristics of poems WRITING: State your message using a positive tone CULTURE: Reflect on music

¡En español!

Level 3 — Scope & Sequence

		COMMUNICATION	GRAMMAR	CULTURE	RECYCLING	STRATEGIES
PRELIMINAR	**Etapa preliminar** p. xxxiv *¡Bienvenidos al mundo hispano!* **UNIT OPENER** **CULTURE NOTES** • *El Instituto de Culturas Tejanas* • *La selva de Darién* • *El Alcázar de Colón* • Joan Miró • *La calle Rincón* • *El teleférico de Monserrate*	• Talk about present activities • Talk about past events and activities			• Present tense of regular verbs • Present tense verbs with irregular *yo* forms • Preterite tense of regular verbs • Spelling changes in the preterite • Stem changes in the preterite • Irregular preterites	
UNIDAD 1 Así somos • Estados Unidos	**Etapa 1** p. 30 *¿Cómo soy?* **UNIT OPENER** **CULTURE NOTES** • Oscar de la Hoya • *Comida mexicana* • *Repertorio Español* • Ellen Ochoa • *La Prensa*	• Describe people • Talk about experiences • List accomplishments	• Present and past perfect	**EN VOCES** Cristina García—*Soñar en cubano* **CONEXIONES** *El arte:* self portrait **NOTAS CULTURALES** • Concept of *barrio* • *Los apodos* • Spanish-speaking immigrants and identity	• *Ser* vs. *estar* • Imperfect tense • Preterite vs. imperfect **Ya sabes:** *Características*	**LISTENING:** Give a clear physical description **SPEAKING:** Add details to descriptions; describe personal characteristics and actions **READING:** Observe how verb tenses reveal time
	Etapa 2 p. 52 *¿Cómo me veo?*	• Describe fashions • Talk about pastimes • Talk about the future • Predict actions	• Future tense • Future of probability	**EN COLORES** *Un gran diseñador:* Oscar de la Renta **CONEXIONES** *Las matemáticas:* create an annual budget **NOTAS CULTURALES** • Araceli Segarra, climber of Mt. Everest • Pet sounds and names	• Verbs like *gustar* • *Por* and *para* **Activity 4:** *De compras* (clothing) **Activity 15:** *¿Dónde estarán?* (wondering about location) **Ya sabes:** *¿De qué es?*	**LISTENING:** Distinguish admiring and critical remarks **SPEAKING:** Use familiar vocabulary in a new setting; brainstorm to get lots of ideas **CULTURE:** Examine the cultural role of fashion
	Etapa 3 p. 74 *¡Hay tanto que hacer!*	• Talk about household chores • Say what friends do • Express feelings	• Reflexives used reciprocally **NOTA** *saber/conocer*	**EN VOCES** Sandra Cisneros—*La casa en Mango Street* **EN COLORES** *El legendario rey del mambo:* Tito Puente **TÚ EN LA COMUNIDAD** **NOTAS CULTURALES** • *El compadrazgo* • Sammy Sosa • Greater Eastside, LA	• Reflexive verbs • Impersonal constructions with *se* **Activity 2:** *¡Hazlo!* (say what you have to do) **Activity 5:** *Un día desastroso* (reflexive verbs) **Activity 9:** *Mi padrino* (imperfect)	**LISTENING:** Make an argument for and against hiring others to maintain a home **SPEAKING:** Identify feelings important in a friendship **READING:** Chart contrasts between dreams and reality **WRITING:** Use details to enrich a description **CULTURE:** Interview, report, and value musical influences

		COMMUNICATION	GRAMMAR	CULTURE	RECYCLING	STRATEGIES
UNIDAD 2 ¡El mundo es nuestro! • México y América Central	**Etapa 1** p. 102 *Pensemos en los demás* **UNIT OPENER CULTURE NOTES:** • María Izquierdo • *¡Protege la selva tropical!* • *Tejidos Guatemaltecos* • *Ruinas de Copán* • *Cebiche mixto* • Oscar Arias	• Say what you want to do • Make requests • Make suggestions	**NOTA** pronoun placement with commands	**EN VOCES** Elizabeth Burgos– *Me llamo Rigoberta Menchú* **TÚ EN LA COMUNIDAD** **NOTAS CULTURALES** • Youth groups in Mexico and C.A. • Young people addressing adults • *Castellano*	• Command forms • *Nosotros* commands • Speculating with the conditional **Activity 2:** *¿Qué vas a hacer?* (say what you are going to do) • **Activity 5:** *La clase de ejercicio (tú, usted o ustedes)* • **Activity 12:** *Costa Rica* (conditional)	**LISTENING:** Anticipate, compare and contrast **SPEAKING:** Name social problems then propose solutions; identify the general ideas, then delegate responsibilities **READING:** Comprehend complex sentences
	Etapa 2 p. 124 *Un planeta en peligro*	• Say what should be done • React to the ecology • React to others' actions	• Present perfect subjunctive **NOTA** *-uir* verbs add a *y* in subjunctive form	**EN COLORES:** *Unidos podemos hacerlo:* literacy in Nicaragua **CONEXIONES** *Las ciencias:* recycling **NOTAS CULTURALES** • Currencies in C.A. and Mexico • *Grupo de los Cien/* international conservation	• Present subjunctives **Activity 2:** *El horario de Ángela* (describe schedules) **Activity 5:** *La ecóloga* (subjunctive) **Ya sabes:** *Es bueno que…* etc.	**LISTENING:** Inventory local efforts to save the environment **SPEAKING:** Consider the effect of words and tone of voice; express support (or lack of) **CULTURE:** Gather and analyze information about literacy
	Etapa 3 p. 146 *La riqueza natural*	• React to nature • Express doubt • Relate events in time	• Subjunctive with *cuando* and other conjunctions of time **NOTA** *-cer* verbs add a *z* in the subjunctive	**EN VOCES** Juan José Arreola– *Baby H.P.* **EN COLORES** *Un país de encanto:* Costa Rican rainforests **CONEXIONES** *Las ciencias:* the products of a rainforest **NOTAS CULTURALES** • *Isla de Ometepe/Lago Nicaragua* • *Reservas naturales en Centroamérica*	• Subjunctive with expressions of emotion • Subjunctive to express doubt and uncertainty **Activity 3:** *¿Has visto…?* (animals) • **Activity 7:** *El mundo de hoy* (expressing emotion) • **Activity 9:** *No te creo* (expressing doubt) • **Activity 12:** *Tan pronto como* • **Activity 13:** *Los quehaceres* (conjunctions of time) **Ya sabes:** Expressions of emotion and doubt	**LISTENING:** Determine your purpose for listening **SPEAKING:** Gain thinking time before speaking; reassure others **READING:** Recognize uses of satire, parody, and irony **WRITING:** Persuade by presenting solutions to problems **CULTURE:** Analyze advantages and disadvantages of ecotourism
UNIDAD 3 Celebración de mi mundo • Caribe	**Etapa 1** p. 174 *¡Al fin la graduación!* **UNIT OPENER CULTURE NOTES:** • *Los Muñequitos de Matanzas* • *Bakeré* • *Frutas tropicales* • Rosario Ferré • Juan Luis Guerra • *Parque ceremonial Taíno, Utuado*	• Describe personal celebrations • Say what people want • Link events and ideas	• Subjunctive with conjunctions • Imperfect subjunctive **NOTA** *-ger* verbs change *g* to *j* in subjunctive	**EN VOCES** Nicolás Guillén– *Ébano Real* **TÚ EN LA COMUNIDAD** **NOTAS CULTURALES** • Graduation ceremony in R.D. • *Fiesta de graduación*	• Subjunctive for expressing wishes **Activity 5:** *Pedro* (subj with impersonal expressions) **Activity 13:** *Los chismes* (expressions of doubt) **Activity 14:** *Permiso* (recreation) **Ya sabes:** *otros verbos, conjunciones, el futuro*	**LISTENING:** Recognize major transitions **SPEAKING:** Give advice and best wishes **READING:** Interpret metaphors
	Etapa 2 p. 196 *¡Próspero Año Nuevo!*	• Talk about holidays • Hypothesize • Express doubt and disagree • Describe ideals	• Subjunctive with nonexistent and indefinite • Conditional sentences **NOTA** *sembrar, recoger, educar* spelling changes in subjunctive	**EN COLORES** *Una tradición de Puerto Rico:* masks **CONEXIONES:** *El arte:* art of the Caribbean **NOTAS CULTURALES** • *Salsa* • *Chayanne*	• Subjunctive for disagreement and denial **Activity 5:** *En la comunidad* (nonexistent and indefinite) **Activity 14:** *Las profesiones* (subj/profession) **Ya sabes:** *dar las gracias, dudar que…* etc.	**LISTENING:** Observe interview techniques **SPEAKING:** Socialize as host or guest; encourage participation **CULTURE:** Recognize and describe uses of disguise
	Etapa 3 p. 218 *Celebraciones de patria*	• Describe historic events • Make suggestions and wishes • Express emotion and doubt • State cause and effect	• Subjunctive vs. indicative **NOTA** *-zer* verbs change *z* to *c* in subjunctive	**EN VOCES:** José Martí– de *Versos sencillos: I.* **EN COLORES:** *Una historia única:* celebrations in the R.D. **CONEXIONES:** *Los estudios sociales:* independence days **NOTAS CULTURALES** • *El naufragio de la Santa Maria* • *El Himno Nacional de la R.D.* • *Guantanamera*	• Summary of the subjunctive **Activity 4:** *Los costumbres* (holidays) **Activity 7:** *¡Santo Domingo!* (subjunctive) **Activity 9:** *La comunidad* (subjunctive) **Ya sabes:** *dudar/creer* etc.	**LISTENING:** Listen and take notes **SPEAKING:** Describe celebrations; express yourself **READING:** Observe what makes poetry **WRITING:** Use transitions to make text flow smoothly **CULTURE:** Analyze national celebrations

		COMMUNICATION	GRAMMAR	CULTURE	RECYCLING	STRATEGIES
UNIDAD 4 Un futuro brillante • Cono Sur	**Etapa 1** p. 246 *El próximo paso* UNIT OPENER CULTURE NOTES • Antonio Berni • Rafael Guarga • *El arpa Andina* • *Mate* • *La bolsa* • *La Universidad de Chile*	• Describe your studies • Ask questions • Say what you are doing • Say what you were doing	• Progressive with *ir, andar,* and *seguir* • Past progressive	EN VOCES Jorge Luis Borges– *Borges y yo* TÚ EN LA COMUNIDAD NOTAS CULTURALES • Hand gestures • Professional titles • First name usage • Borges' blindness	• Interrogative words • Present progressive **Activity 8:** *Las llamadas* (present progressive, reflexives) **Activity 9:** *La limpieza* (present progressive, household chores) **Ya sabes:** question words	LISTENING: Listen and summarize SPEAKING: Establish closer relationships; extend a conversation READING: Analyze the role of identity and fantasy
	Etapa 2 p. 268 *¿Cuál será tu profesión?*	• Talk about careers • Confirm and deny • Express emotions • Hypothesize	• Past perfect subjunctive • Conditional perfect	EN COLORES: *Los jóvenes y el futuro:* career choices CONEXIONES *Los estudios sociales:* what professions interest you NOTAS CULTURALES • Getting into a university • Popular professions in Spanish-speaking world	• Affirmative and negative expressions **Activity 6:** *Necesitas saber* (affirmative/negative) **Activity 8:** *La celebración* (past perfect subjunctive) **Ya sabes:** negatives/ affirmatives	LISTENING: Identify key information for careers SPEAKING: Anticipate what others want to know; conduct an interview CULTURE: Formulate plans for the future
	Etapa 3 p. 290 *Un mundo de posibilidades*	• Learn about Latin American economics • Avoid redundancy • Express possession • Express past probability	• Future perfect	EN VOCES Isabel Allende–*Paula* EN COLORES: *Se hablan… ¡muchos idiomas!:* Spanish language origins CONEXIONES *Los estudios sociales:* ONU / OEA NOTAS CULTURALES • Job-hunting process in South America • Saving money	• Subject and stressed object pronouns • Possessive pronouns **Activity 3:** *Internet* (numbers) **Activity 5:** *¿Quién?* (subject/ stressed object pronouns) **Activity 9:** *¿De Argentina o Chile?* (possessive pronouns) **Ya sabes:** *comparaciones numéricas,* possessive pronouns, subject/object pronouns	LISTENING: Use statistics to evaluate predictions SPEAKING: Guess cognates; speculate about the past READING: Speculate about the author WRITING: Use cause and effect to demonstrate ability CULTURE: Observe how language reflects culture
UNIDAD 5 Artes en España y las Américas • España	**Etapa 1** p. 318 *Tradiciones españolas* UNIT OPENER CULTURE NOTES • Fernando Botero • *Chocolate y churros* • *La reina Isabel* • *Los cantos gregorianos* • Salvador Dalí • *Teatro Colón*	• Identify and specify • Request clarification • Express relationships • Discuss art forms	• *¿Qué? vs. ¿cuál?* • Relative pronouns	EN VOCES Miguel de Unamuno and Ana María Matute CONEXIONES *Los estudios sociales:* create a timeline of the Spanish Civil War NOTAS CULTURALES • El Museo del Prado	• Demonstrative adjectives and pronouns **Activity 7:** *Las respuestas* (*¿qué? vs. ¿cuál?*) **Activity 14:** *Los artistas* (relative pronouns, literature) **Ya sabes:** *La pintura, La literatura*	LISTENING: Use advance knowledge of the topic SPEAKING: Discuss a painting; organize ideas for research READING: Compare famous authors
	Etapa 2 p. 340 *El Nuevo Mundo*	• Refer to people and objects • Express relationships • Make generalizations • Describe arts and crafts	• Relative pronouns • *Lo que*	EN COLORES *Un arquitecto y sus obras:* Mexican architect CONEXIONES *Las matemáticas:* Mayan numerals NOTAS CULTURALES • *Bailes típicos* • *El inca Garcilaso de la Vega* • *Las ruinas de Tikal*	• Direct object pronouns • Indirect object pronouns **Activity 4:** *¿Lo conoces?* (direct object pronouns) **Activity 7:** *Después de la entrevista* (indirect object pronouns, work) **Activity 8:** *El viaje* (indirect object pronouns)	LISTENING: Improve your auditory memory SPEAKING: Maintain a discussion; discuss Latin American dance CULTURE: Use architecture as a cultural text
	Etapa 3 p. 362 *Lo mejor de dos mundos*	• Talk about literature • Talk about film • Avoid redundancy	• Nominalization [box 1] • Nominalization [box 2]	EN VOCES: Federico García Lorca–*La casa de Bernarda Alba* EN COLORES *Tres directores:* Spanish-speaking film directors TÚ EN LA COMUNIDAD NOTAS CULTURALES • Movie titles in Spanish and English • Boom in Latin American fiction	• Double object pronouns **Activity 5:** *El(La) presidente* (double object pronouns) **Activity 12:** *Clarificaciones* (nominalization)	LISTENING: Evaluate discussions SPEAKING: Discuss a novel; critique a film READING: Interpret a drama WRITING: Support an opinion with facts and examples CULTURE: Reflect on the international appeal of movies

UNIDAD 6 ¡Ya llegó el futuro! • Venezuela, Ecuador, Colombia, Bolivia, Perú

	COMMUNICATION	GRAMMAR	CULTURE	RECYCLING	STRATEGIES
Etapa 1 p. 390 *¿Qué quieres ver?* **UNIT OPENER** **CULTURE NOTES** • *Parque de Ciencia y Tecnología Maloka* • Machu Picchu • Simón Bolívar • Armando Reverón • *El teléfono celular* • *Maduritos*	• Narrate in the past • Express doubt and certainty • Report what others say • Talk about television	• Sequence of tenses	**EN VOCES** *Brillo afuera, oscuridad en casa:* Spanish language soap operas **TÚ EN LA COMUNIDAD** **NOTAS CULTURALES** • *Telenovelas* • Invitation implies inviter pays	• Preterite vs. imperfect • Indicative vs. subjunctive • Reported speech **Activity 1:** *¿Por qué no…?* (movies) **Activity 9:** *¡Es dudoso!* (subjunctive with doubt) **Activity 14:** *Abuelo* (reported speech)	**LISTENING:** Keep up with what is said and agreed **SPEAKING:** Negotiate; retell memories **READING:** Distinguish facts from interpretations
Etapa 2 p. 412 *Aquí tienes mi número…*	• Talk about technology • State locations • Make contrasts • Describe unplanned events	• *Pero* vs. *sino* • *Se* for unplanned occurrences	**EN COLORES** *¿Un aparato democrático?:* cell phones in Latin America **CONEXIONES** *El arte:* make an ad for electronics **NOTAS CULTURALES** • Game shows in Spanish	• Conjunctions • Prepositions and adverbs of location **Activity 2:** *¡Voy a ElectroMundo!* (electronics) **Ya sabes:** Prepositions/ adverbs of location; conjunctions with subjunctive	**LISTENING:** Analyze the appeal in radio ads **SPEAKING:** Make excuses; consider the factors for and against an electronic purchase **CULTURE:** Survey technology in daily life
Etapa 3 p. 434 *¡Un viaje al ciberespacio!*	• Compare and evaluate • Express precise relationships • Navigate cyberspace	• Verbs with prepositions	**EN VOCES** Gabriel García Márquez **EN COLORES** *Bolivia en la red:* Bolivian web page **CONEXIONES** *La tecnología:* evaluate computer configurations for your classroom **NOTAS CULTURALES** • Spread of computer technology in Latin America • Searching for Spanish websites • *Macondo* in works by Márquez	• Summary of prepositions • Comparatives and superlatives **Activity 4:** *Comparaciones* (comparatives) **Activity 5:** *Marcos* (comparatives, computers) **Ya sabes:** verbs with prepositions	**LISTENING:** Identify important computer vocabulary **SPEAKING:** Compare and evaluate films; compare and evaluate computer configurations **READING:** Monitor comprehension **WRITING:** Prioritize information in order of importance **CULTURE:** Evaluate the Internet as a means of developing cultural knowledge and understanding

Starting the Year Off Right

REVIEW ReTeach

The extensive Bridge Unit refreshes students' memory of the vocabulary and grammar concepts from the previous year to better prepare them to be successful in Level 1B.

● **Bridge Unit** helps students recall and practice Level 1A concepts.

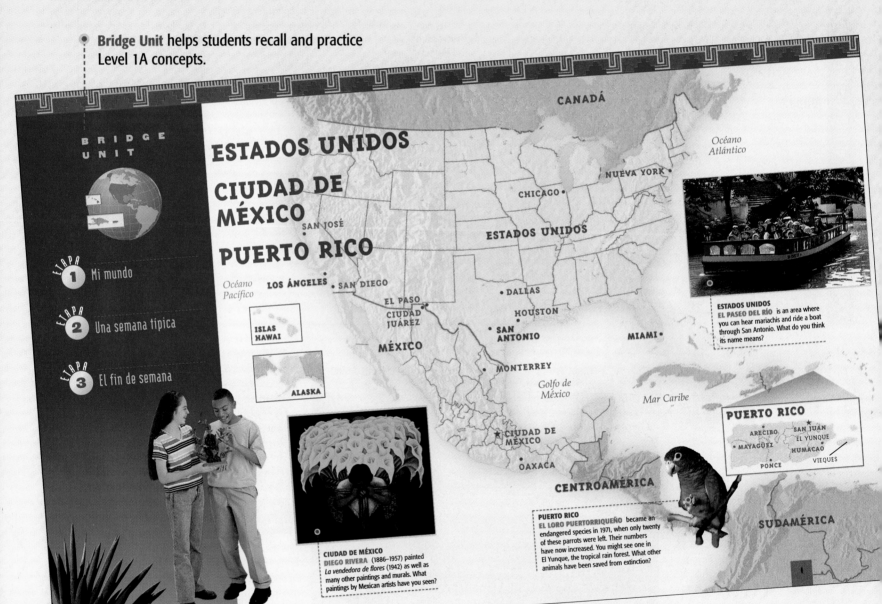

BRIDGE UNIT

ETAPA **1** Mi mundo

ETAPA **2** Una semana típica

ETAPA **3** El fin de semana

ESTADOS UNIDOS

CIUDAD DE MÉXICO

PUERTO RICO

CANADÁ
NUEVA YORK
CHICAGO
ESTADOS UNIDOS
Océano Atlántico
SAN JOSÉ
Océano Pacífico
LOS ÁNGELES • SAN DIEGO
EL PASO
CIUDAD JUÁREZ
DALLAS
HOUSTON
SAN ANTONIO
MIAMI
ISLAS HAWAI
MÉXICO
ALASKA
MONTERREY
Golfo de México
Mar Caribe
CIUDAD DE MÉXICO
OAXACA
CENTROAMÉRICA
SUDAMÉRICA

PUERTO RICO
ARECIBO • SAN JUAN
MAYAGÜEZ • EL YUNQUE
HUMACAO
PONCE • VIEQUES

ESTADOS UNIDOS
EL PASEO DEL RÍO is an area where you can hear mariachis and ride a boat through San Antonio. What do you think its name means?

CIUDAD DE MÉXICO
DIEGO RIVERA (1886–1957) painted *La vendedora de flores* (1942) as well as many other paintings and murals. What paintings by Mexican artists have you seen?

PUERTO RICO
EL LORO PUERTORRIQUEÑO became an endangered species in 1971, when only twenty of these parrots were left. Their numbers have now increased. You might see one in El Yunque, the tropical rain forest. What other animals have been saved from extinction?

● **Practice activities** give students a chance to figure out what they remember as well as find out if they need more help.

"This is one of the best I've seen."

Laura A. Bertrand
Explorer Middle School
Phoenix, AZ

En acción
VOCABULARIO Y GRAMÁTICA

Gramática en vivo

Sr. Estrada: ¡Alma! **¿Cómo estás** hoy?
Alma: Muy bien, señor Estrada, **¿y usted?**

Familiar and Formal Greetings

Familiar:

¿Cómo estás?
is a familiar greeting.

Use with:
* a friend
* a family member
* someone younger

Another familiar greeting: **¿Qué tal?**

Tú is a familiar way to say *you*.

Formal:

¿Cómo está usted?
is a formal greeting.

Use with:
* a person you don't know
* someone older
* someone for whom you want to show respect

Usted is a formal way to say *you*.

 ACTIVIDAD **4**

¿Qué tal?

Hablar/Escribir How would you greet the following people?

1. una amiga
2. un maestro
3. un policía
4. tu mamá
5. un muchacho
6. una señora

ACTIVIDAD **5**

¡Saludos!

Hablar Imagine you run into the following people at the store. Take turns greeting each person and giving a response.

modelo

tu maestro(a) / muy bien
Estudiante A: *¿Cómo está usted?*
Estudiante B: *Estoy muy bien, gracias.*

1. tu doctor(a) / bien
2. un(a) estudiante / regular
3. un(a) amigo(a) / terrible
4. un(a) policía / muy bien

ACTIVIDAD **6**

¿Cómo está usted?

Hablar Imagine your partner is a teacher at your school. Greet him or her and tell each other how you are. Change roles.

Gramática en vivo

Alma: Arturo, te presento a Francisco García. Él **es** mi vecino.

Subject Pronouns and the Verb ser

▶ To discuss people in Spanish, you will often use **subject pronouns**. When you want to describe a person or explain who he or she is, use the verb **ser**.

	Singular	Plural
	yo soy *I am*	**nosotros(as)** somos *we are*
familiar	**tú** eres *you are*	**vosotros(as)** sois *you are*
formal	**usted** es *you are*	**ustedes** son *you are*
	él, ella es *he, she is*	**ellos(as)** son *they are*

▶ If Alma were to say that someone is a neighbor, she would say:
—Él **es** **un** vecino.

However, if she were to say that someone is a policeman, she would say:
—Él **es** policía.

> The word **un** or **una** does not appear before a profession.

ACTIVIDAD **7**

¿Quiénes son?

Leer/Escribir Use subject pronouns to complete the sentences. There may be more than one right answer.

modelo

Ella es una muchacha.

1. _____ es un señor.
2. _____ soy estudiante.
3. _____ somos amigos.
4. _____ son hermanos.
5. _____ eres mi amiga.
6. _____ es una mujer.

ACTIVIDAD **8**

Mi comunidad

Hablar/Escribir Point out the people in your community by telling who everyone is.

modelo

ella / doctora **Ella es doctora.**

1. yo / estudiante
2. tú / amiga
3. nosotros / familia
4. él / maestro
5. ellas / muchachas

● **Gramática en vivo** boxes remind students of Level 1A grammar concepts so they can successfully progress through Level 1B.

MOTIVATE TO COMMUNICATE
¡En español!

Setting the Stage for Communication

Each unit is set in a different Spanish-speaking country to excite students about the new places and new things they're going to learn.

Unit Objectives preview for the students what they will be able to do at the end of the unit.

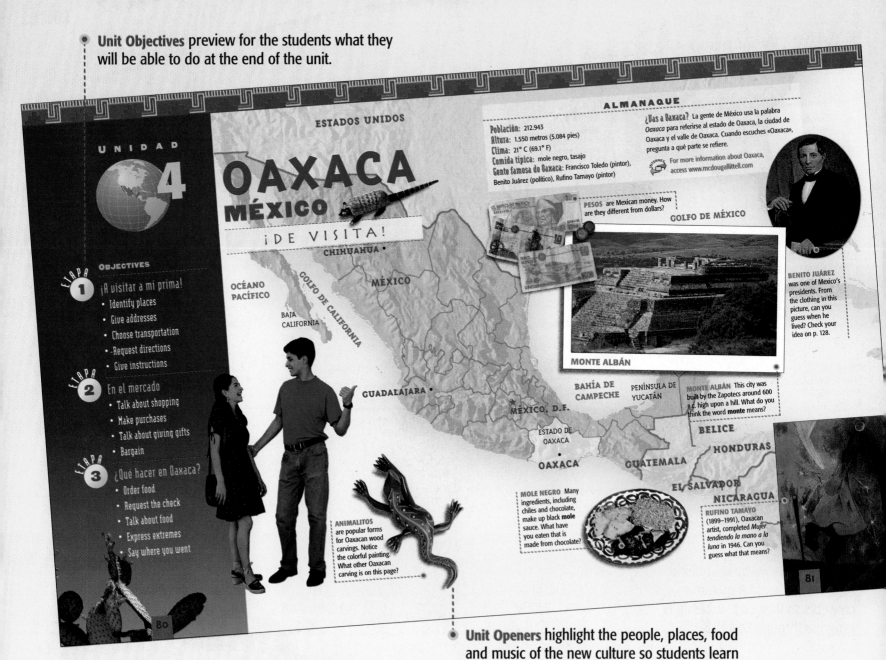

UNIDAD 4

ETAPA 1

OBJECTIVES

¡A visitar a mi prima!

- Identify places
- Give addresses
- Choose transportation
- Request directions
- Give instructions

ETAPA 2

En el mercado

- Talk about shopping
- Make purchases
- Talk about giving gifts
- Bargain

ETAPA 3

¿Qué hacer en Oaxaca?

- Order food
- Request the check
- Talk about food
- Express extremes
- Say where you went

OAXACA MÉXICO
¡DE VISITA!

ESTADOS UNIDOS

OCÉANO PACÍFICO

GOLFO DE CALIFORNIA

BAJA CALIFORNIA

CHIHUAHUA

MÉXICO

GUADALAJARA

MÉXICO, D.F.

ESTADO DE OAXACA

OAXACA

BAHÍA DE CAMPECHE

PENÍNSULA DE YUCATÁN

GOLFO DE MÉXICO

GUATEMALA

BELICE

HONDURAS

EL SALVADOR

NICARAGUA

ALMANAQUE

Población: 212.943
Altura: 1.550 metros (5.084 pies)
Clima: 21° C (69.1° F)
Comida típica: mole negro, tasajo
Gente famosa de Oaxaca: Francisco Toledo (pintor), Benito Juárez (político), Rufino Tamayo (pintor)

¿Vas a Oaxaca? La gente de México usa la palabra *Oaxaca* para referirse al estado de Oaxaca, la ciudad de Oaxaca y el valle de Oaxaca. Cuando escuches «Oaxaca», pregunta a qué parte se refiere.

For more information about Oaxaca, access www.mcdougallittell.com

PESOS are Mexican money. How are they different from dollars?

BENITO JUÁREZ was one of Mexico's presidents. From the clothing in this picture, can you guess when he lived? Check your idea on p. 128.

MONTE ALBÁN

MONTE ALBÁN This city was built by the Zapotecs around 600 b.c. high upon a hill. What do you think the word **monte** means?

ANIMALITOS are popular forms for Oaxacan wood carvings. Notice the colorful painting. What other Oaxacan carving is on this page?

MOLE NEGRO Many ingredients, including chiles and chocolate, make up black **mole** sauce. What have you eaten that is made from chocolate?

RUFINO TAMAYO (1899–1991), Oaxacan artist, completed *Mujer tendiendo la mano a la luna* in 1946. Can you guess what that means?

80

81

Unit Openers highlight the people, places, food and music of the new culture so students learn Spanish in its authentic context.

"Everything ties nicely together. The unit has a good introductory theme so that students can take vocabulary and structures and apply them to talk about themselves."

Elizabeth Torosian
Doherty Middle School
Andover, MA

● **Etapa Openers** remind students of the communicative objectives.

UNIDAD 4

ETAPA

3

¿Qué hacer en Oaxaca?

- Order food
- Request the check
- Talk about food
- Express extremes
- Say where you went

¿Qué ves?

Mira la foto de Monte Albán.

1. ¿Alguien lleva una gorra?
2. ¿Quién es la persona principal?
3. ¿Qué hace?
4. ¿Cuánto cuesta un refresco en el restaurante?

134

Restaurante La Madre Tierra

Nuestra especialidad

Mole negro y tasajo
$32
Ensaladas
$15
Sopas
$12
Enchiladas
$20
Pollo
$25
Bistec (con arroz y frijoles)
$30
Refrescos
$10
Postres
$25

135

● **¿Qué ves?** reviews language for application in the new cultural context.

MOTIVATE TO COMMUNICATE

¡En español!

Strengthen proficiency through meaningful communicative contexts

IMPROVE · COMPREHENSION

Two stages of vocabulary introduction better prepare students for recognition and comprehension.

En contexto visually preteaches active vocabulary in a relevant context.

En contexto

VOCABULARIO

Carlos is at a restaurant in Oaxaca. Take a look at what he likes to eat.

A
Carlos tiene mucha hambre y va a un restaurante. Lee el menú y decide comer una enchilada. Es deliciosa. ¡Pero la salsa es picante! El mesero va a servirle una limonada.

el restaurante

el mesero

la enchilada

la limonada

CASA LITA

ENSALADAS Y SOPAS
Ensalada mixta $25
Sopa de pollo $20

COMIDAS
Servidas con arroz y frijoles
Arroz con pollo $45
Bistec asado $60
Enchiladas $40
Pollo $50
Tacos $35
Tamales $40
Tortas $35

LA ESPECIALIDAD DE LA CASA
Mole negro y tasajo $40

BEBIDAS
Agua mineral $10
Café $12
Limonada $15
Refrescos $15
Té $12

POSTRES
Flan $20
Fruta $15
Pastel $20

el tenedor

el bistec

el arroz

el cuchillo

B
Otras personas comen en el restaurante también. Una persona come arroz y bistec. Usa un tenedor y un cuchillo para comer.

el pollo

la ensalada

la sopa

la cuchara

C
Otra persona come sopa, pollo y ensalada. Usa una cuchara para tomar la sopa.

D
Una persona quiere café con azúcar. Otra quiere una taza de té.

el café

el té

las tazas

el azúcar

E
¿Qué tienen de postre? ¡Un flan muy rico!

el flan

Preguntas personales
1. ¿Te gusta comer comida picante?
2. ¿Prefieres comer en un restaurante o en casa?
3. ¿Prefieres un bistec o pollo?
4. ¿Qué te gusta más: la sopa, la ensalada o el postre?
5. ¿Cuál es tu comida favorita?

ciento treinta y seis
Unidad 4 136

ciento treinta y siete
Etapa 3 137

Preguntas personales encourage students to recognize the active vocabulary and make it meaningful to them.

T28 Walkthrough

> "Early success in Spanish is motivating for students. The combination of <u>En contexto</u> and <u>En vivo</u> provides the perfect means to boost student confidence and desire to learn Spanish."
>
> Sharon Larracoechea
> South Junior High School
> Boise, ID

● **Listening strategies** provide a starting point and focus for the dialog to help comprehension.

En vivo
DIÁLOGO

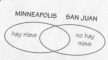

Diana   Roberto   Ignacio

PARA ESCUCHAR · STRATEGY: LISTENING

Sort and categorize details Minneapolis and San Juan are a world apart, yet in at least one way they are similar. How? What does Roberto say? What differences are mentioned? Use a Venn diagram to sort these details.

MINNEAPOLIS   SAN JUAN

hay nieve   no hay nieve

¡Qué tiempo!

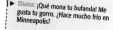

1 ▶ Diana: ¡Qué mona tu bufanda! Me gusta tu gorro. ¿Hace mucho frío en Minneapolis?

2 ▶ Roberto: En el invierno, sí, ¡hace mucho frío! ¡Brrr! Tengo frío cuando pienso en los inviernos de Minneapolis.

3 ▶ Diana: ¿Nieva mucho?
Roberto: Bueno, en el invierno, nieva casi todas las semanas. Pero en verano, es como aquí. Hace mucho calor.

4 ▶ Ignacio: ¿Qué vas a hacer con toda esta ropa de invierno? Aquí nadie la necesita.
Roberto: Tienes razón. Voy a necesitar shorts, trajes de baño y gafas de sol.

5 ▶ Diana: ¡Ay! Pues, ya tienes ropa de verano.
Roberto: Claro que la tengo. ¡En Minneapolis no es invierno todo el año!

6 ▶ Roberto: ¡Qué día bonito! Hace muy buen tiempo. Tengo ganas de ir a El Yunque.
Diana: Perfecto, porque el proyecto de Ignacio para el concurso es sobre el bosque tropical. Y está preparando el proyecto este mes.

7 ▶ Ignacio: Sí, y necesito sacar fotos del bosque. Y las quiero sacar hoy mismo.
Roberto: Tengo suerte, ¿no lo creen?
Diana: Creo que tienes mucha suerte.
Ignacio: Tengo prisa. Es buena hora para sacar fotos porque hay sol.

8 ▶ Ignacio: ¡Qué bonito! Los árboles, las flores…
Roberto: Sí, muy bonita.
Ignacio: No es como Minneapolis, ¿verdad, Roberto?
Roberto: Tienes razón, Ignacio.

9 ▶ Ignacio: Mi proyecto va a estar bien chévere, ¿no creen?… ¿No creen?…
…Sí, Ignacio, creo que tu proyecto va a ser muy impresionante.

10 ▶ Ignacio: ¡Está lloviendo! ¡Y no tengo paraguas!
Roberto: Te estamos esperando, hombre.

248 doscientos cuarenta y ocho
Unidad 3

● **Motivating dialogs** with embedded vocabulary and structures depict real-life situations.

MOTIVATE TO COMMUNICATE
¡En español!

Help Middle School Students Communicate with Confidence

¡En español! helps middle school students conquer their language learning anxieties and support each other to become better communicators.

En acción
VOCABULARIO Y GRAMÁTICA

ACTIVIDAD 1

Mmmm... ¡qué rico!

Escuchar En el restaurante Rosa, Sofía y Carlos hablan de muchos platos. Pero, ¿qué comen? *(Hint: Write the letter of the dishes the friends actually request.)*

1. Rosa come _____ .
   a. el bistec asado
   b. la especialidad de la casa
   c. la ensalada mixta y pollo
   d. el burrito
   e. la hamburguesa

2. Sofía come _____ .
   a. la ensalada mixta y pollo
   b. la especialidad de la casa
   c. el burrito
   d. la hamburguesa
   e. la enchilada

3. Carlos come _____ .
   a. la especialidad de la casa
   b. la hamburguesa
   c. la enchilada
   d. el bistec asado
   e. el burrito

ciento cuarenta
Unidad 4

ACTIVIDAD 2

En el restaurante

Escuchar ¿Quién habla: Sofía, Carlos, Rosa o el mesero? *(Hint: Tell who made the following statements.)*

1. «Yo quiero un plato tradicional.»
2. «Me gustan las enchiladas, pero voy a pedir bistec.»
3. «Una limonada para mí.»
4. «¿Un flan, señoritas? Lo sirvo en dos platos... »
5. «No quiero ningún postre, pero ¿me puede traer la cuenta, por favor?»

Vocabulario

La comida

las bebidas

la carne

la lechuga

el pan

el pan dulce

el pastel

el queso

caliente *hot, warm*
dulce *sweet*
sin *without*
vegetariano(a) *vegetarian*

¿Prefieres una cena con carne o sin carne? ¿Qué te gusta comer?

ACTIVIDAD 3

¿Qué prefieres?

Hablar Pregúntale a un(a) compañero(a) qué comidas prefiere. *(Hint: Ask a classmate what foods he or she prefers.)*

modelo

el flan / el pastel

Estudiante A: ¿Qué prefieres, **el flan** o **el pastel**?

Estudiante B: Prefiero **el flan**. (Prefiero **el pastel**.) (No me gusta nada.) ¿Y tú?

1. el bistec / el pollo
2. la ensalada mixta / la sopa
3. la fruta / el queso
4. el pan dulce / las papas fritas
5. la limonada / el refresco

ciento cuarenta y uno
Etapa 3   **141**

Exceptionally versatile activities are developmentally appropriate to ensure success. The carefully-crafted vocabulary sequence supports the students' learning to ensure confidence and success.

"All the pieces are there for a good text that will bring us to the 21st century."

Janet Wohlers
Weston Middle School
Weston, MA

ACTIVIDAD 4

¿Qué dice?

Escribir/Hablar En una hoja de papel, escribe lo que dice la persona en cada caso. *(Hint: On a separate sheet of paper, write what the person says in each scene. Choose from the expressions listed below.)*

 ¡Qué barato!

 ¡Qué caliente!

 ¡Qué rico!

 ¡Qué picante!

¡Qué dulce!

¡Qué simpático!

ACTIVIDAD 5

¿Qué pasa?

Escuchar Escucha las descripciones. ¿Qué foto se relaciona con cada descripción? *(Hint: Which description matches each photo?)*

a.

b.

c.

d.

ACTIVIDAD 6

♻ Las tiendas y tú

Hablar Habla con otro(a) estudiante sobre las tiendas. Cambien de papel. *(Hint: Talk to a classmate about where you went shopping and what you bought recently.)*

modelo

zapatería

Estudiante A: ¿Fuiste a la **zapatería**?

Estudiante B: Sí, fui a comprar unos zapatos.

Nota

Fui and fuiste are past tense forms of the verb **ir.** Fui means *I went;* fuiste means *you* **(tú)** went.

1. pastelería
2. carnicería
3. panadería
4. librería
5. tienda de música

ACTIVIDAD 7

♻ A poner la mesa

Hablar Trabajas en un restaurante. El (La) nuevo(a) mesero(a) no sabe cómo poner la mesa. Ayúdalo(a). *(Hint: Help the waiter/waitress set the table.)*

modelo

el tenedor

Mesero(a): ¿Dónde pongo **el tenedor**?

Tú: Al lado del plato, a la izquierda.

Nota

Poner means *to put.* It has an irregular **yo** form: **pongo.** The expression poner la mesa means *to set the table.*

1. el cuchillo
2. la cuchara
3. el vaso
4. la taza
5. el plato

También se dice

To describe Mexico's spicy cuisine, picante is used by all Spanish speakers. In Mexico, picoso(a) describes especially spicy food! Spanish speakers use different words for *waiter/waitress.*

- **mesero(a):** Mexico, Puerto Rico
- **camarero(a):** Spain
- **mozo(a):** Argentina, Puerto Rico
- **caballero/señorita:** many countries

salsa picante

MOTIVATE TO COMMUNICATE
¡En español!

Present grammar concepts visually to improve comprehension & retention

Illustrated grammar makes it easier for students to understand, remember, and apply new concepts.

Visual grammar concepts help students see how the language works.

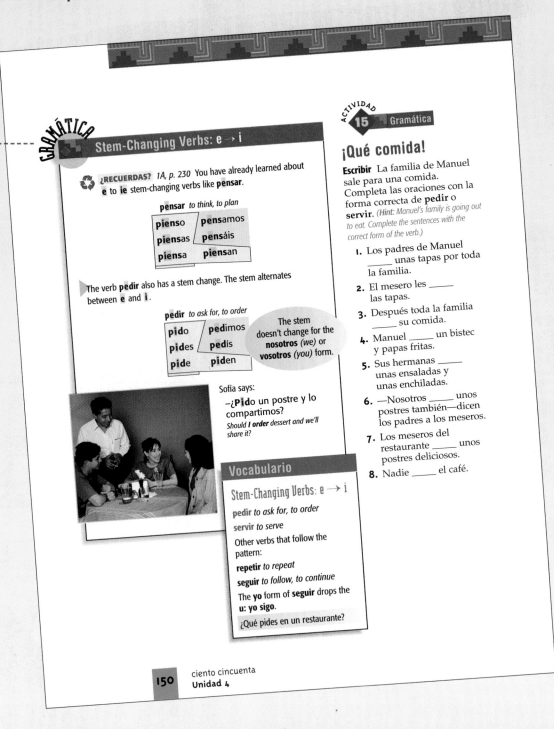

GRAMÁTICA

Stem-Changing Verbs: e → i

¿RECUERDAS? *1A, p. 230* You have already learned about **e** to **ie** stem-changing verbs like **pensar**.

pensar *to think, to plan*

pienso	**pens**amos
piensas	**pens**áis
piensa	**piens**an

The verb **pedir** also has a stem change. The stem alternates between **e** and **i**.

pedir *to ask for, to order*

pido	**ped**imos
pides	**ped**ís
pide	**pid**en

The stem doesn't change for the **nosotros** *(we)* or **vosotros** *(you)* form.

Sofía says:

–¿**Pid**o un postre y lo compartimos?

*Should **I order** dessert and we'll share it?*

Vocabulario

Stem-Changing Verbs: e → i

pedir *to ask for, to order*

servir *to serve*

Other verbs that follow the pattern:

repetir *to repeat*

seguir *to follow, to continue*

The **yo** form of **seguir** drops the **u: yo sigo.**

¿Qué pides en un restaurante?

ACTIVIDAD 15 — Gramática

¡Qué comida!

Escribir La familia de Manuel sale para una comida. Completa las oraciones con la forma correcta de **pedir** o **servir**. *(Hint: Manuel's family is going out to eat. Complete the sentences with the correct form of the verb.)*

1. Los padres de Manuel _____ unas tapas por toda la familia.

2. El mesero les _____ las tapas.

3. Después toda la familia _____ su comida.

4. Manuel _____ un bistec y papas fritas.

5. Sus hermanas _____ unas ensaladas y unas enchiladas.

6. —Nosotros _____ unos postres también—dicen los padres a los meseros.

7. Los meseros del restaurante _____ unos postres deliciosos.

8. Nadie _____ el café.

ciento cincuenta
150 Unidad 4

- **The activity sequence,** from controlled to open-ended activities, guides students through a solid progression that builds vocabulary and grammar skills.

- **Clear models** make it easier for students to understand what they are supposed to do.

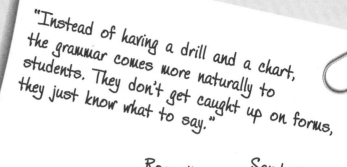

"Instead of having a drill and a chart, the grammar comes more naturally to students. They don't get caught up on forms, they just know what to say."

Sandy Baker
Roswell Kent Middle School
Akron, OH

ACTIVIDAD 18

¿A quién?

Escuchar Carlos y Elena están en un restaurante. ¿Es cierta o falsa cada oración? Corrige las falsas. *(Hint: Decide if each sentence is true or false. Correct the false ones.)*

1. Carlos tiene hambre.
2. Elena va a pedir enchiladas de pollo.
3. Carlos va a pedir un bistec.
4. Los dos van a pedir algún refresco.
5. Carlos no va a pedir ningún postre.

Vocabulario

En el restaurante

Para pedir comida

¿Me ayuda a pedir? *Could you help me order?*

¿Me trae…? *Could you bring me…?*

Quisiera… *I would like…*

Para pedir la cuenta

¿Cuánto es? *How much is it?*

La cuenta, por favor. *The check, please.*

Es aparte. *Separate checks.*

¿Está incluido(a)…? *Is … included?*

¿Cuánto le doy de propina? *How much do I tip?*

¿Cómo pides en un restaurante?

ACTIVIDAD 19

♻ La fiesta

Hablar Trabajas con un(a) compañero(a). Tú haces una fiesta. Tu amigo(a) te pregunta quién trae cada cosa. Cambia de papeles. *(Hint: Your friend asks you who is bringing various things to your party. Use the correct form of traer. Change roles.)*

modelo

Antonio / platos

Estudiante A: *Antonio trae los platos, ¿verdad?*
Estudiante B: *Sí, él los trae.*

Nota

Traer means *to bring.* It has an irregular **yo** form: **traigo.** Its other forms are regular.

1. tú / tenedores
2. Margarita y yo / ensalada mixta
3. Enrique y Pablo / pollo
4. yo / enchiladas

ACTIVIDAD 20

¡Buen provecho!

Escribir Un mesero sirve a unos clientes en un restaurante. Completa la conversación con las palabras de la lista. *(Hint: Complete the conversation with words from the list.)*

| trae | ayuda | pedir |
| fresco | especialidad | pido |

Mesero: Buenas tardes, jóvenes. ¿Listos para __1__?
José: Yo __2__ bistec y una ensalada, por favor. ¿Está __3__ el pan?
Mesero: Sí, señor. ¿Y las señoritas?
Ana: ¿Me __4__ una ensalada de frutas y un refresco?
Janet: Perdón, señor, pero no soy de aquí. ¿Me __5__ a pedir?
Mesero: Con mucho gusto. La __6__ hoy son enchiladas suizas.
Janet: ¡Perfecto! ¡Yo __7__ la especialidad!

ACTIVIDAD 21

En el restaurante

Hablar/Escribir Vas a un restaurante con tu amigo. Trabaja en un grupo de tres para escribir un diálogo en dos partes, usando las expresiones de la lista. Luego, presenten los diálogos a la clase. *(Hint: Work in a group of three. Write a restaurant dialog.)*

Parte 1: Llegan al restaurante. El mesero les trae el menú. Piden la comida.

Parte 2: El mesero les trae la comida. Hablan de la calidad de la comida y del servicio.

modelo

Estudiante A: *¿Nos puede traer el menú, por favor?*
Estudiante B (Mesero[a]): *Sí, lo traigo ahora mismo.*
Estudiante C: *¿Qué vas a pedir?*
Estudiante A: *¿Sirven buenas comidas vegetarianas aquí?*
Estudiante C: *Creo que sí. A mí me gusta la carne.*
Estudiante A: *¿Por qué no pides el arroz con pollo?*
Estudiante C: *¡Buena idea!*
Estudiante B (Mesero[a]): *¿Están listos para pedir?*

■ **MÁS COMUNICACIÓN** p. R3

Pronunciación

Trabalenguas

Pronunciación de la g The letter **g** in Spanish has a soft sound before the vowels **i** and **e**. It sounds somewhat like the *h* in the English word *he*, but a little harder. Practice by pronouncing the following words:

gimnasio   biología   **g**eneral   **G**eraldo

When it precedes other vowels, the **g** has a different sound, like in the word *go*. To produce this sound with **i** or **e**, a **u** must be inserted. Practice the following words:

gato   **g**usto   **g**ordo   abri**g**o   **g**uitarra   hambur**g**uesa

Now try the tongue twister.

Cuando digo «digo» digo «Diego».
Cuando digo «Diego» digo «digo».

- **Pronunciación** is taught through **Trabalenguas** and **Refranes** which make learning Spanish both memorable and fun.

MOTIVATE TO COMMUNICATE
¡En español!

Improve students' reading skills with a variety of high-interest selections

VARIETY OF READINGS

Engaging reading selections, that are read and summarized on audio, provide students a tremendous advantage to increase their literacy in Spanish.

- **Reading strategies** develop students' skills by emphasizing different ways to approach a variety of readings and genres.

En voces

LECTURA

PARA LEER

STRATEGY: READING

Recognizing sequence Charts can help you remember the events of a story in the order they happen. For example, when you read a biography, you can list the events in the person's life chronologically. As you read this selection complete a chart like the one below.

Benito Juárez

Event	Stage in Life
• loses parents	• 5 years old
• worked as a shepherd	• a boy

Benito Juárez, un oaxaqueño por excelencia

En 1806 (mil ochocientos seis), en un pueblo del estado de Oaxaca, nace[1] un niño. Se llama Benito. Cuando Benito tiene sólo cinco años, su mamá y su papá se mueren[2]. Un tío lleva a Benito a vivir a su casa, pero Benito tiene que trabajar porque la familia es pobre[3]. El tío le dice: —Benito, tienes que cuidar a los corderitos[4] en la montaña.

Y entonces, Benito trabaja todos los días de pastorcito[5]. Un día, decide salir del pueblo porque quiere una vida mejor. Llega a la capital

---

¹is born
²die
³poor
⁴young sheep
⁵shepherd

y conoce a un buen hombre, Antonio Salanueva. El señor Salanueva enseña a Benito a hablar español (antes, sólo hablaba zapoteco, el idioma nativo regional). El señor Salanueva también le enseña a leer y a escribir. Después de muchos años de estudio, llega a ser abogado[6]. Se dedica a ayudar a la gente pobre.

Los mexicanos conocen a Benito como un hombre bueno, serio y muy trabajador y ¡lo quieren para gobernador del estado! Trabaja mucho e, increíblemente, llega a ser presidente de toda la República Mexicana.

¡Así es que el humilde Benito va de pastorcito a presidente!

---

⁶lawyer

¿Comprendiste?

1. ¿De dónde es Benito?
2. ¿Cómo trabaja de niño?
3. ¿Cuál es su profesión de adulto?
4. ¿Qué idiomas habla?
5. ¿Qué llega a ser?

¿Qué piensas?

1. ¿Concoces a alguna persona cuya vida es similar a la de Benito Juárez? ¿Cómo son similares las dos personas?
2. ¿Qué te parece esta historia? ¿Crees que mucha gente puede hacer lo mismo que Benito Juárez?

ciento tres **103**
Etapa I

102 **Unidad 4**

- **¿Comprendiste?** checks students' basic understanding of what they've read.

"The strategy boxes will be useful. I'm a true believer in the metacognitive focus of teaching strategies."

Bill Heller
Perry Jr./Sr. High School
Perry, NY

En voces

LECTURA

PARA LEER

STRATEGY: READING
Making a story map To help you remember characters and events in a story, use a story map like the one below. This will help you organize the main ideas in this legend.

Characters:
1. mujer vieja 2. _____ 3. _____
Problem: Los vecinos quieren ...
Solution: El tlacuache ...

Una leyenda oaxaqueña
El fuego y el tlacuache[1]

La gente mazateca, que vive en la región norte de Oaxaca, les cuenta esta leyenda a sus hijos.

Una noche una mujer vieja atrapa la lumbre[2] al caerse de una estrella[3]. Todos sus vecinos[4] van a la casa de la vieja a pedir lumbre. Pero la vieja no quiere darle lumbre a la gente.

En ese momento, llega un tlacuache y les dice a los vecinos: —Yo, tlacuache, voy a darles la lumbre si ustedes prometen no comerme.

Todos se ríen[5] cuando oyen las palabras del tlacuache. Pero el tlacuache les repite que él sí va a compartir la lumbre con todo el mundo.

[1] opossum
[2] fire, light
[3] star
[4] neighbors
[5] laughs

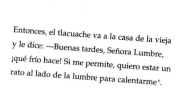

Entonces, el tlacuache va a la casa de la vieja y le dice: —Buenas tardes, Señora Lumbre, ¡qué frío hace! Si me permite, quiero estar un rato al lado de la lumbre para calentarme[6].

La vieja le permite al tlacuache acercarse[7] a la lumbre porque sabe que sí hace un frío terrible. En ese momento el animalito avanza y se pone la cola[8] en la lumbre. Entonces, sale rápidamente de la casa y le da la lumbre a todas las casas de la región.

Es por eso que hasta ahora los tlacuaches tienen la cola pelada[9].

[6] warm myself
[7] approach
[8] tail
[9] hairless

¿Comprendiste?
1. ¿Quién atrapa la lumbre?
2. ¿Quiere darle la lumbre a alguien?
3. ¿Qué dice el tlacuache a los vecinos?
4. ¿Cómo puede el tlacuache entrar a la casa de la vieja? ¿Qué le dice a ella?
5. ¿Cómo es que la gente recibe el fuego?

¿Qué piensas?
1. ¿Cuál es el tema principal de esta leyenda?
   a. Nos dice que los tlacuaches son animales muy generosos.
   b. Es una leyenda de por qué los tlacuaches tienen la cola pelada.
2. ¿Crees que tlacuache es una palabra española o una palabra mazateca? ¿Por qué?
3. ¿Qué otro animal podría haberles traído (could have brought) el fuego a las personas por tener la cola pelada?

● **¿Qué piensas?** asks students to think critically about the reading selection.

MOTIVATE TO COMMUNICATE ¡En español!

Encourage students to experience different cultures

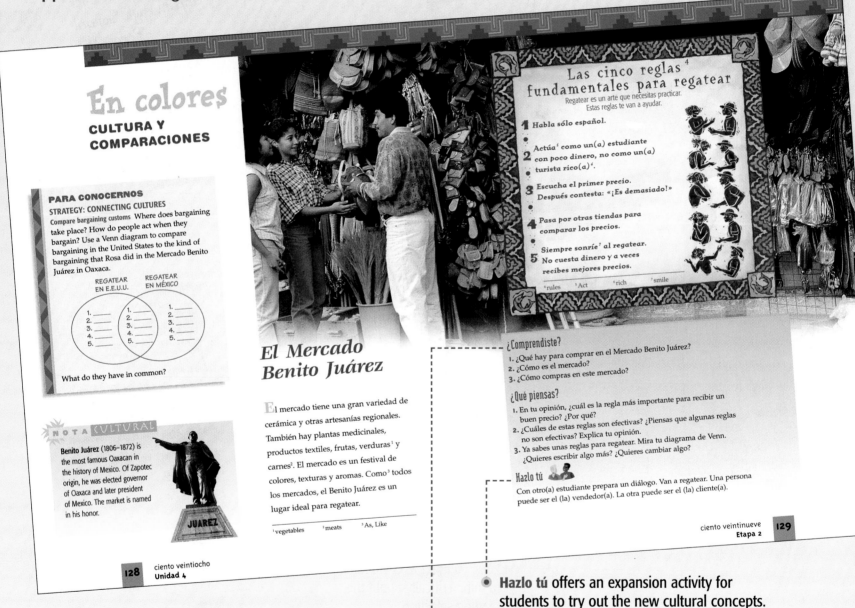

EXPAND · VIEWPOINTS

Focused cultural strategies improve students' ability to understand and appreciate the target culture.

En colores
CULTURA Y COMPARACIONES

PARA CONOCERNOS
STRATEGY: CONNECTING CULTURES
Compare bargaining customs Where does bargaining take place? How do people act when they bargain? Use a Venn diagram to compare bargaining in the United States to the kind of bargaining that Rosa did in the Mercado Benito Juárez in Oaxaca.

REGATEAR EN E.E.U.U.   REGATEAR EN MÉXICO

1. ___   1. ___   1. ___
2. ___   2. ___   2. ___
3. ___   3. ___   3. ___
4. ___   4. ___   4. ___
5. ___   5. ___   5. ___

What do they have in common?

NOTA CULTURAL

Benito Juárez (1806–1872) is the most famous Oaxacan in the history of Mexico. Of Zapotec origin, he was elected governor of Oaxaca and later president of Mexico. The market is named in his honor.

JUAREZ

El Mercado Benito Juárez

El mercado tiene una gran variedad de cerámica y otras artesanías regionales. También hay plantas medicinales, productos textiles, frutas, verduras¹ y carnes². El mercado es un festival de colores, texturas y aromas. Como³ todos los mercados, el Benito Juárez es un lugar ideal para regatear.

¹vegetables   ²meats   ³As, Like

Las cinco reglas⁴ fundamentales para regatear
Regatear es un arte que necesitas practicar. Estas reglas te van a ayudar.

1 Habla sólo español.

2 Actúa⁵ como un(a) estudiante con poco dinero, no como un(a) turista rico(a)⁶.

3 Escucha el primer precio. Después contesta: «¡Es demasiado!»

4 Pasa por otras tiendas para comparar los precios.

5 Siempre sonríe⁷ al regatear. No cuesta dinero y a veces recibes mejores precios.

⁴rules   ⁵Act   ⁶rich   ⁷smile

¿Comprendiste?
1. ¿Qué hay para comprar en el Mercado Benito Juárez?
2. ¿Cómo es el mercado?
3. ¿Cómo compras en este mercado?

¿Qué piensas?
1. En tu opinión, ¿cuál es la regla más importante para recibir un buen precio? ¿Por qué?
2. ¿Cuáles de estas reglas son efectivas? ¿Piensas que algunas reglas no son efectivas? Explica tu opinión.
3. Ya sabes unas reglas para regatear. Mira tu diagrama de Venn. ¿Quieres escribir algo más? ¿Quieres cambiar algo?

Hazlo tú
Con otro(a) estudiante prepara un diálogo. Van a regatear. Una persona puede ser el (la) vendedor(a). La otra puede ser el (la) cliente(a).

ciento veintinueve **129**
Etapa 2

ciento veintiocho **128**
Unidad 4

● **Hazlo tú** offers an expansion activity for students to try out the new cultural concepts.

● **¿Comprendiste?** asks students to recall the information in the selection.

● **Cultural strategies** help students understand their own culture and other cultures to broaden their world view.

"The cultural information is not merely added on at the end of the chapter but is an integral part of the lesson. Great job!"

Colleen Yarbrough
Canon McMillan Middle School
Canonsburg, PA

En colores

CULTURA Y COMPARACIONES

PARA CONOCERNOS

STRATEGY: CONNECTING CULTURES

Analyze and recommend Some areas depend on tourism for income, but sometimes local people are against it. Why is that so? Think of reasons for and against tourism.

Turismo: no	Turismo: sí
1.	1.
2.	2.
3.	3.

Based on your analysis, write three or more rules for being a good tourist.

NOTA CULTURAL

Today many Zapotec Indians support themselves through farming and traditional handicrafts such as weaving.

Monte Albán:

ruinas misteriosas

Para el concurso de Onda Internacional, Carlos visita Monte Albán. Saca fotos y escribe este artículo sobre una de las primeras culturas de Oaxaca.

El estado de Oaxaca es una importante región arqueológica. El lugar más famoso es Monte Albán, una de las primeras ciudades de Mesoamérica[1] y la vieja capital de los zapotecas[2]. Sabemos que la civilización de Monte Albán empieza por el año 500 a.C.[3] Pero los orígenes y el fin de esta civilización son un misterio fascinante.

[1] Middle America (Mexico and Central America)
[2] Zapotec Indians
[3] B.C.

Muchos turistas visitan Monte Albán todos los años para conocer sus pirámides, terrazas, tumbas y esculturas. La parte donde hay más exploración es la Plaza Central, centro de la vida social y religiosa de los zapotecas. Allí hay grandes plataformas, como el Juego de Pelota y la Galería de los Danzantes. Los arqueólogos no saben mucho sobre el Juego de Pelota. Tampoco saben qué representan los Danzantes. ¿Son figuras de hombres que danzan o son prisioneros[4]?

El Juego de Pelota

Aproximadamente entre los años 700 y 800 d.C.[5], los zapotecas abandonan Monte Albán. Luego, los mixtecas[6] usan el lugar. Hoy, descendientes de los dos grupos viven en las montañas y el valle de Oaxaca. Su cultura sigue presente en la lengua y las costumbres[7].

[4] prisoners
[5] A.D.
[6] Mixtec Indians
[7] customs

¿Comprendiste?

1. ¿Qué importancia tiene Monte Albán?
2. ¿Qué sabemos del fin de la civilización de Monte Albán?
3. ¿Qué pueden ver los turistas aquí?
4. ¿Qué saben los arqueólogos del Juego de Pelota o de los Danzantes?
5. ¿Hay zapotecas hoy en Oaxaca?

¿Qué piensas?

Eres un(a) turista en Monte Albán. En una hoja de papel, describe tu visita y tus reacciones. Mira las fotos para inspirarte.

156 ciento cincuenta y seis
Unidad 4

157

● **¿Qué piensas?** helps students to think critically about the target culture as well as their own culture.

MOTIVATE TO COMMUNICATE
¡En español!

Follow up with diagnostic review

The comprehensive review, correlated to the etapa objectives, thoroughly reviews and prepares the students to be successful for assessment.

● **The side column learning channel** helps students self-diagnose and review what they can do and where they can go to get help.

ETAPA 3

En uso
REPASO Y MÁS COMUNICACIÓN

OBJECTIVES
- Order food
- Request the check
- Talk about food
- Express extremes
- Say where you went

Now you can...
- order food.
- request the check.

To review
- affirmative and negative words, see p. 147.

ACTIVIDAD 1 En el restaurante

Lucía y Emilio están en un restaurante. Completa su diálogo con el mesero con la forma correcta de las siguientes palabras: **alguno, ninguno, algo, nada, alguien, nadie**. *(Hint: Lucía and Carlos are in a restaurant. Complete their conversation with the waiter using the correct form of the words given.)*

Lucía: Emilio, conozco a ___1___ que trabaja en este restaurante.
Emilio: ¿De verdad? Yo no conozco a ___2___ aquí. ¿Quién es?
Lucía: Un vecino. Prepara los postres.
Mesero: La especialidad es el bistec. No hay ___3___ bistec tan delicioso como el nuestro. Les doy ___4___ minutos para mirar el menú.

Mesero: ¿Están listos para pedir?
Emilio: Sí, para mí, la especialidad.
Lucía: Y yo quisiera las enchiladas y una ensalada.
Mesero: ¿Quieren ___5___ de tomar?
Emilio: Por ahora, ___6___ más. Después, vamos a compartir ___7___ postre.

Emilio: La cuenta, por favor.
Mesero: Sí, señor. Un momento.
Lucía: ¿Le dejamos ___8___ propina?
Emilio: No. Está incluida.

Now you can...
- talk about food.

To review
- stem-changing verbs: **e → i**, see p. 150.

ACTIVIDAD 2 El nuevo mesero

El nuevo mesero está aprendiendo. ¿Qué sirve? *(Hint: A new waiter is learning. What is he serving?)*

modelo
Isabel: arroz (lechuga)
*Cuando **Isabel** pide **arroz**, el mesero le sirve **lechuga**.*

1. Andrés y yo: enchiladas (pollo)
2. tú: una ensalada (pastel)
3. los señores Gálvez: un flan (pan)
4. yo: carne (un postre)
5. ella: una sopa (un sándwich)
6. nosotros: té (café)

Now you can...
- talk about food.
- express extremes.

To review
- the verb **gustar** + nouns, see p. 144.
- extremes, see p. 149.

ACTIVIDAD 3 ¡La comida es buenísima!

A todos les gusta comer. ¿Qué opinan de la comida? *(Hint: Everyone likes to eat. What is their opinion of the food?)*

modelo
yo / enchiladas / bueno
A mí me gustan **las enchiladas**. Son **buenísimas**.

1. mis hermanos / flan / rico
2. Jaime / papas fritas / bueno
3. tú / salsa / rico
4. yo / limonada / bueno
5. la señorita Anaya / arroz / bueno
6. nosotros / tacos / rico

Now you can...
- talk about food.

To review
- the verb **traer**, see p. 152.

ACTIVIDAD 4 ¡Una fiesta mexicana!

Hay una fiesta mexicana hoy. ¿Qué traen todos? *(Hint: Today is a Mexican celebration. What does everyone bring?)*

modelo
Dolores: salsa
Dolores trae la salsa.

1. yo: tenedores
2. Salvador: platos
3. nosotros: enchiladas
4. el profesor: arroz
5. Alex y Tito: ensalada
6. la directora: flan
7. tú: pastel
8. René y yo: limonada

Now you can...
- say where you went.

To review
- **fui/fuiste**, see p. 143.

ACTIVIDAD 5 ¿Adónde fuiste?

Tu amigo(a) acaba de ir de compras. Escribe tus preguntas y sus respuestas según el modelo. Tiene las siguientes cosas: **un disco compacto, pan, un collar, carne, un pastel, unos artículos de cuero y una novela**. *(Hint: Your friend just went shopping. Write your questions and your friend's answers, following the model and using the items mentioned.)*

modelo
pastelería
Tú: ¿Fuiste a la **pastelería**?
Tu amigo(a): Sí, fui para comprar un pastel.

1. joyería
2. librería
3. panadería
4. carnicería
5. tienda de música
6. mercado

- **Speaking strategies** help students become better communicators by expanding their repertoire of expressions through tone of voice, personalization, gestures, etc.

"En uso is really great.... This is a good way to complete the etapa before testing."

Alma Hernandez
Alamo Junior High School
Midland, TX

- **En tu propia voz** prompts students with a short writing assignment to sharpen their language skills.

ACTIVIDAD 6 ¡Tengo hambre!

PARA CONVERSAR

STRATEGY: SPEAKING

Borrow useful expressions Here are some useful expressions for agreeing and accepting (**está bien, perfecto**) and for refusing (**no quiero…, por ahora nada más**). Use them in your conversation in the restaurant.

Estás en un restaurante. Pide un mínimo de tres cosas. Después, habla de la comida y pide la cuenta. Otro(a) estudiante va a ser el (la) mesero(a). Cambien de papel. *(Hint: You're in a restaurant. Order at least three things from the server. Then talk about the food and ask for the check. Another student will be the server. Change roles.)*

Quisiera…

¿Me trae…?

Me gustaría…

¿Está incluido(a)…?

ACTIVIDAD 7 ¡Una fiesta!

Trabajando en grupos, hablen de dos cosas que cada persona va a traer a una fiesta. *(Hint: Working in groups, talk about two things that each person is going to bring to a party.)*

modelo

Sara: Me gusta la limonada. Traigo limonada y algunos vasos.

José: Me gustan las enchiladas y la música. Traigo enchiladas y una guitarra.

ACTIVIDAD 8 En tu propia voz

Escritura Trabajas en un restaurante mexicano. Escribe un párrafo para una guía turística. *(Hint: You work in a Mexican restaurant. Write a paragraph as a guide for a tourist.)*

modelo

Restaurante Azteca ¿Le gusta la salsa picante? En el restaurante Azteca servimos una salsa deliciosa y muy picante. La especialidad de la casa es…

En la comunidad

Grendale is a high school student in Nevada. He sometimes speaks Spanish with coworkers when he volunteers at a nursing home. At his part-time job, he uses Spanish with Mexican, South American, and Spanish tourists who come to the store. He has a friend from Uruguay who is an exchange student, and they often speak in Spanish. Do you speak Spanish with any of your friends?

En resumen
REPASO DE VOCABULARIO

ORDERING FOOD

¿Me ayuda a pedir?	Could you help me order?
¿Me trae…?	Could you bring me…?
el menú	menu
pedir	to ask for, to order
Quisiera…	I would like…

At the Restaurant

el (la) mesero(a)	waiter (waitress)
el restaurante	restaurant
servir	to serve
traer	to bring

Place Setting

la cuchara	spoon
el cuchillo	knife
la taza	cup
el tenedor	fork

EXPRESSING EXTREMES

riquísimo(a)	very tasty

REQUESTING THE CHECK

¿Cuánto es?	How much is it?
¿Cuánto le doy de propina?	How much do I tip?
la cuenta	bill, check
La cuenta, por favor.	The check, please.
Es aparte.	Separate checks.
¿Está incluido(a)…?	Is… included?
la propina	tip

SAYING WHERE YOU WENT

Fui…/Fuiste…	I went…/You went…

TALKING ABOUT FOOD

caliente	hot, warm
delicioso(a)	delicious
dulce	sweet
picante	spicy
rico(a)	tasty
vegetariano(a)	vegetarian

Food

el arroz	rice
el azúcar	sugar
el bistec	steak
la carne	meat
la enchilada	enchilada
la ensalada	salad
la lechuga	lettuce
el pan	bread
el pollo	chicken
el queso	cheese
la salsa	salsa
la sopa	soup

Beverages

la bebida	beverage, drink
el café	coffee
la limonada	lemonade
el té	tea

Desserts

el flan	caramel custard dessert
el pan dulce	sweet roll
el pastel	cake
el postre	dessert

OTHER WORDS AND PHRASES

algo	something
alguien	someone
alguno(a)	some
desayunar	to have breakfast
el desayuno	breakfast
la lengua	language
listo(a)	ready
nada	nothing
nadie	no one
ninguno(a)	none, not any
poner	to put
poner la mesa	to set the table
el pueblo	town, village
sin	without
tampoco	neither, either
todavía	still, yet

Juego

Cada miembro de la familia Martínez quiere algo diferente. ¡Pobre Pablo, el mesero! Pablo es inteligente y trae lo que quieren. ¿Qué les sirve a 1) Marco, 2) Martina y 3) Marisol?

Marco Martínez: Quiero algo líquido y caliente con proteínas.

Martina Martínez: Quiero algo verde y vegetariano.

Marisol Martínez: Quiero algo dulce para mi café.

Marco   Martina   Marisol

- **En la comunidad,** which occurs once in every unit, features real students using their Spanish in their own community.

MOTIVATE TO COMMUNICATE

¡En español!

Integrates themes and concepts for communication application

Engage students with highly motivating interdisciplinary connections and thematic projects.

- **Conexiones** thematically links and expands to other subject areas for better long term retention.

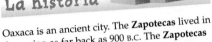

Conexiones
OTRAS DISCIPLINAS Y PROYECTOS

La historia

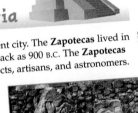

Oaxaca is an ancient city. The **Zapotecas** lived in the region as far back as 900 B.C. The **Zapotecas** were great architects, artisans, and astronomers. They created a number system, a calendar, hieroglyphic writing, and extraordinary ceramics and jewelry.

Around 800 A.D., Zapotecan culture began to decline as a result of the arrival of another civilization, known as the **Mixtecas**. The **Mixtecas** practiced agriculture, hunting, and fishing. They made beautiful ornaments in gold, silver, and copper. Today, in Oaxaca, the presence of both these cultures is still very much alive.

Do you think these **danzantes zapotecas** are ancient or modern? Why do you think so?

What do you think this piece of **mixteca** jewelry is made of? What kind of jewelry is it?

Las matemáticas

Did you know that every country in the world has its own form of money? Did you know that the currencies of all countries are related to each other and that they shift in value?

The following is a list of the currencies of some Spanish-speaking countri and their value per U.S. dollar. This informa changes from day to day, so check on the Internet or with a local bank or newspaper current rates.

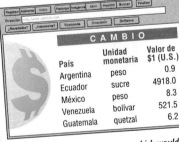

CAMBIO

País	Unidad monetaria	Valor de $1 (U.S.)
Argentina	peso	0.9
Ecuador	sucre	4918.0
México	peso	8.3
Venezuela	bolívar	521.5
Guatemala	quetzal	6.2

1. *According to the chart above, which would b worth the most: 4,000 sucres, 300 bolívares, 10 quetzales?*

2. *If you had a choice between buying a gift f* **pesos argentinos** *or* **cincuenta pesos mex** *which currency would you choose to use?*

162   ciento sesenta y dos
Unidad 4

• **Proyecto cultural** invites students to participate in a cultural scenario and build upon what they've learned.

> "I am so impressed with this program. The interdisciplinary features provide a greater context and bring everything together for the student."
>
> Sally Nickerson
> Broadview Middle School
> Burlington, NC

Proyecto cultural

As a class project, write a short play about market day in Oaxaca. Half the class will be sellers at the market and half will be buyers. Buyers will bargain with the sellers to get the best prices. To prepare for market day, do the following:

1. Use classroom objects or bring in items from home to be "sold." Make a list with realistic prices in pesos for each item.

2. Your teacher will help you make play money in Mexican pesos. Buyers will need enough pesos to purchase one or two items. Sellers will need enough pesos to make change.

3. Write the script and put on the play. You may want to videotape your production to show other Spanish classes or your family.

These woman display their backstrap weaving at a market in Oaxaca.

Objeto	Precio
libro	27 pesos
video	57 pesos
aretes	70 pesos
reloj	120 pesos

ciento sesenta y tres 163
Unidad 4

MOTIVATE TO COMMUNICATE
¡En español!

Implement ideas and lesson plans easily and effectively

CREATIVE AND PRACTICAL

The Ampliación and Etapa Overview in the Teacher's Edition offer outstanding support to make teaching Spanish adaptable to every situation.

● **Ampliación** features multi-modal activities that spark students' excitement with new ways to learn language and culture.

Ampliación

These activities may be used at various points in the Unit 4 sequence.

■ For Block Schedule, you may find that these projects will provide a welcome change of pace while reviewing and reinforcing the material presented in the unit. See the **Block Scheduling Copymasters**.

PROJECTS

Create a tourist guide for Oaxaca. Divide the class into groups, assigning each group research on a particular aspect of the guide:

1. Geography   4. Main tourist attractions
2. History   5. Art and music
3. Museums   6. Crafts

Each group is responsible for writing and illustrating its section of the guide. The completed project may be duplicated and published for display, or shared with other Spanish classes or family members.

PACING SUGGESTION: Have students begin research at the beginning of the unit. Final projects are completed at the end of Unit 4.

Film or record an audiovisual guide for bargaining in a **mercado**. Include at least four different dialogs scripted by the students showing both successful and unsuccessful bargaining interactions.

PACING SUGGESTION: Upon completion of Etapa 2.

STORYTELLING

Rosa al mercado After reviewing bargaining vocabulary, model a mini-story (using puppets, student actors, or pictures from the text) that students will retell and revise:

Rosa va al mercado. Mañana es el cumpleaños de su mamá. Rosa le pregunta al vendedor, "¿Me deja ver un anillo de plata?" El vendedor le deja ver un anillo de plata. Rosa pregunta, "¿Cuánto cuesta el anillo?" El vendedor dice, "100 pesos." Rosa regatea con el vendedor. Rosa le dice, "Quiero comprar el anillo pero es muy caro. Le puedo ofrecer 90 pesos." El vendedor acepta.

Pause as the story is being told so that students may fill in words and act out gestures. Students then write, narrate, and read aloud a longer main story. This new version should include vocabulary from the previous story.

Tú al mercado Ask students to create their own shopping stories. They may imagine shopping in a mall, a market, small shops, or even by phone.

PACING SUGGESTION: Upon completion of Etapa 2.

BULLETIN BOARD/POSTERS

Bulletin Board Plan ahead: Contact local travel agencies for maps and brochures on Oaxaca. To begin the unit, ask students to create mind maps to activate prior knowledge after looking at the bulletin board for 2 minutes. Add the mind maps to the bulletin board.

Posters Have students create •**Travel** posters for Oaxaca •**Museum** or artisan posters •**Magazine/newspaper** posters for stores with items and prices •**Garage sale** posters with items listed

ESTADOS UNIDOS

MÉXICO

OAXACA

GUATEMALA

OAXACA

GAMES

¿Me lo vendes?
Divide the class in half. Give half of the students in the class a total of 100 pesos in play money (bills). Give the other half pictures of items to sell. Have students call a local bank or check the Internet for the current exchange rate. Tell students they must establish a price for each item. The sellers should try to get as much money for their items as possible, while the buyers should try to buy as many items as possible. Give the class 10 minutes to circulate and bargain with one another. At the end of 10 minutes, the seller with the most money and the buyer with the most objects win.

PACING SUGGESTION: Upon completion of Etapa 2.

RECIPE

Chocolate oaxaqueño is a well-known specialty of Oaxaca. It is sold in the form of powder, sticks, or bars and used in cooking as well as in making hot chocolate. Although you may not be able to purchase authentic Oaxacan chocolate locally, you can still prepare a tasty version of **chocolate oaxaqueño** with your students.

El tesoro del centro comercial

Photocopy a map of a local shopping center and give each student a copy. Decide, as a class, on a common starting point (usually the entrance to the mall). Divide the class into pairs. Instruct one of the players in each pair to draw (in pencil) a treasure chest somewhere on the map, without letting the partner see the map or the location of the treasure. Tell the partner who "hid" the treasure that he/she must now guide his/her partner to the treasure by giving directions in Spanish. Once students are familiar with the game, they can erase the original treasure chests and play again as a timed competition between pairs.

PACING SUGGESTION: Use as review of directions at any point in the unit.

MUSIC

An important festival of music and dance is held in Oaxaca every July. The **Guelaguetza** (gay-la-**gay**-tzah), which means "deep and sincere offering" in the Zapotec language, celebrates a ceremony that brought together the people of the seven regions of the state in times of great need. Music samples are available on your *Canciones* Cassette or CD. Videos and recordings are available through the Tourist Board of Oaxaca. Contact www.mcdougallittell.com for more information.

HANDS-ON CRAFTS

Work with the art department to make **animalitos** in clay or homemade play dough. As students paint and decorate their creations, review colors in Spanish, adding new vocabulary if needed. Completed projects may be displayed at your school, at a local elementary school, or at the local library.

Receta

Chocolate oaxaqueño
225 g (1/2 lb.) de chocolate amargo en trozos
2 litros (2 quarts) de leche
1/4 taza de agua
azúcar y canela al gusto

Ponga el agua a hervir en una cacerola pequeña. Añada el chocolate y derrítalo a fuego lento, sin dejar de mezclar. Eche la leche, siga calentando y con una batidora, bata hasta que se forme espuma. Añada azúcar y canela al gusto. Sirva inmediatamente en tazas pequeñas. ¡Mmmmm!—¡qué rico!

● **Easy-to-prepare recipes** give students a delicious opportunity to experience new cultural cuisines.

- **At-a-glance overview** outlines the objectives, strategies and program resources for time-saving support.

"WOW! ¡En español! has it all. I'd love to teach from this book."

Kathleen Gliewe
Helena Middle School
Helena, MT

UNIDAD 4 ETAPA **3** ¿QUÉ HACER EN OAXACA?
pages 134–163

Planning Guide CLASSROOM MANAGEMENT

OBJECTIVES

Communication
- Talk about food *pp. 136–137*
- Order food and request the check *pp. 138–139*
- Express extremes *pp. 138–139, 149*
- Say where you went *pp. 138–139*

Grammar
- Use the verb **poner** *p. 143*
- Use **gustar** to talk about things you like *pp. 144–145*
- Use affirmative and negative words *pp. 147–148*
- Use stem-changing verbs: e → i *pp. 150–151*

Pronunciation
- Pronunciation of **g** *p. 153*
- Dictation *TE p. 153*

Culture
- Oaxacan cuisine *p. 144*
- Zapotec Indians *p. 156*
- Monte Albán *pp. 156–157*

♻ Recycling
- Stores *p. 143*
- Prepositions of location *p. 143*
- Clothing *p. 145*
- Direct object pronouns *p. 152*

STRATEGIES

Listening Strategies
- Integrate your skills *p. 138*

Speaking Strategies
- Vary ways to express preferences *p. 141*
- Borrow useful expressions *p. 160*

Reading Strategies
- Making a story map *p. 154*
- Look for cognates *TE p. 157*

Writing Strategies
- Brainstorm details, then organize your information *TE p. 160*

Connecting Cultures Strategies
- Recognize variations in vocabulary *p. 143*
- Consider the effects of tourism from the point of view of the inhabitants *pp. 156–157*
- Connect and compare what you know about jobs in your community to help you learn about jobs in a new community *pp. 156–157, 160*

PROGRAM RESOURCES

📖 Print
- *Más práctica* Workbook PE *pp. 17–24*
- Block Scheduling Copymasters
- Unit 4 Resource Book
  Más práctica Workbook TE *pp. 103–110*
  Information Gap Activities *pp. 119–122*
- Family Involvement *pp. 123–124*
- Video Activities *pp. 125–127*
- Videoscript *pp. 128–130*
- Audioscript *pp. 131–134*
- Assessment Program, Unit 4 Etapa 3 *pp. 135–178*
- Answer Keys *pp. 179–200*

🎧 Audiovisual
- Audio Program Cassettes 12A, 12B / CD 12
- *Canciones* Cassette / CD
- Video Program Videotape 4 / Videodisc 2B
- Overhead Transparencies M1–M5; GO1–GO5; 106, 127–136

💻 Technology
- Electronic Teacher Tools/Test Generator
- *Intrigas y aventuras* CD-ROM, Disc 1
- www.mcdougallittell.com

✓ Assessment Program Options
- Cooperative Quizzes (Unit 4 Resource Book)
- Etapa Exam Forms A and B (Unit 4 Resource Book)
- *Para hispanohablantes* Etapa Exam (Unit 4 Resource Book)
- Portfolio Assessment (Unit 4 Resource Book)
- Unit 4 Comprehensive Test (Unit 4 Resource Book)
- *Para hispanohablantes* Unit 4 Comprehensive Test (Unit 4 Resource Book)
- Multiple Choice Test Questions (Unit 4 Resource Book)
- Audio Program Testing Cassette T2 / CD T2
- Electronic Teacher Tools/Test Generator

Native Speakers
- *Para hispanohablantes* Workbook PE, *pp. 17–24*
- *Para hispanohablantes* Workbook TE (Unit 4 Resource Book)
- *Para hispanohablantes* Etapa Exam (Unit 4 Resource Book)
- *Para hispanohablantes* Unit 4 Comprehensive Test (Unit 4 Resource Book)
- Audio *Para hispanohablantes* Cassettes 12A, 12B, T2 / CD 12, T2
- Audioscript *Para hispanohablantes* (Unit 4 Resource Book)

133A Planning Guide • UNIDAD 4 Etapa 3

Student Text Listening Activity Scripts

Sofía   Rosa   Carlos   Mesero

📹 Videoscript: Diálogo *pages 138–139*
- Videotape 4 • Videodisc 2B

U4E3 • En vivo (Diálogo)

Search Chapter 7, Play to 8

- Use the videoscript with **Actividades 1, 2** pages 140–141

Sofía: Tienes que decirme. ¿Cómo conoces a Carlos?
Rosa: ¡Es un secreto!
Sofía: ¡Por favor, Rosa!
Rosa: No puedo decirte. Las promesas son promesas.
Sofía: ¡Pero soy tu prima, Rosa! ¡Me tienes que decir!
Rosa: Está bien, está bien. Conozco a Carlos porque fui a la tienda de su papá para pedir direcciones para llegar a tu casa.
Sofía: ¡Ah!, ¿es todo? ¿No son amigos por Internet?
Rosa: No, ¡qué va! Qué imaginación tienes.
Mesero: Buenas tardes, Carlos. Buenas tardes, señoritas. Bienvenidos al restaurante La Madre Tierra. Aquí tienen el menú.
Carlos: ¿Nos puede traer pan, por favor?
Mesero: Sí, cómo no. Enseguida se lo traigo.
Rosa: Yo quiero un plato tradicional de Oaxaca. ¿Qué pido?
Carlos: La especialidad de la casa es una combinación de algunos platos regionales. Tiene mole negro y tasajo. Es riquísima.
Sofía: Yo voy a pedir una ensalada mixta y pollo.
Rosa: Y tú, Carlos, ¿qué pides normalmente?
Carlos: Me gustan las enchiladas, pero ahora tengo ganas de comer carne. Voy a pedir bistec asado. Viene con arroz y frijoles.
Mesero: ¿Listos para pedir?
Sofía: Sí, señor. Para mí, una ensalada mixta y pollo.
Rosa: Para mí, la especialidad de la casa.
Mesero: ¿Y para el señor?
Carlos: Un bistec asado.
Mesero: ¿Algo de tomar?
Sofía: Una limonada para mí.
Rosa: Agua mineral, por favor.
Carlos: Un refresco de naranja.
Mesero: Muy bien. ¿Y de postre? Los postres ricos son otra especialidad de la casa. Son buenísimos.
Sofía: Por ahora, nada más. El postre lo pedimos después, gracias.
Mesero: Para servirles.
Rosa: Oye, Carlos, ¿cómo va tu proyecto para el concurso?
Carlos: Muy bien. Mi proyecto para el concurso es sobre las ruinas de Monte Albán. Es fascinante la historia de México.
Rosa: ¿Ya fuiste a Monte Albán?
Carlos: Sí, fui a Monte Albán el otro día para sacar fotos. Hay mucho que ver: tumbas, altares ceremoniales y pirámides. El Centro Ceremonial es algo increíble. Desde arriba, hay unas vistas fabulosas. Los Danzantes son unas figuras muy curiosas. Y el Juego de Pelota es antiguo e interesante. El Palacio es maravilloso. Las ruinas de Monte Albán son impresionantes. ¡Es un lugar mágico!
Rosa: Estoy segura de que tú vas a ganar el concurso. Tu proyecto va a presentar el pasado fascinante de los mexicanos. Me gusta mucho tu idea para el concurso.
Mesero: ¿Algo más, jóvenes?
Sofía: Qué crees, Rosa, ¿pido un postre y lo compartimos?
Rosa: Bueno, si pedimos algo pequeño.
Mesero: ¿Un flan, señoritas? Lo sirvo en dos platos con dos cucharas.
Sofía: Perfecto, señor. Muchas gracias.
Mesero: ¿Y para usted?
Carlos: No quiero ningún postre, pero ¿me puede traer la cuenta, por favor? Tengo prisa.
Mesero: Sí, cómo no.
Sofía: El mesero es muy amable y sirve muy bien.
Carlos: Sí, el mesero es muy amable. Me gusta la gente de este restaurante. ¡Quisiera comer aquí todos los días!
Rosa: ¡Ah! ¡Un momento! Aquí tienes tu mapa. Gracias.
Carlos: Al contrario.

🎬 ¿Qué pasa? *page 142*

1. Le gusta comer los postres. Está comiendo un flan.
2. No tiene mucha hambre. Prefiere comer sólo fruta.
3. Está enfermo. Quiere comer sopa de pollo.
4. Tiene mucha sed. Está tomando una limonada.

🎬 ¿A quién? *page 152*

Carlos: ¡Qué hambre tengo! ¿Qué vas a pedir, Elena?
Elena: Voy a pedir unas enchiladas de carne.
Carlos: Tú siempre pides enchiladas.
Elena: Sí, tienes razón. Siempre las pido. Me gustan mucho y son riquísimas aquí. ¿Y tú?
Carlos: Voy a pedir un bistec y papas fritas.
Elena: ¿Y para beber?
Carlos: Voy a tomar algún refresco.
Elena: Y yo un té.
Carlos: De postre, voy a pedir un flan. ¿Y tú?
Elena: No tengo tanta hambre como tú. No voy a pedir ningún postre.

Quick Start Review Answers

p. 138 Food vocabulary
1. el plato, el tenedor, el cuchillo, la taza
2. el arroz, el bistec, el pollo, una enchilada
3. la limonada, el café, el té, el refresco

3. A mi mejor amiga le gustan las papas fritas.
4. A mi tía Ana le gusta el pan dulce.
5. A Tomás le gustan las enchiladas.

p. 140 Dialog review
1. tienda
2. mole
3. ensalada
4. postres
5. ningún

p. 150 Affirmative and negative words
1. nadie
2. alguien
3. algo
4. tampoco
5. algún

p. 147 Likes and dislikes
Answers will vary. Answers could include:
1. A mi hermano le gusta la comida picante.
2. A mis padres les gusta la sopa vegetariana.

p. 156 In a restaurant
Answers will vary. Answers could include:
1. el pan
2. la especialidad de la casa
3. la propina
4. la comida picante
5. la carne

Listening Scripts • UNIDAD 4 Etapa 3 133B

- **Listening scripts** in the Teacher's Edition provide practical information needed for easier lesson preparation.

MOTIVATE TO COMMUNICATE
¡En español!

Suggests practical teaching ideas for lesson planning

FLEXIBLE AND EXCEPTIONAL

The comprehensive Teacher's Edition and resource materials provide the support you need to introduce, explain, and expand your lessons.

• **Time-saving lessons** present sequenced teaching suggestions and ideas.

UNIDAD 4 ETAPA 3 Pacing Guide

Sample Lesson Plan - 45 Minute Schedule

DAY 1

Etapa Opener
• Quick Start Review (TE, p. 134) 5 MIN.
• Anticipate/Activate prior knowledge: Have students look at the *Etapa* Opener and answer the *¿Qué ves?* questions, p. 134. 10 MIN.

En contexto: Vocabulario
• Quick Start Review (TE, p. 136) 5 MIN.
• Have students use context and pictures to learn *Etapa* vocabulary. 10 MIN.
• Have students work in pairs to answer the *Preguntas personales*, p. 137. 5 MIN.
• Ask pairs to share each other's answers to *Preguntas personales*, p. 137. 5 MIN.

DAY 2

En vivo: Diálogo
• Quick Start Review (TE, p. 138) 5 MIN.
• Review the Listening Strategy, p. 138. 5 MIN.
• Play audio or show video for the dialog, pp. 138–139. 10 MIN.
• Replay as needed. 5 MIN.
• Read the dialog aloud, having students take the roles of characters. 10 MIN.
• Use the Situational OHTs for additional vocabulary practice. 10 MIN.

Homework Option:
• Video Activities, Unit 4 Resource Book, pp. 125–127.

DAY 3

En acción: Vocabulario y gramática
• Check homework. 5 MIN.
• Quick Start Review (TE, p. 140) 5 MIN.
• Ask students for a summary of the dialog to check recall. 5 MIN.
• Play the video/audio; have students do *Actividades* 1 and 2 orally. 10 MIN.
• Present the *Vocabulario*, p. 141. 5 MIN.
• Present the Speaking Strategy, p. 141. 5 MIN.
• Have students work in pairs to complete *Actividad* 3. 10 MIN.

DAY 4

En acción (cont.)
• Have students work in pairs on *Actividad* 4. 5 MIN.
• Ask selected pairs to recite the captions they wrote for scenes in *Actividad* 4. 5 MIN.
• Play the audio. Have students stay in their pairs to do *Actividad* 5. 5 MIN.
• Keep students in their pairs to do *Actividad* 6. 5 MIN.
• Ask pairs to volunteer to model their conversations from *Actividad* 6. 10 MIN.
• Mix up the pairs and have students do *Actividad* 7. 5 MIN.
• Ask a few pairs to model setting the table, as in *Actividad* 7, naming each item as they place it. 5 MIN.
• Read and discuss the *También se dice*, p. 143. 5 MIN.

DAY 5

En acción (cont.)
• Quick Start Review (TE, p. 144) 5 MIN.
• Present *Gramática:* Using *gustar* to Talk About Things You Like. 10 MIN.
• Work orally with the class to do *Actividad* 8. 5 MIN.
• Model *Actividad* 9 and discuss possible answers. 5 MIN.
• Have students write their answers to *Actividad* 9. 10 MIN.
• Read and discuss the *Apoyo para estudiar*, p. 145. 5 MIN.
• Quick Wrap-up (TE, p. 145) 5 MIN.

Homework Option:
• *Más práctica* Workbook, p. 21. *Para hispanohablantes* Workbook, p. 19.

DAY 6

En acción (cont.)
• Check homework. 5 MIN.
• Quick Start Review (TE, p. 147) 5 MIN.
• Have students work in groups to complete *Actividad* 10. 10 MIN.
• Call on some groups to report their findings from *Actividad* 10 to the class. 5 MIN.
• Present *Gramática:* Affirmative and Negative Words. 10 MIN.
• Assign *Actividad* 11. 5 MIN.
• Ask pairs of students to use their responses to *Actividad* 11 to perform a dialog. 5 MIN.

DAY 7

En acción (cont.)
• Have students work in pairs on *Actividad* 12. 5 MIN.
• Ask selected pairs to model questioning, answering, and changing your mind from *Actividad* 12. 10 MIN.
• Assign *Actividad* 13. 5 MIN.
• Read and discuss the *Conexiones*, p. 149. 5 MIN.
• Have students work in pairs to complete the *Para hacer*, p. 149. 10 MIN.
• Read and discuss the *Nota*, p. 149, and model *Actividad* 14. 5 MIN.
• Have students write their responses to *Actividad* 14. 5 MIN.

Homework Option:
• *Más práctica* Workbook, pp. 22–23. *Para hispanohablantes* Workbook, pp. 20–21.

DAY 8

En acción (cont.)
• Check homework. 5 MIN.
• Quick Start Review (TE, p. 150) 5 MIN.
• Discuss the Language Note, TE, p. 149. 5 MIN.
• Present *Gramática:* Stem-Changing Verbs: $e \rightarrow i$, and the *Vocabulario*, p. 150. 10 MIN.
• Have students write their responses to *Actividad* 15. 5 MIN.
• Ask volunteers to read their responses to *Actividad* 15. 5 MIN.
• Model *Actividad* 16, then ask students write their responses. 10 MIN.

Homework Option:
• *Más práctica* Workbook, p 24. *Para hispanohablantes* Workbook, p. 22

"This program... seems very detailed, well thought out, and offers the teacher many options."

Leela Scanlon
West Middle School
Andover, MA

DAY 9

En acción (cont.)
- Check homework. 5 MIN.
- Read and discuss the *Nota*, p. 151. 5 MIN.
- Have students work in pairs on *Actividad* 17. 5 MIN.
- Ask selected pairs to model their conversations from *Actividad* 17. 5 MIN.
- Play the audio. Assign *Actividad* 18. 5 MIN.
- Present and practice the *Vocabulario*, p. 152. 5 MIN.
- Read and discuss the *Nota*, p. 152. 5 MIN.
- Assign pairs to work on *Actividad* 19. 5 MIN.
- Ask volunteers to model their conversations in *Actividad* 19. 5 MIN.

DAY 10

En acción (cont.)
- Have students work in pairs on *Actividad* 20. 5 MIN.
- Call on pairs to model their completed conversations from *Actividad* 20. 5 MIN.
- Have students work in groups of three to complete *Actividad* 21. 10 MIN.
- Ask groups to volunteer to perform their dialogs from *Actividad* 21 for the class. 5 MIN.
- Use Information Gap Activities, Unit 4 Resource Book, pp. 120–121. 5 MIN.
- *Más comunicación*, p. R12. 5 MIN.
- Play the audio and have students practice the *Trabalenguas*, p. 153. 10 MIN.

DAY 11

En voces: Lectura
- Quick Start Review (TE, p. 154) 5 MIN.
- Present the Reading Strategy, p. 154. 5 MIN.
- Have volunteers read the selection aloud. 15 MIN.
- Work orally with students on the *¿Comprendiste?* questions (Answers, TE, p. 155). 10 MIN.
- Discuss the *¿Qué piensas?* questions, p. 155. 10 MIN.

Homework Option:
- Have students write their answers to the *¿Qué piensas?* questions, p. 155.

DAY 12

En colores: Cultura y comparaciones
- Check homework. 5 MIN.
- Quick Start Review (TE, p. 156) 5 MIN.
- Discuss the Connecting Cultures Strategy, p. 156. 5 MIN.
- Brainstorm some rules for being a good tourist. 5 MIN.
- Have volunteers read the selection aloud. 10 MIN.
- Work orally with students to answer the *¿Comprendiste?* questions. (Answers, TE, p. 157). 10 MIN.
- Discuss the *¿Qué piensas?* questions, p. 157. 5 MIN.

DAY 13

En uso: Repaso y más comunicación
- Quick Start Review (TE, p. 158) 5 MIN.
- Assign *Actividad* 1. 5 MIN.
- Work orally with students to complete *Actividades* 2–3. 10 MIN.
- Have students read and think about *Actividades* 4–5. 5 MIN.
- Call on students to give oral responses to *Actividades* 4–5. 10 MIN.
- Present the Speaking Strategy, p. 160. 5 MIN.
- Have students work in pairs on *Actividad* 6. 5 MIN.

Homework Option:
- Have students review all of the *Gramática* boxes in *Etapa* 3.

DAY 14

En uso (cont.)
- Quick Start Review (TE, p. 161) 5 MIN.
- Review grammar questions as needed. 5 MIN.
- Have students work in groups on *Actividad* 7. 5 MIN.
- Ask groups to share their work from *Actividad* 7. 5 MIN.

En tu propia voz: Escritura
- Have students work independently to complete the writing activity, *Actividad* 8. 10 MIN.
- Ask volunteers to read their work from *Actividad* 8. 5 MIN.

En resumen: Repaso de vocabulario
- Review *Etapa* 3 vocabulary. 10 MIN.

Homework Option:
- Have students study for the *Etapa* exam.

DAY 15

En resumen: Repaso de vocabulario
- Answer questions related to *Etapa* 3 content. 10 MIN.
- Complete *Etapa* exam. 25 MIN.

Conexiones
- Have students read the *Conexiones*, pp. 162–163, as they complete the exam.

Classroom Management Tip

Vary classroom activities Give students opportunities to get information from a variety of sources and combine it into interesting reports or displays.

Set up a computer Learning Center where students can access the Internet and online encyclopedia sources for information about indigenous groups in Mexico. Borrow specialty books from your school or local library that provide visual as well as textual information about Mexico's varied past. Access to these sources of information will enhance students' appreciation of the richness of Mexico's history.

Classroom Management Tips offer teachers practical suggestions for pacing and variety.

Pacing Guide • UNIDAD 4 Etapa 3 **133D**

MOTIVATE
TO COMMUNICATE
¡En español!

Support middle school students' varied learning styles & ability levels

The Middle School Teacher's Edition and ancillaries offer strategies that address the multiple intelligences, different ability levels, and native-speaker needs.

● **Middle School Classroom Community** provides paired, group, and cooperative learning activities to help build your classroom community of Spanish speakers.

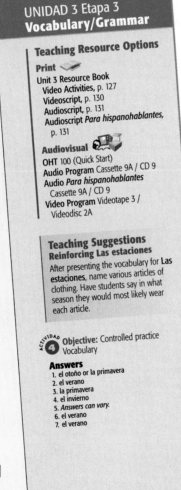

UNIDAD 3 Etapa 3
Vocabulary/Grammar

Teaching Resource Options

Print
Unit 3 Resource Book
  Video Activities, p. 127
  Videoscript, p. 130
  Audioscript, p. 131
  Audioscript *Para hispanohablantes*, p. 131

Audiovisual
OHT 100 (Quick Start)
Audio Program Cassette 9A / CD 9
Audio *Para hispanohablantes*
  Cassette 9A / CD 9
Video Program Videotape 3 /
  Videodisc 2A

Teaching Suggestions
Reinforcing Las estaciones
After presenting the vocabulary for **Las estaciones**, name various articles of clothing. Have students say in what season they would most likely wear each article.

ACTIVIDAD 4 Objective: Controlled practice
  Vocabulary

Answers
1. el otoño or la primavera
2. el verano
3. la primavera
4. el invierno
5. *Answers can vary.*
6. el verano
7. el verano

Vocabulario

Las estaciones

el verano — tomar el sol — el desierto — el bronceador — los shorts

el otoño — el viento — la montaña — el río

el invierno — el lago — cero grados

la primavera — la tormenta — el impermeable

¿Qué actividad te gusta hacer en cada estación?

ACTIVIDAD 4 ¿En qué estación?

Hablar/Leer Identify the season in which the following comments were probably made. Some items may have more than one right answer.

modelo
¡Vamos a la playa!
El verano.

1. Mira los árboles. ¡Qué colores tan bonitos!
2. Pero, ¿dónde está mi bronceador?
3. ¡Por fin no nieva!
4. ¿Quieres ir conmigo al lago a patinar sobre hielo?
5. ¡Ay, llueve otra vez! ¿Dónde está mi impermeable?
6. Vamos al río a nadar, ¿quieres?
7. Como no tengo clases, tengo mucho tiempo libre.

NOTA CULTURAL
El Yunque is a rain forest. All rain forests have four zones. They are (from lowest to highest) the floor, the understory, the canopy, and the emergent layer. Some zones are more humid than others. Some get more sunlight. Each is a habitat for different kinds of animals and plants.

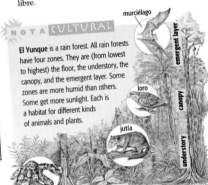

murciélago · emergent layer · loro · canopy · jutía · understory · floor · serpiente

252 doscientos cincuenta y dos
Unidad 3

Middle School Classroom Community

TPR Find or make posters illustrating each season. Have students count off. Tell them to gather at the poster for the most appropriate season for each activity you call out. (Example: **Uno–nadar en el océano**)

Storytelling Student 1 names an item of clothing that can or cannot be worn in a rainforest. Student 2 repeats this and adds his or her own sentence: **Me llevo los shorts. No me llevo el abrigo.**

Portfolio Have students use the information gathered in **Actividad 5** to make a poster showing seasonal activities in your region.

Rubric

Criteria	Scale	
Accuracy of information	1 2 3 4 5	A = 13–15 pts.
Logical organization	1 2 3 4 5	B = 10–12 pts.
Vocabulary use	1 2 3 4 5	C = 7–9 pts.
		D = 4–6 pts.
		F = < 4 pts.

"To me, this is a very smooth and logical etapa It flows well, and there are interesting and relevant activities. It's exciting and motivating!"

Robert Hughes
Martha Brown Middle School
Fairport, NY

UNIDAD 3 Etapa 3
Vocabulary/Gramma

ACTIVIDAD 5 **Objective:** Open-ended practice
Vocabulary/grammar review

Answers
Answers will vary but must include the following activities.
1. jugar al baloncesto
2. andar en bicicleta
3. nadar
4. patinar sobre hielo
5. mirar las plantas/flores

Quick Wrap-up
Write the 4 seasons on the board. Have students choose their favorite one and provide 2–3 sentences, orally or in writing, to describe what they typically do during that season.

Game
¿En que estación? Have students bring in pictures of clothing, accessories, and sports equipment used in **Unidad 3**. Put all the pictures into a bag. Divide a piece of poster board into four equal parts; label each with a season. Students take turns selecting a picture from the bag (no peeking) and making a sentence about it and the season it is used in. For example, gloves are selected. **Cuándo hace frío en el invierno llevo guantes,** is the sentence, and the picture is placed on **invierno.** Play until there are no more pictures. Paste, label, and display pictures on poster board.

Block Schedule
Variety Divide the class into small groups. Give each group a season. Groups must devise a visual (collage, poster, mural, diorama, brochure, etc.) to represent their season.

Vocabulary/Grammar • UNIDAD 3 Etapa 3   **253**

● **Block Scheduling Suggestions** at point-of-use help teachers vary and streamline their lessons.

---

tividades

partner. Find out what activities your
her friends and family like to do throughout
om the following.

cen tus amigos en el invierno?
igos juegan al baloncesto en el invierno.

en la primavera

en el verano

en el otoño

en el invierno

NOTA CULTURAL
The National Puerto Rican Day Parade on Fifth Avenue in New York City is the largest parade in the country. Millions of people watch it, and tens of thousands of people march in it every June.

doscientos cincuenta y tres   **253**
Etapa 3

---

hing Middle School Students

Help Ask yes or no questions related to the
s and seasonal activities.
amos el sol en invierno en *(your country)?*
amos shorts en diciembre en *(your city)?*
emos clases en el verano en *(your school)?*

ve Speaker Ask students to describe the
ns in their country. Ask about typical clothing or
them compare weather in different months.

Multiple Intelligences
Visual Have students collect pictures of actual weather conditions from magazines or newspapers. Ask them to describe these weather conditions to the class.
Kinesthetic Have students work in pairs to develop a mime or dance to act out weather conditions that you assign.

● **Teaching Middle School Students** features numerous creative ideas to address different types of students.

MOTIVATE TO COMMUNICATE
¡En español!

Cultural References

Note: *Page numbers in bold type refer to the Teacher's Edition.*

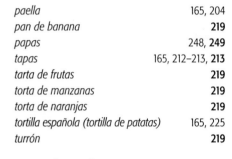

¡En español!

INSERVICE WORKSHOPS

This section of your Teacher's Edition contains professional development materials for reference throughout the school year. You may also access www.mcdougallittell.com for additional information.

Teaching Spanish in Middle School

Sharon Larracoechea
South Junior High School
Boise, ID

Effective language instruction in Middle School addresses the unique set of needs and talents that Middle School students bring to the classroom. Successful Middle School teachers take into account that their students are younger, more energetic and less experienced than their High School counterparts. These teachers use a variety of resources and techniques for language instruction and support the development of Middle School students into confident and successful learners.

Meeting Middle School Students' Needs

Build Confidence Through Success The Middle School student needs to feel confident in what he or she does. The building of self-esteem at this age level is very important to the learning process. Students in Middle School Spanish classes can experience small successes each day by completing activities that motivate them to understand, personalize, and communicate. Multiple opportunities for learning allow students to see their own progress.

Offer Social Interaction Middle School students are quite social, and thrive on interaction with their peers. Communicative activities, including Total Physical Response (TPR), pair and group work, and cooperative learning provide a means for social interaction and allow students to share the excitement of language learning.

Provide Purpose and Meaning Age- and developmentally-appropriate activities that address real-life situations will encourage students to be language learners. When Middle School students can see that language has purpose and meaning, they will be willing to try to communicate in Spanish.

Tell Stories A good story is especially compelling to Middle School students, and really helps to make the language and culture come alive. Initially, you can create the stories and students may respond without speaking. (Total Physical Response is useful for this type of activity.) Eventually, with very specific guidance, students will be able invent their own simple stories using the target language.

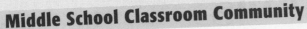

Middle School Classroom Community

TPR Display around the room and on the board phrases with active verbs that students know (**sacar fotos, tomar el sol, escribir,** etc.). Next name or describe places. Students turn to face the verb phrases describing what can be done in the place you named. Then switch: display the places and name the activities.

Storytelling Divide the class into groups of four. Using words written on cards, visuals, etc. give each group a weather expression. The groups have a time limit to prepare a story that incorporates the three components. When time is called, each group tells its story.

Teaching Tips for Success

- Be sure to infuse culture into the curriculum. Students will learn that culture is as important to language study as is the vocabulary and grammar.

- Use more than the textbook: videos, ancillaries and any other type of audio and visual stimulation will provide a more interesting and varied experience.

- Go beyond the classroom. Families and community members can play a valuable role in Middle School learning. Activities that involve parents, families and community members enrich the Middle School curriculum and greatly facilitate learning.

- Include cooperative learning, as well as other types of group and pair work. Give students a variety of opportunities to communicate with their peers in Spanish.

- Monitor students' progress. Check for understanding and adjust instruction accordingly.

- Provide continuous, authentic and appropriate assessment and evaluation. These are essential components of the Middle School learning process.

- Plan a smooth articulation between Middle School and High School. Using a single series that articulates smoothly from 1A to 1B to 2 makes everyone's job easier!

Middle School Tips for Block Schedules

- A routine saves energy and maximizes learning time.

- A daily class agenda helps students know what to expect.

- Use the "10 minute rule." No activity should last longer than 10 minutes. (This is sound advice for any class, but it's especially important not to let activities drag during a longer class period.)

- Include lots of movement.

- Evaluate students regularly, and adapt your plan accordingly.

- Focus on what students can *do*, rather than on what they should "know."

Addressing the Standards in Your Teaching

Ann Tollefson
Natrona County Schools
Caspar, WY

UNIDAD 3
Cultural Opener

Unit Theme
Living in and visiting Puerto Rico, discussing weather, and participating in leisure activities

Communication
- Expressing feelings and emotions
- Discussing what just happened
- Talking on the telephone
- Discussing sports
- Talking about clothes and accessories
- Describing the weather
- Stating preferences and opinions

Cultures
- Learning about regional vocabulary
- Learning about leisure activities in Puerto Rico
- Learning about the history, geography, and wildlife of Puerto Rico
- Learning about some important people from Puerto Rico

Connections
- Connecting to Music: Music and dance in Puerto Rico and in the U.S.
- Connecting to Science: Using the Celsius scale in Spanish-speaking countries and learning the conversion formula

Comparisons
- Comparing music and dance in Puerto Rico and in the U.S.
- Comparing sports traditions in Puerto Rico with sports traditions in the U.S.
- Comparing tourist attractions in Puerto Rico and in the U.S.

Communities
- Using Spanish for personal interest
- Using Spanish to help others

¡En español!, the Spanish program you have selected for your classroom and students, will help you integrate the national Standards for Foreign Language Learning into your Spanish program. It reflects what we know about best practices and has been reviewed by classroom teachers across the country. Like you, they are excited, and a little nervous, about the times in which the profession finds itself, times rife with changes, challenges and opportunities!

The Standards: Essential Knowledge and Skills

Consider the national Standards. For the first time in the history of the profession, we have reached general consensus on the essential knowledge and skills that students progressing through our programs should be able to demonstrate.

The Standards suggest best practices and new pedagogical approaches that will help our students reach higher degrees of facility and competence in a language, but in no way do they imply that classroom teachers should discard everything they have done in the past. Rather, they encourage us to examine what we do in light of the skills and knowledge we have agreed our students should demonstrate, to weave together the best of the new with the best of what we already know. Without implying that we must begin all over again, they suggest to us proven approaches that may improve the opportunities and experiences we offer our students.

Empowering Teachers

In essence we have empowered ourselves as language teachers. With the Standards, we have together established a measure against which we as individual teachers can measure our own programs and students.

With that common vision we have achieved three major milestones in the profession: 1) we are better able to build programs that we know will allow our students to compare favorably with their counterparts across the nation; 2) students going from one program to another will be more likely to succeed because we as a profession can more realistically expect to be working toward similar measures of achievement; 3) we have some consensus to help us as we design and implement extended sequences of study. Now that we know what the destination is, we are better able to design programs to help our students to get there!

Successful Learning Contexts

In addition, the Standards have defined the contexts within which successful language learning occurs. Language teachers have always known that learning another language is far more than mastering a body of words and the rules that tell us how to combine them in a meaningful manner. But describing and communicating the "more" is something with which we have struggled.

In addressing this issue, the Standards have enabled us to come to agreement on the goals and context that give life to those words and rules. The five goals of Communication, Culture, Connections, Comparisons, and Communities have given us a common framework within which to design significant, challenging language experiences for our students.

Consensus: Goals and Products

Teachers now have a number of tools that have never before been available. With both the Standards for Learning Spanish and the generic national Standards we have achieved an important objective: Spanish teachers are no longer faced with the task of deciding independently what the goals and products of each program should be. They are now free to tailor and adapt what we have agreed upon as a profession to what they know about their own schools and students. The new Standards for Heritage Language Speakers go a step further, providing teachers a tool to help them adapt classroom instruction to the needs and abilities of students for whom the Spanish language is part of their cultural heritage.

Teaching Today

Where do we find ourselves as language teachers in the profession today? What is happening to make our jobs easier, to free us to be more creative, to help us become more effective teachers?

With the publication of the national Standards, we have established together what we want for our students: "Knowing how, when and why to say what to who" in the languages we teach. We have agreed upon what our students should know and be able to do at several steps in their sequence of language study.

Further, with the ACTFL Proficiency Guidelines for K-12 Learners we have defined how well our students should be able to achieve those standards. Currently, an anthology of assessments for the Standards is being field-tested nationally.

Classroom teachers now have standard guidelines for how well students should be able to meet them, and sample measurements to see whether or not they have indeed done so. Yet nowhere is there any suggestion that there is only one instructional approach. How we adapt the Standards and assessments to our own classrooms and students is rightly left to us as professionals.

¡En español! and the Standards

¡En español! was designed to help your students meet the national Standards while offering you the same freedom to choose among and to tailor any number of instructional approaches. Each Unit Opener in your Teacher's Edition shows you how the instructional material was written directly to the Standards, leaving you the choice of individualizing to meet your own students' needs.

We are learning together as a profession, working together to build new and ever more effective programs like ¡En español!

What might we consider as we revisit and enliven teaching and learning in our programs? Surely, we may want to consider redesigning assessments as we redesign instruction, developing more holistic assessments that reflect changing practices and expectations for students. *¡En español!* presents a wide variety of assessment options, as well as point-of-use assessment rubrics in your Teacher's Edition.

The Standards movement is a process: there is no one expert to tell us how to transform our classrooms into magical places where all students will effortlessly master the Spanish language. In fact, we are the experts, the professionals best equipped to design instruction for our own classrooms and for our own students. The Standards challenge us to continually revisit and refine the experiences and opportunities we offer our students.

What Exciting Times!

We are learning together as a profession, working together to build new and ever more effective programs like *¡En español!*, yet providing individual teachers the tools and freedom to tailor best practices to their own classrooms. Stay tuned—it is only going to get better!

Integrating Technology in the Language Classroom: A Common-Sense Approach

Willard A. Heller, Jr.
Perry Junior High School
Perry, NY

Language teachers have always been pioneers in using the latest technology to enhance the effectiveness of instruction. The language labs of the sixties were the first large scale integration of a subject curriculum and the latest available technology. Time is the most valuable resource for the language teacher. Language teachers continue to recognize the value of using instructional technology to maximize the effective use of class time.

Teaching Resource Options

Audiovisual

OHT 93, 94, 95, 95A, 96, 96A, 99 (Quick Start)
Audio Program Cassette 9A / CD 9
Audio *Para hispanohablantes* Cassette 9A / CD 9
Video Program Videotape 3 / Videodisc 2A

Search Chapter 6, Play to 7
U3E3 • En contexto (Vocabulary)

Technology

Intrigas y aventuras
CD-ROM, Disc 1

Why Use A Variety of Instructional Technologies?

There are many compelling reasons to motivate the classroom teacher to use a wide variety of technologies. Aside from making most efficient use of class time, judiciously selected computer and multimedia technology can help the language teacher:

- Address multiple learning styles, intelligences and preferences
- Provide variety and interest to the language learning experience
- Encourage multiple repetitions of content in different contexts
- Obtain current cultural information
- Facilitate communication by language learners with classmates and peers

Audiovisual Technology

For many years, language teachers have successfully and skillfully incorporated audiovisual technology into lessons to enrich the learning experience. These "older" technologies still can serve the learning goals of the language classroom.

Overhead Projector Overhead transparencies can be used to introduce vocabulary, practice listening comprehension, and prompt speaking and writing tasks. Students can use overhead transparencies to narrate stories or to summarize readings from the text. The *¡En español!* Overhead Transparencies also contain situational transparencies, maps, fine art, and even graphic organizers.

Audio Program Cassettes/CDs Audio can offer students a sampling of the wide variety of accents and dialects among native speakers in many authentic contexts. Student presentations and dialogues can be taped for diagnosis, instruction, assessment, and portfolios. The *¡En español!* Audio Program contains activities, dialogs, and recorded readings as well as an additional native speaker component.

Videotapes/Videodiscs Video can enhance the listening experience by offering visual cues to the listener and by supplying a culturally authentic setting and context for the language. See the *¡En español!* Videotapes, Videodiscs, and Video Activities.

Video Cameras Student pair and group activities can be recorded. Playing back student work gives a chance to develop listening comprehension and can be used to provide feedback on fluency, accuracy, pronunciation, and accent. These video presentations are also perfect for Parents' Night!

Language Labs Technological advances have transformed the hard-wired language laboratory of the sixties into a flexible solution for meeting the varied needs of learners. In addition to supplying listening practice, language labs allow teachers to monitor and record individual responses to recorded cues. Many modern language labs allow the teacher to pair or group students for participation in dialogs.

Computer Technology

Computers are becoming more commonly available in the classroom and in laboratory settings. They are valuable in giving the type of individualized repetition and feedback necessary to build confidence in language learners. As availability increases, language teachers will be able to more easily integrate this technology into lessons. The most useful applications include:

CD-ROM Programs Compact discs can hold the quantity of programming necessary to be able to provide interactive multimedia practice for listening, reading, speaking and writing, as well as grammar and vocabulary drill and practice. The *¡En español! Intrigas y aventuras* CD-ROM program offers lesson-specific practice in an engaging, student-friendly format.

Integrated Software Word processing, spreadsheet, and page layout software can be used as a tool for students to share writing, research results, and cultural information with classmates.

Presentation Software Students can create their own multimedia presentations in the target language, incorporating text, graphics, sound, and video.

The Internet offers abundant opportunity to take language learning beyond the walls of the classroom and the borders of the community.

Program-specific Software Test Generators and Electronic Teacher Tools, such as those in the *¡En español!* program, allow teachers to individualize assessment and ancillaries to suit the needs of their own classrooms.

Internet Resources

The Internet offers abundant opportunity to take language learning beyond the walls of the classroom and the borders of the community. There are several significant uses of the Internet.

E-mail and "Key Pals" Instant worldwide communication encourages frequent exchanges between Internet pen pals, commonly called "key pals." Many websites and resources are available to connect students with Spanish-speaking pen pals.

World Wide Web The World Wide Web provides a vast source of reading material containing the most up-to-the-minute cultural information and authentic documents in the target language. Newspapers, national and regional tourist offices, and museums have rich websites and provide a good starting place for Internet exploration.

The *¡En español!* website offers program participants a forum for exchanging ideas and additional support and information on a wide variety of topics. (See page T64 for more information.)

 www.mcdougallittell.com

Technology and Professional Enrichment

Technology can also be a valuable tool for individual teachers to continue to develop as scholars of the target language and culture and as classroom practitioners. Particularly through the vast resources of the World Wide Web, teachers can stay current with cultural and linguistic developments in the target culture. Newspapers on the Internet can help the language teacher keep up with current events in target culture countries. In addition, reading popular resources can provide insights into current vocabulary and usage.

Participation in e-mail Mailing Lists (called LISTSERVs) allow the language teacher to contribute to and learn from a worldwide community of L2 educators. One such moderated listserv is FLTEACH. (FLTEACH@LISTSERV.ACSU.BUFFALO.EDU) E-mail messages posted to the list are distributed to each member of the list. Members of the list represent all levels of L2 instruction all over the country and all over the world. Through active participation in the list, participants can discuss current pedagogical issues and share information on all aspects of language instruction. [For more information about this listserv, contact the moderators of the list at FLTEACH@SNYCORVA.CORTLAND.EDU or see page T64.]

Classroom Delivery

The manner in which technology is available is as varied as the technology itself. Teacher-directed lessons can be enriched through incorporation of audiovisual and computer technology to prompt or reinforce vocabulary development or grammar skills, to promote skill building in speaking, listening, reading, and writing, or to deepen cross-cultural understanding. Any phase of a lesson can be enhanced with the use of carefully selected instructional media. When using instructional technology, always (1) give a purpose and strategy for each listening or viewing and (2) provide a way for students to respond to content. The response can be providing non-verbal cues, answering questions, or giving a summary.

Learning Stations can be set up to exploit limited technological resources. Small groups of students can rotate through various activities over the course of one or more classes. Activities can include:

Listening Station Tapes, headsets, and response sheets are available to complete directed listening or music activities.

Computer Station Even one computer in a classroom can be used by a small group to use a CD-ROM, to produce a graph of survey results, to create a newsletter or advertisement integrating text and graphics, or to compose a story.

Games Station Students can play commercial or teacher-made games to reinforce Etapa vocabulary or grammar patterns.

Realia Station Guided reading of posters, city plans, tour brochures or other authentic documents related to the Etapa theme can be done.

Speaking Station Group speaking tasks or prepared dialogs can be recorded for feedback and evaluation.

Puzzle Station Crossword puzzles, word finds, scavenger hunts, and other creative practice activities can be completed.

Cooperative Learning Group activities, projects or productions can incorporate technology by using presentation or page layout software; videotaping, audio taping with sound effects; overhead transparencies or visual aids to liven presentations in the target language.

Language or Computer Lab The entire class can engage in projects using Internet resources, presentation software, word processing and page layout software. Within the lab setting, it is still possible to offer considerable creativity, flexibility, and individualization of student responses.

Planning for the widest possible variety of carefully selected technology resources can maximize the use of scarce class time, increase active involvement of students, address individual needs, and motivate curiosity about the target culture. The *¡En español!* program resources (see pages T8–T9) help both students and teachers easily integrate technology into the learning experience and successfully adapt to varied learning styles and ability levels.

Strategies for Foreign Language Learning

Estella Gahala
Albuquerque, NM

As foreign language educators have reached out to increase numbers of foreign language students, there has been recognition of the need to expand effective instruction. Learners have many different ways of learning. Our well-crafted instruction is a net in which we hope to catch them all, but capable students can sometimes elude our best efforts. How shall we teach different types of students?

One Source of Success

A series of research studies has direct bearing on the question: What distinguishes successful learners of another language from unsuccessful ones? Success is measured by performance in the five skills. Findings include:

- Differences among students are less evident at low-levels of proficiency. As competence increases, more differences emerge. A major difference is in their personal strategies for learning.

- Successful students have a larger repertoire of strategies. They start with "top-down" strategies ("What is the gist?") and resort to "bottom-up" strategies ("What does the word mean?") when completely stymied.

- Unsuccessful students have a smaller repertoire of strategies. They start with "bottom-up" strategies and give up more quickly.

Feedback revealed an impressive array of student-initiated strategies, including memory strategies, cognitive strategies, compensation strategies, metacognitive strategies, affective strategies, and social strategies. Students are inventive in how they learn, including incorporating personal experience and learning from other students.

Definition of Strategies

A strategy is a plan, step, or series of actions toward achievement of a goal. Rebecca Oxford's[1] comprehensive work on language learning strategies explains how strategies help the

---

PARA LEER

STRATEGY: READING

Scan Reading very quickly to get a specific piece of information, like a football score or a movie time, is called scanning. Scan this poster and decide whether Ignacio and Roberto can attend...

PARA CONVERSAR

STRATEGY: SPEAKING

Use your tone to convey meaning Words alone do not reveal meaning. Your tone of voice makes a difference. In both your invitations and answers, express different feelings (happy, nervous, etc.).

PARA CONOCERNOS

STRATEGY: CONNECTING CULTURES

Reflect on sports traditions Can you think of any sports in the U.S. that have players from other countries? What sports are they? Are some countries associated with certain sports more than others? Why do you think that might be true? Use this chart to organize your answers.

Deporte	País 1	País 2	País 3
el béisbol	Cuba	Japón	
el hockey	Canadá	Rusia	

PARA ESCUCHAR • STRATEGY: LISTENING

Listen for a purpose Listening for specific information is like scanning when reading. Practice listening for one idea. What is the exact day and time of an important event for Ignacio? Why is it important?

El evento	El día	La hora

PARA ESCRIBIR • STRATEGY: WRITING

Appeal to the senses A well-constructed poster will entice people to attend the party. One way to do so is to include details that appeal to the senses: sight (**la vista**), hearing (**el oído**), touch (**el tacto**), taste (**el gusto**), and smell (**el ofato**).

classroom teacher become more collaborative with students in the teaching/learning process. Strategies are learner centered. They provide the means to acquire, store, retrieve, and use information. But they also have an emotional connection to learning, making it easier, faster, more enjoyable, more self-directed, more effective, and more transferable to new situations. Otherwise stated, strategies are a significant component of brain-compatible learning.

¡En español!: A Strategic Approach to Learning

¡En español! students encounter strategies as they begin the task of comprehending, communicating, and developing cultural knowledge and awareness. Strategies are not *the* way, but rather *a* way of going about the task. As learners progress, they gain exposure to a full repertory of strategies. Teachers encourage students to reflect on what helps and what doesn't and to exchange ideas on what works best. Such metacognition empowers the teacher to be strategic in the selection of activities and validates successful learning efforts. The teacher can thus select appropriate steps to increase student learning based on a new understanding of student needs.

Strategies for Receiving and Comprehending Language

Listening and reading have in common these characteristics: (a) prior knowledge improves comprehension, (b) the general idea is often sufficient for comprehension, (c) different purposes permit different strategies, (d) authentic input through listening and reading is essential in developing communicative competence.

A major difference is that one can reread a text and extract knowledge through contextual guessing and cognates; whereas opportunities to re-listen may be outside students' control, and recognition of cognates is less likely in listening than in reading.

Listening Listening strategies initially focus on *oral features:* intonation indicating a question or a command, or sounds and short words meaning "Now it's my turn to speak." Throughout Levels 1 and 2, listeners deal with *content*: get the gist, identify related details, sequence events, sort

information. Occasionally they are asked to borrow language relating to useful expressions and social formulas. Gradually they use graphic organizers in *higher order thinking* to organize details, compare two situations, make inferences. Level 3 listening strategies focus on real-world tasks like listening to a music awards show, debates on environmental issues, or job interviews. The strategy activates listener knowledge, focuses on key aspects of the text, then prompts reflection upon their opinions. Periodically, across levels, students *recombine strategies* for a familiar task such as listening to a vacation guide or a lecture in science class.

Reading Reading strategies contain many parallels. Learners *anticipate and predict content* by examining graphics, visuals, or titles. They use skimming and scanning techniques. Attention is directed to the *organization* of the reading text: main ideas, related details, sequence, various narrative devices. They also *recombine strategies.* Graphic organizers guide them in managing larger amounts of text. A major thrust of Level 3 strategies is to build toward reading literature: coping with complicated time sequences, complex sentence structure, and metaphoric texts.

Strategies for Producing and Communicating with Language

Listening gives models of oral language for speaking; reading gives models for writing. Students write what they can say, but since more class time is often spent on writing activities, sometimes their writing may be more polished than their speech.

Speaking A well-known survey of adults reveals that many are extremely afraid of public speaking. We have all had students who seemed to reflect comparable feelings. Before deciding what to say and constructing it with vocabulary, grammar, and pronunciation, they have emotional and social hurdles to leap. So those are the first strategies. *Attitudinal or emotional strategies* urge them not to be afraid of making mistakes, to think positively, take risks, take time, improvise. *Social strategies* show them how to work with others, encourage others, negotiate, brainstorm. With the right mind-set, they can comfortably use the *functional strategies* to express preferences, agree, disagree, encourage, persuade, describe, give advice, borrow and use set expressions, summarize, circumlocute, and use story-telling techniques. Examples or models guide them.

Writing Because novice and intermediate learners write the way they speak, they can apply functional speaking strategies to informal writing activities in *En tu propia voz.* The linguistic elements are the same: spelling is added, and they have more time for reflection, organization, and correction of their postcards, posters, and personal communication.

¡En español! has a carefully sequenced and developmentally appropriate process writing strand that gives students step-by-step instruction in producing a polished finished product. Writing strategies help students to approach their writing tasks in a creative and intelligent fashion, encouraging both individual and group work.

Study Hints *Apoyos para estudiar* focus on difficulties that arise in contrasts between English and Spanish. Students are unaccustomed to thinking about the structure of language and using terms like gender, verb conjugations, and interrogatives. The novice learner gets useful tips about how to practice, to learn, and to remember. In addition, *apoyos* help all learners connect new structures to familiar concepts. *Apoyos* provide a bridge of support between study-friendly grammar explanations and language use in learning activities.

Interrelationships among the linguistic strategies influence each learner's journey toward communicative competence. Yet why learn another language if not to communicate with its speakers and appreciate the richness of their culture? This interrelationship of language and culture is an important aspect of the *¡En español!* program.

Culture Culture is interwoven and embedded throughout *¡En español!* The section *En colores* brings learners into direct contact with practices, products, and perspectives of Spanish-speaking cultures. Our students are scarcely aware that they themselves live in a culture; they perceive their culture as the norm and all else as "weird." As beginners develop intercultural sensitivities, they first recognize the cultural topic in their own milieu, reflect upon it, then explore it in the target culture. Emphasis is on similarities before observing differences. Observe ourselves and then observe "other." In the light of "other," we reexamine self.

Food is one of the most powerful purveyors of cultural experience. One reading is about *tapas* in Spain. The strategy reminds students that fast food chains are a US invention being exported to other countries. They are to think of their favorite one and make personal responses to questions about the foods that are served, reasons for going there, and with whom they go. After reading about *tapas,* they are asked to compare the two eating experiences and then speculate on how the two young Spaniards in the story might feel on a first trip to our student's favorite fast food restaurant. In a post-reading activity, they bring language and culture together in a role-play set in a restaurant where they order *tapas.* The strategy is the first step in opening students to a new experience and developing sensitivity about it. Students begin to understand and appreciate the new culture from an "insider" rather than an "outsider" perspective.

Benefits of Strategic Learning

Student strategies for learning are introspective and not easily observed. By making students aware of different approaches to learning, they become more self-directed and more successful. Because strategies involve social, emotional, reflective, and cognitive dimensions of learning, the whole person is involved and supported in the learning process. Direct teaching of strategies provides the teacher with more diagnostic tools to use in problem solving with students. This problem-solving approach reflects and respects individuality. Everyone benefits by sharing insights and experiences, by building a repertory of learning and strategies, and by building confidence.

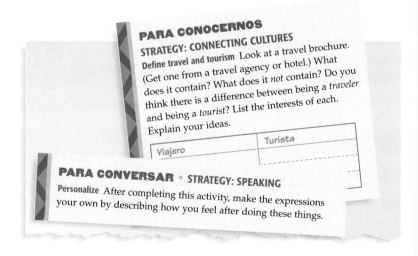

PARA CONOCERNOS
STRATEGY: CONNECTING CULTURES
Define travel and tourism Look at a travel brochure. (Get one from a travel agency or hotel.) What does it contain? What does it *not* contain? Do you think there is a difference between being a *traveler* and being a *tourist*? List the interests of each. Explain your ideas.

Viajero	Turista

PARA CONVERSAR • **STRATEGY: SPEAKING**
Personalize After completing this activity, make the expressions your own by describing how you feel after doing these things.

[1] Oxford, Rebecca. (1990). *Language Learning Strategies: What Every Teacher Should Know.* New York, NY: Newbury House.

Uniting Teaching, Learning and Assessment

Patricia Hamilton Carlin
University of Central Arkansas
Conway, AR

Assessment is an essential component of the teaching-learning process. Assessment helps teachers, students, parents, and administrators measure the progress that is being made toward reaching course objectives and instructional goals. Planning for assessment involves a consideration of national, state, and local guidelines, as well as parental expectations. Also, the teacher must decide how to design appropriate assessment instruments for students with varying interests, abilities, and learning styles. Teachers must also decide how to assign an appropriate "weight" to the various components of the student's grade.

There are several different ways to handle assessment. Here are some basic tips which can help both veteran and novice teachers design a balanced assessment plan for their classes.

PROGRAM RESOURCES

 Assessment Options

- **Cooperative Quizzes** (Unit 2 Resource Book)
- **Etapa Exam** Forms A and B (Unit 2 Resource Book)
- *Para hispanohablantes* Etapa Exam (Unit 2 Resource Book)
- **Portfolio Assessment** (Unit 2 Resource Book)
- **Multiple Choice Test Questions** (Unit 2 Resource Book)
- **Audio Program Testing** Cassette T1 / CD T1
- **Electronic Teacher Tools/Test Generator**

Include Formative and Summative Assessments

Include both formative and summative assessments as components of the student's grade. Formative assessments are the stepping stones that help students build their skills, while summative assessments provide a summation of what has been learned to that point.

Quizzes, a common type of formative assessment, can provide helpful feedback to both teacher and students. Giving quizzes cooperatively in pairs or small groups can be particularly effective and fun. The *¡En español!* Cooperative Quizzes lower students' anxiety level, help students think critically about linguistic structures, and increase retention of the material. (Also, the teacher has fewer papers to grade!)

Include Traditional and Alternative Assessments

Provide opportunities for different types of students to excel in their areas of strength by including both traditional assessments (pencil and paper) and alternative assessments such as portfolios, journals, video/class presentations, visual/audio projects, interviews, etc.

¡En español! provides excellent support in this area. (See pages T8–T9 for a description of the Assessment Program.) The testing program includes contextualized quizzes and tests designed to assess

both discrete and global skills in listening, speaking, reading, writing, and culture at both the Etapa and Unit level, as well as mid-year and final exams. An easy-to-use Test Generator and additional printed Multiple Choice Questions make individualizing assessment convenient. Rubrics for grading projects, writing assignments, and oral activities are provided at point-of-use in the Teacher's Edition as general guidelines. As always, the classroom teacher may expand and specify these rubrics for individual needs.

View Assessment as a Process

Remember that assessment is an ongoing process, and that *you*, the classroom teacher, are in charge. Continually monitor the progress that your students are making, and don't be afraid to make adjustments to your assessment plans, as needed, to enhance the teaching-learning process. For example, assessing the progress of native speakers of Spanish in your classes may begin with the Diagnostic exams, and continue with the *Para hispanohablantes* testing materials. Once you have established a level of performance for students, assessment may expand to include special research projects, reports, and presentations.

Remember that assessment is an ongoing process, and that you, the classroom teacher, are in charge.

Develop a Sense of Community

Finally, look for ways to make assessment more enjoyable for both you and your students. If you are using the *¡En español!* Cooperative Quizzes, you may find that they can provide a non-threatening culmination activity that synthesizes material for students at the end of the class period. As the sense of collaborative learning is reinforced, the classroom can truly become a community of learners. Develop projects that allow students to collaborate and extend the sense of community within the classroom. When assigning grades for these projects, reward students for creativity and effort, as well as for linguistic accuracy. The *¡En español!* program provides Portfolio Assessment materials, as well as suggestions for portfolio projects in the Teacher's Edition.

Assessing a second language involves the careful balance between formative and evaluative instruments, between traditional and alternative formats, and the appropriate assessment of all skills. The *¡En español!* Assessment Program provides a wide range of support materials to allow teachers to choose the most effective tools to manage class time efficiently to reach their course objectives and instructional goals. Designing a balanced assessment plan helps to create a program that *encourages* students to build the skills they need to communicate and interact in the community of Spanish speakers.

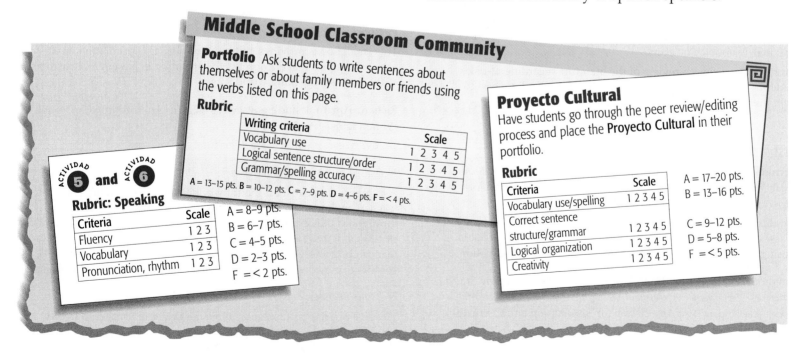

Middle School Classroom Community

Portfolio Ask students to write sentences about themselves or about family members or friends using the verbs listed on this page.

Rubric

Writing criteria	Scale
Vocabulary use	1 2 3 4 5
Logical sentence structure/order	1 2 3 4 5
Grammar/spelling accuracy	1 2 3 4 5

A = 13–15 pts. **B** = 10–12 pts. **C** = 7–9 pts. **D** = 4–6 pts. **F** = < 4 pts.

ACTIVIDAD 5 and **ACTIVIDAD 6**

Rubric: Speaking

Criteria	Scale
Fluency	1 2 3
Vocabulary	1 2 3
Pronunciation, rhythm	1 2 3

A = 8–9 pts.
B = 6–7 pts.
C = 4–5 pts.
D = 2–3 pts.
F = < 2 pts.

Proyecto Cultural

Have students go through the peer review/editing process and place the **Proyecto Cultural** in their portfolio.

Rubric

Criteria	Scale
Vocabulary use/spelling	1 2 3 4 5
Correct sentence structure/grammar	1 2 3 4 5
Logical organization	1 2 3 4 5
Creativity	1 2 3 4 5

A = 17–20 pts.
B = 13–16 pts.
C = 9–12 pts.
D = 5–8 pts.
F = < 5 pts.

Professional Bibliography and Additional Resources

Audrey L. Heining-Boynton
University of North Carolina
Chapel Hill, NC

Part of being a dedicated teacher is committing to life-long learning, keeping abreast of the latest trends and issues. What follows is a synthesis of a variety of texts and articles that will provide you with a starting point to explore pertinent issues and "hot topics," such as: *At-risk Students, Assessment, Culture and Multiculturalism, Foreign Language Standards, Second Language Acquisition, Classroom Management, Multiple Intelligences, and Block Scheduling.*

At-risk Students

• *Readings from Educational Leadership: Students At Risk.* Edited by Ronald S. Brandt (1990). Alexandria, VA: Association for Supervision and Curriculum Development.

For anyone who wants a thorough overview of the problem of at-risk students, this collection of readings is the place to begin. *Educational Leadership,* one of the finest journals for all K-12 teachers, compiles books that are collections of articles from previous editions, and this edition combines over forty articles on this topic.

• Heining-Boynton, A. (1994). "The At-Risk Student in the Foreign Language Classroom." In *Meeting New Challenges in the Foreign Language Classroom.* Edited by Gale K. Crouse. Lincolnwood, IL: National Textbook Company.

This article provides a review of the literature regarding at-risk students, and then provides teaching techniques on how best to meet the needs of these special students.

Assessment

• Herman, J.L., Aschbacher, P.R. and Winters, L. (1992). *A Practical Guide to Alternative Assessment.* Alexandria, VA: Association for Supervision and Curriculum Development.

This text provides teachers with ways to determine the purpose of assessment, select the tasks and set the criteria, ensure reliable scoring, and incorporate interdisciplinary factors in the equation.

• Marzano, R.J., Pickering, D. and McTighe, J. (1993). *Assessing Student Outcomes: Performance Assessment Using the Dimensions of Learning Model.* Alexandria, VA: Association for Supervision and Curriculum Development.

Beginning with a definition of how assessment standards are linked to the five dimensions of learning, the text offers suggestions on how teachers can assess and keep track of student performance.

• Moeller, A. (1994). "Portfolio Assessment: A Showcase for Growth and Learning in the Foreign Language Classroom." In *Meeting New Challenges in the Foreign Language Classroom.* Edited by Gale K. Crouse. Lincolnwood, IL: National Textbook Company.

This article offers a rationale for the process of portfolio assessment and provides a step-by-step method for foreign language teachers to include this as a holistic component to their instruction and assessment.

• *Teaching, Testing, and Assessment: Making the Connection.* (1994). Northeast Conference Reports. Editor, Charles Hancock. Lincolnwood, IL: National Textbook Company.

Besides an overview of conceptualization that connects teaching, testing, and assessment, the chapters offer ideas for assessing all language skills in a variety of ways.

Culture and Multiculturalism

• Noble, J. and Lacasa, J. (1995). *The Hispanic Way.* Lincolnwood, IL: Passport Books.

This small books provides cultural/sociological information on a variety of topics that encompass the attitudes, behavior, and customs of the Spanish-speaking world.

• Richard-Amato, P. and Snow, M. (1992). *The Multicultural Classroom.* White Plains, NY: Longman.

An overview of why we teach culture.

• *Newsweek en español, People en español, etc.*

A number of weekly and monthly publications exist to help Spanish teachers maintain a current knowledge of what is happening throughout the Spanish-speaking world. Publications like *Newsweek en español, People en español,* and daily newspapers from the countries that can be accessed on the WWW are with news from Spanish-speaking countries. Another excellent resource is *National Geographic.*

• *Teaching Tolerance*

This free quarterly publication available from the Southern Poverty Law Center is an outstanding resource for teachers. Write to: Teaching Tolerance, 400 Washington Ave., Montgomery, AL 36014.

Foreign Language Standards

* *National Standards: A Catalyst for Reform.* Edited by Robert C. Lafayette. (1996). Lincolnwood, IL: National Textbook Company.

  This compendium looks at the foreign language standards and how they impact all aspects of foreign language teaching.

* *Standards for Foreign Language Learning: Preparing for the 21st Century.* (1996). American Council on the Teaching of Foreign Languages, 6 Executive Plaza, Yonkers, NY.

  Foreign language teaching and learning is now organized by five principles known as the five C's of foreign language education: communication, cultures, connections, comparisons, and communities.

General Educational Issues

Block Scheduling

* Canady, R.L. & Rettig, M.D. (1995). *Block Scheduling: A catalyst for change in high schools.* Larchmont, NY: Eye on Education.

* Canady, R.L. & Rettig, M.D. (1996). *Teaching in the Block: Strategies for engaging active learners.* Larchmont, NY: Eye on Education.

* Cunningham, R. David. Jr. & Nogle, Sue Ann. (December 1996). "Six keys to block scheduling." *The High School Magazine*, 29–32.

* Elkins, G. (Spring 1996). "Making longer better: Staff development for block scheduling." Arlington, VA: ASCD Professional Development Newsletter.

* Gerking, Janet L. (April 1995). "Building block schedules: A firsthand assessment of restructuring the school day." *The Science Teacher*, 23–27.

* Hottenstein, D.S. (Winter 1996). "Supporting block scheduling: A response to critics." *Alliance* 1(2), 11. Reston, VA: The National Alliance of High Schools, a division of the National Association of Secondary School Principals.

* Wisconsin Association of Foreign Language Teachers. (1995). *Redesigning high school schedules: A report of the Task Force on Block Scheduling by the Wisconsin Association of Foreign Language Teachers.* Madison, WI: WAFLT (can be found on ERIC on the Internet).

Classroom Management

* Johnson, D. and Johnson, R. (1995). *Reducing School Violence Through Conflict Resolution.* Alexandria VA: Association for Supervision and Curriculum Development.

  This text discusses how to teach conflict resolution.

* Jones, F. (1987). *Positive Classroom Discipline.* New York, NY: McGraw Hill.

  Jones has foolproof ways to have the discipline and classroom management we all want and deserve.

* Kohn, A. (1996). *Beyond Discipline: From Compliance to Community.* Alexandria, VA: Association for Supervision and Curriculum Development.

  This text takes a new approach to classroom management/ discipline.

Multiple Intelligences

* Armstrong, Thomas. (1991). *Awakening Your Child's Natural Genius.* Los Angeles: Jeremy P. Tarcher, Inc.

* Armstrong, Thomas. (1987). *Discovering and Encouraging Your Child's Personal Learning Style.* Los Angeles: Jeremy P. Tarcher, Inc., Distributed by St. Martin's Press.

* Armstrong, Thomas. (1994). *Multiple Intelligences in the Classroom.* Alexandria, VA: Association for Supervision and Curriculum Development.

* Gardner, Howard. (1983). *Frames of Mind: The Theory of Multiple Intelligences.* New York, NY: Basic Books.

* Kline, Peter. (1988). *The Everyday Genius: Restoring Children's Natural Joy of Learing, and Your Too.* Arlington, VA: Great Ocean Puublishers.

* Lazear, David. *Seven Pathways of Learning: Teaching Students and Parents about Multiple Intelligences.* Zephyr Press, Tucson, Arizona, 1994.

Second Language Acquisition

* Krashen, S.D. and Terrell, T.D. (1983) *The Natural Approach: Language Acquisition in the Classroom.* Englewood Cliffs, NJ: Prentice-Hall.

  This text provides the philosophy and approach to teaching second language based on research in linguistics, psychology, and psycholinguistics. Its major concepts are the Input Hypothesis and the Affective Filter Hypothesis.

* Larsen-Freeman, D. and Long, M.H. (1992). *An Introduction to Second Language Acquisition Research.* New York, NY: Longman.

  A complete overview of second language theories, this is a sophisticated text that provides a lengthy bibliography and set of references for further investigation.

* *Research in language Learning: Principles, Processes and Prospects.* (1993) Editor, Alice Omaggio Hadley. Lincolnwood, IL: National Textbook Company.

  One of the series of ACTFL Foreign Language Education Series, this text is dedicated to research in language learning, and offers a variety of perspectives on language acquisition research and how it applies to the classroom.

* *TESOL Quarterly*

  This journal provides research articles on second language acquisition.

* Omaggio Hadley, A. (1993) *Teaching Language in Context.* Boston, MA: Heinle and Heinle.

  Omaggio Hadley's text sets the standard for a thorough exploration of the teaching of the four skills and references which are a good place to begin for anyone who wishes additional information on a given topic.

Additional Resources

There are many organizations that can provide a wealth of additional information and support for Spanish teachers. The list below will help you to expand your classroom resources and contact other teachers. Remember, however, that addresses and telephone numbers often change; it is advisable to verify them before sending inquiries.

Professional Organizations

The American Council on
the Teaching of Foreign
Languages (ACTFL)
6 Executive Plaza
Yonkers, NY 10701
(914) 963-8830
http://www.actfl.org/

American Association of
Teachers of Spanish
and Portuguese (AATSP)
Gunter Hall, Room 106
University of Northern Colorado
Greely, CO 80639
(303) 351-1090
http://www.aatsp.org/home.html/

Cultural Offices/Embassies/Consulates/Tourist Offices

Consult the telephone listings in most major cities for a listing of the embassies and consulates of Spanish-speaking countries closest to you.

Tourist Office of Spain
665 Fifth Avenue
New York, NY 10022
(212) 759-8822
http://www.okspain.org/

Mexican Government Tourist Office
2707 N. Loop West, Suite 450
Houston, TX 77008
(713) 880-5153
http://www.mexico-travel.com

Penpal Exchanges

Student Letter Exchange
(League of Friendship)
630 Third Avenue
New York, NY 10017
(212) 557-3312

World Pen Pals
1694 Como Avenue
St. Paul, MN 55108
(612) 647-0191

Travel/Cultural Exchange

CIEE Student Travel Services
205 East 42nd St.
New York, NY 10017
(212) 661-1414
http://www.counciltravel.com/

American Field Service
220 East 42nd St., 3rd Floor
New York, NY 10017
(212) 949-4242
http://www.afs.org/usa/

Periodicals/Films

Subscriptions may be purchased for the school through the companies listed below, or through others in your local area:

EBSCO Subscription Services
P.O. Box 1943
Birmingham, AL 35201-1943

Gessler Publishing Company
55 West 13th St.
New York, NY 10011
(212) 627-0099

Continental Book Company
8000 Cooper Avenue Bldg. 29
Glendale, NY 11385
(718) 326-0572

The International Film Bureau
332 South Michigan Avenue
Chicago, IL 60604-4382
(312) 427-4545

Online Contacts

Many organizations now maintain websites. Since, again, these are subject to change, it is advisable to check before contacting. We encourage you to visit the McDougal Littell website for materials specific to the *¡En español!* program. In addition, FLTEACH provides an additional discussion forum for teacher exchange of ideas and information:

 www.mcdougallittell.com

FLTEACH
To subscribe or obtain information:
LISTSERV@listserv.acsu.buffalo.edu

In your message, put the following:
SUBSCRIBE FLTEACH, first name, last name
(to unsubscribe, send UNSUB FLTEACH,
first name, last name)

To send messages to all FLTEACH subscribers:
FLTEACH@listserv.acsu.buffalo.edu

McDougal Littell

¡En español!

1b

AUTHORS

Estella Gahala

Patricia Hamilton Carlin

Audrey L. Heining-Boynton

Ricardo Otheguy

Barbara J. Rupert

CULTURE CONSULTANT

Jorge A. Capetillo-Ponce

McDougal Littell
A HOUGHTON MIFFLIN COMPANY
Evanston, Illinois • Boston • Dallas

Cover Photography

Center: Large image taken in Otavalo, Ecuador, by Martha Granger/EDGE Productions.

Bottom, from left to right: Keel-billed toucan *(Ramphastos sulfuratus: Ramphastidaej),*
Range: Mexico to Venezuela, Tom Boyden; Hand-painted oxcart in Sarchí, Costa Rica, Brent
Winebrenner/International Stock Photo (also on back cover); Woven baskets in Oaxaca, Mexico,
Martha Granger/EDGE Productions; Detail of Parc Güell by Gaudí in Barcelona, Spain,
Martha Granger/EDGE Productions.

ISBN: 0-395-91079-X   1 2 3 4 5 6 7 8 9 – VJM – 04 03 02 01 00 99

Internet: www.mcdougallittell.com

Contenido

OBJECTIVES

- Greet and introduce others
- Say where people are from
- Express likes and dislikes
- Describe friends and family
- Talk about dates and ages
- Express possession

iii

ETAPA

2

OBJECTIVES

- Talk about school
- Discuss obligations and plans
- Talk about schedules and time
- Ask questions
- Say where you are going
- Request food
- Sequence events

OFICINA

CIUDAD DE MÉXICO: Una semana típica   28

BRIDGE UNIT

ETAPA 3

OBJECTIVES

- Extend invitations
- Talk on the phone
- Express feelings and preferences
- Say what just happened and what is happening
- Talk about sports
- Say what you know
- Make comparisons
- Describe the weather

PUERTO RICO: El fin de semana   54

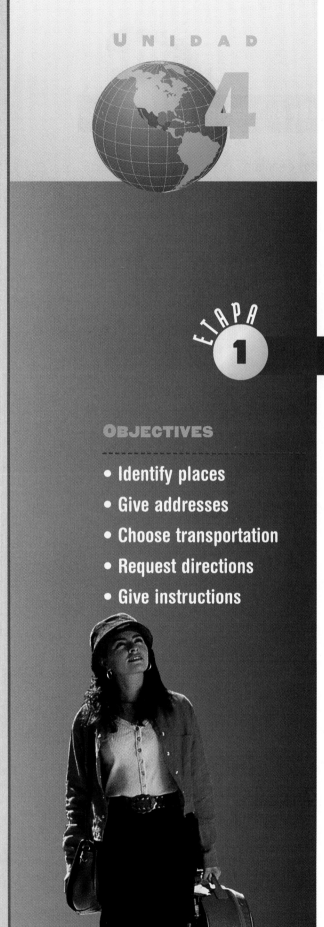

UNIDAD 4

OAXACA
MÉXICO

¡DE VISITA!

Enjoy regional handicrafts and food with Rosa, Carlos, and Sofía.

ETAPA **1**

OBJECTIVES

- Identify places
- Give addresses
- Choose transportation
- Request directions
- Give instructions

ETAPA
2

vii

¿Qué hacer en Oaxaca? 134

OBJECTIVES

- Order food
- Request the check
- Talk about food
- Express extremes
- Say where you went

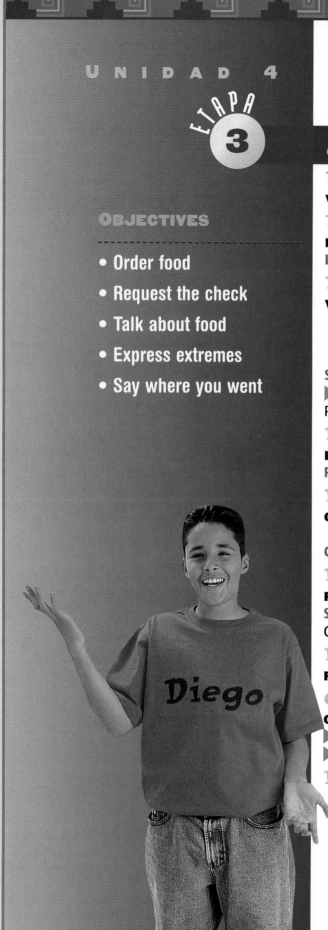

Diego

BARCELONA
ESPAÑA

PREPARACIONES ESPECIALES

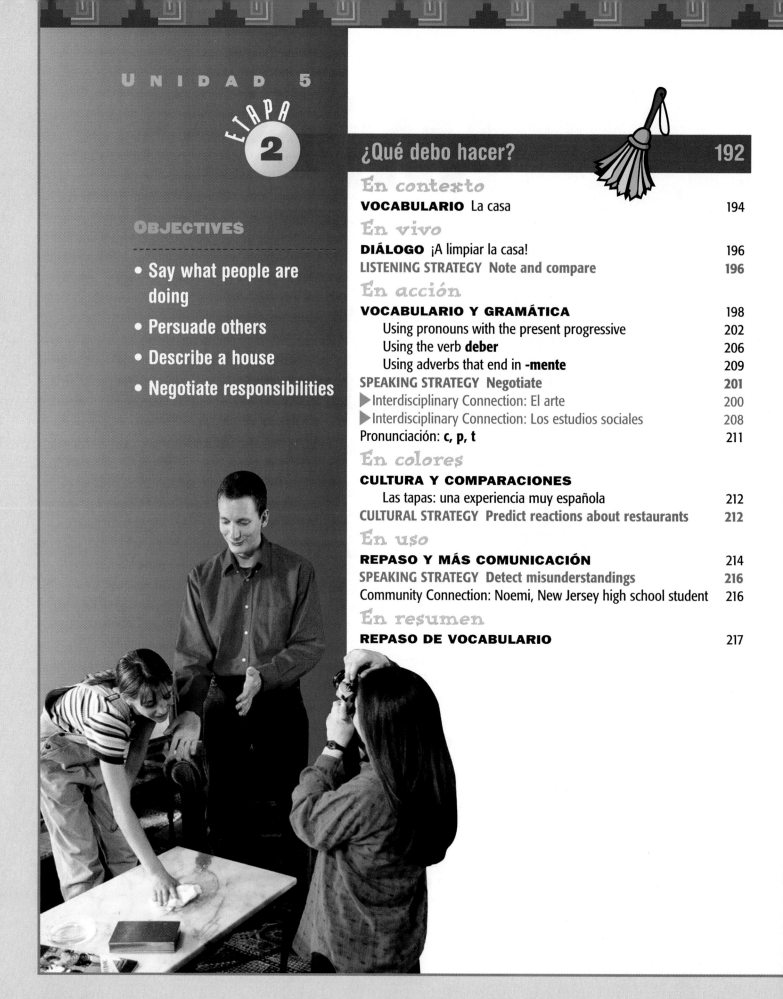

UNIDAD 5

ETAPA 2

¿Qué debo hacer? 192

OBJECTIVES

- Plan a party
- Describe past activities
- Express extremes
- Purchase food

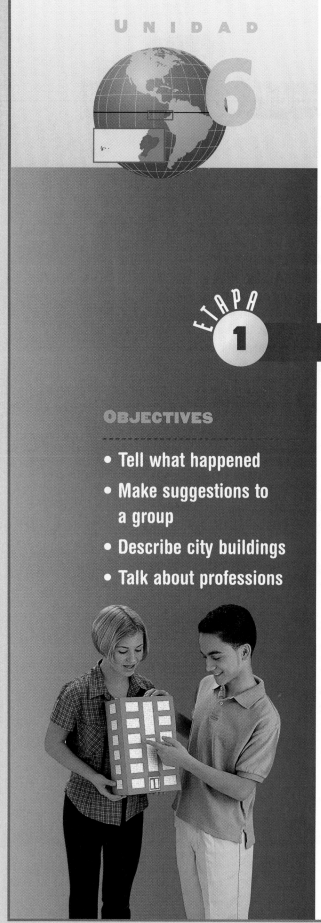

UNIDAD

6

QUITO
ECUADOR

LA CIUDAD Y EL CAMPO

Compare life in the city to life in the countryside with Patricia, Miguel, and his family.

ETAPA
1

OBJECTIVES

- Tell what happened
- Make suggestions to a group
- Describe city buildings
- Talk about professions

UNIDAD 6

ETAPA 2

OBJECTIVES

- Point out specific people and things
- Tell where things are located
- Talk about the past

UNIDAD 6

ETAPA 3

OBJECTIVES

- Talk about the present and future
- Give instructions to someone
- Discuss the past

About the Authors

Estella Gahala holds a Ph.D. in Educational Administration and Curriculum from Northwestern University. A career teacher of Spanish and French, she has worked with a wide range of students at the secondary level. She has also served as foreign language department chair and district director of curriculum and instruction. Her workshops at national, regional, and state conferences as well as numerous published articles draw upon the current research in language learning, learning strategies, articulation of foreign language sequences, and implications of the national Standards for Foreign Language Learning upon curriculum, instruction, and assessment. She has coauthored six basal textbooks.

Patricia Hamilton Carlin completed her M.A. in Spanish at the University of California, Davis, where she also taught as a lecturer. She also holds a Master of Secondary Education with specialization in foreign languages from the University of Arkansas. She has taught preschool through college, and her secondary programs in Arkansas have received national recognition. A coauthor of the *¡DIME! UNO* and *¡DIME! DOS* secondary textbooks, she currently teaches Spanish and methodology at the University of Central Arkansas, where she also supervises student teachers. She is a frequent presenter at local, regional, and national foreign language conferences.

Audrey L. Heining-Boynton received her Ph.D. in Curriculum and Instruction from Michigan State University. She is a Professor of Education and Romance Languages at The University of North Carolina at Chapel Hill, where she is a second language teacher educator and Professor of Spanish. She has also taught Spanish, French, and ESL at the K–12 level. Dr. Heining-Boynton was the president of the National Network for Early Language Learning, has been on the Executive Council of ACTFL, and involved with AATSP, Phi Delta Kappa, and state foreign language associations. She has presented both nationally and internationally, and has published over forty books, articles, and curricula.

Ricardo Otheguy received his Ph.D. in Linguistics from the City University of New York, where he is currently Professor of Linguistics at the Graduate School and University Center. He has written extensively on topics related to Spanish grammar as well as on bilingual education, and the Spanish of the United States. He is coauthor of *Tu mundo: Curso para hispanohablantes,* a Spanish high school textbook for Spanish speakers, and of *Prueba de ubicación para hispanohablantes,* a high school Spanish placement test.

Barbara J. Rupert has taught Level 1 through A.P. Spanish during her many years of high school teaching. She is a graduate of Western Washington University, and has broadened her knowledge and skills base with numerous graduate level courses emphasizing language acquisition, authentic assessment, and educational leadership and reform. She serves as the World Languages Department Chair, District Trainer and Chair of her school's Site Council. Barbara is the author of CD-ROM activities for the *¡Bravo!* series and presents at a variety of foreign language conferences. In 1996, Barbara received the Christa McAuliffe Award for Excellence in Education.

Culture Consultant

Jorge A. Capetillo-Ponce is presently a Ph.D. candidate in Sociology at the New School for Social Research, where he is also Special Consultant to the Dean of The Graduate Faculty. His graduate studies at the New School and El Colegio de México include a diversity of fields such as international relations, sociopolitical analysis, cultural theory, and sociology. He has published a wide range of essays on art, politics, religion, international relations, and society in Latin America, the United States, and the Middle East; as well as being an advisor to a number of politicians and public figures, a researcher and editor, and a college professor and television producer in Mexico, Nicaragua, and the United States.

Consulting Authors

Dan Battisti
Dr. Teresa Carrera-Hanley
Bill Lionetti
Patty Murguía Bohannan
Lorena Richins Layser

Regional Language Reviewers

Dolores Acosta (Mexico)
Jaime M. Fatás Cabeza (Spain)
Grisel Lozano-Garcini (Puerto Rico)
Isabel Picado (Costa Rica)
Juan Pablo Rovayo (Ecuador)

Contributing Writers

Ronni L. Gordon
Christa Harris
Debra Lowry
Sylvia Madrigal Velasco
Sandra Rosenstiel
David M. Stillman
Jill K. Welch

Ad hoc Representatives

Vicki Armstrong
Jane Asano
Kathy Cavers
Dan Griffith
Rita McGuire
Gretchen Toole

Senior Reviewers

O. Lynn Bolton
Dr. Jane Govoni
Elías G. Rodríguez
Ann Tollefson

Middle School Reviewers

Mary Jo Aronica
Springman School
Glenview, IL

Laura Bertrand
Explorer Middle School
Phoenix, AZ

María Corcoran
Sacred Heart Model School
Louisville, KY

Diane Drear
Brown Middle School
Hillsboro, OR

Beverly Fessenden
Carwise Middle School
Palm Harbor, FL

Alma Hernández
Alamo Junior High School
Midland, TX

Robert Hughes
Martha Brown Middle School
Fairport, NY

Nancy Lawrence
Cross Cultural Education Unit
Albuquerque, NM

Lucille Madrid
Taylor Junior High School
Mesa, AZ

Sally Nickerson
Broadview Middle School
Burlington City, NC

Lynn Perdue
Fuller Junior High School
Little Rock, AR

Leela Scanlon
West Middle School
Andover, MA

Kathleen Solórzano
Homestead High School
Mequon, WI

Michael Veraldo
Mason Middle School
Mason, OH

Jaya Vijayasekar
Griswold Middle School
Rocky Hill, CT

Colleen Yarbrough
Canon Mcmillan Middle School
Canonsburg, PA

Teacher Reviewers

Susan Arbuckle
Mahomet-Seymour High School
Mahomet, IL

Silvia Armstrong
Mills High School
Little Rock, AR

Sandra Martín Arnold
Palisades Charter High School
Pacific Palisades, CA

Warren Bender
Duluth East High School
Duluth, MN

Adrienne Chamberlain-Parris
Mariner High School
Everett, WA

Norma Coto
Bishop Moore High School
Orlando, FL

Roberto del Valle
Shorecrest High School
Shoreline, WA

Rubén D. Elías
Roosevelt High School
Fresno, CA

José Esparza
Curie Metropolitan High School
Chicago, IL

Lorraine A. Estrada
Cabarrus County Schools
Concord, NC

Alberto Ferreiro
Harrisburg High School
Harrisburg, PA

Judith C. Floyd
Henry Foss High School
Tacoma, WA

Lucy H. García
Pueblo East High School
Pueblo, CO

Marco García
Lincoln Park High School
Chicago, IL

Raquel R. González
Odessa High School
Odessa, TX

Linda Grau
Shorecrest Preparatory School
St. Petersburg, FL

Deborah Hagen
Ionia High School
Ionia, MI

Sandra Hammond
St. Petersburg High School
St. Petersburg, FL

Bill Heller
Perry Junior/Senior High School
Perry, NY

Jody Klopp
Oklahoma State Department
of Education
Edmond, OK

Richard Ladd
Ipswich High School
Ipswich, MA

Carol Leach
Francis Scott Key High School
Union Bridge, MD

Laura McCormick
East Seneca Senior High School
West Seneca, NY

Rafaela McLeod
Southeast Raleigh High School
Raleigh, NC

Teacher Reviewers (cont.)

Kathleen L. Michaels
Palm Harbor University
   High School
Palm Harbor, FL

Vickie A. Mike
Horseheads High School
Horseheads, NY

Terri Nies
Mannford High School
Mannford, OK

María Emma Nunn
John Tyler High School
Tyler, TX

Lewis Olvera
Hiram Johnson West Campus
   High School
Sacramento, CA

Anne-Marie Quihuis
Paradise Valley High School
Phoenix, AZ

Rita Risco
Palm Harbor University
   High School
Palm Harbor, FL

James J. Rudy, Jr.
Glen Este High School
Cincinnati, OH

Pamela Urdal Silva
East Lake High School
Tarpon Springs, FL

Kathleen Solórzano
Homestead High School
Mequon, WI

Sarah Spiesman
Whitmer High School
Toledo, OH

M. Mercedes Stephenson
Hazelwood Central High School
Florissant, MO

Carol Thorp
East Mecklenburg High School
Charlotte, NC

Elizabeth Torosian
Doherty Middle School
Andover, MA

Wendy Villanueva
Lakeville High School
Lakeville, MN

Helen Webb
Arkadelphia High School
Arkadelphia, AR

Jena Williams
Jonesboro High School
Jonesboro, AR

Janet Wohlers
Weston Middle School
Weston, MA

Student Review Board

Andrea Avila
Fannin Middle School
Amarillo, TX

Maya Beynishes
Edward R. Murrow High School
Brooklyn, NY

James Dock
Guilford High School
Rockford, IL

Richard Elkins
Nevin Platt Middle School
Boulder, CO

Kathryn Finn
Charles S. Pierce Middle School
Milton, MA

Robert Foulis
Stratford High School
Houston, TX

Lorrain Garcia
Luther Burbank High School
Sacramento, CA

Katie Hagen
Ionia High School
Ionia, MI

Steven Hailey
Davis Drive School
Apex, NC

Eli Harel
Thomas Edison
   Intermediate School
Westfield, NJ

Cheryl Kim
Dr. Leo Cigarroa High School
Laredo, TX

Jennifer Kim
Kellogg Middle School
Seattle, WA

Jordan Leitner
Scripps Ranch High School
San Diego, CA

Courtney McPherson
Miramar High School
Miramar, FL

Zachary Nelson
Warsaw Community High School
Warsaw, IN

Diana Parrish
Oak Crest Junior High School
Encinitas, CA

Kimberly Robinson
Perryville Senior High School
Perryville, AR

John Roland
Mountain Pointe High School
Phoenix, AZ

Nichole Ryan
Bermudian Springs High School
York Springs, PA

Ryan Shore
West Miami Middle School
Miami, FL

Tiffany Stadler
Titusville High School
Titusville, FL

Michael Szymanski
West Seneca East High School
West Seneca, NY

Anela Talic
Soldan International Studies
   High School
St. Louis, MO

Gary Thompson
Fort Dorchester High School
Charleston, SC

Bethany Traynor
Glen Este High School
Cincinnati, OH

Gerard White
Paramount High School
Paramount, CA

Nichols Wilson
Waubonsie Valley High School
Aurora, IL

Amy Wyron
Robert Frost Intermediate School
Rockville, MD

Karina Zepeda
West Mecklenburg High School
Charlotte, NC

Teacher Panel

Linda Amour
Highland High School
Bakersfield, CA

Dena Bachman
Lafayette Senior High School
St. Joseph, MO

Sharon Barnes
J. C. Harmon High School
Kansas City, KS

Ben Barrientos
Calvin Simmons
   Junior High School
Oakland, CA

Paula Biggar
Sumner Academy of
   Arts & Science
Kansas City, KS

Edda Cardenas
Blue Valley North High School
Leawood, KS

Joyce Chow
Crespi Junior High School
Richmond, CA

Mike Cooperider
Truman High School
Independence, MO

Judy Dozier
Shawnee Mission South
   High School
Shawnee Mission, KS

Maggie Elliott
Bell Junior High School
San Diego, CA

Dana Galloway-Grey
Ontario High School
Ontario, CA

Nieves Gerber
Chatsworth Senior High School
Chatsworth, CA

Susanne Kissane
Shawnee Mission Northwest
   High School
Shawnee Mission, KS

Ann Lopez
Pala Middle School
San Jose, CA

Beatrice Marino
Palos Verdes Peninsula
   High School
Rolling Hills Estates, CA

Barbara Mortanian
Tenaya Middle School
Fresno, CA

Vickie Musni
Pioneer High School
San Jose, CA

Rodolfo Orihuela
C. K. McClatchy High School
Sacramento, CA

Terrie Rynard
Olathe South High School
Olathe, KS

Beth Slinkard
Lee's Summit High School
Lee's Summit, MO

Rosa Stein
Park Hill High School
Kansas City, MO

Urban Panel

Rebecca Carr
William G. Enloe High School
Raleigh, NC

Norha Franco
East Side High School
Newark, NJ

Kathryn Gardner
Riverside University High School
Milwaukee, WI

Eula Glenn
Remtec Center
Detroit, MI

Jeana Harper
Detroit Fine Arts High School
Detroit, MI

Guillermina Jauregui
Los Angeles Senior High School
Los Angeles, CA

Lula Lewis
Hyde Park Career Academy
   High School
Chicago, IL

Florence Meyers
Overbrook High School
Philadelphia, PA

Vivian Selenikas
Long Island City High School
Long Island City, NY

Sadia White
Spingarn Stay Senior High School
Washington, DC

Block Scheduling Panel

Barbara Baker
Wichita Northwest High School
Wichita, KS

Patty Banker
Lexington High School
Lexington, NC

Beverly Blackburn
Reynoldsburg Senior High School
Reynoldsburg, OH

Henry Foust
Northwood High School
Pittsboro, NC

Gloria Hawks
A. L. Brown High School
Kannapolis, NC

Lois Hillman
North Kitsap High School
Poulsbo, WA

Nick Patterson
Central High School
Davenport, IA

Sharyn Petkus
Grafton Memorial High School
Grafton, MA

Cynthia Prieto
Mount Vernon High School
Alexandria, VA

Julie Sanchez
Western High School
Fort Lauderdale, FL

Marilyn Settlemyer
Freedom High School
Morganton, NC

El mundo

■ Países hispanohablantes

□ Países con alto número de hispanohablantes

OCÉANO ÁRTICO

Mar de Laptev

Mar de Kara

Mar de Barents

Mar de Noruega

ISLANDIA

SUECIA   FINLANDIA

NORUEGA

ESTONIA
LETONIA
LITUANIA

REINO
UNIDO   Mar del
           Norte

IRLANDA

POLONIA   BIELORRUSIA

UCRANIA

MOLDAVIA

ANDORRA

PORTUGAL   ESPAÑA

GIBRALTAR

Islas
Canarias
(Esp.)

MARRUECOS

FRANCIA

ITALIA

GRECIA

TURQUÍA

Mar Negro

GEORGIA

ARMENIA

Mar Caspio

CHIPRE
LÍBANO

SIRIA
IRAQ

ISRAEL

JORDANIA

EGIPTO

BAHREIN

QATAR

E.A.U.

OMÁN

ARABIA
SAUDITA

Mar Rojo

KUWAIT

IRÁN

AFGANISTÁN

PAQUISTÁN

NEPAL

BHUTÁN

INDIA

ARGELIA

LIBIA

SAHARA
OCCIDENTAL

MAURITANIA

MALÍ

NÍGER

CHAD

SUDÁN

SENEGAL

BURKINA
FASO

GUINEA

COSTA
DE MARFIL

BENIN
NIGERIA
TOGO

GHANA

LIBERIA

SIERRA
LEONA

GUINEA
BISSAU

GUINEA
ECUATORIAL

CAMERÚN

GABÓN

CONGO

REP. CENTRO-
AFRICANA

ERITREA

YEMEN

JIBUTI

ETIOPÍA

SOMALIA

UGANDA

REP. DEL
CONGO

KENIA

RUANDA
BURUNDI

TANZANIA

CABINDA
(ANGOLA)

ANGOLA

MALAWI

ZAMBIA

SEYCHELLES

COMORES

MOZAMBIQUE

MAURICIO

NAMIBIA

ZIMBABWE

BOTSWANA

MADAGASCAR

SUAZILANDIA

SUDÁFRICA   LESOTHO

Mar Mediterráneo

ALEMANIA

AUSTRIA

RUMANIA

RUSIA

KAZAKSTÁN

UZBEKISTÁN   KIRGUISTÁN

TURKMENISTÁN   TADJIKISTÁN

MONGOLIA

Lago
Baikal

Mar de
Ojotsk

COREA
DEL NORTE

COREA
DEL SUR

Mar de
Japón

JAPÓN

CHINA

TAIWÁN

Trópico de Cáncer

GUAM
(EE.UU.)

MYANMAR

LAOS

BANGLADESH   TAILANDIA   VIETNAM

CAMBOYA

Mar de
China

FILIPINAS

PALAU   MICRONESIA

BRUNEI

MALAYSIA

Mar
Arábigo

Golfo
de
Bengala

SRI
LANKA

ISLAS
MALDIVAS

SINGAPUR

INDONESIA

Ecuador

PAPUASIA
NUEVA GUINEA

OCÉANO
ÍNDICO

Trópico de Capricornio

AUSTRALIA

1	DINAMARCA	9 ESLOVENIA
2	HOLANDA	10 CROACIA
3	BÉLGICA	11 BOSNIA Y HERZEGOVINA
4	LUXEMBURGO	12 YUGOSLAVIA
5	SUIZA	13 ALBANIA
6	REPÚBLICA CHECA	14 MACEDONIA
7	ESLOVAQUIA	15 BULGARIA
8	HUNGRÍA	16 MALTA

N

0	1000	2000 kilómetros
0	1000	2000 millas

ANTÁRTIDA

30°   60°   90°   120°

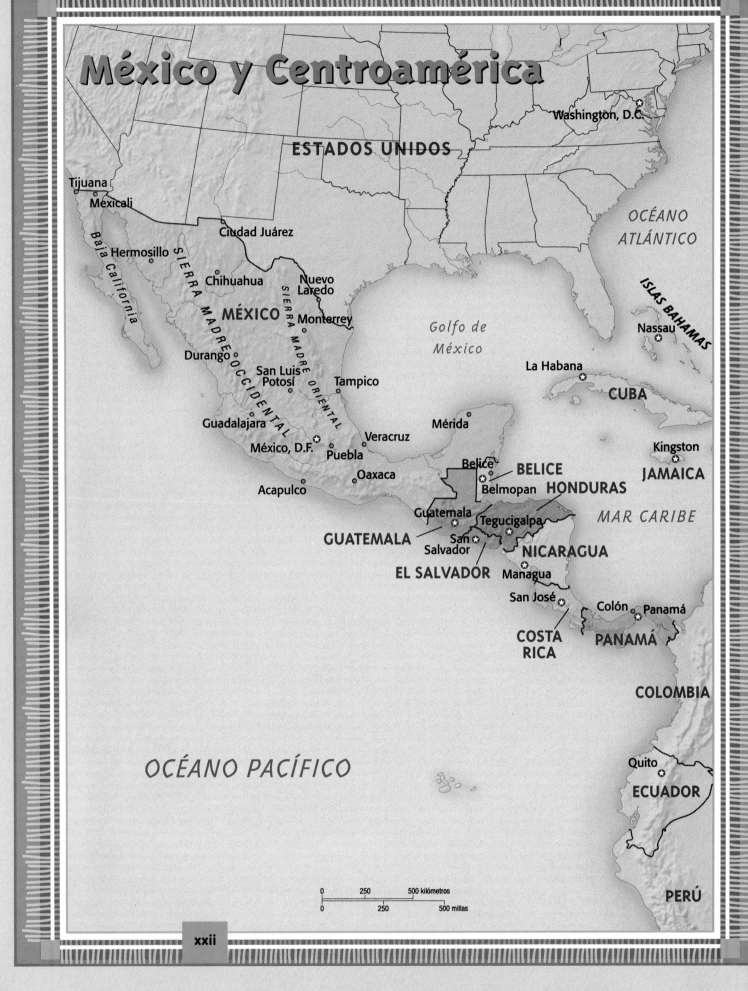

México y Centroamérica

ESTADOS UNIDOS

Washington, D.C.

OCÉANO ATLÁNTICO

Tijuana

Mexicali

Ciudad Juárez

Hermosillo

SIERRA MADRE OCCIDENTAL

Chihuahua

Nuevo Laredo

Baja California

MÉXICO

Monterrey

SIERRA MADRE ORIENTAL

Durango

San Luis Potosí

Golfo de México

ISLAS BAHAMAS

Nassau

La Habana

CUBA

Tampico

Guadalajara

Mérida

México, D.F.

Veracruz

Puebla

Kingston

JAMAICA

Acapulco

Oaxaca

Belice

BELICE

Belmopan

HONDURAS

Guatemala

GUATEMALA

Tegucigalpa

MAR CARIBE

San Salvador

NICARAGUA

EL SALVADOR

Managua

San José

Colón

Panamá

COSTA RICA

PANAMÁ

COLOMBIA

OCÉANO PACÍFICO

Quito

ECUADOR

| 0 | 250 | 500 kilómetros |
| 0 | 250 | 500 millas |

PERÚ

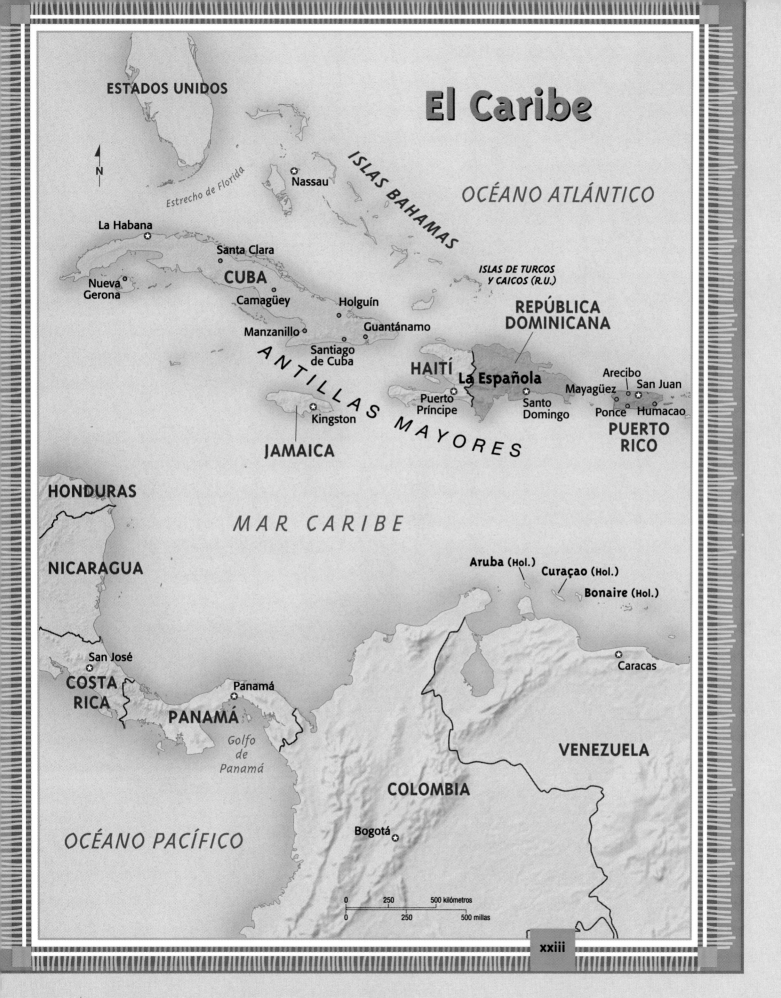

El Caribe

ESTADOS UNIDOS

N

Estrecho de Florida

Nassau

ISLAS BAHAMAS

OCÉANO ATLÁNTICO

La Habana

Santa Clara

CUBA

ISLAS DE TURCOS
Y CAICOS (R.U.)

Nueva
Gerona

Camagüey

Holguín

REPÚBLICA
DOMINICANA

Manzanillo

Guantánamo

Santiago
de Cuba

ANTILLAS

HAITÍ

La Española

Arecibo

San Juan

Mayagüez

Puerto
Príncipe

Santo
Domingo

Ponce

Humacao

Kingston

MAYORES

PUERTO
RICO

JAMAICA

HONDURAS

MAR CARIBE

NICARAGUA

Aruba (Hol.)

Curaçao (Hol.)

Bonaire (Hol.)

San José

Caracas

COSTA
RICA

Panamá

PANAMÁ

Golfo
de
Panamá

VENEZUELA

COLOMBIA

OCÉANO PACÍFICO

Bogotá

0   250   500 kilómetros

0   250   500 millas

Sudamérica

MAR CARIBE

OCÉANO ATLÁNTICO

Barranquilla
Cartagena
Maracaibo
Lago Maracaibo
Caracas
TRINIDAD Y TOBAGO
Puerto España

VENEZUELA

Georgetown
Paramaribo
GUYANA
Cayena
SURINAM
GUYANA FRANCESA (FRANCIA)

Medellín
Manizales
Bogotá
Cali
COLOMBIA

Otavalo
Quito
ECUADOR
Guayaquil
Cuenca

Ecuador

Río Negro
Río Amazonas

PERÚ

Río Madeira
Río Tapajóz
Río Xingú
Río Tocantins

Trujillo

BRASIL

Río São Francisco

Lima
Callao

CORDILLERA

Lago Titicaca

BOLIVIA
La Paz
Cochabamba
Santa Cruz

Sucre

Brasilia

Islas Galápagos
(Ecuador)

Bogotá
COLOMBIA
Quito
ECUADOR
OCÉANO PACÍFICO
PERÚ
0   250 kilómetros
0   250 millas

GRAN CHACO
PARAGUAY
Asunción

Trópico de Capricornio

Salta
San Miguel de Tucumán
Resistencia

CHILE

Córdoba
Mendoza
Rosario
URUGUAY

Valparaíso
Santiago
Buenos Aires
La Plata
Montevideo

OCÉANO PACÍFICO

ARGENTINA

Concepción

Bahía Blanca
Mar del Plata

Temuco

ANDES
PATAGONIA
PAMPAS

OCÉANO ATLÁNTICO

0   250   500 kilómetros
0   250   500 millas

Estrecho de Magallanes

Tierra del Fuego
Islas Malvinas (R.U.)

Cabo de Hornos

N

xxiv

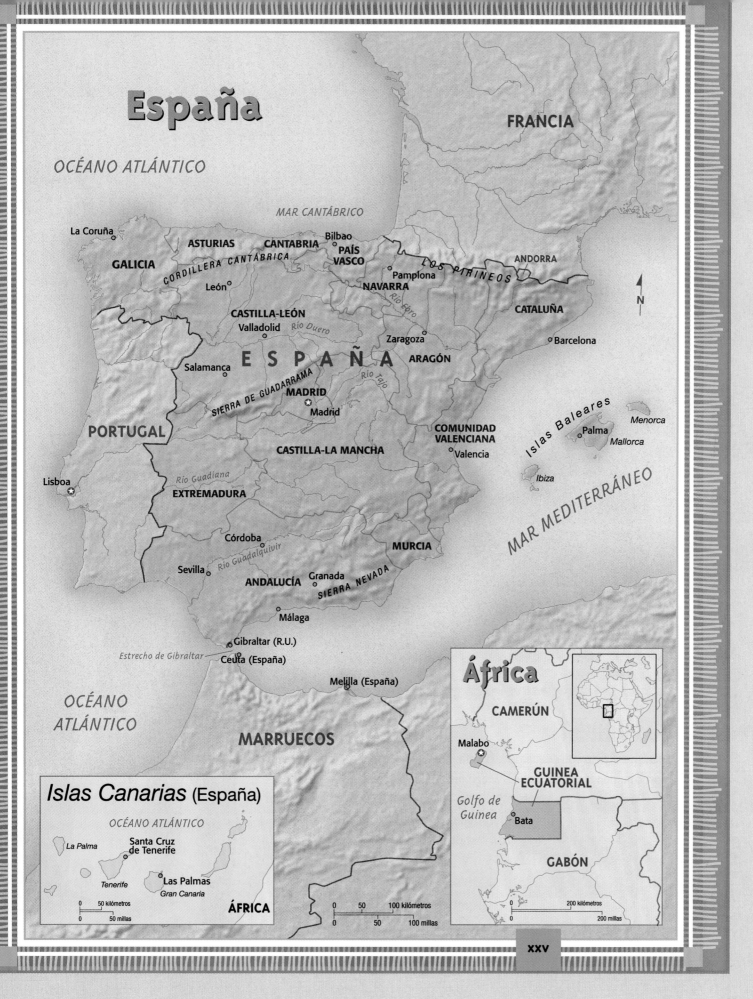

España

OCÉANO ATLÁNTICO

FRANCIA

MAR CANTÁBRICO

La Coruña

ASTURIAS CANTABRIA
GALICIA   CORDILLERA CANTÁBRICA Bilbao
                                  PAÍS
                                  VASCO
León   Pamplona
                                  NAVARRA
CASTILLA-LEÓN
Valladolid   Río Duero
                           Zaragoza
E S P A Ñ A   ARAGÓN
Salamanca
              SIERRA DE GUADARRAMA   Río Tajo
              MADRID
              Madrid

PORTUGAL

LOS PIRINEOS   ANDORRA

CATALUÑA

Barcelona

Islas Baleares   Menorca
                 Palma
                 Mallorca
COMUNIDAD
VALENCIANA
Valencia   Ibiza

CASTILLA-LA MANCHA

Río Guadiana

Lisboa

EXTREMADURA

MAR MEDITERRÁNEO

Córdoba
Río Guadalquivir   MURCIA
Sevilla
        ANDALUCÍA Granada
                   SIERRA NEVADA
        Málaga

Gibraltar (R.U.)
Estrecho de Gibraltar — Ceuta (España)

OCÉANO
ATLÁNTICO

Melilla (España)

MARRUECOS

Islas Canarias (España)

OCÉANO ATLÁNTICO

La Palma   Santa Cruz
            de Tenerife

Tenerife   Las Palmas
            Gran Canaria
ÁFRICA

50 kilómetros
0
50 millas

África

CAMERÚN

Malabo
GUINEA
ECUATORIAL
Golfo de
Guinea
        Bata

GABÓN

50   100 kilómetros
0 50   100 millas

200 kilómetros
0   200 millas

Why Learn Spanish?

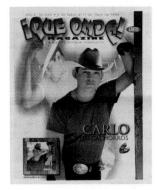

To Appreciate the Importance of Spanish in the U.S.

The influence of Spanish is everywhere. Spanish words like **plaza** and **tornado** have become part of the English language. Just think of U.S. place names that come from Spanish: **Colorado, Florida, Nevada, Los Angeles, San Antonio, La Villita,** etc. You can see Spanish on signs. There are Spanish radio and television stations. Singers such as Jon Secada perform in Spanish as well as English.

To Connect

Spanish will help you **communicate** with other people. Spanish is the second most common language in the U.S. and the third most common in the world. You will be able do things like **ask someone for directions, bargain at a market,** and **order in a restaurant** in Spanish.

To Have Fun

Taking Spanish is a new experience that will expose you to the **food,** the **music,** the **celebrations,** and other aspects of Spanish-speaking cultures. It will make travel to other countries as well as to different places in the United States much more enjoyable and more meaningful.

To Be Challenged

Studying Spanish is a challenge. There is a lot to learn, but it's not just vocabulary and grammar in a textbook. In the future you **will be able to read** Spanish-language **newspapers, magazines,** and **books.** Imagine reading *Don Quijote de la Mancha* by Miguel de Cervantes in the original Spanish someday!

To Help You in the Future

Taking a foreign language like Spanish is an accomplishment to be emphasized on college and job applications. It can also help you fulfill college language requirements. Spanish can be **useful in many careers,** from doctor, bank teller, and social worker to teacher, tour guide, and translator.

How to Study Spanish

Use Strategies

Listening strategies provide a starting point to help you understand.

Speaking strategies will help you express yourself in Spanish.

Reading strategies will show you different ways to approach reading.

Writing strategies help you out with your writing skills.

Cultural strategies help you compare Spanish-speaking cultures of the world to your own culture.

PARA CONVERSAR
STRATEGY: SPEAKING
Saying what is the best and worst After Activity 8, decide which is the best **(el mejor)** or the worst **(el peor)** of these categories: **equipo de baloncesto, grupo musical, película del año.**

Use Study Hints

The **Apoyo para estudiar** feature provides study hints that will help you learn Spanish.

APOYO PARA ESTUDIAR

Preterite Tense

Since the **nosotros** form of an **-ar** verb is the same in the preterite and the present tenses, how can you determine the tense? Use context clues. Look for time indicators, like those in the vocabulary box, and the tense of other verbs.

Build Your Confidence

Everyone learns differently, and there are different ways to achieve a goal. Find out what works for you. Grammar boxes are set up with an explanation, a visual representation, and examples from real-life contexts. Use this combination of words and graphics to help you learn Spanish. Focus on whatever helps you most.

GRAMÁTICA   The Verb **decir**

To talk about what someone says, use the verb **decir**. The verb **decir** means *to say* or *to tell*. It has several irregular forms in the present tense.

digo	decimos
dices	decís
dice	dicen

Only the **nosotros(as)** and **vosotros(as)** forms are regular.

Sofía says:
—Yo **digo que** el mercado tiene las cosas más bonitas.
I say that the market has the prettiest things.

Note that **decir que** means *to say that*...

Have Fun

Taking a foreign language does not have to be all serious work. The dialogs in this book present the Spanish language in **entertaining, real-life contexts.**

- Pair and group activities give you a chance to **interact with your classmates.**
- Vocabulary and grammar puzzles will test your knowledge, but will also be **fun to do.**

Listen to Spanish
Inside and Outside of Class

Hearing Spanish will help you understand it. Pay attention to the **dialogs** and the **listening activities** in class.

Take advantage of opportunities to **hear Spanish outside of class** as well.

- Do you know someone who speaks Spanish?
- Are there any Spanish-language radio and/or television stations in your area?
- Does your video store have any Spanish-language movies?

Take Risks

The goal of studying a foreign language like Spanish is to **communicate.**

Don't be afraid to **speak.**

Everyone makes mistakes, so don't worry if you make a few. When you do make a mistake, **pause and then try again.**

McDougal Littell

¡En español!

Unit Theme
Friends and family at work and at play

Communication
- Greet and introduce others
- Say where people are from
- Express likes and dislikes
- Describe friends and family
- Talk about dates and ages
- Express possession
- Talk about school
- Discuss obligations and plans
- Talk about schedules and time
- Ask questions
- Say where you are going
- Request food
- Sequence events
- Extend invitations
- Talk on the phone
- Express feelings and preferences
- Say what just happened and what is happening
- Talk about sports
- Say what you know
- Make comparisons
- Describe the weather

Teaching Resource Options

Audiovisual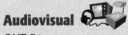
OHT B1

BRIDGE UNIT

ESTADOS UNIDOS

CIUDAD DE MÉXICO

SAN JOSÉ

PUERTO RICO

Océano Pacífico LOS ÁNGELES SAN DIEGO

EL PASO
CIUDAD JUÁREZ

ISLAS HAWAI

MÉXICO

ALASKA

ETAPA 1 Mi mundo

ETAPA 2 Una semana típica

ETAPA 3 El fin de semana

CIUDAD DE MÉXICO
DIEGO RIVERA (1886–1957) painted *La vendedora de flores* (1942) as well as many other paintings and murals. What paintings by Mexican artists have you seen?

Middle School Classroom Community

Paired Activity Ask pairs of students to study the map. Have them list all of the Spanish words on this page for which they know, or can guess, the English equivalent. Have them share their lists and their reasoning with the class.

Game Play **Yo tengo… ¿Quién tiene?** Make a set of alphabet and numeral cards (0–9). Distribute them equally, keeping the leftovers. Hold up a card and say **Yo tengo b, ¿Quién tiene z?** The student with *z* says **Yo tengo z, ¿Quién tiene** (another letter or numeral). The object is to keep going as long as possible without repeating, so students need to keep track of used letters and numerals.

CANADÁ

NUEVA YORK

CHICAGO

Océano Atlántico

ESTADOS UNIDOS

DALLAS

HOUSTON

SAN ANTONIO

MIAMI

MONTERREY

Golfo de México

Mar Caribe

CIUDAD DE MÉXICO

OAXACA

PUERTO RICO

ARECIBO — SAN JUAN

MAYAGÜEZ — EL YUNQUE

HUMACAO

PONCE — VIEQUES

CENTROAMÉRICA

SUDAMÉRICA

ESTADOS UNIDOS
EL PASEO DEL RÍO is an area where you can hear mariachis and ride a boat through San Antonio. What do you think its name means?

PUERTO RICO
EL LORO PUERTORRIQUEÑO became an endangered species in 1971, when only twenty of these parrots were left. Their numbers have now increased. You might see one in El Yunque, the tropical rain forest. What other animals have been saved from extinction?

Culture Highlights

● **EL INTERCAMBIO** Neither Americans nor Europeans can picture their lives without the products exchanged as a consequence of Columbus's voyage. It began a trade network of flora, fauna, and products never imagined by inhabitants of either continent. Today's ordinary tomato (**tomatl**) was feared as poisonous, while chocolate (**xocolatl**) was hoarded by the Versailles court. Sugar, a scarcity in Europe, flourished on Hispaniola; corn, tobacco, potatoes, and chiles sailed to Europe, while wheat, olives, grapes, oranges, and lemons returned. Condors, vultures, parrots, **quetzales,** and turkeys (**guaxolotl**) reached Europe, while chickens, pigs, sheep, horses, cattle, donkeys, mules, mastiffs, bloodhounds, etc., came back.

Teaching Middle School Students

Challenge Encourage students to look up and compare the capitals of the U.S., Puerto Rico, and Mexico.

Multiple Intelligences

Verbal Get students back into thinking in Spanish by having them work in pairs to dictate and spell back words on these pages.

Kinesthetic Have students write words from these pages in the air as you spell them out. After you spell each word, ask students to say it in unison.

Block Schedule

Research Invite students to look at the map and read all of the captions. Have them select one or two places in Mexico or Puerto Rico and research where the name came from. They might also choose a place in the United States that has a Spanish name.

Ampliación

These activities may be used at various points in the Bridge Unit sequence.

For Block Schedule, you may find that these projects will provide a welcome change of pace while reviewing and reinforcing the material presented in the unit. See the **Block Scheduling Copymasters.**

● PROJECTS

Personalidades de nuestro mundo latino Have students create a Latino personalities BIG book, using poster paper for each page. Students form groups according to fields such as Art, Literature, Entertainment, Sports, Politics/Government, and Medicine/Science. Each group is responsible for researching, designing, and illustrating its page and presenting it to the class. They can accompany the presentation with music by a Latino singer, a print by a Latino artist, a video clip from a Latino film, etc. Bind the completed pages together using loose-leaf rings. Finally, your class can share their project with other classes in the school, family members, or friends at a special presentation.

> PACING SUGGESTION: Upon completion of any Etapa. This may be an ongoing project through the school year, after a unit on a specific country.

● STORYTELLING

La quinceañera de Rosalinda Review any pertinent vocabulary before reading this mini-story twice. Next, have students retell the story several times. Then students form pairs or small groups to continue the action with a dialog they write and act out for the class. Their dialog can be set before the party, at it, or even afterward.

> Mary y Helen acaban de recibir invitaciones a la quinceañera de una amiga de su clase de origen mexicano. Es la primera vez que van a una quinceañera y están muy emocionadas y contentas. La fiesta es sábado por la noche el 16 de mayo en el Gran Hall del Hotel River Walk en San Antonio a las 8:30 de la noche. Tienen que llevar vestidos muy elegantes. Hay una cena completa y un baile con música mariachi, etc.

Tape the presentations so that students can critique themselves. Save them for their portfolios and/or compare them with others they present later on so that they can appreciate their progress. After the presentation, listeners describe the conversation they liked the best and see if classmates know which one they are referring to.

> PACING SUGGESTION: Upon completion of Etapa 2.

● BULLETIN BOARD/POSTERS

Latinos todos Have students make signs for each Hispanic country and use them as headings for articles they find in English and Spanish-language publications. Use the bulletin board as a center on Latino social and political issues. When students bring in an article, they summarize it (5 minutes or less) and share it with the class. Then they add it to the bulletin board. Appoint a student to update the board as necessary.

GAMES

Todo está en el nombre

Divide the class into groups according to the states with Spanish names: California, Colorado, New Mexico, Florida, Montana, and Nevada. Furnish each group with a road map of that state. Set a time limit, 6–7 minutes, and have them list the names of as many places as they can that have Spanish names. Give the team another 5 minutes to look up the meanings of any names they are unsure of. When time is up, teams read their lists and discuss any unusual names. Then they compile a class chart by categories (i.e., *Ríos, Lagos, Playas, Montañas, Pueblos, Ciudades, Parques,* etc.).

PACING SUGGESTION: Use at any point in the unit.

MUSIC

Los discos latinos

Because this unit deals with Latino communities in the U.S., Mexico (City), and Puerto Rico, have students form 3 groups, one for each Etapa studied. Students visit record stores and find out what kinds of music come from that area. For example, the Tex-Mex group looks for music typical to that area, writes down titles, listens to some of the music, and then brings examples of it to class to share. They may include facts about when that music was first heard and personalities in its history such as Sal Marquez or the late Selina.

HANDS-ON CRAFTS

Un mural movible

Have the class design a wall hanging of the Hispanic countries. Each student is responsible for the design and execution of a square (18" x 18") on a theme that they decide upon collectively. They'll need 5 yards of felt in any color, plus several pieces of varying colors to cut the shapes from, fabric paint, spray adhesive, an old sheet, and finally, yarn, glitter, embroidery thread, sequins, feathers, or anything they want for decoration. Students consult encyclopedias, tourist guides, books, and magazines for ideas. Themes might include flora and fauna, famous places or people, musical instruments, dances, regional costumes, indigenous groups, products, or crafts. When all the squares are ready, mount them on an old sheet with fabric glue or iron-on webbing. Then students prepare a legend to go with each square so that viewers can understand its symbols. Display this work in a prominent place in the classroom or school where it can be viewed, interpreted, and admired.

RECIPE

Salsa de barbacoa

This barbecue sauce, a specialty of Oaxaca, is delicious with ribs or chicken.

Receta

Salsa de barbacoa

225 g. (1/2 lb.) de chiles chipotles secos (sin tallos y semillas)
2 cucharadas de vinagre de vino
1/2 de taza de mostaza
agua hervida

10 dientes de ajo pelados
2 cucharillas de orégano
2/3 de taza de miel
sal y pimienta negra molida, a gusto

Ponga los chiles en remojo (10 min.). Escúrralos, reservando 1/2 taza de líquido. Eche los chiles, el agua, los ajos, el vinagre y el orégano en una licuadora (1 min.). Cuele todo. Tire los restos. Añada la miel, la mostaza, sal y pimienta. Bata bien. Use la salsa para carne a las brasas. ¡Mmmm!

Planning Guide CLASSROOM MANAGEMENT

OBJECTIVES

Communication
- Greet and introduce others *pp. 4–6, 8*
- Say where people are from *pp. 8–9*
- Express likes and dislikes *pp. 9–10*
- Describe friends and family *pp. 12–18, 20–23*
- Talk about dates and ages *pp. 20–22, 25–26*
- Express possession *pp. 23–25*

Grammar
- Familiar and Formal Greetings *p. 6*
- Subject Pronouns and the Verb **ser** *pp. 7–8*
- Using **ser de** to Express Origin *pp. 8–9*
- Using Verbs to Talk About What You Like to Do *pp. 9–10*
- Using Definite Articles with Specific Things *pp. 14–15*
- Using Indefinite Articles with Unspecified Things *p. 16*
- Using Adjectives to Describe: Gender *p. 17*
- Using Adjectives to Describe: Number *p. 18*
- Saying What You Have: The Verb **tener** *pp. 22–23*
- Expressing Possession Using **de** *pp. 23–24*
- Expessing Possession: Possessive Adjectives *pp. 24–25*
- Giving Dates: Day and Month *pp. 25–26*

PROGRAM RESOURCES

Print
- Activity and Assessment Book
  - Vocabulary Activities *pp. 2, 5, 8–9*
  - Grammar Activities *pp. 3–4, 6–7, 10–11*
  - Information Gap Activities *p. 12*
  - Cooperative Quizzes *pp. 13–16*
  - Audioscripts *pp. 54–58*

Audiovisual
- Bridge Audio Program Cassettes / CD
- Overhead Transparencies B1–B6

Student Text Listening Activity Scripts

 **¿Qué le gusta?** *page 10*

1. A Jorge le gusta nadar.
2. A Diego le gusta comer.
3. A Nina le gusta bailar.
4. A Carmen le gusta cantar.
5. A Marta le gusta patinar.

 **Los cumpleaños** *page 26*

1. El cumpleaños de mi abuela es el doce de marzo.
2. El cumpleaños de Verónica es hoy, el treinta de septiembre.
3. El cumpleaños de Andrés es el primero de julio.
4. El cumpleaños de mi mamá es el catorce de diciembre.
5. El cumpleaños de mi abuelo es el cuatro de noviembre.
6. El cumpleaños de mi papá es el once de junio.
7. El cumpleaños de David es el primero de agosto.
8. El cumpleaños de Javier es el veinticinco de abril.

Pacing Guide

Sample Lesson Plan - 45 Minute Schedule

DAY 1

Unit and Etapa Openers
• Discuss the Openers, pp. 1–3; brainstorm about what students remember from last year. 10 MIN.

En contexto: Vocabulario
• Play the audio. Present the vocabulary, pp. 4–5. 5 MIN.
• Work orally with the class to do *Actividad* 1. 5 MIN.
• Have students work in groups to do *Actividades* 2–3. 5 MIN.

En acción: Vocabulario y gramática
• Quick Start Review (TE, p. 6) 5 MIN.
• Present *Gramática en vivo*: Familiar and Formal Greetings, p. 6. 5 MIN.
• Have students write responses to *Actividad* 4, and then call on them to say their greetings aloud. 5 MIN.
• Have students work in pairs to do *Actividades* 5 and 6. 5 MIN.

Homework Option:
• Activity and Assessment Book, p. 2

DAY 2

En acción (cont.)
• Check homework. 5 MIN.
• Present *Gramática en vivo*: Pronouns and the Verb *ser*, p. 7. 5 MIN.
• Assign *Actividad* 7. 5 MIN.
• Have students write responses to *Actividad* 8, and then call on them to give their responses orally. 5 MIN.
• Assign *Actividad* 9. 5 MIN.
• Have students work in pairs to do *Actividad* 10. 5 MIN.
• Present *Gramática en vivo*: Using *ser de* to Express Origin, p. 8. 5 MIN.
• Assign *Actividad* 11. 5 MIN.
• Have students work in groups on *Actividad* 12. 5 MIN.

Homework Option:
• Activity and Assessment Book, p. 3

DAY 3

En acción (cont.)
• Check homework. 5 MIN.
• Present *Gramática en vivo*: Using Verbs to Talk About What You Like to Do, and the *Vocabulario*, p. 9. 10 MIN.
• Play the audio. Assign *Actividad* 13. 5 MIN.
• Have students work in pairs to do *Actividad* 14. 5 MIN.
• Assign *Actividad* 15. 5 MIN.

En resumen: Ya sabes
• Review vocabulary, p. 11. 10 MIN.
• Complete the *Juego*, p. 11. 5 MIN.

Homework Option:
• Activity and Assessment Book, p. 4

DAY 4

En contexto: Vocabulario
• Check homework. 5 MIN.
• Quick Start Review (TE, p. 12) 5 MIN.
• Play the audio. Present the vocabulary, pp. 12–13. 5 MIN.
• Assign *Actividades* 16–18. 5 MIN.

En acción: Vocabulario y gramática
• Present *Gramática en vivo*: Using Definite Articles with Specific Things, and the *Vocabulario*, p. 14. 5 MIN.
• Assign *Actividad* 19. 5 MIN.
• Have students work in pairs to do *Actividad* 20. 5 MIN.
• Present *Gramática en vivo*: Using Indefinite Articles with Unspecified Things, p. 16. 5 MIN.
• Assign *Actividades* 21–22. 5 MIN.

Homework Option:
• Activity and Assessment Book, pp. 5–6

DAY 5

En acción (cont.)
• Check homework. 5 MIN.
• Have pairs do *Actividad* 23. 5 MIN.
• Present *Gramática en vivo*: Using Adjectives to Describe: Gender, and the *Vocabulario*, p. 17. 5 MIN.
• Assign *Actividad* 24. 5 MIN.
• Have students work in pairs to do *Actividad* 25. 5 MIN.
• Present *Gramática en vivo*: Using Adjectives to Describe: Number, and the *Vocabulario*, p. 18. 5 MIN.
• Assign *Actividades* 26–27. 5 MIN.

En resumen: Ya sabes
• Review vocabulary, p. 19. 5 MIN.
• Do the *Juego*, p. 19. 5 MIN.

Homework Option:
• Activity and Assessment Book, p. 7

DAY 6

En contexto: Vocabulario
• Check homework. 5 MIN.
• Quick Start Review (TE, p. 20) 5 MIN.
• Play the audio. Present the vocabulary, pp. 20–21. 5 MIN.
• Work orally on *Actividad* 28, and then have pairs do *Actividad* 29. 5 MIN.
• Assign *Actividad* 30. 5 MIN.

En acción: Vocabulario y gramática
• Present *Gramática en vivo*: Saying What You Have: The Verb *tener,* and the *Vocabulario*, p. 22. 5 MIN.
• Assign *Actividades* 31–32. 5 MIN.
• Present *Gramática en vivo*: Expressing Possession Using *de*, p. 23. 5 MIN.
• Assign *Actividad* 33. 5 MIN.

Homework Option:
• Activity and Assessment Book, pp. 8–9

DAY 7

En acción (cont.)
• Check homework. 5 MIN.
• Have pairs do *Actividad* 34. 5 MIN.
• Present *Gramática en vivo*: Expressing Possession: Possessive Adjectives, p. 24. 5 MIN.
• Have pairs do *Actividades* 35 and 36. 5 MIN.
• Assign *Actividad* 37. 5 MIN.
• Present *Gramática en vivo*: Giving Dates: Day and Month, p. 25. 5 MIN.
• Review the *Vocabulario*, p. 26, and play the audio. Assign *Actividad* 38. 5 MIN.
• Assign *Actividades* 39 and 40. 5 MIN. .

En resumen: Ya sabes
• Review vocabulary, and do the *Juego*, p. 27. 5 MIN.

Homework Option:
• Activity and Assessment Book, pp. 10–11

Classroom Management Tip

Use technology There is a wealth of information about things Hispanic available on the Internet. Many parents and educators are concerned about students having unsupervised access to the Internet because of the risk of their visiting inappropriate web sites.

Preview all web sites to which you refer your students, but *do* encourage them to use the Internet as a valuable research venue.

You might have students use the Internet to contact the San Antonio Chamber of Commerce, the Tourist Office, Historical Society, and so forth, to find out about the Spanish influence there.

Teaching Resource Options

Audiovisual
OHT B1–B6

Teaching Suggestions
Previewing the Etapa

• Ask students to study the picture on these pages (1 min.).
• Students close books. Ask them to tell what the students in the picture are doing.
• Students reopen books. Ask them to tell which cities are displayed.
• Ask students to name the cities where they were born, where their parents came from, where their grandparents live, etc.
• Ask students what title they would give this bulletin board display.

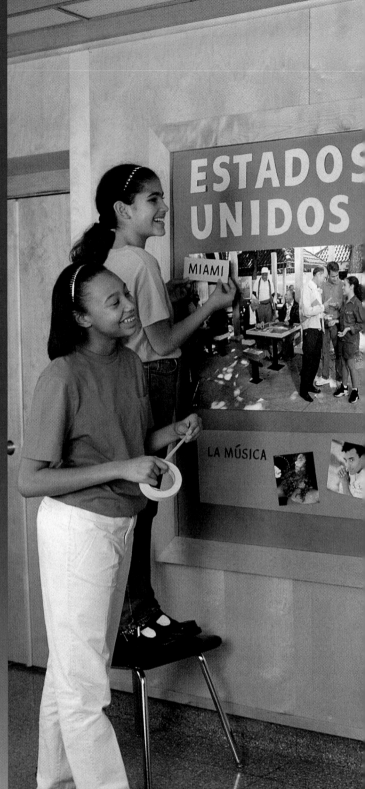

BRIDGE UNIT

ETAPA 1

Mi mundo

• Greet and introduce others

• Say where people are from

• Express likes and dislikes

• Describe friends and family

• Talk about dates and ages

• Express possession

2

Middle School Classroom Management

Cooperative Learning Go over the expectations for working in cooperative groups this year. Make a class list of group roles and words or phrases to use when clarifying or encouraging. The list of roles could include Recorder, Coach, Questioner, Encourager. The list of clarifying and encouraging phrases might include **Cúentame más. Explica, por favor. Bueno. Me gusta esa idea.**

Peer Teaching Ask students to think about what Spanish they remember best. Have them declare themselves experts on these topics and prepare themselves to help others.

Community Connections

Have students work in groups to find statistics on a U.S. city with a large Hispanic population. (These may include Los Angeles, San Antonio, Miami, New York, and Chicago.) Have them make pie charts showing country or region of origin for Hispanics in their cities. The U.S. Census Bureau has a web site where much of this information may be found.

Block Schedule

Gather and Sort Have students study the **Etapa** objectives and then make personal lists under each category, for example, things they like and don't like and birthdays of friends and family members. Students can use this as a reference list as they complete activities throughout the **Etapa**.

Teaching Middle School Students

Extra Help Brainstorm about the objectives on p. 2 so that students are ready to do activities in this **Etapa**.

Native Speakers Ask native speakers to interview family members about their countries of origin so that they're ready to do other Native Speakers activities in this unit.

Multiple Intelligences

Interpersonal Ask students to work in pairs to decide what the theme of the bulletin board in the photo spread is. Ask them to expand on it.

Visual Students may want to construct their own bulletin board of Spanish and Latin American influences and customs in the United States.

Teaching Resource Options

Print

Activity and Assessment Book
  Vocabulary 1.1, p. 2
  Audioscripts, pp. 54–58

Audiovisual

Bridge Audio Program Cassettes / CD
OHT B2

Teaching Suggestions
Reconnecting with Vocabulary

• Read each section of the vocabulary aloud, having students repeat after you.
• Ask for student volunteers to read the mini-dialogs (perhaps for bonus points!).
• Use the TPR activity to reinforce the meaning of individual words.

En contexto

VOCABULARIO

Francisco García Flores has just moved into his new community in Miami. He is getting to know the people there. Look at the illustrations. They will help you understand the meanings of the words in blue.

un policía

una mujer

B El policía vive en el apartamento.

C La mujer vive en un apartamento también. Ella es una amiga de Francisco.

un chico

una chica

A El chico es Francisco García. La chica es Alma Cifuentes.

Alma: ¿Cómo estás?
Francisco: Estoy bien, ¿y tú?
Alma: Regular.

una estudiante una maestra

D La mujer es maestra. La muchacha es estudiante.

Middle School Classroom Community

TPR Read the sentences in the lettered sections out of order. Have students raise their right hands when they hear a word that could describe them.

Game Ask students to work in small groups to make cards with professions and cards with possible dwelling places. Students should take turns choosing one from each pile to form a sentence, such as **El profesor vive en la casa.**

una familia

un señor

una señora

una señorita

un muchacho

E La familia García vive en una casa. La señora García es doctora.

Alma: Bienvenido a la comunidad, Francisco.
Francisco: Gracias, Alma.
Alma: De nada.
Francisco: Te presento a mi familia.
Señor García: Encantado. ¿Cómo estás?
Alma: Muy bien, gracias, ¿y usted?
Señor García: Bien, gracias.

TENEMOS TAMALES HOJA

una muchacha

un hombre

F El hombre es el señor Estrada.

Señor Estrada: Hola, muchacha. ¿Qué tal?
Alma: Le presento a mi amigo Francisco.
Francisco: Mucho gusto. ¿Cómo está usted?
Señor Estrada: No muy bien hoy.
Francisco: ¿No muy bien?
Señor Estrada: ¡Es lunes! Estoy terrible.

ACTIVIDAD 1 — ¿Dónde viven?

Hablar Tell where each of these people lives.

modelo

la maestra / casa

La maestra vive en una **casa**.

1. el policía / casa
2. la muchacha / apartamento
3. la doctora / casa
4. mi familia / ¿?

ACTIVIDAD 2 — Saludos

Hablar/Escribir Complete the conversations. Then work with two classmates to act them out.

Chica: Hola, ¿qué __1__?
Chico: Muy bien. Y tú, ¿ __2__ estás?
Chica: ¡ __3__ terrible!

Señor: Le __4__ a mi amiga, la señora García.
Señorita: Encantada. ¿Cómo __5__ usted?
Señora: Muy __6__, gracias. ¿Y __7__?

ACTIVIDAD 3 — ¡Mucho gusto!

Hablar Find out the name of the student next to you and introduce him or her to another classmate.

ACTIVIDAD 1
Objective: Controlled practice Vocabulary

Answers
1. El policía vive en una casa.
2. La muchacha vive en un apartamento.
3. La doctora vive en una casa.
4. Mi familia vive en…

ACTIVIDAD 2
Objective: Transitional practice Vocabulary

Answers
1. tal
2. cómo
3. Estoy
4. presento
5. está
6. bien
7. usted

ACTIVIDAD 3
Objective: Open-ended practice Vocabulary

Answers will vary.

Quick Wrap-up

Check students' comprehension of names for people by having volunteers circulate around the room identifying persons in the room and saying, for example, **Es un chico; Es una chica; Es un amigo; Es una amiga; Es un hombre (una mujer)** [pointing to you].

Game

Presento a mi gente Have students bring in photos of family members or pictures from magazines, naming the people as they present them to the class. When all the pictures have been displayed, divide the class into 2 teams. A player from Team A chooses any picture except his or her own and reintroduces the people in it. Players from Team A continue reintroducing people, earning a point for each one, until they make a mistake. Play then passes to Team B.

Block Schedule

Process Time Allow students ample time to practice and understand when people should use the familiar form and formal form for greeting one another. Have partners write the names of all the different characters shown in the vocabulary on individual strips of paper. Tell them each to pick a strip and then role-play a greeting to one another using **tú** and **usted** appropriately.

Teaching Middle School Students

Extra Help Ask students to form a circle, and have one student begin by asking the student on his or her right ¿Cómo estás? That student will answer and then ask the next student the same question, and so on until each student has had a chance to ask and answer.

Native Speakers Ask students to share different ways people greet each other in their home countries.

Multiple Intelligences

Logical/Mathematical Have students put the vocabulary from pp. 4–5 into categories. They may choose male/female or profession/description, or any other set of categories that works.

Teaching Resource Options

Audiovisual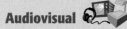

OHT B3 (Quick Start)

 Quick Start Review

♻ Vocabulary

Use OHT B3 or write on the board:
Match each phrase with its response.

1. ¿Qué tal?
2. ¿Cómo está usted?
3. Le presento a mi amiga, Maura.
4. Gracias.
5. La señora Gómez vive en una casa.

a. De nada.
b. Mucho gusto.
c. Muy bien, gracias. ¿Y usted?
d. Es maestra en la escuela.
e. Regular, ¿y tú?

Answers
1. e 2. c 3. b 4. a 5. d

Teaching Suggestions
Familiar and Formal Greetings

• Point out that people often just say
¿Cómo está? and omit **usted**
in the formal greeting.
• To reinforce familiar versus formal,
have a student stand up and state
his or her name; then have another
student give the appropriate greeting:
Señor Taylor → Señor Taylor, ¿cómo
está usted? Ana → Ana, ¿cómo
estás?

 Objective: Controlled practice
Formal/informal greetings

Answers
1. ¿Cómo estás? / ¿Qué tal?
2. ¿Cómo está usted?
3. ¿Cómo está usted?
4. ¿Cómo estás? / ¿Qué tal?
5. ¿Cómo estás? / ¿Qué tal?
6. ¿Cómo está usted?

 Objective: Transitional practice
Greetings

Answers
Answers may vary.
1. ¿Cómo está usted? / Bien, gracias.
2. ¿Qué tal? / Regular, gracias.
3. ¿Cómo estás? / Estoy terrible.
4. ¿Cómo está usted? / Muy bien, gracias.

En acción
VOCABULARIO Y GRAMÁTICA

Gramática en vivo

Sr. Estrada: ¡Alma! **¿Cómo estás** hoy?

Alma: Muy bien, señor Estrada,
¿y usted?

Familiar and Formal Greetings

Familiar:

¿Cómo estás?
is a familiar greeting.

Use with:
• a friend
• a family member
• someone younger

Another familiar greeting: **¿Qué tal?**

Tú is a familiar way to say *you*.

Formal:

¿Cómo está usted?
is a formal greeting.

Use with:
• a person you don't know
• someone older
• someone for whom you
  want to show respect

Usted is a formal way to say *you*.

 ACTIVIDAD **4**

¿Qué tal?

Hablar/Escribir How would you greet the following people?

1. una amiga
2. un maestro
3. un policía
4. tu mamá
5. un muchacho
6. una señora

6 seis
Bridge Unit

ACTIVIDAD **5**

¡Saludos!

Hablar Imagine you run into
the following people at the
store. Take turns greeting each
person and giving a response.

modelo

tu maestro(a) / muy bien

Estudiante A: *¿Cómo está usted?*

Estudiante B: *Estoy muy bien,
gracias.*

1. tu doctor(a) / bien
2. un(a) estudiante / regular
3. un(a) amigo(a) / terrible
4. un(a) policía / muy bien

ACTIVIDAD **6**

¿Cómo está usted?

Hablar Imagine your partner is
a teacher at your school. Greet
him or her and tell each other
how you are. Change roles.

Middle School Classroom Management

Student Self-Check Spend some time introducing
students to the Spanish-English dictionary. Show them
how to use it and where it is kept. Encourage them to
use it often.

Planning Ahead You may want to collect newspaper
or magazine photos of people of all ages to use in a
greetings drill.

Gramática en vivo

Alma: Arturo, te presento a Francisco García. Él es mi vecino.

Subject Pronouns and the Verb ser

▶ To discuss people in Spanish, you will often use **subject pronouns**. When you want to describe a person or explain who he or she is, use the verb **ser**.

	Singular		Plural
	yo soy		**nosotros(as)** somos
	I am		*we are*
familiar	**tú** eres		**vosotros(as)** sois
	you are		*you are*
formal	**usted** es		**ustedes** son
	you are		*you are*
	él, ella es		**ellos(as)** son
	he, she is		*they are*

▶ If Alma were to say that someone is a neighbor, she would say:

—**Él es un vecino.**

However, if she were to say that someone is a policeman, she would say:

—**Él es policía.**

> The word **un** or **una** does not appear before a profession.

¿Quiénes son?

Leer/Escribir Use subject pronouns to complete the sentences. There may be more than one right answer.

modelo

Ella *es una muchacha.*

1. _____ es un señor.
2. _____ soy estudiante.
3. _____ somos amigos.
4. _____ son hermanos.
5. _____ eres mi amiga.
6. _____ es una mujer.

Mi comunidad

Hablar/Escribir Point out the people in your community by telling who everyone is.

modelo

ella / doctora   **Ella es doctora.**

1. yo / estudiante
2. tú / amiga
3. nosotros / familia
4. él / maestro
5. ellas / muchachas

siete **7**
Etapa 1

Objective: Open-ended practice Greetings

Answers will vary.

Teaching Suggestions
Subject Pronouns and the Verb ser

- Point out that when the context is clear, subject pronouns are often omitted. When needed, they may be used to clarify (**Ella** [not **él**] **es de Miami**).
- After presenting **ser** and the pronouns, have students work in pairs to practice giving a pronoun and the corresponding verb form, and then switch roles.

Objective: Controlled practice Subject pronouns

Answers
1. Él/Usted
2. Yo
3. Nosotros
4. Ellos/Ustedes
5. Tú
6. Ella/Usted

Objective: Controlled practice Ser

Answers
1. Yo soy estudiante.
2. Tú eres una amiga.
3. Nosotros somos una familia.
4. Él es maestro.
5. Ellas son muchachas.

Teaching Middle School Students

Extra Help Work with students to make up a mnemonic device that helps them remember when to use formal and familiar forms.

Multiple Intelligences

Intrapersonal Ask students to use **soy** to create as many sentences about themselves as they can.

Visual Provide students with photos from magazines or newspapers and ask them to write as many sentences using the correct forms of **ser** as they can.

Block Schedule

FunBreak Invite small groups to play a game of Charades using all the profession names they know (including **estudiante**). As students pantomime a profession, group members use subject pronouns in their guesses. **Tú eres doctora. Ella es doctora.**

Vocabulary/Grammar • BRIDGE UNIT Etapa 1

Teaching Resource Options

Print

Activity and Assessment Book
Grammar 1.1, p. 3

9 **Objective:** Controlled practice
Ser

Answers

1. es	5. son
2. soy	6. somos
3. eres	7. son
4. es	

10 **Objective:** Open-ended practice
Vocabulary/**ser**

Answers will vary.

Teaching Suggestions
Using ser de to Express Origin

• Have students imagine that they are from a Spanish-speaking country. Then have them prepare a piece of paper with their chosen country of origin written on it in large print (you should make one, too). Starting with yourself, say **Soy de…**, then point to and say your country. Have students follow your example.

• Expand on the activity by asking where different people are from and having students answer: **¿De dónde es Tara? Ella es de México.** Practice all the forms of **ser** and subject pronouns.

11 **Objective:** Controlled practice
Ser de

Answers

1. Pedro y Adrian son de Miami.
2. Yo soy de Estados Unidos.
3. Juan es de Costa Rica.
4. Nosotros somos de Texas.
5. Ella es de Nicaragua.
6. Tú eres de Guatemala.
7. Ustedes son de Argentina.
8. Mercedes es de Chile.
9. Usted es de Bolivia.
10. Marta es de España.

9

Presentaciones

Escribir Complete the conversation between Rosa and her teacher.

Rosa: ¿Usted ___1___ la señora Mendoza?

Señora M: Sí, yo ___2___ la señora Mendoza. Y tú ___3___ Rosa.

Rosa: Sí. Le presento a María. Ella ___4___ mi amiga.

Señora M: Encantada. ¿Ustedes ___5___ mis estudiantes?

Rosa: Sí, nosotras ___6___ sus estudiantes. Estos muchachos también ___7___ sus estudiantes.

Señora M: Muy bien. ¡Bienvenidos!

10

¿Quién?

Hablar Take turns telling your partner about three people you know. Include their profession.

modelo

La señora Garza es una mujer. Es policía.

Gramática en vivo

Alma: Pues, ¿**de** dónde **son** ustedes?

Francisco: Nosotros **somos de** muchos lugares. Mamá **es de** Puerto Rico. Papá **es de** México. Yo **soy de** Puerto Rico y David **es de** San Antonio.

 Using ser de to Express Origin

 To say where a person is from, use: **ser + de + place**

11

¿De dónde son?

Escribir Write sentences describing where everyone is from.

modelo

Luisa / Perú
***Luisa** es de **Perú**.*

1. Pedro y Adrian / Miami
2. yo / Estados Unidos
3. Juan / Costa Rica
4. nosotros / Texas
5. ella / Nicaragua
6. tú / Guatemala
7. ustedes / Argentina
8. Mercedes / Chile
9. usted / Bolivia
10. Marta / España

---

8 ocho
Bridge Unit

Middle School Classroom Community

Paired Activity Ask students to work together to present the dialog in **Actividad 9** to the class. Male students will adjust the nouns and pronouns for their gender.

Portfolio Ask students to choose 3 famous people and write where each comes from.

Rubric

Criteria	Scale	
Accuracy of information	1 2 3 4 5	A = 13–15 pts.
Logical organization	1 2 3 4 5	B = 10–12 pts.
Vocabulary use	1 2 3 4 5	C = 7–9 pts.
		D = 4–6 pts.
		F = < 4 pts.

¿De dónde eres?

Hablar/Escribir Conduct a survey among your classmates. Ask five people where they are from. Fill out a chart like the one below. Write your results as a sentence.

Estudiante	Es de...
Trina	Trina es de Denver.
Luis	Luis es de Springfield.

Gramática en vivo

Alma: A Arturo **le gusta** mucho **correr**. A mí me gusta también. ¿**Te gusta correr**, Francisco?

Francisco: No, **no** me gusta mucho **correr**.

Using Verbs to Talk About What You Like to Do

When you want to talk about what you like to do, use the phrase:

Me gusta + *infinitive*

The infinitive is the basic form of a verb.

Other helpful phrases to talk about what people like:

Te gusta correr. *You like to run.*

Le gusta correr. *He/She likes to run.*

To say someone doesn't like something, use **no** before the phrase.

No me gusta **correr**.
I don't like to run.

Vocabulario

Infinitives ♻ Ya sabes

bailar   **cantar**   **comer**   **escribir**

leer   **nadar**   **patinar**   **trabajar**

¿Qué te gusta?

Objective: Open-ended practice
Ser de

Answers will vary.

Teaching Suggestions
Using Verbs to Talk About What You Like to Do

- Personalize each verb by asking individual students if they like to do the things pictured.
- Practice **le gusta** by asking the entire class ¿**A quién le gusta** ___?; depending on who responds, have students give answers such as: **A Tony le gusta** ___ **pero a Sarah no le gusta.**

Game

El alfabeto infinitivo A player from Team A tells what he or she likes or dislikes to do, spelling out the infinitive. (**Me gusta j-u-g-a-r en el parque.**) A player from Team B repeats the sentence with **le gusta**, saying the infinitive, and adding a new sentence with a spelled-out infinitive. (**A Noah le gusta jugar en el parque. Me gusta c-o-m-e-r en restaurantes.**) If the student who is up misses the verb, play passes to the next person on the other team.

Block Schedule

Journal Have students interview teachers or other staff members in your school. Students then write a brief biography, including where the interviewees are from, where they live, and what they like to do. The information can be written as a journal entry.

Teaching Middle School Students

Extra Help Help students to make up a mnemonic device—a jingle or silly sentence—to remember the connection between **¿De dónde...?** and **ser + de + place.**

Challenge Have students write their own versions of the conversation in **Actividad 9**, with themselves and you as characters.

Multiple Intelligences

Musical/Rhythmic Have students write a rhyming song lyric about what they like and don't like to do.

Interpersonal Ask students to make up sentences about things that they like to do.

Teaching Resource Options

Print

Activity and Assessment Book
Grammar 1.1, p. 4
Audioscripts, pp. 54–58

Audiovisual

Bridge Audio Program Cassettes / CD

13 Objective: Controlled practice
Listening comprehension/**gustar**/
vocabulary

Answers (See script, p. 1C.)
1. e
2. d
3. b
4. c
5. a

14 Objective: Transitional practice
Gustar

Answers should follow the model.

15 Objective: Open-ended practice
Vocabulary/**gustar**

Answers will vary.

ACTIVIDAD 13

¿Qué le gusta?

Escuchar Listen as Francisco tells you what his friends like to do. Match each of Francisco's friends' names with the correct picture.

1. Jorge
2. Diego
3. Nina
4. Carmen
5. Marta

ACTIVIDAD 14

¿Te gusta?

Hablar Ask your partner if he or she likes to do the following things.

modelo

cantar

Estudiante A: *¿Te gusta cantar?*
Estudiante B: *Sí, me gusta cantar.*
o: No, no me gusta cantar.

1. nadar
2. leer
3. bailar
4. comer
5. patinar
6. trabajar
7. escribir
8. hablar español

ACTIVIDAD 15

Me gusta...

Escribir Write a paragraph naming two things you like and two things you don't like to do. Then tell two things your friend likes and two things he or she doesn't like to do.

Middle School Classroom Community

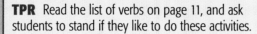

TPR Read the list of verbs on page 11, and ask students to stand if they like to do these activities.

Game Ask pairs to cut out and mount on index cards pictures of activities listed on page 11. Have them both write on the card whether they like or dislike the activity. Then they shuffle and stack the cards and play a game of War. In the first game, **me gusta** outranks **no me gusta**. In the second, the reverse is true.

En resumen

YA SABES ♻

SAYING WHERE PEOPLE ARE FROM

¿De dónde + ser...?	Where is... from?
ser de...	to be from...

People

el (la) amigo(a)	friend
la chica	girl
el chico	boy
la familia	family
el hombre	man
la muchacha	girl
el muchacho	boy
la mujer	woman
el señor	Mr.
la señora	Mrs.
la señorita	Miss

Professions

el (la) doctor(a)	doctor
el (la) estudiante	student
el (la) maestro(a)	teacher
el (la) policía	police officer

Subject Pronouns

yo	I
tú	you (familiar singular)
él	he
ella	she
usted	you (formal singular)
ustedes	you (formal plural)
nosotros(as)	we
vosotros(as)	you (familiar plural)
ellos(as)	they

Places

la comunidad	community
el mundo	world
el país	country

GREETING OTHERS

¿Cómo está usted?	How are you? (formal)
¿Cómo estás?	How are you? (familiar)
¿Qué tal?	How is it going?
Estoy...	I am...
(No muy) Bien, ¿y tú/usted?	(Not very) Well, and you (familiar/ formal)?
Regular.	So-so.
Terrible.	Terrible./Awful.
Gracias.	Thank you.
De nada.	You're welcome.

INTRODUCING OTHERS

Te/Le presento a...	Let me introduce you (familiar/formal) to...

SAYING WHERE YOU LIVE

Vivo en...	I live in...
Vive en...	He/She lives in...
el apartamento	apartment
la casa	house

EXPRESSING LIKES

¿Te gusta...?	Do you like...?
¿Le gusta...?	Does he/she like...?
Me gusta...	I like...
Te gusta...	You like...
Le gusta...	He/She likes...

Activities

bailar	to dance
cantar	to sing
comer	to eat
correr	to run
escribir	to write
leer	to read
nadar	to swim
patinar	to skate
trabajar	to work

OTHER WORDS AND PHRASES

bienvenido(a)	welcome
el concurso	contest
el lugar	place
mucho(a)	much, many
no	not
o	or
pero	but
también	also, too
y	and

Juego

Le gusta bailar pero no le gusta correr. Le gusta leer pero no le gusta cantar. Le gusta nadar pero no le gusta comer mucho. ¿Qué actividades no le gusta hacer a Marisol?

Marisol

correr **cantar** **comer**

Teaching Middle School Students

Extra Help Have students sort the vocabulary into 2 personalized categories: "Words I Know" and "Words I Sometimes Forget". Then have them work in pairs on their hard words.

Native Speakers Ask students to expand **Actividad 15** to a complete paragraph, which they carefully edit and revise before turning it in.

Multiple Intelligences

Visual Students may want to work in pairs to play **Piccionario**. One student will choose a word from this list and do a simple drawing of it. The second student will guess the word in Spanish.

Teaching Suggestions
Vocabulary Review

• Play "Rumba," a variation of Bingo. (1) Have students draw a grid with 5 squares across and 5 down. (2) Have students write in the first 25 vocabulary words from the "People," "Professions," "Places," and "Activities" categories in a scattered order in the squares of the grid. (3) Call out the English definitions and have students mark the corresponding Spanish vocabulary words on the grid. The first person to get five in a row, in any direction, calls out "Rumba!" and wins the game.

• Variations on "Rumba": (1) Allow students to write **gratis** in the middle square just as Bingo has a "free" square. (2) Expand the "Rumba," requiring a Z or an N or a T to win, rather than a straight line as in simple Bingo. (3) Change the categories in the "Rumba." (4) Have students write the English definitions in the squares, and you call out the Spanish words.

Juego

Answer: A Marisol no le gusta hacer las actividades con la letra **c**.

Project

Have pairs of students select a heading from the **Repaso de vocabulario**, preferably one which has 8–10 words. Have them use the words to create a **crucigrama**. They'll need graph paper and a good eraser to plan the word placement. They should put in the numbers and headings **Vertical** and **Horizontal**. Completed puzzles can be illustrated. Distribute them to other pairs to solve.

Block Schedule

Peer Review Allow small groups of students to review the vocabulary and grammar. Each group member can be responsible for making a study sheet for one grammatical concept. Students might also assign appropriate vocabulary categories to particular grammar concepts. They should try to use as much assigned vocabulary as possible in their individual grammar study guides.

Teaching Resource Options

Print

Activity and Assessment Book
Vocabulary 1.2, p. 5
Audioscripts, pp. 54–58

Audiovisual

Bridge Audio Program Cassettes / CD
OHT B3 (Quick Start), B4

Quick Start Review

♻ **Ser**

Use OHT B3 or write on the board:
Complete each sentence with the
correct form of the verb **ser**.

1. Nosotros _____ vecinos.
2. Ellas _____ de Perú.
3. Tú _____ estudiante.
4. Ustedes _____ doctores.
5. María _____ de Guatemala.
6. Yo _____ maestra.

Answers

1. somos   3. eres   5. es
2. son   4. son   6. soy

Teaching Suggestions
Reconnecting with Vocabulary

• Read each section of the vocabulary
  aloud, having students repeat after
  you.
• Ask for student volunteers to read the
  description of each individual and to
  include the additional information in
  short sentences (perhaps for bonus
  points!).
• Use the TPR activity to reinforce the
  meaning of individual words.

En contexto

🎧 VOCABULARIO

Francisco's friends back in San Antonio are waiting to
go to a Tejano music concert. Look at the illustrations.
They will help you understand the meanings of the
words in blue.

A Francisco tiene amigos
simpáticos. ¿Cómo son?

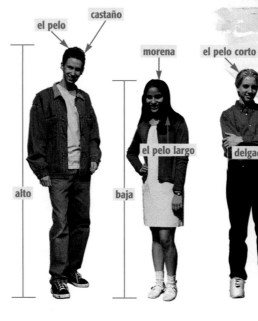

el pelo   castaño

morena   el pelo corto   rubio

la camiseta   los oj

pelirroja

la blusa blanca

el pelo largo   delgado   la falda morada   el

alto   baja   el perro   gordo   la bolsa

Raúl no es muy
serio. ¡Es cómico!

Rosalinda es
inteligente y
bonita.

Bill tiene un perro que se
llama Bud. Bud es gordo.

Graciela es guapa,
alta y pelirroja.

Al final, la chica
es paciente. Ella
es guapa, pero
el gato es feo.

12   doce
Bridge Unit

Middle School Classroom Community

TPR Say short, broad, descriptive sentences using
vocabulary from these pages. Students stand if they
fit your description.

Paired Activity Distribute old clothing catalogs and
ask students to take turns describing the models in the
pictures. Variation: One student chooses a model and
asks another to describe it.

Portfolio Ask students to write descriptions of their
friends.

Rubric

Criteria	Scale	
Creativity	1 2 3 4 5	A = 13–15 pts.
Logical organization	1 2 3 4 5	B = 10–12 pts.
Vocabulary use/spelling	1 2 3 4 5	C = 7–9 pts.
		D = 4–6 pts.
		F = < 4 pts.

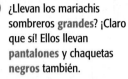

los zapatos

los pantalones

B ¿Llevan los mariachis sombreros **grandes**? ¡Claro que sí! Ellos llevan **pantalones** y chaquetas **negros** también.

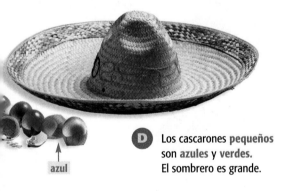

trabajador

C El hombre no es **perezoso**. Es muy **trabajador**. Trabaja en el bote.

azul

D Los cascarones **pequeños** son **azules** y **verdes**. El sombrero es grande.

---

16 Los amigos

Leer Match a description to each of Francisco's friends.

1. Graciela
2. Bill
3. Raúl
4. Rosalinda
5. Bud

a. cómico y alto
b. inteligente y baja
c. pelirroja y guapa
d. gordo
e. rubio y delgado

17 Soy yo

Hablar/Escribir Describe yourself and what you're wearing. Also include one activity you like to do.

Me llamo __1__ . Soy alto(a)/bajo(a). Tengo el pelo __2__ . Tengo los ojos __3__ . Hoy llevo __4__ y __5__ . Mi color favorito es __6__ . Describo mi personalidad con esta palabra: ¡ __7__ !

18 Mi mejor amigo(a)

Escribir Write a description of your best friend. What does he or she look like? What kind of personality does he or she have?

---

16 Objective: Controlled practice
Vocabulary

Answers
1. c
2. e
3. a
4. b
5. d

17 Objective: Transitional practice
Vocabulary

Answers will vary.

18 Objective: Open-ended practice
Vocabulary

Answers will vary.

Quick Wrap-up

Engage in a TPR activity in which you give students certain characteristics (the adjectives presented on these pages) and they mime them. For example: **Marta, eres muy perezosa** (she yawns or looks listless). **Enrique, eres muy trabajador** (he looks very busy). Another option is to have students point to articles of clothing worn by students as you announce them. For example: **una falda blanca, zapatos amarillos…**

Block Schedule

Gather and Sort Challenge partners to make as many categories as possible using characteristics and clothing, such as **pelo castaño** and **lleva camiseta**. Pairs then write their classmates' names under all appropriate categories. You may want to impose a time limit and see which pair has the most correct categories and listings.

Teaching Middle School Students

Extra Help Help students as they work in pairs to write descriptions of what each is wearing.

Native Speakers Ask students to contribute any clothing vocabulary that may be different from that in this lesson.

Multiple Intelligences

Logical/Mathematical Have students make a table to categorize the clothing vocabulary according to the definite article each takes.

Teaching Suggestions
Using Definite Articles with Specific Things

- Point out that *masculine* and *feminine* are just terms to identify the two groups of nouns in Spanish (as in many other languages) and that there is no connection between the noun itself and the idea of male or female: **Camisa** is feminine; whereas **sombrero** is masculine. But a man wears a **camisa**, and a woman can wear a **sombrero**.
- Tell students that to help them remember the gender of nouns, they should memorize the words with **el** or **la**, especially if the noun doesn't end in **-o** or **-a**, such as **el calcetín**, **los calcetines**.
- Give (or dictate to) students a list of nouns ending in **-o, -a, -os, -as**; have students underline the masculine/feminine endings and write **el, la, los,** or **las** before each noun. Avoid masculine nouns ending in **-a** like **mapa** and feminine nouns ending in **-o** like **mano**.

Game

Bingo de ropa Have students fold a sheet of paper to form 16 boxes. Have them write the name of an article of clothing in each box. You, or a class appointee, calls out an article of clothing at random (or shows a picture of it) and uses it in a sentence. Students cross it out if they have it. The first student to cross out four articles of clothing in a row, in any direction, wins.

En acción
VOCABULARIO Y GRAMÁTICA

Gramática en vivo

Alma: Y la chica que lleva la blusa morada, ¿cómo se llama?
Francisco: Ella es mi amiga Rosalinda.
Alma: ¡Tiene el pelo largo!

Using Definite Articles with Specific Things

In Spanish, the **definite article** that accompanies a noun will match its gender and number.

		Definite Article	Noun
Masculine	Singular	el *the*	chico *boy*
	Plural	los *the*	chicos *boys*
Feminine	Singular	la *the*	chica *girl*
	Plural	las *the*	chicas *girls*

matches gender — *matches number*

Usually
- nouns ending with **-o** are masculine.
- nouns ending with **-a** are feminine.

Vocabulario

La ropa ♻ Ya sabes

- los calcetines
- el sombrero
- la camisa
- el suéter
- la chaqueta
- el vestido
- los jeans

¿Cuál es tu ropa favorita?

Middle School Classroom Management

Planning Ahead You may want to collect a supply of old clothing catalogs for later use in class activities.

Organizing Group Work Randomize your groups by having students read the definite articles, one student per article (**el, los, la, las**), starting over after **las**. Then, have all the students who called **el** form a group, and so forth.

ACTIVIDAD 19

Mi ropa

Escribir Write a list of the clothes Alma needs this week.

modelo

los pantalones

1.

2.

3.

4.

5.

6.

7.

8.

9.

ACTIVIDAD 20

¡No me gusta!

Hablar Imagine you are shopping with a friend. Take turns asking your friend if he or she likes the clothes listed below.

modelo

camisa

Estudiante A: *¿Te gusta la camisa?*

Estudiante B: *No, no me gusta la camisa.*

1. falda
2. chaqueta
3. vestido
4. blusa
5. sombrero
6. suéter
7. camiseta

ACTIVIDAD 19 **Objective:** Controlled practice
Vocabulary

Answers

1. los calcetines
2. las blusas
3. el suéter
4. el vestido
5. los jeans
6. la falda
7. las camisetas
8. los zapatos
9. el sombrero

ACTIVIDAD 20 **Objective:** Transitional practice
Definite articles

Answers

1. ¿Te gusta la falda? / Sí, me gusta… *o*: No, no me gusta…
2. ¿Te gusta la chaqueta? / Sí, me gusta… *o*: No, no me gusta…
3. ¿Te gusta el vestido? / Sí, me gusta… *o*: No, no me gusta…
4. ¿Te gusta la blusa? / Sí, me gusta… *o*: No, no me gusta…
5. ¿Te gusta el sombrero? / Sí, me gusta… *o*: No, no me gusta…
6. ¿Te gusta el suéter? / Sí, me gusta… *o*: No, no me gusta…
7. ¿Te gusta la camiseta? / Sí, me gusta… *o*: No, no me gusta…

Game

Me gusta comprar Divide the class into 2 teams. The first player from Team A names a place or an event. The first player from Team B has one minute to create a list of clothing he or she would like to buy for that place or event. The team gets one point for each appropriate item. When time is called, teams switch roles.

Teaching Middle School Students

Extra Help To help students remember clothing vocabulary, have them draw 2 people and label all their clothing. They should keep their drawings in their journals.

Multiple Intelligences

Intrapersonal Have students write descriptions of what they are wearing and what they would like to be wearing.

Interpersonal Ask students to form small groups and exchange ideas about clothing they like.

Block Schedule

Journal Have students write a journal entry each day for one week describing what they wore to school that day. If students change clothing and go places after school, they may want to describe these outfits as well.

Teaching Resource Options

Print

Activity and Assessment Book
Grammar 1.2, p. 6

Teaching Suggestions
Using Indefinite Articles with Unspecified Things

- Point out that indefinite articles refer to any item, not a specific one, such as in **Quiero un lápiz**, meaning *any* pencil, as opposed to **Quiero el lápiz en la mesa**, meaning *the* pencil on the table.
- Point out that **un** can mean "one" or "a" and is a shortened form of **uno**.
- Give (or dictate to) students the same list of nouns ending in **-o**, **-a**, **-os**, **-as** (p. 14); have students underline the masculine/feminine endings and write **un, una, unos,** or **unas** before each noun.

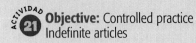 **Objective:** Controlled practice Indefinite articles

Answers
1. unos
2. un
3. unos
4. unas
5. una
6. un
7. una
8. unas

 Objective: Transitional practice Definite articles/vocabulary

Answers will vary.

 Objective: Transitional practice Vocabulary/indefinite articles/**ser**

Answers will vary.

Gramática en vivo

Francisco: Tengo **un** video de mis amigos. ¿Te interesa?
Alma: ¡Claro que sí, cómo no!

Using Indefinite Articles with Unspecified Things

The **indefinite article** that accompanies a noun will also match its gender and number.

		Indefinite Article	Noun
Masculine	Singular	un / *a*	chico / *boy*
	Plural	unos / *some*	chicos / *boys*
Feminine	Singular	una / *a*	chica / *girl*
	Plural	unas / *some*	chicas / *girls*

matches gender · matches number

 ACTIVIDAD 21

¿Qué tiene Carolina?

Leer/Escribir Carolina is describing what she has in her closet. Fill in her description with **un, una, unos,** or **unas**.

Tengo __1__ zapatos, __2__ suéter, __3__ vestidos, __4__ camisas, __5__ chaqueta, __6__ sombrero, __7__ blusa y __8__ faldas.

 **ACTIVIDAD 22**

Tu ropa favorita

Hablar/Escribir Ask three people what their favorite clothes are. Record their answers.

modelo

Estudiante A: *¿Cúal es tu ropa favorita?*

Estudiante B: *Son los jeans y las camisas.*

 **ACTIVIDAD 23**

¿Qué es?

Hablar You and your partner can't agree on anything. Take turns correcting one another.

modelo

zapatos / calcetines

Estudiante A: *¿Qué son?*

Estudiante B: *Son unos zapatos.*

Estudiante A: *No, son unos calcetines.*

1. pantalones / jeans
2. chaqueta / suéter
3. camisas / blusas
4. gato / perro
5. doctora / maestra

Middle School Classroom Community

Game A student from Team A will choose an object in the room and then call on a student from Team B to give the word in Spanish and its indefinite article. If that student is successful, Team B chooses an object.

Learning Scenario Hand out old clothing catalogs. Put students in small groups, and tell them they are ordering clothing for an event. Ask them to decide on an event and what clothing would be best for it. Then have them fill out order forms.

Gramática en vivo

Alma: Es muy **bonit**a.

Francisco: También es muy **intelligent**e. En el colegio, es **seri**a y **trabajador**a.

Using Adjectives to Describe: Gender

▶ **Adjectives** match the gender of the nouns they describe. In Spanish, adjectives usually follow the noun.

Masculine adjectives	Feminine adjectives
often end in **-o**.	often end in **-a**.

Most adjectives that end with **-e** match both genders.

el chic**o** **pacient**e   ◀— *same word* —▶   la chic**a** **pacient**e

Many adjectives that end with a **consonant** match both genders.

el chic**o** **fenomenal**   ◀— *same word* —▶   la chic**a** **fenomenal**

Some add **-a** to become feminine. These adjectives must be learned.

becomes

el chico **trabajador**   ———▶   la chica **trabajador**a
the hard-working boy   *the hard-working girl*

Vocabulario

Adjectives	♻ Ya sabes
aburrido(a)	**fuerte**
bueno(a)	**interesante**
divertido(a)	**malo(a)**
¿Cómo eres?	

ACTIVIDAD 24

¿Cómo son?

Leer/Escribir Describe Francisco's friends. Use two adjectives for each person.

guapo(a)   trabajador(a)

interesante   bueno(a)

fuerte   simpático(a)

alto(a)   moreno(a)

1. Graciela es...
2. Raúl es...
3. Rosalinda es...
4. Bill es...

ACTIVIDAD 25

¡Cuéntame!

Hablar Describe the following people to a partner. Then change roles.

1. El (La) maestro(a) es...
2. Mi amiga es...
3. Mi amigo es...
4. Tú eres...
5. Yo soy...
6. Un(a) buen(a) estudiante es...

---

diecisiete
Etapa 1

17

Teaching Suggestions
Using Adjectives to Describe: Gender

- Point out that many adjectives do not have masculine and feminine forms but only singular and plural (e.g., **fuerte, interesante, paciente**).
- Draw 4 columns on the board with the headings **el chico, la chica, el perro**, and **la clase**. Divide the class into 4 groups, assigning each group a column; then have students go to the board and fill up the columns with as many appropriate adjectives as possible. Remind them to pay attention to adjective endings.

ACTIVIDAD 24 Objective: Transitional practice Vocabulary/adjective agreement

Answers
Answers may vary.
1. guapa y simpática.
2. alto e interesante.
3. morena y trabajadora.
4. bueno y fuerte.

ACTIVIDAD 25 Objective: Open-ended practice Vocabulary/adjective agreement

Answers will vary.

■ Block Schedule

Change of Pace You may wish to do **Actividad 22** with the whole class. As you ask ¿Cuál es tu ropa favorita?, write responses on the chalkboard. You can tally the number of responses for each clothing article (jeans, camisas, faldas, etc.). Students might also show this information in a bar graph or pictograph.

Teaching Middle School Students

Extra Help For the rest of the year, have students keep a page in their journals with 3 lists of adjectives: regular masculine, regular feminine, and exceptions. Occasionally, work with them to practice the words in their exceptions list.

Challenge Have students write their own version of **Actividad 21**, describing items in their own closets.

Multiple Intelligences

Naturalist Ask students to bring in nature scenes and describe them for the class, either in writing or orally.

Teaching Resource Options

Print

Activity and Assessment Book
  Grammar 1.2, p. 7

Teaching Suggestions
Using Adjectives to Describe: Number

- Have students underline all of the number markers (shown here) in the following sentences. 1. **Los calcetines negros son nuevos.** 2. **Mis zapatos viejos son verdes y azules.**
- Point out that adjectives, like nouns, become plural by adding **-s** or **-es,** but verbs do not (i.e., **son** doesn't end in **-s**).
- Ask students to look around the room and make sentences about the color of objects that they can identify: **El lápiz es amarillo.** Have them use plurals when appropriate.

 Objective: Controlled practice
Vocabulary/adjective agreement

Answers
1. rojos
2. simpáticas
3. pacientes
4. cómicos / largos
5. inteligentes
6. trabajadoras
7. verdes
8. negros

Objective: Open-ended practice
Vocabulary/adjective agreement

Answers will vary.

Gramática en vivo

Alma: ¡Qué buen amigo eres! ¡Y qué **buen**os amigos tienes! Pues, ahora tienes una nueva amiga.

Francisco: ¡Sí! ¡A los **nuev**os amigos!

Using Adjectives to Describe: Number

▶ Adjectives must also match the number of the nouns they describe. To make an adjective plural, add **-s** if it ends with a vowel, **-es** if it ends with a consonant.

▶ When an adjective describes a group with both genders, the **masculine** form of the adjective is used.

El chico y la chica son **guap**os.

¡Escríbelo!

Escribir Write these sentences using the correct form of one of the words in parentheses.

modelo

*Mis zapatos son (azul / trabajador).   Mis zapatos son **azules**.*

1. Graciela tiene tres vestidos (rojo / inteligente).
2. Mis amigas son (simpático / verde).
3. Los maestros son muy (paciente / rojo).
4. Me gusta leer libros (cómico / trabajador) y (largo / negro).
5. La chica tiene dos perros (inteligente / azul).
6. Laura y Marisa son muy (trabajador / largo).
7. Mis pantalones son (verde / simpático).
8. La mujer tiene unos sombreros (negro / fuerte).

¿Qué tienes?

Escribir Think about the clothes that you have in your closet or dresser at home. Using the words you have learned, make a list of at least five different items that you have in your closet.

modelo

cinco camisas blancas

dos pantalones marrones

...

Vocabulario

Los colores Ya sabes

Colors are adjectives too.

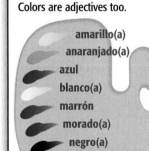

amarillo(a)
anaranjado(a)
azul
blanco(a)
marrón
morado(a)
negro(a)
rojo(a)
rosado(a)
verde

The plural form of **marrón** is **marrones**. Other words for *brown* are **café** and **pardo(a)**.

¿Cuál es tu color favorito?

Middle School Classroom Community

Game Ask the class to choose a rock star, or invent one, and then describe his or her wardrobe: **El (La) cantante de rock tiene 20 jeans verdes.** Some students may want to illustrate this activity.

TPR Call out an article of clothing (and color) and ask all students wearing this article to stand.

Storytelling Have students sit in a circle. Give one student a soft ball. This student starts a story about an imaginary person by describing one feature of this person. He or she then tosses the ball to a classmate who must continue the story and description.

En resumen

YA SABES ♻

DESCRIBING OTHERS

¿Cómo es?	What is he/she like?

Appearance

alto(a)	tall
bajo(a)	short (height)
bonito(a)	pretty
castaño(a)	brown hair
corto(a)	short (length)
delgado(a)	thin
feo(a)	ugly
fuerte	strong
gordo(a)	fat
grande	big, large
guapo(a)	good-looking
largo(a)	long
moreno(a)	dark hair and skin
pelirrojo(a)	redhead
pequeño(a)	small
rubio(a)	blond

Features

Tiene…	He/She has…
los ojos (verdes, azules)	(green, blue) eyes
el pelo (rubio, castaño)	(blond, brown) hair

Personality

aburrido(a)	boring
bueno(a)	good
cómico(a)	funny, comical
divertido(a)	enjoyable, fun
inteligente	intelligent
interesante	interesting
malo(a)	bad
paciente	patient
perezoso(a)	lazy
serio(a)	serious
simpático(a)	nice
trabajador(a)	hard-working

DESCRIBING CLOTHING

What one is wearing

¿De qué color…?	What color…?
Llevo…/Lleva…	I wear…He/She wears…
¿Qué lleva?	What is he/she wearing?

Clothing

la blusa	blouse
el calcetín	sock
la camisa	shirt
la camiseta	T-shirt
la chaqueta	jacket
la falda	skirt
los jeans	jeans
los pantalones	pants
la ropa	clothing
el sombrero	hat
el suéter	sweater
el vestido	dress
el zapato	shoe

Colors

amarillo(a)	yellow
anaranjado(a)	orange
azul	blue
blanco(a)	white
marrón	brown
morado(a)	purple
negro(a)	black
rojo(a)	red
rosado(a)	pink
verde	green

OTHER WORDS AND PHRASES

la bolsa	bag
el (la) gato(a)	cat
el (la) perro(a)	dog
nuevo(a)	new
otro(a)	other, another
pues	well
¡No digas eso!	Don't say that!
¡Qué (divertido)!	How (fun)!
Es verdad.	It's true.

Juego

La mujer alta tiene el pelo corto y negro. Lleva una chaqueta azul y una falda larga. ¿Quién es?

a.

b.

c.

Teaching Suggestions
Vocabulary Review

Have students bring in magazines with photos of famous people. Hold up photos and ask students to describe their appearance and personality and to state what they are wearing: **Michael Jordan es alto y fuerte. Es inteligente y divertido. Lleva pantalones negros y una camiseta blanca.**

Juego

Answer: b

Project

Have students work in groups. First they choose a color. Then they look through magazines for pictures of items in that color. Each group creates a poster to represent its color.

Teaching Middle School Students

Extra Help Help students make up a rhyme that will help them remember the difference between **bajo(a)** and **corto(a)**.

Challenge Choose 10 words from this list and ask students to create an original sentence for each word.

Multiple Intelligences

Verbal Ask a student to be the teacher and quiz the class on the vocabulary.

Kinesthetic Ask students to describe someone else's clothing and then have that person stand. Remind students not to tease anyone about his or her clothing.

Block Schedule

Variety Ask each student to use the vocabulary to create a description of an imaginary character. Students should use words from each vocabulary category. When students complete descriptions, put them in pairs or small groups to introduce their characters to one another.

Quick Start Review

♻ Adjectives

Use OHT B3 or write on the board:
Rewrite the paragraph below, substituting
the adjectives with their opposites.

Mi amigo es muy serio. Es rubio.
Tiene el pelo corto. Es perezoso y
un poco feo, pero es alto. Es un
mal amigo.

Teaching Suggestions
What Have Students Learned?
Reconnecting with Vocabulary

- Read each section of the vocabulary
  aloud, having students repeat after
  you; include the **Otras palabras
  para hablar de la familia.**
- Start a chain by asking a student
  how old his or her brother is. The
  respondent answers or says **No
  tengo hermano** and then asks
  someone else about the age of a
  sibling.
- Use the TPR activity to reinforce the
  meaning of individual words.

En contexto

🎧 VOCABULARIO

Francisco's cousin Verónica is having a party for her
fifteenth birthday. Look at the illustrations. They will help
you understand the meanings of the words in blue.

¡FELICIDADES!
el abuelo | la abuela

A **Francisco:** Hoy es una fecha
especial. Es el cumpleaños de
mi prima Verónica.
Alma: ¿Cuántos años tiene?
Francisco: Ella tiene quince
años de edad.
Alma: ¿Tiene una fiesta?
Francisco: Sí. Está muy feliz.

B Los señores viejos son los García,
los abuelos de Verónica. Javier
y Juan García son sus hijos.

¡FELICIDADES!

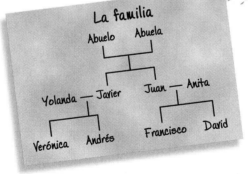

La familia

Abuelo   Abuela

Yolanda — Javier   Juan — Anita

Verónica   Andrés   Francisco   David

Verónica
Yolanda
la madre | la hermana | el hermano
el padre
Javier García
Andrés

C Verónica es la hija y Andrés es el hijo
de Yolanda y Javier García. Verónica es
la hermana mayor de Andrés.

20 veinte
Bridge Unit

Middle School Classroom Community

TPR Have each student choose one of the family
vocabulary words. Now read the sections on pp. 20–21.
Students touch their heads when their word is read.

Storytelling Ask a student to name a character from
a popular television program; the next student must
state that character's relationship to another, and so on.

Portfolio Ask students to make, label, and illustrate
their own (or imaginary) family trees.

Rubric

Criteria	Scale	
Creativity	1 2 3 4 5	A = 13–15 pts.
Logical organization	1 2 3 4 5	B = 10–12 pts.
Vocabulary use/spelling	1 2 3 4 5	C = 7–9 pts.
		D = 4–6 pts.
		F = < 4 pts.

Juan García   Anita

el tío   la tía   el primo

el primo

David   Francisco

D Juan y Anita son **los padres de los hermanos** David y Francisco. También son **los tíos** de Verónica y Andrés. David es muy **joven**. Es **el hermano menor** de Francisco.

Otras palabras para hablar de la familia:

el (la) esposo(a) husband (wife)
el (la) hermanastro(a) stepbrother (stepsister)
la madrastra stepmother
el (la) medio(a) hermano(a) half-brother (half-sister)
el (la) nieto(a) grandson (granddaughter)
el padrastro stepfather

ACTIVIDAD 28 ¿Quién es?

Hablar Tell who the members of Verónica's family are.

modelo

Francisco

Francisco es el primo.

1. Yolanda   4. Andrés
2. David   5. Javier
3. Juan   6. Anita

ACTIVIDAD 29 El cumpleaños

Hablar/Escribir Fill in the following conversation between Francisco and Alma. Then act it out with a partner.

Francisco: Hoy es el __1__ de Verónica. Está muy __2__ .
Alma: Verónica es tu hermana, ¿no?
Francisco: No, es mi __3__ .
Alma: ¿__4__ años tiene?
Francisco: Tiene quince años de __5__ .
Alma: No es muy vieja. Es __6__ .

ACTIVIDAD 30 La familia

Escribir Create a family tree of a real or an imagined family. Name and label each family member in Spanish. Don't forget to include grandparents, aunts, uncles, and cousins!

veintiuno
Etapa 1   21

Teaching Middle School Students

Teaching Suggestions
Saying What You Have: The Verb tener

- Point out that **tener** is an irregular verb and has different spellings; ask students if they see any pattern.

- Point out that in Spanish you do not say how old you are but rather how many years you have.

- Have students hold up sheets of paper with their ages written in large print; then ask who is 12, 13, 14, etc., and have students answer to **¿Quién tiene 12 años? María y Camilo tienen 12 años.**

- Point out that numbers from 16 to 29 ending in the letter **-s** have a written accent: **dieciséis, veintidós, veintitrés,** and **veintiséis;** you may want to show the older, optional written forms of these numbers (**diez y seis, veinte y dos**), and note that they do not require written accents.

ACTIVIDAD 31 Objective: Controlled practice **Tener/numbers**

Answers
1. Yo tengo quince años.
2. Mamá tiene treinta y seis años.
3. Papá tiene cuarenta años.
4. Los abuelos tienen setenta y un años.
5. Tú tienes trece años.
6. Juanita y yo tenemos quince años.

En acción
VOCABULARIO Y GRAMÁTICA

Gramática en vivo

Alma: ¿Qué edad tiene Verónica?
Francisco: Pues, su cumpleaños es en octubre. Así que ahora tiene quince **años.**

Saying What You Have: The Verb tener

yo	tengo	nosotros(as)	tenemos
tú	tienes	vosotros(as)	tenéis
usted, él, ella	tiene	ustedes, ellos(as)	tienen

▶ Tener is also used to talk about how old a person is.

Tiene quince **años.**
She is fifteen years old.

ACTIVIDAD 31

¿Cuántos años tienen?

Hablar/Escribir Help Alma tell her sister how old everyone is in their family.

modelo

mis primos: 22

***Mis primos** tienen veintidós años.*

1. yo: 15
2. mamá: 36
3. papá: 40
4. los abuelos: 71
5. tú: 13
6. Juanita y yo: 15

Vocabulario

Los números de 11 a 100
♻ Ya sabes

once	veinticinco
doce	veintiséis
trece	veintisiete
catorce	veintiocho
quince	veintinueve
dieciséis	treinta
diecisiete	treinta y uno
dieciocho	cuarenta
diecinueve	cincuenta
veinte	sesenta
veintiuno	setenta
veintidós	ochenta
veintitrés	noventa
veinticuatro	cien

For 21, 31, and so on, use **veintiún, treinta y un,** and so on before a masculine noun and **veintiuna, treinta y una,** and so on before a feminine noun.

¿Cuántos años tienes?

Middle School Classroom Management

Planning Ahead You may want to make a calendar with each student's birthday marked on it.

Peer Teaching Have pairs or small groups become experts on one decade of numbers. Have them present the vocabulary by making up a song, poem, or skit to highlight the unique characteristics of their decade (teens, twenties, etc.).

¿Cuántos tienes?

Escribir Fill in the blanks with the correct form of **tener** or with a number.

1. Ella _____ once camisas. Yo tengo _____ camisas. Nosotros _____ veinticuatro camisas.

2. Javier tiene _____ libros. Tú _____ catorce libros. Ustedes _____ ochenta y cuatro libros.

3. Usted _____ dieciocho zapatos. Ellos tienen _____ zapatos. Ustedes _____ cuarenta y ocho zapatos.

4. Mi primo tiene _____ amigos. Yo _____ veinte amigos. Nosotros _____ cuarenta y dos amigos.

5. Yo _____ cuatro plumas. Tú _____ treinta plumas. Nosotros tenemos _____ plumas.

6. Yo tengo _____ maestros. Mis amigos _____ siete maestros. Nosotros _____ dieciséis maestros.

Gramática en vivo

Francisco: Ellos son los hijos **de** mi tío Javier y mi tía Yolanda.

Expressing Possession Using de

▶ In Spanish, you use the preposition **de** to refer to the possessor.

el hermano **de** papá
Dad's brother

los hijos **de** Javier
Javier's children

La familia de Lucía

Escribir Explain how the following people are related to Lucía.

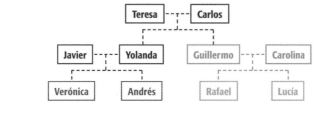

| Teresa | — | Carlos |

| Javier | Yolanda | Guillermo | Carolina |

| Verónica | Andrés | Rafael | Lucía |

modelo
_____

Rafael

Rafael *es el hermano de Lucía.*

1. Javier y Yolanda
2. Guillermo
3. Teresa y Carlos
4. Verónica
5. Andrés

Teaching Middle School Students

Extra Help Have students use **Actividad 31** as a model to write and say the ages of their own family members.

Native Speakers Have native speakers interview family members about the way they write numbers in the teens and twenties.

Multiple Intelligences

Musical/Rhythmic Have students make up a number-word song to the tune of "Twinkle, Twinkle, Little Star."

Objective: Transitional practice **Tener**/numbers

Answers
1. tiene / trece / tenemos
2. setenta / tienes / tienen
3. tiene / treinta / tienen
4. veintidós / tengo / tenemos
5. tengo / tienes / treinta y cuatro
6. nueve / tienen / tenemos

Teaching Suggestions
Expressing Possession Using de
Point out the shirt on a student and state, **Es la camisa de** (student's name). Continue with the same or other articles of clothing on different students, and have students complete the sentences.

Objective: Controlled practice Possessive **de**

Answers
1. Javier y Yolanda son los tíos de Lucía.
2. Guillermo es el padre de Lucía.
3. Teresa y Carlos son los abuelos de Lucía.
4. Verónica es la prima de Lucía.
5. Andrés es el primo de Lucía.

Block Schedule

FunBreak Have students create their own family trees (or have them take out ones they have already made). Put them in small groups to practice making statements about one another. One group member stands up and holds his or her family tree. Other members take turns using numbers and possession concepts to describe the person standing. (**Carolina es la prima de Miguel. Miguel tiene seis primos.**) Suggest that students make 5 statements about each person before changing roles.

Teaching Resource Options

Print

Activity and Assessment Book
Grammar 1.3, p. 10

Objective: Transitional practice
Possessive **de**

Answers

1. No, las primas no son de Paco. Son de Jaime.
2. No, las camisas no son de Andrea. Son de Carmen.
3. No, el abuelo no es de Alma. Es de Francisco.
4. No, los zapatos no son de ustedes. Son de ellos.
5. No, las frutas no son de mí. Son de la muchacha.
6. No, los amigos no son del hombre. Son de la mujer.
7. No, la chaqueta no es de mí. Es de Laura.
8. No, la calculadora no es de Sara. Es de Tomás.

Teaching Suggestions
Expressing Possession: Possessive Adjectives

- Pick up your own book and state, **Es mi libro**; then point to several of your books and state, **Son mis libros**. Do the same with a student's items: **Es tu zapato; son tus zapatos. Es su chaqueta (la chaqueta de ella); son sus chaquetas (las chaquetas de ellos).**
- Clarify that both **su** and **sus** can mean "his," "her," "its," "their," or "your."
- Point out that singular and plural endings of possessive adjectives do not relate to there being one or more owners but rather depend on whether what is being possessed is singular or plural (i.e., "their book" is **su libro** not **sus libro**, and "his books" is **sus libros** not **su libros**).

ACTIVIDAD 34

¡No sé!

Hablar Your partner is confused about who and what belong to whom. Take turns figuring it out.

modelo

Estudiante A: ¿Son los libros de Carla? (Juan)

Estudiante B: No, *los libros* no son *de Carla*. Son *de Juan*.

1. ¿Son las primas de Paco? (Jaime)
2. ¿Son las camisas de Andrea? (Carmen)
3. ¿Es el abuelo de Alma? (Francisco)
4. ¿Son los zapatos de ustedes? (ellos)
5. ¿Son las frutas de ti? (la muchacha)
6. ¿Son los amigos del hombre? (la mujer)
7. ¿Es la chaqueta de ti? (Laura)
8. ¿Es la calculadora de Sara? (Tomás)

Gramática en vivo

Alma: Y tu abuela, ¿cómo es?

Francisco: Mi abuela es muy paciente, especialmente con sus queridos nietos. Ella adora a sus nietos.

Expressing Possession: Possessive Adjectives

Singular Possessive Adjectives		Plural Possessive Adjectives	
mi *my*	nuestro(a) *our*	mis *my*	nuestros(as) *our*
tu *your (familiar)*	vuestro(a) *your (familiar)*	tus *your (familiar)*	vuestros(as) *your (familiar)*
su *your (formal)*	su *your (formal)*	sus *your (formal)*	sus *your (formal)*
su *his, her, its*	su *their*	sus *his, her, its*	sus *their*

▸ The adjectives **nuestro(a)** and **vuestro(a)** must agree in gender with the nouns they describe.

▸ If you need to emphasize, substitute the adjective with:

de + **pronoun** or the person's name

This also helps to clarify the meaning of su and sus.

becomes

Es su tío. → Es el tío **de él**.

de mí	de nosotros(as)
de ti	de vosotros(as)
de usted, él, ella	de ustedes, ellos(as)

Middle School Classroom Community

Paired Activity Ask students to work in pairs, taking turns describing a family member as in the dialog in **Gramática en vivo**.

Cooperative Learning Have students work in groups of 3 to practice vocabulary. The roles are Director, Gatherer, and Guesser. The Guesser covers his or her eyes while the Director silently indicates to the Gatherer 3 items to place on the table. The Guesser now looks at the items and tells to whom each item belongs. Then students switch roles and start again, trying to vary the owners and the items for a well-rounded practice.

ACTIVIDAD 35

¿Cómo es la familia?

Hablar Take turns asking a partner about family members.

modelo

prima / inteligente, bonito

Estudiante A: *¿Cómo es tu **prima**?*

Estudiante B: *Mi prima es* **inteligente** *y* **bonita**.

1. abuelos / viejo, simpático
2. mamá / cómico, joven
3. tíos / alto, moreno
4. hermano / rubio, bajo
5. papá / interesante, pelirrojo
6. hermanas / bueno, delgado

ACTIVIDAD 36

¡La misma cosa!

Hablar/Escribir Read the sentences below. Rewrite them using a possessive adjective.

modelo

Ella es la mamá de Rosa.

Ella es *su* **mamá**.

1. Son los tíos de Ana.
2. Lucía es la abuela de Pedro.
3. Las camisas son de Alma y Corina.
4. La casa es de nosotros.
5. La ropa es de ustedes.

ACTIVIDAD 37

¿Donde está mi ropa?

Escribir There was a mix-up at the laundromat. Everyone is looking for his or her clothes! Write sentences that show who owns which article of clothing.

modelo

la blusa / de Ana

Es **la blusa** *de* **Ana**. *Es su* **blusa**.

1. el suéter / de Paula
2. las chaquetas / de nosotros
3. la falda / de la abuela
4. la blusa / de ti
5. los pantalones / de Marcos
6. las camisetas / de las chicas
7. el sombrero / de mí
8. los zapatos / de la señora

Gramática en vivo

Francisco: Oye, ¿cuál es la fecha de hoy?
Alma: Es el **once** de noviembre.

◆ Giving Dates: Day and Month

▶ When you want to give the date, use the following phrase:

Es el + **number** + **de** + month.

▶ In Spanish, the only date that does not follow this pattern is the first of the month.

Es el **primero** **de** noviembre.
It is *November* ***first***.

veinticinco
Etapa 1

25

Teaching Middle School Students

Challenge Have students make up a version of **Actividad 34** that reflects true relationships among classmates' families.

Multiple Intelligences

Logical/Mathematical Ask students to interview each other, asking what date their birthdays fall on. Then have them create a graph showing the number of birthdays on each date.

ACTIVIDAD 35 Objective: Controlled practice
Possessive adjectives

Answers
1. ¿Cómo son tus abuelos? / Mis abuelos son viejos y simpáticos.
2. ¿Cómo es tu mamá? / Mi mamá es cómica y joven.
3. ¿Cómo son tus tíos? / Mis tíos son altos y morenos.
4. ¿Cómo es tu hermano? / Mi hermano es rubio y bajo.
5. ¿Como es tu papá? / Mi papá es interesante y pelirrojo.
6. ¿Cómo son tus hermanas? / Mis hermanas son buenas y delgadas.

ACTIVIDAD 36 Objective: Transitional practice
Possessive adjectives

Answers
1. Son sus tíos.
2. Es su abuela.
3. Son sus camisas.
4. Es nuestra casa.
5. Es su ropa.

ACTIVIDAD 37 Objective: Transitional practice
Possessive adjectives

Answers
1. Es el suéter de Paula. Es su suéter.
2. Son las chaquetas de nosotros. Son nuestras chaquetas.
3. Es la falda de la abuela. Es su falda.
4. Es la blusa de ti. Es tu blusa.
5. Son los pantalones de Marcos. Son sus pantalones.
6. Son las camisetas de las chicas. Son sus camisetas.
7. Es el sombrero de mí. Es mi sombrero.
8. Son los zapatos de la señora. Son sus zapatos.

Teaching Suggestions
Giving Dates: Day and Month

Have students read the grammar box; point out that in Spanish you do not use the ordinal numbers when giving the date, except for the first **(primero)** of the month.

■ Block Schedule

Variety Have groups of students sit in a circle with some of their own items in front of them (pencils, books, etc.). Students work around the circle, pointing to an item and asking a question: **¿Es la camisa de Ana?** The person to the right answers, **Sí, es su camisa** or **No, es la camisa de Juanita**. The person who answered asks the next question.

Teaching Resource Options

Print

Activity and Assessment Book
Grammar 1.3, p. 11
Information Gap Activities, p. 12
Cooperative Quizzes, pp. 13–16
Audioscripts, pp. 54–58

Audiovisual

Bridge Audio Program Cassettes / CD
OHT B6

Teaching Suggestions
Day and Month

• Read each month aloud, having students repeat after you.
• Using a large calendar, point to dates in different months and have students say the date in a complete sentence: **Es el ocho de noviembre**.
• Point out that the months are written in lowercase letters; dictate some dates and have students write them down.

 Objective: Controlled practice
Listening comprehension/dates

Answers (See script, p. 1C.)
1. g   5. h
2. d   6. f
3. a   7. e
4. b   8. c

 Objective: Transitional practice
Dates

Answers
1. Es el cuatro de octubre.
2. Es el doce de julio.
3. Es el diecisiete de noviembre.
4. Es el primero de mayo.
5. Es el veintidós de septiembre.
6. Es el veinticinco de diciembre.
7. Es el treinta de marzo.
8. Es el nueve de enero.

Quick Wrap-up

Announce a variety of dates, some of which will be holidays (**el cuatro de octubre, el veinticinco de diciembre**, etc.). Have students raise one hand when they hear a non-holiday. Have them raise two hands when they hear a holiday (**el primero de enero**).

Los cumpleaños

Escuchar Listen as Francisco tells you when his family members have birthdays. Then match the correct birthday with each person.

1. abuela
2. Verónica
3. Andrés
4. mi mamá
5. abuelo
6. mi papá
7. David
8. Javier

a. el primero de julio
b. el 14 de diciembre
c. el 25 de abril
d. el 30 de septiembre
e. el primero de agosto
f. el 11 de junio
g. el 12 de marzo
h. el 4 de noviembre

Vocabulario

Los meses del año Ya sabes

¿Cuál es tu mes favorito?

¡Escribe la fecha!

Escribir Read the dates that are expressed in numbers. Then write the dates using words. Don't forget that the day comes first, followed by the month.

modelo

13/6
*Es el **trece** de **junio**.*

1. 4/10   5. 22/9
2. 12/7   6. 25/12
3. 17/11   7. 30/3
4. 1/5   8. 9/1

Tu cumpleaños

Hablar/Escribir Ask ten classmates when their birthday is. List the students you talk with and record their birthdays next to their names.

modelo

Estudiante A: *¿Cuándo es tu cumpleaños?*

Estudiante B: *Es el 12 de octubre.*

Middle School Classroom Community

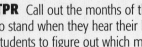

TPR Call out the months of the year, asking students to stand when they hear their birth months. Ask students to figure out which month has the most birthdays.

Portfolio Ask students to write which is their favorite month and explain why.

Rubric

Criteria	Scale	
Creativity	1 2 3 4 5	A = 13–15 pts.
Logical organization	1 2 3 4 5	B = 10–12 pts.
Vocabulary use/spelling	1 2 3 4 5	C = 7–9 pts.
		D = 4–6 pts.
		F = < 4 pts.

En resumen

YA SABES ♻

DESCRIBING FAMILY

Family Members

la abuela	grandmother
el abuelo	grandfather
los abuelos	grandparents
la hermana	sister
el hermano	brother
los hermanos	brother(s) and sister(s)
la hija	daughter
el hijo	son
los hijos	son(s) and daughter(s), children
la madre	mother
el padre	father
los padres	parents
el (la) primo(a)	cousin
la tía	aunt
el tío	uncle
los tíos	uncle(s) and aunt(s)

Descriptions

joven	young
mayor	older
menor	younger
viejo(a)	old

EXPRESSING POSSESSION

¿De quién es…?	Whose is…?
el (la)… de…	(someone)'s…
Es de…	It's…
mi	my
tu	your (familiar)
su	your (formal), his, her, its, their
nuestro(a)	our
vuestro(a)	your (plural familiar)

ASKING AND TELLING AGES

Asking About Age

la edad	age
¿Cuántos años tiene…?	How old is…?
Tiene… años.	He/She is…years old.

Numbers from 11 to 100

once	eleven
doce	twelve
trece	thirteen
catorce	fourteen
quince	fifteen
dieciséis	sixteen
diecisiete	seventeen
dieciocho	eighteen
diecinueve	nineteen
veinte	twenty
veintiuno	twenty-one
treinta	thirty
cuarenta	forty
cincuenta	fifty
sesenta	sixty
setenta	seventy
ochenta	eighty
noventa	ninety
cien	one hundred

GIVING DATES

Asking the Date

el año	year
la fecha	date
¿Cuál es la fecha?	What is the date?
Es el… de…	It's the…of…

Months

el mes	month
enero	January
febrero	February
marzo	March
abril	April
mayo	May
junio	June
julio	July
agosto	August
septiembre	September
octubre	October
noviembre	November
diciembre	December

TALKING ABOUT BIRTHDAYS

el cumpleaños	birthday
felicidades	congratulations
feliz	happy

OTHER WORDS AND PHRASES

ahora	now
la ciudad	city
con	with
dentro	inside
fuera	outside
hay	there is, there are
más	more
muy	very
¡Qué chévere!	How awesome!
¿Quién es?	Who is it?
¿Quiénes son?	Who are they?
sólo	only
tener	to have
todo(a)	all

Juego

El abuelo tiene 24 años más que su hijo Carlos. Carlos tiene 35 años más que su hijo Antonio. Los tres combinados tienen 100 años.
¿Cuántos años tiene…

1. el abuelo?
2. Carlos?
3. Antonio?

veintisiete
Etapa 1
27

Teaching Middle School Students

Extra Help Work with students to form sentences by choosing words from the different categories on p. 27. You start the sentence and let students help each other complete it.

Multiple Intelligences

Verbal Ask a student to be the teacher and quiz the class on the vocabulary.

Naturalist Have students group the months by season north of the equator and again by season south of the equator.

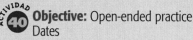

ACTIVIDAD 40 Objective: Open-ended practice
Dates

Answers will vary.

Teaching Suggestions
Vocabulary Review

Ask students to state their birthdays or make a question/answer chain; ask if students can give their mother's (father's, sister's, brother's, etc.) birthday and say how old they are: **El cumpleaños de mi padre es el tres de junio; él tiene cuarenta y dos años.**

Juego

Answers
1. El abuelo tiene 61 años.
2. Carlos tiene 37 años.
3. Antonio tiene 2 años.

Critical Thinking

Tape the name of a season in each corner of the room. Then have students go to the season (corner) that they celebrate their birthdays in. By asking each other **¿Cuándo es tu cumpleaños?**, they line up in birthday order. A scribe lists class birthdays and adds them to the bulletin board. Sing the Birthday Song to each student on his or her special day: **Cumpleaños feliz deseamos a ti, que cumples cien años. Cumpleaños feliz.**

▣ Block Schedule

Variety Create a class calendar. On a large piece of paper or on the bulletin board show a calendar for each month. Ask students to label the calendar with their birthdays. Then discuss each month with the class. Have students describe any special days there are in that month (relatives' birthdays, anniversaries, holidays, special celebrations). Label on the calendar any special days that involve the whole class, such as field trips, vacations, no-school days, and school plays or shows.

Planning Guide CLASSROOM MANAGEMENT

OBJECTIVES

Communication
- Talk about school *pp. 30–35, 38–44*
- Discuss obligations and plans *pp. 35–36, 48–49*
- Talk about schedules and time *pp. 38–44*
- Ask questions *p. 44*
- Say where you are going *pp. 40–41, 46–47*
- Request food *pp. 38–39*
- Sequence events *p. 50*

Grammar
- Saying What You Do: Present of **-ar** Verbs *pp. 32–33*
- Expressing Frequency with Adverbs *pp. 34–35*
- Expressing Obligation with **hay que** and **tener que** *pp. 35–36*
- Saying Where You Are Going: The Verb **ir** *pp. 40–41*
- Telling Time *pp. 41–42*
- Describing Location with the Verb **estar** *p. 43*
- Asking Questions: Interrogative Words *p. 44*
- Saying What You Are Going to Do: **ir a**... *pp. 48–49*
- Present Tense of Regular **-er** and **-ir** Verbs *pp. 49–50*
- Regular Present Tense Verbs with Irregular **yo** Forms *p. 51*
- Using the Verb **oír** *p. 52*

PROGRAM RESOURCES

Print
- Activity and Assessment Book
  - Vocabulary Activities *pp. 17, 20, 23–24*
  - Grammar Activities *pp. 18–19, 21–22, 25–26*
  - Information Gap Activities *p. 27*
  - Cooperative Quizzes *pp. 28–31*
  - Audioscripts *pp. 54–58*

Audiovisual
- Bridge Audio Program Cassettes / CD
- Overhead Transparencies B7–B11

Student Text Listening Activity Scripts

ACTIVIDAD 16 ¡Qué horario! *page 42*

Pablo: Oye, Ricardo. Tengo seis materias. A las siete y media tengo matemáticas, y a las ocho y cuarto tengo ciencias naturales.

Ricardo: Las matemáticas y las ciencias son difíciles, ¿no?

Pablo: Sí. A las nueve tengo inglés, y a las diez menos cuarto tengo receso.

Ricardo: ¿Cuántas clases tienes después del receso?

Pablo: Tengo tres: literatura, arte y estudios sociales.

Ricardo: ¿Cuándo descansas, amigo?

Pablo: Las clases terminan a la una menos cuarto. ¡Qué día!

ACTIVIDAD 29 Por la tarde *page 50*

Alicia va a hacer muchas cosas hoy. Primero tiene que hablar con la profesora de inglés. Antes de salir de la escuela, va a ir a la práctica de voleibol en el gimnasio. Luego, tiene que comprar fruta para la cena. Entonces va a pasar un rato en casa de unos amigos. Por fin, va a ir a casa para cenar.

Pacing Guide

Sample Lesson Plan - 45 Minute Schedule

DAY 1

Etapa Opener
- Discuss the Opener, pp. 28–29. 5 MIN.

En contexto: Vocabulario
- Quick Start Review (TE, p. 30) 5 MIN.
- Play the audio. Have students use context and pictures to review the vocabulary, pp. 30–31. 5 MIN.
- Do *Actividad* 1 orally. 5 MIN.
- Have students work in pairs to do *Actividad* 2. 5 MIN.

En acción: Vocabulario y gramática
- Present *Gramática en vivo*: Saying What You Do: Present of *-ar* Verbs, and the *Vocabulario*, p. 32. 5 MIN.
- Assign *Actividad* 3. 5 MIN.
- Present the *Vocabulario*, p. 33, and then have students work in pairs to do *Actividad* 4. 5 MIN.
- Have students work in pairs to do *Actividad* 5. 5 MIN.

Homework Option:
- Activity and Assessment Book, p. 17

DAY 2

En acción (cont.)
- Check homework. 5 MIN.
- Present *Gramática en vivo*: Expressing Frequency with Adverbs, p. 34. 5 MIN.
- Assign *Actividad* 6. 5 MIN.
- Have students write responses to *Actividad* 7, and then call on them to give their responses orally. 5 MIN.
- Have students work in groups to do *Actividad* 8. 5 MIN.
- Present *Gramática en vivo*: Expressing Obligation with *hay que* and *tener que*, p. 35. 5 MIN.
- Assign *Actividad* 9. 5 MIN.
- Have pairs do *Actividad* 10. 5 MIN.

En resumen: Ya sabes
- Review vocabulary, and do the *Juego*, p. 37. 5 MIN.

Homework Option:
- Activity and Assessment Book, pp. 18–19

DAY 3

En contexto: Vocabulario
- Check homework. 5 MIN.
- Quick Start Review (TE, p. 38) 5 MIN.
- Play the audio. Present vocabulary, pp. 38–39. 5 MIN.
- Assign *Actividad* 11. 5 MIN.
- Have students work in pairs on *Actividad* 12, and then work orally with the class on *Actividad* 13. 5 MIN.

En acción: Vocabulario y gramática
- Present *Gramática en vivo*: Saying Where You Are Going: The Verb *ir*, and the *Vocabulario*, p. 40. 5 MIN.
- Assign *Actividad* 14. 5 MIN.
- Have students work in pairs to complete *Actividad* 15. 5 MIN.
- Present *Gramática en vivo*: Telling Time, p. 41, and the *Vocabulario*, p. 42. 5 MIN.

Homework Option:
- Activity and Assessment Book, pp. 20–21

DAY 4

En acción (cont.)
- Check homework. 5 MIN.
- Play the audio and assign *Actividad* 16. 5 MIN.
- Assign *Actividad* 17. 5 MIN.
- Have students work in pairs to do *Actividad* 18. 5 MIN.
- Present *Gramática en vivo*: Describing Location with the Verb *estar*, p. 43. 5 MIN.
- Assign *Actividades* 19–20. 5 MIN.
- Present *Gramática en vivo*: Asking Questions: Interrogative Words, p. 44. 5 MIN.
- Assign *Actividad* 21. 5 MIN.
- Have pairs do *Actividad* 22. 5 MIN.

Homework Option:
- Activity and Assessment Book, p. 22

DAY 5

En resumen: Ya sabes
- Check homework. 5 MIN.
- Review vocabulary, and do the *Juego*, p. 45. 5 MIN.

En contexto: Vocabulario
- Quick Start Review (TE, p. 46) 5 MIN.
- Play the audio. Present the vocabulary, pp. 46–47. 5 MIN.
- Assign *Actividad* 23. 5 MIN.
- Have pairs do *Actividad* 24. 5 MIN.
- Have groups do *Actividad* 25. 5 MIN.

En acción: Vocabulario y gramática
- Present *Gramática en vivo*: Saying What You Are Going to Do: *ir a...*, and the *Vocabulario*, p. 48. 5 MIN.
- Assign *Actividad* 26. 5 MIN.

Homework Option:
- Activity and Assessment Book, pp. 23–24

DAY 6

En acción (cont.)
- Check homework. 5 MIN.
- Have students work in groups to do *Actividad* 27. 5 MIN.
- Present *Gramática en vivo*: Present Tense of Regular *-er* and *-ir* Verbs, and the *Vocabulario*, p. 49. 5 MIN.
- Work orally on *Actividad* 28, and have students write responses. 5 MIN.
- Present the *Vocabulario*, p. 50. 5 MIN.
- Play the audio, and assign *Actividad* 29. 5 MIN.
- Assign *Actividad* 30. 5 MIN.
- Present *Gramática en vivo*: Regular Present Tense Verbs with Irregular *yo* Forms, p. 51. 5 MIN.
- Assign *Actividad* 31. 5 MIN.

Homework Option:
- Activity and Assessment Book, p. 25

DAY 7

En acción (cont.)
- Check homework. 5 MIN.
- Work orally with the class on *Actividad* 32. 5 MIN.
- Have students write out their answers to *Actividad* 32. 5 MIN.
- Present *Gramática en vivo*: Using the Verb *oír*, p. 52. 5 MIN.
- Assign *Actividad* 33. 5 MIN.
- Have students work in pairs to do *Actividad* 34. 5 MIN.
- Quick Wrap-up (TE, p. 52) 5 MIN.

En resumen: Ya sabes
- Review vocabulary, p. 53. 5 MIN.
- Do the *Juego*, p. 53. 5 MIN.

Homework Option:
- Activity and Assessment Book, p. 26

Classroom Management Tip

Vary classroom activities
Students may need to review the alphabet and numbers. If you assign a task that helps them *and* helps others, they will have a more positive attitude toward review.

You might have students create an illustrated Spanish-alphabet dictionary. Display the finished works in class for a while. Then, take them to a local children's hospital or to The Gift of Life, an organization that provides heart surgery for Latin American children in the U.S.

Teaching Resource Options

Audiovisual

OHT B7–B11

Teaching Suggestions
Previewing the Etapa

- Ask students to study the picture on these pages for one minute.
- Students close books; ask students to tell what the theme of the bulletin board is.
- Reopen books; ask for what class the students might be making the display. Why?
- Ask students if they were making a display about where they live, what categories of items they would include.

Project

Have students find pictures of famous Mexicans and Mexican Americans, one for each student. Have them write a speech balloon for each. Each day, have a few students present their efforts and then add them to the bulletin board. After the bulletin board is set up, play a game with it. Remove all the speech balloons and put them in a bag. Then have each student fish one out, read it aloud, and place it next to the correct picture. If the student is unable to make a correct placement, the next student tries.

BRIDGE UNIT

ETAPA 2

Una semana típica

- Talk about school
- Discuss obligations and plans
- Talk about schedules and time
- Ask questions
- Say where you are going
- Request food
- Sequence events

28

CIUDAD DE MÉXICO

LA COMIDA
EL TACO
AL PASTOR
TORTA
PAPAYA

Middle School Classroom Management

Time Saver Bring to class a kitchen timer. Use it to set a time limit for pair, group, and cooperative learning activities.

Cooperative Learning When you arrange your classroom for group work, you might want to consider the following: members of a group should sit face to face; groups should be far enough apart so that they do not interfere with one another and so that you can easily walk between them. It is easiest in the beginning to work with small groups or pairs.

Community Connections

Have students look into schedules for local movie theaters, transportation, street cleaning, etc. Have them bring as many examples as they can find for use when practicing time and schedule vocabulary later in this **Etapa**.

Teaching Middle School Students

Extra Help Review classroom activities and days of the week by having students make and decorate rule charts and/or calendars for the classroom.

Native Speakers Have students describe in as much detail as possible what the students are doing in the photograph.

Multiple Intelligences

Interpersonal Have pairs brainstorm words in Spanish that would have to do with **una semana típica** (days of the week, activities, school). Which pair has the longest list?

Block Schedule

Variety Have students make a list of weekly activities organized into categories: before-school activities, in-school activities, and after-school activities. Students then write as many of the activities as they can in Spanish and use a dictionary to look up words they don't know.

Teaching Resource Options

Print

Activity and Assessment Book
Vocabulary 2.1, p. 17
Audioscripts, pp. 54–58

Audiovisual

Bridge Audio Program Cassettes / CD
OHT B7, B8 (Quick Start)

Quick Start Review

 Dates

Use OHT B8 or write on the board:
Write the birthdays of your family
or friends and their ages.

Modelo: El cumpleaños de mi
mamá es el primero de abril.
Ella tiene treinta y nueve años.

Answers will vary.

Teaching Suggestions
Reconnecting with Vocabulary

• Read each section of the vocabulary
aloud, having students repeat after
you; use the individual words for a
dictation practice.
• Ask students what they use the
different items for: **¿Para qué usas
el lápiz?**
• Use the TPR activity to reinforce the
meaning of individual words.

En contexto

🎧 VOCABULARIO

Isabel spends most of the week in school. Here Isabel describes
the things she uses there.

A

¿Te gusta mi **escritorio**? Vengo a **la escuela** todos
los días porque me gusta **estudiar**. Yo uso mi
cuaderno mucho, y **un lápiz** y **una pluma** para
escribir. **El libro** grande es mi **diccionario**.

el diccionario   el lápiz
el papel
el escritorio   el cuaderno

una buena nota

la mochila
la pluma
la calculadora

el libro

B Llevo **una mochila** todos los días
también. Siempre necesito **papel**
y mi **calculadora** en **la clase**.

30 treinta
Bridge Unit

Middle School Classroom Community

TPR Play **¿Quién tiene…?** with students. Ask students
if they have certain classroom objects in all shapes and
colors. If students have the object, they should wave it
in the air. **¿Quién tiene un cuaderno azul? ¿Quién
tiene una mochila? ¿Una pluma roja?**

Game Have students work in groups of 4. Have
them make 4 cards for each of the vocabulary words
that are nouns. Then have them play Go Fish!, asking
¿Tienes _____?

el pizarrón

LA TIZA—CHALK

el borrador

C Mi profesor usa **el pizarrón** y **la tiza** mucho cuando **habla**. **Escucho** con atención porque es difícil **sacar una buena nota**.

la computadora

la pantalla

la impresora

el teclado

el ratón

D Uso **la computadora** en la clase de **ciencias**. La computadora tiene **una pantalla**, **un ratón** y **una impresora**. Uso **el teclado** para escribir.

ACTIVIDAD 1 La clase de español

Leer/Escribir Tell whether these statements are true (**sí**) or false (**no**) for your Spanish class. If a statement is false, correct it.

1. El (La) profesor(a) usa el pizarrón.
2. Los estudiantes escuchan al (a la) profesor(a).
3. Hay una computadora e impresora.
4. Hay treinta escritorios.
5. La clase es grande.
6. Hay tiza en el cuaderno.
7. Los estudiantes hablan mucho.
8. Necesitas usar la calculadora.
9. La clase es difícil.
10. Hay un diccionario español-inglés.

ACTIVIDAD 2 Para las clases

Hablar Ask your partner about what people have, need, and use at school.

1. ¿Qué tienes en tu mochila?
2. ¿Qué necesitas para las clases?
3. ¿Qué tienes en tu escritorio?
4. ¿Qué usas para escribir?
5. ¿Qué usa el (la) profesor(a) en la clase?
6. ¿Qué necesitan los estudiantes en la clase de ciencias?
7. ¿Qué son las cosas que no necesitas todos los días?
8. ¿Qué necesitas en la clase de español?

treinta y uno
Etapa 2
31

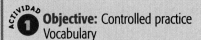
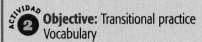

ACTIVIDAD 1 **Objective:** Controlled practice Vocabulary

Answers will vary.

ACTIVIDAD 2 **Objective:** Transitional practice Vocabulary

Answers will vary.

🔔 Quick Wrap-up

Hold a spelling bee using the **Etapa** vocabulary. Start by calling on a student to spell a word. If the student is correct, the student calls on another student. If not, you continue until a student responds correctly.

Game

Necesitamos Have students form two teams. Call out a school subject or activity and give teams 2 minutes to list the supplies needed for that subject. Then call out another subject and repeat the process until the school subjects have been exhausted. Finally, the teams share the lists and cross out any items the other team mentions. In the end, the team with the longest list of items not named by the other team wins.

■ Block Schedule

Change of Pace Have students work in small groups. Ask each group to make a set of cards for each of the school-related vocabulary words on these pages. When cards are completed, challenge groups to try to place each card on an appropriate item in the classroom. See which group can properly place their cards the quickest.

Teaching Middle School Students

Extra Help Have pairs point to each item pictured on pages 30–31 and ask each other if they have the item. Write a question and some responses on the board to serve as a model.

Native Speakers Have students pretend they are writing to a student in a Spanish-speaking country and write a paragraph that describes the general routine at their school.

Multiple Intelligences

Logical/Mathematical Have students organize their school supplies by shape: **redondo** *(round)* or **cuadrado** *(square)*.

Teaching Resource Options

Print

Activity and Assessment Book
Grammar 2.1, p. 18

Teaching Suggestions
Saying What You Do: Present of -ar Verbs

- Provide oral practice of the 6 forms of **estudiar** in the grammar box by pointing to yourself or to students, stating the subject, and asking students to say the corresponding verb form.
- Act out some of the verbs in the vocabulary box (**buscar, entrar, mirar, esperar**) and ask: **¿Qué hago?** Students can practice the **tú** and **usted** forms in their answers. Then have students act out the verbs and ask other students to answer: **¿Qué hace Elena?**
- Remind students that when the context is clear, subject pronouns are often omitted in Spanish (since the verb endings correspond to the subject); subject pronouns may be used to clarify (**él estudia**—not **ella**) or to emphasize (**Yo no llevo sombrero pero tú sí**).
- Tell students that the **vosotros** verb forms are used in Spain but not in Latin America.

Objective: Controlled practice
Regular -ar verbs

Answers
Answers may vary.
1. enseñan / ayudan
2. contestan
3. lleva / busca / necesita
4. prepara / busca / mira
5. miro / uso
6. necesitamos / buscamos / usamos
7. llegas
8. busco / llevo
9. necesitamos / esperamos
10. entra

En acción
VOCABULARIO Y GRAMÁTICA

Gramática en vivo

Isabel: Necesit**o** sacar una buena nota en esta clase.

Ricardo: Yo también. Estudi**o** todos los días, pero la clase es difícil.

Saying What You Do: Present of -ar Verbs

To form the present tense of a regular verb that ends in **-ar**, drop the **-ar** and add the appropriate ending.

estudi ar *to study*

yo	estudi**o**	nosotros(as)	estudi**amos**
tú	estudi**as**	vosotros(as)	estudi**áis**
usted, él, ella	estudi**a**	ustedes, ellos(as)	estudi**an**

Vocabulario

Verbs Ending in -ar ♻ **Ya sabes**

ayudar (a)	esperar	pasar
buscar	llegar	preparar
contestar	llevar	usar
enseñar	mirar	
entrar (a, en)	necesitar	

¿Qué haces cada día?

ACTIVIDAD 3

En la escuela

Escribir What are these people doing? Use the verbs in the vocabulary box. In some cases, there is more than one right way to answer.

1. Los maestros _____ a los estudiantes.
2. Los estudiantes _____ las preguntas.
3. Juan _____ pantalones negros.
4. Julio _____ la tarea.
5. Yo _____ el pizarrón.
6. Nosotros _____ un lápiz para escribir.
7. Tú _____ tarde a la clase.
8. Yo _____ un libro en la mochila.
9. Nosotros _____ usar el ratón con la computadora.
10. Ana _____ en la clase.

Middle School Classroom Management

Time Saver To help students settle down quickly and focus on Spanish class, you might have ready each day a puzzle, game, or math problem (in Spanish) for students to do as soon as they sit down.

Peer Review Consider assigning permanent pairs or small groups whose role is to review and critique each other's portfolio submissions. Expect that students will go through the editing process before being ready to submit work for their portfolios.

¿Quién enseña o estudia...?

Hablar Work with a partner to identify who studies and who teaches these subjects. Change roles.

modelo

arte

Estudiante A: *¿Quién estudia **arte**?*

Estudiante B: *Arturo y Catalina estudian **arte**.*

Estudiante A: *¿Quién enseña **arte**?*

Estudiante B: *El señor Clark enseña **arte**.*

I. ciencias	6. educación física
2. español	7. computación
3. estudios sociales	8. historia
4. matemáticas	9. inglés
5. música	10. literatura

¡Todas las materias!

Hablar/Escribir Write a sentence describing each of your classes. Then switch papers with a friend and compare your opinions.

modelo

La clase de historia es muy difícil pero interesante. Necesito estudiar para el examen de literatura. La lección en la clase de música…

Vocabulario

Las materias ♻ Ya sabes

el arte

la historia

las ciencias

el inglés (Good morning.)

la computación

la literatura

la educación física

las matemáticas
$$x + y = z$$

el español (Buenos días.)

la música

los estudios sociales

For more class subjects, see p. R13.

Here are other words to use to talk about classes.

fácil	el examen	la prueba
difícil	la lección	

Remember that you can use these adjectives you've learned, too.

aburrido(a)   **bueno(a)**

interesante   **malo(a)**

¿Qué clase tiene mucha tarea?

---

treinta y tres
Etapa 2
33

Teaching Middle School Students

Extra Help Write each of the verbs from the **Vocabulario** box on page 32 on a slip of paper. Have students pull out 3 slips and conjugate those verbs. Or, ask individual students simple **sí/no** questions about -ar verbs: **¿Bailas? ¿Estudias mucho? ¿Tocas la guitarra?**

Multiple Intelligences

Verbal How many sentences can students create about their day from the list of verbs on page 32?

Visual Have students create and label their own icons or signs for the classroom subjects on page 33.

Teaching Suggestions
Las materias

- Read all of the vocabulary aloud, having students repeat after you.
- Point out that both "science" and "mathematics" are plural in Spanish, as is "social studies."
- Using the adjectives from the vocabulary, say short sentences, and have students name subjects matching your descriptions: **Es fácil– la música. Son interesantes–las ciencias.**
- Using names of teachers that the students know, ask, for example: **¿Qué enseña el señor Hobart?**

4 **Objective:** Transitional practice Regular -ar verbs/vocabulary

Answers will vary.

5 **Objective:** Open-ended practice Regular -ar verbs/vocabulary

Answers will vary.

▣ Block Schedule

Survey Have students work in groups of about 5 or 6 to design and conduct a survey about school subjects. Groups develop 5 incomplete statements using the subjects and adjectives in the vocabulary box. **La clase de _____ es interesante. La clase de _____ es fácil.** Groups get 10 students to complete the survey. They then compile the data and report the results.

Teaching Resource Options

Print 📖

Activity and Assessment Book
  Grammar 2.1, p. 18

Teaching Suggestions
Expressing Frequency with Adverbs

Point out that **mucho** and **poco** can be both adverbs and adjectives: **Estudia mucho/poco; estudia muchas/pocas materias.**

Objective: Controlled practice
Adverbs of frequency

Answers will vary.

Gramática en vivo

Isabel: ¡Qué vergüenza! **Siempre** escucho con atención en la clase de inglés.

◆ Expressing Frequency with Adverbs

siempre	*always*
todos los días	*every day*
mucho	*often*
a veces	*sometimes*
de vez en cuando	*once in a while*
poco	*a little*
rara vez	*rarely*
nunca	*never*

▶ These expressions are usually placed **before** the **verb**:
  siempre
  rara vez
  nunca

▶ These expressions are usually placed **after** the **verb**:
  mucho
  poco

▶ Longer phrases can be placed at the **beginning** or the **end** of the **sentence**:
  todos los días
  a veces
  de vez en cuando

ACTIVIDAD 6

¿Cierto o falso?

Escribir Tell whether the statements are true or false. If false, make them true.

modelo

A veces contestas en la clase.

Sí, a veces contesto en la clase.

o: Yo siempre contesto en la clase.

1. Tus amigos llegan tarde de vez en cuando.
2. La maestra enseña mucho en la clase.
3. Tú y tus hermanos nunca preparan la tarea.
4. Tu papá rara vez ayuda a tu hermano(a) con la tarea.
5. Te gusta llevar vestidos de vez en cuando.
6. Tú siempre bailas en casa.
7. Te gusta leer todos los días.
8. Tus padres patinan poco.

Middle School Classroom Community

Cooperative Learning Have groups do **Actividad 7** and calculate the percentage of students who answered **siempre** or **nunca** for each entry. *(Hint: They divide the number of answers by the total number of students and multiply by 100.)* Student A is the secretary; B, the encourager; C, the calculator; D, the reporter. Groups can compare results.

Group Activity Give each group a stack of cards. Each card has an adverb of frequency, subject, verb, or direct object on it. Students work together to make sentences out of the cards, making sure they put the adverb in the right place.

ACTIVIDAD 7

¿Siempre o nunca?

Hablar/Escribir Tell how often you do these things.

modelo

trabajar en casa

Trabajo en casa *todos los días.*

1. estudiar
2. bailar
3. nadar
4. patinar
5. llegar tarde
6. contestar en la clase
7. ayudar a los amigos
8. llevar sombrero
9. hablar por teléfono
10. usar la computadora

ACTIVIDAD 8

¿Con qué frecuencia?

Hablar/Escribir Ask three students how often they do the activities listed in the chart. Prepare a summary for the class.

Actividad	Clara	Javier	Tina
llevar zapatos rojos	rara vez	nunca	a veces
usar el diccionario	mucho	de vez en cuando	siempre
tomar un refresco	todos los días	poco	todos los días
usar el teléfono	siempre	mucho	rara vez

modelo

Resumen: *Clara rara vez lleva zapatos rojos pero usa el diccionario mucho. Toma un refresco todos los días y siempre usa el teléfono. Javier nunca lleva zapatos rojos…*

Gramática en vivo

Isabel: Tengo que **sacar** una buena nota. ¡Es muy importante!

Expressing Obligation with hay que and tener que

- Use the impersonal phrase

  hay que + *infinitive*

  if there is **no specific subject.**

- Use a form of **tener** in the phrase

  tener que + *infinitive*

  if there is a specific subject.

Teaching Middle School Students

Extra Help Point out that the columns with children's names in **Actividad 8** are just a model.

Native Speakers Have students provide sentences with **hay que** and **tener que**. You might pair native speakers with non-native speakers.

Multiple Intelligences

Naturalist Suggest that students bring to class pictures of animals, plants, and weather that they might see in your community. Under each picture they write how often they see the object: **Siempre veo "X"; Veo mucho "X"**; etc.

Answers

Answers will vary.

1. estudio	6. contesto
2. bailo	7. ayudo
3. nado	8. llevo
4. patino	9. hablo
5. llego	10. uso

 Objective: Open-ended practice Adverbs of frequency/-**ar** verbs/ vocabulary

Answers will vary.

Teaching Suggestions
Expressing Obligation with hay que and tener que

- Point out that when saying **hay que** the speaker means that the obligation is for everyone; with **tener que** the obligation is specified for a particular person or group: **Hay que ayudar a los amigos. Tengo que ayudar a mi amiga.**
- Emphasize that **hay que** never changes forms, but **tener** does change forms.
- Review the forms of **tener** (Etapa 1, p. 22) to use in the phrase **tener que estudiar.** State the subject and have students finish the sentence (example: **nosotros → tenemos que estudiar**).

Block Schedule

Change of Pace Make separate cards for each of the adverbs of frequency. Also make cards for a variety of verbs. Put the adverbs and verbs in separate piles. Invite students to take a card from each pile and make a sentence. They can also state whether this statement is true or false about themselves.

Teaching Resource Options

Print

Activity and Assessment Book
Grammar 2.1, p. 19

 Objective: Controlled practice
Hay que/tener que

Answers
1. Hay que / tengo que
2. tiene que / hay que
3. hay que / tienen que
4. Hay que / tenemos que

 Objective: Transitional practice
Tener que/vocabulary

Answers
1. Marta tiene que ayudar a su abuela. ¿Tienes que ayudar…? Sí, (No, no) tengo que…
2. Ana tiene que esperar a su amiga. ¿Tienes que esperar…? Sí, (No, no) tengo que…
3. Mis amigos tienen que correr. ¿Tienes que correr? Sí, (No, no) tengo que…
4. Jorge y yo tenemos que usar la computadora. ¿Tienes que usar…? Sí, (No, no) tengo que…

Quick Wrap-up

Engage students in a TPR activity using **tener que**. For example: **Álvaro, tienes que bailar con Elena. Marta, tienes que correr alrededor de la clase dos veces. Yolanda y Miguel, tienen que buscar al estudiante con una camisa verde.**

¡Tienes que decidir!

Leer/Escribir Read the two sentences. Decide in which sentence to use **hay que** and in which to use a form of **tener que**.

modelo

Hay que ayudar en casa.
Ana _tiene que_ ayudar a su hermana en la escuela.

1. _____ escuchar muy bien a los maestros.

   Yo _____ escuchar la radio por la noche.

2. Paula _____ llevar una falda todos los días.

   En diciembre _____ llevar una chaqueta.

3. Para sacar buenas notas _____ estudiar.

   Por las tardes las hermanas _____ estudiar.

4. _____ usar el ratón con la computadora.

   Nosotros _____ usar el diccionario en la clase de inglés.

¿Qué tienen que hacer?

Hablar With a partner, say what the people need to do. Then ask and tell whether you do the activities. Choose from the following activities.

correr   estudiar   ayudar a su abuela

usar la computadora   esperar a su amiga

Juan

modelo

Juan

Estudiante A: _Juan_ tiene que estudiar. ¿Tienes que estudiar también?

Estudiante B: Sí, yo tengo que estudiar también.

1. Marta

2. Ana

3. mis amigos

4. Jorge y yo

Middle School Classroom Community

TPR Warm up with a TPR routine. Tell students that they should touch the objects you name if they have them. Use vocabulary from the **En resumen** (for example, **un lápiz, dos libros, papel**).

Paired Activity Have pairs interview each other to find out each other's classes, class activities, and tastes at school. What school supplies do they need? What class do they like best? Do they talk a lot in class? Pairs then introduce and describe each other to the class. As an extension, students can write the answers to the interview on chart paper and decorate it for the entire class to look at.

En resumen

YA SABES ♻

DESCRIBING CLASSES

At School

la clase	class, classroom
la escuela	school
el examen	test
la lección	lesson
la prueba	quiz
la tarea	homework

School Subjects

el arte	art
las ciencias	science
la computación	computer science
la educación física	physical education
el español	Spanish
los estudios sociales	social studies
la historia	history
el inglés	English
la literatura	literature
las matemáticas	mathematics
la materia	subject
la música	music

Classroom Activities

enseñar	to teach
escuchar	to listen (to)
estudiar	to study
hablar	to talk, to speak
mirar	to watch, to look at
preparar	to prepare
sacar una buena nota	to get a good grade

DESCRIBING CLASS OBJECTS

el borrador	eraser
la calculadora	calculator
el cuaderno	notebook
el diccionario	dictionary
el escritorio	desk
el lápiz	pencil
el libro	book
la mochila	backpack
el papel	paper
el pizarrón	chalkboard
la pluma	pen
la tiza	chalk

At the Computer

la computadora	computer
la impresora	printer
la pantalla	screen
el ratón	mouse
el teclado	keyboard

SAYING HOW OFTEN

a veces	sometimes
de vez en cuando	once in a while
mucho	often
nunca	never
poco	a little
rara vez	rarely
siempre	always
todos los días	every day

DISCUSSING OBLIGATIONS

hay que	one has to, one must
tener que	to have to

Actions

ayudar (a)	to help
buscar	to look for, to search
contestar	to answer
entrar (a, en)	to enter
esperar	to wait for, to expect
llegar	to arrive
llevar	to wear, to carry
necesitar	to need
pasar	to happen, to pass, to pass by
usar	to use

OTHER WORDS AND PHRASES

¡Ahora mismo!	Right now!
Con razón.	That's why.
difícil	difficult, hard
fácil	easy
mismo(a)	same
pronto	soon
la razón	reason
tarde	late

Juego

Jorge tiene que preparar la tarea de cada clase. ¿En qué materias tiene tarea?

1. Usa una calculadora.
2. Estudia un libro sobre computadoras.
3. Busca una palabra en inglés en su diccionario.
4. Canta.

$x + y = z$

Teaching Middle School Students

Challenge Have students write or tell 5 things they need to do in order to do well in math class.

Multiple Intelligences

Musical/Rhythmic Have students create chants that will help them remember when to use **tener que** and **hay que**.

Kinesthetic Write each verb from page 37 on a slip of paper. Students pull 3 slips from a bag and act out the verbs for the class to guess.

Teaching Suggestions
Vocabulary Review

- Ask students to form sentences using words from at least 3 different categories. (**En la prueba de matemáticas a veces uso la calculadora.**)
- Have students write 5 vocabulary words with the letters scrambled. Students then exchange papers, unscramble the words, and also write their meanings.

Juego

Answers
1. matemáticas
2. computación
3. inglés
4. música

Project

Have students design their own class schedule cards, including the day, time, instructors' names, and room numbers. They may use magazine clippings or sketches to illustrate the schedules. You may have these presented orally or in a visual display.

Block Schedule

Peer Review Allow students to review vocabulary words with a partner. Encourage students to share strategies for remembering words or for understanding concepts.

Teaching Resource Options

Print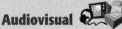

Activity and Assessment Book
  Vocabulary 2.2, p. 20
  Audioscripts, pp. 54–58

Audiovisual

Bridge Audio Program Cassettes / CD
OHT B8 (Quick Start), B9

Quick Start Review

🔄 **Ser**

Numbers 1–100

Use OHT B8 or write on the board:
Give and write out the number to
complete each sentence.

1. Yo tengo _____ años.
2. Tengo _____ clases este semestre.
3. Mi padre (madre) tiene _____ años.
4. Hay _____ estudiantes en la clase de español.
5. Mi cumpleaños es el _____ de _____.

Answers will vary.

Teaching Suggestions
Reconnecting with Vocabulary

• Read each section of the vocabulary aloud, having students repeat after you.
• Ask students at what time Ricardo appears in each place (**¿A qué hora está en el gimnasio?**). Then ask students at what time they are in different classes at school.
• Use the TPR activity to reinforce the meaning of individual words.

En contexto

🎧 VOCABULARIO

Isabel and Ricardo have a lot to do at school today. Let's see where they go at different times during the day.

 A **Isabel:** ¿A qué hora está la maestra en la oficina?
Ricardo: A la una. Son las diez ahora. ¿Quieres tomar un refresco?
Isabel: No. Quiero beber agua.

 B
¿Qué hora es? Es la una. Ricardo está en la biblioteca. ¡Necesita un receso!

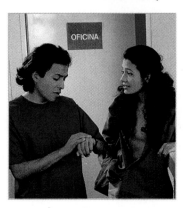

Horario para hoy
10:00 – oficina
11:00 – biblioteca
11:30 – cafetería
4:00 – gimnasio
5:00 – auditorio

la fruta
el refresco
las papas fritas
la hamburguesa
un vaso de agua
la torta

C

Ricardo: Es la una y media. Quiero comer una hamburguesa y unas papas fritas en la cafetería.

Isabel: Y yo quiero comer una torta y tomar un vaso de agua.

38 treinta y ocho
Bridge Unit

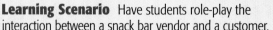

Middle School Classroom Community

TPR Lead students through a TPR routine at different places at school: ¡Buenos días! (Stretch.) **Son las siete. Vamos a la escuela. Son las ocho y media. Estamos en la clase de gimnasio.** (Exercise.) **Son las nueve. Vamos a la biblioteca para leer.** (Read.) **Ahora vamos a la cafetería.** (Eat.)

Learning Scenario Have students role-play the interaction between a snack bar vendor and a customer.

Paired Activity Bring to class clocks with movable hands and have pairs practice asking and telling time.

D

Son las cuatro, y a Ricardo le gusta jugar con sus amigos en **el gimnasio.**

E

A las cinco Ricardo e Isabel **están en el auditorio.** Toman **una merienda** después de practicar.

ACTIVIDAD **11** La merienda

Hablar/Escribir Given a choice, what do you want to eat or drink for a snack?

modelo

fruta / una torta
*Quiero comer **fruta.***

1. unas papas fritas / una fruta
2. un refresco / un vaso de agua
3. una hamburguesa / una torta
4. un taco / una torta

ACTIVIDAD **12** ¿Dónde estás?

Hablar Tell your partner where you are at the following times.

modelo

9:00 / la clase de español
Estudiante A: *¿Dónde estás a **las nueve**?*
Estudiante B: *Estoy en **la clase de español.***

1. 10:30 / el auditorio
2. 1:00 / la biblioteca
3. 5:00 / el gimnasio
4. 12:00 / la cafetería
5. 3:30 / la oficina
6. 7:00 / en casa

ACTIVIDAD **13** Tu horario

Hablar Write five sentences telling where you are at five different times during the day.

modelo

A las ocho estoy en la oficina de la escuela.

treinta y nueve
Etapa 2
39

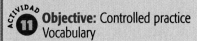

ACTIVIDAD **11** **Objective:** Controlled practice
Vocabulary

Answers will vary.

ACTIVIDAD **12** **Objective:** Transitional practice
Vocabulary

Answers
1. ¿Dónde estás a las diez y media? / Estoy en el auditorio.
2. ¿Dónde estás a la una? / Estoy en la biblioteca.
3. ¿Dónde estás a las cinco? / Estoy en el gimnasio.
4. ¿Dónde estás a las doce (al mediodía)? / Estoy en la cafetería.
5. ¿Dónde estás a las tres y media? / Estoy en la oficina.
6. ¿Dónde estás a las siete? / Estoy en casa.

ACTIVIDAD **13** **Objective:** Open-ended practice
Vocabulary

Answers will vary.

Quick Wrap-up

Take a class survey of food/beverage preferences. Ask for a show of hands as you announce pairs. For example: **¿Qué les gusta más, tomar agua o un refresco?, ¿comer una hamburguesa o una merienda de frutas?,** etc.

Teaching Middle School Students

Native Speakers Pair students together and have them discuss their class schedules and favorite and least favorite classes.

Multiple Intelligences

Musical/Rhythmic Review numbers by working with the class to make up and sing a song about counting something, like students or pencils. Use the tune from "Twinkle, Twinkle, Little Star."

Block Schedule

Change of Pace Have students work in pairs and interview each other. They should ask and answer questions about what they usually do or where they usually are at different times of the day. Then have students describe for the class their partner's typical day.

Teaching Suggestions
Saying Where You Are Going: The Verb ir

• Ask students if they can name the other verb they've learned with the **yo** form ending in **y**. (**ser / soy**)

• Point out that **voy** can mean "I go" or "I'm going." Ask what each of the other forms of the verb can mean.

• Read all of the **vida diaria** vocabulary aloud, having students repeat after you; make sure that they know the meanings of these words.

• Use the vocabulary words to ask students such questions as ¿Adónde vas para (el almuerzo / descansar / una cita, etc.)?

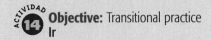

Objective: Transitional practice
Ir

Answers
1. Mis abuelos van a casa.
2. Usted va a la oficina.
3. Vas a la cafetería.
4. Vamos al auditorio.
5. Voy a la biblioteca.

En acción
VOCABULARIO Y GRAMÁTICA

Gramática en vivo

Isabel: ¿Adónde **vas**, Ricardo?
Ricardo: **Voy** a la cafetería. ¿Me acompañas?
Isabel: Sí, **vamos**. Tengo tiempo.

▪ Saying Where You Are Going: The Verb ir

When you talk about where someone is going, use the verb **ir**.

> As a question, **vamos** can mean *Shall we...?* But if stated definitely it means *Let's go!*

The verb **ir** means *to go.*

yo	voy	nosotros(as)	vamos
tú	vas	vosotros(as)	vais
usted, él, ella	va	ustedes, ellos(as)	van

• Use **adónde** to mean *where* when there is a verb indicating motion, such as **ir**.

> **¿Adónde va** Ricardo?
> *(To) Where is Ricardo going?*

• Use **dónde** to ask where someone or something is.

> **¿Dónde** está Ricardo?
> *Where is Ricardo?*

Vocabulario

La vida diaria	♻ Ya sabes
el almuerzo	terminar
la cita	tomar
comprar	visitar
descansar	

¿Qué te gusta hacer cada día?

ACTIVIDAD 14

Vamos a...

Escribir Where do people go to do these things?

la casa   la cafetería

la biblioteca

el gimnasio   la oficina

el auditorio

modelo

ella / correr con sus amigos
Ella va al gimnasio.

1. mis abuelos / preparar el almuerzo
2. usted / hablar con la maestra
3. tú / comprar el almuerzo
4. nosotros / escuchar un concierto
5. yo / buscar libros

40 cuarenta
Bridge Unit

Middle School Classroom Management

Planning Ahead If you haven't done so already, you might bring to class a clock with movable hands or have students make paper-plate clocks.

Peer Review Have students trade papers and correct each other's work for **Actividades 14–17**.

ACTIVIDAD
15

¿Adónde van?

Hablar Imagine where everyone is going. Use the correct form of **ir.**

> a la escuela
> a la ciudad
> al gimnasio
> a la casa
> a la biblioteca
> al apartamento
> al auditorio
> a la cafetería

modelo

los estudiantes

Estudiante A: *¿Adónde van los estudiantes?*

Estudiante B: *Los estudiantes van a la escuela.*

1. tu amiga
2. tus hermanos
3. tú
4. la maestra
5. tú y tus amigos
6. los estudiantes
7. ustedes
8. Esteban

Gramática en vivo

Isabel: Profesora, ¿qué hora es?
Maestra: **Son las once** menos cuarto.

Telling Time

Use:

¿Qué hora es?	to ask what time it is.
Son las + *hour*.	to give the time for every hour except one o'clock.
Es la una.	to say it is one o'clock.

- Use **y + *minutes*** for the number of minutes **after** the hour.
- Use **menos + *minutes*** for the number of minutes **before** the hour.
- Use **cuarto** for a quarter of an hour.
- Use **media** for half an hour.

To talk about when something will happen, use:

¿A qué hora + *verb* + *event*?
  ¿A qué hora es la clase?

A las + *hour*
  A las (dos, tres).

A la + *one o'clock*
  A la una.

cuarenta y uno
Etapa 2

41

ACTIVIDAD
15 **Objective:** Open-ended practice
Ir /places

Answers

Answers will vary but should contain the following verb forms.

1. va
2. van
3. vas / voy
4. va
5. van / vamos
6. van
7. van / vamos
8. va

Teaching Suggestions
Telling Time

- Use or draw a clock with hands to demonstrate telling time.
- Give examples of the items in **Gramática en vivo: Son las cuatro. / Son las cuatro y cuatro. / Son las cuatro y cuarto. / Son las cuatro y media. / Son las cinco menos cuarto.**
- Explain that "it's one o'clock" uses **es la una**, and not **son**, because it is talking about one hour; all the other hours are plural and require **son**.
- Point out that **son las cuatro menos cuarto** means 3:45, not 4:45.
- Point out that **son las ____** tells what time it is, whereas **a las ____** tells at what time something occurs.

Critical Thinking

Have students write a description of an activity they do and the time of day they do the activity. Have them present the description orally, and have classmates guess the time and the activity described. The first student to guess correctly is the next to go.

Block Schedule

Retention To help students understand and remember **menos** + minutes for the number of minutes before the hour, they might make a chart like the following: **1:35—dos menos veinticinco, 1:40—dos menos veinte,** and so on. The chart can be used as a visual tool for time-telling activities.

Teaching Middle School Students

Extra Help Play the role of **Estudiante A** in **Actividad 15** and organize it as a whole-class activity before students do it in pairs.

Native Speakers Have students write a paragraph that tells what they're going to do and where they're going to go over the weekend.

Multiple Intelligences

Kinesthetic Draw a large clock without hands. Tape it to the floor or to the door. Invite students to take turns configuring their bodies to show the time.

Teaching Resource Options

Print

Activity and Assessment Book
  Vocabulary 2.2, p. 21
  Audioscripts, pp. 54–58

Audiovisual

Bridge Audio Program Cassettes / CD

Teaching Suggestions
Para hablar de la hora

- Read all of the vocabulary aloud, having students repeat after you; make sure that students understand the meaning of each word or phrase.
- Point out that in Spain and other Spanish-speaking countries, **la tarde** can stretch up until the supper hour, which may be as late as 9:00 or 10:00 P.M.
- Point out that students often confuse the terms **la hora** and **el tiempo**; **la hora** refers to a specific time, whereas **el tiempo** refers to time in general (**no tengo la hora** = "I don't know the time"; **no tengo tiempo** = "I don't have time").

 Objective: Controlled practice
Listening comprehension/telling time/vocabulary

Answers (See script, p. 27A.)
1. falso; La clase es a las siete y media.
2. falso; Las matemáticas son difíciles.
3. cierto
4. falso; Es a las diez menos cuarto.
5. cierto
6. falso; Descansa a la una menos cuarto.

 Objective: Controlled practice
Telling time

Answers
1. Son las nueve y cuarto de la mañana.
2. Son las ocho de la noche.
3. Son las tres y cuarto de la tarde.
4. Son las siete y media de la mañana.
5. Son las doce y media de la tarde.
6. Son las dos de la mañana.
7. Son las cuatro de la tarde.
8. Son las seis de la tarde.
9. Son las once de la mañana.
10. Son las nueve y media de la noche.

 Objective: Open-ended practice
Telling time

Answers will vary.

 16

¡Qué horario!

Escuchar/Escribir Listen to Pablo and Ricardo talk about Pablo's schedule. Tell whether the statements are true or false. Correct the false statements.

1. La clase de matemáticas es a las siete.
2. Las matemáticas y la literatura son fáciles para Pablo.
3. La clase de inglés es a las nueve.
4. El receso es a las diez y cuarto.
5. Pablo tiene tres clases después del receso.
6. Pablo descansa al mediodía.

Vocabulario

Para hablar de la hora

 Ya sabes

Use these phrases when telling time.

A la una de la
  mañana/tarde/noche
la medianoche
el mediodía
por la mañana/tarde/noche   **el reloj**

¿Cuándo estudias?

 17

¿Qué dice el reloj?

Escribir Write the following times in words, and tell whether it is morning, afternoon, or evening.

modelo

10:30 A.M.

Son las diez y media de la mañana.

1. 9:15 A.M.	**6.** 2:00 A.M.
2. 8:00 P.M.	**7.** 4:00 P.M.
3. 3:15 P.M.	**8.** 6:00 P.M.
4. 7:30 A.M.	**9.** 11:00 A.M.
5. 12:30 P.M.	**10.** 9:30 P.M.

18

¿Qué hora es cuando…?

Hablar Ask a classmate what time it is when he or she is in the following places or does the following things. Change roles.

modelo

Tomas el almuerzo.

Estudiante A: *¿Qué hora es cuando* **tomas el almuerzo**?
Estudiante B: *Son las once y media.*

1. Estás en la clase de español.
2. Estás en el gimnasio.
3. Llegas a casa por la tarde.
4. Estudias.
5. Vas a la escuela por la mañana.
6. Estás en la clase de inglés.
7. Terminas la tarea por la noche.
8. Tomas una merienda en la cafetería de la escuela.
9. ¿?

---

42   cuarenta y dos
Bridge Unit

Middle School Classroom Community

TPR Instruct students to draw different times on a blank clock on the board: **Sarita, escribe la una y media en el reloj. Ricardito, escribe la hora que llegas a casa después de las clases…**

Game Play the **Estoy pensando en…** guessing game about the time and time of day. For example: **Estoy pensando en una hora para comer la merienda. ¿Qué hora es? Son las cuatro de la tarde.**

Portfolio Have students write their school schedules, spelling out the hour. On an additional page, have them write their impressions of 4 of their classes. (You might review adjectives ahead of time.)

Rubric

Criteria	Scale	
Creativity	1 2 3 4 5	A = 13–15 pts.
Logical organization	1 2 3 4 5	B = 10–12 pts.
Vocabulary use/spelling	1 2 3 4 5	C = 7–9 pts.
		D = 4–6 pts.
		F = < 4 pts.

Gramática en vivo

Maestra: A veces la profesora Díaz **está** en su oficina durante el almuerzo, y a las tres.

Describing Location with the Verb estar

To say where people or things are located, use the verb **estar**.

yo	estoy	nosotros(as)	estamos
tú	estás	vosotros(as)	estáis
usted, él, ella	está	ustedes, ellos(as)	están

ACTIVIDAD 19

¿Dónde están?

Escribir Write six sentences to tell where these people are. Choose one element from each column.

modelo

Los estudiantes están en la cafetería.

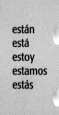

yo		en la clase
mi mamá	están	en casa
tú	está	en una fiesta
Isabel y yo	estoy	en la oficina
mis amigos	estamos	en el gimnasio
la maestra	estás	en el auditorio
los estudiantes		en la cafetería

ACTIVIDAD 20

¿Están en...?

Leer/Escribir Tell where the people are, based on what they're doing.

1. Ana busca libros. Ella…

2. Los chicos juegan al baloncesto. Ellos…

3. Tomo el almuerzo. Yo…

4. Escuchamos un concierto de la banda de la escuela. Nosotros…

5. Visito a mis amigos. Yo…

6. La secretaria habla con el director de la escuela. Ella…

7. Tenemos un examen de matemáticas. Nosotros…

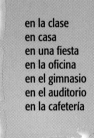

cuarenta y tres
Etapa 2
43

Teaching Suggestions
Describing Location with the Verb estar

- Point out that this is the third verb that students have learned with the **yo** form ending in **-y**; ask them what the other two were. (**ser / ir**)
- Remind students that they have also learned to use **estar** to say how they are feeling. (**¿Cómo estás? Estoy bien.**)
- Again remind students that the subject pronouns are not needed but may be used for clarification or emphasis. (**Ella está en casa, y no él.**)

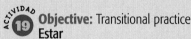

19 Objective: Transitional practice
Estar

Answers will vary.

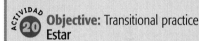

20 Objective: Transitional practice
Estar

Answers

Answers may vary.
1. …está en la biblioteca.
2. …están en el gimnasio.
3. …estoy en la cafetería.
4. …estamos en el auditorio.
5. …estoy en la casa de mis amigos.
6. …está en la oficina.
7. …estamos en la clase.

Block Schedule

FunBreak Have students work in groups to make a map of your school. They should also make a group of cards with subject names (**tú, yo, Ana y Pablo**, etc.). Groups can use the map as a game board to play **¿Dónde está…?** Players take turns rolling a number cube and picking a subject card. They ask where the person on the card is. **¿Dónde están Ana y Pablo?** They then answer their question, naming the spot on the game board where the number cube landed.

Teaching Middle School Students

Challenge Have students write or tell where they are at the times indicated in **Actividad 17: A las diez y media de la mañana, estoy en la clase de ciencias.**

Multiple Intelligences

Verbal Give pairs 2 sets of cards to practice conjugation of **estar** + rooms in school. One set has rooms they have learned. The other set consists of singular and plural subjects. Pairs stack cards facedown in 2 piles. Students take turns drawing cards from the 2 piles. Student A asks: **¿Dónde está "X"?** Student B answers: **Está en…**

Teaching Resource Options

Print

Activity and Assessment Book
   Grammar 2.2, p. 22

Teaching Suggestions
Asking Questions: Interrogative Words

• Model the use of each interrogative word in the following sentence:

¿ _____ estudia?

¿Cómo estudia? (Bien).
¿Por qué estudia? (Tiene examen.)
¿Cuál de las materias estudia? (español)
¿Qué estudia? (inglés, español, historia, etc.)
¿Cuándo estudia? (por la mañana)
¿Quién estudia? (Roberto)
¿Dónde estudia? (en casa)

• Point out that **¿por qué?** means "why" and **porque** means "because."

 Objective: Controlled practice Interrogatives

Answers
1. ¿Cómo te llamas?
2. ¿De dónde eres?
3. ¿Con quién vives?
4. ¿Cuál es tu clase favorita?
5. ¿Quién es tu maestro favorito?
6. ¿Qué te gusta hacer?

 Objective: Open-ended practice Interrogatives

Answers will vary.

 Quick Wrap-up

Prepare beginnings and endings of questions on cards and have students come to the front of the class to assemble them. For example, students might put together the following fragments: ¿Cómo / te llamas? ¿Por qué / tienes que estudiar? ¿Qué / te gusta hacer? ¿Cuándo / es tu cumpleaños?

Gramática en vivo

Ricardo: ¿**Por qué** no vamos a la cafetería para hablar más tranquilos?
Isabel: ¿**Cuándo**?
Ricardo: A las cinco y veinte.

Asking Questions: Interrogative Words

Use rising intonation to signify a question
or
switch the position of the subject and verb to ask a yes / no question.

cómo *how*	**por qué** *why*
cuál(es) *which or what*	**qué** *what*
cuándo *when*	**quién(es)** *who*

Each interrogative word has an **accent** on the appropriate vowel.

Entrevista

Escribir You are working on the Spanish Club's newsletter. You want to print the following interview with a student from Mexico, but somehow all the questions have disappeared! Fill in the questions.

1. ¿_____?
   Me llamo Antonio Solís Guerra.

2. ¿_____?
   Soy de Guadalajara, México.

3. ¿_____?
   Vivo con la familia Jones.

4. ¿_____?
   Mi clase favorita es ciencias naturales.

5. ¿_____?
   Mi maestro favorito es el señor Scott.

6. ¿_____?
   Me gusta patinar, bailar, cantar y ¡practicar el inglés!

44 cuarenta y cuatro
Bridge Unit

Preguntas

Leer/Escribir Read the paragraph. Then write four questions about it. Trade papers with a classmate and answer the questions. Share your responses.

> Después de las clases, Enrique va a la cafetería porque tiene hambre. Su amigo Daniel va con él. Enrique toma una hamburguesa y un refresco. ¡La hamburguesa está deliciosa! Daniel toma fruta.

modelo

Estudiante A: *¿Cuándo va Enrique a la cafetería?*

Estudiante B: *Enrique va a la cafetería después de las clases.*

Middle School Classroom Community

Group Activity Fold a set of 6 index cards in half. Write an interrogative on each one. Stand cards around the room at work stations. Have teams of students work at one table at a time. Set a time limit of 5 minutes. Students write as many questions with that question word as possible. When the timer rings, teams move on to the next station.

Learning Scenario With the class, write on the board a list of people whom students would like to interview if given the chance (actors, athletes, musicians, etc.). Students take turns assuming an identity. The rest of the class asks questions of the "guest." Each student answers as his or her assumed identity would.

En resumen

YA SABES ♻

TALKING ABOUT SCHEDULES

el almuerzo	lunch
la cita	appointment
el horario	schedule
el receso	break
el semestre	semester

Activities

comprar	to buy
descansar	to rest
estar	to be
terminar	to finish
tomar	to take, to eat or drink
visitar	to visit

ASKING AND TELLING TIME

¿A qué hora es…?	(At)What time is…?
¿Qué hora es?	What time is it?
A la(s)…	At… o'clock.
Es la…/Son las…	It is… o'clock.
de la mañana	in the morning
de la noche	at night
de la tarde	in the afternoon
la medianoche	midnight
el mediodía	noon
menos	to, before
por la mañana	during the morning
por la noche	during the evening
por la tarde	during the afternoon
el reloj	clock, watch
y cuarto	quarter past
y media	half past

ASKING QUESTIONS

adónde	(to) where
cómo	how
cuál(es)	which (ones), what
cuándo	when
dónde	where
por qué	why
qué	what
quién(es)	who

REQUESTING FOOD

¿Quieres beber…?	Do you want to drink…?
¿Quieres comer…?	Do you want to eat…?
Quiero beber…	I want to drink…
Quiero comer…	I want to eat…

Snacks

el agua (fem.)	water
la fruta	fruit
la hamburguesa	hamburger
la merienda	snack
las papas fritas	french fries
el refresco	soft drink
la torta	sandwich
el vaso de	glass of

SAYING WHERE YOU ARE GOING

ir	to go
al	to the

Places

el auditorio	auditorium
la biblioteca	library
la cafetería	cafeteria, coffee shop
el gimnasio	gymnasium
la oficina	office

OTHER WORDS AND PHRASES

durante	during
por favor	please
la verdad	truth

Juego

¿Adónde van?

Marco: Me gusta escuchar música.

Maricarmen: Necesito buscar unos libros.

Josefina: Voy a hablar con la maestra.
Ella no está en clase.

¿Adónde va Marco? ¿Maricarmen? ¿Josefina?

Buenos días.

Good morning.

$x + y = z$

Teaching Suggestions
Vocabulary Review

- Draw 5 columns on the board with these headings: **actividades, la hora, comida, preguntas, lugares**.
- Have students close their books. Call on volunteers to come to the board and write a word or phrase that could fit into one of the categories. Continue until all ideas are exhausted.

Juego

Answers may vary slightly.
Marco va al auditorio.
Maricarmen va a la biblioteca.
Josefina va a la oficina.

Game

Buscapalabras Have student pairs select 8–10 words from the vocabulary review and create a word find. They write a clue for each word. (**La última hora del día → medianoche.**) Collect and redistribute the puzzles. The first pair to circle all the words wins. Save the word finds to use for review before an exam.

Teaching Middle School Students

Native Speakers Remind students that all interrogatives carry accent marks. Write a set of sentences that includes interrogatives with their accent marks missing and sentences with the relative pronouns/conjunctions **como, cual, cuando, porque, que,** and **quien(es).** Students must supply the correct accent marks.

Multiple Intelligences

Intrapersonal Have students write 4 or 5 questions about themselves and then answer them.

Block Schedule

Variety Invite students to work in pairs or groups to expand upon the concept in the **Juego.** Groups write statements and then ask questions similar to the ones in the student book. Groups then exchange papers and answer each other's questions.

Teaching Resource Options

Print

Activity and Assessment Book
Vocabulary 2.3, pp. 23–24
Audioscripts, pp. 54–58

Audiovisual

Bridge Audio Program Cassettes / CD
OHT B8 (Quick Start), B10, B11

Quick Start Review

 Ir

Use OHT B8 or write on the board:
Complete each sentence with the
correct form of **ir** to tell where
everyone is going this morning.

1. Antonia _____ a la biblioteca.
2. Ustedes _____ a la cafetería.
3. Pedro y yo _____ a clase.
4. Tú _____ al gimnasio.
5. Yo _____ a la oficina.

Answers
1. va   2. van   3. vamos   4. vas   5. voy

Teaching Suggestions
Reconnecting with Vocabulary

• Read each section of the vocabulary
aloud, having students repeat after
you.
• Ask students to name some of the
things Ricardo likes to do; then ask
students what they like to do at the
park.
• Use the TPR activity to reinforce the
meaning of individual words.

En context

🎧 VOCABULARIO

Ricardo is taking a walk through a park where he
and his friends spend a lot of time after school.

¡**Hola!** Por fin, ¡voy al **parque**!
Voy a visitar con mis amigos y **hacer**
muchas cosas.

A Cuando voy al parque, **paso un rato con mis
amigos**. Ellos **tocan la guitarra** y yo canto.

la guitarra

B También me gusta
andar en bicicleta
o **caminar con el
perro.**

la bicicleta

la revista

el periódico

C A veces nos gusta leer **una revista** o
leemos **el periódico**. Nos gusta ver qué
pasa en **el museo** o **el teatro.**

46 cuarenta y seis
Bridge Unit

Middle School Classroom Community

TPR Have students take turns pantomiming the
activities on pages 46–47: **tocar la guitarra, cantar,
andar en bicicleta, leer, pasear por el parque, tener
hambre/sed, beber, comer, cuidar al hermanito.**

Group Activity As an extension to **Actividad 24,**
have small groups write and act out their own dialogs
that use the vocabulary on these pages.

D Cuando mi amiga tiene que cuidar a su hermano, pasean por el parque.

la tienda

los chicharrones

E Cuando tenemos hambre y sed, vamos a la tienda para comprar y beber un refresco. También nos gusta comer chicharrones.

23 Actividades

Leer Match the following things with an appropriate verb.

1. la guitarra	a. leer
2. el periódico	b. beber
3. el perro	c. comer
4. bicicleta	d. tocar
5. un refresco	e. andar en
6. chicharrones	f. caminar con

24 ¡Vamos!

Hablar/Escribir Complete the conversations. Then work with a partner to act them out.

Ricardo: ¿Qué quieres hacer en el parque hoy?

Isabel: Quiero __1__ . Y tú, ¿qué quieres hacer?

Ricardo: Quiero __2__ porque no tengo mucho tiempo hoy. Tengo que __3__ .

Ricardo: Tengo hambre. Quiero __4__ algo.

Isabel: ¿Por qué no compramos __5__ , entonces?

Ricardo: Sí, y vamos a beber __6__ .

Isabel: Muy __7__ idea. ¡Vamos!

25 ¿A quién le gusta?

Hablar/Escribir Who likes what?

1. Write down six activities on these pages.

2. Ask different classmates if they like to do these activities. When classmates answer **sí**, have them sign their name next to the activity. Get at least six signatures.

cuarenta y siete
Etapa 2 **47**

23 Objective: Controlled practice
Vocabulary

Answers
1. d
2. a
3. f
4. e
5. b
6. c

24 Objective: Transitional practice
Vocabulary

Answers will vary.

25 Objective: Open-ended practice
Vocabulary

Answers will vary.

🔔 Quick Wrap-up

Take a class poll of students' interests in a variety of activities. Write them on the board or announce them. Students stand up if they're interested in doing activities such as the following: **ir al parque, ir a la tienda, comer una hamburguesa, leer una revista, andar en bicicleta, cantar, cuidar a los hermanos, tocar un instrumento, ir al museo, beber un refresco, ir a California (Florida, etc.).** You may wish to count heads and discover the most/least favorite activities.

Teaching Middle School Students

Extra Help Ask individual students: ¿Te gusta cantar? ¿Te gusta andar en bicicleta? ¿Te gusta ir al teatro? etc.

Native Speakers Have pairs talk about their favorite after-school activities. You might have them tell about each other to the class.

Multiple Intelligences

Visual Have students make personality charts or collages of their favorite activities, colors, foods, friends, etc. Suggest they include at least one photo of themselves doing something they like. Students can share their charts with the class.

Block Schedule

Variety Have students write sentences on the topic: **Después de las clases…** They should write about what they like and don't like to do after school, using known vocabulary.

Teaching Suggestions
Saying What You Are Going to Do: ir a...

• Point out that **voy a** + **un lugar** (a place) is used to say where you are going, whereas **voy a** + infinitive is used to say what you are going to do: **Voy al restaurante. Voy a comer.**

• Read all of the vocabulary aloud, having students repeat after you; make sure that students understand the meaning of each word/phrase.

• Ask students what they are going to do after school, encouraging them to use the vocabulary in the box on page 48; after each student answers, ask the others: **¿Qué va a hacer** (student's name)?

Game

¿Qué voy a hacer? Divide the class into 2 teams. A student from Team A pantomimes an activity that he or she will do after school or in the near future. The rest of Team A has 1 minute to guess the activity and earn a point before play passes to Team B.

26 **Objective:** Transitional practice **Ir a** + infinitive

Answers

Answers will vary.
1. Los maestros van a...
2. Mi amigo(a) y yo vamos a...
3. Vas a...
4. Mi amigo(a) va a...
5. Voy a...

En acción
VOCABULARIO Y GRAMÁTICA

Gramática en vivo

Isabel: ¡Voy a **participar** en el concurso!

Saying What You Are Going to Do: ir a...

▶ To talk about activities you are going to do, use the phrase:

ir + a + *infinitive*

yo	voy a...	nosotros(as)	vamos a...
tú	vas a...	vosotros(as)	vais a...
usted, él, ella	va a...	ustedes, ellos(as)	van a...

26

Después de las clases

Escribir Imagine what people are going to do after school. Use the vocabulary box.

modelo

mi amiga	***Mi amiga*** *va a cuidar el perro.*

1. los maestros   **4.** mi amigo(a)

2. mi amigo(a) y yo   **5.** yo

3. tú

Vocabulario

Más para hacer después de clases
♻ Ya sabes

cuidar (a) un animal	pintar
el pájaro	tocar el piano
el pez	ver la televisión
cenar	mandar una carta
hacer ejercicio	preparar
ir al supermercado	la cena
leer	(la) comida
una novela	
un poema	
(la) poesía	

¿Qué haces tú?

Middle School Classroom Management

Cooperative Learning It's very effective to tell groups and pairs of students how much time they will have to do an activity (for example, **Actividad 27,** p. 49). You might even assign a student to be Time Monitor.

Peer Teaching You might group native speakers with non-native speakers to encourage natural cadence and tone of voice.

¿Qué vas a hacer?

Hablar/Escribir Ask three classmates what they and their family or friends are going to do on Saturday (these can be real or imaginary plans). Write a summary of their answers.

modelo

Estudiante A: *¿Qué vas a hacer el sábado?*

Estudiante B: *Voy a hacer ejercicio con mi amiga.*

Estudiante A: *¿Qué van a hacer tú y tu familia?*

Estudiante B: *Vamos a ir al cine.*

Resumen: *Susana va a hacer ejercicio con su amiga. Susana y su familia van a ir al cine. Pablo va a andar en bicicleta con sus amigos.*

Gramática en vivo

Ricardo: ¿Com**emos** unos chicharrones? Esa señora vend**e** unos chicharrones deliciosos.

Present Tense of Regular -er and -ir Verbs

Regular **-er** verbs have the same endings as **-ir** verbs except in the **nosotros(as)** and **vosotros(as)** forms. Notice that the letter change matches the verb ending.

-**e**r verbs = **emos**, **éis**
-**i**r verbs = **imos**, **ís**

com er *to eat*

com**o**	com**emos**
com**es**	com**éis**
com**e**	com**en**

viv ir *to live*

viv**o**	viv**imos**
viv**es**	viv**ís**
viv**e**	viv**en**

Vocabulario

Verbs Ending in -er and -ir ♻ Ya sabes

You have seen the verbs **beber, comer, correr, escribir, leer** before. Here are some others.

Verbs: **-er**

aprender	**vender**
comprender	**ver (yo: veo)**

Verbs: **-ir**

abrir	**recibir**
compartir	**vivir**

¿Qué haces después de las clases?

cuarenta y nueve
Etapa 2
49

Teaching Middle School Students

Extra Help You might first model **Actividad 27** as a pair activity (you being Student A and random students being Student B).

Multiple Intelligences

Verbal To practice **ir a** + infinitive, give pairs 2 sets of cards. One set has pictures or words of activities on pages 46–48. The other set consists of subject pronouns and nouns. Stack cards facedown in 2 piles. Students take turns drawing cards from the different piles. Student A asks: **¿Qué va a hacer "X"?** Student B answers: **Va a...**

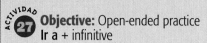
Objective: Open-ended practice
Ir a + infinitive

Answers will vary.

Teaching Suggestions
Present Tense of Regular -er and -ir Verbs

- Provide oral practice of the 6 forms (or 5, if you don't wish to have students use **vosotros**) of **comer** and **vivir** in the grammar box by pointing to yourself or to students, stating the subject, and asking students to say the corresponding verb form.
- Review the **-ar** verb endings; ask students to point out similarities and differences in the patterns of the endings of regular **-ar**, **-er**, and **-ir** verbs. Point out that accents only occur in the **vosotros** forms.

■ Block Schedule

Change of Pace To vary the activity format, do **Actividad 26** with the class. Write the activities from the vocabulary box on the chalkboard. For each item, have 2 students come to the front of the class. One student makes a sentence using the given subject, and then asks: **¿Qué haces tú?** The second student answers the question about himself or herself.

Teaching Resource Options

Print

Activity and Assessment Book
  Grammar 2.3, p. 25
  Audioscripts, pp. 54–58

Audiovisual

Bridge Audio Program Cassettes / CD

Teaching Suggestions
Vocabulary

Have students use the vocabulary in the Sequencing Events box with regular -er and -ir verbs to tell what they do (1) before and after class; (2) first, next, and last in class.

ACTIVIDAD 28 Objective: Controlled practice
Regular -er/-ir verbs

Answers
1. bebe
2. corren (comen)
3. aprendo
4. vemos
5. vives
6. abre (ve)
7. compartimos (comemos)
8. comen (comparten)

ACTIVIDAD 29 Objective: Transitional practice
Listening comprehension/**ir a** + infinitive/vocabulary

Answers (See script, p. 27A.)
1. e
2. a
3. c
4. d
5. b

ACTIVIDAD 30 Objective: Transitional practice
Regular -er/ir verbs/vocabulary

Answers
1. Primero
2. bebo
3. como
4. compartimos (comemos)
5. Luego/Después
6. vamos
7. Entonces
8. escribe
9. Después/Luego
10. comprenden
11. Por fin
12. recibo

ACTIVIDAD 28

¿Qué hacen?

Hablar/Escribir Choose the correct form of a verb from the list to tell what these people are doing.

comer	compartir	aprender
correr	abrir	beber
vivir	ver	escribir

modelo

Yo _escribo_ una carta.

1. Mamá _____ un refresco.
2. Los estudiantes _____ en el parque.
3. Yo _____ español.
4. Mi amigo y yo _____ la televisión.
5. Tú _____ en la ciudad.
6. Papá _____ un libro.
7. Mi hermana y yo _____ una merienda.
8. Mis amigos _____ hamburguesas.

Vocabulario

Sequencing Events Ya sabes

To sequence events, use these words.

| primero | luego | antes |
| entonces | por fin | después |

When a **noun** or an **infinitive** follows **antes** or **después**, use the preposition **de**.

¿Qué haces **después de las clases** y **antes de cenar**?

*What do you do **after** classes and **before** eating dinner?*

¿Qué pasa cada día?

ACTIVIDAD 29

Por la tarde

Escuchar Listen and indicate the order (1–5) in which Alicia plans to do these things.

a. Va a jugar al voleibol.
b. Va a cenar.
c. Va a comprar fruta.
d. Va a pasar un rato con los amigos.
e. Va a hablar con la profesora de inglés.

ACTIVIDAD 30

Una tarde típica

Escribir Amelia is describing a typical afternoon at school. Use the words to fill in the blanks.

por fin	comer	comprender
beber		compartir
después	entonces	escribir	ir
luego	primero	recibir

Me llamo Amelia. Por la tarde tengo que hacer mucho. __1__, yo __2__ un refresco y __3__ una hamburguesa. Es mi almuerzo. A veces mis amigos y yo __4__ papas fritas. __5__, nosotros __6__ a la clase de matemáticas. __7__, la maestra __8__ en el pizarrón. ¡ __9__ los estudiantes __10__ la lección! __11__ yo __12__ una buena nota.

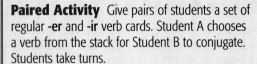

Middle School Classroom Community

Paired Activity Give pairs of students a set of regular -er and -ir verb cards. Student A chooses a verb from the stack for Student B to conjugate. Students take turns.

Storytelling Have pairs or small groups of students write a story about **una tarde típica** that uses some of the words in **Actividad 30** and words of their own choice. The class can vote on the funniest or the most outlandish.

Gramática en vivo

Ricardo: No toco el piano muy bien.
Isabel: ¡Conozco a alguien muy modesto!

Regular Present Tense Verbs with Irregular yo Forms

conocer *to know, to be* *familiar with (a person or a place)*		**hac**er *to do, to make*	
cono**zco**	conocemos	ha**go**	hacemos
conoces	conocéis	haces	hacéis
conoce	conocen	hace	hacen

ACTIVIDAD 31

¿Quién conoce a...?

Hablar/Escribir Tell who knows these people or places. Choose from the two columns and use the verb **conocer**.

modelo

Mi maestra conoce a mi mamá.

1. nosotros	a tu papá
2. Juan y Elena	a la madre de Paco
3. yo	a mi familia
4. Marco	la biblioteca
5. tú	a su tío
6. tus padres	la ciudad

ACTIVIDAD 32

¿Qué hacen todos?

Hablar/Escribir Tell what the following people are doing. Choose words from the list or think of your own activities.

la tarea   un proyecto para una clase
ejercicio   una torta
la cena   el almuerzo   ¿?

modelo

mi hermano   ***Mi hermano** hace la tarea.*

1. tú	4. mi amigo(a)
2. mi abuela	5. mi amigo(a) y yo
3. yo	6. los estudiantes

Teaching Middle School Students

Challenge Using **Actividad 28** as a model, have students make additional regular -er and -ir verb practice sheets for fellow students to complete.

Multiple Intelligences

Intrapersonal Designate time in the classroom so that students can practice the **Etapa** vocabulary and grammar with flash cards or other personalized study devices.

Teaching Suggestions
Regular Present Tense Verbs with Irregular yo Forms
Provide oral practice of the forms of **conocer** and **hacer** by pointing to yourself or to students, stating the subject, and asking students to say the corresponding verb form. Repeat the practice, this time using the verb in a meaningful context.

ACTIVIDAD 31 **Objective:** Transitional practice
Conocer

Answers

Answers will vary but should include the following verb forms.
1. Conocemos…
2. Juan y Elena conocen….
3. Conozco…
4. Marco conoce…
5. Conoces…
6. Tus padres conocen…

ACTIVIDAD 32 **Objective:** Transitional practice
Hacer

Answers

Answers will vary.
1. Haces…
2. Mi abuela hace…
3. Hago….
4. Mi amigo(a) hace…
5. Mi amigo(a) y yo hacemos…
6. Los estudiantes hacen…

Block Schedule

Gather and Sort Have students make a list of activities that they typically do every day. Then have them sort the activities within some time frames, for example, **antes/después del mediodía**, **antes/después de las clases**, **durante la semana/durante el fin de semana**.

Teaching Resource Options

Print

Activity and Assessment Book
  Information Gap Activities, pp. 26–27
  Cooperative Quizzes, pp. 28–31

Teaching Suggestions
Using the Verb oír

• Provide oral practice of the forms of **oír** by pointing to yourself or to students, stating the subject, and asking students to say the corresponding verb form.
• Ask students to look carefully at the spelling of each form; tell them that in Spanish the letter **i** usually changes to **y** between vowels (**oyes, oye, oyen**).
• Point out that **oye** is often used to attract someone's attention. **Oye, Isabel** is equivalent to saying: "Hey, Isabel."

 Objective: Transitional practice Oír

Answers
Answers will vary but should include the following verb forms.
1. oigo   5. oyes
2. oye   6. oye
3. oyen   7. oigo
4. oímos   8. oyen

 Objective: Transitional practice Oír

Answers
1. Susana y Jorge oyen el gato.
2. Mi abuelo oye la televisión.
3. Oigo música (el piano).
4. Oyes el perro.

🔔 Quick Wrap-up

Write on the board in 3 columns the words **hago, oigo,** and **conozco**. As you announce words/phrases that would go with each of them, have volunteers go to the board and write the word/phrase in the appropriate column. For example: **la tarea, a muchas personas, música de...**

Gramática en vivo

Ricardo: ¡O**y**e, Isabel!

Using the Verb oír

The verb **oír** *(to hear)* has an irregular **yo** form in the present tense. Some of its forms also require a spelling change. When Ricardo uses o**y**e as he does above, it means *Hey!*

oi**g**o	oímos
o**y**es	oís
o**y**e	o**y**en

¿Qué oyen?

Hablar/Escribir Indicate what or whom these people hear in the places indicated.

modelo

tú (en la escuela)
Oyes a los estudiantes.

1. yo (en el parque)
2. mi amigo (en casa)
3. mis padres (en la ciudad)
4. mis amigos y yo (en la cafetería)
5. tú (en el gimnasio)
6. mi hermano(a) (en el auditorio)
7. yo (en la clase de música)
8. los estudiantes (en la clase de computación)

52 cincuenta y dos
Bridge Unit

Ellos oyen...

Hablar/Escribir Decide what each of these people is hearing, based on the picture. Then write a sentence using the verb **oír**.

modelo
nosotros
***Nosotros** oímos el pájaro.*

1. Susana y Jorge

2. mi abuelo

3. yo

4. tú

Middle School Classroom Community

Group Activity Spell aloud vocabulary words from page 53 for students to write. Then say the words for students to spell.

Portfolio Have students choose a medium to describe by the hour their typical Saturday routine (writing, video, music, mural, etc.).

Rubric

Criteria	Scale	
Creativity	1 2 3 4 5	A = 13–15 pts.
Logical organization	1 2 3 4 5	B = 10–12 pts.
Vocabulary use/spelling	1 2 3 4 5	C = 7–9 pts.
		D = 4–6 pts.
		F = < 4 pts.

En resumen

YA SABES

DISCUSSING PLANS

ir a...	*to be going to...*

After-school Plans

andar en bicicleta	*to ride a bike*
caminar con el perro	*to walk the dog*
cenar	*to have dinner, supper*
comer chicharrones	*to eat pork rinds*
cuidar (a)	*to take care of*
el animal	*animal*
mi hermano(a)	*my brother (sister)*
el pájaro	*bird*
el pez	*fish*
hacer ejercicio	*to exercise*
ir al supermercado	*to go to the supermarket*
leer	*to read*
la novela	*novel*
el periódico	*newspaper*
el poema	*poem*
la poesía	*poetry*
la revista	*magazine*
mandar una carta	*to send a letter*
pasar un rato con los amigos	*to spend time with friends*
pasear	*to go for a walk*
pintar	*to paint*
preparar	*to prepare*
la cena	*supper, dinner*
la comida	*food, a meal*
tocar el piano	*to play the piano*
tocar la guitarra	*to play the guitar*
ver la televisión	*to watch television*

SEQUENCING EVENTS

antes (de)	*before*
después (de)	*after, afterward*
entonces	*then, so*
luego	*later*
por fin	*finally*
primero	*first*

ACTIVITIES

abrir	*to open*
aprender	*to learn*
beber	*to drink*
compartir	*to share*
comprender	*to understand*
hacer	*to make, to do*
oír	*to hear*
recibir	*to receive*
tener hambre	*to be hungry*
tener sed	*to be thirsty*
vender	*to sell*
ver	*to see*
vivir	*to live*

PLACES AND PEOPLE YOU KNOW

conocer a alguien	*to know, to be familiar with someone*

Places

el museo	*museum*
el parque	*park*
el teatro	*theater*
la tienda	*store*

OTHER WORDS AND PHRASES

cada	*each, every*
el corazón	*heart*
la gente	*people*
el problema	*problem*
la vida	*life*

Juego

¿Qué actividades hacen las personas?

Adriana: Le gusta hacer ejercicio y tiene un perro.

José: Le gusta tocar un instrumento. Jakob Dylan, Mary Chapin Carpenter y Melissa Etheridge tocan este instrumento.

Jorge: Es un hermano muy responsable. Tiene una familia grande.

Teaching Suggestions
Vocabulary Review

Divide the class into 3 groups and ask them to make up 5 sentences telling what they do on a Saturday. Have them use the Sequencing Events vocabulary and the vocabulary from at least one other category. The group that first makes up 5 grammatically correct sentences wins the game.

Juego

Answers
Adriana camina con el perro.
José toca la guitarra.
Jorge cuida a sus hermanos.

Game

Categorías Students play individually, in pairs, or in teams. They are ready to write as you call out a category from the vocabulary review. Give students 2–3 minutes to write as many vocabulary words as they can. Then share the lists as a scribe writes them on chart paper and students cross them off their lists. Those who listed words that no others had listed earn a point. Announce another category and repeat the process.

Teaching Middle School Students

Multiple Intelligences

Musical/Rhythmic You (or students) might make a tape of the sounds pictured in **Actividad 34** and of more sounds the students will easily recognize. Provide a numbered sheet of subjects, and as students listen to the tape, they write what they hear, using **oír** and the subject nouns or pronouns.

Logical/Mathematical Have students poll classmates to find out how many do the after-school activities listed in Column 1 on page 53.

Block Schedule

Variety Have students work in pairs to play **¿Qué oyes?** Students take turns describing a situation and asking **¿Qué oyes? (Estás en el parque. ¿Qué oyes?)** Students answer the question and then switch roles.

pages 54–79

Planning Guide CLASSROOM MANAGEMENT

OBJECTIVES

Communication
- Extend invitations *pp. 56–58*
- Talk on the phone *p. 62*
- Express feelings and preferences *pp. 56–58, 60–62, 68*
- Say what just happened and what is happening *pp. 59–60, 78*
- Talk about sports *pp. 64–70, 77*
- Say what you know *pp. 68–69*
- Make comparisons *pp. 69–70*
- Describe the weather *pp. 72–76*

Grammar
- Expressing Feelings with **estar** and Adjectives *p. 58*
- Saying What Just Happened with **acabar de** *pp. 59–60*
- Saying Where You Are Coming From with **venir** *pp. 60–61*
- Saying What Someone Likes to Do Using **gustar** + infinitive *pp. 61–62*
- Talking About Playing a Sport: The Verb **jugar** *pp. 66–67*
- Stem-Changing Verbs: **e→ie** *pp. 67–68*
- Saying What You Know: The Verb **saber** *pp. 68–69*
- Phrases for Making Comparisons *pp. 69–70*
- Describing the Weather *pp. 74–75*
- Special Expressions Using **tener** *pp. 75–76*
- Direct Object Pronouns *pp. 76–77*
- Saying What Is Happening: Present Progressive *p. 78*

PROGRAM RESOURCES

 Print

- Activity and Assessment Book
  Vocabulary Activities *pp. 32, 35, 38–39*
  Grammar Activities *pp. 33–34, 36–37, 40–41*
  Information Gap Activities *pp. 42–43*
  Cooperative Quizzes *pp. 44–47*
  Comprehensive Unit Test *pp. 50–53*
  Audioscripts *pp. 54–58*

Audiovisual

- Bridge Audio Program Cassettes / CD
- Overhead Transparencies B12–B16

Student Text Listening Activity Scripts

ACTIVIDAD 20 Gimnasia mental *page 70*

1. Ocho y cuatro son…
2. Dieciséis y tres son…
3. Once menos cinco son…
4. Treinta y catorce son…
5. Doce y diecinueve son…
6. Cincuenta y veinte son…
7. Sesenta y treinta son…

ACTIVIDAD 32 ¡Tantas preguntas! *page 77*

1. ¿Compras el bronceador?
2. ¿Quién prepara la comida?
3. ¿Necesitas las gafas de sol?
4. ¿Quién usa los libros?
5. ¿Entiendes la lección?

Pacing Guide

Sample Lesson Plan - 45 Minute Schedule

DAY 1

Etapa Opener
- Discuss the Opener, pp. 54–55; brainstorm about what students remember from last year. 5 MIN.

En contexto: Vocabulario
- Quick Start Review (TE, p. 56) 5 MIN.
- Play the audio. Have students use context and pictures to review *Etapa* vocabulary, pp. 56–57. 5 MIN.
- Do *Actividad* 1 orally. 5 MIN.
- Have students write their responses to *Actividad* 1. 5 MIN.
- Have students work in pairs to do *Actividad* 2. 5 MIN.

En acción: Vocabulario y gramática
- Present *Gramática en vivo*: Expressing Feelings with *estar* and Adjectives, and the *Vocabulario*, p. 58. 5 MIN.
- Assign *Actividad* 3. 5 MIN.
- Have pairs do *Actividad* 4. 5 MIN.

Homework Option:
- Activity and Assessment Book, p. 32

DAY 2

En acción (cont.)
- Check homework. 5 MIN.
- Present *Gramática en vivo*: Saying What Just Happened with *acabar de*, p. 59. 5 MIN.
- Work orally with the class to do *Actividad* 5, and then ask students to write their own responses. 5 MIN.
- Have students work in pairs on *Actividad* 6. 5 MIN.
- Present *Gramática en vivo*: Saying Where You Are Coming From with *venir*, p. 60, and then assign *Actividad* 7. 5 MIN.
- Work orally on *Actividad* 8. 5 MIN.
- Present *Gramática en vivo*: Saying What Someone Likes to Do Using *gustar* + infinitive, p. 61, and the *Vocabulario*, p. 62. 5 MIN.
- Have pairs do *Actividad* 9. 5 MIN.
- Have pairs do *Actividad* 10. 5 MIN.

Homework Option:
- Activity and Assessment Book, pp. 33–34

DAY 3

En resumen: Ya sabes
- Check homework. 5 MIN.
- Review the vocabulary, and do the *Juego*, p. 63. 5 MIN.

En contexto: Vocabulario
- Quick Start Review (TE, p. 64) 5 MIN.
- Play the audio. Present vocabulary, pp. 64–65. 5 MIN.
- Have students work in pairs on *Actividad* 11. 5 MIN.
- Have students work in groups on *Actividades* 12–13. 5 MIN.

En acción: Vocabulario y gramática
- Present *Gramática en vivo*: Talking About Playing a Sport: The Verb *jugar*, and the *Vocabulario*, p. 66. 5 MIN.
- Have students work in pairs on *Actividad* 14. 5 MIN.
- Assign *Actividad* 15. 5 MIN.

Homework Option:
- Activity and Assessment Book, p. 35

DAY 4

En acción (cont.)
- Check homework. 5 MIN.
- Present *Gramática en vivo*: Stem-Changing Verbs: e → ie, and the *Vocabulario*, p. 67. 5 MIN.
- Assign *Actividades* 16–17. 5 MIN.
- Present *Gramática en vivo*: Saying What You Know: The Verb *saber*, p. 68. 5 MIN.
- Have students work in pairs to do *Actividad* 18. 5 MIN.
- Have students work in groups to do *Actividad* 19. 5 MIN.
- Present *Gramática en vivo*: Phrases for Making Comparisons, p. 69, and then play the audio and assign *Actividad* 20. 5 MIN.
- Assign *Actividad* 21. 5 MIN.
- Have pairs do *Actividad* 22. 5 MIN.

Homework Option:
- Activity and Assessment Book, pp. 36–37

DAY 5

En resumen: Ya sabes
- Check homework. 5 MIN.
- Do the *Juego*, p. 71. 5 MIN.

En contexto: Vocabulario
- Quick Start Review (TE, p. 72) 5 MIN.
- Play the audio. Present the vocabulary, pp. 72–73. 5 MIN.
- Have students do *Actividad* 23. 5 MIN.
- Work orally on *Actividad* 24. 5 MIN.
- Assign *Actividad* 25. 5 MIN.

En acción: Vocabulario y gramática
- Present *Gramática en vivo*: Describing the Weather, and the *Vocabulario*, p. 74. 10 MIN.

Homework Option:
- Activity and Assessment Book, pp. 38–39

DAY 6

En acción (cont.)
- Check homework. 5 MIN.
- Work orally with the class on *Actividad* 26, and then have students write their responses. 5 MIN.
- Work orally with the class on *Actividad* 27. 5 MIN.
- Present *Gramática en vivo*: Special Expressions Using *tener*, p. 75. 5 MIN.
- Have students do *Actividad* 28 in pairs. 5 MIN.
- Have students stay in their pairs to do *Actividad* 29. 5 MIN.
- Assign *Actividad* 30. 5 MIN.
- Present *Gramática en vivo*: Direct Object Pronouns, p. 76. 5 MIN.
- Assign *Actividad* 31. 5 MIN.

Homework Option:
- Activity and Assessment Book, p. 40

DAY 7

En acción (cont.)
- Check homework. 5 MIN.
- Play the audio and assign *Actividad* 32. 5 MIN.
- Have pairs do *Actividad* 33. 5 MIN.
- Present *Gramática en vivo*: Saying What Is Happening: Present Progressive, p. 78. 5 MIN.
- Work orally on *Actividad* 34, and then have students write responses. 5 MIN.
- Have students work in pairs to do *Actividad* 35. 5 MIN.
- Quick Wrap-up (TE, p. 78) 5 MIN.

En resumen: Ya sabes
- Review vocabulary, p. 79. 5 MIN.
- Do the *Juego*, p. 79. 5 MIN.

Homework Option:
- Activity and Assessment Book, p. 41

Classroom Management Tip

Make connections Students need to use and practice new vocabulary and skills in order to retain them. One way to use and improve skills is to research related subjects.

You might ask students to find out who **los taínos** were. What happened to them? What legacy did they leave us? These questions could be answered in a **taíno** forum that students present for each other. Have them pay special attention to the words we now have in English because of the **taínos**.

Teaching Resource Options

Audiovisual

OHT B12–B16

Teaching Suggestions
Previewing the Etapa

• Ask students to study the picture on pp. 54–55 (1 min.).
• Close books; ask students to tell what the pictures show people doing.
• Reopen books; ask students what sports might be popular in Puerto Rico. Why?
• Ask students to name different sports according to the seasons and say which is their favorite sport in each season.
• Ask students which sports they like to play and which they like to watch.

BRIDGE UNIT

ETAPA 3

El fin de semana

• Extend invitations

• Talk on the phone

• Express feelings and preferences

• Say what just happened and what is happening

• Talk about sports

• Say what you know

• Make comparisons

• Describe the weather

54

Middle School Classroom Management

Planning Ahead Prepare (or have students help you prepare) an extensive vocabulary picture file so that you'll be ready for a variety of vocabulary practice activities.

Streamlining Post homework assignments for the entire week so that students know ahead of time what work they will be responsible for.

EL YUNQUE

EL COQUÍ   EL LORO PUERTORRIQUEÑO

BÉISBOL

Sandy Alomar, Jr.

MÁS SOBRE PUERTO RICO

PUERTO RICO

55

Interdisciplinary Connection

Have groups choose and investigate aspects of Puerto Rico—the place where Spanish, African, and Taino cultures mingled to form a diverse cultural legacy. One group investigates food, another makes a historical time line, another looks at the statehood issue, etc. Each group mounts a captioned bulletin board collage.

Block Schedule

Process Time Allow students time to read the objectives for this **Etapa** and to look through the pages to review concepts that they will be working on. Encourage students to take this time to recall vocabulary and expressions related to the topics.

Teaching Middle School Students

Extra Help Divide the class into 4 or 5 groups. Assign each group a portion of the illustration and ask them to make as many sentences about their section as they can within 10 minutes. Call time and ask each group to present their sentences to the class.

Native Speakers Ask native speakers about a similar bulletin board display for their countries of origin. What sports, activities, etc., would they choose to advertise the attractions of their home countries?

Multiple Intelligences

Intrapersonal Have students write down the 3 activities in the illustration that they like the best or that interest them the most. If there is one that they really dislike, have them note that, too.

Teaching Resource Options

Print

Activity and Assessment Book
  Vocabulary 3.1, p. 32
  Audioscripts, pp. 54–58

Audiovisual

Bridge Audio Program Cassettes / CD
OHT B12, B13 (Quick Start)

Quick Start Review

♻ **Estar**

Use OHT B13 or write on the board:
Everyone is busy today. Write sentences
to tell where each person is.

Modelo: Carmen come el almuerzo.
            Está en la cafetería.

1. Tú buscas un libro.
2. Nosotros tomamos un examen.
3. Yo compro una camisa.
4. Lisa camina con el perro.
5. Los estudiantes van a hacer
   ejercicio.

Answers
Answers may vary.
1. Estás en la biblioteca.
2. Estamos en clase.
3. Estoy en la tienda.
4. Está en el parque.
5. Están en el gimnasio.

Teaching Suggestions
Reconnecting with Vocabulary

• Read each section of the vocabulary
  aloud, having students repeat after
  you. Ask for student volunteers to
  read the short dialogs (perhaps for
  bonus points!).
• Start a chain by asking a student if he
  or she wants to go somewhere or do
  something (**¿Quieres ir al cine?**). After
  answering, the student should invite
  another student to go somewhere or
  do something, and so on, making a
  chain.
• Use the TPR activity to reinforce the
  meaning of individual words.

En contexto

🎧 VOCABULARIO

Look at the illustrations to see what Diana and Ignacio do
in their free time.

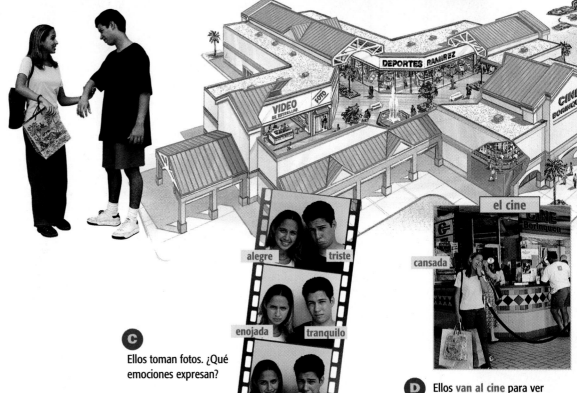

A

Ignacio y Diana están **contentos**
porque tienen **tiempo libre.**

Diana: ¿Quieres **acompañarme** a
comprar unas cosas?
Ignacio: ¡Claro que sí! Me gusta
mucho **ir de compras.**

B **Ignacio:** ¿Quieres **alquilar**
un video?
Diana: Sí, me encantaría.

ocupado

el cine

cansada

alegre   triste

enojada   tranquilo

contenta preocupado

C

Ellos toman fotos. ¿Qué
emociones expresan?

D Ellos **van al cine** para ver
una película. ¡Qué lástima!
Diana está **cansada.**

56 cincuenta y seis
Bridge Unit

Middle School Classroom Community

TPR Assign parts of the room to be stores in a **centro
comercial.** Have students take turns telling their partners
something that they want or have to do in the mall.
The partners go to the correct place. When they return,
they may tell the partners that they have what they
went for.

Portfolio Have the class write a story about someone
who goes to a mall on a Saturday.

Rubric

Criteria	Scale	
Vocabulary use/spelling	1 2 3 4 5	A = 17–20 pts.
Correct sentence structure/grammar	1 2 3 4 5	B = 13–16 pts.
Logical organization	1 2 3 4 5	C = 9–12 pts.
Creativity	1 2 3 4 5	D = 5–8 pts.
		F = < 5 pts.

nervioso

enfermo

E En la tienda Ignacio y Diana ven a un hombre **nervioso** y una madre **preocupada**. Su hijo está **enfermo**.

emocionada

deprimido

F A los chicos les gusta **practicar deportes**. Siempre están **emocionados**, no **deprimidos**. ¿**Te gustaría** practicar con los chicos?

G Ignacio: Te **invito** al **concierto** esta noche.
Diana: ¡Ay! ¡Qué lástima! Estoy **ocupada**. Tengo que estudiar.

ACTIVIDAD 1 **Las emociones**

Hablar/Escribir Tell how you feel in the following situations.

modelo

Cuando voy a un concierto…
Cuando voy a un concierto, *estoy emocionado(a).*

1. Cuando veo un video cómico…
2. Cuando veo una película triste…
3. Cuando tengo un examen…
4. Cuando saco una buena nota…
5. Cuando practico deportes…
6. Cuando estoy enfermo(a)…
7. Cuando no es posible ir a una fiesta…
8. Cuando trabajo mucho…
9. Cuando mi mamá está enferma…
10. Cuando tengo mucho tiempo libre…

ACTIVIDAD 2 **¿Te gustaría…?**

Hablar Invite a classmate to do two activities shown on these pages. Change roles.

modelo

Estudiante A: *¿Te gustaría ir de compras?*
Estudiante B: *Sí, me encantaría.*
　　　　　　　 o: Gracias, pero no puedo.

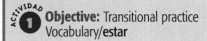

ACTIVIDAD 1 **Objective:** Transitional practice Vocabulary/**estar**

Answers

Answers may vary.
1. …estoy alegre.
2. …estoy triste.
3. …estoy nervioso(a) (preocupado[a]).
4. …estoy contento(a).
5. …estoy emocionado(a).
6. …estoy deprimido(a).
7. …estoy enojado(a).
8. …estoy cansado(a).
9. …estoy triste (preocupado[a]).
10. …estoy alegre.

ACTIVIDAD 2 **Objective:** Open-ended practice Vocabulary

Answers will vary.

Quick Wrap-up

Engage students in a TPR activity in which they show, by exaggerated gestures and facial expressions, their understanding of the adjectives of emotion presented here. For example, **Leonor, estás muuuyyy enferma. Paquito, estás taaannn preocupado…**

Project

Have students work in pairs to list events that make them feel the emotion that you assign. Next, students look for pictures of people feeling that emotion and use them to decorate a poster of events they listed. Finally, pairs write speech balloons for each picture.

Block Schedule

Variety Give students old magazines and newspapers. Have them look for and cut out pictures that represent different emotions. Each picture goes on a different index card to make a deck you can use for games of Concentration and War (for War, each emotion needs to be assigned a priority number).

Teaching Middle School Students

Extra Help Have students brainstorm vocabulary about feelings and emotions. Leave their list on the board. Then divide the class in two and have students take turns miming the emotions for the other team to guess in Spanish.

Native Speakers Ask native speakers to talk about shopping in their countries of origin. Find out what is available and what various stores, malls, etc., are called.

Multiple Intelligences

Verbal Have students work in pairs to practice **Actividad 1**. Ask them to continue the activity by making up their own situations for each other.

Teaching Suggestions
Expressing Feelings with estar and Adjectives

- Tell students that the adjectives used with **estar** show changeable conditions, such as **contento, enfermo, preocupado, nervioso, emocionado, ocupado y deprimido**; the adjectives that they learned with **ser**, such as **inteligente, moreno,** and **cubano,** describe permanent characteristics of personality or appearance.
- To practice the adjective endings and verb endings, ask students to make a sign telling how they feel (remind girls to put the feminine ending on the adjectives). Then have students stand and state **Estoy _____.** When two students have stated that they feel the same way, emphasize the plural forms of the verb and adjectives. (**Marta y Juan están cansados. Carmen y Pilar están contentas.**)
- Read all of the vocabulary (**Para aceptar o no una invitación**) aloud, having students repeat after you. Make sure that students understand the meaning of each word/phrase.

Objective: Transitional practice
Vocabulary/**estar**

Answers
Answers may vary.
1. Antes de una prueba, estoy nervioso(a).
2. Si saco una buena nota, estoy contento(a).
3. Si tengo mucha tarea, estoy preocupado(a).
4. Después de una prueba, estoy alegre.
5. Si saco una mala nota, estoy enojado(a).
6. Cuando hablo por teléfono, estoy contento(a).

Objective: Open-ended practice
Vocabulary

Answers will vary.

En acción
VOCABULARIO Y GRAMÁTICA

Gramática en vivo

Diana: Estás **contento**, ¿no?
Ignacio: Sí, pero también **estoy nervioso**.

Expressing Feelings with estar and Adjectives

Estar is used with **adjectives** to describe how someone feels at a given moment.

agrees

Diana **está preocupada** por Ignacio.
Diana is worried about Ignacio.

agrees

Ignacio **está preocupado** por Roberto.
Ignacio is worried about Roberto.

> Remember that **adjectives** must **agree** in gender and number with the nouns they describe.

¿Cómo estás?

Escribir Write about how you feel in these situations.

modelo

después de la clase de educación física

Después de la clase de educación física, *estoy cansado(a).*

1. antes de una prueba
2. si saco una buena nota
3. si tengo mucha tarea
4. después de una prueba
5. si saco una mala nota
6. cuando hablo por teléfono

58 cincuenta y ocho
Bridge Unit

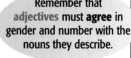

¿Quieres...?

Hablar Work with a partner to create a dialog in which one invites the other to do something. You can accept or not accept, but you need to explain why.

modelo

Estudiante A: *¿Quieres ir al cine mañana?*

Estudiante B: *Gracias, pero no puedo. Estoy muy ocupado.*

Estudiante A: *¡Qué lástima! Tal vez otro día.*

Estudiante B: *Me gustaría ir el sábado. ¿Quieres acompañarme?*

Estudiante A: *Sí, me encantaría. Me gusta mucho ir al cine.*

Vocabulario

Para aceptar o no una invitación
 Ya sabes

Gracias, pero no puedo.	porque
Me gustaría…	solo(a)
¡Qué lástima!	temprano
Tal vez otro día.	

¿Cuándo usas estas frases?

Middle School Classroom Management

Planning Ahead Have a variety of props ready for working with the special verbs in this section (**acabar de, venir [de], gustar,** and **jugar**).

Streamlining Divide the vocabulary among groups of students (feelings, places, activities, telephone expressions, etc.). Have students make lists of the words and expressions, and put them in charge of helping the class practice their vocabulary.

Gramática en vivo

Diana: Acabo **de** comprar unos zapatos.

Saying What Just Happened with acabar de

▶ When you want to say that something just happened, use the present tense of

$$acabar + de + infinitive$$

acabo **de** comer	acabamos **de** comer
I just ate	*we just ate*
acabas **de** comer	acabáis **de** comer
you just ate	*you just ate*
acaba **de** comer	acaban **de** comer
he, she, you just ate	*they, you just ate*

ACTIVIDAD 5

¿Qué acabas de hacer?

Hablar/Escribir Tell what has just happened in each case.

modelo

Llego a casa con muchos libros y revistas.

Acabo de visitar la biblioteca.

1. Llegan a casa con mucha comida.

2. Llegamos a casa con ropa nueva.

3. Llega a casa muy contento(a).

4. Llego a casa con el perro.

5. Llegamos a casa muy tarde.

6. Llegas a casa muy cansado(a).

Teaching Middle School Students

Challenge Ask students to write a paragraph telling what they just did, where they are coming from, how they feel, and what they would like to do tomorrow.

Multiple Intelligences

Kinesthetic Divide the class into groups. Have each student cut a piece of paper into quarters and write an activity on each quarter. Tell them to turn the group's papers over and mix them up. Have a student draw a slip of paper and then pantomime the activity. The other group members take turns guessing what he or she has just done. Have them take turns until all the papers are used.

Teaching Suggestions
Saying What Just Happened with acabar de

Point out that Spanish uses the present tense of **acabar** + **de** + infinitive to say what English uses the word *just* + past tense to say. ("I just arrived." = **Acabo de llegar.**)

ACTIVIDAD 5 **Objective:** Transitional practice **Acabar de**/vocabulary

Answers

Answers may vary.
1. Acaban de ir al supermercado.
2. Acabamos de ir a la tienda.
3. Acaba de ir al cine.
4. Acabo de ir al parque.
5. Acabamos de ir a una fiesta.
6. Acabas de practicar deportes.

Game

Él acaba de... One player from Team A and one from Team B simultaneously pantomime different activities for 1 minute and then stand silently at the front of the room. Members of Team A discuss and decide what their player mimed, while members of Team B do the same for their player. Award points for correct guesses, and then play again with another pair of pantomime artists.

Block Schedule

Retention As a review and practice, have students use their textbooks to make up several test items covering the concepts from this unit. Students exchange tests with a partner and complete the items. After the test has been completed, partners can get together to score their work.

Teaching Resource Options

Print

Activity and Assessment Book
Grammar 3.1, p. 33
Audioscripts, pp. 54–58

Audiovisual

Bridge Audio Program Cassettes / CD

 6 Objective: Controlled practice Acabar de/adjective agreement/ expressing feelings with **estar** + adjectives

Answers

1. ¿Por qué está Raúl cansado? / Acaba de andar en bicicleta.
2. ¿Por qué está Dora contenta? / Acaba de leer la poesía de García Lorca.
3. ¿Por qué está mi madre emocionada? / Acaba de recibir una carta de mi abuela.
4. ¿Por qué estás deprimido(a)? / Acabo de leer una novela muy triste.
5. ¿Por qué están ustedes preocupados(as)? / Acabamos de tener una prueba muy difícil.
6. ¿Por qué estás tranquilo(a)? / Acabo de descansar un rato y escuchar música.

Teaching Suggestions
Saying Where You Are Coming From with venir

- After presenting the forms of **venir**, have students review **tener**. Ask where the verb forms are similar and where they are different (**nosotros** and **vosotros**).
- Have students tell which class they are coming from. (**Vengo de la clase de historia.**) When two students have said that they are coming from the same class, point out the **ellos** form (**Juanita y Pepe vienen de la clase de arte**).

 7 Objective: Transitional practice Venir/vocabulary

Answers

Answers will vary but should contain the following.

1. viene de
2. viene de
3. vienen de
4. vengo de
5. vienen de
6. vienes de
7. vienen de
8. venimos de
9. vienen de

¿Por qué?

Hablar Take turns with a partner asking why these people feel as they do. Answer that it is because they have just done the following things. (Pay attention to the agreement of adjectives and nouns.)

modelo

ustedes / alegre

(ver una película divertida)

Estudiante A: *¿Por qué están **ustedes alegres**?*

Estudiante B: *Acabamos de **ver una película divertida.***

---

1. Raúl / cansado(a) (andar en bicicleta)
2. Dora / contento(a) (leer la poesía de García Lorca)
3. mi madre / emocionado(a) (recibir una carta de mi abuela)
4. tú / deprimido(a) (leer una novela muy triste)
5. ustedes / preocupado(a) (tener una prueba muy difícil)
6. tú / tranquilo(a) (descansar un rato y escuchar música)

Gramática en vivo

Ignacio: Roberto y su familia vienen de Minnesota.

Saying Where You Are Coming From with venir

▶ **Venir** (*to come*) is similar to **tener**, except that the **nosotros(as)** and **vosotros(as)** forms have **-ir** endings, while **tener** uses **-er** endings.

vengo	ven**imos**
vienes	ven**ís**
viene	vienen

¿De dónde vienen?

Escribir Write down where the following people are coming from.

cine	supermercado
tienda	clase de inglés
parque	teatro
escuela	oficina
museo	cafetería

modelo

estudiantes   Los **estudiantes** vienen de la **tienda**.

1. Jorge
2. la maestra
3. mis padres
4. yo
5. ustedes
6. tú
7. Marta y Luis
8. nosotros
9. mis amigos

Middle School Classroom Community

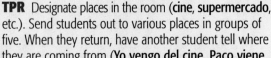

TPR Designate places in the room (**cine, supermercado**, etc.). Send students out to various places in groups of five. When they return, have another student tell where they are coming from (**Yo vengo del cine. Paco viene de la oficina. Ana y Clara vienen del parque**, etc.).

Group Activity Give each group visuals, flash cards, magazine pictures, etc., that show places and activities. Have students separate them into one pile for places and one pile for activities. Students take turns drawing from each pile and making sentences that say where they are coming from and what they like to do there. Some of these sentences will be quite silly.

ACTIVIDAD 8

¿A qué hora?

Hablar Tell at what time these people come from the following places.

modelo

mi padre / trabajo

Mi padre viene del **trabajo** a las seis.

1. mi madre / tienda
2. los estudiantes / clase
3. yo / escuela
4. tú / estadio
5. el doctor / oficina
6. Juan y yo / cine

Gramática en vivo

Ignacio: **A las muchachas** sólo les gusta **ver** las películas de romance, ¿no es verdad?

Diana: ¡No! ¡También nos gusta **ver** otras!

Saying What Someone Likes to Do Using gustar + infinitive

▶ Here are more phrases to use to talk about what more than one person likes to do.

nos gusta **correr**	*we like to run*
os gusta **correr**	*you (familiar) like to run*
les gusta **correr**	*they/you (formal) like to run*

▶ When you want to emphasize or identify the person that you are talking about, use:

a +
- name
- noun
- pronoun

These are the **pronouns** that follow **a**.

a mí →	me gusta		**a nosotros(as)** →	nos gusta
a ti →	te gusta		**a vosotros(as)** →	os gusta
a usted, él, ella →	le gusta		**a ustedes, ellos(as)** →	les gusta

sesenta y uno
Etapa 3
61

Teaching Middle School Students

Extra Help For an intense review of **gustar**, have the class brainstorm activities. Call on 5 students and ask each to say in a sentence something he or she likes to do. When they finish, call out **le** and have students restate what one student said. Call out **les** and have students restate what two students said.

Multiple Intelligences

Visual Have students look at pictures/visuals of places and activities. Ask them to write sentences using forms either of **venir de** or **gustar**. Call time and have students share sentences with the class.

ACTIVIDAD 8

Objective: Transitional practice
Venir/time

Answers

Answers will vary but should contain the following.

1. Mi madre viene de la tienda a la(s)…
2. Los estudiantes vienen de la clase a la(s)…
3. Yo vengo de la escuela a la(s)…
4. Tú vienes del estadio a la(s)…
5. El doctor viene de la oficina a la(s)…
6. Juan y yo venimos del cine a la(s)…

Teaching Suggestions
Saying What Someone Likes to Do Using gustar + infinitive

- After presenting **nos**, **(os)**, and **les** with **gustar** + infinitive, review the **me**, **te**, and **le** forms already learned.
- Point out that in Spanish, rather than directly saying "I like," people say the equivalent of "It is pleasing to me," which explains why they use **me, te, le, nos, os,** and **les** rather than **yo, tú, él,** etc.
- Practice the **a** + pronoun forms by stating a phrase with **gustar** and having students add the corresponding **a** + pronoun when repeating the verb phrase: **Te gusta hablar** → **A ti te gusta hablar.**

Critical Thinking

Have each student survey 3 school friends outside the class regarding their likes and dislikes of food, sports, leisure activities, music, movies, literature, etc. They collect the information in chart form and then write it up in an experience chart, which they present to the class. When all the charts have been presented, display them and ask students to compile a class chart. Have them draw some conclusions about student preferences based on all the data.

Block Schedule

Research Invite students to select a favorite celebrity, perhaps a movie or television personality, a professional athlete, or a singer/musician. Ask them to research where this person was born and some of the person's likes and dislikes. Encourage students to do a written or oral report.

Teaching Resource Options

Print

Activity and Assessment Book
Grammar 3.1, p. 34

Teaching Suggestions
El teléfono

• When reviewing and practicing the telephone vocabulary, use toy phones or used phones.

• Mention that there are various ways to answer the phone, depending on the country. In Mexico, they say **Bueno** when answering; in Spain, the person who answers says **Dígame,** and the caller then says **Oiga.** These are formulas for speaking and should not be translated word for word.

 9 Objective: Open-ended practice Vocabulary/grammar

Answers will vary.

10 Objective: Transitional practice Present tense verbs/**gustar**/ vocabulary

Answers
1. Yo siempre hablo por teléfono porque me gusta.
2. Mis amigos nunca dejan un mensaje porque no les gusta.
3. Mi hermano(a) siempre llama a un amigo porque le gusta.
4. Tú nunca ves la televisión porque no te gusta.
5. Nosotros siempre bebemos agua porque nos gusta.
6. Mis padres nunca practican deportes porque no les gusta.
7. La maestra siempre escucha la máquina contestadora porque le gusta.
8. El maestro nunca va al cine porque no le gusta.

🔔 Quick Wrap-up

How well do your students know each other? How well do you know them? Find out by announcing common activities and asking who likes to do each. Examples: **¿A quién le gusta jugar con videojuegos? Marta, ¿qué te gusta más, comer hamburguesas o frutas? A mí me gusta mucho leer novelas románticas. Samuel, ¿a ti te gusta también?,** etc.

Hablando por teléfono

Hablar Your partner "calls" you on the phone to invite you to do something. Act out different conversations.

modelo

Estudiante A: *¿Te gustaría ir al cine el sábado?*

Estudiante B: *Sí, me gustaría mucho. ¿A qué hora?*

Estudiante A: *La película empieza a las dos.*

Estudiante B: *A las dos tengo que ayudar a mi padre.*

Estudiante A: *Ay, qué lástima. Tal vez otro día.*

¿Qué les gusta hacer?

Hablar Take turns with a partner commenting on people's likes and dislikes.

modelo

Ignacio / nunca comer en la cafetería

Estudiante A: ***Ignacio nunca come en la cafetería*** *porque a él no le gusta.*

Ana / siempre llegar temprano a clase

Estudiante B: ***Ana siempre llega temprano a clase*** *porque a ella le gusta.*

1. yo / siempre hablar por teléfono
2. mis amigos / nunca dejar un mensaje
3. mi hermano(a) / siempre llamar a un amigo
4. tú / nunca ver la televisión
5. nosotros / siempre beber agua
6. mis padres / nunca practicar deportes
7. la maestra / siempre escuchar la máquina contestadora
8. el maestro / nunca ir al cine

Vocabulario

El teléfono ♻ Ya sabes

contestar	llamar
dejar un mensaje	la máquina contestadora
la guía telefónica	marcar
la llamada	

Speaking on the phone:

¿Puedo hablar con…?	Dile/Dígale que me llame.
Un momento.	Quiero dejar un mensaje para…
Regresa más tarde.	Deje un mensaje después del tono.

¿Qué dices cuando hablas por teléfono?

Middle School Classroom Community
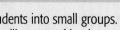

Learning Scenario Put students into small groups. Tell them to imagine they are calling some friends to set up a weekend activity.

Game Divide the class in half. Have a student from Team A start a sentence that involves an emotion (**No quiero estudiar hoy porque estoy muy…**). Have a student from Team B finish the sentence with an emotion (**cansado**). Someone from Team B starts the next sentence. If a team does not complete the sentence or uses an adjective twice, it loses a point. If a team completes a sentence, it gets a point.

En resumen

YA SABES ♻

EXTENDING INVITATIONS

¿Quieres acompañarme a…?	Would you like to come with me to…?
Te invito.	I'll treat you. I invite you.
¿Te gustaría…?	Would you like…?

Accepting

¡Claro que sí!	Of course.
Me gustaría…	I would like…
Sí, me encantaría.	Yes, I would love to.

Declining

Gracias, pero no puedo.	Thanks, but I can't.
¡Qué lástima!	What a shame!
Tal vez otro día.	Maybe another day.

Activities

alquilar un video	to rent a video
el concierto	concert
ir al cine	to go to a movie theater
ir de compras	to go shopping
la película	movie
practicar deportes	to play sports
el tiempo libre	free time

EXPRESSING FEELINGS

alegre	happy
cansado(a)	tired
contento(a)	content, happy, pleased
deprimido(a)	depressed
emocionado(a)	excited
enfermo(a)	sick
enojado(a)	angry
nervioso(a)	nervous
ocupado(a)	busy
preocupado(a)	worried
tranquilo(a)	calm
triste	sad

TALKING ON THE PHONE

contestar	to answer
dejar un mensaje	to leave a message
la guía telefónica	phone book
la llamada	call
llamar	to call
la máquina contestadora	answering machine
marcar	to dial
el teléfono	telephone

Phrases for talking on the phone

Deje un mensaje después del tono.	Leave a message after the tone.
Dile/Dígale que me llame.	Tell (familiar/formal) him or her to call me.
¿Puedo hablar con…?	May I speak with…?
Quiero dejar un mensaje para…	I want to leave a message for…
Regresa más tarde.	He/She will return later.
Un momento.	One moment.

WHERE YOU ARE COMING FROM

del	from the
venir	to come

SAYING WHAT JUST HAPPENED

acabar de…	to have just…

OTHER WORDS AND PHRASES

conmigo	with me
contigo	with you
cuando	when, whenever
¡No te preocupes!	Don't worry!
porque	because
solo(a)	alone
temprano	early
ya no	no longer

Juego

¿Adónde van en su tiempo libre?

1. **A Miguel le gusta escuchar música.**
2. A Mariela le gusta ver las películas de Antonio Banderas.
3. A Martina y a Martín les gusta comprar ropa.

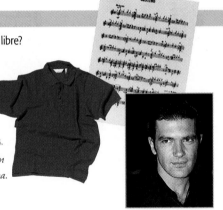

sesenta y tres
Etapa 3

63

Teaching Middle School Students

Extra Help To model **Actividad 9**, set up a telephone dialog between you and the class (**¿Paco no está? ¿Puedo dejarle un mensaje?**). Have the class make up the message.

Multiple Intelligences

Interpersonal Have students relate feelings with activities (**Estoy contenta cuando voy a un concierto.**) and share these emotions with their partners. Partners may then share with the class if appropriate.

BRIDGE UNIT Etapa 3
Review

Teaching Suggestions
Vocabulary Review

Ask students to make sentences using vocabulary from "Expressing Feelings," "Other Words and Phrases," and at least one other category. (**Estoy cansado porque acabo de practicar deportes.**)

Juego

Answers
1. Miguel va al concierto.
2. Mariela va al cine.
3. Martina y Martín van a las tiendas.

Game

¡Cuántas palabras sabes! Give students 2–3 minutes to write all the words they know that begin with the letter of the alphabet that you call out. Have pairs of students compare lists and cross out duplicates on each list. The student in each pair with more words left on his or her list wins.

▉ Block Schedule

Variety Ask students to work in pairs to practice telephone conversations. Each student takes a turn calling the other and extending an invitation to do one of the activities in the vocabulary list. The partner either accepts or declines the offer, expressing feelings or emotions about the activity.

Review • BRIDGE UNIT Etapa 3   **63**

Teaching Resource Options

Print 📖

Activity and Assessment Book
  Vocabulary 3.2, p. 35
  Audioscripts, pp. 54–58

Audiovisual

Bridge Audio Program Cassettes / CD
OHT B13 (Quick Start), B14

Quick Start Review

♻ Regular **-ar, -er,** and **-ir** verbs

Use OHT B13 or write on the board:
Complete each of Julia's sentences
about herself and people in her
school with the correct form of the
corresponding verb:

beber
comprender
enseñar
llevar
vivir

1. Nosotros _____ en una ciudad
   grande.
2. Los maestros _____ sus clases
   bien.
3. Gloria _____ un vestido negro a
   clase.
4. Tú no _____ la lección.
5. Yo _____ un refresco al mediodía.

Answers
1. vivimos   4. comprendes
2. enseñan   5. bebo
3. lleva

Teaching Suggestions
Reconnecting with Vocabulary

• Read each section of the vocabulary
  aloud, having students repeat after
  you.
• Ask students to name indoor sports,
  outdoor sports, water sports, sports
  requiring a lot of equipment, sports
  requiring little or no equipment, etc.
• Name different sports and ask students
  to say a piece of equipment each one
  requires.
• Use the TPR activity to reinforce the
  meaning of individual words.

En contexto

🎧 VOCABULARIO

Diana and Ignacio are looking at equipment in a sporting
goods store.

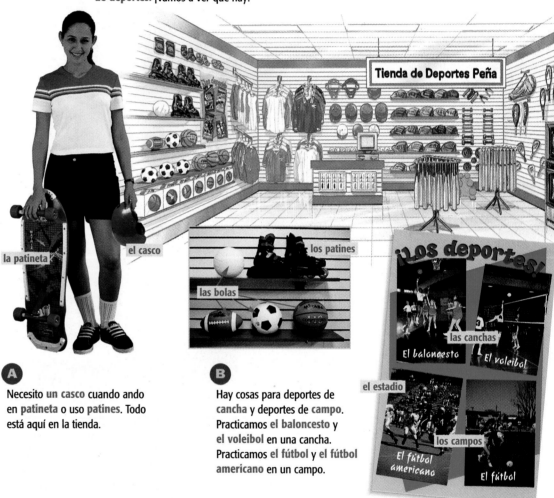

¡Hola! Ignacio y yo estamos en la tienda
de deportes. ¡Vamos a ver qué hay!

Tienda de Deportes Peña

la patineta

el casco

las bolas

los patines

¡Los deportes!

las canchas

El baloncesto   El voleibol

el estadio

El fútbol americano   El fútbol

los campos

A

Necesito un casco cuando ando
en patineta o uso patines. Todo
está aquí en la tienda.

B

Hay cosas para deportes de
cancha y deportes de campo.
Practicamos el baloncesto y
el voleibol en una cancha.
Practicamos el fútbol y el fútbol
americano en un campo.

64   sesenta y cuatro
Bridge Unit

Middle School Classroom Community

TPR Designate parts of the room as areas in a
sporting goods store. Students take turns telling
their partners to go and buy a piece of equipment.

Storytelling Divide the class into groups. Have each
group choose a sport and prepare a "drama" about
someone who plays or wants to play that sport. Have
the groups perform for each other.

la pesa

la raqueta

C Sé **levantar pesas.**

Ignacio usa **una raqueta** y **una bola.** Su deporte favorito es **el tenis.**

el guante

la pelota

el bate

D Ignacio usa **un guante,** **un bate** y **una pelota** cuando juega al **béisbol.** **¡El equipo** practica en **un estadio!**

el equipo

E En Puerto Rico, a mucha gente le gusta **esquiar** en el agua y practicar **el surfing.**

esquiar

el surfing

ACTIVIDAD **11**  **¡Practicamos!**

Hablar Take turns asking what you need to play the sports listed below.

modelo

jugar al fútbol americano

Estudiante A: *Quiero jugar al fútbol americano. ¿Qué necesito?*

Estudiante B: *Necesitas una bola y un casco.*

1. jugar al tenis
2. patinar
3. jugar al fútbol
4. andar en patineta
5. jugar al baloncesto
6. levantar pesas

ACTIVIDAD **12** **¿Qué practicas?**

Hablar/Escribir Ask five classmates which sports they play. Record their names and answers.

modelo

Estudiante A: *¿Qué deportes practicas?*

Estudiante B: *Juego al tenis y levanto pesas.*

Resumen: *Tina juega al tenis y levanta pesas. Marco…*

ACTIVIDAD **13** **Deportes**

Hablar/Escribir Who knows how to play certain sports?

❶ Work in a group of four students.

❷ On paper, write the sports that are listed on these pages. (There are ten!)

❸ Ask group members if they know how to play each one. When classmates answer **sí,** have them sign their name next to the sport.

sesenta y cinco
Etapa 3 **65**

ACTIVIDAD **11** **Objective:** Transitional practice Vocabulary

Answers
Answers will vary.
1. Quiero jugar al tenis. ¿Qué necesito? / Necesitas una bola y una raqueta.
2. Quiero patinar. ¿Qué necesito? / Necesitas patines y un casco.
3. Quiero jugar al fútbol. ¿Qué necesito? / Necesitas una bola.
4. Quiero andar en patineta. ¿Qué necesito? / Necesitas una patineta y un casco.
5. Quiero jugar al baloncesto. ¿Qué necesito? / Necesitas una bola (y una cancha).
6. Quiero levantar pesas. ¿Qué necesito? / Necesitas pesas.

ACTIVIDAD **12** **Objective:** Transitional practice Vocabulary

Answers will vary.

ACTIVIDAD **13** **Objective:** Open-ended practice Vocabulary

Answers will vary.

🔔 **Quick Wrap-up**
Engage students in a TPR activity in which they act out certain sports. For example: **Antonio juega al béisbol con Daniela. Javier esquía muy rápido. Olivia y Patricia jueguan al baloncesto…**

Teaching Middle School Students

Extra Help Have a student call out a sports-related word or expression. Give clues until another student calls out a word related to the first in some way (**la cancha → el baloncesto / jugar,** etc.).

Native Speakers Ask native speakers to talk about sports in their countries of origin. Find out what sports they like, whether they play a sport, and whether they like the sports played in this country.

Multiple Intelligences

Kinesthetic Have the class imagine that they are enrolled in a "multi-athalon" in the Olympics, and that they are engaged in a training session. A student calls out a sport, and everyone pretends to be playing that sport. Ask various students to call out a sport until the list (and the class) is exhausted.

Block Schedule

Challenge Have students select a sport with which they are familiar. Then ask them to write several how-to statements about playing that particular sport. **Para jugar al fútbol, necesitas una bola. Tienes que correr mucho.**

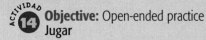
En acción
VOCABULARIO Y GRAMÁTICA

Gramática en vivo

Ignacio: ¿**J**uegas **al** béisbol en Minneapolis?

◆ **Talking About Playing a Sport: The Verb jugar**

▶ When you talk about playing a sport, you use the verb **jugar.** The forms of **jugar** are unique. In some of them, the **u** changes to **ue**.

jugar *to play*	
juego	**jug**amos
juegas	**jug**áis
juega	**jueg**an

▶ When you use **jugar** with the name of a sport, you must use

jugar a + *sport*

Vocabulario

Más sobre los deportes
♻ **Ya sabes**

la gorra

al aire libre	el gol	la piscina
andar en patineta	el hockey	sobre hielo
ganar	el partido	

Use these adjectives and others you know to describe sports.

favorito(a)   **peligroso(a)**

¿Qué frase usas para hablar de tu deporte favorito?

¿Quién juega?

Hablar/Escribir Take turns with a partner asking each other who plays the following sports. Then ask and answer where.

modelo

jugar al béisbol

Estudiante A: *¿Quién juega al béisbol?*

Estudiante B: *Yo juego al béisbol.*

Estudiante A: *¿Dónde juegas?*

Estudiante B: *Juego al aire libre.*

1. jugar al hockey
2. andar en patineta
3. jugar al fútbol americano
4. jugar al baloncesto
5. patinar sobre hielo
6. jugar al tenis
7. nadar en el agua
8. jugar al voleibol

ACTIVIDAD
15

¿Qué hacen?

Escribir Guess which activity the following people are doing. Then write a sentence.

modelo

Víctor hace un gol en el estadio.

Víctor juega al fútbol.

1. Julio usa patines.

2. Ana y yo usamos una raqueta.

3. Marta va a la piscina.

4. Yo uso un guante y una pelota y llevo una gorra.

5. Ganamos porque somos rápidos y altos.

6. José usa un casco y una bola y juega en un campo.

Gramática en vivo

Roberto: Mucha gente en los Estados Unidos p**ie**nsa que el fútbol americano es más interesante que el fútbol.

Stem-Changing Verbs: e → ie

▶ When you use the verb **pensar** (*to think, to plan*), the **e** in its **stem** sometimes changes to **ie**.

stem changes to

p**e**nsar   p**ie**nso

pensar *to think, to plan*

pienso	pensamos
piensas	pensáis
piensa	piensan

Vocabulario

Stem-Changing Verbs: e → ie

♻ Ya sabes

cerrar	perder
empezar	preferir
entender	querer
merendar	

¿Cuándo usas una de estas palabras?

Teaching Middle School Students

Multiple Intelligences

Visual Have students take turns saying what sport their partners are playing. The partners must sketch something to suggest the sport (**Juegas al béisbol**→ the partner draws a bat).

Verbal Divide the class into groups. Have each group member choose a different subject (**yo, Marta, tú, José y yo,** etc.). Have the e→ie verbs written on strips of paper. One student draws a verb and makes a sentence with the verb and his or her subject. All the other members must draw a verb and make a sentence using that subject. Shuffle the verbs and go around again until all the subjects have been used.

ACTIVIDAD
15 **Objective:** Controlled practice
Jugar

Answers

1. Julio patina (juega al hockey).
2. Ana y yo jugamos al tenis.
3. Marta nada.
4. Juego al béisbol.
5. Jugamos al baloncesto.
6. José juega al fútbol americano.

Teaching Suggestions

Stem-Changing Verbs: e→ie

• Point out that **pensar** and the verbs in the vocabulary box are also "boot" verbs. Have students repeat the verbs after you and tell their meanings.

• Make sure that students understand which **e** changes to **ie** in the verbs **empezar, entender, merendar,** and **preferir**.

• Have students think of original sentences with **pensar/preferir/ querer** + infinitive.

Interdisciplinary Connection

Drama Have pairs or groups of 3 use any 5 stem-changing verbs in a play. Have them include dialog on any topic the verbs suggest to them, and with any verb forms they choose. When the plays are ready, they can be read in class, acted out, or turned into books that students illustrate. Vote on the best, funniest, or silliest story.

Block Schedule

Gather and Sort Students can work in pairs or small groups to discuss and compare different sports. They then select some categories that can be used to sort the sports (play inside/ play outside; winter/summer; play with ball/no ball). Have students use the categories they chose to make a Venn diagram or graph.

Teaching Resource Options

Print

Activity and Assessment Book
Grammar 3.2, p. 36
Audioscripts, pp. 54–58

Audiovisual

Bridge Audio Program Cassettes / CD

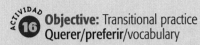 **16 Objective:** Transitional practice
Querer/preferir/vocabulary

Answers

Answers will vary but should contain the following.

1. ¿Por qué no quieren jugar al béisbol? / No quieren jugar al béisbol porque prefieren…
2. ¿Por qué no quiere jugar al fútbol americano? / No quiere jugar al fútbol americano porque prefiere…
3. ¿Por qué no queremos jugar al tenis? / No queremos jugar al tenis porque preferimos…
4. ¿Por qué no quieres jugar al baloncesto? / No quiero jugar al baloncesto porque prefiero…
5. ¿Por qué no quiere Antonia jugar al fútbol? / No quiere jugar al fútbol porque prefiere…

 17 Objective: Controlled practice
Stem-changing verbs

Answers

1. empiezan	5. prefiere
2. pienso	6. pierde
3. quieren	7. cierra
4. entendemos	8. merendamos

Teaching Suggestions
Saying What You Know: The Verb saber

- After presenting all of the forms of **saber**, review the forms of **conocer**, another regular verb with an irregular **yo** form. Point out that **conocer** means "to be acquainted with someone or something," whereas **saber** means "to know a fact or information" or "to know how to do something."
- Give some contrasting examples of **saber** and **conocer** (Conozco a la chica pero no sé dónde vive; Mi mamá conoce México pero no sabe hablar español).
- Have students practice **saber** by telling different things that they and their friends know how to do (Mi amiga y yo sabemos bailar).

 16

¿Por qué no?

Hablar Take turns asking why the following people don't want to play the sport shown. Answer that it is because they prefer to play something else.

modelo

ellos

Estudiante A: *¿Por qué no quieren jugar al fútbol?*

Estudiante B: *No quieren jugar al fútbol porque prefieren el béisbol.*

1. los chicos

2. él

3. nosotros

4. tú

5. Antonia

 17

La rutina de Roberto

Escribir Use the verbs shown to rewrite Ignacio's paragraph, filling in the blanks.

En mi colegio las clases siempre __1__ (pensar / empezar) a las siete y media de la mañana. Yo __2__ (pensar / merendar) que es muy temprano. Muchos estudiantes __3__ (querer / entender) dormir por la mañana. Pero también nosotros __4__ (cerrar / entender) que es necesario estudiar mucho. Mi amigo Roberto __5__ (perder / preferir) estudiar en casa por la tarde. A él le gusta estudiar conmigo porque de vez en cuando __6__ (perder / empezar) su libro. Cuando termina de estudiar, siempre __7__ (querer / cerrar) los libros y escucha música. A veces, yo hago lo mismo. Luego él y yo __8__ (merendar / preferir). Comemos fruta o yogur.

Gramática en vivo

Claudio: ¡Ah! ¿Sabe él a qué hora empieza la práctica?
Ignacio: Sí.

◆ Saying What You Know: The Verb saber

▶ **Saber** is another verb that has an irregular **yo** form. You use **saber** when you talk about factual information you know.

saber *to know*	
sé	sabemos
sabes	sabéis
sabe	saben

▶ To say that someone knows how to do something, use: **saber** + *infinitive*.

Sé patinar muy bien.
I know how to skate very well.

Middle School Classroom Community

Learning Scenario Tell students that they are at the World Series (or at a major sporting event of their choice). Have them compare the team members, say who is playing, comment on the equipment and uniforms, discuss the fans, etc. Encourage students to use the dictionary if they need extra vocabulary.

Paired Activity Have students take turns telling their partners what they, friends, family members, teachers, etc., know how to do. Or they may say what they and others do not know how to do but want to learn.

¿Sabe o no sabe?

Hablar Take turns asking a partner if the following people know how to do the activities listed below. Add an additional comment to each response.

modelo

tu tía / jugar al voleibol

Estudiante A: ***Tu tía*** *sabe* ***jugar al voleibol****, ¿no?*

Estudiante B: *Sí, sabe jugar muy bien.* **o:** *No, no sabe, pero quiere aprender.*

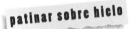

patinar sobre hielo

esquiar

cantar

hablar español

bailar el tango

nadar

pintar

tocar el piano

1. tu amigo(a)
2. tus padres
3. tú
4. tú y tu hermano(a)
5. el (la) maestro(a)
6. tu madre
7. tus primos(as)
8. ustedes

¿Qué sabes hacer?

Hablar/Escribir Work in groups of four. Tell each other what you know how to do well (and not so well). Then choose one person to report to the class.

modelo

Estudiante A: *Sé nadar muy bien.*

Estudiante B: *Yo sé nadar también.*

Estudiante C (a la clase): *Carla y Sara saben nadar...*

Gramática en vivo

Roberto: Me gusta jugar al baloncesto y al tenis. Pienso que el tenis es **menos divertido que** el baloncesto. También me gusta nadar.

Ignacio: Me gusta correr **más que** nadar.

Phrases for Making Comparisons

▶ Several phrases are used when making comparisons and using adjectives.

más... que	**menos... que**	**tan... como**
more... than	*less... than*	*as... as*

▶ These phrases are used when you don't include adjectives.

más que...	**menos que...**	**tanto como...**
more than...	*less than...*	*as much as...*

▶ When you talk about numbers, you must use:

más de	or **menos de**.
más de dos o tres minutos	en **menos de** cinco minutos
more than *two or three minutes*	*in **less than** five minutes*

▶ There are a few irregular comparative words.

mayor	**menor**	**mejor**	**peor**
older	*younger*	*better*	*worse*

sesenta y nueve
Etapa 3 | **69**

BRIDGE UNIT Etapa 3
Vocabulary/Grammar

Objective: Transitional practice Saber

Answers

Answers will vary but should contain the following.

1. sabe
2. saben
3. sabes / sé
4. saben / sabemos
5. sabe
6. sabe
7. saben
8. saben / sabemos

Objective: Open-ended practice Saber/vocabulary

Answers will vary.

Teaching Suggestions
Phrases for Making Comparisons

• When presenting comparisons, provide a variety of visually stimulating examples—the sillier the better.

• Have students pronounce and pay close attention to **mayor** and **mejor**, as they often confuse these two words. Give examples using the irregular comparative words. (**José es mi mejor amigo. Yo soy mayor que él.**)

Teaching Middle School Students

Extra Help Have students brainstorm comparison words. Start them off by naming 2 things to compare. Have students volunteer sentences, and ask several students to take turns writing them on the board or on the overhead. Encourage students to name things to be compared.

Multiple Intelligences

Intrapersonal Give students 5 categories (**carros, actores/actrices, equipos,** etc.), and ask them to write a sentence comparing 2 items from each category.

Block Schedule

Journal Have students prepare a journal entry on the topic "My feelings about sports." They may decide to comment on a particular sport or express some feelings about sports in general. They might also use comparison phrases to explain their preferences.

Teaching Resource Options

Print

Activity and Assessment Book
Grammar 3.2, p. 37
Audioscripts, pp. 54–58

Audiovisual

Bridge Audio Program Cassettes / CD

 Objective: Controlled practice
Listening comprehension/numbers/
comparisons

Answers (See script, p. 53A.)
1. más de
2. menos de
3. tanto como
4. menos de
5. más de
6. más de
7. menos de

Objective: Open-ended practice
Comparisons/vocabulary

Answers will vary.

Objective: Transitional practice
Comparisons

Answers

Answers will vary but should contain the following.
1. ¿Cuál es más difícil, el béisbol o el fútbol?
2. ¿Cuál es peor, el fútbol americano o el baloncesto?
3. ¿Cuál es más aburrido, el voleibol o el tenis?
4. ¿Cuál es más interesante, el baloncesto o el béisbol?
5. ¿Cuál es mejor, el fútbol o el fútbol americano?
6. ¿Cuál es más peligroso, el voleibol o el surfing?

 **Quick Wrap-up**

Announce pairs of celebrities and have students compare them. For example:
¿Quién juega mejor al tenis, Pete Sampras o Monica Seles?

Gimnasia mental

Escuchar Listen to the following numbers being added or subtracted. In the chart, indicate whether the number is more than, less than, or the same as the number listed in each case.

menos de	tanto como	más de
	once	
	veinte	
	seis	
	cuarenta y cinco	
	treinta	
	sesenta	
	cien	

Famosos o familiares

Escribir Make a list of pairs of people you know—famous or familiar. Then compare them using one of the suggested characteristics below.

alto(a)	simpático(a)
cómico(a)	serio(a)
inteligente	trabajador(a)
paciente	

modelo

mi hermano / mi hermana

alto(a)

Mi hermano *es más* **alto** *que* **mi hermana**.

¿Qué piensas?

Hablar With a partner, compare the following sports in terms of the words indicated. Take turns asking and giving opinions.

modelo

Estudiante A: *¿Cuál es más* **divertido**, *el tenis o el béisbol?*

Estudiante B: *Para mí, el tenis es más* **divertido** *que el béisbol.* **o:** *Para mí, el tenis es tan* **divertido** *como el béisbol.*

divertido

1. **difícil**   2. **malo**

3. **aburrido**   4. **interesante**

5.   6.

bueno   **peligroso**

---

70   setenta
Bridge Unit

Middle School Classroom Community

Cooperative Learning The task is to work in groups to review sports vocabulary, using visuals, pictures, flash cards, etc. The roles are:

• a student to review names of sports

• a student to review verbs associated with sports: **jugar, andar, ganar, perder, esquiar, levantar pesas**

• a student to review sports equipment

• a student to review locations of sports and ways of talking about sports

When the review is complete, students must write 4 sentences that contain each of the items reviewed.

En resumen

YA SABES ♻

TALKING ABOUT SPORTS

el equipo	team
ganar	to win
el gol	goal
jugar (a)	to play
el partido	game
la tienda de deportes	sporting goods store

Sports

andar en patineta	to skateboard
el baloncesto	basketball
el béisbol	baseball
esquiar	to ski
el fútbol	soccer
el fútbol americano	football
el hockey	hockey
levantar pesas	to lift weights
el surfing	surfing
el tenis	tennis
el voleibol	volleyball

Equipment

el bate	bat
la bola	ball
el casco	helmet
la gorra	baseball cap
el guante	glove
los patines	skates
la patineta	skateboard
la pelota	baseball
la raqueta	racket

Locations

al aire libre	outdoors
el campo	field
la cancha	court
el estadio	stadium
la piscina	swimming pool
sobre hielo	on ice

EXPRESSING PREFERENCES

preferir	to prefer
querer	to want

SAYING WHAT YOU KNOW

saber	to know

MAKING COMPARISONS

más de	more than
más... que	more…than
mayor	older
mejor	better
menor	younger
menos de	less than
menos... que	less…than
peor	worse
tan... como	as…as
tanto como	as much as

OTHER WORDS AND PHRASES

cerrar	to close
empezar	to begin
entender	to understand
favorito(a)	favorite
loco(a)	crazy
merendar	to have a snack
peligroso(a)	dangerous
pensar	to think, to plan
perder	to lose

Juego

A Ángela, a Marco y a Juanito les gusta practicar diferentes deportes. ¿Cuáles son? Busca sus nombres. Con las otras letras, identifica su deporte preferido.

1. ALSAEGSPENARALEVANT
2. GINAMURFSOCR
3. NIAUJOTTBLOFU

Teaching Suggestions
Vocabulary Review

Divide the class into 2 groups and have individual team members play sports Charades in front of their group. The team must guess the sport and name either the equipment or the place related to it.

Juego

Answers
1. Ángela–levantar pesas
2. Marco–surfing
3. Juanito–fútbol

Game

Compara las categorías Use the vocabulary categories of "Sports," "Equipment," and "Locations" to make comparisons. Have pairs select a category and write as many comparisons as they can with words in that category in 6–8 minutes. **El estadio es más grande que la cancha. Me gusta levantar pesas mejor que esquiar.** Then, each pair shares its comparisons. The pair with the most valid comparisons wins. Offer a bonus for using stem-changing verbs in the comparisons.

▮ Block Schedule

Variety After students have completed **Actividad 22**, have them use the illustrations to make as many different comparisons as they can. **Me gusta jugar al voleibol más que jugar al tenis. Un equipo de fútbol americano es más grande que un equipo de baloncesto.**

Teaching Middle School Students

Multiple Intelligences

Interpersonal Have pairs of students research and discuss Latin American or Spanish sports figures. Ask them to find one they agree is a good role model and prepare a short report on him or her.

Logical/Mathematical Have students take turns with partners making statements about sports—which are more interesting, harder, more fun, etc. Share with the class and have students take a poll to survey the whole class.

Teaching Resource Options

Print 📖

Activity and Assessment Book
  Vocabulary 2.1, p. 17
  Audioscripts, pp. 54–58

Audiovisual 📼

Bridge Audio Program Cassettes / CD
OHT B13 (Quick Start), B15, B16

Quick Start Review

🔄 **Hacer** and **tener**

Use OHT B13 or write on the board:
What does Gustavo have to say about
his family? Complete his sentences with
correct forms of **hacer** or **tener**.

1. Mis padres _____ ejercicio todos
   los días.
2. Mi padre _____ cuarenta y cinco
   años.
3. Yo _____ trece años.
4. Mi hermano y yo _____ que
   estudiar mucho para las clases.
5. De vez en cuando yo _____ mi
   tarea en el autobús.

Answers
1. hacen 2. tiene 3. tengo 4. tenemos 5. hago

Teaching Suggestions
Reconnecting with Vocabulary

• Read each section of the vocabulary
  aloud, having students repeat after
  you.
• Not following any order, ask students
  what the weather is in pictures A
  through D. Then ask students what
  the person is wearing.
• Ask students what the weather is
  normally like in **El Yunque** and what
  they should wear there.
• Use the TPR activity to reinforce the
  meaning of individual words.

En contexto

🎧 VOCABULARIO

Roberto has experienced all kinds of weather in
Minnesota and Puerto Rico, as you can see from the
pictures in his scrapbook.

yo

yo en el invierno
el gorro
la bufanda
el abrigo   la nieve

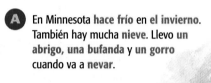

A En Minnesota **hace frío** en **el invierno**.
También hay mucha **nieve**. Llevo **un
abrigo, una bufanda** y **un gorro**
cuando va a **nevar**.

mamá con paraguas
el paraguas
de cuadros

B ¿Qué tiempo hace? Hace mal
tiempo. Va a llover. Por eso, mi
mamá lleva un paraguas de
cuadros. No le gusta la lluvia.

C Es verano y mi primo
está en la playa.
Hace calor, y él va a
nadar en el mar.

mi primo en el verano
el mar
el traje de baño
la playa

Middle School Classroom Community

TPR Designate parts of the room as seasons and
include Puerto Rico and Minnesota in each season.
Have visuals, flash cards, etc., showing weather and
seasonal clothing at each station. Have students take
turns sending their partners to a season and place.
The partners must return with an appropriate item
of clothing.

Storytelling Divide the class into groups and have
them create a story about a student from a Latin
American country who comes to the United States and
has to learn about differences in climate and clothing.
Have each group present their story to the class.

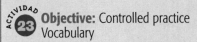

mi amiga María

las gafas de sol

con rayas

D Mi amiga María lleva **las gafas de sol**. Las lleva cuando **hay sol**. No las lleva cuando llueve. También lleva una camisa **con rayas**.

EL TIEMPO

el sol

Temperaturas
9 de marzo

	Alta	Baja
San Juan	87°	73°
Minneapolis	30°	15°

el bosque

la planta

la flor

EL YUNQUE

el árbol

E Saco fotos en **el bosque** tropical El Yunque. Me gusta ver **los árboles** grandes, **las flores** bonitas y **las plantas** interesantes.

 23 **Las fotos de Roberto**

Hablar/Leer Say if the following statements are true (**sí**) or false (**no**).

1. María lleva una camisa de cuadros.
2. El primo de Roberto está en la playa.
3. Hay árboles y plantas en el bosque.
4. Roberto lleva una bufanda y un gorro cuando hace calor.
5. María lleva gafas de sol cuando hace mal tiempo.
6. La mamá de Roberto necesita un paraguas cuando va a llover.
7. Nieva en los veranos de Minnesota.
8. Hace frío en los inviernos de Minnesota.

 24 **¿Cuándo?**

Hablar Tell which season, winter or summer, you associate with the following words. Be careful. Some words may be appropriate to both seasons.

1. la nieve
2. el calor
3. la playa
4. el sol
5. la bufanda
6. las gafas de sol
7. el abrigo
8. la lluvia

 25 **Una tarjeta postal**

Escribir Write a postcard to a pen pal in another country. Tell him or her what the weather is like in the winter and summer where you live. Also include what your pen pal should wear while visiting during those seasons.

setenta y tres
Etapa 3 **73**

23 **Objective:** Controlled practice
Vocabulary

Answers
1. no
2. sí
3. sí
4. no
5. no
6. sí
7. no
8. sí

24 **Objective:** Transitional practice
Vocabulary

Answers
1. el invierno
2. el verano
3. el verano
4. el invierno o el verano
5. el invierno
6. el invierno o el verano
7. el invierno
8. el invierno o el verano

25 **Objective:** Open-ended practice
Vocabulary

Answers will vary.

Teaching Middle School Students

Extra Help Divide the class into 4 groups. Assign each group a season and the subheads "Puerto Rico" and "Minnesota." Have them list the weather expressions appropriate for their season, and then have groups trade lists and write the clothing appropriate for their seasons.

Native Speakers Ask native speakers to talk about the climate and weather in their countries of origin.

Multiple Intelligences

Naturalist Divide the class into groups and provide pictures showing different weather scenes. A student begins by showing a picture to the group. Another student names a season or gives a weather expression. The next adds to that or mentions an appropriate item of clothing, etc.

Block Schedule

Research Have students research **El Yunque** in Puerto Rico. Encourage them to find out such information as climate, average rainfall, types of vegetation, and animals that are found there. Invite a student to present a few pieces of information. Then continue to ask volunteers to provide facts that have not yet been stated.

Teaching Suggestions
Describing the Weather

- Read all of the weather expressions aloud, having students repeat after you. Include **llueve** and **nieva** (pointing out that they are stem-changing verbs but almost always use the "it" form).
- Ask students to describe today's weather.
- Read the additional words from the **Vocabulario**, having students repeat after you. Ask students what words and phrases go with each season of the year.

Objective: Open-ended practice Weather expressions

Answers will vary.

En acción
VOCABULARIO Y GRAMÁTICA

Gramática en vivo

Diana: ¿N ie va mucho?
Roberto: Bueno, en el invierno, n ie va casi todas las semanas. Pero en el verano, es como aquí. Hace mucho calor.

Describing the Weather

To talk about weather, you will often use the verb hacer.

¿Qué tiempo hace?
What's it like out?

Hace... *It's...*	**(mucho) calor.** *(very) hot.*	**(muy) buen tiempo.** *(very) nice outside.*
	(mucho) frío. *(very) cold.*	**(muy) mal tiempo.** *(very) bad outside.*
	(mucho) sol. *(very) sunny.*	**(mucho) fresco.** *(very) cool.*
	(mucho) viento. *(very) windy.*	

When you talk about wind or sun, you can also use hay.

Hay... *It's...*	**(mucho) sol.** *(very) sunny.*
	(mucho) viento. *(very) windy.*

Use the verbs ll o ver and n e var to say it is raining (ll ue ve) or it is snowing (n ie va). They are verbs with stem changes, just like j u gar and p e nsar.

To say that it's cloudy, use the expression está nublado.

¡Para hoy y mañana!

Hablar/Escribir Prepare and deliver the weather report for your area, including the forecast for today and for tomorrow.

modelo

Hoy está nublado. La temperatura está a sesenta grados. Por la tarde va a llover. Mañana va a hacer más frío y...

Vocabulario

Las estaciones	Ya sabes
el invierno	**la primavera**
el otoño	**el verano**
Otras palabras	
el bronceador	**el río**
el desierto	**los shorts**
el grado	**tomar el sol**
el impermeable	**la tormenta**
el lago	**el viento**
la montaña	

¿Qué actividad te gusta hacer en cada estación?

Middle School Classroom Management

Planning Ahead Anticipate the review of direct object pronouns and begin working them in as soon as you can. **Actividad 27**, or any conversation that features noun objects, can be recycled for this purpose.

Time Saver Have the materials relating to weather in a specific location so that students can get them for practice or class activities.

ACTIVIDAD 27

¿Qué tiempo hace?

Hablar Describe what the weather might be like from the hints given.

modelo

Necesitas llevar paraguas.
Llueve mucho. No hay sol.

1. Necesitas usar bronceador.
2. Piensas esquiar en la montaña.
3. Llevas abrigo y bufanda.
4. Buscas tu traje de baño.
5. No es posible sacar fotos.
6. Quieres jugar al tenis.
7. Vas a patinar sobre hielo.
8. Llevas un suéter para caminar con el perro.
9. No quieres ir al parque.
10. No necesitas gafas de sol.

Gramática en vivo

Diana: Creo que *tienes* mucha *suerte*.

Ignacio: *Tengo prisa.* Es buena hora para sacar fotos porque hay sol.

Special Expressions Using *tener*

▶ You can use the verb *tener* in many expressions.

tener...	calor	prisa	tener ganas de...	bailar
to be...	*hot*	*in a hurry*	*to feel like...*	*dancing*
	cuidado	razón		cantar
	careful	*right*		*singing*
	frío	sueño		
	cold	*sleepy*		
	miedo	suerte		
	afraid	*lucky*		

ACTIVIDAD 28

¿Y tú?

Hablar Describe situations to your partner where you might feel cold, hot, afraid, lucky, or sleepy. Then ask about his or her experiences.

modelo

Cuando nieva, yo tengo frío. ¿Y tú?

Teaching Middle School Students

Extra Help After reviewing **tener** expressions, have students tell you how they feel in response to visuals or to statements or to brief scenarios that you describe for them. **(Es la una y media de la mañana y tú haces la tarea. → Tengo mucho sueño.)**

Multiple Intelligences

Musical/Rhythmic Have students write a song or poem about a particular weather condition and how it makes them feel.

ACTIVIDAD 27

Objective: Open-ended practice Weather expressions/vocabulary

Answers

Answers may vary.
1. Hace calor. Hay sol.
2. Nieva.
3. Hace frío.
4. Hace calor.
5. Llueve. / Está nublado.
6. Hace buen tiempo/calor.
7. Hace frío.
8. Hace fresco.
9. Llueve.
10. Está nublado. / Llueve.

Teaching Suggestions
Special Expressions Using tener

• Review the forms of **tener** before presenting the expressions.
• Give students circumstances and have them use an appropriate expression with **tener**. (**Es la medianoche/ tengo sueño. La música es buena/tengo ganas de bailar.**)

ACTIVIDAD 28

Objective: Open-ended practice Expressions with **tener**

Answers will vary.

Block Schedule

Change of Pace Divide the class into 6 groups. Each of 5 groups will be responsible for completing a written weather summary for its assigned day. The report must include the date, weather conditions, and high and low temperatures for the day. The sixth group takes all 5 written reports and creates a weather summary for the week.

Teaching Resource Options

Print

Activity and Assessment Book
 Grammar 3.3, p. 40
 Audioscripts, pp. 54–58

Audiovisual

Bridge Audio Program Cassettes / CD

---

29 Objective: Transitional practice
Expressions with **tener**

Answers

Answers will vary but should contain the following.
1. ¿Dónde tienes cuidado? / Tengo cuidado…
2. ¿Cuándo tienes calor? / Tengo calor…
3. ¿Quién tiene suerte? / _____ tiene suerte.
4. ¿Por qué tienes prisa? / Tengo prisa porque…
5. ¿Quién tiene…?

30 Objective: Open-ended practice
Expressions with **tener**

Answers

Answers will vary.
1. Cuando llueve, nosotros tenemos ganas de…
2. Cuando hace frío, Juanita tiene ganas de…
3. Cuando hace buen tiempo, tú tienes ganas de…
4. Cuando hace mal tiempo, ellas tienen ganas de…
5. Cuando hace fresco, Daniel tiene ganas de…
6. Cuando nieva, Cristina y Ana tienen ganas de…

Teaching Suggestions
Direct Object Pronouns

- Practice the **lo/la/los/las** forms before the conjugated verb by asking students if they want something and having them answer using the corresponding direct object pronoun. (¿Quieres la pizza? Sí, la quiero. ¿Quieres los libros? Sí, los quiero.)
- Practice the same object pronoun forms with an infinitive by asking students if they want to buy something and having them answer using the corresponding direct object pronoun. (¿Quieres comprar la pizza? Sí, quiero comprarla. ¿Quieres comprar los libros? Sí, quiero comprarlos. o: Sí, la quiero comprar. Sí, los quiero comprar.)

29

Cuéntame

Hablar Ask a classmate questions using the words below. Change roles.

modelo

cuándo / tener sueño

Estudiante A: ¿Cuándo tienes sueño?

Estudiante B: Tengo sueño *por la mañana.*

1. dónde / tener cuidado
2. cuándo / tener calor
3. quién / tener suerte
4. por qué / tener prisa
5. quién / tener ¿?

30

Tengo ganas de...

Escribir Tell what these people do and don't feel like doing in certain weather.

modelo

Hace calor. / yo

*Cuando **hace calor**, tengo ganas de ir a la playa. No tengo ganas de correr.*

1. Llueve. / nosotros
2. Hace frío. / Juanita
3. Hace buen tiempo. / tú
4. Hace mal tiempo. / ellas
5. Hace fresco. / Daniel
6. Nieva. / Cristina y Ana

Gramática en vivo

Diana: ¡Ay! Pues, ya **tienes** ropa de verano.
Roberto: Claro que la **tengo**.

▶ Direct Object Pronouns

▶ The **direct object** in a sentence receives the action of the verb. Nouns used as **direct objects** can be replaced by pronouns.

Singular	Plural
me	**nos**
me	*us*
te	**os**
you (familiar)	*you (familiar)*
lo *masculine*	**los** *masculine*
you (formal), him, it	*you (formal), them*
la *feminine*	**las** *feminine*
you (formal), her, it	*you (formal), them*

▶ The **direct object noun** is placed after the **conjugated verb**.

replaced by

—Pues, ya **tienes** ropa de verano.　　—Claro que la **tengo**.
*You already have **summer clothing**.*　　*Of course I have **it**.*

▶ The **direct object** pronoun is placed directly before the **conjugated verb**.

▶ When an infinitive follows the conjugated verb, the **direct object** pronoun can be placed:

before the **conjugated verb** or attached to the **infinitive**

Middle School Classroom Community

Game (Whole class or small groups) Choose a student, and tell the class that they must guess what this student has. Their only clue is the object pronoun. Write down the item (**la camisa**) and say, **Carlos la tiene**. When a student guesses correctly, show what you wrote down. The student who guessed is the next to say (and write down) what another student has.

Learning Scenario Tell students to imagine that they are in a sporting goods store. Identify several students as clerks, and one as a manager. The rest are customers. Tell them to talk about what they need in the way of equipment and clothing, to request help from the employees, to ask the manager about where things are, etc.

ACTIVIDAD 31

¿Qué objeto?

Escribir Rewrite the sentence by replacing the highlighted words with a direct object pronoun.

modelo

Yo quiero comprar **el gorro**.   _Yo **lo** quiero comprar._

1. Lilia escribe **las cartas.**
2. Pablo come **la torta.**
3. Yo veo a **mis abuelos.**
4. Ustedes leen **libros.**
5. Tú tomas **el examen.**
6. Ana prepara **la comida.**

ACTIVIDAD 32

¡Tantas preguntas!

Escuchar/Leer Someone is asking you the following questions. Listen and select the most appropriate answer.

1. **a.** Sí, la compro.
   b. Sí, los compro.
   c. Sí, lo compro.

2. **a.** Mamá lo prepara.
   b. Mamá la prepara.
   c. Mamá las prepara.

3. **a.** Sí, los necesito.
   b. Sí, las necesito.
   c. Sí, la necesito.

4. **a.** Marta los usa.
   b. Marta lo usa.
   c. Marta las usa.

5. **a.** La entiendo un poco.
   b. Los entiendo un poco.
   c. Las entiendo un poco.

ACTIVIDAD 33

¿Quién los usa?

Hablar Take turns with a classmate asking who uses these items. Answer and then change roles. (Pay attention to the direct object pronouns!)

modelo

Estudiante A: _¿Quién usa el guante?_

Estudiante B: _Mi hermano lo usa._

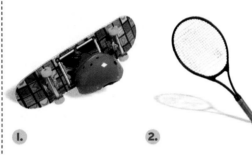

1.   2.

3.   4.

5.   6.

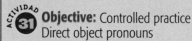

ACTIVIDAD 31 Objective: Controlled practice
Direct object pronouns

Answers
1. Lilia las escribe.
2. Pablo la come.
3. Yo los veo.
4. Ustedes los leen.
5. Tú lo tomas.
6. Ana la prepara.

ACTIVIDAD 32 Objective: Controlled practice
Listening comprehension/direct object pronouns

Answers (See script, p. 53A.)
1. c
2. b
3. b
4. a
5. a

ACTIVIDAD 33 Objective: Transitional practice
Direct object pronouns

Answers
Answers will vary but should contain the following.
1. ¿Quién usa la patineta y el casco? / …los usa.
2. ¿Quién usa la raqueta? / …la usa.
3. ¿Quién usa las pelotas? / …las usa.
4. ¿Quién usa el bate? / …lo usa.
5. ¿Quién usa las pesas? / …las usa.
6. ¿Quién usa el traje de baño? / …lo usa.

Teaching Middle School Students

Challenge Ask students to write a short play with 4 characters. In the dialog, the play writer must include all direct object pronouns.

Multiple Intelligences

Verbal Ask students to write 6 short yes/no questions involving something that someone does (**¿Escribes cartas? ¿Lees libros? ¿Comes pizza?**, etc.). Tell students they must respond using direct object pronouns (**Sí, las escribo. No, no los leo. Sí, la como,** etc.). Have them interview several students and then count how many said yes or no to their questions.

Block Schedule

FunBreak Students can work in pairs to describe a particular weather/seasonal situation and then ask about wearing an article of clothing. **Es invierno y hay nieve. ¿Llevo un traje de baño?** The partner provides an answer using a direct object pronoun. **No, no lo llevas.**

Teaching Resource Options

Print

Activity and Assessment Book
Grammar 3.3, p. 41
Information Gap Activities, pp. 42–43
Cooperative Quizzes, pp. 44–47

Audiovisual

OHT B16

Teaching Suggestions
Saying What Is Happening: Present Progressive

• Emphasize that the present progressive in Spanish is only used to say what is in progress at the moment. Whereas in English we might say, "I'm studying in Spain next year," in Spanish we would say, **Voy a estudiar en España el año que viene.** We cannot say, **Estoy estudiando en España el año que viene.**

• Point out that nothing ever comes between **estar** and the present participle. Also, the ending of the present participle always ends in **-o** and never changes for masculine or feminine. (**Ellas están comiendo.**)

 Objective: Open-ended practice Present progressive

Answers will vary.

 Objective: Open-ended practice Present progressive

Answers will vary.

Quick Wrap-up

Give TPR statements for individuals or pairs of students to act out. Examples: **Marcos esquía en el agua.** (He acts out skiing.) **Tina y Luz leen libros.** (They act out reading books.)

Gramática en vivo

Ignacio: ¡Está **llov**iendo! ¡Y no tengo paraguas!
Roberto: Te estamos esper**ando**, hombre.

Saying What Is Happening: Present Progressive

▶ When you want to say that an action is happening now, use the present progressive.

estoy **esperando**	estamos **esperando**
estás **esperando**	estáis **esperando**
está **esperando**	están **esperando**

▶ To form this tense, use:

the present tense of estar + **present participle**

▶ To form the **present participle** of a verb, drop the **ending** of the infinitive and add **-ando** or **-iendo**.

-ar verbs	esperar ← ar/ar	ando	esperando
-er verbs	comer ← er/er	iendo	comiendo
-ir verbs	escribir ← ir/ir	iendo	escribiendo

▶ When the **stem** of an **-er** or **-ir** verb ends in a vowel, change the **-iendo** to **-yendo**.

leer ⟶ le**y**endo

Llama la abuela

Hablar/Escribir Your house is full of friends and relatives. Your grandmother calls to find out what everyone is doing. Mention five people.

modelo

Papá está hablando con el tío Alberto. Mi hermana está comiendo…

¿Qué?

Hablar Work in pairs. Act out an activity that you have learned to say in Spanish, and have your partner guess what you are doing. Then change roles. Or turn this activity into "charades" for the class.

modelo

Estudiante A: *¿Qué estoy haciendo?*
Estudiante B: *¡Estás nadando!*

Middle School Classroom Community

Cooperative Learning The task is to work in groups to review seasons and weather expressions. The roles are:

• a student in charge of weather visuals, who will pass them out and collect them

• a student to conduct an oral review using the visuals

• a student in charge of showing pictures of clothing/accessories and asking students to say when the items would be worn

• a student in charge of assigning each member of the group to write a short paragraph about one of the seasons or the weather for that day, and also in charge of collecting the papers

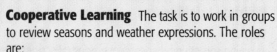

En resumen

YA SABES ♻

DESCRIBING THE WEATHER

¿Qué tiempo hace?	What is the weather like?
Está nublado.	It is cloudy.
Hace…	It is…
buen tiempo	nice outside
calor	hot
fresco	cool
frío	cold
mal tiempo	bad outside
sol	sunny
viento	windy
Hay…	It's…
sol	sunny
viento	windy
el grado	degree
llover	to rain
la lluvia	rain
nevar	to snow
la nieve	snow
el sol	sun
la temperatura	temperature
el tiempo	weather
la tormenta	storm
el viento	wind

Seasons

las estaciones	seasons
el invierno	winter
el otoño	fall
la primavera	spring
el verano	summer

DESCRIBING HOW YOU FEEL

tener…	to be…
calor	hot
cuidado	careful
frío	cold
miedo	afraid
prisa	in a hurry
razón	right
sueño	sleepy
suerte	lucky
tener ganas de…	to feel like…

STATING AN OPINION

creer	to think, to believe
Creo que sí/no.	I think so. / I don't think so.

CLOTHING AND ACCESSORIES

Clothing

el abrigo	coat
la bufanda	scarf
el gorro	cap
el impermeable	raincoat
los shorts	shorts
el traje de baño	bathing suit

Styles

con rayas	striped
de cuadros	plaid, checked

Accessories

el bronceador	suntan lotion
las gafas de sol	sunglasses
el paraguas	umbrella

OTHER WORDS AND PHRASES

sacar fotos	to take pictures
tomar el sol	to sunbathe

Places

el bosque	forest
el desierto	desert
el lago	lake
el mar	sea
la montaña	mountain
la playa	beach
el río	river

Vegetation

el árbol	tree
la flor	flower
la planta	plant

Juego

Es julio. Hace frío y nieva mucho. Mucha gente esquía en las montañas. ¿En qué país están?

a. **México**

b. **Estados Unidos**

c. **Chile**

Teaching Suggestions
Vocabulary Review

Divide the class into 4 groups. Group 1 names a season, Group 2 names a place, Group 3 tells the weather for that place in that season, and Group 4 tells the appropriate clothing or accessories. After doing the 4 seasons, shift the categories of the groups clockwise and repeat.

Juego

Answer: Chile

Project

Have student pairs write an oversized postcard (8 1/2" x 11") to a friend or relative about an imaginary trip to one of the places mentioned in the vocabulary review. They earn a point for each vocabulary word they include. Have them carefully edit and prepare a final draft of the card before completing it with an illustration of that vacation spot. Display the cards.

Teaching Middle School Students

Native Speakers Have students write a **juego** similar to the one on p. 79 about a place in their country of origin.

Multiple Intelligences

Naturalist After reviewing vocabulary for "Places" and "Vegetation," ask students to choose one of those items and, working with another student who chose the same topic, write a description, dialog, skit, etc., about the place or plant, the weather, and the season.

▪ Block Schedule

Journal Ask students to select a place from the word list (**bosque, desierto…**) and a season during which they would like to visit that place. Encourage students to write a journal entry about what the place would be like and what they would do if they took a trip there.

Unit Theme
Visiting a city (Oaxaca, Mexico), making purchases, and ordering in a restaurant

Communication
- Asking for and giving directions
- Identifying places to visit in the city
- Choosing means of transportation
- Talking about shopping
- Making purchases and bargaining
- Discussing gift ideas
- Ordering food
- Saying where you went

Cultures
- Learning about the history of Oaxaca and its surroundings
- Learning about traditional arts, crafts, and architecture in Oaxaca
- Learning about regional foods
- Learning about bargaining in a marketplace

Connections
- Connecting to Physical Education: Mexican folk dancing
- Connecting to Mathematics: Calculating prices in a Mexican **mercado**

Comparisons
- Comparing shopping in Mexico and in the U.S.
- Comparing modes of transportation
- Comparing city/town structure

Communities
- Using Spanish in the workplace
- Using Spanish in volunteer activities

Teaching Resource Options

Print
Block Scheduling Copymasters

Audiovisual
OHT M1, M2; 103, 104
Canciones Audiocassette/CD
Video Program Videotape 4 / Videodisc 2B

Search Chapter 1, Play to 2
U4 Cultural Introduction

UNIDAD

4

OAXACA
MÉXICO

¡DE VISITA!

ESTADOS UNIDOS

CHIHUAHUA •

OCÉANO PACÍFICO

GOLFO DE CALIFORNIA

BAJA CALIFORNIA

MÉXICO

GUADALAJARA •

OBJECTIVES

ETAPA **1**
¡A visitar a mi prima!
- Identify places
- Give addresses
- Choose transportation
- Request directions
- Give instructions

ETAPA **2**
En el mercado
- Talk about shopping
- Make purchases
- Talk about giving gifts
- Bargain

ETAPA **3**
¿Qué hacer en Oaxaca?
- Order food
- Request the check
- Talk about food
- Express extremes
- Say where you went

ANIMALITOS are popular forms for Oaxacan wood carvings. Notice the colorful painting. What other Oaxacan carving is on this page?

Middle School Classroom Community

Group Activity Divide the class into small groups. Give each group a map of Mexico. Ask students to pretend they are tourists. Have them choose two cities in Oaxaca and then trace the route between them with a highlighter. Then have them make individual maps of Mexico, highlighting Oaxaca, the region to be visited in this **Unidad**.

Game Give each student a small, detailed map of Mexico. Form a circle with the entire class. Student A chooses a city, river, mountain range, etc., and says its name. Student B has to choose one whose name begins with the last letter of the previous name (Acapulco → Oaxaca, and so on). The game is over when a new match cannot be found.

ALMANAQUE

Población: 212.943

Altura: 1.550 metros (5.084 pies)

Clima: 21° C (69.1° F)

Comida típica: mole negro, tasajo

Gente famosa de Oaxaca: Francisco Toledo (pintor), Benito Juárez (político), Rufino Tamayo (pintor)

¿Vas a Oaxaca? La gente de México usa la palabra *Oaxaca* para referirse al estado de Oaxaca, la ciudad de Oaxaca y el valle de Oaxaca. Cuando escuches «Oaxaca», pregunta a qué parte se refiere.

INTERNET For more information about Oaxaca, access www.mcdougallittell.com

PESOS are Mexican money. How are they different from dollars?

GOLFO DE MÉXICO

MONTE ALBÁN

BAHÍA DE CAMPECHE

PENÍNSULA DE YUCATÁN

MÉXICO, D.F.

MONTE ALBÁN This city was built by the Zapotecs around 600 B.C. high upon a hill. What do you think the word **monte** means?

BENITO JUÁREZ was one of Mexico's presidents. From the clothing in this picture, can you guess when he lived? Check your idea on p. 128.

ESTADO DE OAXACA

OAXACA

GUATEMALA

BELICE

HONDURAS

EL SALVADOR

NICARAGUA

MOLE NEGRO Many ingredients, including chiles and chocolate, make up black **mole** sauce. What have you eaten that is made from chocolate?

RUFINO TAMAYO (1899–1991), Oaxacan artist, completed *Mujer tendiendo la mano a la luna* in 1946. Can you guess what that means?

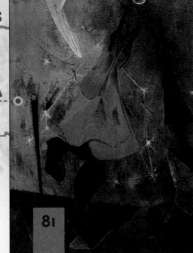

81

Teaching Middle School Students

Challenge Ask students to research the work of other Mexican artists, such as Fernando Toledo, Leonora Carrington, Jesús Gallardo, or José Chávez Morado. Have them write a short report and share their information and examples of the artist's work with the class.

Multiple Intelligences

Logical/Mathematical Ask students to find the current value of the Mexican **peso** as compared to the dollar. They may use the Internet or the financial section of the newspaper. Interested students may want to pretend to convert $100 into **pesos**, then wait a week, find the new value, and convert their **pesos** back into dollars.

Teaching Suggestions
Previewing the Unit

Tell students that this unit centers on Oaxaca, Mexico. Ask students to scan these two pages for 15 seconds, then close their books. Then ask them to tell you what they remember. You may wish to use the introduction to the video to preview the unit.

Culture Highlights

● **ARTESANÍAS DE OAXACA** The wood carvings seen here are called **alebrije**. Pottery, jewelry, and **tapetes** (rugs) are also made in Oaxaca.

● **PESOS** The name **peso** is also used for currency in Argentina, Chile, Colombia, the Dominican Republic, and Uruguay.

● **MOLE NEGRO** Oaxaca's traditional cuisine is a fusion of Spanish and Native American flavors. **Mole negro** contains **chiles mulatos, chiles chilhuacles,** chocolate, oregano, and onions.

● **BENITO JUÁREZ** Benito Juárez is among the most revered presidents in Mexican history. In 1857, he implemented major reforms in Mexico's constitution. During his presidency, he led Mexico's fight against the French in the 1860s. **El Cinco de Mayo**, a Mexican holiday also celebrated by Mexican-Americans, commemorates Juárez's victory over the French at the Battle of Puebla in 1862.

● **MONTE ALBÁN** Monte Albán offers the best view of the city of Oaxaca. Monte Albán contains temples, tombs, a ball court, and areas that might have been used for astronomical observation.

● **RUFINO TAMAYO** Rufino Tamayo, born in Oaxaca, gave his personal collection of pre-Columbian art to Oaxaca in 1974.

Block Schedule

Variety Have students compare and contrast the population and geography of Oaxaca with their own town or city.

Ampliación

These activities may be used at various points in the Unit 4 sequence.

For Block Schedule, you may find that these projects will provide a welcome change of pace while reviewing and reinforcing the material presented in the unit. See the **Block Scheduling Copymasters.**

ESTADOS UNIDOS

● PROJECTS

Create a tourist guide for Oaxaca. Divide the class into groups, assigning each group research on a particular aspect of the guide:

1. Geography   4. Main tourist attractions
2. History   5. Art and music
3. Museums   6. Crafts

Each group is responsible for writing and illustrating its section of the guide. The completed project may be duplicated and published for display, or shared with other Spanish classes or family members.

PACING SUGGESTION: Have students begin research at the beginning of the unit. Final projects are completed at the end of Unit 4.

Film or record an audiovisual guide for bargaining in a **mercado.** Include at least four different dialogs scripted by the students showing both successful and unsuccessful bargaining interactions.

PACING SUGGESTION: Upon completion of Etapa 2.

MÉXICO

● STORYTELLING

Rosa al mercado After reviewing bargaining vocabulary, model a mini-story (using puppets, student actors, or pictures from the text) that students will retell and revise:

> Rosa va al mercado. Mañana es el cumpleaños de su mamá. Rosa le pregunta al vendedor, "¿Me deja ver un anillo de plata?" El vendedor le deja ver un anillo de plata. Rosa pregunta, "¿Cuánto cuesta el anillo?" El vendedor dice, "100 pesos." Rosa regatea con el vendedor. Rosa le dice, "Quiero comprar el anillo pero es muy caro. Le puedo ofrecer 90 pesos." El vendedor acepta.

★ MÉXICO, D.F.

Pause as the story is being told so that students may fill in words and act out gestures. Students then write, narrate, and read aloud a longer main story. This new version should include vocabulary from the previous story.

Tú al mercado Ask students to create their own shopping stories. They may imagine shopping in a mall, a market, small shops, or even by phone.

PACING SUGGESTION: Upon completion of Etapa 2.

OAXACA

● BULLETIN BOARD/POSTERS

Bulletin Board Plan ahead: Contact local travel agencies for maps and brochures on Oaxaca. To begin the unit, ask students to create mind maps to activate prior knowledge after looking at the bulletin board for 2 minutes. Add the mind maps to the bulletin board.

Posters Have students create •**Travel** posters for Oaxaca •**Museum** or artisan posters •**Magazine/newspaper** posters for stores with items and prices •**Garage sale** posters with items listed

OAXACA
la ciudad y sus alrededores

GAMES

¿Me lo vendes?

Divide the class in half. Give half of the students in the class a total of 100 pesos in play money (bills). Give the other half pictures of items to sell. Have students call a local bank or check the Internet for the current exchange rate. Tell students they must establish a price for each item. The sellers should try to get as much money for their items as possible, while the buyers should try to buy as many items as possible. Give the class 10 minutes to circulate and bargain with one another. At the end of 10 minutes, the seller with the most money and the buyer with the most objects win.

PACING SUGGESTION: Upon completion of Etapa 2.

El tesoro del centro comercial

Photocopy a map of a local shopping center and give each student a copy. Decide, as a class, on a common starting point (usually the entrance to the mall). Divide the class into pairs. Instruct one of the players in each pair to draw (in pencil) a treasure chest somewhere on the map, without letting the partner see the map or the location of the treasure. Tell the partner who "hid" the treasure that he/she must now guide his/her partner to the treasure by giving directions in Spanish. Once students are familiar with the game, they can erase the original treasure chests and play again as a timed competition between pairs.

PACING SUGGESTION: Use as review of directions at any point in the unit.

MUSIC

An important festival of music and dance is held in Oaxaca every July. The **Guelaguetza** (*gay•la•gay•tzah*), which means "deep and sincere offering" in the Zapotec language, celebrates a ceremony that brought together the people of the seven regions of the state in times of great need. Music samples are available on your *Canciones* Cassette or CD. Videos and recordings are available through the Tourist Board of Oaxaca. Contact www.mcdougallittell.com for more information.

HANDS-ON CRAFTS

Work with the art department to make **animalitos** in clay or homemade play dough. As students paint and decorate their creations, review colors in Spanish, adding new vocabulary if needed. Completed projects may be displayed at your school, at a local elementary school, or at the local library.

GUATEMALA

RECIPE

Chocolate oaxaqueño is a well-known specialty of Oaxaca. It is sold in the form of powder, sticks, or bars and used in cooking as well as in making hot chocolate. Although you may not be able to purchase authentic Oaxacan chocolate locally, you can still prepare a tasty version of **chocolate oaxaqueño** with your students.

Receta

Chocolate oaxaqueño
225 g (1/2 lb.) de chocolate amargo en trozos
2 litros (2 quarts) de leche
1/4 taza de agua
azúcar y canela al gusto

Ponga el agua a hervir en una cacerola pequeña. Añada el chocolate y derrítalo a fuego lento, sin dejar de mezclar. Eche la leche, siga calentando y con una batidora, bata hasta que se forme espuma. Añada azúcar y canela al gusto. Sirva inmediatamente en tazas pequeñas. ¡Mmmmm!—¡qué rico!

Planning Guide CLASSROOM MANAGEMENT

OBJECTIVES

Communication
- Identify places *pp. 84–85*
- Give addresses *pp. 86–87*
- Choose transportation *pp. 86–87*
- Request directions *pp. 86–87, 100*
- Give instructions *pp. 86–87*

Grammar
- Use the verb **decir** *pp. 92–93*
- Use prepositions of location *pp. 95–96*
- Use regular affirmative **tú** commands *pp. 97–99*

Pronunciation
- Pronunciation of **r** *p. 101*
- Dictation *TE p. 101*

Culture
- Oaxaca, Mexico—its history and culture *pp. 80–81, 99, 102–103*

♻ Recycling
- Seasons, weather *p. 90*
- **Hay** *p. 90*
- Free-time activities *p. 97*
- Direct object pronouns *p. 98*
- Sequencing events *p. 98*

STRATEGIES

Listening Strategies
- Listen and follow directions *p. 86*

Speaking Strategies
- Recognize and use set phrases *p. 96*
- Use variety to give directions *p. 106*

Reading Strategies
- Recognize sequence *p. 102*

Writing Strategies
- Organize information by category *TE p. 106*

Connecting Cultures Strategies
- Recognize variations in vocabulary *p. 94*
- Learn about Oaxaca, Mexico *pp. 80–81, 99, 102–103*
- Connect and compare what you know about streets and places in your community to help you learn about streets and places in a new community *pp. 84–85*

PROGRAM RESOURCES

Print

- *Más práctica* Workbook PE *pp. 1–8*
- Block Scheduling Copymasters *pp. 81–88*
- Unit 4 Resource Book
  Más práctica Workbook TE *pp. 1–8*
  Information Gap Activities *pp. 17–20*

- Family Involvement *pp. 21–22*
- Video Activities *pp. 23–25*
- Videoscript *pp. 26–28*
- Audioscript *pp. 29–32*
- Assessment Program, Unit 4 Etapa 1 *pp. 33–51; 170–178*
- Answer Keys *pp. 179–200*

Audiovisual

- **Audio Program** Cassettes 10A, 10B / CD 10
- *Canciones* Cassette / CD
- **Video Program** Videotape 4 / Videodisc 2B
- **Overhead Transparencies** M1–M5; 103–104, 107–116

Technology

- Electronic Teacher Tools/Test Generator
- *Intrigas y aventuras* CD-ROM, Disc 1
- www.mcdougallittell.com

Assessment Program Options

- **Cooperative Quizzes** (Unit 4 Resource Book)
- **Etapa Exam** Forms A and B (Unit 4 Resource Book)
- *Para hispanohablantes* Etapa Exam (Unit 4 Resource Book)
- **Portfolio Assessment** (Unit 4 Resource Book)
- **Multiple Choice Test Questions** (Unit 4 Resource Book)
- **Audio Program** Testing Cassette T2 / CD T2
- **Electronic Teacher Tools/Test Generator**

Native Speakers

- *Para hispanohablantes* Workbook PE, *pp. 1–8*
- *Para hispanohablantes* Workbook TE (Unit 4 Resource Book)
- *Para hispanohablantes* Etapa Exam (Unit 4 Resource Book)
- Audio *Para hispanohablantes* Cassettes 10A, 10B, T2 / CD 10, T2
- Audioscript *Para hispanohablantes* (Unit 4 Resource Book)

Rosa | Carlos | Sofía

Student Text Listening Activity Scripts

 Videoscript: Diálogo *pages 86–87*

• Videotape 4 • Videodisc 2B

Search Chapter 3, Play to 4
U4E1 • En vivo (Dialog)

• Use the videoscript with **Actividades 1, 2** *pages 88–89*

Rosa: Perdone, ¿puede usted decirme dónde queda la calle Morelos?

Hombre: ¿Cómo dice, señorita?

Rosa: ¿Si sabe dónde está la calle Morelos?

Hombre: No, señorita. Perdone, pero no sé dónde queda esa calle.

Rosa: Gracias.
¡Disculpe!

Carlos: ¿Sí? Buenos días.

Rosa: Buenos días. Vengo de la Ciudad de México para visitar a mi prima y su familia. No sé donde queda su nueva casa. Ella no sabe que vengo. No quiero llamar. Busco esta dirección.

Carlos: Ah, sí, claro, la calle Morelos. Desde aquí es muy fácil llegar.

Rosa: ¡Ay, qué bueno! ¿Queda lejos de aquí?

Carlos: No, no está lejos. Son unas cuatro o cinco cuadras. A pie, llegas en diez minutos. Pero llegas más rápido en taxi.

Rosa: Como es un día bonito, prefiero caminar. ¿Puedes decirme cómo llego?

Carlos: ¡Sí, claro que sí!
Ésta es la avenida Constitución. Camina derecho una cuadra por esta calle. Allí vas a ver un banco.

Rosa: ¿Dices que hay un banco?

Carlos: Sí, hay un banco al lado de una farmacia.

Rosa: Y ahí, ¿qué hago?

Carlos: Vas a llegar a un parque. Cruza el parque. Enfrente de la estatua está la calle Morelos.

Rosa: Muchas gracias, eh...

Carlos: Carlos, me llamo Carlos.

Rosa: Muchas gracias, Carlos.

Carlos: De nada, eh...

Rosa: Rosa, soy Rosa.

Carlos: Encantado, Rosa.

Rosa: Igualmente, Carlos.

Carlos: Si tienes tiempo durante tu visita, pasa por la tienda. Salgo del trabajo a las siete. Si quieres, salimos a comer con tu prima.

Rosa: Me gustaría. Bueno, si hay tiempo. A ver qué dice mi prima. ¡Ah! ¿Puedo llevar el mapa?

Carlos: Sí, claro que sí. ¡Hasta luego, Rosa!

Rosa: Hasta luego. ¡Gracias!

Sofía: ¡Rosa!

Rosa: ¡Sofía, prima! ¿Cómo estás?

Sofía: ¡Qué sorpresa! ¿Qué haces por aquí?

Rosa: ¡Vengo a visitarte!

Sofía: ¡Qué gusto de verte! Pasa, pasa, prima.

Rosa: ¡Qué bonita es la nueva casa de tu familia!

Sofía: Gracias.

Rosa: ¿Dónde está mi tía?

Sofía: Está haciendo algunas compras.

Rosa: Ah, yo también quiero ir de compras. Es el cumpleaños de mi mamá y quiero comprar algo bonito para ella aquí en Oaxaca.

Sofía: Yo digo que el mercado tiene las cosas más bonitas. ¿Por qué no vamos mañana por la mañana? ¿Qué dices?

Rosa: Me encantaría. Además, tú sabes dónde venden cosas buenas y bonitas.

Sofía: Entonces, mañana, ¡al mercado! Y después, salimos a pasear por la plaza.

Rosa: ¡Ay, qué bueno! ¿Y qué más podemos hacer?

Sofía: Podríamos ir al cine.

ACTIVIDAD 4 ¿En qué estación? *page 90*

1. Rosa está de vacaciones. Visita a su amiga Ana en Vermont. Van a las montañas con la familia de Ana a esquiar. Hace mucho frío y nieva mucho.

2. Ana manda una carta. Describe sus vacaciones. Es julio. Hace mucho calor. Va a la playa por dos semanas. Nada mucho y toma el sol.

3. Llega otra carta de Ana. Describe el tiempo. Unos días hay mucha lluvia y hace fresco. Otros días hay mucho sol y también hace fresco. Hay unas flores muy bonitas.

4. Ana describe el tiempo en otra carta. Hace fresco y hay mucho viento. Unos días llueve, otros no. No hay muchas flores. Los colores de los árboles son bonitos.

ACTIVIDAD 20 ¿Puede usted decirme...? *page 101*

Rosa: Perdone, señor. ¿Puede usted decirme dónde está la librería?

Policía: ¡Sí! ¡Cómo no! Queda muy cerca. Camina derecho una cuadra por la calle Reforma. Allí vas a ver una plaza.

Rosa: ¿Veo una plaza?

Policía: Sí. Allí, dobla a la derecha y camina una cuadra más. La librería está a la izquierda en la esquina de la avenida Juárez.

Rosa: ¿Y puede usted decirme si hay una papelería cerca de aquí?

Policía: Sí. Cuando sales de la librería, dobla a la derecha y camina dos cuadras. La papelería está a la izquierda.

Rosa: Ah, por favor, ¿puede usted decirme si el correo está por aquí?

Policía: Sí, está a la derecha de la papelería en la misma cuadra.

Rosa: ¡Qué bueno! Muchas gracias, señor.

Quick Start Review Answers

p. 88 Video review
1. queda
2. dirección
3. A pie
4. al lado de
5. Enfrente de

p. 92 Verbs with irregular yo forms
1. Yo sé hablar español.
2. Yo hago mi tarea en la biblioteca.
3. Yo oigo a mi hermano.
4. Yo tengo quince años.
5. Yo conozco a un muchacho de Puerto Rico.
6. Yo vengo del cine.

p. 95 Transportation
Answers will vary.
Answers could include:
en autobús, en carro, en taxi, a pie, en metro
1. Voy a la escuela en autobús.
2. Voy al centro commercial en carro.
3. Voy al aeropuerto en taxi.
4. Voy a la tienda de videos a pie.
5. Voy a la joyería en metro.

p. 97 Vocabulary
caminar, correr, pasear, ir a pie

Sample Lesson Plan - 45 Minute Schedule

DAY 1

Unit Opener
- Anticipate/Activate prior knowledge: Present the *Almanaque* and the cultural notes. Use Map OHTs as needed. **10** MIN.

Etapa Opener
- Quick Start Review (TE, p. 82) **5** MIN.
- Have students look at the *Etapa* Opener and answer the *¿Qué ves?* questions, p. 82. **5** MIN.

En contexto: Vocabulario
- Quick Start Review (TE, p. 84) **5** MIN.
- Have students use context and pictures to learn *Etapa* vocabulary. **15** MIN.
- Have students answer the *Preguntas personales*, p. 85. **5** MIN.

DAY 2

En vivo: Diálogo
- Quick Start Review (TE, p. 86) **5** MIN.
- Review the Listening Strategy, p. 86. **5** MIN.
- Play audio or show video for the dialog, pp. 86–87. **10** MIN.
- Replay the audio or video, then have students take the roles of the characters. **10** MIN.

En acción: Vocabulario y gramática
- Quick Start Review (TE, p. 88) **5** MIN.
- Have students open to the *En Contexto*, pp. 84–85, for reference. Use OHT 5 and 6 to review vocabulary. **10** MIN.

Homework Option:
- Video Activities, Unit 4 Resource Book, pp. 23–25.

DAY 3

En acción (cont.)
- Check homework. **5** MIN.
- Play the video/audio. **5** MIN.
- Have students do *Actividad* 1 orally. **5** MIN.
- Do *Actividad* 2 orally. **5** MIN.
- Have students work in groups to do *Actividad* 3. **10** MIN.
- Read and discuss the *Nota Cultural*, p. 89. **5** MIN.
- Play the audio and do *Actividad* 4. **5** MIN.
- Read and discuss the *Nota cultural*, p. 90. **5** MIN.

DAY 4

En acción (cont.)
- Quick Start Review (TE, p. 92) **5** MIN.
- Have students work in pairs to do *Actividad* 5. **5** MIN.
- Ask volunteers to model their work on *Actividad* 5. **5** MIN.
- Present the *Vocabulario*, p. 91. **5** MIN.
- Do *Actividad* 6 orally. **5** MIN.
- Present *Gramática:* The Verb *decir*, p. 92. **5** MIN.
- Do *Actividad* 7 orally. **5** MIN.
- Have students work independently on *Actividad* 8. **5** MIN.
- Ask volunteers to share their work on *Actividad* 8. **5** MIN.

Homework Option:
- *Más práctica* Workbook, p. 5. *Para hispanohablantes* Workbook, p. 3.

DAY 5

En acción (cont.)
- Check homework. **5** MIN.
- Present the *Vocabulario*, p. 93. **5** MIN.
- Work with students to do *Actividad* 9 orally. **5** MIN.
- Ask students to write answers to *Actividad* 9. **5** MIN.
- Have students do *Actividad* 10 in pairs. **5** MIN.
- Call on some pairs to act out the roles in *Actividad* 10. **10** MIN.
- Read and discuss the *También se dice*, p. 94. **5** MIN.
- Read and discuss the *Conexiones*, p. 94. **5** MIN.

DAY 6

En acción (cont.)
- Quick Start Review (TE, p. 95) **5** MIN.
- Present *Gramática*: Using Prepositional Phrases to Express Location. **10** MIN.
- Do *Actividad* 11 orally with the class. **5** MIN.
- Have students write their answers to *Actividad* 11. **5** MIN.
- Have students work in pairs and present their work on *Actividad* 12. **10** MIN.
- Discuss the Speaking Strategy, p. 96. **5** MIN.
- Have students work in pairs to complete *Actividad* 13. **5** MIN.

Homework Option:
- *Más práctica* Workbook, pp. 6–7. *Para hispanohablantes* Workbook, pp. 4–5.

DAY 7

En acción (cont.)
- Check homework. **5** MIN.
- Quick Start Review (TE, p. 97) **5** MIN.
- Present *Gramática*: Regular Affirmative *tú* Commands, p. 97. **10** MIN.
- Have students write their responses to *Actividad* 14. **5** MIN.
- Have students work in pairs to do *Actividad* 15. **10** MIN.
- Call on some pairs to share their work on *Actividad* 15. **5** MIN.
- Read and discuss the *Conexiones*, p. 98. **5** MIN.

Homework Option:
- *Más práctica* Workbook, p. 8. *Para hispanohablantes* Workbook, p. 6.

DAY 8

En acción (cont.)
- Check homework. **5** MIN.
- Have students work in pairs on *Actividad* 16. **5** MIN.
- Have volunteer pairs model their work on *Actividad* 16. **5** MIN.
- Keep students in pairs to do *Actividad* 17. **5** MIN.
- Ask volunteers to present their conversations for *Actividad* 17. **5** MIN.
- Keep students in pairs to do *Actividad* 18. **5** MIN.
- Ask pairs to read their work for *Actividad* 18. **10** MIN.
- Read and discuss the *Nota Cultural*, p. 99. **5** MIN.

DAY 9

En acción (cont.)
- Present the *Vocabulario*, p. 100. **5 MIN.**
- Practice asking for directions. **5 MIN.**
- Have students work in groups to do *Actividad* 19. **5 MIN.**
- Ask groups to volunteer to model asking directions as assigned in *Actividad* 19. **10 MIN.**
- Play the audio and have students do *Actividad* 20. **10 MIN.**
- Sketch the map on p. 101 on the board, and ask students to mark the places in *Actividad* 20 on it. **10 MIN.**

DAY 10

En acción (cont.)
- Discuss the *Nota*, p. 101. Decide as a class how to say your school address in Spanish. **5 MIN.**
- Have students work independently to do *Actividad* 21. **10 MIN.**
- Ask students to volunteer to read their invitations from *Actividad* 21 for the class. **5 MIN.**
- Use Information Gap Activities, Unit 4 Resource Book, pp. 18–19; *Más comunicación*, p. R1. **10 MIN.**
- Discuss and demonstrate the *Pronunciación*, p. 101. **10 MIN.**
- Have students work in pairs to practice the *refrán*, p. 101. **5 MIN.**

DAY 11

En voces: Lectura
- Quick Start Review (TE, p. 102) **5 MIN.**
- Review the Reading Strategy, p. 102. **5 MIN.**
- Ask students to predict what the story is about. **5 MIN.**
- Have students read Benito Juárez, *un oaxaqueño por excelencia*, pp. 102–103 silently. **10 MIN.**
- Ask volunteers to read the story orally. **10 MIN.**
- Have students answer the *¿Comprendiste?* questions for the *Lectura*. (Answers, TE, p. 103) **5 MIN.**
- Work orally with students to answer the *¿Qué piensas?* questions for the *Lectura*, p. 103. **5 MIN.**

Homework Option:
- Have students review all of the *Gramática* boxes in *Etapa* 1 to prepare for *En uso*.

DAY 12

En uso: Repaso y más comunicación
- Answer grammar questions arising from the homework review. **5 MIN.**
- Quick Start Review (TE, p. 104) **5 MIN.**
- Present the *Repaso y más comunicación* using the Teaching Suggestions (TE, p. 104). **10 MIN.**
- Have students write *Actividad* 1. **10 MIN.**
- Check answers for *Actividad* 1 with the whole class. **5 MIN.**
- Work with students to do *Actividad* 2 orally. **10 MIN.**

DAY 13

En uso (cont.)
- Have students read and prepare to answer *Actividades* 3 and 4. **10 MIN.**
- Ask pairs of students to take the roles in *Actividad* 3. **10 MIN.**
- Present the Speaking Strategy, p. 106. **5 MIN.**
- Display a map and practice giving directions. **5 MIN.**
- Have students work in pairs to do *Actividad* 5. **5 MIN.**
- Ask some pairs to volunteer to share their work on *Actividad* 5 orally. **5 MIN.**
- Read and discuss the *Conexiones*, p. 106. **5 MIN.**

Homework Option:
- Have students complete the questions in the *Conexiones*, p. 106.

DAY 14

En resumen: Repaso de vocabulario
- Check homework. **5 MIN.**
- Quick Start Review (TE, p. 107) **10 MIN.**

En tu propia voz: Escritura
- Have students do the writing activity, *Actividad* 6, independently. **10 MIN.**
- Call on selected students to read their work from *Actividad* 6. **5 MIN.**
- Put students in groups of 3 and follow the Teaching Suggestions (TE, p. 107). **5 MIN.**
- Review grammar questions, etc., as necessary. **5 MIN.**
- Have students solve the *Juego*, p. 107 (Answer, TE, p. 107). **5 MIN.**

Homework Option:
- Have students study for the *Etapa* exam.

DAY 15

En resumen: Repaso de vocabulario
- Answer questions related to *Etapa* 1 content. **10 MIN.**
- Complete *Etapa* exam. **25 MIN.**

Ampliación
- Use a suggested project, game, or activity (TE, pp. 81A–81B) as students complete the exam.

Classroom Management Tip

Create Spanish-only situations
Provide plenty of situations in which students can display what they have learned. Give them a chance to learn and practice in private, and ask them to speak in front of the group when they are ready.

Have students research a typical Mexican town organized around a **zócalo** with **iglesia, ayuntamiento,** etc. Groups can create a movable town of shoe-box buildings. When the town is complete, students take turns describing where things are and giving directions for getting around.

Etapa Theme

Identifying places in a city, choosing transportation, and asking for and giving directions

Grammar Objectives

• Using the verb **decir**
• Using prepositions of location
• Using regular affirmative **tú** commands

Teaching Resource Options

Print

Block Scheduling Copymasters

Audiovisual

OHT 104, 113 (Quick Start)

Quick Start Review

♻ Vocabulary review

Use OHT 113 or write on board:
Write at least 3 items/expressions associated with these geographic regions (weather, clothing, activities, etc.):

1. la playa   3. el bosque
2. las montañas   4. el desierto

Answers

Answers will vary. Answers could include:
1. el verano, el traje de baño, esquiar en el agua, tomar el sol
2. hace frío, la nieve, esquiar, los árboles
3. hace calor, los shorts, sacar fotos, las plantas
4. hace/hay sol, el sombrero, las gafas de sol, tener sed

Teaching Suggestions
Previewing the Etapa

• Ask students to study the photo on pp. 82–83 (1 min.).
• Close books; ask students to share at least 3 things that they noticed.
• Reopen books and look at the picture again (1 min.); close books and share 3 more details.
• Ask students where the girl might be coming from and where she might be going.
• Use the **¿Qué ves?** questions to focus the discussion.

UNIDAD 4

ETAPA 1

¡A visitar a mi prima!

• Identify places

• Give addresses

• Choose transportation

• Request directions

• Give instructions

¿Qué ves?

Mira la foto del Zócalo de Oaxaca.

1. ¿La chica vive en Oaxaca o está visitando Oaxaca?
2. ¿Qué tiempo hace?
3. ¿Cuántos museos ves en el mapa?

OAXACA

- Museo Rufino Tamayo
- Museo de Arte Contemporáneo
- Av. Morelos
- Av. Independencia
- Catedral de Oaxaca
- Tinoco y Palacios
- 5 de Mayo
- Av. Juárez
- Zócalo
- Las Casas
- Palacio de Gobierno
- Mercado Juárez
- a Monte Albán

82

Middle School Classroom Management

Planning Ahead Collect floor plans of local museums or ask students to make maps of your school for use in the activities in this **Etapa**.

Peer Review Divide the class into small groups. Ask each group to come up with three more questions about the picture. Remind them that each member of the group is responsible for the accuracy of all of the questions. Have each group ask the rest of the class their questions. You may want to ask them to write their questions on the chalkboard.

Cross Cultural Connections

El mapa de Oaxaca Ask students to compare the map of Oaxaca to a map of their town. How does the street organization compare? Which buildings are the same? Which are different?

Culture Highlights

● **OAXACA** The region of Oaxaca, located in southeast Mexico, has a population of more than 3 million people, including many native groups. During pre-Columbian times, the region was inhabited by diverse ethnic groups, such as the Mixtecs and Zapotecs. Toward the middle of the 15th century, the Aztecs conquered the area and established a number of military points to control the transportation of merchandise.

● **LA CATEDRAL DE OAXACA** Construction of the cathedral in Oaxaca began in 1640, but suffered a series of setbacks and reconstructions after earthquakes and pillages. Inside the cathedral, there is an altar made of bronze imported from Italy, an antique pipe organ, and paintings from the 18th century.

● **MUSEO DE ARTE CONTEMPORÁNEO** The Museum of Contemporary Art, which opened in 1992, is located in a house that once belonged to an aristocratic family in Oaxaca. It contains the most important collections of Mexican modern art, including a retrospective of the work of the Oaxacan artist Rufino Tamayo.

Supplementary Vocabulary

la fuente	fountain
el mirador	gazebo
los globos	balloons
el (la) vendedor(a)	vendor
la maleta	suitcase

83

Teaching Middle School Students

Extra Help Ask yes/no questions about the photo. Help students to respond with full sentences, starting with **Sí** or **No**.

Native Speakers Ask native speakers to prepare their own collage like the one on pp. 80–81. Theirs should reflect their native country.

Multiple Intelligences

Interpersonal Have students imagine what the girl in the photo may be thinking. Ask them to write down their thoughts and then share them with the class.

Block Schedule

Retention Have students write down as many things as they can remember about Mexico from **Unidad 2**. Compile the lists to form a more complete review of Mexico. (For additional activities, see **Block Scheduling Copymasters**.)

Teaching Resource Options

Print

Unit 4 Resource Book
Video Activities, pp. 23–24
Videoscript, p. 26
Audioscript, p. 29
Audioscript *Para hispanohablantes,*
   p. 29

Audiovisual

OHT 107, 108, 109, 109A, 110, 110A,
113 (Quick Start)
Audio Program Cassette 10A / CD 10
Audio *Para hispanohablantes*
   Cassette 10A / CD 10
Video Program Videotape 4 / Videodisc
2B

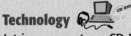

Search Chapter 2, Play to 3
U4E1 • En contexto (Vocabulary)

Technology

Intrigas y aventuras CD-ROM, Disc 1

🔔 Quick Start Review

♻️ Verb review

Use OHT 113 or write on the board:
Complete each sentence with the
correct form of the verb:

1. Mañana, yo ____ al bosque. (ir)
2. ¿Cuándo ____ Alma el museo?
   (visitar)
3. ¿A qué hora ____ las niñas? (llegar)
4. Nosotros ____ todos los días por
   el parque. (pasear)
5. ¿Te gusta ____ en el parque?
   (caminar)
6. ¿ ____ usted dónde está el teatro?
   (saber)
7. La maestra ____ la puerta. (cerrar)
8. Yo ____ de San Antonio. (venir)

Answers

1. voy	3. llegan	5. caminar	7. cierra
2. visita	4. paseamos	6. Sabe	8. vengo

Language Note

Point out that the word **farmacia** is like
familia, with the stress on the next-to-last
syllable. Both words end in a *-ya* sound,
unlike the word **día,** in which you hear
both vowels separately.

En contexto

VOCABULARIO

Rosa is taking a walk through the city of Oaxaca. She looks at a map
in order to find her way around.

el correo

la iglesia

la plaza

el café

B Allí está **el correo,** de donde mando
cartas. **La iglesia** es muy bonita.

A Hay mucho que ver en Oaxaca.
¡Mira **el mapa**! Es divertido
pasear. Primero, voy a **una
plaza.** Después, descanso en
un café y tomo un refresco.

la farmacia

C Si estoy enferma y necesito medicina, voy a
la farmacia. Está en **la calle** Bustamante.

84 ochenta y cuatro
Unidad 4

Middle School Classroom Community

TPR Ask students to look at the illustration on pages
84–85. As you name different features (**parque,
iglesia, plaza,** etc.), have students point to them.

Portfolio Ask students to draw and label maps of
their school with as much detail as possible.

Rubric

Criteria	Scale	
Accuracy of information	1 2 3 4 5	**A** = 13–15 pts.
Logical organization	1 2 3 4 5	**B** = 10–12 pts. **C** = 7–9 pts.
Vocabulary use	1 2 3 4 5	**D** = 4–6 pts. **F** = < 4 pts.

el banco

el hotel

la estación
de autobuses

D Voy al **banco** por la tarde. Si quieres visitar la ciudad, hay **un hotel** muy bonito para pasar la noche.

E Llego a **la estación de autobuses** de Oaxaca. Acabo de venir de la capital.

la esquina

F Para ir del **centro** al **aeropuerto** voy por esta **avenida**. Hay un taxi en **la esquina**.

Preguntas personales

1. ¿Te gusta ir al centro?
2. ¿Usas la estación de autobuses o el aeropuerto?
3. ¿Prefieres pasar un rato en un café o en una plaza?
4. ¿Dónde compras medicina?
5. ¿Adónde vas si estás en otra ciudad y tienes sueño?

ochenta y cinco
Etapa 1

85

Teaching Suggestions
Introducing Vocabulary

• Have students look at pages 84–85. Use OHT 107 and 108 and Audio Cassette 10A / CD 10 to present the vocabulary.

• Ask the Comprehension Questions in order of yes/no (questions 1–3), either/or (questions 4–6), and simple word or phrase (questions 7–10). Expand by adding similar questions.

• Use the TPR activity to reinforce the meaning of individual words.

• Use the video vocabulary presentation for review and reinforcement.

Comprehension Questions

1. ¿Hay mucho que ver en Oaxaca? (Sí.)
2. ¿Es posible pasear en Oaxaca? (Sí.)
3. ¿Va Rosa primero a un café? (No.)
4. ¿Quiere Rosa tomar una merienda o un refresco? (un refresco)
5. ¿De dónde manda cartas, del correo o de la iglesia? (del correo)
6. Cuando Rosa está enferma, ¿va a la farmacia o a la plaza? (a la farmacia)
7. ¿En qué calle está la farmacia? (en la calle Bustamante)
8. ¿Adónde va Rosa por la tarde? (al banco)
9. Si quieres visitar a Oaxaca, ¿dónde puedes pasar la noche? (en un hotel)
10. ¿Cómo puedes ir del centro al aeropuerto? (en un taxi)

Supplementary Vocabulary

el edificio	building
la acera	sidewalk
el semáforo	traffic light
la estación de policía	police station
la estación de bomberos	fire station
el hospital	hospital
la estación de metro	subway station
la estación de tren	train station

■ Block Schedule

Retention Expand the vocabulary by having students write definitions in Spanish for the new words. For example: **el correo es donde mando cartas.**

Teaching Middle School Students

Challenge Ask students to devise additional questions about visiting a new city.

Multiple Intelligences

Visual Students may want to find pictures of Oaxaca on the Internet or through a travel agency. Ask students to share their pictures with the class, identifying each one.

Verbal Have pairs of students play **Más calor, más frío.** Student A secretly picks an intersection on the map. Student B starts at the corner of **5 de Mayo** and **Murguia** and guesses a route through the city as Student A indicates whether he or she is getting warmer or colder. They can gesture with their hands to indicate no change.

Teaching Resource Options

Print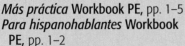

Más práctica Workbook PE, pp. 1–5
Para hispanohablantes Workbook
PE, pp. 1–2
Block Scheduling Copymasters
Unit 4 Resource Book
  Más práctica Workbook TE, pp. 1–4
  Para hispanohablantes Workbook
  TE, pp. 9–10
  Video Activities, pp. 23–24
  Videoscript, p. 27
  Audioscript, p. 29
  Audioscript *Para hispanohablantes,*
  p. 29

Audiovisual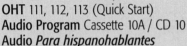

OHT 111, 112, 113 (Quick Start)
Audio Program Cassette 10A / CD 10
Audio *Para hispanohablantes*
  Cassette 10A / CD 10
Video Program Videotape 4 /
  Videodisc 2B

Search Chapter 3, Play to 4
U4E1 • En vivo (Dialog)

Technology

Intrigas y aventuras CD-ROM, Disc 1

Quick Start Review

🔄 Greetings

Use OHT 113 or write on the board:
Write a brief dialog between 2 people
meeting for the first time.

Answers
Answers will vary. Answers could include:

A: Hola, me llamo Carlos.
B: Encantada, Carlos.
A: Y tú, ¿cómo te llamas?
B: Me llamo Elena.
A: Mucho gusto, Elena.
B: El gusto es mío, Carlos.

Gestures

Before reading the **Diálogo**, have students
pay close attention to scenes 3, 4, 5, 6, 8,
and 10. Ask them if the gestures pictured
help them predict what is going to be
said in the **Diálogo**. Discuss students'
predictions.

   DIÁLOGO

Visita a Oaxaca

Rosa   Carlos   Sofía

PARA ESCUCHAR • STRATEGY: LISTENING

Listen and follow directions How you remember directions gives
clues about the ways you prefer to learn. Listen to Carlos's
directions. Which is most natural for you, to (1) repeat key words,
(2) write key words, (3) use gestures, (4) draw a map, or (5) do
something else? Your choices indicate how you prefer to learn.
Use them to help you follow directions as you listen.

1▶ Rosa: Perdone, ¿puede usted
decirme dónde queda la calle
Morelos?
Hombre: No, señorita. Perdone,
pero no sé dónde queda esa calle.

5▶ Carlos: Ésta es la avenida
Constitución. Camina por esta
calle. Allí vas a ver un banco.
Rosa: ¿Dices que hay un banco?
Carlos: Sí, hay un banco al lado
de una farmacia.

6▶ Carlos: Vas a llegar a un parque. Cruza
el parque. Enfrente de la estatua está la
calle Morelos.
Rosa: Muchas gracias, eh…
Carlos: Carlos, me llamo Carlos.
Rosa: Rosa, soy Rosa.

7▶ Carlos: Salgo del trabajo a las siete.
Si quieres, salimos a comer con tu
prima.
Rosa: Me gustaría. A ver qué dice
mi prima. ¿Puedo llevar el mapa?
Carlos: Sí, claro que sí.

86 ochenta y seis
Unidad 4

Middle School Classroom Community

TPR Write school destinations on index cards. Ask
volunteers to choose a card and mime going to the
destination. As the mime makes each change of
direction, he or she stops and waits for the class to say
what has just been done. When the mime "arrives" at
the destination, the class guesses where it is.

Group Activity After reading the dialog, ask groups
of 3 students to work together to create their own

mini-dialog, asking how to get to a location in your
school or town. Ask them to act it out for the class.

Learning Scenario Assign one student the role of a
new, native Spanish speaker in your school and another
student the role of principal of the school. Have the
principal call on different students in the class to help
the newcomer find his way. The newcomer may ask,
"Perdone, ¿puede usted decirme dónde queda…?"

2 ▶ Rosa: Buenos días. Vengo a visitar a mi prima. No sé dónde queda su nueva casa. Busco esta dirección.

3 ▶ Carlos: ¡Ah, sí!, claro, la calle Morelos. Desde aquí es muy fácil llegar.
Rosa: ¡Ay, qué bueno! ¿Queda lejos de aquí?

4 ▶ Carlos: A pie llegas en diez minutos. Pero llegas más rápido en taxi.
Rosa: Prefiero caminar. ¿Puedes decirme cómo llego?

8 ▶ Sofía: ¡Rosa!
Rosa: ¡Sofía! ¿Cómo estás?
Sofía: ¡Qué sorpresa! ¿Qué haces por aquí?
Rosa: ¡Vengo a visitarte!
Sofía: Pasa, pasa, prima.

9 ▶ Rosa: ¡Qué bonita es la nueva casa de tu familia! ¿Dónde está mi tía?
Sofía: Está haciendo algunas compras.
Rosa: Yo también quiero ir de compras. Es el cumpleaños de mi mamá y quiero comprar algo bonito para ella.

10 ▶ Sofía: Yo digo que el mercado tiene las cosas más bonitas. ¿Por qué no vamos mañana por la mañana? ¿Qué dices?
Rosa: Me encantaría.
Sofía: Entonces, mañana, ¡al mercado! Y después, salimos a pasear por la plaza.

ochenta y siete **87**
Etapa 1

Teaching Middle School Students

Multiple Intelligences

Kinesthetic Ask a student to stand and respond as you give directions for walking around the classroom. Have the rest of the class monitor his or her progress. Any student who thinks a mistake has been made stands and shows where he or she believes the walker should be. If correct, this student takes over as walker.

Verbal Ask students to work in small groups to act out the dialog. Ask them to work in pairs using the map on pages 84–85 and ask directions to a location on that map.

• Prepare students for listening by focusing on the dialog context. Reintroduce the characters and the setting by asking yes/no, either/or, or simple answer questions, such as: **¿Cómo se llama la chica? ¿Está Rosa en la Ciudad de México? ¿De dónde viene Rosa, de Miami o de la Ciudad de México?**

• Use the video, audio cassette, or CD to present the dialog. The expanded dialog on video offers additional listening practice opportunities.

Video Synopsis

• Rosa goes to Oaxaca to visit her cousin Sofía. She asks people for directions to Sofía's house. For a complete transcript of the video dialog, see p. 81D.

Comprehension Questions

1. ¿Sabe el hombre dónde queda la calle Morelos? (No.)
2. ¿Viene Rosa a visitar a su prima? (Sí.)
3. ¿Es difícil llegar a la calle Morelos desde la tienda? (No.)
4. ¿Llegas en diez minutos a pie? (Sí.)
5. ¿Prefiere Rosa ir en taxi o a pie? (a pie)
6. ¿Está el banco en la avenida Constitución o en la calle Morelos? (en la avenida Constitución)
7. ¿Qué hay al lado del banco, un hotel o una farmacia? (una farmacia)
8. ¿Qué hay en el parque? (una estatua)
9. ¿Dónde está la tía de Rosa? (Está haciendo algunas compras.)
10. ¿Por qué quiere Rosa ir de compras con Sofía? (Porque es el cumpleaños de su mamá.)

Block Schedule

Variety First, have students write a 2-sentence description of each character: Rosa, Carlos, and Sofía. Then have them write a 3–5 sentence summary of the dialog. Combine the best descriptions and summaries to come up with a dialog résumé. (For additional activities, see **Block Scheduling Copymasters.**)

Teaching Resource Options

Print 📖

Unit 4 Resource Book
Video Activities, p. 25
Videoscript, p. 28
Audioscript, pp. 29–30
Audioscript *Para hispanohablantes*,
   pp. 29–30

Audiovisual 🎧

OHT 114 (Quick Start)
Audio Program Cassettes 10A, 10B /
   CD 10
Audio *Para hispanohablantes*
   Cassette 10A / CD 10
Video Program Videotape 4 /
   Videodisc 2B

🔔 Quick Start Review

 Video review

Use OHT 114 or write on the board:
Complete the sentences according to
the video.

1. ¿Puede usted decirme dónde ____
   la calle Morelos?
2. No sé dónde queda su nueva
   casa. Busco esta ____.
3. ____ ____ llegas en diez minutos.
4. Sí, hay un banco ____ ____ ____
   una farmacia.
5. ____ ____ la estatua está la calle
   Morelos.

Answers *See p. 81D.*

 Objective: Controlled practice
Listening comprehension/vocabulary

Answers (See script, p. 81D.)
1. c
2. a
3. e
4. b
5. d

En acción

VOCABULARIO Y GRAMÁTICA

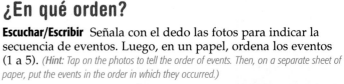

OBJECTIVES

- Identify places
- Give addresses
- Choose transportation
- Request directions
- Give instructions
- *Use the verb* **decir**
- *Use prepositions of location*
- *Use regular affirmative* **tú** *commands*

1 ¿En qué orden?

Escuchar/Escribir Señala con el dedo las fotos para indicar la secuencia de eventos. Luego, en un papel, ordena los eventos (1 a 5). *(Hint: Tap on the photos to tell the order of events. Then, on a separate sheet of paper, put the events in the order in which they occurred.)*

a. Rosa habla con Carlos.

b. Rosa llega a la casa de su prima.

c. Rosa habla con un hombre en la calle.

d. Rosa habla con Sofía sobre el mercado.

e. Rosa recibe el mapa de Carlos.

88 ochenta y ocho
Unidad 4

Middle School Classroom Management

Organizing Group Work When students work in groups, the class noise level can get very high. Brainstorm with the class to make a list of group work guidelines that keeps the noise to a manageable level, then test this list as students work on **Actividad 3**.

Peer Review When students have completed **Actividades 1–3**, have them trade papers with a partner. Ask them to review the answers and discuss any discrepancies with each other before correcting their own work.

ACTIVIDAD 2

La visita

Escuchar/Leer Rosa busca la casa de su prima. Completa las oraciones. *(Hint: Rosa is looking for her cousin's new house. Complete the sentences.)*

modelo

Rosa visita (Guanajuato / Oaxaca).

Rosa visita Oaxaca.

1. Rosa busca (la calle Morelos / el Zócalo).
2. Rosa prefiere (caminar / ir en taxi).
3. Al lado del banco hay (una iglesia / una farmacia).
4. La calle Morelos está enfrente de (un banco / una estatua).
5. Sofía (no sabe / sabe) que Rosa viene a visitarla.

ACTIVIDAD 3

¿Dónde queda?

Hablar Estás en una ciudad que no conoces bien. Escoge un lugar de la lista. Pregunta a tu compañero(a) dónde queda el lugar. Cambien de papel. *(Hint: You are in a new city. Choose a place from the list. Ask your partner where it is. Change roles.)*

modelo

Estudiante A: *¿Puede usted decirme dónde queda la farmacia?*

Estudiante B: *La farmacia queda al lado del hotel.*

el aeropuerto	la farmacia
el banco	el hotel
la iglesia	el parque
la estación	el mercado

NOTA CULTURAL

Large supermarkets exist in cities in Spanish-speaking countries, but small, independent shops are more popular. Most shoppers prefer to buy their groceries at neighborhood shops rather than at supermarkets because they enjoy the personal attention they receive from the staff. Some also believe the produce is fresher in small shops.

ochenta y nueve
Etapa 1 **89**

ACTIVIDAD 2 Objetive: Controlled practice Listening comprehension/vocabulary

Answers (See script, p. 81D.)
1. la calle Morelos
2. caminar
3. una farmacia
4. una estatua
5. no sabe

ACTIVIDAD 3 Objetive: Transitional practice Vocabulary

Answers will vary.

Language Note

Cognados y cognados falsos After studying the cognates in **Unidad 4**, have each student look up five more in a bilingual dictionary, share their finds, and add them to **El diccionario de cognados españoles** begun in **Unidad 1**. Whenever they find another cognate, have them take note of its origin, when it came into use, and whether it has the same meaning both in Spanish and English today. Explain the idea of false cognates; give examples, such as **colegio, profesor,** and **original** and ask students which one they think may be false (**colegio** does not mean "college").

Teaching Middle School Students

Extra Help Ask students to change the subject in **Actividad 2** to **Rosa y yo** and help them work with the **nosotros** form.

Multiple Intelligences

Visual Ask students to make a poster for the class illustrating the cognates in **Actividad 3**. They will write only the Spanish word and indicate the meaning with drawings or cutouts.

Verbal Ask students to work in pairs to create a dialog that takes place in a shop.

Interpersonal Ask students to describe to each other where a shop, bank, etc., are in relation to each other in your neighborhood. Encourage them to politely interrupt when they need clarification on a point.

Block Schedule

Variety Do a variation of **Actividad 3** related to your town or city. Working in pairs, one student plays a Spanish-speaking visitor. He or she asks the other student whether certain places or stores are found in your town or city. Students should take turns playing each role.

Teaching Resource Options

Print

Unit 4 Resource Book
Video Activities, p. 25
Videoscript, p. 28
Audioscript, p. 29–30
Audioscript, *Para hispanohablentes*,
p. 29–30

Audiovisual

Audio Program Cassettes 10A, 10B /
CD 10
Audio *Para hispanohablentes* 4 / 10B
Videodisc 2B

4 Objective: Transitional practice
Listening comprehension/vocabulary

 Seasons, weather

Answers (See script, p. 81D.)
1. d
2. b
3. a
4. c

5 Objective: Controlled practice
Vocabulary

Hay

Answers
1. ¿Hay una farmacia por aquí?
2. ¿Hay un banco por aquí?
3. ¿Hay un mercado por aquí?
4. ¿Hay una iglesia por aquí?
5. ¿Hay un parque por aquí?
6. ¿Hay un hotel por aquí?

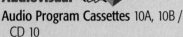

¿En qué estación?

Escuchar Escucha las descripciones. ¿Qué estación describe cada una? *(Hint: Listen to the descriptions. What season does each describe?)*

a. la primavera
b. el verano
c. el otoño
d. el invierno

NOTA CULTURAL

In Mexico you can get almost everywhere by bus. There are first- and second-class services. If you travel on a first-class bus, there is an attendant who serves snacks and beverages. On some major routes, you can even watch videos. Train travel is also popular, although the service is not as extensive or as reliable as bus travel.

La nueva comunidad

Hablar Una muchacha quiere saber qué hay en su nueva comunidad. ¿Qué pregunta? *(Hint: A girl wants to know what is in her new community. What does she ask?)*

modelo

¿Hay un correo por aquí?

Nota

The word **por**, which most often means *for*, has many uses and meanings.

Camina **por** esta calle.	Walk **along/down** this street.
Pasa **por** la tienda.	Come (Pass) **by** the store.
¿Qué haces **por** aquí?	What are you doing **around** here?

Middle School Classroom Community

Learning Scenario Ask students to work in small groups to plan a shopping trip. Have them make a list of school supplies and school clothes, then plan which shops they will need to visit to make all of their purchases.

Portfolio Ask students to illustrate and label each of the place names they have learned.

Rubric

Criteria	Scale	
Creativity	1 2 3 4 5	A = 13–15 pts.
Logical organization	1 2 3 4 5	B = 10–12 pts.
Vocabulary use/spelling	1 2 3 4 5	C = 7–9 pts.
		D = 4–6 pts.
		F = < 4 pts.

ACTIVIDAD
6

¿Adónde van?

Hablar Rosa y Sofía van de compras. Di adónde van para comprar las siguientes cosas. *(Hint: Rosa and Sofía are shopping. Say where they go to buy things.)*

modelo

Van a la pastelería.

 1.

 2.

 3.

 4.

 5.

 6.

 7.

 8.

Vocabulario

Las tiendas

el centro comercial

la carnicería

la joyería

la librería

la panadería

la papelería

la pastelería

la tienda de música y videos

la zapatería

¿A qué tiendas vas de compras?

Teaching Middle School Students

Native Speakers Ask students to describe a store that might be different from one in your town, such as a bakery or a stationer's.

Multiple Intelligences

Kinesthetic Bring in objects from different stores and display them. Ask students to come up, choose an object, hold it up, and say what store it comes from.

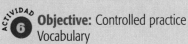

ACTIVIDAD
6
Objective: Controlled practice
Vocabulary

Answers

1. Van a la tienda de música y videos.
2. Van a la joyería.
3. Van a la zapatería.
4. Van a la carnicería.
5. Van al café.
6. Van a la papelería.
7. Van a la farmacia.
8. Van al correo.

Teaching Suggestions
Teaching Vocabulary

Have students practice the **Vocabulario** in pairs. One student names a familiar store in their town/city. The other says what kind of store it is.

Critical Thinking

Ask students what they notice about the names of the stores listed in the **Vocabulario**, and have them prepare a presentation about the origins of the words. (The store names end in **-ía**, and the names come from the items the stores sell.)

Block Schedule

FunBreak Ask each student to write the name of an item on each of 6 index cards. Have them write the names of shops where the items might be found on 6 more cards. Then have pairs of students play Go Fish with their cards. They shuffle all their cards together and deal 6 cards to each player. The rest are the Go Fish pile. Players ask each other for cards that will give them pairs (a shop and an item that can be purchased there). If the opponent hasn't got the requested card, the player must pick another from the Go Fish pile.

Teaching Resource Options

Print 📖

Más práctica Workbook PE, p. 5
Para hispanohablantes Workbook PE, p. 3
Block Scheduling Copymasters
Unit 4 Resource Book
  Más práctica Workbook TE, pp. 6–7
  Para hispanohablantes Workbook
    TE, pp. 12–13
  Information Gap Activities, p. 17

Audiovisual 📽️

OHT 114 (Quick Start)

Technology 💻

Intrigas y aventuras CD-ROM, Disc 1

Quick Start Review

♻️ Verbs with irregular **yo** forms

Use OHT 114 or write on the board:
Write sentences using the elements
given:

1. yo / saber / hablar español
2. yo / hacer / mi tarea en la
   biblioteca
3. yo / oír / a mi hermano
4. yo / tener / quince años
5. yo / conocer / a un muchacho
   de Puerto Rico
6. yo / venir / del cine

Answers *See p. 81D.*

Teaching Suggestions
Teaching the Verb decir

Point out that **decir** means *to say* or
to tell. Give examples: **A ver qué dice
mi prima. ¿Puedes decirme dónde
queda la calle Morelos?**

Actividad 7 Objective: Controlled practice
Decir

Answers
1. Ella dice que en la ciudad hay calles bonitas.
2. Rosa y Sofía dicen que en el Zócalo hay gente interesante.
3. Nosotras decimos que en el parque hay música.
4. Yo digo que en los restaurantes hay comida regional.
5. Tú dices que en los museos hay artículos antiguos.
6. Las primas dicen que en el centro comercial hay muchas tiendas.

GRAMÁTICA

The Verb decir

To talk about what someone says, use the verb **decir**. The verb **decir**
means *to say* or *to tell.* It has several irregular forms in the present tense.

digo	**decimos**
dices	**decís**
dice	**dicen**

Only the **nosotros(as)** and
vosotros(as) forms are regular.

Sofía says:
—Yo **digo que** el mercado
tiene las cosas más bonitas.
I say that the market has the prettiest things.

Note that **decir que**
means *to say that…*

Actividad 7 Gramática

¿Qué dicen?

Hablar La gente dice que hay
mucho para hacer en Oaxaca.
¿Quién dice qué? *(Hint: People say
that there are many things to do in Oaxaca.
Who says what?)*

modelo

Carlos / las iglesias / arte regional

Carlos dice que en **las iglesias** hay
arte regional.

1. Ella / la ciudad /
   calles bonitas

2. Rosa y Sofía / el Zócalo /
   gente interesante

3. nosotras / el parque /
   música

4. yo / los restaurantes /
   comida regional

5. tú / los museos /
   artículos antiguos

6. las primas / el centro
   comercial/ muchas tiendas

92 noventa y dos
Unidad 4

Middle School Classroom Community

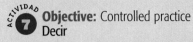

Paired/Group Activity Ask students to work in
pairs or small groups to write captions or a dialog to
go with the photos in **Actividad 7**.

Portfolio Have students interview each other, asking
¿Qué dices hoy? They should write and date the
responses. Have them come back to this activity on
later dates and compare responses. Example: **Jennie**

dice que hoy es su cumpleaños. Carlos dice que hoy
está contento porque…

Rubric

Criteria	Scale	
Vocabulary use	1 2 3 4 5	A = 13–15 pts.
Logical sentence structure/order	1 2 3 4 5	B = 10–12 pts.
Grammar/spelling accuracy	1 2 3 4 5	C = 7–9 pts.
		D = 4–6 pts.
		F = < 4 pts.

ACTIVIDAD 8 Gramática

¿De dónde salen?

Escribir Rosa y Sofía ven a la gente que sale de varios lugares. ¿De dónde sale cada persona? *(Hint: Rosa and Sofía see people coming out of various places. Where does each person come from?)*

Nota

Salir means *to leave* or *to go out*. It has an irregular **yo** form: **salgo**. Its other forms are regular.

1. Beatriz _____ del cine.
2. Juan y Pedro _____ de la librería.
3. Yo _____ de la panadería.
4. Nosotros _____ de la farmacia.
5. Tú _____ del correo.
6. Ustedes _____ del banco.
7. Carlos _____ de la tienda de música y videos.
8. Rosa y Sofía _____ del café.

■ **MÁS PRÁCTICA** *cuaderno* p. 5
■ **PARA HISPANOHABLANTES** *cuaderno* p. 3

ACTIVIDAD 9

¿Qué modo?

Hablar/Escribir La gente sale para varios lugares. ¿Qué modo de transporte usan? *(Hint: People are leaving for various places. What means of transportation are they using?)*

modelo

Miguel / el museo

Miguel *sale para* **el museo.** *Va* **en taxi.**

en autobús
en tren
en barco
en avión
en taxi
a pie

1. Rosa y Sofía / el centro comercial
2. nosotros /la Ciudad de México
3. usted / San Juan
4. Félix / Miami
5. tú / el correo
6. yo / ¿?

Vocabulario

De viaje

manejar *to drive*
viajar *to travel*
el viaje *trip*

a pie
en autobús
en avión
en barco
en carro
en metro
en moto(cicleta)
en taxi
en tren

¿Cómo prefieres viajar?

noventa y tres
Etapa 1 **93**

Teaching Middle School Students

Extra Help If students have not yet made a set of verb flash cards, have them start now with **decir** and **salir**. They write the infinitive on one side of the card and the present-tense forms on the back. As you (or they) discover troublesome verbs, have them add to the collection. Ask each student to find a practice buddy to work with regularly, using the flash cards.

Multiple Intelligences

Logical/Mathematical Ask students to interview classmates about how they get to school. Summarize findings on a graph showing how many come by car, bus, subway, bicycle, or on foot.

ACTIVIDAD 8 **Objective:** Controlled practice
Salir

Answers
1. sale
2. salen
3. salgo
4. salimos
5. sales
6. salen
7. sale
8. salen

ACTIVIDAD 9 **Objective:** Transitional practice
Salir/ir/vocabulary

Answers
Modes of transportation may vary.
1. Rosa y Sofía salen para el centro comercial. Van en autobús / a pie.
2. Nosotras salimos para la Ciudad de México. Vamos en avión.
3. Usted sale para San Juan. Va en avión.
4. Félix sale para Miami. Va en tren.
5. Tú sales para el correo. Vas en taxi.
6. Yo salgo para... Voy en / a...

Language Notes

- Students may use the word **motocicleta** or the shortened form **moto** to refer to a motorcycle. Both are feminine.
- **Manejar** is usually used in Latin America to talk about driving. **Conducir** is usually used in Spain. **Guiar** is used in Puerto Rico.

▮ Block Schedule

FunBreak In groups, have students create 3-D cities to use throughout the **Etapa.** Use posterboard for the base and have students draw the streets and empty spots for buildings, parks, etc. For the buildings, use either houses from board games or cutouts. For the parks, student can make trees from art supplies. They should also make labels for each building, park, etc. Use the cities to practice vocabulary and giving directions. Students can change the location of the buildings and the labels to add variety to their activities. (For additional activities, see **Block Scheduling Copymasters.**)

Teaching Resource Options

Print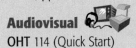

Más práctica Workbook PE, pp. 6–7
Para hispanohablantes Workbook PE, pp. 4–5
Block Scheduling Copymasters
Unit 4 Resource Book
  Más práctica Workbook TE, pp. 6–7
  Para hispanohablantes Workbook TE, pp. 12–13

Audiovisual

OHT 114 (Quick Start)

Technology

Intrigas y aventuras CD-ROM, Disc 1

ACTIVIDAD 10 Objective: Open-ended practice
Vocabulary/**gustar**/**decir**

Answers

Answers will vary but must contain the following elements.

1. ¿Cómo le gusta viajar a tu hermano(a)? Mi hermano(a) dice que le gusta viajar...
2. ¿Cómo te gusta viajar? Yo digo que me gusta viajar...
3. ¿Cómo les gusta viajar a tus amigos? Mis amigos dicen que les gusta...
4. ¿Cómo les gusta viajar a ti y a tu familia? Decimos que nos gusta...
5. ¿Cómo le gusta viajar a tu maestro(a)? Mi maestro(a) dice que le gusta...
6. ¿Cómo les gusta viajar a tus padres? Dicen que les gusta...
7. ¿Cómo le gusta viajar a tu abuelo? Mi abuelo dice que le gusta viajar...
8. ¿Cómo le gusta viajar a tu tía? Mi tía dice que le gusta viajar...
9. ¿Cómo les gusta viajar a tus primas? Mis primas dicen que les gusta...
10. ¿Cómo les gusta viajar a ti y a tu amigo? Decimos que nos gusta...

Para hacer

Answers

2–11–75, 2–08–58,
2–10–10, 2–30–92,
2–10–01

Teaching Note

Extend the **Conexiones** by noting that in some countries there is a person on the **farmacia** staff with special medical expertise who will make house calls in cases of need.

¿Cómo les gusta viajar?

Hablar Con un(a) compañero(a), hablen sobre cómo les gusta viajar a estas personas. *(Hint: With a classmate, talk about how these people like to travel.)*

modelo

tus primos

Estudiante A: *¿Cómo les gusta viajar a **tus primos**?*
Estudiante B: *Mis primos dicen que les gusta viajar en moto.*

1. tu hermano(a)
2. tú
3. tus amigos
4. tú y tu familia
5. tu maestro(a)
6. tus padres
7. tu abuelo
8. tu tía
9. tus primas
10. tú y tu amigo

También se dice

There are different ways to talk about cars and driving.

CARS
- el auto(móvil): many countries
- el coche: Spain, parts of South America
- el carro: Mexico, Central America

DRIVING
- conducir: Spain
- manejar: Latin America
- guiar: Puerto Rico

Conexiones

La salud In Spanish-speaking countries, **farmacias** are linked together to offer 24-hour service. If one is closed during late-night hours, it will post a sign indicating a nearby establishment that is open.

PARA HACER: What telephone numbers would you write down to call these *farmacias*?

¡YO MANEJO EL CARRO!

¡YO CONDUZCO EL COCHE!

Middle School Classroom Community

Cooperative Learning Ask students to work in groups of 4 to prepare and use a list of survey questions about free time using **gustar**. Student 1 writes 5 questions. Student 2 duplicates the survey. Student 3 distributes and collects the surveys. Student 4 compiles the results. Then the entire group plans how to report their results to the class.

Storytelling Ask students to make up a character who has silly tastes and tell a short story about him or her. You may want to allow thinking/outlining time instead of requiring extemporaneous stories.

GRAMÁTICA

Using Prepositional Phrases to Express Location

When you talk about where things are located, use **prepositions**. Here are some common ones.

detrás del **taxi**

al lado del **banco**

a la izquierda de **la carnicería**

entre **la farmacia y la panadería**

lejos de **esta calle**

cerca del **taxi**

enfrente del **banco**

a la derecha de **la carnicería**

PUERTO ANGEL
AEROPUERTO 200 km

- **Rosa está cerca del taxi.**
  Rosa is near the taxi.

- **El banco está detrás del taxi.**
  The bank is behind the taxi.

- **El taxi está enfrente del banco.**
  The taxi is in front of the bank.

- **El policía está al lado del banco.**
  The policeman is beside the bank.

- **La farmacia está a la izquierda de la carnicería.**
  The pharmacy is to the left of the butcher's shop.

- **La carnicería está entre la farmacia y la panadería.**
  The butcher's shop is between the pharmacy and the bakery.

- **La panadería está a la derecha de la carnicería.**
  The bakery is to the right of the butcher's shop.

- **El aeropuerto está lejos de esta calle.**
  The airport is far from this street.

> Use **de** when the preposition is followed by a **specific location**.

ACTIVIDAD 11 Gramática ¿Dónde está?

Hablar/Escribir Explica dónde están las tiendas de la foto.
(Hint: Explain where the stores from the photo are.)

1. La carnicería está (a la izquierda / a la derecha) de la farmacia.
2. El taxi está (cerca / lejos) de Rosa.
3. El banco está (enfrente / detrás) del taxi.
4. La panadería está (cerca / lejos) del aeropuerto.
5. La carnicería está (a la izquierda / a la derecha) de la panadería.

■ **MÁS PRÁCTICA** *cuaderno pp. 6–7*   ■ **PARA HISPANOHABLANTES** *cuaderno pp. 4–5*

noventa y cinco
Etapa 1   **95**

Teaching Middle School Students

Extra Help Give each student 5 small pieces of paper, each in a different color for which students have the Spanish word. Ask them to work in pairs, taking turns telling each other where to put their pencils in relation to their slips of paper.

Native Speakers Ask your native speakers to share new vocabulary that names kinds of shops that have not yet been studied in this course.

Multiple Intelligences

Visual Ask students to draw and label cartoons illustrating the prepositions of location. You may want to display them in the class.

Teaching Suggestions
Teaching Using Prepositional Phrases to Express Location
Explain that these words are important for communicating where things are. Use manipulatives to reinforce the meanings of the prepositions.

ACTIVIDAD 11 Objective: Controlled practice
Vocabulary

Answers
1. a la derecha   4. lejos
2. cerca   5. a la izquierda
3. detrás

Quick Wrap-up
Do a brief TPR activity to practice prepositions of locations. Give commands such as the following:
Paco, dale tu lápiz al estudiante que está cerca de la puerta. Oscar, dale la mano a la estudiante que está detrás de Nora…

Block Schedule
Change of Pace Have students draw a map with their house/apartment as the central location. The map can be of your town/city, of your state, or even of the world. Have them add pictures and labels of stores, monuments, places they are interested in going to, etc. Then have them write sentences saying how they go to each place. For example: **Voy al centro comercial a pie. Voy a Argentina en avión.** (For additional activities, see **Block Scheduling Copymasters.**)

Teaching Resource Options

Print

Block Scheduling Copymasters
Unit 4 Resource Book
  Information Gap Activities, pp. 18–19
  Audioscript, p. 30
  Audioscript *Para hispanohablantes*,
    p. 30

Audiovisual

OHT 115 (Quick Start)
Audio *Para hispanohablantes*
  Cassette 10A / CD 10
Audio Program Cassettes 10A, 10B /
  CD 10

Technology

Intrigas y aventuras CD-ROM, Disc 1

 Objective: Transitional practice
Vocabulary

Answers

Answers may vary.
1. ¿Dónde está el banco? Está al lado del hotel.
2. ¿Dónde está el café? Está entre la joyería y la papelería.
3. ¿Dónde está la panadería? Está a la izquierda de la zapatería.
4. ¿Dónde está el correo? Está enfrente de la librería.
5. ¿Dónde está la papelería? Está al lado del café.
6. ¿Dónde está la joyería? Está detrás del banco.
7. ¿Dónde está el hotel? Está entre el banco y la librería.
8. ¿Dónde está la librería? Está a la derecha del hotel.

Objective: Open-ended practice
Vocabulary

Answers will vary.

¿Dónde está?

Hablar Tu compañero(a) y tú están en el centro comercial. Conversen sobre dónde están estas tiendas. *(Hint: You and a classmate are at the mall. Talk about where these stores are.)*

modelo

la zapatería

Estudiante A: ¿Dónde está **la zapatería**?

Estudiante B: *Está a la derecha de la panadería, a la izquierda del correo.*
    o: *Está entre la panadería y el correo.*

1. banco
2. café
3. panadería
4. correo
5. papelería
6. joyería
7. hotel
8. libería

 **Las tiendas**

PARA CONVERSAR
STRATEGY: SPEAKING
Recognize and use set phrases
Think of the expressions you use as a whole instead of constructing them a word at a time. This helps you think in Spanish instead of translating from English.

Hablar/Escribir ¿Dónde están estos lugares en tu comunidad? ¿Cómo vas? *(Hint: Tell where these places are in your community. How do you get to each one?)*

a pie	en carro
en autobús	en moto
en metro	en bicicleta
en taxi	

modelo

la librería

La librería *está lejos de mi casa. Está al lado de una farmacia grande. Voy a la librería en autobús.*

1. farmacia
2. librería
3. zapatería
4. joyería
5. pastelería
6. centro comercial
7. tienda de música y videos

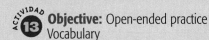 **MÁS COMUNICACIÓN** p. R1

Middle School Classroom Community

Game Make a set of poster boards with the names of shops and other buildings on them. Divide the class into 2 teams and clear the center of the room. Teams will take turns moving the posters around and then asking their opponents to say where the shops are in relation to one another. Each correct description earns the team a point.

Portfolio Ask students to make a map of an imaginary place. Ask them to write 5 sentences describing where things are in relation to each other.

Rubric

Criteria	Scale	
Vocabulary use/spelling	1 2 3 4 5	A = 17–20 pts.
Correct sentence structure/grammar	1 2 3 4 5	B = 13–16 pts.
Logical organization	1 2 3 4 5	C = 9–12 pts.
Creativity	1 2 3 4 5	D = 5–8 pts.
		F = < 5 pts.

GRAMÁTICA

Regular Affirmative tú Commands

To tell a person to do something, use an affirmative command. **Tú commands** are used with friends or family. The regular affirmative **tú command** is the same as the **él/ella** form of the present tense.

Infinitive	Simple Present	Affirmative tú Command
caminar	(él, ella) **camina**	¡Camina!
comer	(él, ella) **come**	¡Come!
abrir	(él, ella) **abre**	¡Abre!

Carlos says:

—**Camina** por esta calle… **Cruza** el parque…
***Walk** down this street… **Cross** the park…*

If you use a **command** with a **direct object pronoun**, attach the pronoun to the end of the command.

Cruza el parque. ➡ **¡Crúzalo!**
***Cross** the park.* ➡ ***Cross** it!*

If needed, add an **accent** when you attach a pronoun to retain the original stress.

Vocabulario

Las direcciones

cruzar *to cross*

doblar *to turn*

quedar (en) *to stay, to be (in a specific place), to agree on*

la cuadra *city block*

derecho *straight ahead*

desde *from*

hasta *until, as far as*

¿Cómo vas a la escuela?

14 Gramática

♻ ¡Hay mucho para hacer en Oaxaca!

Escribir Escribe seis actividades que debe hacer tu compañero(a) en Oaxaca. *(Hint: Write six activities that a classmate should do while in Oaxaca.)*

modelo

jugar al tenis
Juega al tenis.

Escribir tarjetas postales

visitar los museos

escuchar música regional

pasear por las plazas

comer bien

sacar muchas fotos

hablar con la gente

leer revistas en español

noventa y siete
Etapa 1 **97**

Teaching Middle School Students

Extra Help Prepare a list of either/or questions, **¿Practico el piano o estudio para mi examen?**, etc. Work with students to help them make a choice and express it with affirmative **tú** commands.

Native Speakers Ask students to rewrite **Actividad 14** to reflect their home communities. Share these with the rest of the class.

Multiple Intelligences

Visual Ask students to write out a simple skit using commands (such as following a recipe), then act it out while another student videotapes it. Have students show their final production to the class.

Quick Start Review
♻ **Vocabulary**
Use OHT 115 or write on the board: Write the words from the following list that refer to traveling on foot.
caminar / correr / cerrar / pasear / decir / nadar / manejar / ir a pie
Answers *See p. 81D.*

Teaching Suggestions
Regular Affirmative tú Commands
Affirmative **tú** command forms of one syllable do not need an accent when a pronoun is attached: **velo** *(see it)*.

Language Note
Emphasize the difference between **derecho** *(straight ahead)* and **derecha** *(right)*.

14 Objective: Controlled practice
Regular affirmative **tú** commands
♻ Free-time activities

Answers
1. Escucha…
2. Saca…
3. Escribe…
4. Pasea…
5. Habla…
6. Visita…
7. Come…
8. Lee…

Block Schedule
Variety In pairs, have students make a list of affirmative **tú** commands they would hear at a variety of locations, such as at home, at school, or around town. Then have them work with another pair. One pair reads their items and the other pair guesses the possible location. (For additional activities, see **Block Scheduling Copymasters**.)

Teaching Resource Options

Print

Más práctica Workbook PE, p. 8
Para hispanohablantes Workbook PE, p. 6
Block Scheduling Copymasters
Unit 4 Resource Book
 Más práctica Workbook TE, p. 8
 Para hispanohablantes Workbook TE, p. 9

Technology

Intrigas y aventuras CD-ROM, Disc 1

 ACTIVIDAD 15 **Objective:** Controlled practice
Informal commands/direct object pronouns

♻ **Direct object pronouns**

Answers

Reasons for inviting will vary.
1. ¿Invito a María? Sí, ¡invítala!...
2. ¿Invito a Rafael, Gabriela y Tomás? Sí, ¡invítalos!...
3. ¿Invito a Rubén? Sí, ¡invítalo!...
4. ¿Invito a mis primos? Sí, ¡invítalos!...
5. ¿Invito a Julio y Luis? Sí, ¡invítalos!...
6. ¿Invito a Mónica? Sí, ¡invítala!...

 ACTIVIDAD 16 **Objective:** Transitional practice
Informal commands

♻ **Sequencing events**

Answers

Answers may vary.
1. ¿Qué hago primero? ¿Veo la televisión o termino la tarea? Primero, termina la tarea. Después, ve la televisión.
2. ¿Qué hago primero? ¿Abro la tienda o corro por el parque? Primero, abre la tienda. Después, corre...
3. ¿Qué hago primero? ¿Escribo una carta o leo un libro? Primero, escribe... Después, lee...
4. ¿Qué hago primero? ¿Estudio para un examen o ceno? Primero, cena. Después, estudia...
5. ¿Qué hago primero? ¿Visito un museo o saco fotos? Primero, visita un museo. Después, saca fotos.

Para hacer
Answers
1. a	4. e
2. b	5. c
3. d	

 **ACTIVIDAD 15 Gramática**

¿Quién invitamos?

Hablar Conversa con tu compañero(a) sobre las personas que van a invitar a una fiesta. *(Hint: Take turns with a classmate asking about the people you are going to invite to a party.)*

modelo

Pedro

Estudiante A: *¿Invito a **Pedro**?*

Estudiante B: *Sí, ¡invítalo! Es muy divertido y simpático. (Sabe bailar bien, etc.)*

1. María
2. Rafael, Gabriela y Tomás
3. Rubén
4. mis primos
5. Julio y Luis
6. Mónica

■ **MÁS PRÁCTICA** *cuaderno* p. 8

■ **PARA HISPANOHABLANTES** *cuaderno* p. 6

 ACTIVIDAD 16

♻ ¿Qué hago primero?

Hablar Carlos tiene que hacer muchas cosas hoy. Le pregunta a Rosa qué debe hacer primero. *(Hint: Carlos has many things to do. He asks Rosa what to do first.)*

modelo

¿trabajar en la tienda o comer?

Carlos: *¿Qué hago primero? ¿Trabajo en la tienda o como?*

Rosa: *Primero, come. Después, trabaja en la tienda.*

1. ¿ver la televisión o terminar la tarea?
2. ¿abrir la tienda o correr por el parque?
3. ¿escribir una carta o leer un libro?
4. ¿estudiar para un examen o cenar?
5. ¿visitar un museo o sacar fotos?

Conexiones

Los estudios sociales Spanish-speaking countries use international road signs to guide drivers. Why? The signs use symbols instead of words, so foreign visitors who don't know Spanish can easily understand them.

a. b. c.

d. 40 e.

PARA HACER:
Match the signs with the messages.
1. Prohibido la entrada.
2. No se permite doblar a la izquierda.
3. Límite de velocidad: 40 kilómetros por hora
4. Circular por la derecha.
5. No se permiten bicicletas.

98 noventa y ocho
Unidad 4

Middle School Classroom Community

TPR Ask students to sit in a circle. Student A will give a command. If the sentence is formed properly, the student to his or her right will perform the action, then give a command, and so on around the circle.

Paired Activity Ask pairs of students to make "traffic signs" for the classroom (**Camina despacio. Al entrar, dobla a la derecha…**).

Group Activity Ask students to work in small groups and use commands to come up with a recipe for classroom success (**¡Estudia mucho!**, etc.) Or, reverse the coin and have them give the recipe for disaster (**Ve la tele toda la noche. Llega a clase tarde…**).

¡No tenemos tiempo!

Hablar Tu compañero(a) y tú tienen mucho que hacer pero no tienen tiempo en este momento. Conversen sobre cuándo van a hacer cada cosa. *(Hint: You and a classmate have many things to do, but you do not have time at the moment. Take turns telling each other when to do an activity.)*

el viernes · esta tarde · el lunes · miércoles · el sábado · mañana · ahora mismo · martes · el jueves · esta noche

modelo

comprar unos jeans

Estudiante A: *Quiero **comprar unos jeans,** pero no tengo tiempo.*

Estudiante B: *¡Cómpralos el lunes!*

1. buscar las gafas de sol
2. visitar el museo del centro
3. leer un libro sobre un viaje
4. escribir una carta
5. preparar el almuerzo para la familia

¡De fiesta!

Hablar/Escribir Tú organizas una fiesta. Tu compañero(a) te pregunta cómo llegar a tu casa. *(Hint: You are having a party. Your classmate needs directions. Use direct object pronouns when necessary.)*

modelo

Estudiante A: *¿Camino derecho tres cuadras por la calle González Ortega? ¿Cruzo la calle?*

Estudiante B: *Sí, camina derecho tres cuadras por la calle González Ortega. Luego, crúzala.*

1. ¿Doblo a la izquierda y camino seis cuadras?
2. ¿Cruzo la plaza y camino una cuadra más?
3. Entonces, llego a la avenida Hidalgo. ¿La cruzo?
4. ¿Cruzo el parque?

NOTA CULTURAL

Oaxaca means "place of the **guaje**" in Nahuatl, a language of Mexico. The **guaje** is a large tree with pods and flowers. The pods sometimes look like gourds. Some say *Oaxaca* means "place of the gourds."

Teaching Middle School Students

Multiple Intelligences

Naturalist Ask students to state things that we all should do to protect the environment. Give them a dictionary and guide them in the correct usage of vocabulary. For example, **Protege los animales en peligro de extinción. Recicla. Separa la basura…**

Musical/Rhythmic Ask students to prepare a rap, chant, poem, or song telling someone else to do a series of actions.

ACTIVIDAD 17 Objective: Transitional practice Informal commands/direct object pronouns

Answers

Time elements will vary.

1. Quiero buscar las gafas de sol, pero no tengo tiempo. ¡Búscalas…!
2. Quiero visitar el museo del centro, … ¡Visítalo…!
3. Quiero leer un libro sobre un viaje, … ¡Léelo…!
4. Quiero escribir una carta, … ¡Escríbela…!
5. Quiero preparar el almuerzo para la familia, … ¡Prepáralo…!

ACTIVIDAD 18 Objective: Open-ended practice Informal commands

Answers will vary.

Quick Wrap-up

Give commands (or have students give commands) and ask students to respond. **Enrique, ve a María. Invítala a bailar (merendar, nadar, etc.). Verónica, dale tu número de teléfono a Marta. Marta, dale tu dirección a Paco. Oscar, maneja tu coche…**

Block Schedule

Variety Have each student write an unnumbered step-by-step list of instructions. These could tell how to get somewhere or how to make something. Have them cut the list into separate items and put the pieces into an envelope. Write a title for the list on the outside. Every so often during the day, pick an envelope. Read the title and the items, and ask, **"¿Qué hago primero?"**

Teaching Resource Options

Print
Block Scheduling Copymasters
Unit 4 Resource Book
  Information Gap Activities, pp. 18–19
  Audioscript, p. 30
  Audioscript *Para hispanohablantes,*
    p. 30

Audiovisual
Audio Program Cassettes 10A, 10B /
CD 10
Audio *Para hispanohablantes*
  Cassette 10A / CD 10

Technology
Intrigas y aventuras CD-ROM, Disc 1

Teaching Suggestions
Teaching Vocabulary
Have students look back at the **Diálogo** to find where and in what context some of these expressions are used.

Language Note
Perdona is the familiar form. **Perdone** is the formal form.

Objective: Open-ended practice
Informal commands

Answers
Answers may vary.
1. Camina por la avenida 20 de Noviembre. Dobla a la izquierda en la calle Las Casas. El mercado está a la derecha.
2. Dobla a la derecha y camina por la calle Las Casas. En la calle Miguel Cabrera dobla a la izquierda. Cruza la calle Guerrero y la avenida Hidalgo. La catedral está en la derecha.
3. Dobla a la izquierda en la calle Macedonio Alcalá. Dobla a la derecha en la calle Murguía. La tienda está a la derecha.
4. Dobla a la izquierda en la calle García Vigil. La iglesia está a la derecha en la esquina de la calle Guerrero.
5. Vuelve por la calle Miguel Cabrera y dobla a la izquierda. El parque está a la izquierda.
6. Dobla a la izquierda en la avenida 5 de Mayo. Dobla derecha en la avenida de la Independencia. Sigue tres cuadras. El correo está a la izquierda, en la esquina con la avenida 20 de Noviembre.

ACTIVIDAD 19

Una visita a Oaxaca

Hablar Trabaja en un grupo de tres. Tú estás en Oaxaca. Quieres saber cómo llegar a varios lugares. Preguntas a dos jóvenes mexicanos (tus compañeros). *(Hint: Work in a group of three. You are in Oaxaca. You want to find out how to get to various places. You ask two Mexican teenagers.)*

modelo
el parque → el teatro (Estás en el parque. Vas al teatro.)

Estudiante A: *Perdona. ¿Cómo llego al teatro?*

Estudiante B: *Lo siento, pero no sé. No vivo por aquí.*

Estudiante A: *Perdona. ¿Puedes decirme dónde queda el teatro?*

Estudiante C: *Cómo no. Camina derecho dos cuadras por la avenida Independencia hasta la calle 5 de Mayo. El teatro está en la esquina.*

1. el correo → el mercado
2. el mercado → la catedral
3. el Zócalo → la tienda de artesanías
4. la catedral → la iglesia
5. la iglesia → el parque
6. la tienda de artesanías → el correo

Vocabulario

Direcciones, por favor
Perdona(e), ¿cómo llego a…? *Pardon, how do I get to…?*

¿Puedes (Puede usted) decirme dónde queda…? *Could you tell me where…is?*

¿Queda lejos? *Is it far?*

Las respuestas
¡Cómo no! *Of course!*

Lo siento… *I'm sorry…*

acá/aquí *here*

allá/allí *there*

el camino *road*

la dirección *address, direction*

¿Cómo explicas las direcciones?

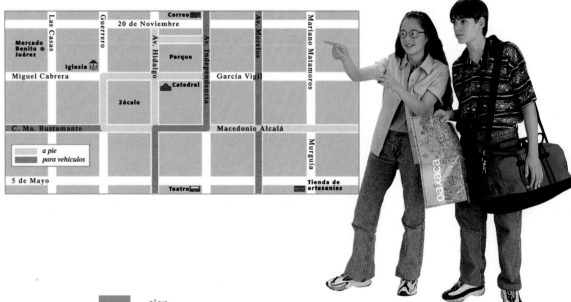

100 cien
Unidad 4

Middle School Classroom Community

TPR Ask a pair of students to direct each other to a place in the classroom. Student A will give directions to a place in the classroom. Student B will follow them. Repeat the activity with other pairs of students.

Portfolio Ask students to copy the map in **Actividad 19,** changing the locations of the 8 places of interest.

Then have them write the answers to **Actividad 19** using the new map.

Rubric

Criteria	Scale
Accuracy of information	1 2 3 4 5
Logical organization	1 2 3 4 5
Vocabulary use	1 2 3 4 5

A = 13–15 pts.
B = 10–12 pts.
C = 7–9 pts.
D = 4–6 pts.
F = < 4 pts.

¿Puede usted decirme...?

Escuchar Rosa le pregunta a un policía cómo llegar a la librería. Escucha la conversación. Indica dónde están la librería, la papelería y el correo. *(Hint: Rosa asks a police officer how to get to the bookstore. Listen to the conversation to tell on which blocks **la librería**, **la papelería**, and **el correo** are.)*

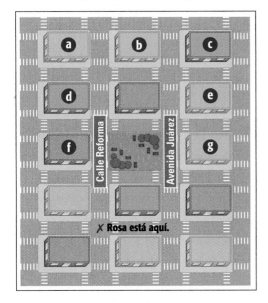

¿Quieres venir?

Escribir Invitas a un(a) amigo a tu casa después de las clases. Escríbele instrucciones (reales o imaginarias) para llegar a tu casa. *(Hint: You invite a new friend to visit you at home after school. Write directions [real or imaginary] for how to get to your house from school.)*

modelo

Mi casa está cerca de la escuela. Cuando sales de la escuela, camina a la derecha. Después de dos cuadras, vas a ver una casa blanca y grande. Dobla a la derecha y camina por la calle Río Grande por tres cuadras. Nuestra casa es a la izquierda. Es una casa azul.

Nota

Addresses with numbers that have more than two digits can be expressed by pairing digits.

284 Connecticut Avenue

—Vivo en la avenida Connecticut, dos ochenta y cuatro.

1340 Main Street

—Vivo en la calle Main, trece cuarenta.

■ **MÁS COMUNICACIÓN** p. R1

Pronunciación

Refrán

Pronunciación de la r When the letter **r** occurs in the middle of a word and between two vowels, it is pronounced by a single tap of your tongue just behind your teeth. It feels like the English *d* when you say the words *buddy* or *ladder*. To practice the tap **r**, pronounce these words. Then try the **refrán**. Can you guess what it means?

la joyería   la panadería   la papelería   la pastelería   la zapatería

Hay que ver para creer.

ciento uno
Etapa I   **101**

Teaching Middle School Students

Extra Help Use the maps you collected at the beginning of this **Etapa** (see "Planning Ahead," TE, p. 82). Use these maps to help students work on asking for and giving directions.

Multiple Intelligences

Verbal Ask students to try the following tongue twister:

Erre con erre, guitarra,

erre con erre, barril;

rápido corren los carros,

los carros del ferrocarril.

---

 20 Objective: Transitional practice Listening comprehension/informal commands

Answers (See script, p. 81D.)
librería (g)
papelería (b)
correo (c)

 21 Objective: Open-ended practice Informal commands/vocabulary

Answers will vary.

Language Note

Point out that **calle** and **avenida** are not capitalized even when they are used to identify specific streets.

Dictation

After students have read the **refrán** in the **Pronunciación,** have them close their books. Dictate the **refrán** in two segments while students write it.

🔔 Quick Wrap-up

Have students list all the words from the **Vocabulario,** pp. 84–85, and the **Diálogo,** pp. 86–87, that have the letter **r** in the middle of a word and between two vowels. Then have them practice pronouncing them.

▨ Block Schedule

Research Have students research the history of Mexico and Oaxaca to find the significance of some of the street names on the map of Oaxaca on p. 100. Some are historical events and others are important people. (For additional activities, see **Block Scheduling Copymasters.**)

Teaching Resource Options

Print

Unit 4 Resource Book
  Audioscript, p. 31
  Audioscript *Para hispanohablantes*,
    p. 31

Audiovisual

Audio Program Cassette
Audio *Para hispanohablantes*
  Cassette 10A / CD 10
OHT M4; 115 (Quick Start)
Canciones Cassette / CD

Quick Start Review

♻ Oaxaca

Use OHT 115 or write on the board:
Make a list of at least 10 places or
buildings you would expect to see
on a visit to Oaxaca.

Answers

Answers will vary. Answers could include:
el Zócalo, Monte Albán, un parque, un correo,
un mercado, una farmacia, una iglesia, un
banco, un hotel, un aeropuerto, una estación
de autobuses, una carnicería, una joyería,
una librería, una panadería, una papelería,
una pastelería, una tienda de música y videos,
una zapatería

Teaching Suggestions

- **Prereading** To place this reading in
  its historical/cultural context, you may
  wish to have students read the
  Conexiones (La historia) on page
  162 of this **Unidad**.
- **Strategy** Point out the use of the
  dash in Spanish (instead of quotation
  marks) to indicate direct speech.
  Have students scan the reading to
  find an instance of this usage.
- **Reading** As usual, ask students to
  look for cognates as they read.
- **Post-reading** Juárez was born in
  a town in the state of Oaxaca. Tell
  students that, as in the U.S., Mexico
  is divided into states. If possible, show
  them a map with states' boundaries
  outlined. Have them count how many
  states there are.

En voces

LECTURA

PARA LEER
STRATEGY: READING

Recognizing sequence Charts can
help you remember the events
of a story in the order they
happen. For example, when you
read a biography, you can list
the events in the person's life
chronologically. As you read this
selection complete a chart like
the one below.

Benito Juárez	
Event	Stage in Life
• loses parents	• 5 years old
• worked as a shepherd	• a boy

Benito Juárez,

En 1806 (mil ochocientos seis), en un pueblo
del estado de Oaxaca, nace[1] un niño. Se llama
Benito. Cuando Benito tiene sólo cinco años, su
mamá y su papá se mueren[2]. Un tío lleva a
Benito a vivir a su casa, pero Benito tiene que
trabajar porque la familia es pobre[3]. El tío
le dice: —Benito, tienes que cuidar a los
corderitos[4] en la montaña.

Y entonces, Benito trabaja todos los días de
pastorcito[5]. Un día, decide salir del pueblo
porque quiere una vida mejor. Llega a la capital

---

[1] is born   [3] poor   [5] shepherd
[2] die   [4] young sheep

102   **Unidad 4**

Middle School Classroom Community

Storytelling After reading the **Lectura**, have
students retell the story. Student A will begin with one
sentence, Student B will follow, and so on throughout
the room until the whole story is retold.

Portfolio Ask students to rewrite the story of Benito
Juárez as if they were Benito, beginning with **Yo...**

Rubric

Criteria	Scale	
Vocabulary use	1 2 3 4 5	**A** = 13–15 pts.
Logical sentence structure/order	1 2 3 4 5	**B** = 10–12 pts. **C** = 7–9 pts.
Grammar/spelling accuracy	1 2 3 4 5	**D** = 4–6 pts. **F** = < 4 pts.

un oaxaqueño por excelencia

y conoce a un buen hombre, Antonio Salanueva. El señor Salanueva enseña a Benito a hablar español (antes, sólo hablaba zapoteco, el idioma nativo regional). El señor Salanueva también le enseña a leer y a escribir. Después de muchos años de estudio, llega a ser abogado[6]. Se dedica a ayudar a la gente pobre.

Los mexicanos conocen a Benito como un hombre bueno, serio y muy trabajador y ¡lo quieren para gobernador del estado! Trabaja mucho e, increíblemente, llega a ser presidente de toda la República Mexicana.

¡Así es que el humilde Benito va de pastorcito a presidente!

[6] lawyer

¿Comprendiste?

1. ¿De dónde es Benito?
2. ¿Cómo trabaja de niño?
3. ¿Cuál es su profesión de adulto?
4. ¿Qué idiomas habla?
5. ¿Qué llega a ser?

¿Qué piensas?

1. ¿Concoces a alguna persona cuya vida es similar a la de Benito Juárez? ¿Cómo son similares las dos personas?
2. ¿Qué te parece esta historia? ¿Crees que mucha gente puede hacer lo mismo que Benito Juárez?

ciento tres
Etapa 1 **103**

Language Note

By now, students have probably begun to realize that the pronunciation of the **b** and the **v** are alike in many cases. Tell students that substituting a **v** for a **b** in some Spanish words may lead them to recognize related words in English and, hence, make word recognition in Spanish easier. For example, in this reading the words **pobre**, **abogado**, and **gobernador** could lead to the English counterparts *poverty*, *advocate*, and *governor*.

¿Comprendiste?
Answers
Answers may vary.
1. Es de un pueblo del estado de Oaxaca.
2. Trabaja de pastor.
3. Es abogado.
4. Habla español y zapoteco.
5. Llega a ser presidente de México.

Teaching Middle School Students

Challenge Ask students to research more details on Juárez's life and to share them with the class. Ask students to find out who is the president of Mexico today.

Multiple Intelligences

Intrapersonal Ask students to list the main events in the life of Benito Juárez and to write down how they feel about each one.

 Block Schedule

Variety Have students think about and identify their heroes. Who are they? Why do they admire them? What are their accomplishments? If students don't already know, have them research their heroes' beginnings. What were they like as children? As adolescents?

Teaching Resource Options

Print

Para hispanohablantes Workbook PE,
  pp. 7–8
Unit 4 Resource Book
  Para hispanohablantes Workbook
    TE, pp. 15–16
  Information Gap Activities, p. 20
  Family Involvement, pp. 21–22
  Multiple Choice Test Questions,
    pp. 170–178

Audiovisual

OHT 116 (Quick Start)
Audio Program Testing Cassette T2 /
  CD T2

Technology

Electronic Teacher Tools/Test
  Generator
Intrigas y aventuras CD-ROM, Disc 1

Quick Start Review

♻ **Requesting directions**

Use OHT 116 or write on the board:
Write 5 questions you would ask while
finding your way around a Spanish-
speaking city for the first time.

Answers
Answers will vary. Answers could include:
¿Puede usted decirme dónde está [el banco]?
¿Hay [un hotel] cerca de aquí?
¿Cómo llego [al correo]?
¿Queda lejos?
¿Dónde está [el centro comercial]?
¿Cruzo la calle?

✔ **Teaching Suggestions**
What Have Students Learned?

Have students look at the "Now you
can…" notes and give examples of
each category. Have them spend extra
time reviewing categories they feel they
are weak in, by consulting the "To
review" notes.

ETAPA 1

Now you can…
• identify places.
• give addresses.

To review
• prepositions
  of location,
  see p. 95.

Now you can…
• give instructions.

To review
• regular affirmative
  tú commands,
  see p. 97.

En uso

REPASO Y MÁS COMUNICACIÓN

OBJECTIVES
• Identify places
• Give addresses
• Choose transportation
• Request directions
• Give instructions

ACTIVIDAD 1 ¡Al centro!

Explícale al nuevo estudiante adónde vas cuando quieres hacer
las siguientes cosas. (*Hint: Explain to the new student where you go when you want
to do the following things.*)

modelo

comprar zapatos (detrás de)

*Cuando quiero **comprar zapatos**, voy a la zapatería. Está **detrás de** la tienda
de música y videos. La dirección es avenida Flores, setenta y nueve.*

1. comprar papel (a la derecha de)
2. comprar jeans (a la izquierda de)
3. tomar un refresco (entre)
4. comprar medicina (detrás de)
5. mandar una carta (al lado de)
6. comprar un libro (a la derecha de)
7. alquilar un video (entre)
8. comprar zapatos (a la izquierda de)

ACTIVIDAD 2 Para sacar buenas notas…

Tu amigo(a) quiere sacar buenas notas. Contesta sus preguntas
con mandatos afirmativos. (*Hint: Your friend wants to get good grades. Answer
the questions with affirmative commands.*)

modelo

¿Uso el diccionario?   Sí, úsalo.

1. ¿Preparo la tarea?
2. ¿Leo el libro?
3. ¿Miro los videos?
4. ¿Aprendo el vocabulario?
5. ¿Estudio las lecciones?
6. ¿Escribo un poema?
7. ¿Compro una calculadora?
8. ¿Tomo los exámenes?

104 ciento cuatro
Unidad 4

Middle School Classroom Community

TPR Ask students to work in small groups imagining
that they are taking group photos and giving each other
commands as to where each should stand or sit.
Provide the commands **ponte** and **siéntate**. (Juanito,
siéntate entre Mari y Jorge.)

Paired Activity Have pairs of students share a book
and do **Actividad 2** as an oral exercise. Student A
opens the book and asks the first four questions while
Student B responds. They switch roles for the last four
questions.

Now you can...

• request directions.

To review

• prepositions of location, see p. 95.

ACTIVIDAD **3** **¿Dónde queda?**

Estás visitando un pueblo y necesitas direcciones para llegar a un banco. Hablas con un policía. Completa la conversación con las expresiones correctas. *(Hint: You are visiting a town and you need directions to get to the bank. You speak with a police officer. Complete the conversation with the correct expressions.)*

Tú: (Oye / Perdone). Señor, ¿(puede / puedo) usted decirme dónde está el banco?

Policía: ¡Cómo (no / sí)! El banco no queda (cerca / lejos). Está a sólo tres (lados / cuadras) de aquí. Primero, hay que caminar (derecho / detrás) por la avenida Olmos hasta llegar a la plaza. Allí, (dobla / llega) a la derecha en la calle San Juan y (queda / camina) una cuadra. Entonces, (cruza / camina) la calle Sonora. El banco queda en la esquina.

Tú: Muchas gracias, señor. ¿Y (hay / puede) un café cerca del banco?

Policía: Sí. El Café Romano está (al lado / entre) del banco. Es excelente. Y si necesitas mandar cartas, el correo queda (derecho / a la izquierda) del café.

Now you can...

• choose transportation.

To review

• the verb **decir**, see p. 92.

• the verb **salir**, see p. 93.

ACTIVIDAD **4** **¡Salgo hoy!**

Todos salen para diferentes lugares. Explica adónde van, qué dicen del lugar adónde van y cómo van a viajar. *(Hint: Everyone is going someplace different. Explain where they are going, what they say about the place they are going, and how they are going to travel.)*

modelo

mi vecino: México (es muy interesante)

Mi vecino sale para **México**. Dice que **es muy interesante**. Va en carro.

1. mi primo: España (es muy especial)

2. nosotros: Los Ángeles (es fantástico)

3. ustedes: la Ciudad de México (es muy divertida)

4. yo: Puerto Rico (es muy bonito)

5. Marta y Ramón: la playa (es divertida)

6. usted: el centro (no es aburrido)

ciento cinco
Etapa 1 105

1. Cuando quiero comprar papel, voy a la papelería. Está a la derecha de la tienda de música y videos. La dirección es calle Colón, treinta y ocho.
2. Cuando quiero comprar jeans, voy a la tienda de ropa. Está a la izquierda de la tienda de música y videos. La dirección es calle Colón, treinta y cuatro.
3. Cuando quiero tomar un refresco, voy al café. Está entre la zapatería y el correo. La dirección es avenida Flores, ochenta y uno.
4. Cuando quiero comprar medicina, voy a la farmacia. Está detrás de la tienda de ropa. La dirección es avenida Flores, setenta y siete.
5. Cuando quiero mandar una carta, voy al correo. Está al lado del café. La dirección es avenida Flores, ochenta y tres.
6. Cuando quiero comprar un libro, voy a la librería. Está a la derecha de la papelería. La dirección es calle Colón, cuarenta.
7. Cuando quiero alquilar un video, voy a la tienda de música y videos. Está entre la tienda de ropa y la papelería. La dirección es calle Colón, treinta y seis.
8. Cuando quiero comprar zapatos, voy a la zapatería. Está a la izquierda del café. La dirección es avenida Flores, setenta y nueve.

ACTIVIDAD **2** **Answers**

1. Sí, prepárala.
2. Sí, léelo.
3. Sí, míralos.
4. Sí, apréndelo.
5. Sí, estúdialas.
6. Sí, escríbelo.
7. Sí, cómprala.
8. Sí, tómalos.

ACTIVIDAD **3** **Answers**

Tú: Perdone / puede
Policía: no / lejos / cuadras / derecho / dobla / camina / cruza
Tú: hay
Policía: al lado / a la izquierda

ACTIVIDAD **4** **Answers**

1. Mi primo sale para España. Dice que es muy especial. Va en avión.
2. Nosotros salimos para Los Ángeles. Decimos que es fantástico. Vamos en tren.
3. Ustedes salen para la Ciudad de México. Dicen que es muy divertida. Van en autobús.
4. Yo salgo para Puerto Rico. Digo que es muy bonito. Voy en barco.
5. Marta y Ramón salen para la playa. Dicen que es divertida. Van en moto(cicleta).
6. Usted sale para el centro. Dice que no es aburrido. Va en taxi.

Teaching Middle School Students

Extra Help Work with selected students on **Actividad 2**. Have them identify the verb infinitive for each sentence. Then help them identify the direct objects and choose the corresponding direct object pronoun.

Native Speakers Ask your native speakers to sketch simple maps of places they know in their country of origin. Duplicate and hand them out so that pairs of students can practice giving and receiving directions.

Challenge Ask students to find maps of Latin America on the Internet and list in Spanish whatever landmarks they can identify (**el río Amazonas, la cordillera de los Andes,** etc.)

■ Block Schedule

Variety Alternate between giving the **Repaso** as homework and having students do it in class. In either case, go over the answers with the group.

Teaching Resource Options

Print

Unit 4 Resource Book
Cooperative Quizzes, pp. 33–34
Etapa Exam, Forms A and B,
   pp. 35–44
Para hispanohablantes Etapa Exam,
   pp. 45–49
Portfolio Assessment, pp. 50–51
Multiple Choice Test Questions,
   pp. 170–178

Audiovisual

OHT 116 (Quick Start)
Audio Program Testing Cassette T2 /
CD T2

Technology

Electronic Teacher Tools/Test
Generator

www.mcdougallittell.com

ACTIVIDAD 5

Rubric: Speaking

Criteria	Scale	
Sentence structure	1 2 3 4 5	A = 17–20 pts.
Vocabulary use	1 2 3 4 5	B = 13–16 pts.
Originality	1 2 3 4 5	C = 9–12 pts.
Fluency	1 2 3 4 5	D = 5–8 pts.
		F = < 5 pts.

ACTIVIDAD 6 En tu propia voz

Rubric: Writing

Criteria	Scale	
Vocabulary use	1 2 3 4 5	A = 13–15 pts.
Accuracy	1 2 3 4 5	B = 10–12 pts.
Creativity, appearance	1 2 3 4 5	C = 7–9 pts.
		D = 4–6 pts.
		F = < 4 pts.

Teaching Note: En tu propia voz

Have students use a town map to indicate where the activities take place, using the writing strategy "Organize information by category" to group contiguous activities.

ACTIVIDAD 5 ¿Cómo llego?

PARA CONVERSAR • STRATEGY: SPEAKING

Use variety to give directions When you give directions, don't just speak. Make your directions clear by using gestures, pointing to a map, and repeating key information. This helps others make sense of your words.

Trabajas en la tienda de música y videos. Explícale a un(a) joven turista cómo llegar a tres lugares. Antes de explicar, haz un mapa como ayuda. Cambien de papel. *(Hint: You work in a music and video store. Explain to a young tourist how to get three places. Before you explain, make a map to help you. Change roles.)*

modelo

Turista: *Perdone, señor(ita), ¿cómo llego a la iglesia?*

Tú: *Camina tres cuadras por la avenida Juárez. La iglesia está a la izquierda en la esquina.*

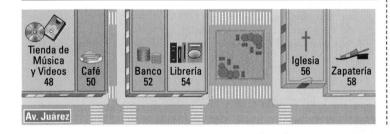

ACTIVIDAD 6

En tu propia voz

Escritura Hay una nueva estudiante que no conoce tu comunidad. Usa las siguientes expresiones para darle siete recomendaciones. *(Hint: There's a new student who doesn't know the community. Use the following phrases to make six suggestions.)*

comer	caminar
visitar	practicar deportes
nadar	jugar
correr	ver películas
patinar	alquilar videos
comprar	mandar cartas
pasear	buscar libros

modelo

Compra ropa en el centro comercial Park Plaza.

Conexiones

La educación física Different regions in Mexico have their own special folk music, dances, and costumes. For example, in one Oaxacan folk dance, women balance filled glasses on their heads! Research other Mexican folk dances in the library and/or on the Internet. Then teach a dance to your class. Answer these questions about the dance.

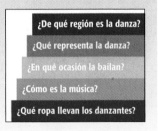

- ¿De qué región es la danza?
- ¿Qué representa la danza?
- ¿En qué ocasión la bailan?
- ¿Cómo es la música?
- ¿Qué ropa llevan los danzantes?

106 ciento seis
Unidad 4

Middle School Classroom Community

TPR Ask pairs of students to take turns forming commands using the verbs in **Actividad 6** and acting them out.

Group Activity Have students work in small groups to quiz each other on the **Repaso de vocabulario**. One student acts as "teacher." He or she opens the book and names a category. The others give words and expressions in that category. The "teacher" may need to give hints in order to elicit all the vocabulary for the category. Have students rotate the "teacher" role until all categories have been covered.

En resumen

REPASO DE VOCABULARIO

IDENTIFYING PLACES

el aeropuerto	airport
el banco	bank
el café	café
la carnicería	butcher's shop
el centro	center, downtown
el centro comercial	shopping center
el correo	post office
la estación de autobuses	bus station
la farmacia	pharmacy, drugstore
el hotel	hotel
la iglesia	church
la joyería	jewelry store
la librería	bookstore
la panadería	bread bakery
la papelería	stationery store
la pastelería	pastry shop
la plaza	town square
la tienda de música y videos	music and video store
la zapatería	shoe store

GIVING ADDRESSES

la avenida	avenue
la calle	street
el camino	road
la dirección	address, direction

CHOOSING TRANSPORTATION

a pie	on foot
el autobús	bus
el avión	airplane
el barco	ship
el carro	car
el metro	subway
la moto(cicleta)	motorcycle
el taxi	taxi, cab
el tren	train

REQUESTING DIRECTIONS

Requesting

Perdona(e), ¿cómo llego a...?	Pardon, how do I get to...?
¿Puedes (Puede usted) decirme dónde queda...?	Could you tell me where ... is?
¿Queda lejos?	Is it far?
acá/aquí	here
allá/allí	there

Replying

¡Cómo no!	Of course!
Lo siento...	I'm sorry...
cerca (de)	near (to)
cruzar	to cross
la cuadra	city block
a la derecha (de)	to the right (of)
derecho	straight ahead
desde	from
detrás (de)	behind
doblar	to turn
enfrente (de)	in front (of)
entre	between
la esquina	corner
hasta	until, as far as
a la izquierda (de)	to the left (of)
al lado (de)	beside, next to
lejos (de)	far (from)
quedar (en)	to stay, to be (in a specific place), to agree on

OTHER WORDS AND PHRASES

la cosa	thing
decir	to say, to tell
manejar	to drive
el mapa	map
por	for, by, around
salir	to go out, to leave
viajar	to travel
el viaje	trip

Juego

¿Adónde van los jóvenes?

Viajo en avión. ¿Adónde voy?

Adriana

No estoy bien y necesito medicina. ¿Adónde voy?

Andrés

Necesito pesos. No tengo suficiente en casa. ¿Adónde voy?

Arturo

ciento siete
Etapa 1   **107**

Community Connections

Have students look in the arts/cultural section of area newspapers. Can they find any performances of Hispanic dancers? They might also look on the Internet. In addition, a few students could call local dance studios to see what dance classes are offered that have their roots in Hispanic culture.

Interdisciplinary Connection

Physical Education Work with the Physical Education teacher to devise an aerobic workout based on traditional Mexican folk dance.

Quick Start Review

🔄 **Etapa** vocabulary

Use OHT 116 or write on the board: Write a mini-dialog that contains at least one word/expression from each of the following categories:

1. Identifying places
2. Giving addresses
3. Choosing transportation
4. Requesting directions

Answers will vary.

Teaching Suggestions
Vocabulary Review

Have students make flash cards of the vocabulary words/expressions and quiz each other in groups of 2 or 3. After 5–10 minutes have students give dictations to each other and check spelling.

Juego

Answers: Adriana va al aeropuerto. Andrés va a la farmacia. Arturo va al banco.

Block Schedule

FunBreak Using the list in the **Repaso de vocabulario**, have students play an alphabet game. Go around the room, naming a letter of the alphabet. (Do not use the letters g, k, n, o, r, u, w, x, y.) Students must name a word beginning with the given letter. Refer to the list for letters that can be used more than once.

Teaching Middle School Students

Native Speakers Have students talk to the class about traditional dances in their home communities. Be prepared to help the rest of the class with vocabulary.

Multiple Intelligences

Interpersonal Ask students to choose five words to give to another student who must then use each word in a separate sentence.

Musical/Rhythmic Ask students to choose words from this list and chant them, exaggerating the stressed syllable, while tapping on their desks. You may also allow students to bring in certain percussion instruments as accompaniment.

Planning Guide CLASSROOM MANAGEMENT

OBJECTIVES

Communication	• Talk about shopping *pp. 110–111* • Make purchases *pp. 112–113* • Talk about giving gifts *pp. 112–113* • Bargaining *pp. 110–111, 112–113, 128–129*
Grammar	• Stem-changing verbs: **o → ue** *pp. 118–119* • Indirect object pronouns *pp. 121–122* • Placement of indirect object pronouns *pp. 124–125*
Pronunciation	• Pronunciation of **rr** *p. 127* • Dictation *TE p. 127*
Culture	• The **artesanías** of Oaxaca *pp. 110–111* • Shopping and making purchases *pp. 128–129* • Benito Juárez *p. 128*
♻ **Recycling**	• Numbers *p. 117* • Places *p. 119* • Telling time *p. 119* • Transportation *p. 119*

STRATEGIES

Listening Strategies	• Observe as you listen *p. 112*
Speaking Strategies	• Express emotion *p. 120* • Disagree politely *p. 132*
Reading Strategies	• Preview graphics *TE p. 128*
Writing Strategies	• Brainstorm details, then organize your information *TE p. 132*
Connecting Cultures Strategies	• Recognize variations in regional vocabulary *p. 115* • Learn about an important person in Mexican history *p. 128* • Connect and compare what you know about bargaining customs in your community to help you learn about bargaining customs in a new community *pp. 110–111, 112–113, 128–129*

PROGRAM RESOURCES

Print

• *Más práctica* Workbook PE *pp. 9–16*
• Block Scheduling Copymasters *pp. 89–96*
• Unit 4 Resource Book
  Más práctica Workbook TE *pp. 52–59*
  Information Gap Activities *pp. 68–71*

Family Involvement *pp. 72–73*
Video Activities *pp. 74–76*
Videoscript *pp. 77–79*
Audioscript *pp. 80–83*
Assessment Program, Unit 4 Etapa 2 *pp. 84–102; 170–178*
Answer Keys *pp. 179–200*

 Audiovisual

• Audio Program Cassettes 11A, 11B / CD 11
• *Canciones* Cassette / CD
• Video Program Videotape 4 / Videodisc 2B
• Overhead Transparencies M1–M5; 105; 117–126

Technology

• Electronic Teacher Tools/Test Generator
• *Intrigas y aventuras* CD-ROM, Disc 1
 www.mcdougallittell.com

✓ Assessment Program Options

• **Cooperative Quizzes** (Unit 4 Resource Book)
• **Etapa Exam** Forms A and B (Unit 4 Resource Book)
• *Para hispanohablantes* **Etapa Exam** (Unit 4 Resource Book)
• **Portfolio Assessment** (Unit 4 Resource Book)
• **Multiple Choice Test Questions** (Unit 4 Resource Book)
• **Audio Program** Testing Cassette T2 / CD T2
• **Electronic Teacher Tools/Test Generator**

Native Speakers

• *Para hispanohablantes* Workbook PE, *pp. 9–16*
• *Para hispanohablantes* Workbook TE (Unit 4 Resource Book)
• *Para hispanohablantes* Etapa Exam (Unit 4 Resource Book)
• Audio *Para hispanohablantes* Cassettes 11A, 11B, T2 / CD 11, T2
• Audioscript *Para hispanohablantes* (Unit 4 Resource Book)

Student Text
Listening Activity Scripts

 Videoscript: Diálogo *pages 112–113*

• Videotape 4 • Videodisc 2B

Search Chapter 5, Play to 6
U4E2 • En vivo (Dialog)

• Use the videoscript with **Actividades 1, 2** *pages 114–115*

Sofía: Bueno, ¿qué le vas a comprar a tu mamá?

Rosa: Quiere una olla de barro negro. ¡Qué mercado tan bonito, Sofía! Venden de todo. En la ciudad voy a los centros comerciales, no a los mercados.

Sofía: ¿Y cuál prefieres?

Rosa: No sé... los centros comerciales son más modernos, pero los mercados son muy interesantes y puedes regatear.
Mira, es el nuevo disco compacto de mi grupo favorito.

Sofía: Pero tienes que comprarle un regalo a tu mamá. ¿Tienes suficiente dinero para un disco compacto?

Rosa: No sé. Vuelvo si me queda dinero.

Carlos: ¡Sofía!

Sofía: ¡Carlos! ¡Qué sorpresa! Carlos, te presento a mi prima Rosa. Es de la Ciudad de México. ¡Carlos!

Carlos: Sí, ya lo sé. Hola, Rosa. ¿Qué onda?

Sofía: Tú... ¿Tú conoces a Rosa? ¿Cómo?

Carlos: Es nuestro secreto, ¿verdad?

Rosa: Sí, es nuestro secreto.

Carlos: Bueno, tengo que ir a trabajar. Pero ¿almorzamos juntos mañana? Podemos ir a mi restaurante favorito para comer sus especialidades oaxaqueñas. Almuerzo allí cada ocho días.

Rosa: Nos encantaría, ¿no, Sofía?

Sofía: Claro que sí.

Carlos: Voy a participar en un concurso y quiero sus opiniones.

Rosa: Me parece ideal.

Carlos: Entonces hasta mañana, a la una, en el restaurante La Madre Tierra. Está cerca de la tienda donde trabajo. ¿Recuerdas cómo llegar al restaurante, Sofía?

Sofía: Sí, Carlos, recuerdo dónde está. Hasta mañana.

Carlos: ¡Adiós!

Rosa: ¡Hasta mañana! ¡Ah! ¡Y te doy el mapa!

Sofía: ¿Qué mapa?

Vendedor: Tenemos de todo... ollas, platos, jarras. Tenemos aquí una selección muy grande. Aquí usted encuentra el regalo perfecto...

Rosa: ¿Me deja ver esta olla grande?

Vendedor: Sí, cómo no.

Rosa: Es muy bonita. ¿Cuánto cuesta?

Vendedor: Las ollas grandes cuestan 70 pesos cada una.

Sofía: Son preciosas, ¿no?

Rosa: ¡Es muy cara! Le puedo ofrecer 50 pesos.

Vendedor: Ay, señorita, tengo que ganarme la vida, ¿no? Le dejo la olla en 65.

Rosa: ¿Por qué no me da la olla por 60?

Vendedor: Muy bien, señorita. Quedamos en 60.

Rosa: Muchísimas gracias, muy amable.

Vendedor: De nada.

Sofía: Muy bien, Rosa. Ahora tienes el regalo para tu mamá. ¿Tienes dinero suficiente para el disco compacto?

Rosa: Sí, creo que sí. ¿Sabes? Quiero comprarle un regalo a Carlos. Le doy el disco compacto mañana. ¿Por qué no volvemos a esa tienda de música?

 **¿Qué usa?** *page 119*

Como está cerca, voy a la escuela a pie.

Si tengo prisa, voy a mi clase de piano en taxi.

El Parque Chapultepec es muy bonito. Voy allí los domingos en metro.

Mi familia y yo visitamos a mis abuelos en carro.

Hay un museo interesante en el centro. Para ir, voy en autobús.

Regalos para todos *page 123*

La tienda de música y videos es el lugar ideal para comprar regalos. A mis hermanas les gusta ver videos. Por eso les compro dos. A mi hermano le compro un videojuego. Juega todo el fin de semana. Para mis amigos, los mejores regalos están en la sección de música. A mi amiga Amanda le gusta mucho bailar, entonces le compro un disco compacto de salsa. Mi amigo Pablo va a celebrar su cumpleaños. Le compro un radio. ¡A la profesora Díaz le compro un casete de rock en español! ¡No te preocupes, Sofía! ¡Te compro un casete a ti también!

Quick Start Review Answers

p. 112 Shopping vocabulary
artículos de cuero:
   el cinturón / las botas / la cartera / la bolsa
joyas:
   la pulsera / el collar / los aretes / el anillo
cerámica:
   la olla / la jarra / el plato

p. 114 Dialog review
1. Rosa y Sofía son primas.
2. Sofía y Carlos son amigos.
3. Rosa quiere un regalo para su madre.
4. Rosa quiere comprarle un regalo a Carlos.

p. 128 Bargaining vocabulary
6 Muy bien, quedamos en 80. Muchas gracias.
2 Cuesta 100 pesos.
3 ¡Es demasiado! Le puedo ofrecer 70.
4 ¡Es demasiado barato! Se la dejo en 90.
1 Es muy bonita esta jarra. ¿Cuánto cuesta?
5 No puedo. ¿Me la deja en 80?

Sample Lesson Plan - 45 Minute Schedule

DAY 1

Etapa Opener
- Quick Start Review (TE, p. 108) 5 MIN.
- Anticipate/Activate prior knowledge: Have students look at the *Etapa* Opener and answer the *¿Qué ves?* questions, p. 108. 10 MIN.

En contexto: Vocabulario
- Quick Start Review (TE, p. 110) 5 MIN.
- Have students use context and pictures to learn *Etapa* vocabulary. 10 MIN.
- Uses the Situational OHTs for additional practice. 10 MIN.
- Have students work in pairs to answer the *Preguntas personales*, p. 111. 5 MIN.

DAY 2

En vivo: Diálogo
- Quick Start Review (TE, p. 112) 5 MIN.
- Discuss Gestures (TE, p. 112). 5 MIN.
- Review the Listening Strategy, p. 112. 5 MIN.
- Play audio or show video for the dialog, pp. 112–113. 10 MIN.
- Replay as needed. 5 MIN.
- Read the dialog aloud, having students take the roles of characters. 10 MIN.

Homework Option:
- Video Activities, Unit 4 Resource Book, pp. 74–76.

DAY 3

En acción: Vocabulario y gramática
- Check homework. 5 MIN.
- Quick Start Review (TE, p. 114) 5 MIN.
- Use OHT 15 and 16 to review the *En contexto* vocabulary. Ask students for a summary of the dialog to check recall. 10 MIN.
- Play the video/audio; do *Actividad* 1 orally with the class. 10 MIN.
- Do *Actividad* 2 orally. 5 MIN.
- Have students work in groups to complete *Actividad* 3. 5 MIN.
- Call on some groups to report the results of their work on *Actividad* 3. 5 MIN.

DAY 4

En acción (cont.)
- Quick Start Review (TE, p. 118) 5 MIN.
- Have students work independently on *Actividad* 4. 5 MIN.
- Ask volunteer pairs to read their letter to Emiliana from *Actividad* 4 to the class. 5 MIN.
- Have students work in pairs to do *Actividad* 5. 5 MIN.
- Ask pairs to volunteer to model their conversations from *Actividad* 5. 5 MIN.
- Present *Gramática*: Stem-Changing Verbs: *o → ue* and the *Vocabulario*. 10 MIN.
- Have students write the answers to *Actividad* 6. 5 MIN.
- Call on selected students to share their completed paragraph from *Actividad* 6. 5 MIN.

Homework Option:
- Have students read the *Conexiones*, p. 117, and complete the *Para hacer.*

DAY 5

En acción (cont.)
- Check homework. 5 MIN.
- Have students complete *Actividad* 7 and then give their answers orally. 10 MIN.
- Have students work in pairs to do *Actividad* 8. 5 MIN.
- Play the audio; do *Actividad* 9. 5 MIN.
- Have students work in pairs to do *Actividad* 10 then report their results. 10 MIN.
- Discuss the Speaking Strategy, p. 120, then present the *Vocabulario*. 5 MIN.
- Have students work in pairs to complete *Actividad* 11. 5 MIN.

Homework Option:
- *Más práctica* Workbook, p. 13. *Para hispanohablantes* Workbook, p. 11.

DAY 6

En acción (cont.)
- Check homework. 5 MIN.
- Quick Start Review (TE, p. 121) 5 MIN.
- Present *Gramática*: Indirect Object Pronouns, p. 121. 10 MIN.
- Have students write their answers to *Actividad* 12. 5 MIN.
- Ask selected students to share their responses to *Actividad* 12 orally. 5 MIN.
- Have students work independently to complete *Actividad* 13. 5 MIN.
- Ask volunteers to write their sentences for *Actividad* 13 on the board. 5 MIN.
- Present and practice the *Vocabulario*, p. 123. 5 MIN.

Homework Option:
- *Más práctica* Workbook, pp. 14–15. *Para hispanohablantes* Workbook, pp. 12–13.

DAY 7

En acción (cont.)
- Check homework. 5 MIN.
- Quick Start Review (TE, p. 124) 5 MIN.
- Have students complete *Actividad* 14. 5 MIN.
- Ask volunteers to write their answers to *Actividad* 14 on the board. 10 MIN.
- Have students work in pairs on *Actividad* 15. 5 MIN.
- Call on selected pairs to share their work on *Actividad* 15 with the class. 5 MIN.
- Present *Grámatica*: Placement of Indirect Object Pronouns, p. 124. 10 MIN.

DAY 8

En acción (cont.)
- Assign *Actividad* 16. 5 MIN.
- Call on students to write their completed sentences from *Actividad* 16 on the board. 10 MIN.
- Play the audio; do *Actividad* 17. 5 MIN.
- Have students work in pairs to complete *Actividad* 18. 5 MIN.
- Ask pairs to volunteer to model their story from *Actividad* 18. 5 MIN.
- Read and discuss the *Conexiones*, p. 126. 5 MIN.
- Draw a quick copy of the map in the *Conexiones*, p. 126, on the board. Work with the class to do the *Para hacer* orally. 10 MIN.

Homework Option:
- Have students write answers to the *Para hacer*, p. 126.

DAY 9

En acción (cont.)
- Check homework. 5 MIN.
- Have students work in pairs to do *Actividad* 19. 5 MIN.
- Call on pairs to report their findings from *Actividad* 19. 5 MIN.
- Have students work in pairs to do *Actividad* 20. 5 MIN.
- Call on selected pairs to share their work from *Actividad* 20. 5 MIN.
- Use Information Gap Activities, Unit 4 Resource Book, pp. 69–70. 10 MIN.
- *Más comunicación*, p. R11. 5 MIN.
- Play the audio. Have students practice the *Trabalenguas*, p. 127. 5 MIN.

DAY 10

En colores: Cultura y comparaciones
- Quick Start Review (TE, p. 128) 5 MIN.
- Discuss the Connecting Cultures Strategy, p. 128. 5 MIN.
- Complete the Venn diagram, p. 128. 5 MIN.
- Have volunteers read *El Mercado Benito Juárez*, pp. 128–129, aloud. 10 MIN.
- Work orally with students to answer the *¿Comprendiste?* questions, p. 129 (Answers, TE, p. 129). 5 MIN.
- Discuss the *¿Qué piensas?* questions, p. 129. 5 MIN.
- Have students work in pairs to do the *Hazlo tú*, p. 129. 5 MIN.
- Ask selected pairs of students to share their dialog from the *Hazlo tú*. 5 MIN.

Homework Option:
- Have students prepare written answers to the *¿Qué piensas?* questions, p. 129.

DAY 11

En uso: Repaso y más comunicación
- Check homework. 5 MIN.
- Quick Start Review (TE, p. 130) 5 MIN.
- Work orally with students to complete *Actividad* 1. 10 MIN.
- Have students write their answers to *Actividad* 2 independently. 5 MIN.
- Call on pairs of students to perform the conversation in *Actividad* 2. 10 MIN.
- Work orally with the class on *Actividad* 3. 10 MIN.

DAY 12

En uso (cont.)
- Have students write out answers to *Actividad* 4. 5 MIN.
- Call on students to play the parts in *Actividad* 4, using their own written responses. 10 MIN.
- Present the Speaking Strategy, p. 132. 5 MIN.
- Have students work in pairs on *Actividad* 5. 10 MIN.
- Call on selected pairs to model their conversations from *Actividad* 5 for the class. 10 MIN.
- Read and discuss the *Conexiones*, p. 132. 5 MIN.

Homework Option
- Have students collect items for the mock *mercado* suggested in the *Conexiones*, p. 132.

DAY 13

En uso (cont.)
- Use objects students have brought in to set up the mock *mercado* suggested in the *Conexiones*, p. 132. Practice *regatear*. 10 MIN.
- Have students work in groups on *Actividad* 6. 10 MIN.
- Ask volunteers to write their sentences from *Actividad* 6 on the board. 5 MIN.

En tu propria voz: Escritura
- Have students work independently on the writing activity in *Actividad* 7. 10 MIN.
- Ask volunteers to read their work from *Actividad* 7 to the class. 10 MIN.

Homework Option:
- Have students review all of the *Gramática* boxes in *Etapa* 2 as preparation for the exam.

DAY 14

En resumen: Repaso de vocabulario
- Review grammar questions as necessary. 10 MIN.
- Quick Start Review (TE, p. 133) 5 MIN.
- Put students in groups and follow the Teaching Suggestion, TE, p. 133. 5 MIN.
- Call on students to share their vocabulary sentences orally. 10 MIN.
- Ask students to solve the *Juego*, p. 133. 10 MIN.
- Answer the *Juego* orally (Answers, TE, p. 133). 5 MIN.

Homework Option:
- Have students study for the *Etapa* exam.

DAY 15

En resumen: Repaso de vocabulario
- Answer questions related to *Etapa* 2 content. 10 MIN.
- Complete *Etapa* exam. 25 MIN.

Ampliación
- Use a suggested project, game, or activity (TE, pp. 81A–81B) as students complete the exam.

Classroom Management Tip

Make connections Learning anything is easier if you can connect what you are learning with your personal experience. Role-playing allows students to personalize different situations.

In the upcoming **Etapa**, students will have an opportunity to role-play different bargaining situations. Collect objects, photographs, and play money for students to use during these role-play activities.

UNIDAD 4 Etapa 2
Opener

Etapa Theme
Making purchases in Oaxaca and bargaining in the Mercado Benito Juárez

Grammar Objectives
- Using stem-changing verbs: o → ue
- Using indirect object pronouns

Teaching Resource Options
Print 📖
Block Scheduling Copymasters

Audiovisual 🎧📽️
OHT 105, 123 (Quick Start)

Quick Start Review
♻ Places
Use OHT 123 or write on board:
List at least 5 items in each category:

1. Places in a city
2. Modes of transportation
3. Prepositions to express location
4. Giving directions/addresses

Answers
Answers will vary. Answers could include:
1. el banco, el café, el centro comercial, la farmacia, la iglesia, la plaza
2. a pie, en autobús, en barco, en carro, en metro, en taxi
3. cerca (de), detrás (de), a la derecha (de), a la izquierda (de), al lado (de), lejos (de)
4. la calle, la dirección, cruzar, la cuadra, derecho, doblar, la esquina

Teaching Suggestions
Previewing the Etapa
- Ask students to study the picture on pp. 108–109 (1 min.).
- Have them close their books and share at least 3 items that they noticed.
- Have them reopen their books and look at the picture again (1 min.). Have them close their books again and share 3 more details.
- Use the **¿Qué ves?** questions to focus the discussion.

UNIDAD 4

ETAPA 2

En el mercado

- Talk about shopping
- Make purchases
- Talk about giving gifts
- Bargain

¿Qué ves?

Mira la foto del centro de Oaxaca.
1. ¿Hace buen tiempo?
2. ¿Quiénes llevan camisetas azules?
3. ¿Quiénes llevan vestidos?
4. ¿Qué hace la mujer?

108

Middle School Classroom Management

Streamlining Ask students to bring to class large-sized pictures of people, animals, places, things, situations, weather, transportation, food, etc. Mount each picture on tag board to add to the class picture file. The pictures can be used in many ways throughout the year—as story prompts, vocabulary review, or just for fun and games.

Time Saver Designate an area of the room where you can display student work. When an assignment is ready for viewing, students can take care of making the display themselves.

Cross Cultural Connections

Ask students to read the restaurant sign in the upper left corner of the photo: **La Casa de la Abuela.** What kind of cooking might they expect at this restaurant? (**La Casa de la Abuela** serves traditional Oaxacan dishes.)

Culture Highlights

● **EL MERCADO** The **mercados** in Oaxaca have become popular tourist attractions. Artisans sell their products, such as rugs, pottery, wood carvings, and jewelry. **Mercados** are also good places to eat and try out a great variety of Oaxacan traditional dishes.

Explain that there are several types of markets in Latin American cities; there are artisans' markets, produce markets, and flower markets. Ask students if they can guess what **supermercado** or **hipermercado** mean.

● **ALEBRIJE** Wood carving has been practiced since Zapotec times by artisans and their families. You might mention that **alebrije** means "something that is jumbled, confused, or fantastic." The carvings are usually done with a knife, then painted to create imaginary figures such as **cabras** (goats), **armadillos**, **asnos** (donkeys), **coyotes**, **serpientes** (snakes), **unicornios** (unicorns), and even **marcianos** (Martians)!

Supplementary Vocabulary

el dulce de algodón	cotton candy
el líquido para pompas (burbujas) de jabón	bubble soap
el cangrejo	crab
la jirafa	giraffe
el ciervo	deer

Teaching Middle School Students

Extra Help Ask students about the picture on pp. 108–109. Use yes/no and either/or questions, such as ¿Está el mercado en el centro de Oaxaca? ¿Qué vende la mujer, animales o vestidos?, etc.

Native Speakers Ask your native speakers to ask and answer their own ¿Qué ves? questions about the photograph.

Multiple Intelligences

Logical/Mathematical Ask students to compare shopping at the **Mercado Benito Juárez** to shopping where they like to shop. They can present their results in a table or Venn diagram.

Block Schedule

Setting the Theme Play Mexican music and ask students to close their eyes and pretend they are in Oaxaca. Have them describe what they might see and what they imagine themselves to be doing. (For additional activities, see **Block Scheduling Copymasters**.)

Teaching Resource Options

Print

Unit 4 Resource Book
Video Activities, pp. 74–75
Videoscript, p. 77
Audioscript, p. 80
Audioscript *Para hispanohablantes*,
   p. 80

Audiovisual

OHT 117, 118, 119, 119A, 120, 120A,
123 (Quick Start)
Audio Program Cassette 11A / CD 11
Audio *Para hispanohablantes*
   Cassette 11A / CD 11
Video Program Videotape 4 / Videodisc
   2B

Search Chapter 4, Play to 5
U4E2 • En contexto (Vocabulary)

Technology

Intrigas y aventuras CD-ROM, Disc 1

Quick Start Review

♻ Stores

Use OHT 123 or write on board:
List at least 5 types of stores.

Answers

Answers will vary. Answers could include:
la carnicería, la farmacia, la joyería, la librería,
la panadería, la papelería, la tienda de música
y videos, la zapatería

Teaching Suggestions
Introducing Vocabulary

• Have students look at pages 110–111.
  Use OHT 117 and 118 and Audio
  Cassette 11A /CD 11 to present the
  vocabulary.
• Ask the Comprehension Questions
  in order of yes/no (questions 1–3),
  either/or (questions 4–6), and simple
  word or phrase (questions 7–10).
  Expand by adding similar questions.
• Use the TPR activity to reinforce the
  meaning of individual words.
• Use the video vocabulary presentation
  for review and reinforcement.

En contexto · ARTESANÍAS

 VOCABULARIO

Sofía is going shopping at the market in Oaxaca. She sees all
kinds of things. Find out what items interest her the most.

el mercado

A ¡Hola! Voy al Mercado
Benito Juárez. Allí compro el regalo
perfecto.

el regalo

los artículos de cuero

las botas
la bolsa
el cinturón
la cartera

las joyas

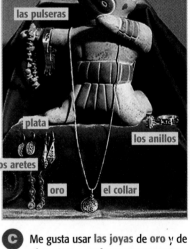

las pulseras
plata
los anillos
los aretes
oro   el collar

B Hay artículos de cuero, como
botas, una bolsa, un cinturón y
una cartera. ¿Qué voy a comprar?

C Me gusta usar las joyas de oro y de
plata. Voy a poder comprar aretes,
anillos, pulseras y collares aquí.

110 ciento diez
Unidad 4

Middle School Classroom Community

TPR As you call out the leather and jewelry
vocabulary words, have students stand up if they are
wearing one of the items (**aretes, cinturón,** etc.).

Game Play ¿Quién tiene...? with students. Ask who
in the class has some of the vocabulary items, such as:
¿Quién tiene unas botas negras? Everyone with the
item stands. Have standing students volunteer to keep
asking questions until the entire class is standing.

CERÁMICA

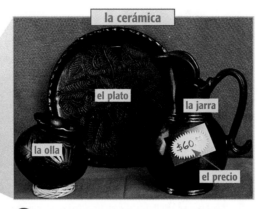

la cerámica

la jarra

el plato

la olla

$60

el precio

D Hay muchas **artesanías** aquí. Hay **cerámica**, como **jarras**, **ollas** y **platos. El precio** de la jarra es 60 pesos.

pagar

el dinero

JARRAS $75⁰⁰

E En el mercado es divertido **regatear**.

Sofía: ¿**Me deja ver** la jarra? ¿**Cuánto cuesta**?
Vendedor: Cincuenta pesos.
Sofía: ¡**Es muy cara**! No tengo suficiente **dinero**. **Le puedo ofrecer** treinta y cinco pesos.
Vendedor: **Le dejo** la jarra **en** cuarenta pesos.
Sofía: Bueno.
Vendedor: ¿Cómo va a **pagar**?

Preguntas personales

1. ¿Te gustan las artesanías?
2. ¿Prefieres las joyas o las artesanías?
3. Cuando vas a un mercado, ¿regateas o pagas el precio?
4. ¿Qué joya quieres comprar?
5. ¿Tienes un artículo de cuero? ¿Cuál?

ciento once
Etapa 2

III

Comprehension Questions

1. ¿Busca Sofía el regalo perfecto? (Sí.)
2. ¿Ella va al correo? (No.)
3. ¿Es una cartera un artículo de cuero? (Sí.)
4. ¿Es el collar de plata o de oro? (de plata)
5. En la foto C, ¿hay un anillo o dos anillos? (dos)
6. ¿Cuál es el precio de la jarra en la foto D, sesenta pesos o setenta pesos? (sesenta pesos)
7. ¿Qué es divertido hacer en el mercado? (regatear)
8. ¿Cuánto cuesta la jarra originalmente? (cincuenta pesos)
9. ¿Cuánto ofrece Sofía? (treinta y cinco pesos)
10. ¿Cuánto paga? (cuarenta pesos)

Culture Highlights

● **JOYERÍA DE OAXACA** Oaxacan jewelry reflects Mesoamerican traditions dating back to 1500 B.C. In pre-Columbian times, Mixtec and Zapotec jewelry was used for religious purposes and burial ceremonies. Mixtec jewelry can be found in the Museum of the American Indian in New York. Reproductions of the valuable gold, silver, jade, and pearl artifacts that Dr. Alfonso Caso discovered at Monte Albán in 1932 are in the Museum of Oaxaca.

Language Notes

• In **joyas de oro y de plata**, the word **de** is used to say what the jewelry is made of.
• There are other Spanish words for the different kinds of jewelry. **Sortija** is another word for *ring*. **Pendiente(s)** also means *earring(s)*. Another way to say *bracelet* is **brazalete**.

Block Schedule

Variety Try to offer students as many different intelligence approaches as possible. Note which students respond to which approaches. It is not necessary to do each approach yourself; encourage individual students to choose their own intelligence preference.

Teaching Middle School Students

Extra Help Make a nicely decorated gift box with a removable lid. Place picture-word cards in the box and encourage pairs of students to drill each other on **Etapa** vocabulary by borrowing the box during free time or study hall.

Multiple Intelligences

Musical To help reinforce the new vocabulary, have students link words with people's names to devise a chant. For example: ¿Qué tiene Pilar? Pilar tiene un collar. ¿Qué tiene Cata? Cata tiene algo de plata. ¿Qué tiene señor Buero? Señor Buero tiene una cartera de cuero…

Kinesthetic Set up a station where students mold the objects on the page out of clay, labeling each to prepare a 3-D vocabulary display.

Teaching Resource Options

Print

Más práctica Workbook PE, pp. 9–12
Para hispanohablantes Workbook PE,
 pp. 9–10
Block Scheduling Copymasters
Unit 4 Resource Book
 Más práctica Workbook TE, pp. 52–55
 Para hispanohablantes Workbook
  TE, pp. 60–61
 Video Activities, p. 76
 Videoscript, p. 78
 Audioscript, p. 80
 Audioscript *Para hispanohablantes*,
  p. 80

Audiovisual

OHT 121, 122, 123 (Quick Start)
Audio Program Cassette 11A / CD 11
Audio *Para hispanohablantes*
 Cassette 11A / CD 11
Video Program Videotape 4 / Videodisc
 2B

Search Chapter 5, Play to 6
U4E2 • En vivo (Dialog)

Technology

Intrigas y aventuras **CD-ROM,** Disc 1

Quick Start Review

♻ Shopping vocabulary

Use OHT 123 or write on board:
Write each word in the correct column.

**la olla / la pulsera / el collar /
el cinturón / la jarra / las botas /
los aretes / la cartera / el plato /
el anillo / la bolsa**

artículos de cuero	joyas	cerámica

Answers *See p. 107B.*

Gestures

Ask students to look at scenes 8–9 and identify facial expressions that show how the vendor feels about Rosa's offer. Remind students that nonverbal communication clues can increase comprehension.

En vivo

  ## DIÁLOGO

¡A regatear!

Rosa

Sofía

Carlos

Vendedor

PARA ESCUCHAR • STRATEGY: LISTENING

Observe as you listen Look carefully as you listen to understand meaning from visual cues. Look for items that belong in specific categories. Write the items in the appropriate column in a chart.

cerámica	cuero	música	joyas

1 ▶ Sofía: ¿Qué le vas a comprar a tu mamá?
Rosa: Quiere una olla de barro negro. Los mercados son muy interesantes y puedes regatear.

5 ▶ Carlos: ¿Almorzamos juntos mañana? Podemos ir a mi restaurante favorito. Almuerzo allí cada ocho días. Voy a participar en un concurso y quiero sus opiniones.
Rosa: Me parece ideal.

6 ▶ Carlos: Entonces hasta mañana, a la una, en el restaurante La Madre Tierra. ¿Recuerdas cómo llegar al restaurante?
Sofía: Sí, Carlos, recuerdo dónde está.
Carlos: ¡Adiós!
Rosa: ¡Hasta mañana!

7 ▶ Vendedor: ¡Ollas, platos, jarras! Aquí encuentra el regalo perfecto…
Rosa: ¿Me deja ver esta olla grande? ¿Cuánto cuesta?
Vendedor: Las ollas grandes cuestan 70 pesos cada una.

112 ciento doce
Unidad 4

Middle School Classroom Community

TPR Organize the class into 4 groups. Assign each group the role of one of the actors in the dialog. Turn off the sound as you play the video and have each group stand as their character speaks, reciting his or her lines in unison.

Group Activity Tell the class that they are going shopping for gifts. Each student writes one purchase on a slip of paper. Clear the center of the room and lay out 3 large overlapping string circles labeled **para mujeres, para hombres,** and **para chicos.** Students place their slips of paper in the appropriate circle. If an article fits in more than one circle, it goes in the overlap. For example, **el anillo** would go in the overlap of all 3 circles.

2 ▶ **Rosa:** Mira, es el nuevo disco compacto de mi grupo favorito.
Sofía: Tienes que comprarle un regalo a tu mamá.

3 ▶ **Rosa:** Vuelvo si me queda dinero.
Sofía: ¡Carlos! ¡Qué sorpresa! Te presento a mi prima. Es de la Ciudad de México.

4 ▶ **Carlos:** Sí, ya lo sé. Hola, Rosa. ¿Qué onda?
Sofía: ¿Tú conoces a Rosa? ¿Cómo?
Carlos: Es nuestro secreto, ¿verdad?

8 ▶ **Rosa:** ¡Es muy cara! Le puedo ofrecer 50 pesos.
Vendedor: Ay, señorita, tengo que ganarme la vida, ¿no? Le dejo la olla en 65.

9 ▶ **Rosa:** ¿Por qué no me da la olla por 60?
Vendedor: Muy bien. Quedamos en 60.
Rosa: Muchísimas gracias, muy amable.
Vendedor: De nada.
Sofía: Muy bien, Rosa. Ahora tienes el regalo para tu mamá.

10 ▶ **Sofía:** ¿Tienes dinero suficiente para el disco compacto?
Rosa: Sí, creo que sí. ¿Sabes?, quiero comprarle un regalo a Carlos. Le doy el disco compacto mañana. ¿Por qué no volvemos a esa tienda de música?

ciento trece
Etapa 2 | **113**

Teaching Middle School Students

Native Speakers Ask students to give a verbal summary of the video.

Multiple Intelligences

Visual As students move through the **Etapa**, have them create a picture dictionary of the vocabulary introduced in the **Etapa**. They may use drawings or cutouts from magazines.

Teaching Suggestions
Presenting the Dialog

• Prepare students for listening by focusing on the dialog context using yes/no or either/or questions. Reintroduce the characters and the setting: **¿El muchacho se llama Carlos? ¿La muchacha que lleva el vestido azul se llama Rosa? ¿Cuál es el nombre de la otra muchacha, Ana o Rosa? ¿Quién lleva un sombrero, el vendedor o Carlos?**

• Use the video, audio cassette, or CD to present the dialog. The expanded dialog on video offers additional listening practice opportunities.

Video Synopsis

• Rosa and Sofía meet Carlos while shopping at the open-air market. For a complete transcript of the video dialog, see p. 107B.

Comprehension Questions

1. ¿Están Rosa y Sofía en el mercado? (Sí.)
2. ¿Rosa va de compras? (Sí.)
3. ¿Quiere Rosa un disco compacto para su madre? (No.)
4. ¿Compra Rosa el disco compacto o espera hasta más tarde? (Espera hasta más tarde.)
5. ¿Es Rosa la prima o la hermana de Sofía? (la prima)
6. ¿Es Rosa de Oaxaca o de la Ciudad de México? (de la Ciudad de México)
7. ¿Quiénes tienen un secreto, Carlos y Rosa o Carlos y Sofía? (Carlos y Rosa)
8. ¿Adónde van Carlos y las muchachas mañana? (al restaurante La Madre Tierra)
9. ¿Qué cosas tiene el vendedor? (ollas, platos, jarras)
10. ¿Cuánto cuestan las ollas grandes? (setenta pesos)

Block Schedule

Process Time Watch out for that overloaded look! Remind students that they don't have to understand every word. To facilitate comprehension, suggest that they concentrate on the dialog in sections. (For additional activities, see **Block Scheduling Copymasters**.)

Teaching Resource Options

Print

Unit 4 Resource Book
  Videoscript, p. 76
  Audioscript, p. 80
  Audioscript *Para hispanohablantes*,
    p. 80

Audiovisual

OHT 124 (Quick Start)
Audio Program Cassette 11A / CD 11
Audio *Para hispanohablantes*
  Cassette 11A / CD 11
Video Program Videotape 4 / Videodisc
  2B

Quick Start Review

♻ Dialog review

Use OHT 124 or write on board:
Unscramble the words to make sentences
about the dialog.

1. primas / y / Rosa / Sofía / son
2. amigos / Sofía / son / y / Carlos
3. para / Rosa / regalo / madre /
   un / quiere / su
4. un / comprarle / regalo /quiere /
   a / Rosa / Carlos

Answers *See p. 107B.*

Teaching Suggestions
Comprehension Check

Use **Actividades 1** and **2** to assess
retention after the dialog. Have students
close their books. Act out the phrases
in **Actividad 2** and see if students can
comprehend and answer correctly.

 Objective: Controlled practice
Listening comprehension/vocabulary

Answers (See script, p. 107B.)
  1. b
  2. b
  3. b
  4. c
  5. b

En acción

VOCABULARIO Y GRAMÁTICA

ACTIVIDAD
1

¿Qué pasa?

Escuchar Completa las oraciones sobre el
diálogo. *(Hint: Complete the statements about the dialog.)*

1. Rosa va a comprarle un regalo a _____.
   a. su prima Sofía
   b. su madre
   c. su tía

2. La _____ de Sofía es de la Ciudad
   de México.
   a. mamá
   b. prima
   c. amiga

3. Mañana Sofía va a _____ con Carlos y Rosa.
   a. escuchar música
   b. almorzar
   c. comprar ollas

4. Rosa paga _____ pesos por la olla grande
   para su mamá.
   a. 75
   b. 50
   c. 60

5. Rosa piensa comprarle _____ a Carlos.
   a. una olla
   b. un disco compacto
   c. un plato

OBJECTIVES

- Talk about shopping
- Make purchases
- Talk about giving gifts
- Bargain
- *Use stem-changing verbs: o→ue*
- *Use indirect object pronouns*

114 ciento catorce
Unidad 4

Middle School Classroom Management

Planning Ahead Prepare for discussing purchases
by starting a collection of catalogs that feature jewelry,
leather goods, and ceramics.

Time Saver Focus on a quick whole-class review of
the dialog, done as a continuing story. You start by
saying, **Rosa y Sofía van al mercado.** Each student, in
turn, adds a sentence in the sequence.

ACTIVIDAD 2

¿Quién?

Escuchar ¿Quién habla en cada caso: Carlos, Rosa, Sofía o el vendedor? *(Hint: Who is speaking in each case: Carlos, Rosa, Sofía, or the vendor?)*

| Carlos | Rosa | Sofía | Vendedor |

1. «Mira, es el nuevo disco compacto de mi grupo favorito.»
2. «¡Carlos! ¡Qué sorpresa!»
3. «¿Tú conoces a Rosa? ¿Cómo?»
4. «¡Ollas, platos, jarras!»
5. «Muy bien, Rosa. Ahora tienes el regalo para tu mamá.»
6. «¿Almorzamos juntos mañana?»

ACTIVIDAD 3

¿Quién lo tiene?

Hablar ¿Quién tiene qué?
(Hint: Who owns what?)

1. On a sheet of paper, write down five items from the list below.

2. Then ask different classmates if they own any of these items.

3. When classmates answer **sí**, have them sign their name next to the item. How fast can you get five signatures?

- un video de *(name of movie)*
- un disco compacto de *(name of musician/s)*
- un anillo de *(oro o plata)*
- una pulsera *(roja, azul, etc.)*
- unos aretes *(negros, etc.)*
- una cartera *(nueva o vieja)*
- unas botas *(viejas o nuevas)*

También se dice

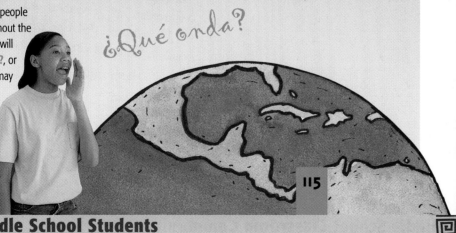

There are many ways to ask people how they are doing. Throughout the Spanish-speaking world you will hear **¿Qué tal?, ¿Qué pasa?,** or **¿Qué hay?** In Mexico, you may also hear **¿Qué onda?** or **¿Qué hubo?**

¿Qué onda?

115

Teaching Middle School Students

Challenge Have students write their own **Querida Emiliana** letters, leaving blanks for at least five vocabulary words. Then have them exchange papers with a friend and try to complete the friend's letter.

Native Speakers Have students pretend they are travel-magazine writers writing about the scene pictured in the **También se dice**. They should write a catchy title and write or tell an "article" of four to five sentences about the scene.

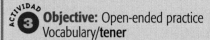

ACTIVIDAD 2 Objective: Controlled practice
Listening comprehension/vocabulary

Answers (See script, p. 107B.)
1. Rosa
2. Sofía
3. Sofía
4. Vendedor
5. Sofía
6. Carlos

ACTIVIDAD 3 Objective: Open-ended practice
Vocabulary/**tener**

Answers will vary.

Game

En orden alfabético Have students form three teams. Appoint a scorekeeper. Then, call a category: **verbos,** for example. A student from the first team must say an **a** verb (**abrir**), a student from the second, a **b** verb (**bailar**), and a student from the third team, a **c** verb (**comer**), etc. Teams play until they reach the end of the alphabet. If a team misses, the next team tries a verb beginning with that letter. Teams get one point if they can't respond. The team with the fewest points wins.

Block Schedule

Variety Have each student choose a Spanish-speaking country. Then have them research the currency of that country and find out the exchange rate. They should find out the names of the bills and coins, and draw illustrations of them.

Teaching Resource Options

Print ✏️

Unit 4 Resource Book
 Videoscript, p. 76
 Audioscript, p. 80
 Audioscript *Para hispanohablantes,*
  p. 80

Audiovisual 📺

OHT 124 (Quick Start)
Audio Program Cassette 11A / CD 11
Audio *Para hispanohablantes*
 Cassette 11A / CD 11
Video Program Videotape 4 / Videodisc
 2B

Objective: Controlled practice
Vocabulary

Answers
1. mercado
2. regalo
3. para
4. olla
5. precio
6. pagar
7. para
8. artículos de cuero
9. cartera
10. cinturón

Interdisciplinary Connection

Science Have students research animals native to Mexico (**mariposa monarca, jaguar, águila,** etc.) or those most represented in Mexican arts and crafts. Then, have them design a toy animal, pin, or necklace that they might expect to find in a Mexican market.

NOTA CULTURAL

These little animals are an example of crafts that are sold in Oaxaca.

ACTIVIDAD 4

Los planes

Leer/Escribir Completa la carta de Rosa con una de las expresiones. *(Hint: Complete Rosa's letter.)*

artículos de cuero	mercado	para
cartera	olla	precio
cinturón	pagar	regalo

Nota

Use **para** *(for, in order to)* to indicate…

• the recipient of items … el regalo **para** tu mamá.

• purpose Vamos al restaurante **para** comer.

• implied purpose Tengo dinero **para** [comprar] algo.

Querida Emiliana:

 Hoy voy al ___1___ con mi prima Sofía.
Tengo que comprar un ___2___ de cumpleaños
___3___ mi mamá. Ella quiere una ___4___ negra.
No sé qué ___5___ tiene una olla, pero Sofía
dice que no voy a ___6___ más de setenta
pesos. Si Sofía tiene razón, voy a tener
suficiente dinero ___7___ comprar algo para
mi papá también. Él prefiere los ___8___.
Entonces, voy a comprar una ___9___ o un
___10___ para él. ¡Ay! Son las ocho. Me tengo
que ir. Sofía me está esperando.

 Hasta pronto,

 Rosa

---

116 ciento dieciséis
Unidad 4

Middle School Classroom Community

Group Activity Write the vocabulary used in **Actividad 5** on the board. Have students count off by tens. Say, "**La bolsa cuesta setenta pesos. ¿Quién tiene setenta pesos?**" The student whose number you called stands and responds, then applies a price to another item and asks who has that amount. **Yo tengo setenta pesos. Las botas cuestan noventa pesos…**

Learning Scenario Give students pictures of objects and prices (from the catalogs mentioned in "Planning Ahead," TE, p. 114). Have them work in small groups to model a scenario about making a purchase.

ACTIVIDAD 5

♻ En la tienda

Hablar Trabajas en una tienda. Una persona quiere saber los precios de unas cosas. ¿Qué dices? Cambien de papel. *(Hint: You work in a shop. Someone wants to know the prices. Take turns asking and giving the prices of different items.)*

modelo

aretes / $75

Estudiante A: *¿Cuánto cuestan los aretes?*

Estudiante B: *Cuestan setenta y cinco pesos.*

Nota

When asking or giving the price of a single item, use **cuesta**. When asking or giving the price of more than one item, use **cuestan**.

¿Cuánto cuesta el anillo?
¿Cuánto cuestan los aretes?

1. pulsera / $84
2. collar / $98
3. anillo / $60
4. bolsa / $75
5. cinturón / $32
6. botas / $95

Conexiones

La historia/La artesanía The region of Oaxaca was civilized long before the Spanish arrived. People have been living there since 900 B.C. Oaxaca's population has kept much of its original heritage intact. The region is known worldwide for the work of its artisans.

> **PARA HACER:**
> Name some examples of handicrafts, such as jewelry, leather goods, or ceramics, that you would find in Oaxaca today.

ciento diecisiete
Etapa 2   **117**

Teaching Middle School Students

Extra Help Act out the letter in **Actividad 4** for the class. Use props (money, pitcher) and exaggerated gestures.

Challenge Extend **Actividad 5** by having students ask each other about the clothes they are wearing or items they have in class.

Multiple Intelligences

Naturalist Ask how many animals students can identify in the **Nota Cultural** photo. What words can they use to describe the animals in Spanish?

Visual Have students draw their own Oaxacan animals. Review adjectives by having students describe each other's work.

ACTIVIDAD 5

Objective: Controlled practice Vocabulary/numbers

♻ **Numbers**

Answers
1. ¿Cuánto cuesta la pulsera? Cuesta ochenta y cuatro pesos.
2. ¿Cuánto cuesta el collar? Cuesta noventa y ocho pesos.
3. ¿Cuánto cuesta el anillo? Cuesta sesenta pesos.
4. ¿Cuánto cuesta la bolsa? Cuesta setenta y cinco pesos.
5. ¿Cuánto cuesta el cinturón? Cuesta treinta y dos pesos.
6. ¿Cuánto cuestan las botas? Cuestan noventa y cinco pesos.

Game

¿Cuál es el precio correcto? Have students gather ads for **Etapa 2** items (**botas, cinturón, anillo,** etc.) with their prices. Students obscure the price, write a whole-number price between $10 and $300 on the back of the ad, and tape the ad to the board. Students take turns bidding for two items that they did not contribute. For example: **Quiero el cinturón de cuero marrón y el collar de oro a lado de él. Pienso que el cinturón cuesta $25 y el collar $300.** A scribe writes each bidder's name and bids near the items. When all bids are in, reveal the real prices. The closest bidder "wins" the item.

Para hacer

Answers
Answers may include: anillos, aretes, collares, pulseras, artículos de cuero, artesanía, bolsas, carteras, cerámicas, cinturones, jarras, ollas, platos.

■ Block Schedule

Variety Have students study the **Nota,** p. 116, and work in pairs or small groups to prepare a mnemonic sentence or rhyme to help them remember the uses of **para.** For example, **Tengo dinero para el metro para ir al mercado y comprar el regalo para mi hija.**

Teaching Resource Options

Print

Más práctica Workbook PE, p. 13
Para hispanohablantes Workbook PE,
  p. 11
Block Scheduling Copymasters
Unit 4 Resource Book
  Más práctica Workbook TE, p. 56
  Para hispanohablantes Workbook
    TE, p. 62
  Audioscript, p. 81
  Audioscript *Para hispanohablantes*,
    p. 82

Audiovisual

OHT 124 (Quick Start)
Audio Program Cassettes 11A, 11B /
  CD 11
Audio *Para hispanohablantes*
  Cassette 11A / CD 11

Technology

Intrigas y aventuras CD-ROM, Disc 1

Quick Start Review

♻ **e → ie verbs**

Use OHT 124 or write on board:
Write the correct form of the verb.

1. María ____ comprar unos aretes.
   (querer)
2. Ellos ____ ir al concierto. (pensar)
3. Yo ____ la jarra roja. (preferir)
4. ¿A qué hora ____ la clase de
   historia? (empezar)
5. Tú siempre ____ la lección de
   matemáticas. (entender)

Answers
1. quiere   4. empieza
2. piensan   5. entiendes
3. prefiero

Teaching Suggestions
Presenting Stem-Changing
Verbs: o → ue

Activating prior knowledge: Focus on
the ¿Recuerdas? note. Ask students to
write or draw a description of the new
o → ue verbs using their own words.
Point out that o → ue stem-changing
verbs are also "boot" verbs. Remind
students to double-check infinitive
endings when conjugating.

GRAMÁTICA

Stem-Changing Verbs: o → ue

♻ **¿RECUERDAS?** *1A, p. 230* Remember verbs like **pensar**,
where the stem alternates between **e** and **ie**?

pensar *to think, to plan*

pie**nso**	**pensamos**
pie**nsas**	**pensáis**
pie**nsa**	**pi**e**nsan**

Something similar happens with verbs like **almorzar** *(to eat lunch)*.
The stem alternates between **o** and **ue**.

almorzar *to eat lunch*

almue**rzo**	**alm**o**rzamos**
almue**rzas**	**alm**o**rzáis**
almue**rza**	**alm**ue**rzan**

The stem
doesn't change for the
nosotros *(we)* or
vosotros *(you)* form.

Carlos says:
—**Alm**ue**rzo** allí cada ocho días.
I eat lunch there every week.

Many other verbs have this same kind of change
in their stem.

The vendor says:
—Aquí **enc**ue**ntra** el regalo perfecto...
*Here **you'll find** the perfect gift...*

—Las ollas grandes **c**ue**stan** 70 pesos...
*The big pots **cost** 70 pesos...*

Vocabulario

Stem-Changing Verbs: o → ue

almorzar *to eat lunch*
contar *to count, to tell or retell*
costar *to cost*
devolver *to return (an item)*
dormir *to sleep*
encontrar *to find, to meet*
poder *to be able, can*
recordar *to remember*
volver *to return, to come back*
¿Qué haces cada día? ¿Cada
semana?

118   ciento dieciocho
      Unidad 4

Middle School Classroom Community

Cooperative Learning Divide the class into groups
of 4. Student 1 writes a question using a stem-changing
verb. Student 2 responds and writes his or her own
question on the same paper. Student 3 reviews the
questions for accuracy, and Student 4 records answers.

TPR Write vocabulary words from p. 118 on cards.
Shuffle them, then call on a student to pick one and
mime the word for classmates to guess.

Portfolio Have students write about their favorite
CD/cassette, video, or video game.

Rubric

Criteria	Scale	
Vocabulary use	1 2 3 4 5	A = 13–15 pts.
Logical sentence structure/order	1 2 3 4 5	B = 10–12 pts. C = 7–9 pts.
Grammar/spelling accuracy	1 2 3 4 5	D = 4–6 pts. F = < 4 pts.

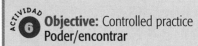

ACTIVIDAD 6 Gramática

¿Dónde vive?

Escribir Completa las oraciones con la forma correcta del verbo **poder** o **encontrar** *(Hint: Use the correct form of poder or encontrar.)*

Enrique no _____ recordar donde vive Luis. Le _____ a Luis en la clase. —¿ _____ darme otra vez tu dirección? —le pide. —Sí, _____ darle mi dirección, pero nosotros _____ encontrarnos después de la escuela. —Bien. Es mejor si te _____ después de la escuela. Hasta las tres.

ACTIVIDAD 7 Gramática

¿Adónde van?

Leer/Escribir Sofía y Rosa hablan con la mamá de Sofía. Completa la conversación con la forma correcta de cada verbo. *(Hint: Complete the conversation with the correct verb and verb form.)*

Rosa: Vamos al mercado para ver si yo __1__ (encontrar / poder) un regalo.

Mamá: ¿ __2__ (volver / recordar) ustedes para almorzar?

Sofía: No. Nosotras __3__ (contar / almorzar) en un café. Y tú, ¿adónde vas?

Mamá: Voy a la zapatería para ver cuanto __4__ (poder / costar) los zapatos.

Sofía: Tia, si yo __5__ (recordar / dormir) bien, la zapatería está cerca del correo, ¿no?

Mamá: Sí, tú __6__ (almorzar / recordar) bien.

■ **MÁS PRÁCTICA** *cuaderno* p. 13

■ **PARA HISPANOHABLANTES** *cuaderno* p. 11

ACTIVIDAD 8

♻ ¿Pedir permiso?

Hablar Tus primos te visitan. Ustedes tienen que pedirle permiso a tu mamá para salir. Ella pregunta a qué hora van a volver ustedes. *(Hint: You have to ask your mother for permission to go out. She wants to know what time you will return.)*

modelo

mis primos y yo → cine 8:30
Estudiante A: *Mamá, ¿podemos ir al cine?*
Estudiante B: *¿A qué hora vuelven?*
Estudiante A: *Volvemos a las ocho y media.*

1. yo → almacén 3:30
2. los primos → centro comercial 4:00
3. Miguel y yo → mercado 5:30
4. Marta → joyería 2:30
5. las primas → farmacia 4:30

ACTIVIDAD 9

♻ ¿Qué usa?

Escuchar Rosa le explica a Sofía cómo va a varios lugares en la capital. ¿Qué transporte usa para ir a cada lugar? *(Hint: Say what transportation Rosa uses.)*

1. carro
2. metro
3. taxi
4. a pie
5. autobús

a. la escuela
b. la clase de piano
c. el parque
d. el museo
e. la casa de los abuelos

ciento diecinueve
Etapa 2
119

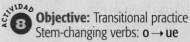

ACTIVIDAD 6
Objective: Controlled practice
Poder/encontrar

Answers
1. puede
2. encuentra
3. Puedes
4. puedo
5. podemos
6. encuentro

ACTIVIDAD 7
Objective: Transitional practice
Stem-changing verbs: o → ue

Answers
1. encuentro
2. Vuelven
3. almorzamos
4. cuestan
5. recuerdo
6. recuerdas

ACTIVIDAD 8
Objective: Transitional practice
Stem-changing verbs: o → ue
♻ Places, telling time

Answers
1. Mamá, ¿puedo ir al almacén? ¿A qué hora vuelves? Vuelvo a las tres y media.
2. Mamá, ¿pueden los primos ir al centro comercial? ¿A qué hora vuelven? Vuelven a las cuatro.
3. Mamá, ¿Miguel y yo podemos ir al mercado? ¿A qué hora vuelven? Volvemos a las cinco y media.
4. Mamá, ¿puede Marta ir a la joyería? ¿A qué hora vuelve? Vuelve a las dos y media.
5. Mamá, ¿pueden las primas ir a la farmacia? ¿A qué hora vuelven? Vuelven a las cuatro y media.

ACTIVIDAD 9
Objective: Transitional practice
Listening comprehension/vocabulary
♻ Transportation

Answers (See script, p. 107B.)
1. e
2. c
3. b
4. a
5. d

Teaching Middle School Students 回

Extra Help Bring to class some shoes (or borrow some from your students!). Ask: What do these shoes and the verbs **pensar** and **almorzar** have in common? (They are "shoe" verbs.) Conjugate **pensar** on the board and outline a shoe around the stem-changing forms (see p. 118 for model). Review and contrast the endings of a regular -ar verb next to **pensar**. Ask: Which forms of **pensar** do not change to -ie?

Multiple Intelligences

Musical Teach the Spanish version of "Frère Jacques": Fray Felipe, fray Felipe, ¿duermes tú? ¿duermes tú? Tocan las campanas, tocan las campanas. Din, dan, don; din, dan, don. Substitute other verbs for duermes. For example: ¿almuerzas tú?, ¿vuelves tú?

▊ Block Schedule

Change of Pace Have one student pantomime a simple sentence using a stem-changing verb (**Él/Ella almuerza a las once y media.**) while the rest of class guesses. The student who guesses, pantomimes a new sentence. (For additional activities, see **Block Scheduling Copymasters.**)

Teaching Resource Options

Print
Block Scheduling Copymasters
Unit 4 Resource Book
  Information Gap Activities, p. 68

Audiovisual
OHT 125 (Quick Start)

Technology
Intrigas y aventuras CD-ROM, Disc 1

 Objective: Open-ended practice **ue** stem-changing verbs

Answers will vary.

 Objective: Open-ended practice Vocabulary

Answers will vary.

🔔 Quick Wrap-up

Using **poder,** have students work in pairs and tell each other 3 things they can do well and 3 things they cannot do well.

Teaching Suggestions
Presenting Vocabulary

• Before assigning **Actividad 11,** have students work in pairs and use the new vocabulary to comment on the photos of the items and their prices. Remember that the prices represent **pesos,** not dollars.

• Have students repeat the new vocabulary words. Encourage them to use associated gestures when appropriate.

¿Qué tienen en común?

Hablar Circula por la clase. Pregunta a tus compañeros estas preguntas. Toma apuntes. Explica a la clase las cosas que tienen en común. *(Hint: Ask classmates these questions. Take notes. Report to the class what you have in common.)*

modelo

Estudiante A: *¿A qué hora vuelves a casa los sábados por la noche?*

Estudiante B: *Generalmente vuelvo a las diez. ¿Y tú?*

Estudiante C: *Vuelvo a las diez también.*

(A la clase:) *Susana y yo volvemos a casa a las diez los sábados por la noche.*

1. ¿A qué hora almuerzas?
2. ¿Dónde encuentras tus libros en casa?
3. ¿Qué les cuentas a tus amigos? ¿Secretos? ¿Información importante?
4. ¿A qué hora vuelves a casa después de las clases?
5. ¿Cuantas horas duermes cada noche?

 ## Le puedo ofrecer...

PARA CONVERSAR STRATEGY: SPEAKING

Express emotion Bargaining is the art of compromise with a little emotion.

React: ¡Qué bonito! ¡Qué chévere! ¡Qué bien!

Get someone's attention: Perdone...

Agree: Creo que sí. Claro que sí. Está bien.

Disagree: Creo que no. Gracias, pero no puedo.

Hablar Estás en un mercado. Necesitas comprar unas cosas. Con otro(a) estudiante, regatea. Cambien de papel. ¡La conversación puede variar mucho! *(Hint: Bargain with a classmate.)*

modelo

Estudiante A: *¿Cuánto cuestan los aretes?*

Estudiante B: *Ochenta pesos.*

Estudiante A: *¡Es demasiado! Le puedo ofrecer setenta pesos.*

Estudiante B: *¡Son muy baratos! Son de buena calidad. Le dejo los aretes en setenta y cinco pesos.*

Estudiante A: *Bueno, los llevo. Pago en efectivo.*

■ **MÁS COMUNICACIÓN** p. R2

Vocabulario

Expresiones para regatear

barato(a) *cheap, inexpensive*
la calidad *quality*
cambiar *to change, to exchange*
el cambio *change, money exchange*
¿Qué palabras usas cuando regateas?

caro(a) *expensive*
demasiado(a) *too much*
el dólar *dollar*

el efectivo *cash*
perfecto(a) *perfect*
la tarjeta de crédito *credit card*

---

120 ciento veinte
Unidad 4

Middle School Classroom Community

Learning Scenario Have students imagine they and a sister or brother plan on pooling their money to buy a gift for their grandmother. Have them argue about which of two items to buy, trying to come to agreement.

Portfolio Have students write about a recent purchase using **Etapa** vocabulary. Encourage partners to review each other's work before the final edit.

Rubric

Criteria	Scale	
Vocabulary use	1 2 3 4 5	A = 13–15 pts.
Logical sentence structure/order	1 2 3 4 5	B = 10–12 pts.
Grammar/spelling accuracy	1 2 3 4 5	C = 7–9 pts.
		D = 4–6 pts.
		F = < 4 pts.

GRAMÁTICA

Indirect Object Pronouns

 ¿RECUERDAS? *1A, p. 259* You learned that **direct object pronouns** can be used to avoid repetition of the noun and answer the question *who?* or *what?*

replaces

—Pues, ya tienes **ropa** de verano.   —Claro que **la** tengo.
*You already have summer **clothing**.*   *Of course I have **it**.*

Indirect objects are **nouns** that tell *to whom/what* or *for whom/what.*
Indirect object pronouns replace or accompany **indirect objects.**

Singular	Plural
me	nos
me	*us*
te	os
you (familiar)	*you (familiar)*
le	les
you (formal), him, her	*you (formal), them*

Notice that **indirect object pronouns** use the same words as **direct object pronouns** except for **le** and **les**.

accompanies   *replaces*

Rosa **le** compra una olla **a su madre.**   Rosa **le** compra una olla.
*Rosa buys a pot **for her mother**.*   *Rosa buys a pot **for her**.*

The pronouns **le** and **les** can refer to different **indirect objects.** To clarify what they mean, they are often accompanied by:

a + **name, noun,** or **pronoun**

Rosa **le** compra una olla.
*Rosa buys a pot **for her**.*

Rosa **le** compra una olla **a** su madre.
*Rosa buys a pot **for her mother**.*

ciento veintiuno   **121**
Etapa 2

Teaching Middle School Students

Extra Help Before beginning **Actividad 11,** quickly review the characters in the dialog, pp. 112–113.

Multiple Intelligences

Verbal Have student volunteers practice the intonation patterns in **Actividad 11.**

Logical/Mathematical Have groups of students tabulate the results in **Actividad 11,** and calculate class percentages for each item.

Quick Start Review
♻ Direct object pronouns

Use OHT 125 or write on board: Write the direct object pronouns you would use to answer these questions.

1. ¿Necesitas el mapa?
2. ¿Vas a comprar las botas?
3. ¿Quieres el disco compacto de Selena?
4. ¿Recibe Julia los regalos de cumpleaños?
5. ¿Tenemos la jarra de mamá?

Answers
1. lo   2. las   3. lo   4. los   5. la

Teaching Suggestions
♻ **Direct object pronouns**

• Focus students' attention on the note on direct object pronouns. Ask for 5 sample sentences.

Presenting Indirect Object Pronouns

• Using gestures, present the verb **dar** *(to give).* Then pass out some classroom objects to students, describing as you go: **Le doy un lápiz verde a Carolina. Les doy papeles a Juan y Chucho.** Reaching for someone's book, ask: **¿Me das tu libro? Gracias.** Have students pass the items to other students and describe: **Carolina te da el lápiz verde, Dani.**

• Point out that there are only two basic differences between direct object pronouns and indirect object pronouns: the key questions, *to whom?* or *for whom?* and the two pronouns **le** and **les.** Also point out that there must be an indirect object pronoun in a sentence with an indirect object.

• Remind students that they have already used indirect object pronouns with **gustar.**

Block Schedule
Process Time To give students more processing time before presenting indirect object pronouns, try the storytelling activity from **Ampliación,** p. 81A. (For additional activities, see **Block Scheduling Copymasters.**)

Teaching Resource Options

Print

Más práctica Workbook PE, pp. 14–15
Para hispanohablantes Workbook PE, pp. 12–13
Block Scheduling Copymasters
Unit 4 Resource Book
  Más práctica Workbook TE, pp. 57–58
  Para hispanohablantes Workbook TE, pp. 63–64
  Audioscript, p. 81
  Audioscript *Para hispanohablantes*, p. 82

Audiovisual

Audio Program Cassettes 11A, 11B / CD 11
Audio *Para hispanohablantes* Cassette 11A / CD 11

Technology

Intrigas y aventuras CD-ROM, Disc 1

Teaching Suggestions
Reinforcing Object Pronouns

For additional practice, write these sentences on the board: **Rosa le compra una olla a su mamá.** *Buys what?* (una olla) *To whom or for whom?* (su mamá) Sí, Rosa le compra una olla a su mamá. Yo les busco zapatos nuevos a mis primos. *Looks for what?* (zapatos nuevos) *To whom or for whom?* (mis primos) ¡Bueno! Les busco zapatos nuevos a mis primos.

 Objective: Controlled practice Indirect object pronouns

Answers
1. le
2. le
3. me
4. nos
5. te
6. les
7. le
8. nos
9. te
10. me

 Objective: Controlled practice Indirect object pronouns/**dar**

Answers
1. Su esposo le da un collar de oro.
2. Nosotros le damos una bolsa.
3. Sus hijos le dan...
4. Su hermano le da...
5. Yo le doy...
6. Tú le das...
7. Sofía le da...

De compras

Hablar/Escribir Completa las oraciones con **me, te, le, les** o **nos**. *(Hint: Complete the sentences with me, te, le, los, o nos.)*

1. A la mamá de Rosa ____ encantan las ollas de barro negro.
2. Rosa ____ pide el precio de la olla al vendedor.
3. A mí no ____ gusta regatear.
4. A nosotros ____ encantan las tiendas de video.
5. ¿A ti ____ gustan los mercados?
6. A Rosa y a Carlos ____ encanta tener un secreto.
7. El vendedor ____ deja un buen precio a Rosa.
8. A nosotros ____ encanta ir de compras.
9. ¿Quieres que ____ compro una jarra cuando voy a Oaxaca?
10. Pero señor, a mí ____ parece muy caro.

¡Cuántos regalos!

Escribir Es el cumpleaños de la mamá de Rosa. Muchas personas le dan regalos. ¿Qué le dan? *(Hint: It is Rosa's mother's birthday. Many people give her gifts. What do they give?)*

modelo

Rosa: un collar de plata
Rosa le da **un collar de plata**.

Nota

Dar means *to give*. It has an irregular **yo** form: **doy**. Its other forms are regular, except the **vosotros** form has no accent.

1. su esposo: un collar de oro
2. nosotros: una bolsa
3. sus hijos: una pulsera
4. su hermano: una jarra de barro negro
5. yo: un disco compacto
6. tú: un video
7. Sofía: unos aretes

■ **MÁS PRÁCTICA** *cuaderno* p. 14–15
■ **PARA HISPANOHABLANTES** *cuaderno* p. 12–13

Juego

¿Lidia le da la lila a Lola, o quiere darle Lola la lila a Lidia?

Middle School Classroom Community

Group Activity Use pictures from the picture file created in "Streamlining," TE, p. 108. Have students pretend they are on a home shopping TV show. One student describes an item and its price while another students holds it up and demonstrates the item.

Cooperative Learning Students can work on **Actividad 13** cooperatively. Write the words from the activity on index cards. Divide the class into groups of four and distribute cards. Student A is responsible for **dar**; Student B, the subjects; Student C, the indirect pronouns; and Student D, the nouns. Students use the cards to form the sentences in the **Actividad.**

Regalos para todos

Escuchar Rosa va a la tienda de música y videos. ¡Compra muchos regalos! Escucha a Rosa y escribe lo que les compra a las personas. *(Hint: Rosa goes to the music and video store. She buys a lot of gifts! Write what she buys for everyone.)*

> *modelo*
>
> Rosa le compra **un casete** a la profesora Díaz.

a.

b.

c.

d.

e.

Para tu cumpleaños

Hablar Conversa con tu compañero(a) sobre los regalos que reciben de estas personas en sus cumpleaños. *(Hint: Talk about the gifts you received for your birthday.)*

> *modelo*
>
> tus padres
>
> **Estudiante A:** ¿Qué te dan **tus padres**?
>
> **Estudiante B:** Me dan casetes.

1. tu hermano(a)
2. tus amigos
3. tu tío(a)
4. tus abuelos
5. tu primo(a)

Vocabulario

En la tienda de música y videos

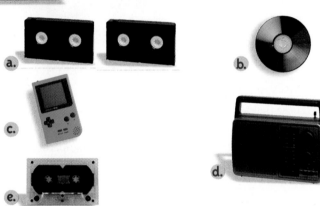

el casete   el disco compacto   el radio   el radiocasete

el video   la videograbadora

el videojuego

¿Qué te gusta usar?

ciento veintitrés
Etapa 2   **123**

Teaching Middle School Students

Extra Help Photocopy **Actividad 12**. Help students first identify the indirect object by underlining the indirect object phrase in each sentence.

Multiple Intelligences

Musical Have individuals or groups make up a song with **Etapa** vocabulary and record it on a tape recorder to share with the class.

Intrapersonal Have each student list the music and video vocabulary in order of importance in his or her daily life (1 = highest; 7 = lowest).

Juego

Answer: Lola quiere darle la lila a Lidia.

Objective: Transitional practice Vocabulary/verb endings/indirect object pronouns

Answers (See script, p. 107B.)
a. los videos, las hermanas
b. el disco compacto, Amanda
c. el videojuego, el hermano
d. el radio, Pablo
e. el casete, Sofía

Objective: Open-ended practice Vocabulary/verb endings/indirect object pronouns

Answers will vary.

Quick Wrap-up

Have students name items they would like to buy in the following stores:
una joyería / una tienda de cerámica / una tienda de música y videos / una tienda de artículos de cuero

Teaching Suggestions
Presenting Vocabulary
Present the vocabulary using the text or objects in the classroom, if available. Ask questions. Progress from yes/no questions (**¿Escuchas música con un casete? ¿Tienes muchos discos compactos?**), to either/or questions (**¿Te gusta escuchar música con un casete o un disco compacto?**), to questions using interrogatives (**¿En cuál pones videos, en un videograbadora o en un radiocasete? ¿Dónde pones casetes?**).

Block Schedule

Change of Pace Have students work in pairs. One student closes his/her eyes while the other places an object (identifiable in Spanish) in the partner's hands, saying: **¿Qué te doy?** The partner guesses, responding **Me das...** Variation: Have students hand you objects to guess. (For additional activities, see **Block Scheduling Copymasters.**)

Teaching Resource Options

Print

Más práctica Workbook PE, p. 16
Para hispanohablantes Workbook PE, p. 14
Block Scheduling Copymasters
Unit 4 Resource Book
  Más práctica Workbook TE, p. 59
  Para hispanohablantes Workbook TE, p. 65

Audiovisual

OHT 125 (Quick Start)

Technology

Intrigas y aventuras CD-ROM, Disc 1

Quick Start Review

♻ Indirect object pronouns

Use OHT 125 or write on the board:
Match the indirect object pronoun with its corresponding phrase:

1. les   a. a mí
2. nos   b. a ella
3. te   c. a Juan y a mí
4. le   d. a los niños
5. me   e. a ti

Answers
1. d   2. c   3. e   4. b   5. a

Teaching Suggestions
Reinforcing Placement of Indirect Object Pronouns

For additional practice, have students complete these sentences:

1. Mi mejor amigo acaba de salir de vacaciones. Voy a escribir___ pronto.
2. Tengo información interesante para ti. Voy a decir___ esta noche.
3. Mi cumpleaños es mañana. Mis padres van a comprar___ un radiocasete.
4. Nuestro profesor de español es excelente. Va a enseñar___ una canción mexicana.
5. Mis primos buscan un coche. Quiero vender___ mi coche viejo.

Answers
1. escribirle   4. enseñarnos
2. decirte   5. venderles
3. comprarme

 GRAMÁTICA

Placement of Indirect Object Pronouns

How do you know where indirect object pronouns go in a sentence? They work just like **direct object pronouns.**

• When the pronoun accompanies a **conjugated verb**, the pronoun comes before the verb.

  before

  Rosa le **quiere comprar** una olla a su madre.
  Rosa wants to buy her mother a pot.

• But when the pronoun accompanies a sentence with an **infinitive**, it can either go before the **conjugated verb** or be attached to the end of the **infinitive**:

  attached

  Rosa **quiere comprar**le una olla a su madre.
  Rosa wants to buy her mother a pot.

ACTIVIDAD 16 Gramática

¿Qué debo regalarles?

Escribir Todos quieren dar los regalos a otros. Completa las oraciones. *(Hint: Everyone wants to give someone a present. Complete the sentences.)*

modelo

Rosa / una jarra a su mamá
Rosa _quiere darle_ una jarra.
o: Rosa _le quiere dar_ una jarra.

1. Yo / unos aretes a mis primas
   Yo _____ unos aretes.
2. Mis padres / un video a Luis
   Mis padres _____ un video.
3. Carlos / un libro a tí
   Carlos _____ un libro.
4. Mi amiga / una bolsa a mí
   Mi amiga _____ una bolsa.

■ **MÁS PRÁCTICA** *cuaderno* p. 16

■ **PARA HISPANOHABLANTES** *cuaderno* p. 14

ACTIVIDAD 17

En la tienda

Hablar/Escribir Carlos está muy ocupado hoy. Acaba de vender muchas cosas en la tienda de su papá. ¿A quiénes les vendió cosas? *(Hint: Carlos is very busy today. He has just sold a lot in his father's store. To whom has Carlos sold things?)*

modelo

Carlos acaba de venderle una revista a Rosa.
o: Carlos le acaba de vender una revista a Rosa.

un refresco   Rosa
un mapa   Rosa y Sofía
un periódico   mí
una revista   su vecino
¿?   ¿?

---

124   ciento veinticuatro
            Unidad 4

Middle School Classroom Community

Learning Scenario Designate an area of the classroom as **El mercado** to use throughout the **Etapa.** You might have students help create the **mercado** by contributing wares, writing signs, creating price tags in **pesos**, making fake money, etc.

Divide the class into groups. Hand out role cards to all but one member of each group. These roles might include the following: (1) **Tienes que devolver una** cosa. (2) **No puedes recordar lo que quieres comprar. No te gusta gastar dinero. Pregunta cuánto cuestan las cosas.** (3) **Tienes hambre. Quieres saber dónde puedes almorzar.** Designate a vendor and have students role-play their scenarios at **el mercado.**

ACTIVIDAD 18

¿Qué pasa?

Hablar Trabaja con un(a) compañero. Explica lo que pasa en estas escenas. Túrnense para describir cada escena. *(Hint: Work with a classmate to tell the story. Take turns describing each scene.)*

¿Quieres venir a mi fiesta de cumpleaños?

María Luisa   Daniel

modelo

María Luisa llama a Daniel por teléfono. Le invita a su fiesta de cumpleaños.

¡Sí! Gracias.

¡Qué bueno!

¿Cuándo es?

El sábado a las ocho.

95 pesos, por favor.

¡Muchas gracias, Daniel! Son tan bonitos.

¿Quieres ir al cine mañana?

ciento veinticinco
Etapa 2   **125**

ACTIVIDAD 16 **Objective:** Controlled practice
Verb endings/indirect object pronouns

Answers
1. quiero darles / les quiero dar
2. quieren darle / le quieren dar
3. quiere darte / te quiere dar
4. quiere darme / me quiere dar

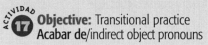

ACTIVIDAD 17 **Objective:** Transitional practice
Acabar de/indirect object pronouns

Answers will vary.

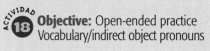

ACTIVIDAD 18 **Objective:** Open-ended practice
Vocabulary/indirect object pronouns

Answers will vary.

Project

Cuentos cómicos cortitos Have students use **Etapa 2** vocabulary to create shopping story comics. These are 5- or 6-frame comic strips with characters, speech balloons, and captions drawn on 8 ½" x 11" paper folded in half lengthwise. Have pairs use their comics as scripts and perform their stories for the class. Display all the comics and/or vote on the funniest, best, etc.

Block Schedule

Retention Use TPR commands to review **ue** stem-changing verbs. Give commands such as: **Micaela, almuerza. Paco y Marcos, duerman en el suelo...** Then, follow up by asking students to tell what they or classmates are doing: **¿Qué hace Micaela? Paco, ¿qué hacen tú y Marcos?**

Teaching Middle School Students

Extra Help Label the columns in **Actividad 17**, **Cosas** and **Personas**. Point out that only the indirect object pronoun, **cosa**, and **persona** change.

Multiple Intelligences

Intrapersonal Designate some quiet time in the classroom so that students with intrapersonal strengths might study and memorize the forms and placement of indirect object pronouns.

Teaching Resource Options

Print

Block Scheduling Copymasters
Unit 4 Resource Book
  Information Gap Activities, pp. 69–70

Audiovisual

OHT 125 (Quick Start)

Technology

Intrigas y aventuras CD-ROM, Disc 1

 Objective: Open-ended practice
Indirect object pronouns/vocabulary

Answers will vary.

Game

Write **lugares (Etapa 1)** on index cards.
Write items that can be purchased in the
lugares (Etapa 2) on another set of index
cards. Use more items than places, but
have enough cards for all students. Clear
the center of the room. Mix the cards and
distribute them randomly, one to each
student. They circulate around the room
showing their cards, looking for a match
(2 min.). Each matched pair makes a
sentence, uniting place and item: **Compro
aretes en una joyería.** Anyone without a
match is out. Return all cards to the pack
and play more rounds.

Para hacer

Answers
Etla (el miércoles); Oaxaca (el sábado);
Ocotlán (el viernes); Miahuatlán (el lunes).

Conexiones

Los estudios sociales Each of the towns and villages
surrounding Oaxaca has a special market day. On Mondays the village of
Miahuatlán features bread and leather goods.
Etla's market day is Wednesday. People buy
meat, cheese, and flowers. On Friday sellers
in Ocotlán display their flowers, pottery,
and textiles. And on
Oaxaca's market
day, Saturday,
nearly everything
imaginable is sold.

PARA HACER:
As you point to each
town, tell which day
of the week you would
go to market and what
you would buy there.
(In Spanish, of course.)

 **N O T A CULTURAL**

When you are in Mexico and
want to buy yourself something,
you can get the most for your
peso if you pay attention to
which shops and stores are
having sales. How can you do
this? Look for advertisements
in the newspaper or signs in
store windows.

 ¡GRAN OFERTA! ¡LIQUIDACIÓN!
¡Grandes rebajas!

ACTIVIDAD 19

¡Cuéntame!

Hablar/Escribir Trabaja con un(a) compañero(a). Cada persona le
hace estas preguntas a la otra persona. Toma apuntes. Explica a la
clase las cosas que tienen ustedes dos en común. *(Hint: Ask your partner
the following questions. Take notes. Report to the class what you have in common.)*

1. ¿Quién te ayuda cuando tienes problemas?
2. ¿Quién te ayuda cuando no entiendes una tarea?
3. ¿Quién te da dinero cuando lo necesitas?
4. ¿Quién te da magníficos regalos?
5. ¿Quién te envía una carta interesante?
6. ¿Quién te escribe mucho correo electrónico?
7. ¿Quién te llama mucho por teléfono?

126 ciento veintiséis
Unidad 4

Middle School Classroom Community

TPR Write some sentences on the board that include
indirect object pronouns. Tell students to go to the
board, find the pronoun, and do one of the following
to it: (**Tócalo, Escribe una "X" sobre el pronombre,
Bórralo,** etc.)

Game Bring a ball to class and practice the
clarification of indirect object pronouns. Have students
sit in a circle. Model the game by saying, **"Le tiro la
bola…¿a quién? Pues, ¡a…**(name of student)**!"**
Throw the ball to said student. Model the game several
times before students start playing.

Almacén SuperGanga

Hablar Trabaja con un(a) compañero(a). Necesitas decidir qué regalos vas a comprar para tu familia. También necesitas saber los precios. *(Hint: You want to buy some gifts for your family. Talk about items and prices with a partner.)*

modelo

Estudiante A: *Quiero comprarle el videojuego «El dragón gigante» a mi hermanito.*

Estudiante B: *¿Cuánto cuesta?*

Estudiante A: *Cuesta sesenta y siete pesos.*

■ **MÁS COMUNICACIÓN** p. R2

ALMACÉN SUPERGANGA
mayo
Especiales

Vídeo
El futuro del planeta
94 pesos

Disco compacto
Las tortugas locas
40 pesos

Reloj Galaxia
85 pesos

Radio Juvenil
Arco iris
94 pesos

Casete Super Estrella
35 pesos

Videojuego
El dragón gigante
67 pesos

Pronunciación

Erre con erre, guitarra, erre con erre, barril;
¡qué rápido corren los carros, los carros del ferrocarril!

Trabalenguas

Pronunciación de la *rr* The sound of the **rr** in Spanish is produced by rapidly tapping the roof of the mouth with the tip of the tongue.

Practice **rr** by repeating this tongue twister aloud. Use the pictures to help you figure out what it means.

ciento veintisiete
Etapa 2
127

ACTIVIDAD 20

Objective: Open-ended practice Indirect object pronouns/vocabulary/numbers

Answers will vary.

🔔 Quick Wrap-up

Dictation: To reinforce comprehension of indirect object pronoun placement, dictate the following four items.

1. Mi tío me compra un libro.
2. Mi tío quiere comprarme un libro.
3. Raúl le escribe una carta a María.
4. Raúl va a escribirle una carta a María.

Dictation

After students have read the tongue twister in the **Pronunciación,** have them close their books. Dictate the tongue twister in segments while students write them.

Block Schedule

Peer Teaching Now that you are at the end of the **En acción** activities, have students choose a concept that they are struggling with. Divide the class into groups. Have students brainstorm for 5 minutes to come up with suggestions for an easy way to remember the concept. Have groups share ideas with the class. (For additional activities, see **Block Scheduling Copymasters.**)

Teaching Middle School Students

Extra Help You might do a quick substitution drill with clothing or other items to review the agreement of direct object pronouns: ¿Ya tienes zapatos? Sí, los tengo. ¿Ya tienes camisa? Sí, la tengo, etc.

Challenge Have students add three more questions to the survey in **Actividad 19.**

Native Speakers Have students write sentences with the expressions from the **Nota cultural.**

Multiple Intelligences

Logical/Mathematical Some students might find it helpful to organize their notes from **Actividad 19** in a Venn diagram.

Teaching Resource Options

Print

Unit 4 Resource Book
  Audioscript, p. 81
  Audioscript *Para hispanohablantes,*
    p. 82

Audiovisual

Audio Program Cassette 11A / CD 11
Audio *Para hispanohablantes*
  Cassette 11A / CD 11
OHT 125 (Quick Start)
Canciones Cassette / CD

🔔 Quick Start Review

♻️ Bargaining vocabulary

Use OHT 125 or write on the board:
Reassemble the following bargaining
conversation by numbering the
following sentences in a logical order.

____ Muy bien, quedamos en 80.
      Muchas gracias.
____ Cuesta 100 pesos.
____ ¡Es demasiado! Le puedo
      ofrecer 70.
____ ¡Es demasiado barato! Se la
      dejo en 90.
____ Es muy bonita esta jarra.
      ¿Cuánto cuesta?
____ No puedo. ¿Me la deja en 80?

Answers *See p. 107B.*

Teaching Suggestions
Presenting Cultura y comparaciones

• Begin by asking students to guess the
  topic of the culture section. Write the
  list of possibilities on the board.
• Then have students suggest their own
  strategies for working on the material.
• Note that in **Para conocernos,**
  creating a Venn diagram is a retrieval
  strategy that assists in learning and
  remembering.

Reading Strategy

Preview graphics Based on what
students see in the visuals, have them
predict the subject of this article. After
reading the passage, have them decide
if their prediction was on target.

En colores

CULTURA Y COMPARACIONES

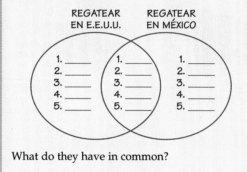

PARA CONOCERNOS

STRATEGY: CONNECTING CULTURES

Compare bargaining customs Where does bargaining
take place? How do people act when they
bargain? Use a Venn diagram to compare
bargaining in the United States to the kind of
bargaining that Rosa did in the Mercado Benito
Juárez in Oaxaca.

REGATEAR   REGATEAR
EN E.E.U.U.   EN MÉXICO

1. ____   1. ____   1. ____
2. ____   2. ____   2. ____
3. ____   3. ____   3. ____
4. ____   4. ____   4. ____
5. ____   5. ____   5. ____

What do they have in common?

NOTA CULTURAL

Benito Juárez (1806–1872) is
the most famous Oaxacan in
the history of Mexico. Of Zapotec
origin, he was elected governor
of Oaxaca and later president
of Mexico. The market is named
in his honor.

JUAREZ

El Mercado Benito Juárez

El mercado tiene una gran variedad de
cerámica y otras artesanías regionales.
También hay plantas medicinales,
productos textiles, frutas, verduras[1] y
carnes[2]. El mercado es un festival de
colores, texturas y aromas. Como[3] todos
los mercados, el Benito Juárez es un
lugar ideal para regatear.

_____

[1] vegetables   [2] meats   [3] As, Like

ciento veintiocho
Unidad 4

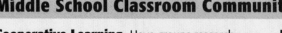
Middle School Classroom Community

Cooperative Learning Have groups research
where gold, silver, copper (optional), leather, and clay
are exported from in South America and Mexico. Each
group member is responsible for one of the above
items. The group secretary records information. All
groups share information and create whole-class
posters with the central visual being a map showing
the countries in question.

Paired Activity Give pairs two sets of cards. One
set has pictures of singular and plural nouns. The other
set consists of prices. Stack cards face down. Students
take turns drawing cards from the different stacks.
Student A asks the price: **¿Cuánto cuesta(n) "X"?**
Student B tells the price **Cuesta(n) "X" pesos.** Each
must use the correct form of **costar.**

Las cinco reglas[4] fundamentales para regatear

Regatear es un arte que necesitas practicar.
Estas reglas te van a ayudar.

1 Habla sólo español.

2 Actúa[5] como un(a) estudiante con poco dinero, no como un(a) turista rico(a)[6].

3 Escucha el primer precio. Después contesta: «¡Es demasiado!»

4 Pasa por otras tiendas para comparar los precios.

5 Siempre sonríe[7] al regatear. No cuesta dinero y a veces recibes mejores precios.

[4] rules   [5] Act   [6] rich   [7] smile

¿Comprendiste?

1. ¿Qué hay para comprar en el Mercado Benito Juárez?
2. ¿Cómo es el mercado?
3. ¿Cómo compras en este mercado?

¿Qué piensas?

1. En tu opinión, ¿cuál es la regla más importante para recibir un buen precio? ¿Por qué?
2. ¿Cuáles de estas reglas son efectivas? ¿Piensas que algunas reglas no son efectivas? Explica tu opinión.
3. Ya sabes unas reglas para regatear. Mira tu diagrama de Venn. ¿Quieres escribir algo más? ¿Quieres cambiar algo?

Hazlo tú

Con otro(a) estudiante prepara un diálogo. Van a regatear. Una persona puede ser el (la) vendedor(a). La otra puede ser el (la) cliente(a).

Teaching Middle School Students

Multiple Intelligences

Interpersonal Have pairs of students discuss the ¿Qué piensas? questions, p. 129. If they're comfortable with their work, they may volunteer to model their conversation for the class.

Visual After students have read the article and examined the photo, have them demonstrate their comprehension by making a picture or series of drawings of things that can be sold at the Oaxacan market.

Supplementary Vocabulary

¿Cuánto vale?	How much is it?
No puedo.	I can't.
Sólo tengo ___ pesos	I only have ____ pesos.
¡Es una ganga!	It's a bargain!

Cross Cultural Connections

Explain to students that if they visit a market, they should ask if they may touch items for sale before doing so. Some vendors do not want the customers touching the merchandise! (This includes foods.) Ask if students have had similar experiences at stores/markets in the U.S.

Interdisciplinary Connection

Social Studies Have students list places in their town, city, or state that are named after famous Americans. Then have them list places in other parts of the U.S.

Critical Thinking

Ask students to think of a bargaining situation from their own lives and either say which of the **Cinco reglas** they used, or write a new rule that was effective.

¿Comprendiste?

Answers
1. Hay una gran variedad de cerámica y otras artesanías regionales, plantas medicinales, productos textiles, frutas, verduras y carne.
2. Es un festival de colores, texturas y aromas.
3. Es un lugar para regatear.

Hazlo tú

Students may refer to the video dialog, but should try to expand on it incorporating the "rules" given here. Remind students to think about previous dialogs they have practiced before beginning to write.

Block Schedule

FunBreak Try out the recipe for **Chocolate oaxaqueño** found in the **Ampliación** on p. 81B.

Teaching Resource Options

Print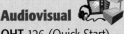

Para hispanohablantes Workbook PE,
pp. 15–16
Block Scheduling Copymasters
Unit 4 Resource Book
  Para hispanohablantes Workbook
  TE, pp. 66–67
  Information Gap Activities,
  p. 71
  Family Involvement, pp. 72–73
  Multiple Choice Test Questions,
  pp. 170–178

Audiovisual

OHT 126 (Quick Start)
Audio Program Testing Cassette T2 /
CD T2

Technology

Electronic Teacher Tools/Test
Generator
Intrigas y aventuras CD-ROM, Disc 1

🔔 Quick Start Review

♻ Stem-changing verbs

Use OHT 126 or write on the board:
Write out the conjugation of 3 stem-
changing verbs. Then outline the
"boot" shape of each.

Answers will vary.

✔ Teaching Suggestions
What Have Students Learned?

- Have students look at the "Now you
  can…" notes listed on the left side of
  pages 130–131. Tell students to think
  about which areas they might not be
  sure of. For those areas, they should
  consult the "To review" notes.
- Use the video to review vocabulary
  and structures.

Now you can...

- talk about
  shopping.

To review

- indirect object
  pronouns, see
  p. 121 and p. 124.

Now you can...

- make purchases.

To review

- stem-changing
  verbs: **o → ue**,
  see p. 118.

En uso

REPASO Y
MÁS COMUNICACIÓN

OBJECTIVES
- Talk about shopping
- Make purchases
- Talk about giving gifts
- Bargain

ACTIVIDAD 1 ¿Qué nos va a comprar?

La abuela de Carlos conoce bien a su familia. ¿Qué les va a comprar?
(Hint: Carlos's grandmother knows her family well. What is she going to buy them?)

modelo

Héctor y Eloísa: ver películas

A **Héctor y a Eloísa** les gusta **ver películas**. Entonces, ella
va a comprarles un video. Cuesta **cincuenta y tres pesos.**

1. yo: usar artículos de cuero
2. mamá: llevar joyas
3. nosotros: escuchar música
4. tú: leer
5. papá: jugar al béisbol
6. los vecinos: tener cosas de cerámica

ACTIVIDAD 2 ¡De compras!

Rosa y Sofía están de compras. Completa su conversación con el
vendedor. *(Hint: Rosa and Sofía are shopping. Complete the conversation with the vendor.)*

  Rosa: ¿Cuánto __1__ (costar) los aretes?
Vendedor: __2__ (recordar, yo) el precio. Los aretes __3__ (costar) sólo
  75 pesos.
  Sofía: Rosa, ¿por qué no __4__ (volver, nosotras) más tarde? __5__
  (poder, nosotras) almorzar en el café Sol.
  Rosa: ¿El café Sol otra vez? Tú y yo siempre __6__ (almorzar) allí.
Vendedor: Yo les __7__ (poder) recomendar el nuevo Café Florida.
  Rosa: Gracias, señor. Compro los aretes.
  Sofía: ¡Qué suerte! Tú siempre __8__ (encontrar) regalos baratos.

130 ciento treinta
Unidad 4

Middle School Classroom Community

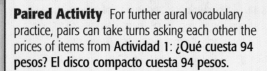

Paired Activity For further aural vocabulary
practice, pairs can take turns asking each other the
prices of items from **Actividad 1**: ¿Qué cuesta 94
pesos? El disco compacto cuesta 94 pesos.

Storytelling Have students work in pairs to make up
and practice a funny story about bargaining. When
they're ready, have them tell their story to the class.

Now you can...
- talk about giving gifts.

To review
- the verb **dar**, see p. 122.
- indirect object pronouns, see p. 121 and p. 124.

3 **¡Feliz cumpleaños!**

Hoy la señora Juárez celebra su cumpleaños. ¿Qué le dan todos?
(Hint: Today is Mrs. Juárez's birthday. What does everyone give her?)

modelo

Gustavo

Gustavo *le da* **una bolsa.**

1. yo **2.** su esposo **3.** tú

4. Sara y yo **5.** sus hijos **6.** nosotros

Now you can...
- bargain.

To review
- vocabulary for bargaining, see p. 111 and p. 120.
- stem-changing verbs: **o → ue**, see p. 118.
- indirect object pronouns, see p. 121 and p. 124.

4 **A regatear!**

Tú quieres comprar un cinturón en el mercado y tienes que regatear. Completa la conversación. *(Hint: You want to buy a belt in the market and you have to bargain. Complete the conversation.)*

Tú: Perdone, señora. ¿(Te / Me) deja ver el cinturón de cuero, por favor?

Vendedora: ¡Cómo no! Usted (podemos / puede) ver que es de muy buena (calidad / oro).

Tú: Es muy bonito. Busco un (precio / regalo) para mi papá, a quien (les / le) gusta usar artículos de cuero. ¿Cuánto (cuesta / cuestan) el cinturón?

Vendedora: Para usted, joven, sólo cien pesos.

Tú: ¡Uy! ¡Es muy (barato / caro)! (Le / Nos) puedo ofrecer setenta pesos.

Vendedora: Bueno, (me / le) dejo el cinturón en ochenta y cinco.

Tú: No (puedes / puedo) pagar tanto. ¿Por qué no (me / les) da el cinturón por ochenta?

Vendedora: Está bien. Quedamos en ochenta.

Answers

1 **Answers**

1. A mí me gusta usar artículos de cuero. Entonces, ella va a comprarme una cartera. Cuesta setenta y seis pesos.
2. A mamá le gusta llevar joyas. Entonces, ella va a comprarle una pulsera. Cuesta ochenta y siete pesos.
3. A nosotros nos gusta escuchar música. Entonces, ella va a comprarnos un disco compacto. Cuesta noventa y cuatro pesos.
4. A ti te gusta leer. Entonces, ella va a comprarte un libro. Cuesta sesenta pesos.
5. A papá le gusta jugar al béisbol. Entonces, ella va a comprarale una gorra. Cuesta cuarenta y dos pesos.
6. A los vecinos les gusta tener objetos de cerámica. Entonces, ella va a comprarles una olla. Cuesta setenta y dos pesos.

2 **Answers**

1. cuestan 5. Podemos
2. Recuerdo 6. almorzamos
3. cuestan 7. puedo
4. volvemos 8. encuentras

3 **Answers**

1. Yo le doy unos aretes.
2. Su esposo le da un anillo.
3. Tú le das un cinturón.
4. Sara y yo le damos una olla.
5. Sus hijos le dan un radiocasete.
6. Nosotros le damos un plato.

4 **Answers**

Me / puede / calidad / regalo / le / cuesta / caro / Le / le / puedo / me

Block Schedule

Change of Pace Bingo with stem changing verbs o→ue. Review verb forms with the class. Before playing, write all of the possible infinitives to be used on the board. Have students fill out their cards with conjugated verb forms. Give clues as follows: subject pronoun, infinitive. (Ex: **yo** form of **poder**) When a student says "bingo," ask him/her to recite the conjugated verbs. (For additional activities, see **Block Scheduling Copymasters**.)

Teaching Middle School Students

Challenge Have students rewrite **Actividad 4** with a twist: they want to buy a **pulsera de plata** for their mother, and they want to pay with a credit card. Volunteers can dramatize the skit.

Multiple Intelligences

Intrapersonal Designate time in the classroom so that students can practice the **Etapa** vocabulary and grammar with flash cards or any other personalized study device.

Teaching Resource Options

Print

Unit 4 Resource Book
  Cooperative Quizzes, pp. 84–85
  Etapa Exam, Forms A and B,
    pp. 86–95
  Para hispanohablantes Etapa Exam,
    pp. 96–100
  Portfolio Assessment, pp. 101–102
  Multiple Choice Test Questions,
    pp. 170–178

Audiovisual

OHT 126 (Quick Start)
Audio Program Testing Cassette T2 /
  CD T2

Technology

Electronic Teacher Tools/Test
  Generator

www.mcdougallittell.com

ACTIVIDAD 5

Rubric: Speaking

Criteria	Scale	
Sentence structure	1 2 3 4 5	A = 17–20 pts.
Vocabulary use	1 2 3 4 5	B = 13–16 pts.
Originality	1 2 3 4 5	C = 9–12 pts.
Fluency	1 2 3 4 5	D = 5–8 pts.
		F = < 5 pts.

ACTIVIDAD 6 Answers will vary.

ACTIVIDAD 7 **En tu propia voz**

Rubric: Writing

Criteria	Scale	
Vocabulary use	1 2 3 4 5	A = 13–15 pts.
Accuracy	1 2 3 4 5	B = 10–12 pts.
Creativity, appearance	1 2 3 4 5	C = 7–9 pts.
		D = 4–6 pts.
		F = < 4 pts.

Teaching Note: En tu propia voz

Suggest that students make a chart similar to the one in **Actividad 6** in order to implement the writing strategy "Brainstorm details, then organize your information" in the paragraph they will write for the visitor from Oaxaca.

ACTIVIDAD 5  **El mercado**

PARA CONVERSAR

STRATEGY: SPEAKING

Disagree politely Find ways to disagree with the seller about the quality of the article or how it compares with another one. You can contradict politely or express a negative opinion in these ways: **no me gusta/gustaría…, no puedo…, no pienso…**

Estás en un mercado al aire libre. Compra tres cosas. Regatea para el mejor precio. Después, cambien de papel.
(Hint: You're at a market. Buy three things. Bargain for the best price. Change roles.)

¿Cuánto cuesta(n)?

¿Me deja ver…?

Le dejo… en…

¡Es muy caro! Le puedo ofrecer…

ACTIVIDAD 6  **¡A comprar regalos!**

Completa la tabla con los regalos que vas a comprar. No puedes pagar más de cien dólares. Luego, en grupos de tres, hablen de sus compras. *(Hint: Fill in the table with the gifts you are going to buy. You can't pay more than $100. Then, in groups of three, tell about your purchases.)*

modelo

Voy a comprarle un videojuego a mi amigo Daniel. Lo puedo encontrar en la tienda Super Max. Cuesta veinte dólares.

¿Para quién?	¿Qué?	¿Dónde?	¿Cuánto?
mi amigo(a) Daniel	un videojuego	Super Max	$20
todos mis amigos			
el (la) profesor(a)			
mi familia y yo			
yo			

ACTIVIDAD 7 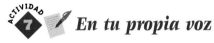 **En tu propia voz**

Escritura Una joven de Oaxaca está de visita. En un párrafo, explícale dónde y cómo comprar regalos para cinco personas.
(Hint: In a paragraph, explain where and how to buy gifts for five members of a visitor's family.)

modelo

Puedes encontrar joyas bonitas en la joyería Sparkles. Queda en la calle Main. Venden collares muy baratos. No puedes regatear, pero puedes pagar con…

Conexiones

Las matemáticas Create your own **mercado** in your Spanish classroom with objects donated by your classmates. You will **regatear**. Make a chart of the objects for sale and the prices they sell for. Calculate the total amount of money raised. Donate all proceeds to a community organization on behalf of the Spanish classes in your school.

Objeto	Precio
disco compacto	$5

132 ciento treinta y dos
Unidad 4

Middle School Classroom Community

TPR Hide objects representing vocabulary words in your classroom. Hand out a scavenger-hunt list and have students look for the items within a specified amount of time.

Portfolio As the activities on pp. 130–131 reflect a variety of learning styles, you might ask students to make up a new activity similar to any **Actividad** on these pages.

Rubric

Criteria	Scale	
Vocabulary use/spelling	1 2 3 4 5	A = 17–20 pts.
Correct sentence structure/grammar	1 2 3 4 5	B = 13–16 pts.
Logical organization	1 2 3 4 5	C = 9–12 pts.
Creativity	1 2 3 4 5	D = 5–8 pts.
		F = < 5 pts.

En resumen
REPASO DE VOCABULARIO

MAKING PURCHASES

Jewelry

el anillo	ring
el arete	earring
el collar	necklace
las joyas	jewelry
el oro	gold
la plata	silver
la pulsera	bracelet

Music and Videos

el casete	cassette
el disco compacto	compact disc
el radio	radio
el radiocasete	radio-tape player
el video	video
la videograbadora	VCR
el videojuego	video game

Handicrafts

la artesanía	handicraft
los artículos de cuero	leather goods
la bolsa	handbag
las botas	boots
la cartera	wallet
la cerámica	ceramics
el cinturón	belt
la jarra	pitcher
la olla	pot
el plato	plate

BARGAINING

¿Cuánto cuesta(n)…?	How much is (are) …?
¡Es muy caro(a)!	It's very expensive!
Le dejo… en…	I'll give … to you for …
Le puedo ofrecer…	I can offer you …
¿Me deja ver…?	May I see …?
regatear	to bargain

TALKING ABOUT GIVING GIFTS

dar	to give
el regalo	gift

TALKING ABOUT SHOPPING

barato(a)	cheap, inexpensive
la calidad	quality
cambiar	to change, to exchange
caro(a)	expensive
demasiado(a)	too much
el mercado	market
perfecto(a)	perfect

Money and Payment

el cambio	change, money exchange
el dinero	money
el dólar	dollar
el efectivo	cash
pagar	to pay
el precio	price
la tarjeta de crédito	credit card

OTHER WORDS AND PHRASES

juntos	together
para	for, in order to

Stem-Changing Verbs: o → ue

almorzar	to eat lunch
contar	to count, to tell or retell
costar	to cost
devolver	to return (an item)
dormir	to sleep
encontrar	to find, to meet
poder	to be able, can
recordar	to remember
volver	to return, to come back

Juego

¿Qué cosa compras por pocos pesos, una olla de plata o un plato barato?

ciento treinta y tres
Etapa 2   **133**

Interdisciplinary Connection

Math   Give students a list of currencies for several Spanish-speaking countries. Have them look up the exchange rate for these currencies in the financial pages of a newspaper. Then have them convert the prices in **Actividad 1,** p. 130, into various currencies.

Community Connections

Have students look around their homes for articles (jewelry, handicrafts, etc.) made in Spanish-speaking countries and make a list. Compile a class list and categorize the items.

Quick Start Review

♻ **Etapa** vocabulary

Use OHT 126 or write on the board: Make flash cards of the **Repaso de vocabulario.** These will be used later as vocabulary review.

Teaching Suggestions
Vocabulary Review

Using flash cards of the words from the Quick Start, break students into groups of 3. Deal 5 cards per group. In 3 minutes, see how many sentences they can make using one card per sentence. The team with the most grammatically correct sentences wins.

Juego

Answer: Compro un plato barato.

Block Schedule
Projects

Assign the following out-of-class projects:
• Check the current exchange rate for the Mexican **peso**/U.S. dollar in the newspaper.
• Find a Mexican recipe.
• Find out about at least one current event in Mexico (Internet, etc.).
• Find realia (travel agencies, etc.).

Teaching Middle School Students

Extra Help   Prepare a handout of the table in **Actividad 6**. Students can write the responses directly on the handout.

Multiple Intelligences

Logical/Mathematical   Have students organize and list **Etapa** vocabulary by shape: **redondo(a)** or **cuadrado(a)**.

Interpersonal   Have students rank ten purchases in order of interest (1 = most interest, 10 = least interest). Pairs can compare wish lists.

Planning Guide CLASSROOM MANAGEMENT

OBJECTIVES

Communication
- Talk about food *pp. 136–137*
- Order food and request the check *pp. 138–139*
- Express extremes *pp. 138–139, 149*
- Say where you went *pp. 138–139*

Grammar
- Use the verb **poner** *p. 143*
- Use **gustar** to talk about things you like *pp. 144–145*
- Use affirmative and negative words *pp. 147–148*
- Use stem-changing verbs: **e → i** *pp. 150–151*

Pronunciation
- Pronunciation of **g** *p. 153*
- Dictation *TE p. 153*

Culture
- Oaxacan cuisine *p. 144*
- Zapotec Indians *p. 156*
- Monte Albán *pp. 156–157*

♻ Recycling
- Stores *p. 143*
- Prepositions of location *p. 143*
- Clothing *p. 145*
- Direct object pronouns *p. 152*

STRATEGIES

Listening Strategies
- Integrate your skills *p. 138*

Speaking Strategies
- Vary ways to express preferences *p. 141*
- Borrow useful expressions *p. 160*

Reading Strategies
- Making a story map *p. 154*
- Look for cognates *TE p. 157*

Writing Strategies
- Brainstorm details, then organize your information *TE p. 160*

Connecting Cultures Strategies
- Recognize variations in vocabulary *p. 143*
- Consider the effects of tourism from the point of view of the inhabitants *pp. 156–157*
- Connect and compare what you know about jobs in your community to help you learn about jobs in a new community *pp. 156–157, 160*

PROGRAM RESOURCES

 Print
- *Más práctica* Workbook PE *pp. 17–24*
- Block Scheduling Copymasters
- Unit 4 Resource Book
  Más práctica Workbook TE *pp. 103–110*
  Information Gap Activities *pp. 119–122*
- Family Involvement *pp. 123–124*
- Video Activities *pp. 125–127*
- Videoscript *pp. 128–130*
- Audioscript *pp. 131–134*
- Assessment Program, Unit 4 Etapa 3 *pp. 135–178*
- Answer Keys *pp. 179–200*

 Audiovisual
- **Audio Program** Cassettes 12A, 12B / CD 12
- *Canciones* Cassette / CD
- **Video Program** Videotape 4 / Videodisc 2B
- **Overhead Transparencies** M1–M5; GO1–GO5; 106, 127–136

 Technology
- **Electronic Teacher Tools/Test Generator**
- *Intrigas y aventuras* CD-ROM, Disc 1
- www.mcdougallittell.com

 Assessment Program Options
- **Cooperative Quizzes** (Unit 4 Resource Book)
- **Etapa Exam** Forms A and B (Unit 4 Resource Book)
- *Para hispanohablantes* Etapa Exam (Unit 4 Resource Book)
- **Portfolio Assessment** (Unit 4 Resource Book)
- **Unit 4 Comprehensive Test** (Unit 4 Resource Book)
- *Para hispanohablantes* **Unit 4 Comprehensive Test** (Unit 4 Resource Book)
- **Multiple Choice Test Questions** (Unit 4 Resource Book)
- **Audio Program** Testing Cassette T2 / CD T2
- **Electronic Teacher Tools/Test Generator**

Native Speakers
- *Para hispanohablantes* Workbook PE, *pp. 17–24*
- *Para hispanohablantes* Workbook TE (Unit 4 Resource Book)
- *Para hispanohablantes* Etapa Exam (Unit 4 Resource Book)
- *Para hispanohablantes* Unit 4 Comprehensive Test (Unit 4 Resource Book)
- Audio *Para hispanohablantes* Cassettes 12A, 12B, T2 / CD 12, T2
- Audioscript *Para hispanohablantes* (Unit 4 Resource Book)

Student Text Listening Activity Scripts

Sofía | Rosa | Carlos | Mesero

 Videoscript: Diálogo *pages 138–139*

• Videotape 4 • Videodisc 2B

Search Chapter 7, Play to 8
U4E3 • En vivo (Dialog)

• Use the videoscript with **Actividades 1, 2** *pages 140–141*

Sofía: Tienes que decirme. ¿Cómo conoces a Carlos?

Rosa: ¡Es un secreto!

Sofía: ¡Por favor, Rosa!

Rosa: No puedo decirte. Las promesas son promesas.

Sofía: ¡Pero soy tu prima, Rosa! ¡Me tienes que decir!

Rosa: Está bien, está bien. Conozco a Carlos porque fui a la tienda de su papá para pedir direcciones para llegar a tu casa.

Sofía: ¡Ah!, ¿es todo? ¿No son amigos por Internet?

Rosa: No, ¡qué va! Qué imaginación tienes.

Mesero: Buenas tardes, Carlos. Buenas tardes, señoritas. Bienvenidos al restaurante La Madre Tierra. Aquí tienen el menú.

Carlos: ¿Nos puede traer pan, por favor?

Mesero: Sí, cómo no. Enseguida se lo traigo.

Rosa: Yo quiero un plato tradicional de Oaxaca. ¿Qué pido?

Carlos: La especialidad de la casa es una combinación de algunos platos regionales. Tiene mole negro y tasajo. Es riquísima.

Sofía: Yo voy a pedir una ensalada mixta y pollo.

Rosa: Y tú, Carlos, ¿qué pides normalmente?

Carlos: Me gustan las enchiladas, pero ahora tengo ganas de comer carne. Voy a pedir bistec asado. Viene con arroz y frijoles.

Mesero: ¿Listos para pedir?

Sofía: Sí, señor. Para mí, una ensalada mixta y pollo.

Rosa: Para mí, la especialidad de la casa.

Mesero: ¿Y para el señor?

Carlos: Un bistec asado.

Mesero: ¿Algo de tomar?

Sofía: Una limonada para mí.

Rosa: Agua mineral, por favor.

Carlos: Un refresco de naranja.

Mesero: Muy bien. ¿Y de postre? Los postres ricos son otra especialidad de la casa. Son buenísimos.

Sofía: Por ahora, nada más. El postre lo pedimos después, gracias.

Mesero: Para servirles.

Rosa: Oye, Carlos, ¿cómo va tu proyecto para el concurso?

Carlos: Muy bien. Mi proyecto para el concurso es sobre las ruinas de Monte Albán. Es fascinante la historia de México.

Rosa: ¿Ya fuiste a Monte Albán?

Carlos: Sí, fui a Monte Albán el otro día para sacar fotos. Hay mucho que ver: tumbas, altares ceremoniales y pirámides. El Centro Ceremonial es algo increíble. Desde arriba, hay unas vistas fabulosas. Los Danzantes son unas figuras muy curiosas. Y el Juego de Pelota es antiguo e interesante. El Palacio es maravilloso. Las ruinas de Monte Albán son impresionantes. ¡Es un lugar mágico!

Rosa: Estoy segura de que tú vas a ganar el concurso. Tu proyecto va a presentar el pasado fascinante de los mexicanos. Me gusta mucho tu idea para el concurso.

Mesero: ¿Algo más, jóvenes?

Sofía: Qué crees, Rosa, ¿pido un postre y lo compartimos?

Rosa: Bueno, si pedimos algo pequeño.

Mesero: ¿Un flan, señoritas? Lo sirvo en dos platos con dos cucharas.

Sofía: Perfecto, señor. Muchas gracias.

Mesero: ¿Y para usted?

Carlos: No quiero ningún postre, pero ¿me puede traer la cuenta, por favor? Tengo prisa.

Mesero: Sí, cómo no.

Sofía: El mesero es muy amable y sirve muy bien.

Carlos: Sí, el mesero es muy amable. Me gusta la gente de este restaurante. ¡Quisiera comer aquí todos los días!

Rosa: ¡Ah! ¡Un momento! Aquí tienes tu mapa. Gracias.

Carlos: Al contrario.

 **¿Qué pasa?** *page 142*

1. Le gusta comer los postres. Está comiendo un flan.
2. No tiene mucha hambre. Prefiere comer sólo fruta.
3. Está enfermo. Quiere comer sopa de pollo.
4. Tiene mucha sed. Está tomando una limonada.

¿A quién? *page 152*

Carlos: ¡Qué hambre tengo! ¿Qué vas a pedir, Elena?

Elena: Voy a pedir unas enchiladas de carne.

Carlos: Tú siempre pides enchiladas.

Elena: Sí, tienes razón. Siempre las pido. Me gustan mucho y son riquísimas aquí. ¿Y tú?

Carlos: Voy a pedir un bistec y papas fritas.

Elena: ¿Y para beber?

Carlos: Voy a tomar algún refresco.

Elena: Y yo un té.

Carlos: De postre, voy a pedir un flan. ¿Y tú?

Elena: No tengo tanta hambre como tú. No voy a pedir ningún postre.

🔔 **Quick Start Review Answers**

p. 138 Food vocabulary
1. el plato, el tenedor, el cuchillo, la taza
2. el arroz, el bistec, el pollo, una enchilada
3. la limonada, el café, el té, el refresco

p. 140 Dialog review
1. tienda
2. mole
3. ensalada
4. postres
5. ningún

p. 147 Likes and dislikes
Answers will vary. Answers could include:
1. A mi hermano le gusta la comida picante.
2. A mis padres les gusta la sopa vegetariana.

3. A mi mejor amiga le gustan las papas fritas.
4. A mi tía Ana le gusta el pan dulce.
5. A Tomás le gustan las enchiladas.

p. 150 Affirmative and negative words
1. nadie
2. alguien
3. algo
4. tampoco
5. algún

p. 156 In a restaurant
Answers will vary. Answers could include:
1. el pan
2. la especialidad de la casa
3. la propina
4. la comida picante
5. la carne

Sample Lesson Plan - 45 Minute Schedule

DAY 1

Etapa Opener
- Quick Start Review (TE, p. 134) 5 MIN.
- Anticipate/Activate prior knowledge: Have students look at the *Etapa* Opener and answer the *¿Qué ves?* questions, p. 134. 10 MIN.

En contexto: Vocabulario
- Quick Start Review (TE, p. 136) 5 MIN.
- Have students use context and pictures to learn *Etapa* vocabulary. 10 MIN.
- Have students work in pairs to answer the *Preguntas personales*, p. 137. 5 MIN.
- Ask pairs to share each other's answers to *Preguntas personales*, p. 137. 5 MIN.

DAY 2

En vivo: Diálogo
- Quick Start Review (TE, p. 138) 5 MIN.
- Review the Listening Strategy, p. 138. 5 MIN.
- Play audio or show video for the dialog, pp. 138–139. 10 MIN.
- Replay as needed. 5 MIN.
- Read the dialog aloud, having students take the roles of characters. 10 MIN.
- Use the Situational OHTs for additional vocabulary practice. 10 MIN.

Homework Option:
- Video Activities, Unit 4 Resource Book, pp. 125–127.

DAY 3

En acción: Vocabulario y gramática
- Check homework. 5 MIN.
- Quick Start Review (TE, p. 140) 5 MIN.
- Ask students for a summary of the dialog to check recall. 5 MIN.
- Play the video/audio; have students do *Actividades* 1 and 2 orally. 10 MIN.
- Present the *Vocabulario*, p. 141. 5 MIN.
- Present the Speaking Strategy, p. 141. 5 MIN.
- Have students work in pairs to complete *Actividad* 3. 10 MIN.

DAY 4

En acción (cont.)
- Have students work in pairs on *Actividad* 4. 5 MIN.
- Ask selected pairs to recite the captions they wrote for scenes in *Actividad* 4. 5 MIN.
- Play the audio. Have students stay in their pairs to do *Actividad* 5. 5 MIN.
- Keep students in their pairs to do *Actividad* 6. 5 MIN.
- Ask pairs to volunteer to model their conversations from *Actividad* 6. 10 MIN.
- Mix up the pairs and have students do *Actividad* 7. 5 MIN.
- Ask a few pairs to model setting the table, as in *Actividad* 7, naming each item as they place it. 5 MIN.
- Read and discuss the *También se dice*, p. 143. 5 MIN.

DAY 5

En acción (cont.)
- Quick Start Review (TE, p. 144) 5 MIN.
- Present *Gramática:* Using *gustar* to Talk About Things You Like. 10 MIN.
- Work orally with the class to do *Actividad* 8. 5 MIN.
- Model *Actividad* 9 and discuss possible answers. 5 MIN.
- Have students write their answers to *Actividad* 9. 10 MIN.
- Read and discuss the *Apoyo para estudiar*, p. 145. 5 MIN.
- Quick Wrap-up (TE, p. 145) 5 MIN.

Homework Option:
- *Más práctica* Workbook, p. 21. *Para hispanohablantes* Workbook, p. 19.

DAY 6

En acción (cont.)
- Check homework. 5 MIN.
- Quick Start Review (TE, p. 147) 5 MIN.
- Have students work in groups to complete *Actividad* 10. 10 MIN.
- Call on some groups to report their findings from *Actividad* 10 to the class. 5 MIN.
- Present *Gramática:* Affirmative and Negative Words. 10 MIN.
- Assign *Actividad* 11. 5 MIN.
- Ask pairs of students to use their responses to *Actividad* 11 to perform a dialog. 5 MIN.

DAY 7

En acción (cont.)
- Have students work in pairs on *Actividad* 12. 5 MIN.
- Ask selected pairs to model questioning, answering, and changing your mind from *Actividad* 12. 10 MIN.
- Assign *Actividad* 13. 5 MIN.
- Read and discuss the *Conexiones*, p. 149. 5 MIN.
- Have students work in pairs to complete the *Para hacer*, p. 149. 10 MIN.
- Read and discuss the *Nota*, p. 149, and model *Actividad* 14. 5 MIN.
- Have students write their responses to *Actividad* 14. 5 MIN.

Homework Option:
- *Más práctica* Workbook, p. 22–23. *Para hispanohablantes* Workbook, pp. 20–21.

DAY 8

En acción (cont.)
- Check homework. 5 MIN.
- Quick Start Review (TE, p. 150) 5 MIN.
- Discuss the Language Note, TE, p. 149. 5 MIN.
- Present *Grámatica:* Stem-Changing Verbs: *e → i*, and the *Vocabulario*, p. 150. 10 MIN.
- Have students write their responses to *Actividad* 15. 5 MIN.
- Ask volunteers to read their responses to *Actividad* 15. 5 MIN.
- Model *Actividad* 16, then ask students to write their responses. 10 MIN.

Homework Option:
- *Más práctica* Workbook, p 24. *Para hispanohablantes* Workbook, p. 22

DAY 9

En acción (cont.)
- Check homework. **5 MIN.**
- Read and discuss the *Nota*, p. 151. **5 MIN.**
- Have students work in pairs on *Actividad* 17. **5 MIN.**
- Ask selected pairs to model their conversations from *Actividad* 17. **5 MIN.**
- Play the audio. Assign *Actividad* 18. **5 MIN.**
- Present and practice the *Vocabulario*, p. 152. **5 MIN.**
- Read and discuss the *Nota,* p. 152. **5 MIN.**
- Assign pairs to work on *Actividad* 19. **5 MIN.**
- Ask volunteers to model their conversations in *Actividad* 19. **5 MIN.**

DAY 10

En acción (cont.)
- Have students work in pairs on *Actividad* 20. **5 MIN.**
- Call on pairs to model their completed conversations from *Actividad* 20. **5 MIN.**
- Have students work in groups of three to complete *Actividad* 21. **10 MIN.**
- Ask groups to volunteer to perform their dialogs from *Actividad* 21 for the class. **5 MIN.**
- Use Information Gap Activities, Unit 4 Resource Book, pp. 120–121. **5 MIN.**
- *Más comunicación*, p. R12. **5 MIN.**
- Play the audio and have students practice the *Trabalenguas*, p. 153. **10 MIN.**

DAY 11

En voces: Lectura
- Quick Start Review (TE, p. 154) **5 MIN.**
- Present the Reading Strategy, p. 154. **5 MIN.**
- Have volunteers read the selection aloud. **15 MIN.**
- Work orally with students on the *¿Comprendiste?* questions (Answers, TE, p. 155). **10 MIN.**
- Discuss the *¿Qué piensas?* questions, p. 155. **10 MIN.**

Homework Option:
- Have students write their answers to the *¿Qué piensas?* questions, p. 155.

DAY 12

En colores: Cultura y comparaciones
- Check homework. **5 MIN.**
- Quick Start Review (TE, p. 156) **5 MIN.**
- Discuss the Connecting Cultures Strategy, p. 156. **5 MIN.**
- Brainstorm some rules for being a good tourist. **5 MIN.**
- Have volunteers read the selection aloud. **10 MIN.**
- Work orally with students to answer the *¿Comprendiste?* questions. (Answers, TE, p. 157). **10 MIN.**
- Discuss the *¿Qué piensas?* questions, p. 157. **5 MIN.**

DAY 13

En uso: Repaso y más comunicación
- Quick Start Review (TE, p. 158) **5 MIN.**
- Assign *Actividad* 1. **5 MIN.**
- Work orally with students to complete *Actividades* 2–3. **10 MIN.**
- Have students read and think about *Actividades* 4–5. **5 MIN.**
- Call on students to give oral responses to *Actividades* 4–5. **10 MIN.**
- Present the Speaking Strategy, p. 160. **5 MIN.**
- Have students work in pairs on *Actividad* 6. **5 MIN.**

Homework Option:
- Have students review all of the *Gramática* boxes in *Etapa* 3.

DAY 14

En uso (cont.)
- Quick Start Review (TE, p. 161) **5 MIN.**
- Review grammar questions as needed. **5 MIN.**
- Have students work in groups on *Actividad* 7. **5 MIN.**
- Ask groups to share their work from *Actividad* 7. **5 MIN.**

En tu propia voz: Escritura
- Have students work independently to complete the writing activity, *Actividad* 8. **10 MIN.**
- Ask volunteers to read their work from *Actividad* 8. **5 MIN.**

En resumen: Repaso de vocabulario
- Review *Etapa* 3 vocabulary. **10 MIN.**

Homework Option:
- Have students study for the *Etapa* exam.

DAY 15

En resumen: Repaso de vocabulario
- Answer questions related to *Etapa* 3 content. **10 MIN.**
- Complete *Etapa* exam. **25 MIN.**

Conexiones
- Have students read the *Conexiones*, pp. 162–163, as they complete the exam.

Classroom Management Tip

Vary classroom activities Give students opportunities to get information from a variety of sources and combine it into interesting reports or displays.

Set up a computer Learning Center where students can access the Internet and online encyclopedia sources for information about indigenous groups in Mexico. Borrow specialty books from your school or local library that provide visual as well as textual information about Mexico's varied past. Access to these sources of information will enhance students' appreciation of the richness of Mexico's history.

Etapa Theme
Ordering food in a restaurant, talking about food, and requesting the check

Grammar Objectives
• Using the verb **gustar** with nouns
• Using affirmative and negative words
• Using stem-changing verbs: **e→i**

Teaching Resource Options
Print
Block Scheduling Copymasters

Audiovisual
OHT 106, 133 (Quick Start)

🔔 Quick Start Review
♻ **Gustar**/Free-time activities
Use OHT 133 or write on board: Complete the following sentences with **gustar** and activities that you and your friends like to do after school and on weekends.

1. A mí...
2. A mi mejor amigo(a)...
3. A ti...
4. A mi mejor amigo(a) y a mí...
5. A muchos de mis amigos...

Answers
Answers will vary. Answers could include:
1. me gusta practicar deportes
2. le gusta ver la televisión
3. te gusta andar en patineta
4. nos gusta jugar al tenis
5. les gusta ir al cine

Teaching Suggestions
Previewing the Etapa
• Ask students to study the picture on pp. 134–135 (1 min.).
• Close books; ask students to talk about what the people are wearing, what they are doing, where they are, etc.
• Reopen books and look at the picture again (1 min.); close books and share 3 details about the picture.
• Use the **¿Qué ves?** questions to focus the discussion.

UNIDAD 4

ETAPA **3**

¿Qué hacer en Oaxaca?

• Order food

• Request the check

• Talk about food

• Express extremes

• Say where you went

¿Qué ves?
Mira la foto de Monte Albán.
1. ¿Alguien lleva una gorra?
2. ¿Quién es la persona principal?
3. ¿Qué hace?
4. ¿Cuánto cuesta un refresco en el restaurante?

134

Restaurante La Madre Tierra
Nuestra especialidad
Mole negro y tasajo
$32
Ensaladas
$15
Sopas
$12
Enchiladas
$20
Pollo
$25
Bistec (con arroz y frijoles)
$30
Refrescos
$10
Postres
$25

Middle School Classroom Management

Planning Ahead Collect menus from Mexican restaurants or Mexican cookbooks, articles about Mexican foods, etc. Check with Mexican restaurants or with people who cook Mexican foods to see if they would help your classes cook if you decide to let them have some "real" Mexican food as part of the unit.

Time Saver To save time when presenting vocabulary and doing the activities, make a file of magazine cutouts and simple drawings of food items and tableware covered in this **Etapa**. Also, collect some paper and plastic tableware.

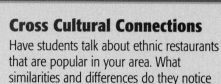
Cross Cultural Connections

Have students talk about ethnic restaurants that are popular in your area. What similarities and differences do they notice between those restaurants and typical U.S. restaurants? Would they be willing to go to a Mexican restaurant and order in Spanish?

Culture Highlights

● **MONTE ALBÁN** The photo on these pages is of Monte Albán. Archaeological excavations, begun in 1931, revealed that an advanced civilization flourished here around 200 B.C. At one time, there were 25,000 inhabitants. No one knows why the city was abandoned about 1400 A.D.

In the South Platform of Monte Albán, archaeologists discovered hidden carvings. The foundation stones in the four corners of the building have carvings on their bottom ends. They were seen only by those who carved them and those who worked on their placement. They were not intended for public enjoyment but were offerings to the Earth.

Supplementary Vocabulary

una pirámide	pyramid
una excavación	archaeological dig
unas ruinas	ruins
una cámara	camera
una diapositiva	slide
una videocámara	video camera

Critical Thinking

Ask students if they recall any information about Monte Albán from the Unit Opener. Assign research groups to gather additional information and present it to the class. What are the theories about why the city was abandoned?

▣ Block Schedule

Preview Have students leaf through the **Etapa.** What do they already know related to what they see? What do they expect to learn? Have them write down their expectations. At the end of the **Etapa,** have them look back and see if they learned what they had expected to. (For additional activities, see **Block Scheduling Copymasters.**)

Teaching Middle School Students

Extra Help Have students study the picture for a minute, then close their books. Give them a list of 10 items, some of which are in the picture, and ask them to check the items that are in the picture.

Native Speakers Encourage students to identify or to display examples of the monetary unit in their country.

Multiple Intelligences

Logical/Mathematical Let students find out about and report on the rate of exchange for **pesos** and dollars and what causes the rates to go up or down.

Teaching Resource Options

Print

Unit 4 Resource Book
Video Activities, pp. 125–126
Videoscript, p. 128
Audioscript, p. 131
Audioscript *Para hispanohablantes,*
    p. 131

Audiovisual

OHT 127, 128, 129, 129A, 130, 130A,
133 (Quick Start)
Audio Program Cassette 12A / CD 12
Audio *Para hispanohablantes*
    Cassette 12A / CD 12
Video Program Videotape 4 / Videodisc
2B

Search Chapter 6, Play to 7
U4E3 • En contexto (Vocabulary)

Technology

Intrigas y aventuras CD-ROM, Disc 1

Quick Start Review

♻ Food vocabulary

Use OHT 133 or write on board:
Make a list of 5 snacks and drinks
in Spanish.

Answers
Answers will vary. Answers could include:
la fruta, la hamburguesa, las papas fritas,
la torta, los chicharrones, el agua, el refresco,
los tacos, el sándwich, las tortillas

Culture Highlights

● **LA COCINA DE OAXACA** The names
of traditional Oaxacan dishes are as
creative as the dishes themselves. There is,
for example, **caldo de gato** (cat broth),
which is made with beef and vegetables.
The names of other dishes come from the
Indian tradition that influenced them; for
example, **tlayudas** (giant tortillas).

En contexto

 VOCABULARIO

Carlos is at a restaurant in Oaxaca. Take
a look at what he likes to eat.

A

Carlos tiene mucha hambre y va a **un
restaurante**. Lee **el menú** y decide
comer **una enchilada**. Es **deliciosa**.
¡Pero **la salsa** es **picante**! **El mesero**
va a **servirle una limonada**.

el restaurante

el mesero

la enchilada

la limonada

CASA LINDA

ENSALADAS Y SOPAS

Ensalada mixta	$25
Sopa de pollo	$20

COMIDAS

Servidas con arroz y frijoles

Arroz con pollo	$45
Bistec asado	$60
Enchiladas	$40
Pollo	$50
Tacos	$35
Tamales	$40
Tortas	$35

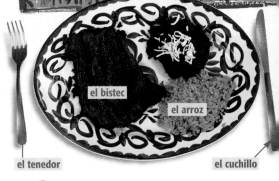

el bistec

el arroz

el tenedor

el cuchillo

B

Otras personas comen en el restaurante
también. Una persona come **arroz** y **bistec**.
Usa **un tenedor** y **un cuchillo** para comer.

Middle School Classroom Community

TPR Hand out paper and plastic tableware to
students. If you wish, include tea bags and sugar
packets. Then, as you name the different items,
ask students to raise their hands and display the
correct item.

Storytelling Tell the students that they are going to
paraphrase *The Three Bears* (**Los Tres Osos**). Choose
four students to pantomime the characters as the

students make up the story. Instead of hot porridge,
use **enchiladas picantes**, or a choice of their own.

Group Activity Give students materials to design
and make a menu for a Mexican restaurant. The
objective is to make them familiar with different types
of foods in general and Mexican dishes in particular.
The groups share the menus with each other and put
them on display in the classroom.

D Una persona quiere **café** con **azúcar**. Otra quiere **una taza** de **té**.

el café

las tazas

el té

el azúcar

la sopa

E ¿Qué tienen de **postre**? ¡Un **flan** muy **rico**!

el flan

la cuchara

el pollo

la ensalada

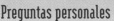

Preguntas personales

1. ¿Te gusta comer comida picante?
2. ¿Prefieres comer en un restaurante o en casa?
3. ¿Prefieres un bistec o pollo?
4. ¿Qué te gusta más: la sopa, la ensalada o el postre?
5. ¿Cuál es tu comida favorita?

C Otra persona come **sopa, pollo** y **ensalada**. Usa **una cuchara** para tomar la sopa.

LA ESPECIALIDAD DE LA CASA

Mole negro y tasajo $40

BEBIDAS

Agua mineral $10
Café $12
Limonada $15
Refrescos $15
Té $12

POSTRES

Flan $20
Fruta $15
Pastel $20

ciento treinta y siete
Etapa 3   **137**

Teaching Suggestions
Introducing Vocabulary

- Have students look at pages 136–137. Use OHT 127 and 128 and Audio Cassette 12A / CD 12 to present the vocabulary.
- Ask the Comprehension Questions below in order of yes/no (questions 1–3), either/or (questions 4–6), and simple word or phrase (questions 7–10). Expand by adding similar questions.
- Use the TPR activity to reinforce the meaning of individual words.
- Use the video vocabulary presentation for review and reinforcement.

Comprehension Questions

1. ¿Tiene hambre Carlos? (Sí.)
2. ¿Va Carlos a una cafetería? (No.)
3. ¿Tiene el restaurante un menú? (Sí.)
4. ¿Va Carlos a comer una enchilada o un sándwich? (una enchilada)
5. ¿Va el mesero a servirle un vaso de agua o una limonada? (una limonada)
6. ¿Está Carlos solo en el restaurante o hay otras personas? (Hay otras personas.)
7. ¿Qué come una persona con su bistec? (arroz y frijoles)
8. ¿Qué usa otra persona para tomar la sopa? (una cuchara)
9. ¿Qué pone otra persona en su café? (azúcar)
10. ¿Qué tienen de postre? (flan)

Supplementary Vocabulary

el jugo de naranja	orange juice
los huevos fritos	fried eggs
los huevos revueltos	scrambled eggs
el cereal	cereal
la leche	milk

Block Schedule

Change of Pace Have students draw a picture of the meal they would have at **Casa Linda** (all courses). Then have them describe their meals to a partner.

Teaching All Students

Extra Help Every so often during the day, take a break to practice vocabulary. Mime a troublesome vocabulary word and have students write it down. Then say the word and let them self-correct.

Multiple Intelligences

Kinesthetic Use the vocabulary illustrations and tableware prepared for "Time Saver," TE, p. 134. Have students arrange the pictures on paper plates, along with appropriate utensils, and offer their plate to another student, naming plate, utensils, and food as they do it. Let them exchange plates and repeat the process with other students.

Teaching Resource Options

Print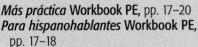

Más práctica Workbook PE, pp. 17–20
Para hispanohablantes Workbook PE, pp. 17–18
Block Scheduling Copymasters
Unit 4 Resource Book
  Más práctica Workbook TE, pp. 103–106
  Para hispanohablantes Workbook TE, pp. 111–112
  Video Activities, pp. 125–126
  Videoscript, p. 129
  Audioscript, p. 131
  Audioscript *Para hispanohablantes*, p. 131

Audiovisual

OHT 131, 132, 133 (Quick Start)
Audio Program Cassette 12A / CD 12
Audio *Para hispanohablantes*
  Cassette 12A / CD 12
Video Program Videotape 4 / Videodisc 2B

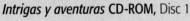

Search Chapter 7, Play to 8
U4E3 • En vivo (Dialog)

Technology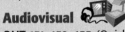

Intrigas y aventuras CD-ROM, Disc 1

Quick Start Review

♻ Food vocabulary

Use OHT 133 or write on board:
List 4 items for each category:

1. Place setting
2. Food
3. Drinks

Answers See p. 133B.

Language Note

Point out that the waiter addresses the customers formally, using **usted**. The customers do the same when speaking to the waiter. Have students use **usted** when role-playing scenes in restaurants, stores, etc.

Gestures

In most Spanish-speaking countries, it is considered impolite to lean over others at the table and reach for something. You should ask for items and wait for them to be passed.

En vivo

 DIÁLOGO

¡Al restaurante!

 Sofía Rosa Carlos  Mesero

PARA ESCUCHAR • STRATEGY: LISTENING

Integrate your skills Combine what you know.

1. Identify the main idea. Is it (1) explaining relationships, (2) ordering in a restaurant, or (3) learning about Oaxaca?
2. Listen for specifics. What word(s) describe(s) Monte Albán?
3. Listen for feelings. Who expresses curiosity? Pleasure? Other emotions?

1► Sofía: Tienes que decirme. ¿Cómo conoces a Carlos?
Rosa: ¡Es un secreto!
Sofía: ¡Por favor, Rosa!

5► Carlos: Un bistec asado.
Mesero: ¿Algo de tomar?
Sofía: Una limonada para mí.
Rosa: Agua mineral, por favor.
Carlos: Un refresco de naranja.

6► Mesero: Muy bien. ¿Y de postre? Los postres ricos son otra especialidad de la casa. Son buenísimos.
Sofía: Por ahora, nada más. El postre lo pedimos después, gracias.
Mesero: Para servirles.

7► Sofía: Oye, Carlos, ¿cómo va tu proyecto para el concurso?
Carlos: Muy bien. Es sobre las ruinas de Monte Albán.
Rosa: ¿Ya fuiste a Monte Albán?
Carlos: Sí, fui para sacar fotos.

138 ciento treinta y ocho
Unidad 4

Middle School Classroom Community

TPR Replay the video. When a food is mentioned, students raise their hands. When a drink is mentioned, students stand up/sit down.

Learning Scenario Have groups of students role-play a visit to a restaurant. Ask groups to volunteer to present their role-plays to the class.

Game Give each group of students a list of a subset of the **Etapa** vocabulary. Each group scrambles each of its words and writes them in a different order. Groups exchange lists for unscrambling. The first group to write the unscrambled words from its list under the correct pictures wins.

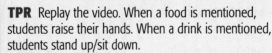

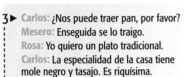

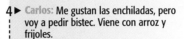

2 ▶ Rosa: Está bien. Conozco a Carlos porque fui a la tienda de su papá para pedir direcciones para llegar a tu casa.

3 ▶ Carlos: ¿Nos puede traer pan, por favor?
Mesero: Enseguida se lo traigo.
Rosa: Yo quiero un plato tradicional.
Carlos: La especialidad de la casa tiene mole negro y tasajo. Es riquísima.

4 ▶ Carlos: Me gustan las enchiladas, pero voy a pedir bistec. Viene con arroz y frijoles.
Mesero: ¿Listos para pedir?
Sofía: Para mí, una ensalada mixta y pollo.
Rosa: Para mí, la especialidad.

8 ▶ Carlos: Hay unas vistas fabulosas. Y el juego de pelota es antiguo e interesante.
Rosa: ¡Me gusta mucho tu idea para el concurso!

9 ▶ Mesero: ¿Algo más, jóvenes?
Sofía: ¿Pido un postre y lo compartimos?
Mesero: ¿Un flan, señoritas? Lo sirvo en dos platos con dos cucharas.
Sofía: Perfecto, señor. Muchas gracias.
Mesero: ¿Y para usted?

10 ▶ Carlos: No quiero ningún postre, pero ¿me puede traer la cuenta, por favor?
Mesero: Sí, cómo no.
Sofía: El mesero sirve muy bien.
Carlos: Me gusta este restaurante. ¡Quisiera comer aquí todos los días!

ciento treinta y nueve
Etapa 3

139

Teaching Suggestions
Presenting the Dialog

• Prepare students for listening by focusing on the dialog context using simple questions. Reintroduce the characters: **¿Cómo se llaman las dos chicas? ¿Son amigas, primas o hermanas? ¿Cómo se llama el chico? ¿Conoce él a las dos chicas?**
• Use the video, audio cassette, or CD to present the dialog. The expanded dialog on video offers additional listening practice opportunities.

Video Synopsis

• Sofía and Rosa meet Carlos for lunch at a restaurant. Carlos discusses his plans for the contest. For a complete transcript of the video dialog, see p. 133B.

Comprehension Questions

1. ¿Van las primas a un restaurante? (Sí.)
2. ¿Conoce Rosa a Carlos por Internet? (No.)
3. ¿Quieren pan los jóvenes? (Sí.)
4. ¿Quiere Carlos la especialidad de la casa o un bistec? (un bistec)
5. ¿Viene el bistec con arroz o con papas fritas? (con arroz)
6. ¿Quién quiere una ensalada mixta, Rosa o Sofía? (Sofía)
7. ¿Qué prefiere tomar Rosa? (agua mineral)
8. ¿Cómo son los postres? (Son ricos y buenísimos.)
9. ¿Sobre qué es el proyecto de Carlos? (sobre las ruinas de Monte Albán)
10. ¿Quiénes quieren postre? (Rosa y Sofía)

Block Schedule

Time Saver The day before working with the **Diálogo,** assign previewing it for homework. Students should look at the photos and read the text, trying to get the general idea. Have them write a 2–3 sentence description. (For additional activities, see **Block Scheduling Copymasters.**)

Teaching Middle School Students

Multiple Intelligences

Interpersonal Have students make a chart with the headings **Me gusta** and **No me gusta.** Tell students to write each of the foods they are studying underneath one of the categories. Have students compare lists with a friend.

Verbal Divide students into groups of four and ask them to take the roles of the video characters and read the dialog with as much expression as possible.

Teaching Resource Options

Print 📖

Unit 4 Resource Book
  Video Activities, p. 127
  Videoscript, p. 130
  Audioscript, pp. 131–132
  Audioscript *Para hispanohablantes,*
    pp. 131–132

Audiovisual 🎧

OHT 134 (Quick Start)
Audio Program Cassettes 12A, 12B /
  CD 12
Audio *Para hispanohablantes*
  Cassette 12A / CD 12
Video Program Videotape 4 / Videodisc
  2B

🔔 Quick Start Review

♻ Dialog review

Use OHT 134 or write on the board:
Complete the following sentences from
the dialog:

1. Conozco a Carlos porque fui a
   la ___ de su papá.
2. La especialidad de la casa tiene
   ___ negro y tasajo.
3. Para mí, una ___ mixta y pollo.
4. Los ___ ricos son otra
   especialidad de la casa.
5. No quiero ___ postre.

Answers *See p. 133B.*

Teaching Suggestions
Comprehension Check

Use **Actividades 1** and **2** to assess
retention after the dialog. Have
students close their books. Read the
items and see if students can answer
correctly. Use as many gestures as
necessary to help students.

Objective: Controlled practice
Listening comprehension/vocabulary

Answers (See script, p. 133B.)
  1. b
  2. a
  3. d

En acción
VOCABULARIO Y GRAMÁTICA

OBJECTIVES

- Order food
- Request the check
- Talk about food
- Express extremes
- Say where you went
- *Use the verb **gustar** with nouns*
- *Use affirmative and negative words*
- *Use stem-changing verbs: **e→i***

ACTIVIDAD 1

Mmmm... ¡qué rico!

Escuchar En el restaurante Rosa, Sofía y Carlos
hablan de muchos platos. Pero, ¿qué comen?
(Hint: Write the letter of the dishes the friends actually request.)

1. Rosa come _____ .
   a. el bistec asado
   b. la especialidad de la casa
   c. la ensalada mixta y pollo
   d. el burrito
   e. la hamburguesa

2. Sofía come _____ .
   a. la ensalada mixta y pollo
   b. la especialidad de la casa
   c. el burrito
   d. la hamburguesa
   e. la enchilada

3. Carlos come _____ .
   a. la especialidad de la casa
   b. la hamburguesa
   c. la enchilada
   d. el bistec asado
   e. el burrito

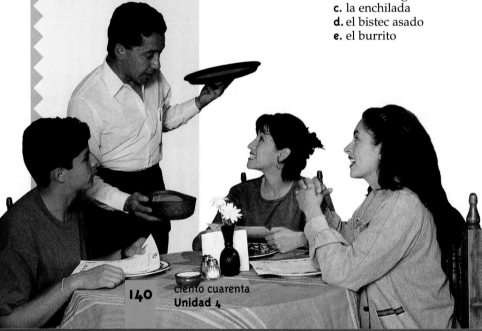

140 ciento cuarenta
Unidad 4

Middle School Classroom Management

Time Saver Use the overhead projector. While
you're taking attendance or moving around the room
to check homework, the students can be doing the
Quick Start Review, correcting their homework,
reviewing vocabulary, taking a mini-quiz, doing a verb
practice, etc. When you need to focus their attention
on you, turn off the projector.

Peer Review Have students work in groups to write
sentences about the new vocabulary. Ask them to use
a variety of verbs to express their preferences: **gustar,**
preferir, and **querer.** Have students read their
sentences to the group and make corrections based
on group feedback.

ACTIVIDAD 2

En el restaurante

Escuchar ¿Quién habla: Sofía, Carlos, Rosa o el mesero? *(Hint: Tell who made the following statements.)*

1. «Yo quiero un plato tradicional.»
2. «Me gustan las enchiladas, pero voy a pedir bistec.»
3. «Una limonada para mí.»
4. «¿Un flan, señoritas? Lo sirvo en dos platos... »
5. «No quiero ningún postre, pero ¿me puede traer la cuenta, por favor?»

Vocabulario

La comida

las bebidas

el pan dulce

la carne

el pastel

la lechuga

el queso

el pan

caliente *hot, warm*
dulce *sweet*
sin *without*
vegetariano(a) *vegetarian*

¿Prefieres una cena con carne o sin carne? ¿Qué te gusta comer?

ACTIVIDAD 3

¿Qué prefieres?

PARA CONVERSAR
STRATEGY: SPEAKING
Vary ways to express preferences Use **querer** or **preferir** to vary your sentences about their choices.

Hablar Pregúntale a un(a) compañero(a) qué comidas prefiere. *(Hint: Ask a classmate what foods he or she prefers.)*

modelo

el flan / el pastel

Estudiante A: ¿Qué prefieres, **el flan** o **el pastel**?

Estudiante B: Prefiero **el flan**. (Prefiero **el pastel**.) (No me gusta nada.) ¿Y tú?

1. el bistec / el pollo
2. la ensalada mixta / la sopa
3. la fruta / el queso
4. el pan dulce / las papas fritas
5. la limonada / el refresco

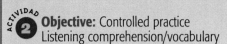

UNIDAD 4 Etapa 3
Vocabulary/Grammar

ACTIVIDAD 2

Objective: Controlled practice Listening comprehension/vocabulary

Answers (See script, p. 133B.)
1. Rosa
2. Carlos
3. Sofía
4. el mesero
5. Carlos

ACTIVIDAD 3

Objective: Transitional practice Vocabulary

Answers will vary.

Teaching Suggestions
Presenting Vocabulary

After presenting the vocabulary for **La comida**, name various foods and drinks. Have students classify them as **Es dulce** or **No es dulce**.

Block Schedule

Variety Have students research Mexican restaurants in your area. They should obtain menus and calculate the total cost of a class lunch at several of the restaurants. If possible, plan a class trip to one of the restaurants. If a class trip is not possible, plan a potluck supper with a Mexican theme.

Teaching Middle School Students

Challenge Suggest to students who are interested in cooking that they prepare a Mexican recipe and share the preparation and the food with the class.

Native Speakers Ask your native speakers to expand the list of foods presented in the **Vocabulario**. Have them model pronunciation for the other students.

Multiple Intelligences

Logical/Mathematical Have students look in Hispanic cookbooks to find out about weights and measurements in preparing recipes. Have them make a presentation to the class, and perhaps prepare a printout of the basic information to give to classmates for their notebooks.

Teaching Resource Options

Print

Unit 4 Resource Book
Video Activities, p. 127
Videoscript, p. 130
Audioscript, pp. 131–132
Audioscript *Para hispanohablantes*,
   pp. 131–132

Audiovisual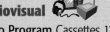

Audio Program Cassettes 12A, 12B /
CD 12
Audio *Para hispanohablantes*
Cassette 12A / CD 12
Video Program Videotape 4 / Videodisc
2B

 Objective: Transitional practice
Vocabulary

Answers
1. ¡Qué rica! or ¡Qué dulce!
2. ¡Qué caliente!
3. ¡Qué barato!
4. ¡Qué picante!
5. ¡Qué simpático!

 Objective: Transitional practice
Listening comprehension/vocabulary

Answers (See script, p. 133B.)
1. b
2. d
3. a
4. c

¿Qué dice?

Escribir/Hablar En una hoja de papel, escribe lo que dice la persona
en cada caso. *(Hint: On a separate sheet of paper, write what the person says in each
scene. Choose from the expressions listed below.)*

¿Qué pasa?

Escuchar Escucha las
descripciones. ¿Qué foto
se relaciona con cada
descripción? *(Hint: Which
description matches each photo?)*

a.

b.

c.

d.

Middle School Classroom Community

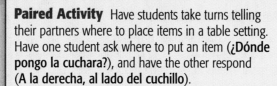

Paired Activity Have students take turns telling
their partners where to place items in a table setting.
Have one student ask where to put an item (**¿Dónde
pongo la cuchara?**), and have the other respond
(**A la derecha, al lado del cuchillo**).

Game Do a brief warm-up on how to use **¡Qué +
adjective!** as an exclamation. Have students work in
groups. One student will name a food, or some other
appropriate item, and the others will respond with an
exclamation, using facial expressions and exaggerated
gestures. Students take turns naming items.

🔄 Las tiendas y tú

Hablar Habla con otro(a) estudiante sobre las tiendas. Cambien de papel. *(Hint: Talk to a classmate about where you went shopping and what you bought recently.)*

modelo

zapatería

Estudiante A: *¿Fuiste a la zapatería?*

Estudiante B: *Sí, fui a comprar unos zapatos.*

Nota

Fui and **fuiste** are past tense forms of the verb **ir. Fui** means *I went;* **fuiste** means *you (tú) went.*

1. pastelería
2. carnicería
3. panadería
4. librería
5. tienda de música

🔄 A poner la mesa

Hablar Trabajas en un restaurante. El (La) nuevo(a) mesero(a) no sabe cómo poner la mesa. Ayúdalo(a). *(Hint: Help the waiter/waitress set the table.)*

modelo

el tenedor

Mesero(a): *¿Dónde pongo el tenedor?*

Tú: *Al lado del plato, a la izquierda.*

Nota

Poner means *to put.* It has an irregular **yo** form: **pongo.** The expression **poner la mesa** means *to set the table.*

1. el cuchillo
2. la cuchara
3. el vaso
4. la taza
5. el plato

También se dice

To describe Mexico's spicy cuisine, **picante** is used by all Spanish speakers. In Mexico, **picoso(a)** describes especially spicy food!

Spanish speakers use different words for *waiter/waitress.*

- **mesero(a):** Mexico, Puerto Rico
- **camarero(a):** Spain
- **mozo(a):** Argentina, Puerto Rico
- **caballero/señorita:** many countries

salsa picante

Teaching Middle School Students

Extra Help To help students remember the difference between **cuchillo** and **cuchara**, point out that there are two long and straight letters in the middle of **cuchillo**, like the flatware.

Native Speakers Ask native speakers to talk about table service items they commonly use in their country. Find out if they call them by a different name, or use different items.

Multiple Intelligences

Musical/Rhythmic Play a recording of some lively Mexican music and have the students move around the room in a large circle. Stop the music and hold up an item of table service. Tell the students to move and repeat the name of the item in rhythm as you play more music. Continue until you have called out all the items.

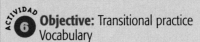

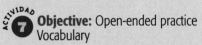 **Objective:** Transitional practice
Vocabulary

Answers

Answers may resemble the following.

1. ¿Fuiste a la pastelería? Sí, fui a comprar pasteles.
2. ¿Fuiste a la carnecería? Sí, fui a comprar carne.
3. ¿Fuiste a la panadería? Sí, fui a comprar pan.
4. ¿Fuiste a la librería? Sí, fui a comprar libros.
5. ¿Fuiste a la tienda de música? Sí, fui a comprar discos.

Objective: Open-ended practice
Vocabulary

🔄 Prepositions of location

Answers

1. Al lado del plato, a la derecha.
2. Al lado del cuchillo, a la derecha.
3. Al lado de la taza, a la izquierda.
4. Al lado del vaso, a la derecha.
5. Entre el tenedor y el cuchillo.

Game

¿Qué hay de comer? Prepare a photocopied drawing of a place setting for each student, adding a soup bowl, bread dish, and dessert dish. Each student receives a copy and plans a 6-item meal. Then, have students play in pairs, each guessing the other's items from clues. For example: **En mi vaso hay algo claro y fresco.** Answer: **En el vaso tienes agua fresco.** If the answer is correct, the same partner gets to guess another item, otherwise, that partner gives clues. The first student to "finish" the meal wins.

■ Block Schedule

Variety Assign a different table-setting item to each small group. Have the group brainstorm a series of 4 clues as to the identity of their item, graduated from hard to dead giveaway. Put out as many lettered boxes as there are groups and assign one to each group. Have them post their hardest clue on the box. Meanwhile, each student starts a guess list, with 4 numbered spaces under the letter of each box *not* belonging to his or her group. Students write guesses as to the contents of the boxes. Guessers may hold their previous guess or write a new one next to the clue number.

Teaching Resource Options

Print 📖

Más práctica Workbook PE, p. 21
Para hispanohablantes Workbook PE, p. 19
Block Scheduling Copymasters
Unit 4 Resource Book
  Más práctica Workbook TE, p. 107
  Para hispanohablantes Workbook TE, p. 113

Audiovisual 📺

OHT 134 (Quick Start)

Technology 💻

Intrigas y aventuras CD-ROM, Disc 1

Quick Start Review

♻ Foods and drinks

Use OHT 134 or write on the board:
Unscramble the following words:

1. elugcha
2. soeuq
3. tosper
4. psoa
5. crúaaz
6. ercan
7. lseapt
8. zrora

Answers

1. lechuga
2. queso
3. postre
4. sopa
5. azúcar
6. carne
7. pastel
8. arroz

Teaching Suggestions
Teaching Using gustar to Talk About Things You Like

Point out that **le** and **les** + **gusta/gustan** can be ambiguous. Therefore, it is helpful to specify to whom an item is pleasing by using the appropriate clause; for example: **A mi amigo, A mis padres,** etc.

NOTA CULTURAL

Mexican cuisine blends pre-Hispanic and Spanish traditions. Oaxaca is known for its many **mole** sauces. Some have more than 20 ingredients. In Veracruz, **chiles rellenos** are popular.

mole

chile relleno

GRAMÁTICA

Using **gustar** to Talk About Things You Like

♻ **¿RECUERDAS?** *1A, p. 209* Remember how to express what **activities** people like to do? You use these phrases with an infinitive.

me gusta…	nos gusta…
te gusta…	os gusta…
le gusta…	les gusta…

▶ When you want to talk about **things** that people like, change the form of **gustar** to match the **singular** or **plural** nouns for those things.

Singular

me gusta **la idea**	nos gusta **la idea**
te gusta **la idea**	os gusta **la idea**
le gusta **la idea**	les gusta **la idea**

Plural

me gustan **las personas**	nos gustan **las personas**
te gustan **las personas**	os gustan **las personas**
le gustan **las personas**	les gustan **las personas**

Rosa says:
matches singular noun
—¡**Me gusta** mucho tu **idea** para el concurso!
I like your idea for the contest a lot!

Carlos says:
matches plural noun
—**Me gustan las enchiladas.**
I like enchiladas.

Notice that the form of **gustar** matches the **noun**, not the speaker.

Middle School Classroom Community

Cooperative Learning Have groups find out what foods the members like and dislike. They divide up the roles but then work together to plan a class presentation.

• Make a chart with group names across the top and food vocabulary down the side.
• Fill in chart cells with **le gusta** or **no le gusta** by interviewing all group members.
• Summarize the results.

Game Have students list ten food items on the board. Ask the class to write one item from the list that they like. Name a student; ask him or her to give a hint about the chosen food (**Es una fruta**). Then ask another student to guess. If the guesser is correct, he or she gets a point, then gives a hint and play continues. If the guesser is incorrect, the hinter gets a point and gives another hint to someone else.

ACTIVIDAD 8 Gramática

¿Qué les gusta(n)?

Hablar Rosa habla de la comida que les gusta a ella y a sus amigos. ¿Qué dice? *(Hint: Rosa is talking about the food that she and her friends like. Tell what she says.)*

modelos

a mí / enchiladas

Me gustan las enchiladas.

a Pedro y a Juan / flan

Les gusta el flan.

1. a Diego /arroz
2. a ustedes / postres
3. a mí / pollo
4. a los chicos /pan dulce
5. a ti / ensaladas
6. a nosotras / tacos
7. a Arturo / flan
8. a Paco y a Enrique / comida picante
9. a nosotras / papas fritas
10. a Carlos / mole negro

MÁS PRÁCTICA *cuaderno p. 21*

PARA HISPANOHABLANTES
cuaderno p. 19

ACTIVIDAD 9

♻ ¡La ropa favorita!

Hablar/Escribir Estás en una tienda de ropa. Di a quiénes les gustan varios artículos. *(Hint: You are in a clothing store. Explain who likes or does not like various clothing items.)*

modelos

a mí: Me gustan los zapatos negros.

a mi primo: A mi primo no le gusta la camiseta.

1. a mí
2. a mi amigo(a)
3. a mis padres
4. a mí y mi madre
5. a mi abuelo
6. a mis amigos
7. a mi hermano(a)
8. a mi prima
9. a mi tía
10. a mí y mi hermana

APOYO PARA ESTUDIAR

¿Me gusta o me gustan?

How do you say *I like it* or *I like them* when talking about nouns? When you use **gustar** with nouns, think of the phrase *to please* in English. *I like something* means *Something is pleasing to me.* So, how do you say *I like it* or *I like them*? Look at the title of this study hint!

ciento cuarenta y cinco
Etapa 3 145

Answers
1. (A Diego) le gusta el arroz.
2. (A ustedes) les gustan los postres.
3. (A mí) me gusta el pollo.
4. (A los chicos) les gusta el pan dulce.
5. (A ti) te gustan las ensaladas.
6. (A nosotros) nos gustan los tacos.
7. (A Arturo) le gusta el flan.
8. (A Paco y a Enrique) les gusta la comida picante.
9. (A nosotros) nos gustan las papas fritas.
10. (A Carlos) le gusta el mole negro.

ACTIVIDAD 9 Objective: Transitional practice **Gustar** and indirect object pronouns

♻ Clothing

Answers
Answers will vary but must contain the following direct object pronouns.
1. me
2. le
3. les
4. nos
5. le
6. les
7. le
8. le
9. le
10. nos

🔔 Quick Wrap-up

Ask students to name people that are of interest to them; they may be people they actually know (friends, relatives, neighbors) or celebrities whose careers they follow. Write the names on the board and ask volunteers to name things that they like: **mi prima: A mi prima le gusta la música de…**

Block Schedule

Change of Pace Have students poll their classmates regarding their favorite foods. To report their findings, have them create a visual, such as a paper plate pie chart. Using **Actividad 8** as a model, they should also write 5–7 sentences to accompany their visual. (For additional activities, see **Block Scheduling Copymasters**.)

Teaching Middle School Students

Extra Help Write on the board

1 = yo	4 = ella
2 = tú	5 = nosotros
3 = usted	6 = ustedes

Roll a die. Choose a student to use the number on the die to decide what form of **gustar** to use with a noun of his or her choice to make a sentence.

Multiple Intelligences

Visual Give students small round stickers. Have them put a happy face on one side of a coin and a sad face on the other side. Ask them to flip their coins 6 times and write a sentence about likes or dislikes to go with the face that landed up on each flip.

Teaching Resource Options

Print

Block Scheduling Copymasters

Audiovisual

OHT 134 (Quick Start)

Technology

Intrigas y aventuras CD-ROM, Disc 1

ACTIVIDAD **10** **Objective:** Open-ended practice
Gustar/vocabulary

Answers will vary.

Game

Comida de colores Select a scorekeeper. Have students form teams by row and select a scribe. Teams may use a Spanish-English dictionary during the game. Say a color, **rojo**. Teams have 3 minutes to write foods that are red. When time is up, each team reads off its red foods (**tomates, fresas, sandía**, etc.). The other teams cross each food off their list. Teams get a point for each food not mentioned by the other teams.

NOTA CULTURAL

Did you know that you sometimes speak Nahuatl (na wá tal), the language of the ancient Aztecs? Anytime you ask for chocolate milk or a bacon, lettuce, and tomato sandwich, you are using words derived from the Nahuatl language. The word *chocolate* comes from two Nahuatl words **xocol** and **atl**. These words mean "dirty water," because the Aztecs mixed their chocolate in water. *Tomato* comes from **tomatl** or **jitomatl**. Other words of Nahuatl origin you might know are *avocado, coyote,* and *cocoa!*

xocolatl

avocatl

tomatl

146 ciento cuarenta y seis
Unidad 4

ACTIVIDAD **10**

Entrevistas

Hablar Escoge tres comidas. Pregunta a tres compañeros(as) si les gusta cada una. Infórmale a la clase. *(Hint: Choose three foods. Interview three students to find out if they like those foods. Report your findings to the class.)*

los postres   el flan

las papas fritas   las hamburguesas

el arroz con pollo

la carne

la salsa

modelo

Estudiante A: *¿Te gustan las hamburguesas?*

Estudiante B: *No, no me gustan mucho.*

(A la clase): *A dos personas les gustan las hamburguesas. A una persona no le gustan.*

Middle School Classroom Community

Group Activity Have the groups write four extremely negative sentences. Have the groups read their sentences aloud and let the groups vote on the four "best most negative sentences."

Game Divide the class into two teams. Say one of the negative/affirmative counterparts and ask a student to give the opposite. If he or she is correct, give the team one point. For "double jeopardy" (two points), the team must make up a sentence using the word. If the answer is incorrect, someone from the other team may give the word to earn the point.

GRAMÁTICA

Affirmative and Negative Words

When you want to talk about an indefinite or negative situation, you use an **affirmative** or a **negative** word.

Affirmative Words		Negative Words	
algo	*something*	**nada**	*nothing*
alguien	*someone*	**nadie**	*no one*
algún/alguno(a)	*some*	**ningún/ninguno(a)**	*none, not any*
siempre	*always*	**nunca**	*never*
también	*also*	**tampoco**	*neither, either*

The waiter asks:
—¿**Algo** de tomar?
***Something** to drink?*

Sofía says:
—Por ahora, **nada** más.
*For now, **nothing** more.*

Notice that **alguno(a)** and **ninguno(a)** must match the gender of the noun they replace or modify. **Alguno** and **ninguno** have different forms when used before masculine singular nouns.

alguno ➡ **algún**   **ninguno** ➡ **ningún**

Las chicas quieren **algún** postre, pero Carlos no quiere **ningún** postre.
*The girls want **some** dessert, but Carlos **doesn't** want **any** dessert.*

When a verb is preceded by **no**, words that follow it must also be negative. A **double negative** is required in Spanish when **no** comes before the verb.

No quiero **nada**.
*I **don't** want **anything**.*

Carlos **no** quiere **ninguno** (de los postres).
*Carlos does **not** want **any** (of the desserts).*

However, if a sentence **begins** with a negative word, such as **nunca** or **nadie**, a second negative is not needed.

Nadie quiere postre.
***No one** wants dessert.*

Nunca comen en casa.
*They **never** eat at home.*

ciento cuarenta y siete
Etapa 3   **147**

Teaching Middle School Students

Challenge As a follow-up to the **Nota cultural**, challenge interested students to find out more about the **Nahuatl** language. Suggest they investigate other words we know that come from that language.

Multiple Intelligences

Verbal Have student pairs take turns asking each other whether they like certain foods or drinks. The partner answers, and adds a follow-up sentence using one of the negative/affirmative counterparts. (**Sí, me gustan mucho las hamburguesas. Siempre las como. / No, no me gusta la carne. Nunca la como.**)

Quick Start Review

♻ **Likes and dislikes**

Use OHT 134 or write on the board: Tell which of your friends or relatives like the following foods. Write complete sentences using **gustar**.

1. la comida picante
2. la sopa vegetariana
3. las papas fritas
4. el pan dulce
5. las enchiladas

Answers *See p. 133B.*

Teaching Suggestions
Presenting Affirmative and Negative Words

• Refer to the **Diálogo,** pp. 138–139. Have students identify the affirmative and negative words.
• Make up a short scenario using several of the words. When students hear one of these words, they should raise their hands or write down the word.

Block Schedule

Recycle Have students look back through the Bridge Unit for sentences using adjectives. Have them rewrite and illustrate the sentences using exaggeration. (For additional activities, see **Block Scheduling Copymasters**.)

Teaching Resource Options

Print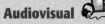

Más práctica Workbook PE,
pp. 22–23

Para hispanohablantes Workbook PE,
pp. 20–21

Block Scheduling Copymasters

Unit 4 Resource Book
Más práctica Workbook TE,
pp. 108–109
Para hispanohablantes Workbook
TE, pp. 114–115
Information Gap Activities, p. 119

Audiovisual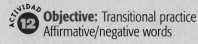

OHT 134 (Quick Start)

Technology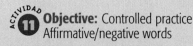

Intrigas y aventuras CD-ROM, Disc 1

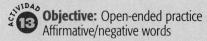 **Objective:** Controlled practice
Affirmative/negative words

Answers

1. algunas	6. ningún
2. ninguna	7. algunas
3. algunos	8. ninguna
4. ningún	9. alguna
5. algunos	10. ninguna

Objective: Transitional practice
Affirmative/negative words

Answers

*Answers will vary but should contain the
following affirmative or negative words.*
1. algo / nada
2. alguien / nadie
3. algo / nada
4. alguien / nadie
5. alguien / nadie
6. alguien / nadie

Objective: Open-ended practice
Affirmative/negative words

Answers will vary.

 **11** Gramática

No quiero...

Leer Tu amigo(a) te invita a
hacer varias cosas, pero no
quieres hacer nada. Completa
la conversación. *(Hint: Your friend
invites you to do a variety of things, but you
don't want to do anything. Complete the
conversation with the correct forms of
alguno(a) or **ninguno(a)**.)*

modelo

*¿Quieres comer **algunos** chocolates?*

*No quiero comer **ningún** chocolate.*

Nota

Ningunos(as) is almost never used. It
is used only with items that are usually
plural, such as **pantalones**.

No tengo **ningunos** pantalones.

1. ¿Quieres ir a _____ tiendas?
2. No quiero ir a _____ tienda.
3. ¿Quieres alquilar _____ videos?
4. No quiero alquilar _____ video.
5. ¿Quieres escuchar _____ discos compactos?
6. No quiero escuchar _____ disco compacto.
7. ¿Quieres leer _____ revistas?
8. No quiero leer _____ revista.
9. ¿Quieres comer _____ fruta?
10. No quiero comer _____ fruta.

 **12** Gramática

¿Que sí o que no?

Hablar Pregúntale a un(a) compañero(a) qué va a hacer el sábado
por la noche. Contesta con **sí** y **no**. *(Hint: Ask another student what he or she is
going to do on Saturday night. Answer both **yes** and **no**, as if you changed your mind.)*

modelo

invitar a alguien a un baile

Estudiante A: *¿Vas a **invitar a alguien a un baile?***

Estudiante B: *Sí, voy a **invitar a alguien a un baile**.*

Estudiante A: *¿Es verdad?*

Estudiante B: *No, no voy a invitar a nadie a un baile.*

1. leer algo	4. caminar con alguien
2. escribir a alguien	5. escuchar a alguien
3. comprar algo	6. regalar algo a alguien

■ **MÁS PRÁCTICA** *cuaderno* pp. 22–23

■ **PARA HISPANOHABLANTES** *cuaderno* pp. 20–21

 **13** ¡No lo hago!

Escribir Lee la lista de Rosa. Luego, escribe cinco cosas que tú
no haces. *(Hint: Read Rosa's list. Then, write five things that you don't do, using the
words listed.)*

1. nada
2. nadie
3. ningún(a)
4. nunca
5. tampoco

> Las cosas que no hago
> No como nada picante.
> No conozco a nadie aburrido.
> No tengo ningún libro interesante.
> Nunca hablo en clase.
> Tampoco escribo en mis libros.

---

148 ciento cuarenta y ocho
Unidad 4

Middle School Classroom Community

Storytelling Have students tell a story about "señor
Positivo" and "señorita Negativa." Let students list
the positive/negative counterparts as an organizer.
Depending on the class, students may contribute
individually or as small groups. You may wish to start
them out: El señor Positivo y la señorita Negativa son
muuuuuy diferentes. A él le gusta todo; a ella no le
gusta nada. Por ejemplo, el señor Positivo siempre
come mucho. Pero la señorita Negativa nunca come
nada. A ella no le gustan ni las frutas, ni el postre, ni
el queso...

Conexiones

La salud Because of its warm climate, Mexico produces a vast variety of fruits–some that we never see in the United States. Besides eating the fruit, Mexicans blend it into delicious drinks **(licuados)**, freeze it into popsicles **(paletas)**, and turn it into soft drinks **(refrescos)** that contain a high percentage of real fruit juice.

PARA HACER:
Think of five of your favorite fruits. Use a dictionary, or ask your teacher, to find out how to say them in Spanish.

ACTIVIDAD 14

¡Es buenísimo!

Hablar/Escribir Todos reaccionan con gran entusiasmo. Describe cada persona o cosa.
(Hint: Everybody is reacting very enthusiastically. Describe each person or item, following the model.)

modelo

el postre (bueno)

El postre es **buenísimo**.

Nota

Some adjectives can express extremes by dropping the final vowel and adding the ending **-ísimo(a)**. The adjective must agree in gender and number with the noun it modifies.

La idea de Rosa es **interesantísima**.

*Rosa's idea is **very (extremely) interesting**.*

Los postres son **buenísimos**.

*The desserts are **really good**.*

When the root of the word ends in **c**, the **c** changes to **qu** before the ending.

rico(a) → ri**qu**ísimo(a)

1. la maestra (bueno)
2. las enchiladas (rico)
3. el perro (malo)
4. la película (triste)
5. los estudiantes (inteligente)
6. la idea (loco)

■ **MÁS COMUNICACIÓN** p. R3

ACTIVIDAD 14

Objective: Controlled practice
Superlative suffixes

Answers
1. La maestra es buenísima.
2. Las enchiladas son riquísimas.
3. El perro es malísimo.
4. La película es tristísima.
5. Los estudiantes son inteligentísimos.
6. La idea es loquísima.

Language Note
To express extremes with adjectives, there is another spelling change. When the last consonant is **g**, the **g** changes to **gu**: largo(a) → larguísimo(a).

Para hacer
Answers will vary.

■ Block Schedule
FunBreak Use the food vocabulary cards prepared for "Time Saver," TE, p. 134. Give one to each student, then ask them to sort themselves into 3 categories: **dulce, picante,** and **otro**. Now, ask them to re-sort into 3 different categories, for example **para el desayuno, para el almuerzo,** and **para la cena**. How many students think they could go to more than one group?

Teaching Middle School Students

Native Speakers Have native speakers name and describe some uncommon fruits they have seen or eaten.

Multiple Intelligences

Visual To get a better feel for the effect of -ísimo adjectives, have students draw several items and label them with an adjective. Tell them to exchange their papers with another student, who draws the same type of items, intensified, and changes the adjective to the -ísimo form.

Vocabulary/Grammar • UNIDAD 4 Etapa 3 **149**

Teaching Resource Options

Print

Más práctica Workbook PE, p. 24
Para hispanohablantes Workbook PE,
   p. 22
Unit 4 Resource Book
   Más práctica Workbook TE, p. 110
   Para hispanohablantes Workbook
   TE, p. 116

Audiovisual

OHT 135 (Quick Start)

Technology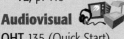

Intrigas y aventuras CD-ROM, Disc 1

Quick Start Review

♻ **Affirmative and negative words**

Use OHT 135 or write on the board:
Rewrite the sentences using the correct
word.
1. No hay ___ aquí hoy. (alguien / nadie)
2. ¿Hay ___ en tu clase que no tiene
   hermanos? (alguien / nadie)
3. Quiero darte ___ después de clase.
   (alguno / algo)
4. Yo no quiero ir ___. (tampoco / también)
5. ¿Quieres ___ postre? (alguna / algún)

Answers *See p. 133B.*

Teaching Suggestions
Teaching Stem-Changing Verbs:
e→i

• Review stem-changing e→i verbs.
  List the verbs and have students
  provide original sentences of each.
• Practice e→i and e→i verbs with a
  soft ball. Toss the ball to a student as
  you say a verb infinitive and a subject
  noun/pronoun. The student must
  give the correct conjugated form as
  he/she tosses the ball back.

 Objective: Controlled practice
15 Pedir

Answers
1. piden
2. sirve
3. pide
4. pide
5. piden
6. pedimos
7. piden
8. pide

GRAMÁTICA

Stem-Changing Verbs: e → i

♻ **¿RECUERDAS?** *1A, p. 230* You have already learned about
e to **ie** stem-changing verbs like **pensar**.

pensar *to think, to plan*

pienso	**pens**amos
piensas	**pens**áis
piensa	**piens**an

The verb **pedir** also has a stem change. The stem alternates
between **e** and **i**.

pedir *to ask for, to order*

pido	**ped**imos
pides	**ped**ís
pide	**pid**en

The stem
doesn't change for the
nosotros *(we)* or
vosotros *(you)* form.

Sofía says:

–¿**Pid**o un postre y lo
compartimos?
*Should I order dessert and we'll
share it?*

Vocabulario

Stem-Changing Verbs: e → i

pedir *to ask for, to order*

servir *to serve*

Other verbs that follow the
pattern:

repetir *to repeat*

seguir *to follow, to continue*

The **yo** form of **seguir** drops the
u: yo sigo.

¿Qué pides en un restaurante?

ACTIVIDAD 15 Gramática

¡Qué comida!

Escribir La familia de Manuel
sale para una comida.
Completa las oraciones con la
forma correcta de **pedir** o
servir. *(Hint: Manuel's family is going out
to eat. Complete the sentences with the
correct form of the verb.)*

1. Los padres de Manuel
   _____ unas tapas por toda
   la familia.
2. El mesero les _____
   las tapas.
3. Después toda la familia
   _____ su comida.
4. Manuel _____ un bistec
   y papas fritas.
5. Sus hermanas _____
   unas ensaladas y
   unas enchiladas.
6. —Nosotros _____ unos
   postres también—dicen
   los padres a los meseros.
7. Los meseros del
   restaurante _____ unos
   postres deliciosos.
8. Nadie _____ el café.

Middle School Classroom Community

Group Activity Have students fold a paper in
two and label the top **La escuela** and the bottom **El
restaurante**. They write a sentence using **servir** on
each half and pass their paper to the right. (**La escuela:
La cafetería sirve las hamburguesas. El restaurante:
El restaurante sirve comida deliciosa.**) Students write
different sentences and pass the papers again. Have
them compare papers and make corrections.

Learning Scenario Tell students that they are to
imagine a restaurant where famous people eat. Each
student chooses the name of a famous person. Call on
students to tell who they are and what they order at
the restaurant. For example, **Soy Madonna. Pido café.
/ Soy Sammy Sosa. Mark McGwire está conmigo.
Pedimos bistec y arroz.**

16 Gramática

Sirven...

Hablar/Escribir Carlos come en casa de sus amigos a menudo. ¿Qué le sirven? *(Hint: Carlos often eats at his friends' homes. What do they serve?)*

modelo

Antonio / hamburguesas

Antonio sirve **hamburguesas**.

1. yo / enchiladas
2. nosotros / tortas
3. usted / frutas
4. tú / pollo
5. Patricia y Carla / ensaladas
6. la señora Ruiz / carne
7. mi hermano y yo / mole negro
8. ustedes / tacos
9. Rosa / bistec
10. nosotros / pan

■ **MÁS PRÁCTICA** *cuaderno* p. 24

■ **PARA HISPANOHABLANTES** *cuaderno* p. 22

17

¡Tengo sed!

Hablar Conversa con un(a) compañero(a) sobre las bebidas que toman ustedes. *(Hint: Take turns with a classmate asking and answering questions about what you drink at various times.)*

modelo

desayunas

Estudiante A: *¿Qué bebida pides cuando* **desayunas**?

Estudiante B: *Pido una taza de chocolate.*

Nota

Desayunar means *to have breakfast.* **El desayuno** is *breakfast.*

ESTUDIANTE A

¿Qué bebida pides cuando...?
1. desayunas
2. tienes mucha sed
3. estás enfermo(a)
4. no puedes dormir
5. cenas con tu familia en un restaurante
6. tienes frío
7. tienes calor
8. estás con tus amigos

ESTUDIANTE B

Pido...

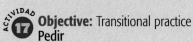

16 **Objective:** Controlled practice
Servir

Answers
1. Yo sirvo enchiladas.
2. Nosotros servimos tortas.
3. Usted sirve frutas.
4. Tú sirves pollo.
5. Patricia y Carla sirven ensaladas.
6. La señora Ruiz sirve carne.
7. Mi hermano y yo servimos mole negro.
8. Ustedes sirven tacos.
9. Rosa sirve bistec.
10. Nosotros servimos pan.

17 **Objective:** Transitional practice
Pedir

Answers will vary.

🔔 Quick Wrap-up
Have a volunteer go to the board and write the **ellos** form of **pedir** on one side and the **nosotros** form on the other. Have students tell what their elders usually order when they go out to eat and what they and their peers/ friends order. For example, **Mis padres (abuelos, vecinos) piden carne, ensaladas... Mi amigo y yo pedimos pizza, hamburguesas, pollo…**

Critical Thinking
Using vocabulary from **Unidad 4**, create four categories. For example: **Lugares, Transporte, Comida,** and **Compras.** Students form four equal teams, one per category. Then, each student writes a different scrambled word from the category on a slip of paper. Shuffle the scrambled words, redistribute them face down, and assign a corner of the room to each category. When you call out, **¡Preparados, listos, ya!**, students unscramble their word, write it on the other side, and run to the corner that the word belongs in.

Teaching Middle School Students

Challenge Ask students to write and illustrate a short restaurant scene using **pedir** and **servir**.

Native Speakers Ask students to list drinks that are associated with each meal and share any new vocabulary with the rest of the class.

Multiple Intelligences

Kinesthetic Have students take turns asking their partner simple questions using **pedir** and **servir**. When students answer, they must pantomime what they say: **¿Qué sirves? Sirvo bebidas.**

▨ Block Schedule
Change of Pace Write all stem-changing verbs on individual cards and put them in a bag. Have students pull out 2 cards. Have them write mini-paragraphs using both words. Ask volunteers to present their work.

Teaching Resource Options

Print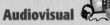

Block Scheduling Copymasters
Unit 4 Resource Book
  Information Gap Activities, pp. 120–121
  Audioscript, p. 132
  Audioscript *Para hispanohablantes*,
    p. 132

Audiovisual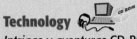

Audio Program Cassettes 12A, 12B /
CD 12
Audio *Para hispanohablantes*
  Cassette 12A / CD 12

Technology

Intrigas y aventuras CD-ROM, Disc 1

 Objective: Controlled practice
Listening comprehension/cumulative
vocabulary and grammar

Answers (See script, p. 133B.)
1. c
2. f (Va a pedir enchiladas de carne.)
3. c
4. f (Carlos va a pedir algún refresco.)
5. f (Va a pedir un flan.)

Teaching Suggestions
Presenting Vocabulary

Before beginning the activities, you
might wish to conduct "mesero(a)
training." Each trainee must demonstrate
his or her knowledge of the typical
questions and statements that a server
needs to know. Include props.

 Objective: Transitional practice
Direct object pronouns/**traer**

♻ Direct object pronouns

Answers
1. Tú traes los tenedores, ¿verdad? Sí, los traigo.
2. Margarita y yo traemos la ensalada mixta,
   ¿verdad? Sí, la traen.
3. Enrique y Pablo traen el pollo, ¿verdad?
   Sí, lo traen.
4. Yo traigo las enchiladas, ¿verdad?
   Sí, las traes.

¿A quién?

Escuchar Carlos y Elena están
en un restaurante. ¿Es cierta o
falsa cada oración? Corrige las
falsas. *(Hint: Decide if each sentence is
true or false. Correct the false ones.)*

1. Carlos tiene hambre.
2. Elena va a pedir
   enchiladas de pollo.
3. Carlos va a pedir
   un bistec.
4. Los dos van a pedir
   algún refresco.
5. Carlos no va a pedir
   ningún postre.

Vocabulario

En el restaurante

Para pedir comida

¿Me ayuda a pedir? *Could you
help me order?*

¿Me trae...? *Could you bring
me...?*

Quisiera... *I would like...*

Para pedir la cuenta

¿Cuánto es? *How much is it?*

La cuenta, por favor. *The check,
please.*

Es aparte. *Separate checks.*

¿Está incluido(a)...? *Is ...
included?*

¿Cuánto le doy de propina?
How much do I tip?

¿Cómo pides en un restaurante?

♻ La fiesta

Hablar Trabajas con un(a) compañero(a). Tú haces una fiesta. Tu
amigo(a) te pregunta quién trae cada cosa. Cambia de papeles.
*(Hint: Your friend asks you who is bringing various things to your party. Use the correct form of
traer. Change roles.)*

modelo

Antonio / platos

Estudiante A: *Antonio* trae los **platos**, ¿verdad?

Estudiante B: *Sí, él los trae.*

Nota

Traer means *to bring*. It has an irregular **yo** form: **traigo.** Its other forms
are regular.

1. tú / tenedores
2. Margarita y yo / ensalada mixta

3. Enrique y Pablo / pollo
4. yo / enchiladas

¡Buen provecho!

Escribir Un mesero sirve a unos clientes en un restaurante.
Completa la conversación con las palabras de la lista. *(Hint: Complete
the conversation with words from the list.)*

trae	ayuda	pedir
fresco	especialidad	pido

Mesero: Buenas tardes, jóvenes. ¿Listos para __1__ ?

José: Yo __2__ bistec y una ensalada, por favor. ¿Está __3__ el pan?

Mesero: Sí, señor. ¿Y las señoritas?

Ana: ¿Me __4__ una ensalada de frutas y un refresco?

Janet: Perdón, señor, pero no soy de aquí. ¿Me __5__ a pedir?

Mesero: Con mucho gusto. La __6__ hoy son enchiladas suizas.

Janet: ¡Perfecto! ¡Yo __7__ la especialidad!

---

152 ciento cincuenta y dos
Unidad 4

Middle School Classroom Community

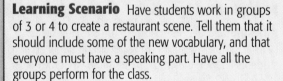

Learning Scenario Have students work in groups
of 3 or 4 to create a restaurant scene. Tell them that it
should include some of the new vocabulary, and that
everyone must have a speaking part. Have all the
groups perform for the class.

TPR Place students in groups of 5. Use the menus
collected for "Planning Ahead," and tableware collected
for "Time Saver," TE, p. 134. Tell students that they are
either customers or waiters in a restaurant. Each group
chooses a director to call out the actions the waiters
and customers must perform: **Píde(le) comida a
Antonia. "Quisiera bistec con papas fritas, por
favor." Sírvele el bistec... Trae un cuchillo para
Marcos... Dale la cuenta a José...**

ACTIVIDAD 21

En el restaurante

Hablar/Escribir Vas a un restaurante con tu amigo. Trabaja en un grupo de tres para escribir un diálogo en dos partes, usando las expresiones de la lista. Luego, presenten los diálogos a la clase. *(Hint: Work in a group of three. Write a restaurant dialog.)*

Parte 1: Llegan al restaurante. El mesero les trae el menú. Piden la comida.

Parte 2: El mesero les trae la comida. Hablan de la calidad de la comida y del servicio.

modelo

Estudiante A: *¿Nos puede traer el menú, por favor?*

Estudiante B (Mesero[a]): *Sí, lo traigo ahora mismo.*

Estudiante C: *¿Qué vas a pedir?*

Estudiante A: *¿Sirven buenas comidas vegetarianas aquí?*

Estudiante C: *Creo que sí. A mí me gusta la carne.*

Estudiante A: *¿Por qué no pides el arroz con pollo?*

Estudiante C: *¡Buena idea!*

Estudiante B (Mesero[a]): *¿Están listos para pedir?*

■ **MÁS COMUNICACIÓN** p. R3

Pronunciación

Trabalenguas

Pronunciación de la *g* The letter **g** in Spanish has a soft sound before the vowels **i** and **e**. It sounds somewhat like the *h* in the English word *he*, but a little harder. Practice by pronouncing the following words:

gimnasio   biolo**gí**a   **ge**neral   **Ge**raldo

When it precedes other vowels, the **g** has a different sound, like in the word *go*. To produce this sound with **i** or **e**, a **u** must be inserted. Practice the following words:

gato   **gu**sto   **go**rdo   abri**go**   **gui**tarra   hambur**gue**sa

Now try the tongue twister.

> Cuando digo «*digo*»
> digo «Diego».
> Cuando digo «Diego» digo «*digo*».

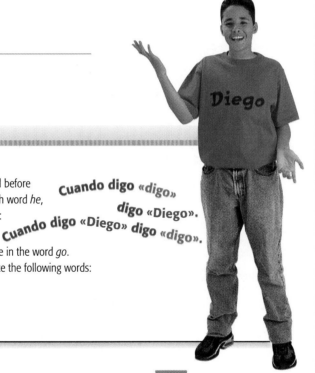

Diego

Teaching Middle School Students

Extra Help To give students more practice with **traer**, tell them to pretend that the class is having a potluck dinner and to say who is bringing what. For more variety, tell them that they have to use a different type of subject from the one previously mentioned: **Ana trae bebidas. Yo traigo enchiladas. Josefina y Carlos traen pan.**

Multiple Intelligences

Verbal In groups of four, have students read aloud **Actividad 20** with expression. Have them reread it substituting other food and drink items and adding more dialog.

ACTIVIDAD 20 Objective: Transitional practice
Pedir/vocabulary

Answers
1. pedir
2. pido
3. fresco
4. trae
5. ayuda
6. especialidad
7. pido

Language Note

Aparte is an adverb, not an adjective, so its form does not change.

ACTIVIDAD 21 Objective: Open-ended practice
Cumulative vocabulary and grammar

Answers will vary.

Dictation

After presenting the **Pronunciación,** have students close their books. Dictate the **Trabalenguas** in segments while students write it.

Block Schedule

Variety Have the class plan a Mexican lunch for students and/or staff. Students will select and prepare food items, design a menu, write invitations, provide decorations, and supply appropriate music. (For additional activities, see **Block Scheduling Copymasters**.)

Teaching Resource Options

Print

Block Scheduling Copymasters
Unit 4 Resource Book
  Audioscript, p. 133
  Audioscript *Para hispanohablantes*,
  p. 133

Audiovisual

OHT 135 (Quick Start)
Audio Program Cassette 12A / CD 12
Audio *Para hispanohablantes*
  Cassette 12A / CD 12
Canciones Cassette / CD

Quick Start Review

♻ **School and after-school activities**

Use OHT 135 or write on the board:
Write 3 activities that you participate in
during school and 3 activities that you
participate in after school.

Answers
Answers will vary. Answers could include:
Voy a mis clases. Hablo con mis profesores.
Estudio en la biblioteca.
Voy al centro comercial. Juego al fútbol
americano. Paso un rato con mis amigos.

✓ Teaching Suggestions

- **Prereading** Have students scan the
  visuals, and based on the content,
  guess what the word **leyenda** means.
  As an advance organizer, have them
  think of legends they know that
  highlight animals.
- **Strategy** As usual, have students
  scan for cognates. Then work with
  students to complete their story
  maps.
- **Reading** In order to focus students
  on the reading, have them review the
  ¿**Comprendiste?** questions. Then
  have volunteers read paragraphs
  aloud.
- **Post-reading** Provide students with
  Spanish/English dictionaries and have
  them look up the names of their
  favorite animals. Have them create an
  illustrated animal dictionary for their
  portfolios.

En voces

LECTURA

PARA LEER
STRATEGY: READING
Making a story map To help
you remember characters and
events in a story, use a story
map like the one below. This
will help you organize the
main ideas in this legend.

> Characters:
> 1. *mujer vieja* 2. _____ 3. _____
> Problem: *Los vecinos quieren ...*
> Solution: *El tlacuache ...*

Una leyenda oaxaqueña
El fuego y el tlacuache[1]

La gente mazateca, que vive en la región norte de Oaxaca,
les cuenta esta leyenda a sus hijos.

Una noche una mujer vieja atrapa la lumbre[2] al caerse de
una estrella[3]. Todos sus vecinos[4] van a la casa de la vieja
a pedir lumbre. Pero la vieja no quiere darle lumbre a
la gente.

En ese momento, llega un tlacuache y les dice
a los vecinos: —Yo, tlacuache, voy a darles la
lumbre si ustedes prometen no comerme.

Todos se ríen[5] cuando oyen las palabras del
tlacuache. Pero el tlacuache les repite que él sí
va a compartir la lumbre con todo el mundo.

---

[1] opossum
[2] fire, light
[3] star
[4] neighbors
[5] laughs

154

ciento cincuenta y cuatro
Unidad 4

Middle School Classroom Community

Learning Scenario Have the class pretend they are
characters in the **leyenda**. Have small groups prepare
their version of the action and videotape it.

Storytelling Have students create a similar **leyenda**
with their own theme and characters. You might start
the story, or have a creative student do so. Let students
add to the story as they wish. Tape the story and let
students edit and illustrate it.

Interdisciplinary Connection
Science Interested students may want to research the practical function of the opossum's hairless tail.

Project
You may also wish to have language-oriented students guess at English words related, via Latin, to the Spanish words **calentarse** (calorie), **frío** (refrigerator, frigid), **lumbre** (illuminate), **compartir** (compartment of a train, shared by several passengers), and **pelado** (peel, pelt).

¿Comprendiste?
Answers
1. Una mujer vieja la atrapa.
2. No, no quiere darle la lumbre a nadie.
3. El tlacuache ofrece traer la lumbre, pero sólo si la gente no lo come.
4. Le dice que tiene mucho frío y que quiere calentarse al lado de la lumbre.
5. Se mete la cola en la lumbre y sale de la casa. Reparte la lumbre a la gente.

Entonces, el tlacuache va a la casa de la vieja y le dice: —Buenas tardes, Señora Lumbre, ¡qué frío hace! Si me permite, quiero estar un rato al lado de la lumbre para calentarme[6].

La vieja le permite al tlacuache acercarse[7] a la lumbre porque sabe que sí hace un frío terrible. En ese momento el animalito avanza y se pone la cola[8] en la lumbre. Entonces, sale rápidamente de la casa y le da la lumbre a todas las casas de la región.

Es por eso que hasta ahora los tlacuaches tienen la cola pelada[9].

---

[6] warm myself [8] tail
[7] approach [9] hairless

¿Comprendiste?
1. ¿Quién atrapa la lumbre?
2. ¿Quiere darle la lumbre a alguien?
3. ¿Qué dice el tlacuache a los vecinos?
4. ¿Cómo puede el tlacuache entrar a la casa de la vieja? ¿Qué le dice a ella?
5. ¿Cómo es que la gente recibe el fuego?

¿Qué piensas?
1. ¿Cuál es el tema principal de esta leyenda?
   a. Nos dice que los tlacuaches son animales muy generosos.
   b. Es una leyenda de por qué los tlacuaches tienen la cola pelada.
2. ¿Crees que tlacuache es una palabra española o una palabra mazateca? ¿Por qué?
3. ¿Qué otro animal podría haberles traído (could have brought) el fuego a las personas por tener la cola pelada?

Teaching Middle School Students

Native Speakers Ask native speakers to tell about stories and legends in their country, especially ones about animals.

Multiple Intelligences

Naturalist Have interested students do additional research on the **tlacuache** and its habitat. They may want to find out how long it has been in the Americas.

Block Schedule
Time Saver Assign the reading as homework so that students can get a head start on comprehension. (For additional activities, see **Block Scheduling Copymasters.**)

Teaching Resource Options

Print 📖

Unit 4 Resource Book
  Audioscript, p. 133
  Audioscript *Para hispanohablantes*,
  p. 133

Audiovisual 🎧

Audio Program Cassette 12A / CD 12
Audio *Para hispanohablantes*
  Cassette 12A / CD 12
OHT 135 (Quick Start)
Video Program Videotape 4 / Videodisc
2B

Search Chapter 8, Play to 9
U4E3 • En colores (Culture)

🔔 Quick Start Review

♻️ **In a restaurant**

Use OHT 135 or write on the board:
You and a friend are customers in a
Mexican restaurant. Complete the
following sentences:

Al mesero/A la mesera
  1. ¿Me trae... ?
  2. Quisiera...
  3. ¿Está incluido(a)... ?

A tu amigo(a)
  4. Me gusta mucho...
  5. No me gusta...

Answers *See p. 133B.*

Teaching Suggestions
**Presenting Cultura y
comparaciones**

• Have students read the Connecting
  Cultures Strategy and discuss.
• Have students read the passage to
  themselves, listing any words they
  don't know. Then have volunteers
  read the passage aloud. Ask students
  to see if they might be able to guess
  the meanings of the words on their
  lists. Go over context clues to help
  them with any they still do not know.
• Expand the cultural information by
  showing the video culture presentation.

En colores

CULTURA Y COMPARACIONES

PARA CONOCERNOS
STRATEGY: CONNECTING CULTURES

Analyze and recommend Some areas depend
on tourism for income, but sometimes local
people are against it. Why is that so?
Think of reasons for and against tourism.

Turismo: no	Turismo: sí
1.	1.
2.	2.
3.	3.

Based on your analysis, write three or more
rules for being a good tourist.

N O T A CULTURAL

Today many Zapotec Indians
support themselves through
farming and traditional
handicrafts such as weaving.

Monte Albán:

Para el concurso de Onda Internacional,
*Carlos visita Monte Albán. Saca fotos y escribe
este artículo sobre una de las primeras culturas
de Oaxaca.*

El estado de Oaxaca es una importante
región arqueológica. El lugar más famoso es
Monte Albán, una de las primeras ciudades
de Mesoamérica [1] y la vieja capital de los
zapotecas [2]. Sabemos que la civilización de
Monte Albán empieza por el año 500 a.C. [3]
Pero los orígenes y el fin de esta civilización
son un misterio fascinante.

---

[1] Middle America (Mexico and Central America)
[2] Zapotec Indians
[3] B.C.

156 ciento cincuenta y seis
Unidad 4

Middle School Classroom Community

TPR Have students mime their responses to the **Para
conocernos**, p. 156. Viewers raise their hands to
indicate that they think the mime is an argument for
tourism. They cover their eyes to signal an argument
against tourism.

Group Activity Tell the groups that they are to
design the site of an ancient civilization. They will have
to name the civilization, design buildings, and show
other achievements of their civilization. Have each
group present information about their ancient
civilization.

Los Danzantes

ruinas misteriosas

Muchos turistas visitan Monte Albán todos los años para conocer sus pirámides, terrazas, tumbas y esculturas. La parte donde hay más exploración es la Plaza Central, centro de la vida social y religiosa de los zapotecas. Allí hay grandes plataformas, como el Juego de Pelota y la Galería de los Danzantes. Los arqueólogos no saben mucho sobre el Juego de Pelota. Tampoco saben qué representan los Danzantes. ¿Son figuras de hombres que danzan o son prisioneros[4]?

El Juego de Pelota

Aproximadamente entre los años 700 y 800 d.C.[5], los zapotecas abandonan Monte Albán. Luego, los mixtecas[6] usan el lugar. Hoy, descendientes de los dos grupos viven en las montañas y el valle de Oaxaca. Su cultura sigue presente en la lengua y las costumbres[7].

---

[4] prisoners
[5] A.D.
[6] Mixtec Indians
[7] customs

¿Comprendiste?

1. ¿Qué importancia tiene Monte Albán?
2. ¿Qué sabemos del fin de la civilización de Monte Albán?
3. ¿Qué pueden ver los turistas aquí?
4. ¿Qué saben los arqueólogos del Juego de Pelota o de los Danzantes?
5. ¿Hay zapotecas hoy en Oaxaca?

¿Qué piensas?

Eres un(a) turista en Monte Albán. En una hoja de papel, describe tu visita y tus reacciones. Mira las fotos para inspirarte.

157

Language Note

The abbreviations **a.C.** and **d.C.** stand for **antes de Cristo** and **después de Cristo**.

Reading Strategy

Ask students to look for and list all cognates in the reading. Compile a class list. Do students notice any spelling patterns for close cognates (for example, **-ción** = *-tion*, **-oso[a]** = *-ous)?*

Culture Highlights

● **LAS TUMBAS DE MONTE ALBÁN**
During the excavations performed in Monte Albán, nearly 170 tombs were found. Some of these tombs were decorated by mural paintings, and most contained many rich offerings. The famous Tomb 7 was filled with marvelous objects made by the Mixtec Indians.

Cross Cultural Connections

Strategy Have students think again about the differences between travel and tourism. If there are archaeological sites in your area, ask students to think about their own reactions to visitors and compare them to possible Zapotec and Mixtec reactions in Monte Albán.

¿Comprendiste?

Answers
1. Monte Albán es una de las primeras ciudades de Mesoamérica y la vieja capital de los zapotecas.
2. El fin de la civilización de Monte Albán es un misterio.
3. Los turistas pueden ver pirámides, terrazas, tumbas y esculturas.
4. Los arqueólogos no saben mucho del Juego de Pelota o de los Danzantes.
5. Sí, hay hoy en Oaxaca.

Block Schedule

Research Have students research more information about Monte Albán, using the Internet or library resources. Some students might also research Mitla, another major archaeological site located 24 miles southwest of Oaxaca.

Teaching Middle School Students

Native Speakers Ask your native speakers to present a short report on an archaeological site in their home countries.

Multiple Intelligences

Kinesthetic Have students design a ball game or a dance based on what they know about the civilization at Monte Albán. They should be prepared to demonstrate and to teach the class how to play the game or perform the dance.

Interpersonal Have students imagine that they are part of the Monte Albán civilization. Ask them to write one or two paragraphs in which they tell who they are and something about the kind of life they lead based on what they know about Monte Albán.

Quick Start Review

🔔 **Verb review**

Use OHT 136 or write on the board:
Give the correct present tense forms
of the following verbs:

1. (yo) poner   4. (nosotros) servir
2. (tú) traer   5. (ustedes) pensar
3. (usted) pedir

Answers .
1. pongo   4. servimos
2. traes   5. piensan
3. pide

Teaching Suggestions
What Have Students Learned?

Have students look at the "Now you
can…" notes listed on the left side of
pages 158–159. Remind them to
review the material in the "To review"
notes before doing the activities or
taking the test.

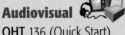 **Answers**

1. alguien   5. algo
2. nadie   6. nada
3. ningún   7. algún
4. algunos   8. alguna

Now you can...
• order food.
• request the check.

To review
• affirmative and
negative words,
see p. 147.

Now you can...
• talk about food.

To review
• stem-changing
verbs: **e → i**,
see p. 150.

En uso
REPASO Y
MÁS COMUNICACIÓN

ACTIVIDAD 1 En el restaurante

Lucía y Emilio están en un restaurante. Completa su diálogo con
el mesero con la forma correcta de las siguientes palabras: **alguno,
ninguno, algo, nada, alguien, nadie.** *(Hint: Lucía and Carlos are in a restaurant.
Complete their conversation with the waiter using the correct form of the words given.)*

Lucía: Emilio, conozco a ___1___ que trabaja en este restaurante.

Emilio: ¿De verdad? Yo no conozco a ___2___ aquí. ¿Quién es?

Lucía: Un vecino. Prepara los postres.

Mesero: La especialidad es el bistec. No hay ___3___ bistec tan delicioso
como el nuestro. Les doy ___4___ minutos para mirar el menú.

Mesero: ¿Están listos para pedir?

Emilio: Sí, para mí, la especialidad.

Lucía: Y yo quisiera las enchiladas y una ensalada.

Mesero: ¿Quieren ___5___ de tomar?

Emilio: Por ahora, ___6___ más. Después, vamos a compartir ___7___ postre.

Emilio: La cuenta, por favor.

Mesero: Sí, señor. Un momento.

Lucía: ¿Le dejamos ___8___ propina?

Emilio: No. Está incluida.

ACTIVIDAD 2 El nuevo mesero

El nuevo mesero está aprendiendo. ¿Qué sirve? *(Hint: A new waiter
is learning. What is he serving?)*

modelo

Isabel: arroz (lechuga)

*Cuando **Isabel** pide **arroz**, el mesero le sirve **lechuga**.*

1. Andrés y yo: enchiladas (pollo)   4. yo: carne (un postre)
2. tú: una ensalada (pastel)   5. ella: una sopa (un sándwich)
3. los señores Gálvez: un flan (pan)   6. nosotros: té (café)

Middle School Classroom Community

TPR Have students work in pairs to prepare props
representing items purchased in **Actividad 5**.
Have them complete the **Actividad** together, and
be prepared to use their props to mime their
conversations for the class.

Portfolio Have students write a short paragraph
about where they went yesterday and why.

Rubric

Criteria	Scale	
Vocabulary use	1 2 3 4 5	A = 13–15 pts.
Logical sentence structure/order	1 2 3 4 5	B = 10–12 pts.
Grammar/spelling accuracy	1 2 3 4 5	C = 7–9 pts.
		D = 4–6 pts.
		F = < 4 pts.

Now you can...

• talk about food.

• express extremes.

To review

• the verb **gustar** + nouns, see p. 144.

• extremes, see p. 149.

Now you can...

• talk about food.

To review

• the verb **traer**, see p. 152.

Now you can...

• say where you went.

To review

• **fui/fuiste**, see p. 143.

ACTIVIDAD 3 ¡La comida es buenísima!

A todos les gusta comer. ¿Qué opinan de la comida? *(Hint: Everyone likes to eat. What is their opinion of the food?)*

modelo

yo / enchiladas / bueno

A mí me gustan **las enchiladas.** Son **buenísimas.**

1. mis hermanos / flan / rico
2. Jaime / papas fritas / bueno
3. tú / salsa / rico
4. yo / limonada / bueno
5. la señorita Anaya / arroz / bueno
6. nosotros / tacos / rico

ACTIVIDAD 4 ¡Una fiesta mexicana!

Hay una fiesta mexicana hoy. ¿Qué traen todos? *(Hint: Today is a Mexican celebration. What does everyone bring?)*

modelo

Dolores: salsa

Dolores trae **la salsa.**

1. yo: tenedores
2. Salvador: platos
3. nosotros: enchiladas
4. el profesor: arroz
5. Alex y Tito: ensalada
6. la directora: flan
7. tú: pastel
8. René y yo: limonada

ACTIVIDAD 5 ¿Adónde fuiste?

Tu amigo(a) acaba de ir de compras. Escribe tus preguntas y sus respuestas según el modelo. Tiene las siguientes cosas: **un disco compacto, pan, un collar, carne, un pastel, unos artículos de cuero** y **una novela.** *(Hint: Your friend just went shopping. Write your questions and your friend's answers, following the model and using the items mentioned.)*

modelo

pastelería

Tú: *¿Fuiste a la **pastelería**?*

Tu amigo(a): *Sí, fui para comprar un pastel.*

1. joyería
2. librería
3. panadería
4. carnicería
5. tienda de música
6. mercado

ACTIVIDAD 2 Answers

1. Cuando Andrés y yo pedimos enchiladas, el mesero nos sirve pollo.
2. Cuando tú pides una ensalada, el mesero te sirve un pastel.
3. Cuando los señores Gálvez piden un flan, el mesero les sirve pan.
4. Cuando yo pido carne, el mesero me sirve un postre.
5. Cuando ella pide una sopa, el mesero le sirve un sándwich.
6. Cuando nosotros pedimos té, el mesero nos sirve café.

ACTIVIDAD 3 Answers

1. A mis hermanos les gusta el flan. Es riquísimo.
2. A Jaime le gustan las papas fritas. Son buenísimas.
3. A ti te gusta la salsa. Es riquísima.
4. A mí me gusta la limonada. Es buenísima.
5. A la señorita Anaya le gusta el arroz. Es buenísimo.
6. A nosotros nos gustan los tacos. Son riquísimos.

ACTIVIDAD 4 Answers

1. Yo traigo los tenedores.
2. Salvador trae los platos.
3. Nosotros traemos las enchiladas.
4. El profesor trae el arroz.
5. Alex y Tito traen la ensalada.
6. La directora trae el flan.
7. Tú traes el pastel.
8. René y yo traemos la limonada.

ACTIVIDAD 5 Answers

1. A: ¿Fuiste a la joyería?
   B: Sí, fui para comprar un collar.
2. A: ¿Fuiste a la librería?
   B: Sí, fui para comprar una novela.
3. A: ¿Fuiste a la panadería?
   B: Sí, fui para comprar pan.
4. A: ¿Fuiste a la carnicería?
   B: Sí, fui para comprar carne.
5. A: ¿Fuiste a la tienda de música?
   B: Sí, fui para comprar un disco compacto.
6. A: ¿Fuiste al mercado?
   B: Sí, fui para comprar unos artículos de cuero.

Block Schedule

FunBreak Have students work in groups of 3–4 to play a scavenger hunt. Provide each group with a different list of items, using vocabulary from units 1–4. Be sure you have these items (or pictures of these items) in your classroom. The first group to gather all items gets extra credit points or a small prize. (For additional activities, see **Block Scheduling Copymasters**.)

Teaching Middle School Students

Multiple Intelligences

Verbal Have students work in groups of three to read aloud **Actividad 1**. Let them read it a second time and personalize the dialog.

Intrapersonal Ask students what they would serve at a party for the Spanish club at school. Have them write up a menu and then list the stores they would go to for the supplies and food they would need.

Teaching Resource Options

Print

Unit 4 Resource Book
Cooperative Quizzes, pp. 135–136
Etapa Exam, Forms A and B,
pp. 137–146
Para hispanohablantes Etapa Exam,
pp. 147–151
Portfolio Assessment, pp. 152–153
Unit 4 Comprehensive Test,
pp. 154–161
Para hispanohablantes Unit 4
Comprehensive Test, pp. 162–169
Multiple Choice Test Questions,
pp. 170–178

Audiovisual

OHT 136 (Quick Start)
Audio Program Testing Cassette T2 /
CD T2

Technology

Electronic Teacher Tools/Test
Generator

 www.mcdougallittell.com

 6

Rubric: Speaking

Criteria	Scale	
Vocabulary use	1 2 3 4 5	A = 13–15 pts.
Sentence structure	1 2 3 4 5	B = 10–12 pts.
Ease, fluency	1 2 3 4 5	C = 7–9 pts.
		D = 4–6 pts.
		F = < 4 pts.

7 Answers will vary.

 8 *En tu propia voz*

Rubric: Writing

Criteria	Scale	
Vocabulary use	1 2 3 4 5	A = 13–15 pts.
Accuracy	1 2 3 4 5	B = 10–12 pts.
Creativity, appearance	1 2 3 4 5	C = 7–9 pts.
		D = 4–6 pts.
		F = < 4 pts.

Teaching Note: En tu propia voz

Remind students to review the writing
strategy "Use different kinds of descriptive
words" before beginning the paragraph
describing the Mexican restaurant.

---

6  **¡Tengo hambre!**

PARA CONVERSAR
STRATEGY: SPEAKING
Borrow useful expressions Here are some useful
expressions for agreeing and accepting (**está
bien, perfecto**) and for refusing (**no quiero…,
por ahora nada más**). Use them in your
conversation in the restaurant.

Estás en un restaurante. Pide un mínimo de
tres cosas. Después, habla de la comida y pide
la cuenta. Otro(a) estudiante va a ser el (la)
mesero(a). Cambien de papel. *(Hint: You're in
a restaurant. Order at least three things from the server. Then talk
about the food and ask for the check. Another student will be the
server. Change roles.)*

Quisiera…

¿Me trae…?

Me gustaría…

¿Está incluido(a)…?

7 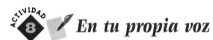 **¡Una fiesta!**

Trabajando en grupos, hablen de dos cosas que
cada persona va a traer a una fiesta. *(Hint: Working
in groups, talk about two things that each person is going to bring
to a party.)*

modelo

Sara: *Me gusta la limonada. Traigo limonada y algunos
vasos.*

José: *Me gustan las enchiladas y la música. Traigo
enchiladas y una guitarra.*

8 *En tu propia voz*

Escritura Trabajas en un restaurante mexicano.
Escribe un párrafo para una guía turística.
*(Hint: You work in a Mexican restaurant. Write a paragraph as
a guide for a tourist.)*

modelo

Restaurante Azteca *¿Le gusta la salsa picante? En el
restaurante Azteca servimos una salsa deliciosa y muy
picante. La especialidad de la casa es…*

En la comunidad

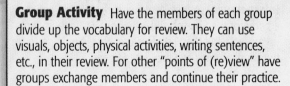

Grendale is a high school student in Nevada. He sometimes
speaks Spanish with coworkers when he volunteers at a nursing
home. At his part-time job, he uses Spanish with Mexican, South
American, and Spanish tourists who come to the store. He has a
friend from Uruguay who is an exchange student, and they often
speak in Spanish. Do you speak Spanish with any of your friends?

Middle School Classroom Community

Group Activity Have the members of each group
divide up the vocabulary for review. They can use
visuals, objects, physical activities, writing sentences,
etc., in their review. For other "points of (re)view" have
groups exchange members and continue their practice.

Game Start by saying that you are thinking of
something in a restaurant. Have students ask you
questions, to which you answer only **sí** or **no**. Let the
student who guesses correctly think of the next word
to be guessed.

En resumen

REPASO DE VOCABULARIO

ORDERING FOOD

¿Me ayuda a pedir?	Could you help me order?
¿Me trae...?	Could you bring me...?
el menú	menu
pedir	to ask for, to order
Quisiera...	I would like...

At the Restaurant

el (la) mesero(a)	waiter (waitress)
el restaurante	restaurant
servir	to serve
traer	to bring

Place Setting

la cuchara	spoon
el cuchillo	knife
la taza	cup
el tenedor	fork

EXPRESSING EXTREMES

riquísimo(a)	very tasty

REQUESTING THE CHECK

¿Cuánto es?	How much is it?
¿Cuánto le doy de propina?	How much do I tip?
la cuenta	bill, check
La cuenta, por favor.	The check, please.
Es aparte.	Separate checks.
¿Está incluido(a)...?	Is... included?
la propina	tip

SAYING WHERE YOU WENT

Fui.../Fuiste...	I went.../You went...

TALKING ABOUT FOOD

caliente	hot, warm
delicioso(a)	delicious
dulce	sweet
picante	spicy
rico(a)	tasty
vegetariano(a)	vegetarian

Food

el arroz	rice
el azúcar	sugar
el bistec	steak
la carne	meat
la enchilada	enchilada
la ensalada	salad
la lechuga	lettuce
el pan	bread
el pollo	chicken
el queso	cheese
la salsa	salsa
la sopa	soup

Beverages

la bebida	beverage, drink
el café	coffee
la limonada	lemonade
el té	tea

Desserts

el flan	caramel custard dessert
el pan dulce	sweet roll
el pastel	cake
el postre	dessert

OTHER WORDS AND PHRASES

algo	something
alguien	someone
alguno(a)	some
desayunar	to have breakfast
el desayuno	breakfast
la lengua	language
listo(a)	ready
nada	nothing
nadie	no one
ninguno(a)	none, not any
poner	to put
poner la mesa	to set the table
el pueblo	town, village
sin	without
tampoco	neither, either
todavía	still, yet

Juego

Cada miembro de la familia Martínez quiere algo diferente. ¡Pobre Pablo, el mesero! Pablo es inteligente y trae lo que quieren. ¿Qué les sirve a 1) Marco, 2) Martina y 3) Marisol?

Marco Martínez: Quiero algo líquido y caliente con proteínas.

Martina Martínez: Quiero algo verde y vegetariano.

Marisol Martínez: Quiero algo dulce para mi café.

Marco   Martina   Marisol

Community Connections
Ask students if they used Spanish outside of school in the past few weeks. Make a class list and continue to add to it during the year. Students might also investigate the number of ways Spanish could be used on a daily basis in your community. You may wish to organize a field trip to one of these sites, or invite someone to come to your class and talk about how Spanish can be used on a daily basis.

Quick Start Review
♻ **Etapa** vocabulary

Use OHT 136 or write on the board: Choose 5 new words from this **Etapa** vocabulary and write a short paragraph containing these words.

Answers will vary.

Teaching Suggestions
Vocabulary Review
Reinforce the food vocabulary and the use of **gustar.** Write singular and plural food and drink words on the board. Have students say if they like them or not.

Juego
Answers
1. Le sirve sopa a Marco.
2. Le sirve ensalada a Martina.
3. Le sirve azúcar a Marisol.

Block Schedule
Change of Pace Have students use unit 4 vocabulary to play a variation of Jeopardy!™, where you provide the answers and students provide the questions. For example: (1) **un lugar que vende libros** = ¿Qué es una **librería**? (2) **un artículo que ponemos a la izquierda de un plato** = ¿Qué es un **tenedor**?

Teaching Middle School Students

Extra Help Whenever you get a chance, ask students questions that require them to agree, accept, or refuse. For example, ¿Quieres pedir la especialidad de la casa? ¿Quieres compartir un postre?

Multiple Intelligences

Verbal Have students study the **Repaso de vocabulario** for a few minutes, then put their books away. Write the different categories of vocabulary on the board, then call out a word from the list and a student's name. The student goes to the board and writes the word or expression in the appropriate category.

Review • UNIDAD 4 Etapa 3   161

Teaching Resource Options

Print
Block Scheduling Copymasters

Audiovisual
OHT GO1–GO5; 136 (Quick Start)

Technology
Intrigas y aventuras CD-ROM, Disc 1

www.mcdougallittell.com

Quick Start Review
 Vacation activities

Use OHT 136 or write on the board:
Write 3 sentences about things you
like to do on vacation and 3 sentences
about things you do *not* like to do on
vacation.

Answers
Answers will vary. Answers could include:
Me gusta viajar en avión. Me gusta sacar
fotos. Me gusta ir de compras. No me gusta
viajar en tren. No me gusta visitar los museos.
No me gusta caminar mucho.

Teaching Suggestions
La historia

- Have volunteer students do research in
the library or on the Internet to find
pictures of some of the Zapotecs' and
Mixtecs' accomplishments, particularly
in the areas of archeology, ceramics,
and jewelry.
- Have students find out who the original
settlers of your region were. Why did
they choose the site? How did they
make a living there? Has the source of
livelihood changed since the days the
area was first settled?

Conexiones
OTRAS DISCIPLINAS Y PROYECTOS

La historia

Oaxaca is an ancient city. The **Zapotecas** lived in
the region as far back as 900 B.C. The **Zapotecas**
were great architects, artisans, and astronomers.
They created a
number system,
a calendar,
hieroglyphic
writing, and
extraordinary
ceramics and
jewelry.

Around 800 A.D.,
Zapotecan culture began
to decline as a result of
the arrival of another
civilization, known as the
Mixtecas. The **Mixtecas**
practiced agriculture, hunting, and fishing. They
made beautiful ornaments in gold, silver, and
copper. Today, in Oaxaca, the presence of both
these cultures is still very much alive.

Do you think these **danzantes zapotecas** are ancient or modern? Why do you think so?

What do you think this piece of **mixteca** jewelry is made of? What kind of jewelry is it?

Las matemáticas π

Did you know that every country in the world
has its own form of money?
Did you know that the
currencies of all countries are
related to each other and that
they shift in value?

The following is a list of the
currencies of some Spanish-speaking countries
and their value per U.S. dollar. This information
changes from day to day, so check on the
Internet or with a local bank or newspaper for
current rates.

País	Unidad monetaria	Valor de $1 (U.S.)
Argentina	peso	0.9
Ecuador	sucre	4918.0
México	peso	8.3
Venezuela	bolívar	521.5
Guatemala	quetzal	6.2

1. *According to the chart above, which would be worth the most: 4,000 sucres, 300 bolívares, or 10 quetzales?*

2. *If you had a choice between buying a gift for* **siete pesos argentinos** *or* **cincuenta pesos mexicanos**, *which currency would you choose to use? Why?*

Middle School Classroom Community

Cooperative Learning Have students work in
groups of 3 using a newspaper. Student 1 finds
advertisements with prices of various types of goods.
Student 2 finds the exchange rates for five Hispanic
countries. Student 3 makes a chart showing the items
from the advertisements and how much money would
be needed to buy those items in the five countries.
Ask them to present the information to the class.

Storytelling Have students work in groups to make
up a story about market day. Let them illustrate the
story by using frames as is done with the videos in the
text. (If the class does the **Proyecto cultural**, the story
may be about students in the class and their market
day.) Have the groups share their stories with the class.

Proyecto cultural

As a class project, write a short play about market day in Oaxaca. Half the class will be sellers at the market and half will be buyers. Buyers will bargain with the sellers to get the best prices. To prepare for market day, do the following:

1. Use classroom objects or bring in items from home to be "sold." Make a list with realistic prices in pesos for each item.

2. Your teacher will help you make play money in Mexican pesos. Buyers will need enough pesos to purchase one or two items. Sellers will need enough pesos to make change.

3. Write the script and put on the play. You may want to videotape your production to show other Spanish classes or your family.

These woman display their backstrap weaving at a market in Oaxaca.

Objeto	Precio
libro	27 pesos
video	57 pesos
aretes	70 pesos
reloj	120 pesos

ciento sesenta y tres
Unidad 4 | **163**

Teaching Middle School Students

Native Speakers Ask native speakers to talk about markets and market day in their region. Let students ask about what kinds of things are sold in a market and how shopping there is different from shopping in a supermarket.

Multiple Intelligences

Musical/Rhythmic Have the students imagine that they are visiting Oaxaca on market day. Play Mexican music and let students wander around the room, pretending to look at things for sale. Stop the music periodically and ask a student what he or she is seeing, hearing, buying, etc.

Unit Theme
Carrying out one's daily routine in Barcelona, doing chores, and planning a party

Communication
- Describing daily routines, grooming, and chores
- Telling others to do something
- Saying what people are doing
- Persuading others
- Describing a house
- Negotiating responsibilities
- Planning a party and purchasing food
- Describing past activities
- Expressing extremes

Cultures
- Learning about Barcelona and its architecture
- Learning about well-known people from Barcelona
- Learning about regional foods
- Learning how to cook

Connections
- Connecting to Art: Comparing painting styles
- Connecting to Health: Planning a meal

Comparisons
- Comparing daily routines and chores in Spain and in the U.S.
- Comparing homes in Spain and in the U.S.
- Comparing appetizers

Communities
- Using Spanish in the workplace
- Using Spanish with family and friends

Teaching Resource Options

Print

Block Scheduling Copymasters

Audiovisual

OHT M5; 137, 138
Canciones Audiocassette/CD
Video Program Videotape 5 / Videodisc 3A

Search Chapter 1, Play to 2
U5 Cultural Introduction

UNIDAD 5

BARCELONA
ESPAÑA

PREPARACIONES ESPECIALES

OBJECTIVES

ETAPA 1
¿Cómo es tu rutina?
- Describe daily routine
- Talk about grooming
- Tell others to do something
- Discuss daily chores

ETAPA 2
¿Qué debo hacer?
- Say what people are doing
- Persuade others
- Describe a house
- Negotiate responsibilities

ETAPA 3
¡Qué buena celebración!
- Plan a party
- Describe past activities
- Express extremes
- Purchase food

MIGUEL DE CERVANTES SAAVEDRA (1574–1616) is the most well-known Spanish author. His classic *Don Quijote de la Mancha* is considered to be the first modern novel. What plays or movies are based on this book?

Océano Atlántico

ISLAS CANARIAS

PORTUGAL

JOAN MIRÓ (1893–1983) is one of Barcelona's most famous artists. You can see his surrealist works at the **Fundación Miró.** How would you describe this piece by Miró?

Tapestry of the Foundation, Miró Foundation on Montjuic

Middle School Classroom Community

Group Activity Ask students to work in small groups to brainstorm what they already know about Spain. Ask them to make a list of cities, exports, unique customs, famous citizens (politicians, painters, singers, actors), etc. You may want to give them a five-minute time limit.

Portfolio Have students make individual maps of Spain, listing principal cities.

Rubric

Criteria	Scale	
Accuracy of information	1 2 3 4 5	A = 13–15 pts.
Logical organization	1 2 3 4 5	B = 10–12 pts.
Vocabulary use	1 2 3 4 5	C = 7–9 pts.
		D = 4–6 pts.
		F = < 4 pts.

ALMANAQUE

Población: 1.630.867

Altura: 12 metros (39 pies)

Clima: 10°C (54°F), invierno; 25°C (75°F), verano

Comida típica: mariscos, tapas, paella

Gente famosa de Barcelona: José Carreras (cantante), Antonio Gaudí (arquitecto), Joan Miró (pintor), Pablo Picasso (pintor), Arantxa Sánchez Vicario (tenista)

¿Vas a Barcelona? Barcelona es la capital de Cataluña, una región de España. Tiene una identidad catalana muy fuerte. La gente habla catalán y español.

For more information about Barcelona, access www.mcdougallittell.com

EL MONUMENTO DE CRISTÓBAL COLÓN commemorates Columbus's meeting with the king and queen of Spain after his first voyage to the Americas. They met in Barcelona in 1493. Who were the king and queen of Spain then?

ACEITUNAS are one of Spain's most important products. Their oil is used to cook Spanish specialties such as **paella** and **tortilla española.** They are also often eaten as **tapas.** What dishes made with olives or olive oil have you eaten?

LA SAGRADA FAMILIA is a church begun by architect Antonio Gaudí (1852–1926). It is not yet finished. What do you think about the style of architecture you see in the photo?

LAS RAMBLAS is a well-known street in the heart of Barcelona that has it all! Artisans, performers, and vendors sell everything from parakeets to newspapers here. Where might you find something similar in the U.S.?

FRANCIA
ANDORRA
ESPAÑA
BARCELONA
MADRID
VALENCIA
ISLAS BALEARES
SEVILLA
GIBRALTAR (R.U.)
CEUTA
Mar Mediterráneo
ARGELIA
MELILLA
MARRUECOS

165

Teaching Middle School Students

Challenge Interested students may want to research Cervantes and Don Quixote. Ask them to present their findings to the class.

Multiple Intelligences

Verbal Ask students to research the Catalonian language (**catalán**), making an oral presentation of some simple phrases along with the Spanish equivalents.

Musical/Rhythmic Ask students to research the contributions of the guitar to Spanish music. You may want to suggest they find compositions by Joaquín Rodrigo (particularly well known is his **Concierto de Aranjuez**), or music played by Andrés Segovia. Some students may want to perform themselves.

Naturalist Ask students to research and make a climate map of Spain.

Teaching Suggestions
Previewing the Unit
Tell students that this unit centers on Barcelona, Spain. Ask students to scan these two pages for 15 seconds, then close their books. Then ask them to tell you what they remember. You may wish to use the introduction to the video to preview the unit.

Culture Highlights

● **CERVANTES** The tumultuous life of Cervantes was the inspiration for his humor and satire. He lost the use of his left hand in battle, he was captured by pirates and held as a slave for 5 years, and he was imprisoned by the Spanish government for suspicious tax-collecting activities. It was during his imprisonment that he conceived the idea for *Don Quijote.*

● **JOAN MIRÓ** The surrealist style of Joan Miró is based on subject matter from the realm of memory and fantasy.

● **EL MONUMENTO DE CRISTÓBAL COLÓN** This monument is a tribute to the adventuresome spirit as well as to Christopher Columbus. The design on the column includes the continents of Europe, Asia, Africa, and the Americas.

● **ACEITUNAS** Olives, one of Spain's major exports, are harvested both when they are green and later when they turn black.

● **LA SAGRADA FAMILIA** This great church, a blend of neo-Gothic and Art Nouveau styles, was Gaudí's greatest project and dream. He wanted it to be large enough for a choir of 1500 singers, 700 children, and 5 organs.

● **LAS RAMBLAS** Rambla means *torrent* in Arabic. The location of the current street is thought to be a former streambed outside the old city walls.

Block Schedule

Preview Have students look through the unit to see what they will be learning. As they do this, they should write a list of words they know that apply to what they see. Compile a class list for reference as students work through the unit. (For additional activities, see **Block Scheduling Copymasters**.)

Ampliación

These activities may be used at various points in the Unit 5 sequence.

For Block Schedule, you may find that these projects will provide a welcome change of pace while reviewing and reinforcing the material presented in the unit. See the **Block Scheduling Copymasters.**

● PROJECTS

Organize tours of Barcelona. Have students work in groups of 4–5 to organize a tour of Barcelona for one of the following groups:

- a group of high school students from the U.S.
- a group of senior citizens from the U.S.
- a group interested in science
- a group interested in art or theater

Each group should plan the length of each tour, an itinerary, the transportation, meals, and the estimated costs. Each group will create a brochure, including a map, and prepare a presentation.

> PACING SUGGESTION: Have students begin research at the beginning of the unit. Final projects are completed at the end of Unit 5.

Film a self-help video with suggestions for being organized, especially for getting ready quickly in the morning. The video should include at least 4 scenes scripted by students showing what to do as well as what not to do.

> PACING SUGGESTION: Upon completion of Etapa 1.

● STORYTELLING

Diego desastre After reviewing vocabulary for daily routines and chores, model a mini-story (using puppets, student actors, or photos from the text) that students will retell and revise:

> Diego no es muy organizado y es un poco perezoso en casa. Sus padres siempre tienen que darle órdenes: «Diego, lávate los dientes antes de ir a la escuela.» «Diego, quita la mesa después de la cena.» Un día llega tarde a clase para un examen. No hace el examen. Sus amigos también le dan órdenes a Diego. «Diego, limpia tu habitación. ¡Es un desastre!»

Pause as the story is being told so that students may fill in words and act out gestures. Students then write, narrate, and read aloud a longer main story. This new version should include vocabulary from the previous story.

Otros quehaceres y rutinas Have students create their own routine/chore stories. They might expand on the model story by centering it around a specific day or event, or they can create their own characters.

> PACING SUGGESTION: Upon completion of Etapa 2.

● BULLETIN BOARD/POSTERS

Bulletin Board Have students research the history of Barcelona to create time lines that show different civilizations, cultures, architecture, events, etc., related to the development of the city. Students should illustrate their time lines with Internet printouts and/or drawings.

Posters Have students create •**Museum** posters for museums in Barcelona •**Restaurant** fliers showing hours, specialties, and prices of Barcelona restaurants •**Chore charts** for a typical household

GAMES

Dibujorama

FRANCIA

Prepare ahead: Bring in a timer, an easel, a large writing pad, and markers. Prepare 20–30 index cards with grooming and chore commands. Each card should include 1 command; some should be negative commands. Divide the class into 2–3 teams. Give a member of the first team a card. He/She silently reads the card. Set the timer to 30 seconds. The group member draws—no speaking or gestures allowed!—to elicit the command on the card. When guessing, only Spanish may be used or the team forfeits its turn. If students on the team guess the command correctly before the time is up, they score, and the next team has a turn. If not, the next team picks a new card. If that team guesses the correct command, they score, and they get another turn.

PACING SUGGESTION: Upon completion of Etapa 2.

ALENCIA

Monopolio

Prepare ahead: Bring to class pieces of sturdy cardboard, slips of paper to make fake money, odds and ends for tokens. Have students work in groups of 4 to create Monopoly®-style boards featuring attractions and streets in Barcelona. Encourage them to be creative with the kinds of spaces they create for the board (shopping, restaurants, etc.), and to include spaces with real estate purchases, expenses (shopping, eating out), fines, and prizes. Then have them make pesetas. Each group can make up their own rules for purchasing, selling, and winning, but the rules should be straightforward and simple. Have students play their game in groups of 4.

PACING SUGGESTION: Upon completion of Etapa 3.

MUSIC

Show students photos of people dancing the **sardana**—the regional dance of Cataluña. Point out that outside cathedrals in that region on Sunday afternoons, circles of people, young and old, hold hands with raised arms and step in unison to the beat of a **sardana** song. Play a **sardana** in class and have students join hands with raised arms and move in a circle, following the steps of a designated leader. More music samples are available on your *Canciones* Cassette or CD.

HANDS-ON CRAFTS

Display examples of paintings in the following styles: realism, surrealism, impressionism, and cubism. Have students formulate a description of each style. Then have students do an art study on one person. They will paint that person in the four different styles. Choose one medium and provide supplies for all students (large posterboards and paint) or have students bring their own supplies. Set up a museum to display the studies.

RECIPE

Postre con naranjas

is an attractive dessert served around the end-of-year holidays. Ask students what special foods they eat on occasions such as Thanksgiving and the Fourth of July. Have them brainstorm foods that are closely linked to special holidays.

Prepare ahead: Prepare the filling the day before. Bring the filling, cream, cherries, and chilled orange halves to class and allow students to prepare their desserts as you read the final instructions. Point out the importance of color and presentation when preparing foods.

Receta

Postre con naranjas
6 naranjas tipo «navel» grandes
un poco de azúcar
2 cucharadas de harina de maíz (la típica Maizena)
nata montada

Parta las naranjas. Exprima el zumo cuidadosamente, sin romper la cáscara. Añada al zumo, un poco de agua, azúcar al gusto y 2 cucharadas de harina de maíz. Cocine la mezcla a fuego muy bajo y remuévala mientras va espesando. Cuando la mezcla esté espesa, como una crema, retírela del fuego y póngala en la nevera. Rellene las medias naranjas vacías con la crema enfriada. Encima ponga un poco de nata y una cereza confitada. (Sirve a 12.)

Planning Guide CLASSROOM MANAGEMENT

OBJECTIVES

Communication
- Describe daily routine *pp. 168–169*
- Talk about grooming *pp. 168–169, 170–171*
- Tell others to do something *pp. 170–171*
- Discuss daily chores *pp. 170–171*

Grammar
- Use reflexive verbs *pp. 175–176*
- Use irregular affirmative **tú** commands *pp. 177–179*
- Use negative **tú** commands *pp. 180–181*
- Use correct pronoun placement with commands *pp. 182–183*

Pronunciation
- Pronunciation of **s, z, c** *p. 185*
- Dictation *TE p. 185*

Culture
- History and culture of Barcelona, Spain *pp. 164–165*
- **Catalán** *p. 179*
- **Las Ramblas** *p. 181*
- **Rock con raíces** *p. 183*
- Pablo Picasso *p. 184*
- **La Tomatina** *pp. 186–187*

♻ Recycling
- Telling time *p. 173*
- Object pronouns *p. 182*

STRATEGIES

Listening Strategies
- Listen for a mood or a feeling *p. 170*

Speaking Strategies
- Sequence events *p. 176*
- Use gestures *p. 190*

Reading Strategies
- Predict *p. 186*

Writing Strategies
- Organize information chronologically and by category *TE p. 190*

Connecting Cultures Strategies
- Learn about Barcelona, Spain *pp. 164–165*
- Recognize variations in vocabulary *pp. 172, 182*
- Learn about the Spanish **rock con raíces** *p. 183*
- Learn about Pablo Picasso *p. 184*
- Connect and compare what you already know about artists and art styles to help you learn about different artists and art styles *pp. 164–165, 190*

PROGRAM RESOURCES

 Print
- *Más práctica* Workbook PE, *pp. 25–32*
- Block Scheduling Copymasters, *pp. 105–112*
- Unit 5 Resource Book
  Más práctica Workbook TE, *pp. 1–8*
  Information Gap Activities *pp. 17–20*
- Family Involvement *pp. 21–22*
- Video Activities *pp. 23–25*
- Videoscript *pp. 26–28*
- Audioscript *pp. 29–32*
- Assessment Program, Unit 5 Etapa 1 *pp. 33–51, 170–178*
- Answer Keys *pp. 179–200*

 Audiovisual
- Audio Program Cassettes 13A, 13B / CD 13
- *Canciones* Cassette / CD
- Video Program Videotape 5 / Videodisc 3A
- Overhead Transparencies M1–M5; 137, 140–150

 **Technology**
- Electronic Teacher Tools/Test Generator
- *Intrigas y aventuras* CD-ROM, Disc 1
- 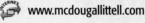 www.mcdougallittell.com

 Assessment Program Options
- Cooperative Quizzes (Unit 5 Resource Book)
- Etapa Exam Forms A and B (Unit 5 Resource Book)
- *Para hispanohablantes* Etapa Exam (Unit 5 Resource Book)
- Portfolio Assessment (Unit 5 Resource Book)
- Multiple Choice Test Questions (Unit 5 Resource Book)
- Audio Program Testing Cassette T2 / CD T2
- Electronic Teacher Tools/Test Generator

Native Speakers
- *Para hispanohablantes* Workbook PE, *pp. 25–32*
- *Para hispanohablantes* Workbook TE (Unit 5 Resource Book)
- *Para hispanohablantes* Etapa Exam (Unit 5 Resource Book)
- Audio *Para hispanohablantes* Cassettes 13A, 13B, T2 / CD 13, T2
- Audioscript *Para hispanohablantes* (Unit 5 Resource Book)

| Luis | Carmen | Mercedes | Juan Carlos | Lourdes |

Student Text Listening *Activity Scripts*

 **Videoscript: Diálogo** *pages 170–171*

• Videotape 5 • Videodisc 3A

Search Chapter 3, Play to 4
U5E1 • En vivo (Dialog)

• Use the videoscript with **Actividades 1, 2** *pages 172–173*

Juan Carlos: ¡Luis, Luis! ¡Mercedes llega en diez minutos!

Luis: ¡Sí, ya lo sé! ¡Ahora me ducho y salgo!

Juan Carlos: ¡Vale!

Lourdes: ¡Luis! ¡Mercedes llega en cinco minutos!

Luis: ¡Sí, sí, ya lo sé, mamá! ¡Pero primero necesito lavarme los dientes!

Carmen: ¡Luis! ¡Luis! ¡Mercedes está aquí!

Luis: ¡Sí, sí, sí! ¡Pero primero me pongo la ropa! ¡Ya voy!
¡Hola, Mercedes! ¿Cómo estás?

Mercedes: Bien, Luis. ¡Y feliz cumpleaños! ¿Qué tal tu mañana?

Luis: Muy tranquila, gracias. Mercedes, ¿qué haces? ¿Por qué me estás sacando fotos? ¡No hagas eso!

Mercedes: No te pongas así. Las fotos son para un concurso.

Luis: ¿Un concurso? Pues dime, ¿para qué concurso son?

Mercedes: Luego, te digo luego. Bueno, Álvaro nos espera en una hora. ¿Estás listo?

Luis: No, no estoy listo. Todavía necesito secarme el pelo. Salgo en diez minutos. Espérame aquí.

Carmen: ¡Ponte otra camisa! Mírate en el espejo, ¡esta camisa está muy fea!

Luis: Muchas gracias, Carmen.

Carmen: Ah, y ¡no uses mi secador de pelo! ¡Por favor, no lo uses!

Luis: Bueno, ya estoy listo. ¿Vamos?

Juan Carlos: Hijo.

Luis: ¿Sí, papá?

Juan Carlos: Necesito tu ayuda. Por favor, haz todo lo que está en esta lista.

Luis: Pero, papá, yo voy a salir. ¿Tengo que hacerlo todo hoy?

Juan Carlos: Sí, hijo. Primero haz los quehaceres.

Luis: ¡Pero, papá!

Lourdes: Luis, necesitamos leche y varias cosas. Ve a la tienda. Aquí tienes mi lista.

Luis: Papá, mamá, es que tengo otros planes. Me espera Álvaro.

Lourdes: Sí, hijo, ya lo sabemos, pero esto es importante.

Luis: ¡No es justo! ¡Es mi cumpleaños!

Juan Carlos: Sí, pero también puedes celebrarlo después. Aquí tienes. Ah, también, cuida a tu hermana.

Luis: ¡No puede ser!

Carmen: ¡Ja, ja! ¡Me tienes que cuidar!

Luis: Voy a llamar a Álvaro. Nunca vamos a llegar a tiempo.

Mercedes: No te preocupes. Él nos espera. ¡Pobre Luis! ¡No seas tan dura con él! ¡Es su cumpleaños!

Carmen: ¡Le quiero ver la cara al llegar a su fiesta!

Luis: Está ocupado. Lo llamo más tarde. Bueno, vamos. Tenemos muchas cosas que hacer. Carmen, Mercedes, ¿me ayudáis con los quehaceres?

 ⑥ Se lavan... *page 176*

1. Carmen se lava la cabeza.
2. Mis padres se lavan las manos.
3. Mercedes y yo nos lavamos los pies.
4. Yo me lavo las piernas.
5. Álvaro se lava la cara.

㉑ La rutina de Álvaro *page 184*

Andrés: Oye, Álvaro, ¿a qué hora te despiertas los sábados?

Álvaro: Bueno, normalmente me despierto entre las ocho y las ocho y media.

Andrés: ¿Usas un despertador?

Álvaro: No, no me gustan los despertadores.

Andrés: ¿Y a qué hora te levantas?

Álvaro: Pues, como me gusta quedarme un rato en la cama, no me levanto antes de las nueve y media.

Andrés: ¿Qué haces después de levantarte?

Álvaro: Me lavo la cara y los dientes.

Andrés: ¿No te bañas los sábados?

Álvaro: ¡Claro que sí! Me baño por la noche antes de salir. También me afeito y me lavo la cabeza.

Quick Start Review Answers

p. 170 Morning routine
Answers will vary. Answers could include:
1. Antes de las siete.
2. Después de las siete.
3. Sí, uso un despertador.
4. Uso dos mantas.
5. Mi champú favorito se llama "Pert Plus". Mi jabón favorito se llama "Dove".

p. 172 Dialog review
1. Carmen   4. Luis
2. Luis   5. Mercedes
3. Lourdes   6. Juan Carlos

p. 177 Reflexive verbs
1. se lava   5. *Answers*
2. te despiertas   *may vary.*
3. secarme   [me acuesto]
4. lavarnos

p. 180 Affirmative **tú** commands
1. Haz tu tarea.
2. Pon el libro en tu escritorio.
3. Di la verdad.
4. Ponte otra camisa.
5. Ven aquí.

p. 182 Negative **tú** commands
1. No escribas tu nombre aquí.
2. No hagas la cena esta noche.
3. No pongas el jabón al lado de la toalla.
4. No compres el regalo hoy.
5. No leas la novela.

p. 191 Etapa vocabulary
Answers will vary. Answers could include:
1. Me despierto a las seis y cuarto pero me levanto a las seis y media.
2. Me ducho todos los días.
3. Me lavo la cabeza con champú.
4. Me lavo los dientes.
5. Me pongo una camisa y unos jeans.

Sample Lesson Plan - 45 Minute Schedule

DAY 1

Unit Opener
- Anticipate/Activate prior knowledge: Present the *Almanaque* and the cultural notes. Use Map OHTs as needed. 10 MIN.

Etapa Opener
- Quick Start Review (TE, p. 166) 5 MIN.
- Have students look at the *Etapa* Opener and answer the *¿Qué ves?* questions, p. 166. 10 MIN.

En contexto: Vocabulario
- Quick Start Review (TE, p. 168) 5 MIN.
- Have students use context and pictures to learn *Etapa* vocabulary. 10 MIN.
- Have students answer the *Preguntas personales*, p. 169. 5 MIN.

DAY 2

En vivo: Diálogo
- Quick Start Review (TE, p. 170) 5 MIN.
- Review the Listening Strategy, p. 170. 5 MIN.
- Play audio or show video for the dialog, pp. 170–171. 5 MIN.
- Replay the audio or video, then have students take the roles of the characters. 10 MIN.
- Work with students to answer the Comprehension Questions (TE, p. 171). 5 MIN.

En acción: Vocabulario y gramática
- Quick Start Review (TE, p. 172) 5 MIN.
- Have students open to *En contexto*, pp. 168–169, for reference. Use OHTs to review vocabulary. 10 MIN.

Homework Option:
- Video Activities, Unit 5 Resource Book, pp. 23–25.

DAY 3

En acción (cont.)
- Check homework. 5 MIN.
- Play the video/audio. 5 MIN.
- Have students do *Actividad* 1 orally. 5 MIN.
- Read and discuss the *También se dice*, p. 172. 5 MIN.
- Do *Actividad* 2 orally. 5 MIN.
- Work orally with students on *Actividad* 3. 5 MIN.
- Have students work in pairs to do *Actividad* 4. 5 MIN.
- Ask volunteers to model their conversations from *Actividad* 4. 5 MIN.
- Have students stay in their pairs to do *Actividad* 5. 5 MIN.

DAY 4

En acción (cont.)
- Quick Start Review (TE, p. 175) 5 MIN.
- Present *Gramática*: Describing Actions That Involve Oneself: Reflexive Verbs, and the *Vocabulario*, p. 175. 10 MIN.
- Play the audio and assign *Actividad* 6. 5 MIN.
- Have students work in pairs to do *Actividad* 7. 5 MIN.
- Call on selected pairs to model their work on *Actividad* 7. 5 MIN.
- Present the Speaking Strategy, p. 176. 5 MIN.
- Have students work in pairs to do *Actividad* 8. 5 MIN.
- Call on selected pairs to share their conversations from *Actividad* 8. 5 MIN.

Homework Option:
- *Más práctica* Workbook, p. 29. *Para hispanohablantes* Workbook, p. 27.

DAY 5

En acción (cont.)
- Check homework. 5 MIN.
- Quick Start Review (TE, p. 177) 5 MIN.
- Have students work in pairs to do *Actividad* 9. 5 MIN.
- Ask pairs to volunteer to read their summaries from *Actividad* 9. 5 MIN.
- Present *Gramática*: Irregular Affirmative *tú* Commands, p. 177. 10 MIN.
- Have students stay in their pairs to work on the *Juego* (Answer, TE, p. 177). 5 MIN.
- Present the *Vocabulario*, p. 178. 5 MIN.
- Work on *Actividad* 10 orally. 5 MIN.

Homework Option:
- *Más práctica* Workbook, p. 30. *Para hispanohablantes* Workbook, p. 28.

DAY 6

En acción (cont.)
- Check homework. 5 MIN.
- Quick Start Review (TE, p. 180) 5 MIN.
- Have students work in pairs to do *Actividad* 11. 5 MIN.
- Call on pairs to act out their responses to *Actividad* 11. 5 MIN.
- Work on *Actividad* 12 orally. 5 MIN.
- Have students write their responses to *Actividad* 12. 5 MIN.
- Read and discuss the *Conexiones*, p. 179. 5 MIN.
- Present *Gramática*: Negative *tú* Commands, p. 180. 5 MIN.
- Work orally with the class on *Actividad* 13. 5 MIN.

Homework Option:
- *Más práctica* Workbook, p. 31. *Para hispanohablantes* Workbook, p. 29.

DAY 7

En acción (cont.)
- Check homework. 5 MIN.
- Work orally with the class on *Actividad* 14. 5 MIN.
- Have students write their responses to *Actividad* 14. 5 MIN.
- Read and discuss the *Nota cultural*, p. 181. 5 MIN.
- Have students work in pairs to do *Actividad* 15. 5 MIN.
- Call on selected pairs to model their conversations from *Actividad* 15 for the class. 5 MIN.
- Have students work in groups on *Actividad* 16. 5 MIN.
- Ask groups to share their results from *Actividad* 16. 10 MIN.

DAY 8

En acción (cont.)
- Quick Start Review (TE, p. 182) 5 MIN.
- Present *Gramática*: Using Correct Pronoun Placement with Commands, p. 182. 10 MIN.
- Assign *Actividad* 17. 5 MIN.
- Have volunteers write their answers to *Actividad* 17 on the board. 5 MIN.
- Read and discuss the *También se dice*, p. 182. 5 MIN.
- Have pairs do *Actividad* 18. 5 MIN.
- Call on selected pairs to model their conversations for *Actividad* 18 for the class. 5 MIN.
- Read and discuss the *Nota cultural*, p. 183. 5 MIN.

Homework Option:
- *Más práctica* Workbook, p. 32. *Para hispanohablantes* Workbook, p. 30.

DAY 9

En acción (cont.)
- Check homework. 5 MIN.
- Have students work in groups to do *Actividad* 19. 5 MIN.
- Ask groups to volunteer to model their conversations from *Actividad* 19. 10 MIN.
- Play the audio and have students do *Actividad* 20. 5 MIN.
- Ask volunteers to give their responses to *Actividad* 20. 5 MIN.
- Read and discuss the *Conexiones,* p. 184. 5 MIN.
- Have students work individually on the *Para hacer,* p. 184. 5 MIN.
- Ask students to read their descriptions of Picasso (*Para hacer,* p. 184). 5 MIN.

DAY 10

En acción (cont.)
- Have students work in pairs to do *Actividad* 21. 10 MIN.
- Ask students to volunteer to read their ads from *Actividad* 21 for the class. 5 MIN.
- Use Information Gap Activities, Unit 5 Resource Book, pp. 18–19. 5 MIN.
- *Más comunicación,* p. R4. 5 MIN.
- Discuss and demonstrate the *Pronunciación,* p. 185. 10 MIN.
- Have students work in pairs to practice the tongue twister, p. 185. 5 MIN.
- Have students work in pairs to create their own tongue twisters, modeled on the *Trabalenguas,* p. 185. 5 MIN.

DAY 11

En voces: Lectura
- Quick Start Review (TE, p. 186) 5 MIN.
- Review the Reading Strategy, p. 186. 5 MIN.
- Ask students to predict what the story is about. 5 MIN.
- Have students read the *Lectura,* pp. 186–187, silently. 10 MIN.
- Ask volunteers to read the story orally. 10 MIN.
- Have students answer the *¿Comprendiste?* questions for the *Lectura* (Answers, TE, p. 187). 5 MIN.
- Work orally with students to answer the *¿Qué piensas?* questions for the *Lectura,* p. 187. 5 MIN.

Homework Option:
- Have students review all of the *Gramática* boxes in *Etapa* 1 to prepare for *En uso.*

DAY 12

En uso: Repaso y más comunicación
- Answer grammar questions arising from the homework review. 5 MIN.
- Quick Start Review (TE, p. 188) 5 MIN.
- Present the *Repaso y más comunicación* using the Teaching Suggestions (TE, p. 188). 10 MIN.
- Have students write their responses to *Actividad* 1. 5 MIN.
- Check answers for *Actividad* 1 with the whole class. 5 MIN.
- Work with students to do *Actividad* 2 orally. 5 MIN.
- Have students read and prepare to respond orally to *Actividad* 3. 5 MIN.
- Work orally with the class on *Actividad* 3. 5 MIN.

DAY 13

En uso (cont.)
- Have students read and prepare to answer *Actividad* 4. 5 MIN.
- Ask pairs of students to take the roles in *Actividad* 4. 5 MIN.
- Present the Speaking Strategy, p. 190. 5 MIN.
- Have students work in pairs to do *Actividad* 5. 5 MIN.
- Have volunteer pairs model their work for *Actividad* 5. 5 MIN.
- Have students work in groups to do *Actividad* 6. 10 MIN.
- Ask groups to volunteer to share their work from *Actividad* 6. 5 MIN.
- Discuss the *Conexiones,* p. 190. 5 MIN.

Homework Option:
- Have students complete the Venn diagram in the *Conexiones,* p. 190.

DAY 14

En tu propia voz: Escritura
- Quick Start Review (TE, p. 191) 5 MIN.
- Check homework. 5 MIN.
- Have students do the writing activity, *Actividad* 7, independently. 10 MIN.
- Call on selected students to read their work from *Actividad* 7. 5 MIN.

En resumen: Repaso de vocabulario
- Follow the Teaching Suggestions (TE, p. 191). 10 MIN.
- Review grammar questions, etc., as necessary. 5 MIN.
- Have students solve the *Juego* (Answers, TE, p. 191). 5 MIN.

Homework Option:
- Have students study for the *Etapa* exam.

DAY 15

En resumen: Repaso de vocabulario
- Answer questions related to *Etapa* 1 content. 10 MIN.
- Complete *Etapa* exam. 25 MIN.

Ampliación
- Use a suggested project, game, or activity (TE, pp. 165A–165B) as students complete the exam.

Classroom Management Tip

Make connections If your students make connections among their subjects and between Spanish and the real world, they will learn faster and have better retention. Look for opportunities to help students make these connections. A good Spanish–art connection is Pablo Picasso.

Guernica is Picasso's painting about the bombing of a Basque town. Use an overhead projector to help students enlarge and create a mural based on the painting. Assign a section to each student to work on as they complete this **Etapa**. Each artist should also be researching facts about the work and the artist.

Etapa Theme
Talking about one's daily routine, grooming, and chores

Grammar Objectives
- Using reflexive verbs
- Using irregular affirmative **tú** commands
- Using negative **tú** commands
- Using correct pronoun placement with commands

Teaching Resource Options

Print

Block Scheduling Copymasters

Audiovisual

OHT 138, 147 (Quick Start)

Quick Start Review

🔄 Vocabulary review

Use OHT 147 or write on the board: Write what means of transportation you might use to get to each place.

1. la escuela
2. el centro comercial
3. San Antonio, Texas
4. Oaxaca, México
5. España

Answers
Answers will vary. Answers could include:
1. a pie, en autobús
2. en carro, en metro
3. en carro, en avión
4. en autobús, en avión
5. en barco, en avión

Teaching Suggestions
Previewing the Etapa
- Ask students to study the photo on pp. 166–167 (1 min.).
- Close books; ask students to share at least 3 things that they noticed.
- Reopen books and look at the picture again (1 min.); close books and share 3 more details.
- Have students describe the people in the photo and the weather.
- Use the **¿Qué ves?** questions to focus the discussion.

UNIDAD 5

ETAPA 1

¿Cómo es tu rutina?

- Describe daily routine
- Talk about grooming
- Tell others to do something
- Discuss daily chores

¿Qué ves?

Mira la foto del Parque Güell en Barcelona.

1. ¿Es interesante o no el parque?
2. ¿Qué hace la chica?
3. ¿Qué lleva la mujer?
4. ¿De qué color es el animal?
5. ¿Cómo se llama el parque de atracciones de Barcelona?

Barcelona

Parque Güell

Avenida Diagonal

Sagrada Familia

Parque de Joan Miró

Estación del Norte

Estación Barcelona Sants

Gran Vía de las Cortes Catalanas

Avenida del Paralelo

BARRIO GÓTICO

Las Ramblas

Parque de atracciones de Montjuic

Puerto

PLAYA

Paseo de Colón

166

Middle School Classroom Management

Planning Ahead You may want to acquire an assortment of magazines from Spain to display in your class library or reference section. Also, now is a good time to add to your vocabulary picture file by collecting magazine ads showing people brushing teeth, washing hair, and going through personal care routines.

Peer Teaching Consider assigning permanent pairs for vocabulary acquisition activities. One member of the pair becomes the expert on **Etapa** verbs while the other pays particular attention to other new vocabulary. This pair takes mutual responsibility for helping each other learn vocabulary.

Cross Cultural Connections

Survey students to see how many read the international news in the newspaper and/or watch international news programs. Explain that, in general, Spaniards tend to know more about U.S. culture than people in the U.S. know about Spain. Discuss why that might be. Ask students what they could do to learn more about Spain.

Culture Highlights

● **BARCELONA** Barcelona has 4 major sections: **Montjuic, Las Ramblas, El Ensanche,** and **El Barrio Gótico. Montjuic** is a high hill outside the city proper. It has been the site of a temple, a lighthouse, and a military fort. Today it is popular for its amusement park, museums (one displaying works by Joan Miró), the 1992 Olympic Stadium, and a botanical garden.

The city of Barcelona has a great interest in the enjoyment of the outdoors. In the last 20 years, close to 100 parks and plazas have been constructed or remodeled.

● **EL PARQUE GÜELL** El Parque Güell was created by Antonio Gaudí and named after his patron, industrialist Eusebio Güell. The park contains stone trees, reptilian fountains, and mosaics of broken ceramic pieces set in concrete.

● **ANTONIO GAUDÍ** Some of Gaudí's other works include **Casa Viçens** (a private home in Barcelona), **Casa Batlló** and **Casa Milà** (2 apartment buildings), and **Palacio Güell.**

Supplementary Vocabulary

la estatua	statue
el lagarto	lizard
la escalera	stairway
subir	to go up

Teaching Middle School Students

Extra Help Students work in groups of 3. Each student makes a list of vocabulary words. One is of people. One is of adjectives. One is of infinitives. Have students use all 3 lists to help them describe the people in the photo.

Native Speakers Ask native speakers whether they have a relative who came from Spain whom they can describe to the class.

Multiple Intelligences

Logical/Mathematical Have students use the map of Barcelona to describe locations in relationship to each other.

Intrapersonal Ask students to write their personal impressions of Gaudí's design.

Block Schedule

Variety Have students sketch and color an **Etapa** opener for their town/city. Have them share their artwork by telling the location, its significance, and what any people in their pictures are doing. (For additional activities, see **Block Scheduling Copymasters.**)

Teaching Resource Options

Print

Unit 5 Resource Book
Video Activities, pp. 23–24
Videoscript, p. 26
Audioscript, p. 29
Audioscript *Para hispanohablantes,*
   p. 29

Audiovisual

OHT 141, 142, 143, 143A, 144, 144A,
147 (Quick Start)
Audio Program Cassette 13A / CD 13
Audio *Para hispanohablantes*
Cassette 13A / CD 13
Video Program Videotape 5 /
Videodisc 3A

Search Chapter 2, Play to 3
U5E1 • En contexto (Vocabulary)

Technology
Intrigas y aventuras CD-ROM, Disc 1

Quick Start Review

♻ Verb review

Use OHT 147 or write on the board:
Use the verb **ir** and a word from each
column to create 5 original sentences.

Modelo: Todos los días, mi mamá va
a la panadería.

los viernes	la panadería
los sábados	el parque
los domingos	el centro comercial
todos los días	la playa
los lunes	el banco
los jueves	la iglesia
	la tienda de videos

Answers
Answers will vary. Answers could include:
Los sábados voy al centro comercial.
Los domingos mi tía va a la iglesia.
Todos los días mi hermano va al parque.
Los viernes Arturo va a la tienda de videos.
Los jueves mi papá va al banco.

Teaching Note

Students are not expected to produce the
reflexive construction at this point. For the
Preguntas personales, they may answer
with phrases rather than complete sentences.

En contexto

 ## VOCABULARIO

Luis is following his morning routine. Watch him get
ready for the day.

A Luis oye **el despertador**. Pero está en
la cama. ¡Quiere dormir más!

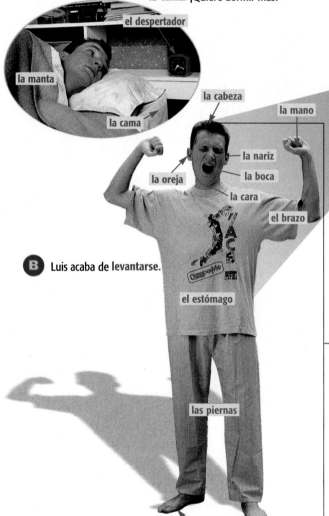

el despertador

la manta

la cabeza

la mano

la nariz

la oreja

la boca

la cara

el brazo

B Luis acaba de **levantarse**.

el estómago

el cuerpo

las piernas

los pies

la cama

168 ciento sesenta y ocho
Unidad 5

Middle School Classroom Community

TPR Introduce a new definition for the verb **tocar:** *to
touch.* Then organize a game of **"Simón dice...,"** calling
out the names of different body parts as students stand
and respond to your instructions. (**Simón dice: —Toca
los pies.**)

Paired Activity Give pairs of students old
magazines, and ask them to construct a "body" using
parts from several different pictures. They must then
label the parts. Ask students to share their work on
class bulletin boards.

C Luis va a **lavarse**. Se lava **la cara** con **jabón** y va a **secarse** con **una toalla**.

el jabón

la toalla

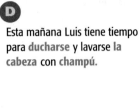

D Esta mañana Luis tiene tiempo para **ducharse** y lavarse **la cabeza** con **champú**.

el espejo

el secador de pelo

el champú

la pasta de dientes

E Luis se lava **los dientes** con **el cepillo de dientes**. Después, va a **peinarse** con **un peine**. ¡Ya está listo!

los dientes

el cepillo de dientes

el peine

Preguntas personales

1. ¿Usas un despertador?
2. ¿Te lavas la cara por la mañana o por la noche?
3. ¿Usas un secador de pelo o una toalla para secarte el pelo?
4. ¿A qué hora te levantas?
5. ¿Cuándo te lavas los dientes?

ciento sesenta y nueve

169

Etapa 1

Teaching Suggestions
Introducing Vocabulary

• Have students look at pages 168–169. Use OHT 141 and 142 and Audio Cassette 13A / CD 13 to present the vocabulary.
• Ask the Comprehension Questions |in order of yes/no (questions 1–3), either/or (questions 4–6), and simple word or phrase (questions 7–10). Expand by adding similar questions.
• Use the TPR activity to reinforce the meaning of individual words.
• Use the video vocabulary presentation for review and reinforcement.

Comprehension Questions

1. En la foto A, ¿está Luis en la cama? (Sí.)
2. ¿Oye Luis el despertador? (Sí.)
3. ¿Tiene Luis 3 mantas? (No.)
4. ¿Quiere Luis levantarse o dormir más? (dormir más)
5. ¿Luis va a lavarse o comer? (lavarse)
6. ¿Usa una camisa o una toalla para secarse? (una toalla)
7. ¿Con qué se lava Luis la cara? (con jabón)
8. ¿Con qué se lava Luis la cabeza? (con champú)
9. ¿Con qué se lava Luis los dientes? (con un cepillo de dientes)
10. ¿Con qué va a peinarse? (con un peine)

Supplementary Vocabulary

el mentón, la barbilla	chin
el codo	elbow
la rodilla	knee
los dedos	fingers
la muñeca	wrist
el tobillo	ankle
la frente	forehead
la barba	beard
el bigote	mustache

Teaching Middle School Students

Extra Help Ask students to list each verb presented on these pages and illustrate them with drawings, stick figures, or cutouts.

Native Speakers Ask native speakers if they can provide other ways to express **manta (frazada)**, **lavarse la cabeza (lavarse el pelo/cabello)**, **lavarse los dientes (cepillarse los dientes)**.

Multiple Intelligences

Logical/Mathematical Ask students to interview classmates about the brand of toothpaste or shampoo they use. Students may wish to make a graph or pie chart showing their results.

■ Block Schedule

FunBreak Working in groups, have students play a word association game. The first student gives a word **(los dientes)** and the next student gives a related word **(lavarse)**. The next student gives a word associated with the second word **(jabón)**, and so on.

Teaching Resource Options

Print

Más práctica Workbook PE,
pp. 25–28

Para hispanohablantes Workbook PE,
pp. 25–26

Block Scheduling Copymasters

Unit 5 Resource Book
Más práctica Workbook TE, pp. 1–4
Para hispanohablantes Workbook
TE, pp. 9–10
Video Activities, pp. 23–24
Videoscript, p. 27
Audioscript, p. 29
Audioscript *Para hispanohablantes*,
p. 29

Audiovisual

OHT 145, 146, 147 (Quick Start)
Audio Program Cassette 13A / CD 13
Audio *Para hispanohablantes*
Cassette 13A / CD 13
Video Program Videotape 5 /
Videodisc 3A

Search Chapter 3, Play to 4
U5E1 • En vivo (Dialog)

Technology

Intrigas y aventuras CD-ROM, Disc 1

🔔 Quick Start Review

♻ Morning routine

Use OHT 147 or write on the board:
Answer the following questions about
your morning routine.

1. ¿Cuándo te levantas los lunes:
   antes o después de las siete?
2. ¿Cuándo te levantas los sábados:
   antes o después de las siete?
3. ¿Usas un despertador?
4. ¿Cuántas mantas usas en la cama?
5. ¿Cómo se llama tu champú
   favorito? ¿Tu jabón favorito?

Answers *See p. 165D.*

Gestures

Assign groups of students specific
characters from the dialog. As you read
the dialog, have them make the gestures
that correspond to their characters.

En vivo
 DIÁLOGO

Muchos quehaceres

Luis   Carmen   Mercedes   Juan Carlos   Lourdes

PARA ESCUCHAR • STRATEGY: LISTENING

Listen for a mood or a feeling Nothing is going right for Luis.
What does he say to show frustration? Jot down some of his
expressions for protesting. When would you use them?

1 ▶ Juan Carlos: ¡Luis! ¡Mercedes llega
en diez minutos!
Luis: ¡Sí, ya lo sé! ¡Ahora me ducho
y salgo! ¡Necesito lavarme los
dientes!

5 ▶ Luis: Necesito secarme el pelo.
Carmen: ¡Ponte otra camisa!
Mírate en el espejo, ¡esta camisa
está muy fea! ¡Y no uses mi
secador de pelo! ¡Por favor, no
lo uses!

6 ▶ Juan Carlos: Hijo. Por favor, haz todo lo
que está en esta lista.
Luis: Pero, ¿tengo que hacerlo todo hoy?
Juan Carlos: Sí, hijo. Primero haz los
quehaceres.
Luis: ¡Pero, papá!

7 ▶ Lourdes: Necesitamos varias cosas.
Ve a la tienda. Aquí tienes mi lista.
Luis: Mamá, me espera Álvaro.
Lourdes: Pero esto es importante.
Luis: ¡No es justo! ¡Es mi
cumpleaños!

170 ciento setenta
Unidad 5

Middle School Classroom Community

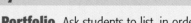

TPR In a quick rhythm, say the grooming-related
vocabulary words. For each word, students touch the
relevant body part.

Portfolio Ask students to list, in order, the grooming
activities they perform every day.

Rubric

Criteria	Scale	
Accuracy of information	1 2 3 4 5	A = 13–15 pts.
Logical organization	1 2 3 4 5	B = 10–12 pts.
Vocabulary use	1 2 3 4 5	C = 7–9 pts.
		D = 4–6 pts.
		F = < 4 pts.

2 ▶ Carmen: ¡Luis! ¡Luis! ¡Mercedes está aquí!
Luis: ¡Sí, sí, sí! ¡Pero primero me pongo la ropa! ¡Ya voy!

3 ▶ Luis: ¡Hola, Mercedes! ¿Cómo estás?
Mercedes: Bien, Luis. ¡Y feliz cumpleaños! ¿Qué tal tu mañana?
Luis: Muy tranquila, gracias.

4 ▶ Luis: ¿Qué haces? ¿Por qué me estás sacando fotos? ¡No hagas eso!
Mercedes: Son para un concurso.
Luis: ¿Para qué concurso son?
Mercedes: Te digo luego. Álvaro nos espera en una hora. ¿Estás listo?

8 ▶ Juan Carlos: Sí, pero también puedes celebrarlo después. También cuida a tu hermana.
Luis: ¡No puede ser!
Carmen: ¡Ja, ja! ¡Me tienes que cuidar!

9 ▶ Luis: Voy a llamar a Álvaro. Nunca vamos a llegar a tiempo.
Mercedes: ¡Pobre Luis! ¡No seas tan dura con él! Es su cumpleaños.
Carmen: ¡Le quiero ver la cara al llegar a su fiesta!

10 ▶ Luis: Está ocupado. Lo llamo más tarde. Bueno, vamos. Tenemos muchas cosas que hacer. ¡Carmen, Mercedes!, ¿me ayudáis con los quehaceres?

Teaching Middle School Students

Extra Help Have students work in pairs. Each writes 5 false statements about the dialog. Then they exchange papers and correct the statements.

Native Speakers Have native speakers make a list of commands, some from the dialog and some not. Have them act out these commands as the class guesses their meaning.

Multiple Intelligences

Verbal Read expressions from the dialog that can be mimed. Call on individual students to stand and act out what they hear.

Teaching Suggestions
Presenting the Dialog

• Prepare students for listening by focusing on the dialog context. Reintroduce Luis and review reflexive verb infinitives. Have students act out the following verbs: **levantarse, lavarse la cara, lavarse los dientes, secarse, ducharse, peinarse.**

• Use the video, audio cassette, or CD to present the dialog. The expanded dialog on video offers additional listening practice opportunities.

Video Synopsis

• It is Luis's birthday and he is getting ready to spend the day with his friends. But first he must do some chores for his parents and take care of his sister. For a complete transcript of the video dialog, see p. 165D.

Comprehension Questions

1. ¿Llega Mercedes en cinco minutos? (No.)
2. ¿Está listo Luis? (No.)
3. ¿Necesita Luis lavarse los dientes? (Sí.)
4. ¿Es hoy el cumpleaños de Mercedes? (No.)
5. ¿Saca Mercedes fotos para una clase o para un concurso? (para un concurso)
6. ¿A Carmen le gusta o no le gusta la camisa de Luis? (no le gusta)
7. ¿Quién tiene que hacer todo lo que está en la lista? (Luis)
8. ¿A quiénes espera Álvaro? (a Luis y a Mercedes)
9. ¿A quién tiene que cuidar Luis? (a su hermana Carmen)
10. ¿Quiénes van a ayudar a Luis con los quehaceres? (Carmen y Mercedes)

Block Schedule

Variety Have each student choose one character from the dialog and write a short paragraph describing that person. They can add imaginary details as well. Have volunteers read their descriptions. (For additional activities, see **Block Scheduling Copymasters.**)

Teaching Resource Options

Print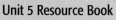

Unit 5 Resource Book
Video Activities, p. 25
Videoscript, p. 28
Audioscript, p. 29
Audioscript *Para hispanohablantes*,
p. 29

Audiovisual

OHT 148 (Quick Start)
Audio Program Cassette 13A / CD 13
Audio *Para hispanohablantes*
Cassette 13A / CD 13
Video Program Videotape 5 /
Videodisc 3A

Quick Start Review

♻ **Dialog review**

Use OHT 148 or write on the board:
Identify the speaker of each quote.

1. Mírate en el espejo, ¡esta camisa está muy fea!
2. ¿Por qué me estás sacando fotos?
3. Aquí tienes mi lista.
4. ¡Necesito lavarme los dientes!
5. Álvaro nos espera en una hora.
6. Primero haz los quehaceres.

Answers *See p. 165D.*

Teaching Suggestions
Comprehension Check

Use **Actividades 1** and **2** to assess retention after the dialog. After students have successfully completed both activities, have them add items to **Actividad 2** and quiz each other.

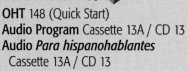

Objective: Transitional practice
Listening comprehension/vocabulary

Answers (See script, p. 165D.)
1. no; Está en el baño.
2. sí
3. no; Piensa que es fea.
4. sí
5. sí

En acción

VOCABULARIO Y GRAMÁTICA

OBJECTIVES

- Describe daily routine
- Talk about grooming
- Tell others to do something
- Discuss daily chores
- *Use reflexive verbs*
- *Use irregular affirmative tú commands*
- *Use negative tú commands*
- *Use correct pronoun placement with commands*

¿Sí o no?

Escuchar Según el diálogo, ¿son ciertos o falsos estos comentarios? Si un comentario es falso, corrígelo. *(Hint: Are the comments true or false? Correct the false ones.)*

1. Cuando Mercedes llega, Luis está listo para salir.
2. Mercedes saca fotos de Luis.
3. A Carmen le gusta la camisa de Luis.
4. A Luis no le gusta cuidar a su hermana Carmen.
5. Cuando Luis llama a Álvaro, no contesta nadie.

También se dice

In this unit you will see and hear language that is typical of Spain. Did you notice that Luis uses the word **ayudáis** instead of **ayudan** when he asks Mercedes and Carmen to help him with the chores? Remember that in Spain the **vosotros(as)** form of verbs is usually used with people one knows well.

172

Middle School Classroom Management

Organizing Pair Work Assign pairs of students to help each other correct **Actividades 1–5**. Ask them to be responsible for making sure that both of them have answered all of the exercises correctly.

Time Saver Sometimes there is not enough time to complete all of the exercises you'd like to cover in a day. In this case, when activities cover the same or similar objectives, assign one activity to half the class and the next activity to the other half of the class. Then encourage discussion of answers when they are presented orally to the class.

2 En la casa de Luis

Escuchar/Leer Escoge la palabra o frase que mejor describe los eventos del diálogo. *(Hint: Choose the best word or phrase.)*

modelo

Juan Carlos dice que Mercedes llega a la casa de Luis en (media hora / diez minutos).

*Juan Carlos dice que Mercedes llega a la casa de Luis en **diez minutos**.*

1. Cuando Mercedes llega a la casa, Luis acaba de (ponerse la ropa / ducharse).

2. Mercedes saca fotos para (un concurso / el cumpleaños).

3. Luis tiene que ir (al colegio / a la tienda).

4. Luis tiene planes para salir con Mercedes y (una amiga / Álvaro).

5. Luis (está / no está) contento con lo que ocurre esa mañana.

3 Antonio va a...

Hablar/Escribir Hoy va a ser un día típico para Antonio, un amigo de Carmen. Explica a qué hora va a hacer cada actividad, según los dibujos. *(Hint: Explain when he is going to do each activity.)*

modelo

*Antonio va a **levantarse** a las **siete y cuarto**.*

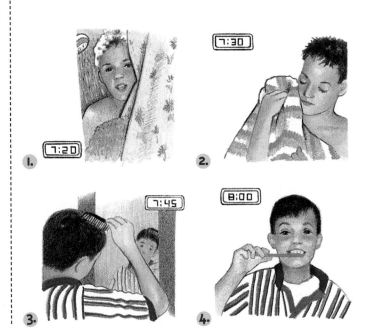

1.
2.
3.
4.

Teaching Middle School Students

Challenge Collect personal care items and items from the classroom for which students have vocabulary. Place these in a box. Call on individual students to close their eyes and pick an item from the box. Ask them to identify and describe their item.

Multiple Intelligences

Visual Ask students to go through old magazines looking for ads that illustrate some of the personal care vocabulary. Have students cut them out and label them in Spanish to make their own flash cards.

ACTIVIDAD 2 Objective: Transitional practice
Listening comprehension/vocabulary

Answers (See script, p. 165D.)
1. ducharse
2. un concurso
3. a la tienda
4. Álvaro
5. no está

ACTIVIDAD 3 Objective: Transitional practice
Vocabulary
Telling time

Answers
1. Va a ducharse a las siete y veinte.
2. Va a secarse a las siete y media.
3. Va a peinarse a las ocho menos cuarto.
4. Va a lavarse los dientes a las ocho.

Block Schedule

FunBreak Have students create Bingo cards with words for parts of the body, personal care items, and daily routine vocabulary. Instead of calling out the words, provide clues. For example: **Es para lavarse los dientes = la pasta de dientes,** or **el cepillo de dientes.**

Teaching Resource Options

Print

Unit 5 Resource Book
Video Activities, p. 25
Videoscript, p. 28
Audioscript, p. 29
Audioscript *Para hispanohablantes*,
  p. 29

Audiovisual

OHT 148 (Quick Start)
Audio Program Cassette 13A / CD 13
Audio *Para hispanohablantes*
  Cassette 13A / CD 13
Video Program Videotape 5 /
  Videodisc 3A

Objective: Transitional practice
Vocabulary

Answers

1. ¿Necesita Luis algo para lavarse? Luis necesita jabón.
2. ¿Necesitan Luis y Carmen algo para secarse? Luis y Carmen necesitan toallas.
3. ¿Necesita Carmen algo para lavarse la cabeza? Carmen necesita champú.
4. ¿Necesita Luis algo para lavarse los dientes? Luis necesita pasta de dientes y un cepillo de dientes.
5. ¿Necesitan Carmen y Luis algo para secarse el pelo? Carmen y Luis necesitan un secador.

Objective: Open-ended practice
Vocabulary

Answers

1. ¿Cómo comes? Para comer, uso dos bocas.
2. ¿Cómo bailas? Para bailar, uso seis piernas.
3. ¿Cómo oyes? Para oír, uso dos orejas.
4. ¿Cómo escribes? Para escribir, uso cuatro manos.
5. ¿Cómo piensas? Para pensar, uso dos cabezas.
6. ¿Cómo nadas? Para nadar, uso cuatro brazos y seis piernas.
7. ¿Cómo caminas? Para caminar, uso seis piernas.
8. ¿Cómo tocas el piano? Para tocar el piano, uso dieciséis dedos (cuatro manos).
9. ¿Cómo ves la televisión? Para ver la televisión, uso cuatro ojos.
10. ¿Cómo juegas al béisbol? Para jugar al béisbol, uso cuatro brazos y seis piernas.

Lo que necesitan

Hablar Ustedes necesitan comprar unas cosas para Luis y Carmen. Hablen de lo que necesitan. ¿Qué dicen?
(*Hint: Say what Luis and Carmen need.*)

modelo

Carmen / peinarse

Estudiante A: ¿Necesita **Carmen** algo para **peinarse**?

Estudiante B: Carmen necesita **un peine** y **un espejo**.

1. Luis / lavarse

2. Luis y Carmen / secarse

3. Carmen / lavarse la cabeza

4. Luis / lavarse los dientes

5. Carmen y Luis / secarse el pelo

Para correr...

Hablar Imagínate que un extraterrestre llega a tu casa. Pregúntale cómo hace las siguientes actividades.
(*Hint: Ask how the extraterrestrial does these activities.*)

modelo

correr

Tú: ¿Cómo **corres**?

Extraterrestre: Para **correr**, uso seis piernas y seis pies.

1. comer
2. bailar
3. oír
4. escribir
5. pensar
6. nadar
7. caminar
8. tocar el piano
9. ver la televisión
10. jugar al béisbol

---

174 ciento setenta y cuatro
Unidad 5

Middle School Classroom Community

TPR Write the verbs found in **Actividad 4** on slips of paper. Ask a student to choose a slip of paper and read it for the whole class to act out.

Learning Scenario Ask students to work in groups of 4 to simulate an interaction at a hair salon. Two group members are hairstylists and the other two are customers.

GRAMÁTICA

Describing Actions That Involve Oneself: Reflexive Verbs

To describe people doing things for themselves, use reflexive verbs. Examples of reflexive actions are *brushing one's teeth* or *combing one's hair*. **Reflexive pronouns** are used with **reflexive verbs** to indicate that the subject of the sentence receives the action of the verb.

lavarse *to wash oneself*

me lavo	**nos** lavamos
te lavas	**os** laváis
se lava	**se** lavan

Many verbs can be used with or without **reflexive pronouns**. When there is **no** reflexive pronoun, the person doing the action does **not** receive the action.

reflexive	*not reflexive*
Pepa **se lava**.	Pepa **lava** el carro.
Pepa washes herself.	*Pepa washes the car.*

Luis says:

—¡Primero **me pongo** la ropa!
First I put on my clothes!

> Notice he says **la ropa**, not **mi ropa**, because reflexive pronouns include the concept of possession.

When you use the **infinitive form** of a reflexive verb **after** a **conjugated verb**, be sure to use the correct **reflexive pronoun**.

Quiero levantarme temprano.
I want to get up early.

Me quiero levantar temprano.

> You can also put the **reflexive pronoun in front** of the **conjugated verb.**

Some verbs have different meanings when used reflexively.

dormir *to sleep*	**dormirse** *to fall asleep*
ir *to go*	**irse** *to leave, to go away*
poner *to put*	**ponerse** *to put on (clothes)*

Vocabulario

Reflexive Verbs

acostarse: o→ue

lavarse la cabeza

afeitarse

lavarse los dientes

bañarse

maquillarse

despertarse: e→ie

ponerse la ropa

Notice that **acostarse** and **despertarse** are stem-changing verbs.

¿Cuándo haces estas actividades, por la mañana o por la noche?

ciento setenta y cinco
Etapa 1 **175**

Quick Start Review
♻ Personal care items

Use OHT 148 or write on the board: List 5 items you use when getting ready in the morning. Tell what part of the body is involved with each one.

Answers
Answers will vary. Answers could include:
1. el jabón: las manos, la cara
2. el champú: la cabeza, el pelo
3. el cepillo de dientes: los dientes
4. el espejo: la cara, el pelo
5. la toalla: la cara, el pelo

Teaching Suggestions
Teaching Reflexive Verbs
• Explain to students that they have been using one reflexive verb for a long time: **llamarse** (Me llamo...).
• Point out that many reflexive verbs describe physical actions.

Teaching Middle School Students

Extra Help Draw two boxes on the board. Call on students to write subject pronouns in one box. Have other students write reflexive verbs in the other box. Then help students use one word from each box to write a sentence.

Multiple Intelligences

Intrapersonal Ask students to make an illustrated clock diagramming their morning activities.

Logical/Mathematical Ask students to survey each other as to what time they go to bed. Have them show their results in a table or graph.

Block Schedule

Change of Pace Have students create small posters depicting related reflexive and nonreflexive actions, such as **Me baño por la mañana** and **Baño el perro los domingos**. (For additional activities, see **Block Scheduling Copymasters**.)

Teaching Resource Options

Print

Más práctica Workbook PE, p. 29
Para hispanohablantes Workbook PE, p. 27
Block Scheduling Copymasters
Unit 5 Resource Book
  Más práctica Workbook TE, p. 5
  Para hispanohablantes Workbook TE, p. 11
  Audioscript, p. 30
  Audioscript *Para hispanohablantes*, p. 30

Audiovisual

OHT 148 (Quick Start)
Audio Program Cassettes 13A, 13B / CD 13
Audio *Para hispanohablantes* Cassette 13A / CD 13

Technology

Intrigas y aventuras CD-ROM, Disc 1

---

6 **Objective:** Controlled practice Listening comprehension/reflexive verbs/vocabulary

Answers (See script, p. 165D.)
1. Carmen se lava la cabeza.
2. Los padres de Luis se lavan las manos.
3. Mercedes y Luis se lavan los pies.
4. Luis se lava las piernas.
5. Álvaro se lava la cara.

7 **Objective:** Controlled practice Estar/**tener que**/adjective-noun agreement/reflexive verbs

Answers
1. ¿Por qué no estás listo(a)? Tengo que peinarme. *o:* Me tengo que peinar.
2. ¿Por qué no están listos sus primos? Tienen que ducharse. *o:* Se tienen que duchar.
3. ¿Por qué no estáis listos(as)? Tenemos que lavarnos la cara. *o:* Nos tenemos que lavar la cara.
4. ¿Por qué no están listas Mercedes y Elena? Tienen que ponerse la ropa nueva. *o:* Se tienen que poner la ropa nueva.
5. ¿Por qué no está listo Luis? Tiene que afeitarse. *o:* Se tiene que afeitar.
6. ¿Por qué no está lista Emiliana? Tiene que maquillarse. *o:* Se tiene que maquillar.
7. ¿Por qué no están listos Álvaro y su hermano? Tienen que lavarse los dientes. *o:* Se tienen que lavar los dientes.
8. ¿Por qué no está lista tu hermana? Tiene que secarse el pelo. *o:* Se tiene que secar el pelo.

Se lavan...

Escuchar/Escribir Luis explica que todos tienen que lavarse después de trabajar mucho. ¿Qué se lavan? *(Hint: Who is washing what?)*

1. Carmen / lavarse / ¿?
2. los padres de Luis / lavarse / ¿?
3. Mercedes y Luis / lavarse / ¿?
4. Luis / lavarse / ¿?
5. Álvaro / lavarse / ¿?

¡No están listos!

Hablar Luis y sus amigos van a una fiesta. Nadie está listo. ¿Qué tiene que hacer cada uno? *(Hint: Say what people have to do.)*

modelo

Marta: lavarse la cabeza

Estudiante A: ¿Por qué no está lista **Marta**?

Estudiante B: **Marta** tiene que **lavarse la cabeza**.
  o: **Marta** se tiene que **lavar la cabeza**.

1. tú: peinarse
2. sus primos: ducharse
3. vosotros(as): lavarse la cara
4. Mercedes y Elena: ponerse la ropa nueva
5. Luis: afeitarse
6. Emiliana: maquillarse
7. Álvaro y su hermano: lavarse los dientes
8. tu hermana: secarse el pelo

■ **MÁS PRÁCTICA** *cuaderno* p. 29
■ **PARA HISPANOHABLANTES** *cuaderno* p. 27

 Primero...

PARA CONVERSAR

STRATEGY: SPEAKING

Sequence events When telling about more than one event, make the order in which they occurred clear. Remember these expressions: **primero, entonces, luego, después, antes de..., después de..., por la mañana/tarde.**

To show your acting talents, mime the activities of your daily routine.

Hablar Pregúntale a otro(a) estudiante qué hace primero. *(Hint: Which activity do you do first?)*

modelo

¿ducharse o lavarse los dientes?

Estudiante A: ¿Qué haces primero, **te duchas** o **te lavas los dientes**?

Estudiante B: Primero **me ducho** y luego **me lavo los dientes.**

1. ¿lavarse la cabeza o lavarse la cara?
2. ¿bañarse o lavarse los dientes?
3. ¿afeitarse / maquillarse o peinarse?
4. ¿lavarse la cara o ponerse la ropa?
5. ¿ponerse la ropa o peinarse?

Middle School Classroom Community

Paired Activity Ask students to work in pairs to rewrite **Actividad 7**, substituting **nosotros** for each of the subjects given.

Game Split the class into 2 teams. Read the game rules and give each team time to plan a strategy for getting the best possible score for each round. Then ask a student to be a leader and call out an infinitive.

Game rules:
- Each player takes each infinitive and writes one sentence with it.
- A round is 6 infinitives; scoring is done after each round.
- Scoring: 1 point for each verb form used by the team in a correct sentence. Duplicate forms do not add points.

ACTIVIDAD 9

Todos los días

Hablar/Escribir Pregúntale a otro(a) estudiante qué hace todos los días. Usa los verbos reflexivos para escribir un resumen de las actividades de esta persona. *(Hint: Ask another student to describe his or her daily routine. Write a summary of the activities using reflexive verbs.)*

modelo

Amelia se levanta todos los días a las siete. Se pone la ropa. No tiene tiempo para lavarse la cabeza pero se peina. También se lava los dientes…

Juego

Beto se despierta, se levanta, se ducha, desayuna y sale para la escuela.

¿Qué más necesita hacer esta mañana?

GRAMÁTICA

Irregular Affirmative tú Commands

♻ **¿RECUERDAS?** *p. 97* You've already learned how to give instructions to someone by using the **affirmative tú commands** of regular verbs.

caminar	¡Camina!
comer	¡Come!
abrir	¡Abre!

Some verbs have **irregular affirmative tú commands**. Here are the irregular affirmative **tú commands** of some verbs you know.

Infinitive	Affirmative tú Command
decir	di
hacer	haz
ir	ve
poner	pon
salir	sal
ser	sé
tener	ten
venir	ven

Luis's father says:

—Primero **haz** los quehaceres.
*First **do** the chores.*

Remember that when you use a **pronoun** with an **affirmative command**, the **pronoun attaches** to the **command**.

Carmen says:

—¡Pon**te** otra camisa!
***Put on** (yourself) another shirt!*

Teaching Middle School Students

Native Speakers Ask native speakers if they address their parents, or other relatives, as **tú** or **usted**. How do they perceive the difference? Ask them to share their impressions with the class.

Multiple Intelligences
Kinesthetic Ask students to work in pairs to compose several sentences using the irregular affirmative **tú** commands. Have them take turns giving and responding to these commands.

Visual Ask students to create posters illustrating commands that give good advice (**¡Haz la tarea!**, etc.).

ACTIVIDAD 8
Objective: Transitional practice
Reflexive verbs

Answers
Answers will vary but should contain some of the following verb forms.
1. te lavas / me lavo
2. te bañas, te lavas / me baño, me lavo
3. te afeitas, te maquillas, te peinas / me afeito, me maquillo, me peino
4. te lavas, te pones / me lavo, me pongo
5. te pones, te peinas / me pongo, me peino

ACTIVIDAD 9
Objective: Open-ended practice
Reflexive verbs/vocabulary

Answers will vary.

Juego
Answer: Necesita peinarse.

Quick Start Review
♻ **Reflexive verbs**
Use OHT 148 or write on the board: Complete each sentence with the appropriate form of a reflexive verb.
1. Mi amigo ___ la cabeza con el champú.
2. Tú ___ con un despertador, ¿no?
3. A mí me gusta ___ con una toalla grande.
4. Necesitamos un cepillo de dientes para ___ los dientes.
5. Yo ___ todos los días a las diez de la noche.

Answers *See p. 165D.*

Teaching Suggestions
Teaching Irregular Affirmative tú Commands
Point out to students that they can now use all regular and irregular verbs in their affirmative **tú** command forms. In other words, they can tell a friend or a family member what to do.

Block Schedule
FunBreak Ask students to write and illustrate their own **Juegos** with a flavor similar to the one on this page.

Teaching Resource Options

Print

Más práctica Workbook PE, p. 30
Para hispanohablantes Workbook PE, p. 28
Block Scheduling Copymasters
Unit 5 Resource Book
  Más práctica Workbook TE, p. 6
  Para hispanohablantes Workbook TE, p. 12
  Information Gap Activities, p. 17

Technology

Intrigas y aventuras CD-ROM, Disc 1

Objective: Controlled practice
Informal commands

Answers
1. Di la verdad.
2. Haz la tarea.
3. Pon la mesa.
4. Sé amable.
5. Ven a casa después de las clases.
6. Ve a la tienda.
7. Sal a jugar.
8. Ten paciencia.

🔔 Quick Wrap-up
Give commands such as the following and have students mime a response: **Haz un taco. Pon tu lápiz en el escritorio de Marisa. Ve al escritorio de Raúl y dale tu libro. Prepara espaguetis, cómelos, lava los platos…**

Teaching Suggestions
Presenting Vocabulary
Personalize the chores by asking students who does what chores at home. For example: **En tu casa, ¿quién quita la mesa? ¿Haces tu cama? ¿La haces todos los días?**

10 Gramática

¡Ay, los hermanos mayores!

Hablar/Escribir Luis le dice a Carmen qué hacer. ¿Qué le dice?
(Hint: What does Luis tell Carmen to do?)

modelo

poner la tarea en la mochila
Pon la tarea en la mochila.

1. decir la verdad
2. hacer la tarea
3. poner la mesa
4. ser amable
5. venir a casa después de las clases
6. ir a la tienda
7. salir a jugar
8. tener paciencia

■ **MÁS PRÁCTICA** *cuaderno* p. 30

■ **PARA HISPANOHABLANTES** *cuaderno* p. 28

Vocabulario

Para hablar de los quehaceres

hacer la cama

lavar los platos

limpiar el cuarto

quitar la mesa

estar limpio(a)

estar sucio(a)

En tu familia, ¿quién hace estos quehaceres?

---

178 ciento setenta y ocho
Unidad 5

Middle School Classroom Community

TPR Ask students to place a book, a pencil, and a piece of paper on their desks. Then give commands related to these items (**Pon tu libro en la cabeza**). Have students respond appropriately.

Storytelling Ask students to sit in a circle to revise the story of Cinderella (**La Cenicienta**) in Spanish. Each must pretend to be a family member and give a different command to Cinderella.

¿Ayudan en casa?

Hablar Trabaja con otro(a) estudiante. Hablen sobre los quehaceres de la casa que tienen que hacer. *(Hint: Take turns asking and answering questions about chores you have to do.)*

modelo

Estudiante A: ¿Lavo **la ropa sucia**?

Estudiante B: Sí, lávala.

1.

2.

3.

4.

5. ¿?

¡Feliz cumpleaños!

Hablar/Escribir Imagínate que hoy es tu cumpleaños y puedes decirles a tus familiares y amigos qué deben hacer. *(Hint: It's your birthday and you can tell your family and friends what to do.)*

modelo

quitar la mesa

Hermanita, quita la mesa, por favor.

1. hacer mi cama
2. preparar mi desayuno
3. poner los libros en mi mochila
4. ir al mercado
5. tener paciencia
6. limpiar mi cuarto
7. ser bueno(a)
8. ¿?

MÁS COMUNICACIÓN p. R4

Conexiones

Los estudios sociales The people of Cataluña speak both **español** and **catalán**. In other parts of Spain, people speak **vascuence** (Basque) and **gallego** (Galician) in addition to Spanish.

PARA HACER:
Write as many sentences as you can to tell about your friends (real or imaginary) who speak two languages. Use the languages listed at the right.

Idiomas (Languages)

alemán	francés	polaco
árabe	griego	portugués
camboyano	hindi	ruso
cantonés	italiano	tagalo
coreano	japonés	vietnamita
español	mandarín	

ciento setenta y nueve
Etapa 1
179

Teaching Middle School Students

Native Speakers Ask native speakers to discuss how household chores are distributed among family members.

Multiple Intelligences

Intrapersonal Ask students to make a list of chores they have to do today.

Kinesthetic Ask students to work in pairs to list situations in which they are usually corrected (for example, some waste paper on the floor, some books spilling out of a knapsack). Students must then create commands to correct the situation and act them out.

UNIDAD 5 Etapa 1
Vocabulary/Grammar

Objective: Transitional practice
Informal commands/direct object pronouns/vocabulary

Answers
1. ¿Hago la cama? Sí, hazla.
2. ¿Limpio el cuarto? Sí, límpialo.
3. ¿Quito la mesa? Sí, quítala.
4. ¿Lavo los platos? Sí, lávalos.
5. *Answers will vary.*

Objective: Open-ended practice
Informal commands

Answers
Answers will vary but should include the following commands.
1. Haz mi cama.
2. Prepara mi desayuno.
3. Pon los libros en mi mochila.
4. Ve al mercado.
5. Ten paciencia.
6. Limpia mi cuarto.
7. Sé bueno(a).
8. *Answers will vary.*

Para hacer
Answers will vary.

Project
Have students keep a household helper diary for a week. They should include every chore they did and note whether the chore was something they're always expected to do, or one they did on their own.

Block Schedule
Variety First have students write a series of 3 affirmative **tú** commands, using regular and irregular verbs. The commands should follow one theme (getting ready in the morning, doing chores, etc.). Then have students work in pairs and take turns giving each other the orders and acting them out. Then have the pairs give their commands to another pair of students. (For additional activities, see **Block Scheduling Copymasters.**)

Teaching Resource Options

Print

Más práctica Workbook PE, p. 31
Para hispanohablantes Workbook PE, p. 29
Block Scheduling Copymasters
Unit 5 Resource Book
  Más práctica Workbook TE, p. 7
  Para hispanohablantes Workbook TE, p. 13

Audiovisual
OHT 149 (Quick Start)

Technology
Intrigas y aventuras CD-ROM, Disc 1

Quick Start Review

♻ **Affirmative tú commands**

Use OHT 149 or write on the board:
Write **tú** command sentences using the following elements:

1. hacer / tu tarea
2. poner / el libro en tu escritorio
3. decir / la verdad a tu madre
4. ponerse / otra camisa
5. venir / aquí

Answers See p. 165D.

Teaching Suggestions
Teaching Negative tú Commands

Note that when verbs ending in **-car**, **-gar**, and **-zar** are used in negative **tú** commands, they require spelling changes: **practiques, juegues, cruces.** Exercises avoid the production of these forms. If students attempt to use verbs with these endings in open discussion, they should be made aware of this.

 Objective: Controlled practice Negative **tú** commands

Answers
1. No comas muchos dulces.
2. No mires mis videos.
3. No bebas tantos refrescos.
4. No veas la televisión toda la noche.
5. No vayas al parque por la noche.
6. No hables tanto por teléfono.
7. No uses mi computadora.
8. No cantes en la biblioteca.
9. No escribas en un libro.
10. No escuches la radio en clase.
11. No corras con el perro.
12. No abras mi libro.

GRAMÁTICA

Negative tú Commands

When you tell someone what **not** to do, use a **negative command**. **Negative tú commands** are formed by taking the **yo** form of the present tense, dropping the **-o**, and adding the appropriate ending.

hablo̶ ⟵ **-es** for **-ar** verbs

vuelvo̶ ⟵ **-as** for **-er** and **-ir** verbs

Infinitive	Yo Form	Negative tú Command
hablar	hablo	¡No hables!
volver	vuelvo	¡No vuelvas!
venir	vengo	¡No vengas!

Carmen says:
—¡Y **no uses** mi secador de pelo!
And **don't use** my hair dryer!

A few verbs have **irregular negative tú commands**. Notice that none of the **yo** forms of these verbs end in **-o**.

Infinitive (yo form)	Negative tú Command
dar (doy)	**No le des** mi dirección a nadie. *Don't give my address to anyone.*
estar (estoy)	**No estés** triste. *Don't be sad.*
ir (voy)	**No vayas** a la tienda. *Don't go to the store.*
ser (soy)	**No seas** mala. *Don't be bad.*

180   ciento ochenta
Unidad 5

¡No, no, no!

Hablar/Escribir A veces Carmen hace cosas que no debe hacer. Luis siempre le dice que no.
(Hint: What does Luis tell Carmen not to do?)

modelo

patinar en la casa
Carmen, no **patines en la casa**.

1. comer muchos dulces
2. mirar mis videos
3. beber tantos refrescos
4. ver la televisión toda la noche
5. ir al parque por la noche
6. hablar tanto por teléfono
7. usar mi computadora
8. cantar en la biblioteca
9. escribir en un libro
10. escuchar la radio en clase
11. correr con el perro
12. abrir mi libro

▪ **MÁS PRÁCTICA** *cuaderno* p. 31

▪ **PARA HISPANOHABLANTES** *cuaderno* p. 29

Middle School Classroom Community

Cooperative Learning Ask students to work together in small groups to make a poster of golden rules for your classroom. Students will brainstorm together. Student 1 will record. Student 2 will search the dictionary. Student 3 will plan what materials to use and obtain them. Student 4 will illustrate the commands.

Portfolio Ask students to make a list of things not to do in certain situations (in Spanish class, at the dinner table, etc.).

Rubric

Criteria	Scale	
Vocabulary use/spelling	1 2 3 4 5	A = 17–20 pts.
Correct sentence structure/grammar	1 2 3 4 5	B = 13–16 pts.
Logical organization	1 2 3 4 5	C = 9–12 pts.
Creativity	1 2 3 4 5	D = 5–8 pts.
		F = < 5 pts.

ACTIVIDAD 14

Instrucciones

Hablar/Escribir Imagínate que estás cuidando a un niño de seis años. ¿Qué instrucciones le das? *(Hint: What do you tell a six-year-old to do?)*

modelo

nadar solo

*No **nades solo**. **Nada** con un amigo.*

1. salir de la casa solo
2. correr en la casa
3. decir malas palabras
4. dormir en el sofá
5. ser malo
6. estar triste
7. comer mucho
8. caminar en la calle
9. llevar ropa sucia
10. lavar el gato

N O T A *CULTURAL*

Some of the most interesting sights on **Las Ramblas,** Barcelona's shopping street, are the "living statues": these costumed people can remain completely still for hours.

ACTIVIDAD 15

¿Que haces?

Hablar Quieres hacer algunas actividades, pero tu amigo(a) tiene otras ideas. ¿Qué dicen? *(Hint: You want to do several activities, but your friend has other plans. What do you say?)*

modelo

leer una novela

Estudiante A: *¿Leo una novela?*

Estudiante B: *No, no **leas una novela**. Limpia el cuarto, por favor.*

preparar la cena

quitar la mesa

limpiar el cuarto

hacer la cama

lavar los platos

lavarse los dientes

1. comer un dulce
2. patinar
3. descansar

4. visitar a un amigo
5. pasear por el parque
6. ir al cine

ACTIVIDAD 16

Bienvenido a la escuela

Hablar/Escribir Estás en una nueva escuela. Pregúntales a varios estudiantes qué hay que hacer para ser un buen estudiante. Cada estudiante dice un mínimo de dos instrucciones. ¿Cuáles son las cinco instrucciones más comunes? *(Hint: What instructions do other students give you in order to do well in a new school? Survey classmates and note the five most common instructions given.)*

modelo

Estudiante A: *¿Qué hago para ser buen estudiante en esta escuela?*

Estudiante B: *Haz la tarea todos los días. No llegues tarde a clase.*

Persona	Instrucciones afirmativas	Instrucciones negativas
Estudiante B	Haz la tarea todos los días.	No llegues tarde a clase.

ciento ochenta y uno
Etapa 1

181

Teaching Middle School Students

Multiple Intelligences

Visual Have students create a "product" and make their owns ads using affirmative or negative **tú** commands.

Verbal Ask students to work with a partner to do a follow-up to **Actividad 14,** telling each other one thing to do and one thing not to do in certain situations.

Naturalist Ask students to make posters with several commands about what to do/not do to protect the environment. Encourage them to use the dictionary if they need to.

14 Objective: Transitional practice
Tú commands

Answers

Answers will vary.
1. No salgas de la casa solo. Sal con amigos.
2. No corras en la casa. Corre en el parque.
3. No digas malas palabras. Di palabras amables.
4. No duermas en el sofá. Duerme en tu cama.
5. No seas malo. Sé bueno.
6. No estés triste. Está feliz.
7. No comas mucho. Come poco.
8. No camines en la calle. Camina en la plaza.
9. No lleves ropa sucia. Lleva ropa limpia.
10. No laves el gato. Lava el carro.

15 Objective: Transitional practice
Tú commands

Answers

Answers will vary but must contain the following.
1. ¿Como un dulce? No, no comas…
2. ¿Patino? No, no patines…
3. ¿Descanso? No, no descanses…
4. ¿Visito a un amigo? No, no visites…
5. ¿Paseo por el parque? No, no pasees…
6. ¿Voy al cine? No, no vayas…

Alternatives must contain one of the following:
prepara la cena, quita la mesa, limpia el cuarto, haz la cama, lava los platos, lávate los dientes.

16 Objective: Open-ended practice
Tú commands

*Answers will vary but should include appropriate affirmative and negative **tú** commands.*

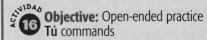

Block Schedule

Change of Pace Have groups of 3 present "good guy/bad guy" skits. Two students stand on either side of the third student, who is trying to make a decision (**¿Hago la tarea?**). The "good guy" side tells him/her a good thing to do (**Haz tu tarea**). The "bad guy" side tells him/her the opposite (**No hagas tu tarea. Ve al parque**). (For additional activities, see **Block Scheduling Copymasters**.)

Teaching Resource Options

Print

Más práctica Workbook PE, p. 32
Para hispanohablantes Workbook PE, p. 30
Block Scheduling Copymasters
Unit 5 Resource Book
  Más práctica Workbook TE, p. 8
  Para hispanohablantes Workbook TE, p. 14
  Information Gap Activities, pp. 18–19
  Audioscript, p. 30
  Audioscript *Para hispanohablantes*, p. 30

Audiovisual

OHT 149 (Quick Start)
Audio Program Cassettes 13A, 13B / CD 13
Audio *Para hispanohablantes* Cassette 13A / CD 13

Technology

Intrigas y aventuras CD-ROM, Disc 1

🔔 Quick Start Review

♻ Negative **tú** commands

Use OHT 149 or write on the board:
Change the following to negative commands:

1. Escribe tu nombre aquí.
2. Haz la cena esta noche.
3. Pon el jabón al lado de la toalla.
4. Compra el regalo hoy.
5. Da los libros al profesor.

Answers *See p. 165D.*

Objective: Controlled practice
Tú commands

♻ Direct object pronouns

Answers
1. Sí, léelo.
2. Sí, cómelos.
3. No, no lo compartas conmigo.
4. No, no lo pidas.
5. Sí, págala.
6. No, no la dejes.
7. *Answers will vary.*

GRAMÁTICA

Using Correct Pronoun Placement with Commands

♻ **¿RECUERDAS?** *pp. 97, 177* Remember that when you use an **object pronoun** with an **affirmative command**, you **attach** the pronoun to the end of the command.

Cruza el parque. ➡ ¡Crúza**lo**!
Cross the park. ➡ *Cross it!*

Remember, you may need to add an **accent** when you attach a pronoun.

▶ **Object pronouns** precede negative commands, just as with other conjugated verbs.

Carmen says: —¡No **lo** uses!
Don't use it (the hair dryer)!

ACTIVIDAD 17 Gramática

♻ ¿Qué hacer?

Escribir Tu amigo(a) no puede decidir qué hacer en el restaurante. Contesta sus preguntas. *(Hint: Answer your friend's questions.)*

modelos

¿Tomo mi limonada ahora? (sí)
Sí, **tómala** ahora.

¿Pido enchiladas? (no)
No, no **las pidas**. ¡Estamos en España ahora!

1. ¿Leo el menú? (sí)
2. ¿Como todos los frijoles? (sí)
3. ¿Comparto el pollo contigo? (no)
4. ¿Pido un postre? (no)
5. ¿Pago la cuenta? (sí)
6. ¿Dejo la propina? (no)
7. ¿?

■ **MÁS PRÁCTICA** *cuaderno* p. 32
■ **PARA HISPANOHABLANTES** *cuaderno* p. 30

También se dice

In Spain, people use certain expressions for daily routine. You may hear other expressions in other countries.

to wash one's hair
• lavarse la cabeza: Spain
• lavarse el pelo: many countries
• lavarse el cabello: many countries

---

182 ciento ochenta y dos
Unidad 5

Middle School Classroom Community

Storytelling Ask students to sit in a circle. Tell them they are each going to add one command to a class recipe for happiness. Ask a recorder to keep track of the recipe so that a class poster can be made.

Group Activity Ask a Spanish-speaking restaurant server to speak to the class about how to behave in a restaurant. Allow plenty of time for students to ask questions and to model his or her suggestions.

ACTIVIDAD 18

¡Hazlo más tarde!

Hablar Tu amigo(a) quiere salir, pero tú tienes muchos quehaceres. ¿Qué te dice? *(Hint: Your friend wants to go out, but you have a lot to do. What does your friend tell you?)*

modelo

Estudiante A: *Tengo que **lavar los platos**.*

Estudiante B: *No **los laves** ahora. **Lávalos** más tarde.*

1.

2.

3.

4.

5.

6.

NOTA CULTURAL

Rock con raíces, or Root-Rock, has become popular with urban youth in Spain. This Spanish version of rock blends the traditional elements of **flamenco,** such as the rhythm, castanets, and hand claps, with electric guitars and synthesizers.

ciento ochenta y tres
Etapa 1 183

Quick Wrap-up

Write on the chalkboard questions about eating establishments in your community. Ask students to give their opinions to a classmate: **¿Comer la pizza de la cafetería de la escuela?** → **Sí, cómela. Es muy buena. No, no la comas. Es muy mala.**

ACTIVIDAD 18 Objective: Controlled practice Tú commands/direct object pronouns/vocabulary

Answers
1. Tengo que hacer la cama.
   No la hagas ahora. Hazla más tarde.
2. Tengo que preparar la comida.
   No la prepares ahora. Prepárala más tarde.
3. Tengo que poner la mesa.
   No la pongas ahora. Ponla más tarde.
4. Tengo que limpiar el cuarto.
   No lo limpies ahora. Límpialo más tarde.
5. Tengo que cuidar las plantas.
   No las cuides ahora. Cuídalas más tarde.
6. Tengo que hacer la tarea.
   No la hagas ahora. Hazla más tarde.

Critical Thinking

Have students think about the information in the **Gramática** box. Ask them to list at least 5 verbs they would use in commands and decide whether they would need to add an accent when attaching the pronoun to an affirmative command. Ask them to explain why or why not in each case.

Block Schedule

Variety Play recordings of flamenco music and ask students to write descriptions of how they feel while listening to the music.

Teaching Middle School Students

Extra Help Have students open to the **Diálogo,** pp. 170–171. Have them list all the commands they find. Then work with them to write the infinitive form of each verb.

Native Speakers Ask students to tell whether Spanish is the only official language in their countries of origin. Ask them to name other official and unofficial languages.

Multiple Intelligences

Kinesthetic Ask students to work with a partner. Each will list several affirmative and negative **tú** commands and then tell the other to perform the activity.

Interpersonal Ask students to work with a partner making a list of activities they have to do but want the other to do for them.

Teaching Resource Options

Print

Block Scheduling Copymasters
Unit 5 Resource Book
Más práctica Workbook TE, p. 8
Para hispanohablantes Workbook
  TE, p. 14
Information Gap Activities, pp. 18–19
Audioscript, p. 30
Audioscript *Para hispanohablantes*,
  p. 30

Audiovisual

Audio Program Cassettes 13A, 13B /
  CD 13
Audio *Para hispanohablantes*
  Cassette 13A / CD 13

Technology

Intrigas y aventuras CD-ROM, Disc 1

 Objective: Transitional practice
19 Tú commands

Answers

*Answers will vary but should contain the
following verb forms.*
• voy / ve / no vayas / regateo / regatea /
  no regatees
• veo / ve / no veas / hago / haz / no hagas
• me acuesto / no te acuestes / acuéstate /
  estudio / estudia / no estudies

 Objective: Transitional practice
20 Listening comprehension/reflexive
verbs/vocabulary

Answers (See script, p. 165D.)
1. falso; Se despierta entre las ocho y las ocho
   y media.
2. cierto
3. cierto
4. falso; Se baña por la noche.
5. cierto

Para hacer

Answers will vary.

¡Tantas decisiones!

Hablar Tienes varios planes pero también tienes
obligaciones. Escoge dos situaciones de la lista y
pregúntales a dos estudiantes qué hacer. *(Hint:
Choose two situations and ask what to do.)*

modelo

*Quieres cenar en un restaurante pero tienes que preparar
la cena para la familia.*

Estudiante A: *¿Ceno en un restaurante o preparo la cena?*

Estudiante B: *No cenes en un restaurante. Prepara la cena.*

Estudiante C: *Cena en un restaurante pero prepara la cena
antes de salir.*

• Quieres ir a una tienda pero puedes regatear
  en el mercado.

• Quieres ver la televisión pero tienes tarea.

• Quieres acostarte pero tienes que estudiar
  para un examen.

La rutina de Álvaro

Escuchar Lee las oraciones. Luego, escucha el
diálogo y di si las oraciones son ciertas o falsas.
Corrige las falsas. *(Hint: Say what is true or false. Correct the
false statements.)*

1. Álvaro se despierta a las nueve los sábados.
2. Álvaro se queda en la cama un rato después
   de despertarse.
3. Álvaro se lava la cara y los dientes después
   de levantarse.
4. Álvaro no se baña los sábados.
5. Álvaro se afeita y se lava la cabeza por
   la noche.

Conexiones

El arte Spain has produced many
famous artists throughout the centuries.
Perhaps the most famous of all is
Pablo Picasso (1881–1973),
who moved to Barcelona in 1895
with his family. Picasso revolutionized
the way we look at art and had
a profound influence on the artists of
the twentieth century who followed
him. He was a master of painting,
sculpture, and ceramics.

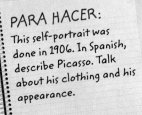

PARA HACER:
This self-portrait was
done in 1906. In Spanish,
describe Picasso. Talk
about his clothing and his
appearance.

Middle School Classroom Community

TPR Have the class stand. Name an object. Students
must decide whether they can sit on this object. When
you say ¡Siéntate!, they either sit or respond ¡No me
siento!

Group Activity Divide the class into 4 groups, and
give each group a season of the year. Each group
brainstorms things they should do during their season
and then writes appropriate commands.

ACTIVIDAD 21

La Farmacia VendeTodo

Escribir Tu amigo(a) y tú trabajan en una farmacia. Escriban un anuncio sobre algunos productos. Usen verbos reflexivos para describir los productos. Usen mandatos para decirles a los clientes qué comprar. ¡Ilustren su anuncio! *(Hint: With your partner, write an ad for a pharmacy describing various products. Tell the customers what to buy. Illustrate your ad!)*

modelo

¡Ve a la Farmacia VendeTodo! Tenemos muy buenos precios, especialmente para los peines y los champús. Cómpralos hoy. No vayas a una farmacia donde cuestan más…

■ **MÁS COMUNICACIÓN** p. R4

Farmacia VendeTodo

¿Te lavas los dientes cada mañana?

¡Usa nuestros cepillos de dientes!

¿Te peinas mucho?

¡Compra nuestros peines!

Tenemos de todo a los mejores precios.

Pronunciación 🎧

Trabalenguas

Pronunciación de la *s*, la *z* y la *c* In the Spanish spoken in Latin America and southern Spain, the **s** and **z** always sound like the *s* in the English word *miss*. When **c** is followed by the vowel **i** or **e**, it has the same sound. In central and northern Spain, the **z** and **c** are not pronounced like an *s*, but like the *th* sound in the English word *thin*, when they are followed by **i** or **e**. So if you go to Barcelona, you may want to try the *th* sound! Practice the sounds by repeating the following words. Then try the tongue twister. From the picture, can you guess what it means?

cabeza
cepillo
lápiz
pasta de dientes
secador

¡El sapo del centro sirve zumo sabroso!

Teaching Middle School Students

Native Speakers Give native speakers an opportunity to read the audio script to **Actividad 20** orally for the class.

Multiple Intelligences

Musical/Rhythmic Have students make up their own jingle for the pharmacy ad in **Actividad 21**.

Kinesthetic Ask students to draw a hidden item, such as a comb or toothbrush, from a bag and then make up a sentence about it. (**Me peino todos los días.**)

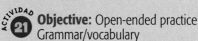
ACTIVIDAD 21 **Objective:** Open-ended practice Grammar/vocabulary

Answers will vary.

Language Note
Note that the plural of **champú** can be **champús** or **champúes**.

🔔 Quick Wrap-up
Have students look back at the **Etapa** opener, pp. 166–167 and give 3 commands Mercedes might give to Luis and 3 commands Luis might give to Mercedes.

Dictation
After students have read the **trabalenguas** in the **Pronunciación,** have them close their books. Dictate the **trabalenguas** in two segments while students write it.

■ Block Schedule
Variety Have students write their own **trabalenguas**. They should refer to the **Repaso de vocabulario** at the end of each **Etapa** for help in remembering vocabulary. Have students present their **trabalenguas** and see how well the class does at pronouncing them. (For additional activities, see **Block Scheduling Copymasters**.)

Teaching Resource Options

Print 📖

Unit 5 Resource Book
  Audioscript, p. 31
  Audioscript *Para hispanohablantes*,
  p. 31

Audiovisual

Audio Program Cassette 13A / CD 13
Audio *Para hispanohablantes*
  Cassette 13A / CD 13
OHT 149 (Quick Start)
Canciones Cassette / CD

🔔 Quick Start Review

  ♻ Barcelona

Use OHT 149 or write on the board:
Imagine that you are on vacation in
Barcelona. Write 2 activities you could
do at each of the following locations:

1. un mercado
2. un parque
3. un restaurante
4. la playa

Answers
Answers will vary. Answers could include:
1. regatear, comprar regalos
2. pasear, sacar fotos
3. tomar un refresco, cenar
4. nadar, tomar el sol

Teaching Suggestions

• **Prereading** Have students look at
the illustrations, and then direct them
to the title of the reading. Can they
figure out the meaning of the cognate
rara (*rare → strange, unusual*)?

• **Strategy: Predict** Discuss what
clues students can find on the pages
to help them predict what the
Lectura is about. Have them fill out
the first part of their organizer.

• **Reading** Have students take turns
reading sentences in the **Lectura**,
trying for smooth transitions between
readers.

• **Post-reading** Have students fill in
the second part of their organizer.
Then discuss their results.

En voces
LECTURA

PARA LEER
STRATEGY: READING

Predict Look at the title and the
illustrations that go with this reading
selection. What do you think this piece
might be about? Write your ideas in
a grid like this. After you've completed
the reading, fill out the other side.

Prediction	What I Found Out
1.	1.
2.	2.
3.	3.

LA TOMATINA:
UNA RARA TRADICIÓN ESPAÑOLA

¿Qué haces cuando hay demasiados tomates en
el jardín[1]? A ver... puedes regalárselos a los vecinos.
Puedes hacer salsa para la pasta. Tal vez haces salsa
ranchera mexicana, ¿verdad?

Pues, en el pueblo español
de Buñol, con el exceso de
tomates la gente hace
la «Tomatina». Llega un
camión[2] lleno de tomates
maduros[3] que se depositan en el centro del pueblo.
¡Y todo el mundo se cubre[4] con ellos! Ocurre al
final de una fiesta que se celebra cada
año a fin de agosto. Durante una hora

---
[1] garden   [3] ripe
[2] truck   [4] is covered

186   ciento ochenta y seis
        Unidad 5

Middle School Classroom Community

Paired Activity Ask students to take turns making
up commands about things to do or not to do during
La Tomatina. Have them share their favorites with the
class.

Group Activity Ask students to create travel
advertisements for **La Tomatina**. These may be posters,
radio or television commercials, etc.

Portfolio Ask students to draw an image from this
reading and describe it.

Rubric

Criteria	Scale	
Creativity	1 2 3 4 5	A = 13–15 pts.
Logical organization	1 2 3 4 5	B = 10–12 pts.
Vocabulary use/spelling	1 2 3 4 5	C = 7–9 pts.
		D = 4–6 pts.
		F = < 4 pts.

hay una verdadera guerra[5] de tomates. Esta locura[6] empezó[7] en Buñol hace más de 50 años[8] entre unos jóvenes del pueblo. Pero ahora llega gente de todas partes—¡vienen más de 20.000 personas!

¿Cómo queda el pueblo después de todas estas festividades? Todo el mundo empieza a limpiar y el pueblo queda bonito y limpio como siempre. ¡Olé!

---

[5] war
[6] madness
[7] began
[8] *hace… años* more than 50 years ago

¿Comprendiste?

1. ¿Dónde se hace la Tomatina?
2. ¿Qué hace la gente del pueblo con los tomates?
3. ¿De dónde vienen los participantes?
4. ¿Cómo está el pueblo después de esta fiesta?

¿Qué piensas?

1. ¿Por qué piensas que esta fiesta se celebra en agosto?
2. ¿Qué piensas de esta fiesta? ¿Te gustaría participar o no? ¿Por qué?
3. ¿Por qué piensas que esta tradición empezó entre jóvenes?

ciento ochenta y siete
Etapa 1
187

Culture Highlights

● Valencia is best known for its celebration of its patron saint, San José, on March 19. The nearly week-long celebration is called **"Las Fallas"** and culminates in the middle of the city with the burning of huge satiric figures made of wood and other materials. Pictures of these would surely be of interest to students.

Community Connections

Does your community have a fair in which local produce is displayed and awarded? Students may wish to visit this fair and then look up the Spanish names of local produce.

Language Note

Students may recognize the cognate **madura** (*ripe*) via the Latin-related English word *mature.* Some Latin and English words containing *t* developed in Spanish with a *d*. Other Spanish words familiar to students that follow this linguistic pattern are **tienda** → *tent*; **mercado** → *market*; **emocionado** → *emotional*; **aprender** → *apprentice*; **calidad** → *quality*.

¿Comprendiste?

Answers
1. Se hace en Buñol.
2. Todo el mundo se cubre en ellos.
3. Vienen de todas partes.
4. Está limpio.

Block Schedule

FunBreak Ask students if they would enjoy participating in **La Tomatina**. Have them speculate on what other foods they would enjoy throwing, and have them look up the Spanish names.

Teaching Middle School Students

Extra Help Help students to summarize the reading by prompting them with questions. (**¿Hacen salsa con el exceso de tomates en Buñol? ¿Qué hacen? ¿Dónde ocurre esta tradición? ¿Es popular?**)

Native Speakers Ask students to report on an interesting celebration in their hometown.

Multiple Intelligences

Logical/Mathematical Ask students to hypothesize how many pounds of tomatoes might be used in this festival.

Naturalist Ask students to research the origins of the tomato and report back to the class.

UNIDAD 5 Etapa 1
Review

Teaching Resource Options

Print

Para hispanohablantes Workbook PE, pp. 31–32

Unit 5 Resource Book
Para hispanohablantes Workbook TE, pp. 15–16
Information Gap Activities, p. 20
Family Involvement, pp. 21–22
Multiple Choice Test Questions, pp. 170–178

Audiovisual

OHT 150 (Quick Start)
Audio Program Testing Cassette T2 / CD T2

Technology

Electronic Teacher Tools/Test Generator
Intrigas y aventuras CD-ROM, Disc 1

🔔 Quick Start Review

♻ Daily routine

Use OHT 150 or write on the board: Answer the following questions in complete sentences.

1. ¿A qué hora te levantas los lunes? ¿los sábados?
2. ¿Te despiertas con un despertador?
3. ¿Comes el desayuno antes o después de bañarte?
4. ¿Te secas el pelo con un secador de pelo?
5. ¿A qué hora te acuestas normalmente?

Answers
Answers will vary. Answers could include:
1. Los lunes me levanto a las seis. Los sábados me levanto a las nueve.
2. Sí, me despierto con un despertador.
3. Como el desayuno después de bañarme.
4. No, no me seco el pelo con un secador de pelo.
5. Normalmente me acuesto a las diez.

✓ Teaching Suggestions
What Have Students Learned?

Have students look at the "Now you can…" notes and give examples of each category. Have them spend extra time reviewing categories they feel they are weak in, by consulting the "To review" notes.

188 Review • UNIDAD 5 Etapa 1

ETAPA 1

Now you can…
• describe daily routine.

To review
• reflexive verbs, see p. 175.

En uso

REPASO Y MÁS COMUNICACIÓN

OBJECTIVES
• Describe daily routine
• Talk about grooming
• Tell others to do something
• Discuss daily chores

ACTIVIDAD 1 Nuestra rutina diaria

Un amigo de Luis describe la rutina diaria de su familia. ¿Qué dice? *(Hint: A friend of Luis describes his family's daily routine. What does he say?)*

modelo
Todos los días yo <u>me despierto</u> a las siete.

1. Mis padres _____ a las seis y media.
2. Yo _____ después de levantarme.

3. Papá _____ a las siete menos cuarto.
4. Mamá _____ antes de prepararnos el desayuno.

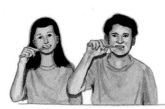 

5. Nosotros _____ los dientes después del desayuno.
6. Mi hermana _____ por la noche.

188 ciento ochenta y ocho
Unidad 5

Middle School Classroom Community

Paired Activity Have students pair up to do **Actividades 1–4**. They can split even- and odd-numbered exercises but must discuss and agree on all their answers.

Group Activity Have students work in groups of 4. Each group chooses a location from a list you write on the board and writes a list of 3 affirmative and 3 negative **tú** commands appropriate to their location. When the groups are finished, ask them to read their commands to the class and ask other groups to guess their location.

¡De viaje!

Luis y su familia van a hacer un viaje. ¿Qué necesitan llevar todos? *(Hint: Luis and his family are taking a trip. What do they need?)*

modelo

lavarse la cara (yo)

Yo *necesito jabón para* **lavarme la cara.**

1. maquillarse (mamá)
2. lavarse los dientes (tú)
3. despertarse (nosotros)
4. secarse (tú)
5. lavarse la cabeza (yo)
6. secarse el pelo (Carmen y yo)
7. peinarse (papá)
8. lavarse las manos (ustedes)

A casa de los abuelos

Vas a pasar el fin de semana con tus abuelos. ¿Qué te dice tu mamá? *(Hint: You're spending the weekend with your grandparents. What does your mother say?)*

modelo

ser simpático(a)	*levantarte muy tarde*
Sé simpático(a).	*No te levantes muy tarde.*

1. hacer los quehaceres
2. ser perezoso(a)
3. salir con tus abuelos y no con tus amigos
4. ir a fiestas con tus amigos
5. decir cosas interesantes
6. ser bueno(a)
7. ponerte otra camisa
8. llevar ropa sucia
9. ir al supermercado con tu abuela
10. tener paciencia con tus abuelos

¡A trabajar!

Un(a) amigo(a) quiere ayudarte con los quehaceres. Contesta sus preguntas. *(Hint: A friend wants to help you with your chores. Answer the friend's questions.)*

modelo

¿Compro los refrescos? (sí)	*¿Preparo la cena? (no)*
Sí, cómpralos.	*No, no la prepares.*

1. ¿Hago las camas? (sí)
2. ¿Lavo los platos sucios? (sí)
3. ¿Cuido a tu hermano? (no)
4. ¿Quito la mesa? (no)
5. ¿Mando las cartas? (sí)
6. ¿Contesto el teléfono? (no)

Now you can...
- talk about grooming.

To review
- reflexive verbs, see p. 175.

Now you can...
- tell others to do something.

To review
- irregular affirmative **tú** commands, see p. 177.
- negative **tú** commands, see p. 180.

Now you can...
- tell others to do something.
- discuss daily chores.

To review
- pronoun placement with commands, see p. 182.

 Answers

1. se levantan
2. me ducho
3. se afeita
4. se peina
5. nos lavamos
6. se baña

 Answers

1. Mamá necesita el espejo para maquillarse.
2. Tú necesitas el cepillo de dientes y la pasta de dientes para lavarte los dientes.
3. Nosotros necesitamos el despertador para despertarnos.
4. Tú necesitas la toalla para secarte.
5. Yo necesito el champú para lavarme la cabeza.
6. Carmen y yo necesitamos el secador de pelo para secarnos el pelo.
7. Papá necesita el peine para peinarse.
8. Ustedes necesitan jabón para lavarse las manos.

Answers

Answers will vary.
1. Haz los quehaceres.
2. No seas perezoso(a).
3. Sal con tus abuelos y no con tus amigos.
4. No vayas a fiestas con tus amigos.
5. Di cosas interesantes.
6. Sé bueno(a).
7. Ponte otra camisa.
8. No lleves ropa sucia.
9. Ve al supermercado con tu abuela.
10. Ten paciencia con tus abuelos.

 Answers

1. Sí, hazlas.
2. Sí, lávalos.
3. No, no lo cuides.
4. No, no la quites.
5. Sí, mándalas.
6. No, no lo contestes.

Teaching Middle School Students

Extra Help Suggest that students review the grooming and daily routine vocabulary on pp. 168–169 before working on **Actividad 2**.

Challenge Have students write their own questions for **Actividad 4** and share them with the class.

Multiple Intelligences

Interpersonal Ask students to work together to make a list of what a good friend should do when he or she comes to visit.

Block Schedule

Variety Use a toy clock or draw a clock on the board. Use a sun and moon to indicate day and night. Give students a time and elicit commands they might hear at that time of day. For example, for 8 A.M.: **Son las ocho de la mañana. ¡Ve a clase!**

Teaching Resource Options

Print

Unit 5 Resource Book
Cooperative Quizzes, pp. 33–34
Etapa Exam, Forms A and B,
pp. 35–44
Para hispanohablantes Etapa Exam,
pp. 45–49
Portfolio Assessment, pp. 50–51
Multiple Choice Test Questions,
pp. 170–178

Audiovisual

OHT 150 (Quick Start)
Audio Program Testing Cassette T2 /
CD T2

Technology

Electronic Teacher Tools/Test
Generator

www.mcdougallittell.com

ACTIVIDAD 5

Rubric: Speaking

Criteria	Scale	
Sentence structure	1 2 3 4 5	A = 17–20 pts.
Vocabulary use	1 2 3 4 5	B = 13–16 pts.
Originality	1 2 3 4 5	C = 9–12 pts.
Ease, fluency	1 2 3 4 5	D = 5–8 pts.
		F = < 5 pts.

ACTIVIDAD 6 *Answers will vary.*

ACTIVIDAD 7 **En tu propia voz**

Rubric: Writing

Criteria	Scale	
Vocabulary use	1 2 3 4 5	A = 13–15 pts.
Accuracy	1 2 3 4 5	B = 10–12 pts.
Creativity, appearance	1 2 3 4 5	C = 7–9 pts.
		D = 4–6 pts.
		F = < 4 pts.

Teaching Note: En tu propia voz

Suggest that students brainstorm a list of
activities and times in order to implement
the writing strategy "Organize information
chronologically and by category" in the
paragraph describing their typical Saturday.

ACTIVIDAD 5  **Todos los días...**

PARA CONVERSAR

STRATEGY: SPEAKING

Use gestures Physical actions, gestures, and
body language convey meaning too. Watch
your partner's actions. Do they convey
meaning? Observe others, especially native
speakers, and mimic body language to
enhance meaning when you speak.

Describe tu rutina diaria. Explica a qué hora
haces las actividades. Mientras hablas, otro(a)
estudiante tiene que hacer las acciones. Cambien
de papel. *(Hint: Describe your daily routine. Tell the time you do
things. A classmate will act out your activities. Change roles.)*

modelo

*Me levanto a las seis de la mañana. Después de
levantarme, siempre me ducho. A las seis y media...*

despertarse   bañarse   afeitarse

levantarse   lavarse la cabeza   maquillarse

ducharse   peinarse   ponerse la ropa

ACTIVIDAD 6 **¡Necesito consejos!**

Imagínate que tienes uno de los problemas de la
lista. ¿Qué consejo van a darte tus compañeros?
*(Hint: Imagine you have a problem from the list. What advice do
your friends give?)*

modelo

Tú: *Siempre tengo sueño en mis clases. Estoy cansado(a)
todo el día.*

Estudiante A: *Acuéstate más temprano.*

Estudiante B: *No te levantes hasta las siete.*

- Tu casa es un desastre y tus padres tienen una
  fiesta esta noche.
- Estás enfermo(a).
- Siempre tienes sueño en tus clases.
- Sacas malas notas en la clase de español.
- Comes mucho y no haces ejercicio.
- Estás muy sucio(a) después de trabajar
  mucho.
- ¿?

ACTIVIDAD 7 *En tu propia voz*

Escritura Describe un sábado típico en tu casa.
Incluye las rutinas y los quehaceres de los
miembros de tu familia. *(Hint: Describe a typical Saturday
at your house. Include the routines and chores of your family.)*

Conexiones

El arte Which kind of art do you prefer?
Modern? Traditional? Still life? Portraits? Who is your
favorite painter? Paint (or draw) a portrait
(**un retrato**) or a still life (**una naturaleza
muerta**) in the style you prefer. Then explain
to a partner what is in your painting. Compare
your painting (in terms of style, subject, and colors)
with your partner's. Complete a Venn diagram.

Mi cuadro   El cuadro
                 de Teresa

Middle School Classroom Community

Paired Activity Have students choose an activity
and act it out in pantomime. Partners will then write
out a complete sentence using that verb.

Storytelling Ask students to sit in a circle. One
student will create a situation in which someone needs
advice. Each student will then give that advice in either
an affirmative or negative **tú** command.

Portfolio Ask students to write some advice to
themselves on how to be a better Spanish student.

Rubric

Criteria	Scale	
Creativity	1 2 3 4 5	A = 13–15 pts.
Logical organization	1 2 3 4 5	B = 10–12 pts.
Vocabulary use/spelling	1 2 3 4 5	C = 7–9 pts.
		D = 4–6 pts.
		F = < 4 pts.

En resumen

REPASO DE VOCABULARIO

DESCRIBING DAILY ROUTINE

acostarse	to go to bed
afeitarse	to shave oneself
bañarse	to take a bath
despertarse	to wake up
dormirse	to fall asleep
ducharse	to take a shower
lavarse	to wash oneself
lavarse la cabeza	to wash one's hair
lavarse los dientes	to brush one's teeth
levantarse	to get up
maquillarse	to put on makeup
peinarse	to comb one's hair
ponerse la ropa	to get dressed
secarse	to dry oneself

TALKING ABOUT GROOMING

Items

el cepillo (de dientes)	brush (toothbrush)
el champú	shampoo
el espejo	mirror
el jabón	soap
la pasta de dientes	toothpaste
el peine	comb
el secador de pelo	hair dryer
la toalla	towel

Parts of the Body

la boca	mouth
el brazo	arm
la cabeza	head
la cara	face
el cuerpo	body
el diente	tooth
el estómago	stomach
la mano	hand
la nariz	nose
la oreja	ear
el pie	foot
la pierna	leg

DISCUSSING DAILY CHORES

hacer la cama	to make the bed
lavar los platos	to wash the dishes
limpiar el cuarto	to clean the room
limpio(a)	clean
los quehaceres	chores
quitar la mesa	to clear the table
sucio(a)	dirty

OTHER WORDS AND PHRASES

la cama	bed
el despertador	alarm clock
duro(a)	hard, tough
irse	to leave, to go away
la manta	blanket
ponerse	to put on (clothes)

Juego

Ya son las siete. ¿Qué necesitan estos chicos para prepararse y llegar a tiempo a la escuela?

ciento noventa y uno
Etapa 1

191

…

Critical Thinking

Ask students to discuss the reasons behind their art preferences. Did they go to museums when they were young? Do personal color preferences play a role?

Community Connections

Have students look in the arts/cultural section of major area newspapers. Can they find any exhibits of Spanish-speaking artists? They might also look on the Internet.

Interdisciplinary Connection

Art Work with the Art department to help students compile a list of well-known Spanish-speaking artists. Have each student choose one artist to research and present.

Quick Start Review

♻ **Etapa** vocabulary

Use OHT 150 or write on the board: Use reflexive verbs to write 5 things you do in the morning before school.

Answers See p. 165D.

Teaching Suggestions
Vocabulary Review

First, name items associated with different parts of the body and have students identify what part (**el champú = la cabeza**). Then give commands and have students identify the parts of the body associated with them (**Ponte los zapatos. = los pies**).

Juego

Answers: un despertador, un secador de pelo, un peine, un espejo

Block Schedule

Retention Without looking back at the **Diálogo**, first have students write a summary of Luis's day. Then tell them to open their books to pp. 170–171 to see how accurate they were. They should correct any errors. Then have students write a paragraph about what might happen after scene 10.

Teaching Middle School Students

Challenge Ask students to write sentences using as many vocabulary words in one sentence as they can within a time limit.

Multiple Intelligences

Visual Show portraits by the Spanish artists Pablo Picasso and Joan Miró and, as a visual challenge, have students try to locate and name the different body parts.

pages 192–217

Planning Guide CLASSROOM MANAGEMENT

OBJECTIVES

Communication
- Saying what people are doing *pp. 194–195, 212–213*
- Persuading others *pp. 196–197*
- Describing a house *pp. 194–195*
- Negotiating responsibilities *pp. 196–197*

Grammar
- Pronouns with the present progressive *pp. 202–205*
- The verb **deber** *pp. 206–208*
- Adverbs that end in **-mente** *pp. 209–210*

Pronunciation
- Pronunciation of **c, p, t** *p. 211*
- Dictation *TE p. 211*

Culture
- Regional vocabulary *pp. 199, 210*
- Floors of buildings *p. 201*
- Spanish **paella** *p. 204*
- **Tapas** *pp. 212–213*

♻ Recycling
- Daily chores *p. 200*
- Reflexive verbs *p. 204*
- Irregular affirmative **tú** commands *p. 207*
- Interrogative words *p. 211*

STRATEGIES

Listening Strategies
- Note and compare *p. 196*

Speaking Strategies
- Negotiate *p. 201*
- Detect misunderstandings *p. 216*

Reading Strategies
- Scan for crucial details *TE p. 212*

Writing Strategies
- Use different kinds of descriptive words *TE p. 212*

Connecting Cultures Strategies
- Recognize variations in regional vocabulary *pp. 199, 210*
- Learn about **paella** in Spain *p. 204*
- Predict reactions about restaurants *p. 212*
- Connect and compare what you know about eating experiences in your community to help you learn about eating experiences in a new community *pp. 212–213*

PROGRAM RESOURCES

 Print
- *Más práctica* Workbook PE *pp. 33–40*
- Block Scheduling Copymasters *pp. 113–120*
- Unit 5 Resource Book
  Más práctica Workbook TE *pp. 52–59*
  Information Gap Activities *pp. 68–71*

- Family Involvement *pp. 72–73*
- Video Activities *pp. 74–76*
- Videoscript *pp. 77–79*
- Audioscript *pp. 80–83*
- Assessment Program, Unit 5 Etapa 2 *pp. 84–102, 170–178*
- Answer Keys *pp. 179–200*

 Audiovisual
- Audio Program Cassettes 14A, 14B / CD 14
- *Canciones* Cassette / CD
- Video Program Videotape 5 / Videodisc 3A
- Overhead Transparencies M1–M5; 139; 151–160

 Technology
- Electronic Teacher Tools/Test Generator
- *Intrigas y aventuras* CD-ROM, Disc 1
- www.mcdougallittell.com

 Assessment Program Options
- **Cooperative Quizzes** (Unit 5 Resource Book)
- **Etapa Exam** Forms A and B (Unit 5 Resource Book)
- *Para hispanohablantes* **Etapa Exam** (Unit 5 Resource Book)
- **Portfolio Assessment** (Unit 5 Resource Book)
- **Multiple Choice Test Questions** (Unit 5 Resource Book)
- **Audio Program** Testing Cassette T2 / CD T2
- **Electronic Teacher Tools/Test Generator**

Native Speakers
- *Para hispanohablantes* Workbook PE, *pp. 33–40*
- *Para hispanohablantes* Workbook TE (Unit 5 Resource Book)
- *Para hispanohablantes* Etapa Exam (Unit 5 Resource Book)
- Audio *Para hispanohablantes* Cassettes 14A, 14B, T2 / CD 14, T2
- Audioscript *Para hispanohablantes* (Unit 5 Resource Book)

Student Text
Listening Activity Scripts

 Videoscript: Diálogo *pages 196–197*

• Videotape 5 • Videodisc 3A

Search Chapter 5, Play to 6
U5E2 • En vivo (Dialog)

• Use the videoscript with **Actividades 1, 2** *pages 198–199*

Luis: Carmen, Mercedes, ¿me ayudáis con los quehaceres?

Carmen: ¿Por qué te debo ayudar?

Luis: A ver. ¿Porque eres una hermana muy maja?
Porque si limpias la sala, te llevo al cine mañana.

Carmen: ¿Eso es todo?

Luis: Te doy un regalo.

Carmen: ¿Qué me vas a dar? ¡Dámelo ahora!

Luis: No, no, después. Primero quita el polvo de la mesa.

Carmen: Ya, ya, estoy quitándolo.

Luis: Mercedes, ¿todavía estás sacando fotos?

Mercedes: Sí, estoy sacándolas para algo muy importante.

Luis: ¿No ves que estoy barriendo el suelo?

Mercedes: Claro, veo que estás barriéndolo. Pero necesito las fotos.

Luis: En vez de sacar fotos, debes ayudarme. Si no me ayudas, vamos a llegar tarde a casa de Álvaro. ¡Me estás volviendo loco con esa cámara!

Mercedes: Está bien, Luis. Ahora te estoy ayudando.

Luis: Carmen, ¿qué estás haciendo? ¿Por qué no estás pasando la aspiradora?

Carmen: Sí, sí, mira, estoy pasándola.

Luis: Pero, Carmen, debes pasarla cuidadosamente. Mira, hazlo como lo estoy haciendo yo, lentamente.

Carmen: Ay, pero Luis, quiero terminar rápidamente.

Luis: Lentamente.
Todavía hay que lavar los platos y sacar la basura.

Mercedes: Tú debes sacar la basura. Yo ayudo a Carmen a lavar los platos. ¿Está bien, Carmen?

Carmen: ¡Sí, perfecto!

Luis: Bueno. Y después vamos a la tienda.
Pero, ¿qué hacéis? ¿Y los platos?

Carmen: Estamos lavándolos, ¿no ves?

11 ¡Qué inteligente! *page 204*

Álvaro: ¡Hola! Ana. ¿Quieres ir al cine esta tarde?

Ana: Gracias, Álvaro, pero no puedo. Estoy ayudando a mi mamá.

Álvaro: ¿Qué están haciendo?

Ana: Estamos limpiando la casa.

Álvaro: ¡Ay! ¡Qué trabajo! ¿Están ayudándote tus hermanos?

Ana: ¡Claro que están ayudándome!

Álvaro: ¿Qué están haciendo?

Ana: Pues, Felipe y Paco están barriendo el suelo.

Álvaro: ¿Y tus hermanas?

Ana: Marta está quitando el polvo y Lucía está pasando la aspiradora.

Álvaro: ¿Y tú? ¿Qué estás haciendo?

Ana: Yo... pues... yo estoy ¡diciéndoles qué hacer!

16 ¿En qué orden? *page 208*

Mi familia y yo vamos a hacer una fiesta para mi abuelo. Él va a cumplir setenta años. ¡Ay! ¡Es mucho trabajo! ¿Cómo empezamos? Bueno, primero debemos mandar las invitaciones. Luego, debo comprar un regalo. A mi abuelo le gustan los artículos de cuero. Le compro una cartera o un cinturón. Después, mi mamá debe hacer una tarta. Y como a él le gustan los dulces, ¡le va a hacer una tarta muy grande! Luego, el día de la fiesta, debemos preparar la comida: chorizo, calamares, jamón... ¡Sí! ¡Va a ser una fiesta fenomenal!

Quick Start Review Answers

p. 198 Dialog review
1. Primero quita el polvo de la mesa.
2. Tú debes sacar la basura.
3. ¿Porque eres una hermana muy maja?
4. Estoy barriendo el suelo.

p. 202 Household chores
1. barrer el suelo
2. sacar la basura
3. quitar el polvo
4. hacer la cama
5. pasar la aspiradora

p. 209 Vocabulary review
1. llave
2. reciente
3. tapas
4. deber
5. baño

Sample Lesson Plan - 45 Minute Schedule

DAY 1

Etapa Opener
- Quick Start Review (TE, p. 192) **5** MIN.
- Anticipate/Activate prior knowledge: Discuss the *Etapa* Opener. **5** MIN.
- Present the Supplementary Vocabulary (TE, p. 193). **5** MIN.
- Answer the *¿Qué ves?* questions, p. 192. **5** MIN.

En contexto: Vocabulario
- Quick Start Review (TE, p. 194) **5** MIN.
- Discuss the Language Note (TE, p. 194). **5** MIN.
- Have students use context and pictures to learn *Etapa* vocabulary. **5** MIN.
- Uses the Situational OHTs for additional practice. **5** MIN.
- Have students work in pairs to answer the *Preguntas personales,* p. 195. **5** MIN.

DAY 2

En vivo: Diálogo
- Quick Start Review (TE, p. 196) **5** MIN.
- Review the Listening Strategy, p. 196. **5** MIN.
- Play audio or show video for the dialog, pp. 196–197. **10** MIN.
- Work orally with the class to fill in the table, p. 196. **5** MIN.
- Discuss Gestures (TE, p. 196). **5** MIN.
- Replay the audio/video as needed. **5** MIN.
- Read the dialog aloud, having students take the roles of characters. **10** MIN.

Homework Option:
- Video Activities, Unit 5 Resource Book, pp. 74–76.

DAY 3

En acción: Vocabulario y gramática
- Check homework. **5** MIN.
- Quick Start Review (TE, p. 198) **5** MIN.
- Use OHTs to review *En contexto* vocabulary. Ask students for a summary of the dialog to check recall. **10** MIN.
- Play the video/audio; do *Actividad* 1 orally with the class. **5** MIN.
- Do *Actividad* 2 orally. **5** MIN.
- Discuss *Actividad* 3. **5** MIN.
- Have students write their responses to *Actividad* 3. **5** MIN.
- Ask volunteers to share their work on *Actividad* 3. **5** MIN.

DAY 4

En acción (cont.)
- Read and discuss the *También se dice,* p. 199. **5** MIN.
- Discuss *Actividad* 4. **5** MIN.
- Have students write their responses to *Actividad* 4. **5** MIN.
- Ask volunteers to share their responses to *Actividad* 4 with the class. **5** MIN.
- Have students work in pairs to do *Actividad* 5. **5** MIN.
- Ask pairs to volunteer to model their conversations from *Actividad* 5. **5** MIN.
- Read and discuss the *Conexiones,* p. 200. **5** MIN.
- Have students write responses to the *Para hacer,* p. 200. **5** MIN.
- Make a class list of all of the adjectives students found for the *Para hacer,* p. 200. **5** MIN.

DAY 5

En acción (cont.)
- Have students work in groups to complete *Actividad* 6. **10** MIN.
- Ask groups to share their tables from *Actividad* 6. **5** MIN.
- Read and discuss the *Nota cultural,* p. 201. **5** MIN.
- Present the Supplementary Vocabulary (TE, p. 201). **5** MIN.
- Discuss the Speaking Strategy, p. 201. **5** MIN.
- Read and discuss the *Nota,* p. 201. **5** MIN.
- Have students work in pairs to complete *Actividad* 7. **5** MIN.
- Ask pairs to volunteer to model their conversations from *Actividad* 7. **5** MIN.

DAY 6

En acción (cont.)
- Quick Start Review (TE, p. 202) **5** MIN.
- Present *Gramática:* Using Pronouns with the Present Progressive, p. 202. **10** MIN.
- Have students work in pairs to do *Actividad* 8. **5** MIN.
- Ask pairs to volunteer to model their conversations from *Actividad* 8. **5** MIN.
- Present the *Vocabulario,* p. 203. **5** MIN.
- Practice new vocabulary. **5** MIN.
- Have students work in pairs to do *Actividad* 9. **5** MIN.
- Call on selected pairs to model their conversations for *Actividad* 9. **5** MIN.

Homework Option:
- *Más práctica* Workbook, pp. 37–38. *Para hispanohablantes* Workbook, pp. 35–36.

DAY 7

En acción (cont.)
- Check homework. **5** MIN.
- Read and discuss the *Nota,* p. 204. **5** MIN.
- Have students work in pairs to complete *Actividad* 10. **5** MIN.
- Ask volunteer pairs to model their answers to *Actividad* 10. **5** MIN.
- Play the audio. Do *Actividad* 11 orally with the class. **5** MIN.
- Read and discuss the *Nota cultural,* p. 204. **5** MIN.
- Present the *Vocabulario,* p. 205. **5** MIN.
- Have students work in pairs to do *Actividad* 12. **5** MIN.
- Call on pairs to present their conversation from *Actividad* 12. **5** MIN.

DAY 8

En acción (cont.)
- Quick Start Review (TE, p. 206) **5** MIN.
- Present *Gramática:* Using the Verb *deber,* p. 206. **10** MIN.
- Present the *Vocabulario,* p. 206. **5** MIN.
- Assign *Actividad* 13. **5** MIN.
- Call on students to write their completed sentences from *Actividad* 13 on the board. **5** MIN.
- Have students work in pairs to complete *Actividad* 14. **5** MIN.
- Ask pairs to volunteer to model their conversation from *Actividad* 14. **5** MIN.
- Quick Wrap-up (TE, p. 207) **5** MIN.

Homework Option:
- *Más práctica* Workbook, p. 39. *Para hispanohablantes* Workbook, p. 37.

DAY 9

En acción (cont.)
- Check homework. **5 MIN.**
- Quick Start Review (TE, p. 209) **5 MIN.**
- Have students work in pairs to do *Actividad* 15. **5 MIN.**
- Call on pairs to model their conversations from *Actividad* 15. **5 MIN.**
- Play the audio. Assign *Actividad* 16. **5 MIN.**
- Ask volunteers to share their answers to *Actividad* 16. **5 MIN.**
- Have students work in groups to do *Actividad* 17. **5 MIN.**
- Call on groups to share their work from *Actividad* 17. **5 MIN.**
- Present *Gramática:* Using Adverbs That End in *-mente,* p. 209. **5 MIN.**

DAY 10

En acción (cont.)
- Quick Start Review (TE, p. 212) **5 MIN.**
- Assign *Actividad* 18. **5 MIN.**
- Work orally with the class on *Actividad* 19. **5 MIN.**
- Have students write their answers to *Actividad* 19. **5 MIN.**
- Assign *Actividad* 20. **5 MIN.**
- Have students work in pairs to complete *Actividad* 21. **5 MIN.**
- Read and discuss the *Pronunciación,* p. 211. **5 MIN.**

En colores: Cultura y comparaciones
- Discuss the Connecting Cultures Strategy, p. 212. **5 MIN.**
- Have volunteers read *Las tapas,* pp. 212–213, aloud. **5 MIN.**

Homework Option:
- *Más práctica* Workbook, p. 40. *Para hispanohablantes* Workbook, p. 38.

DAY 11

En colores (cont.)
- Check homework. **5 MIN.**
- Quick Start Review (TE, p. 214) **5 MIN.**
- Discuss the *¿Comprendiste?* and *¿Qué piensas?* questions, p. 213. **10 MIN.**
- Have students work in groups to complete the *Hazlo tú,* p. 213. **5 MIN.**

En uso: Repaso y más comunicación
- Have students work in pairs to complete *Actividad* 1. **10 MIN.**
- Call on students to share their work from *Actividad* 1. **5 MIN.**
- Have students write their answers to *Actividad* 2 independently. **5 MIN.**

DAY 12

En uso (cont.)
- Work orally with the class on *Actividad* 3. **5 MIN.**
- Have students write out answers to *Actividad* 4. **5 MIN.**
- Call on students to read their responses to *Actividad* 4. **5 MIN.**
- Present the Speaking Strategy, p. 216. **5 MIN.**
- Practice the Speaking Strategy. **5 MIN.**
- Have students work in pairs on *Actividad* 5. **10 MIN.**
- Call on selected pairs to model their conversations from *Actividad* 5 for the class. **10 MIN.**

DAY 13

En uso (cont.)
- Have students work in groups on *Actividad* 6. **10 MIN.**
- Call on selected groups to model their work from *Actividad* 6. **5 MIN.**
- Read and discuss *En la comunidad,* p. 216. **5 MIN.**

En tu propia voz: Escritura
- Discuss the *modelo* for *Actividad* 7. **5 MIN.**
- Have students work independently on the writing activity in *Actividad* 7. **10 MIN.**
- Ask volunteers to read their work from *Actividad* 7 to the class. **10 MIN.**

Homework Option:
- Have students review all of the *Gramática* boxes in *Etapa* 2 as preparation for the exam.

DAY 14

En resumen: Repaso de vocabulario
- Review grammar questions as necessary. **5 MIN.**
- Quick Start Review (TE, p. 217) **5 MIN.**
- Follow the Teaching Suggestion (TE, p. 217). **5 MIN.**
- Call on students to read their vocabulary sentences aloud. **10 MIN.**
- Discuss the Community Connection (TE, p. 217). **5 MIN.**
- Ask students to solve the *Juego,* p. 217. **10 MIN.**
- Answer the *Juego* orally (Answers, TE, p. 217). **5 MIN.**

Homework Option:
- Have students study for the *Etapa* exam.

DAY 15

En resumen: Repaso de vocabulario
- Answer questions related to *Etapa* 2 content. **10 MIN.**
- Complete *Etapa* exam. **25 MIN.**

Ampliación
- Use a suggested project, game, or activity (TE pp. 165A–165B) as students complete the exam.

Classroom Management Tip

Vary classroom activities One way to keep things fresh is to provide a variety of activities. Students don't often do time lines for language classes, but now would be a great time to do one.

Have students work in groups of 4 to do this **Etapa**-long project. Ask each group to prepare part of a time line of Spanish history from 800,000 B.C., when *Homo erectus* appeared, through Phoenician, Greek, Carthaginian, Celtic, Iberian, Roman, Visigoth, Gypsy, and Muslim times, to the present.

Etapa Theme
Doing chores at home and negotiating responsibilities

Grammar Objectives
• Using pronouns with the present progressive
• Using the verb **deber**
• Using adverbs that end in **-mente**

Teaching Resource Options
Print
Block Scheduling Copymasters

Audiovisual
OHT 139, 157 (Quick Start)

Quick Start Review
♻ **Commands**
Use OHT 157 or write on the board: Your friend made the following statements. Give some advice, using a **tú** command:

1. Estoy muy cansado.
2. Necesito un libro sobre Picasso.
3. Esta comida no me gusta.
4. Hay una fiesta esta noche pero no quiero ir.
5. No sé dónde está mi libro.

Answers
Answers will vary. Answers could include:
1. Duerme más.
2. Ve a la biblioteca.
3. No la comas.
4. No vayas a la fiesta.
5. Búscalo.

Teaching Suggestions
Previewing the Etapa
• Ask students to study the picture on pp. 192–193 (1 min.).
• Have them close their books and share at least 3 items that they noticed.
• Have students identify the location of the 3 people and describe what they see.
• Use the **¿Qué ves?** questions to focus the discussion.

UNIDAD 5

ETAPA **2**

¿Qué debo hacer?

• Say what people are doing

• Persuade others

• Describe a house

• Negotiate responsibilities

¿Qué ves?

Mira la foto de la tienda.
1. ¿La tienda vende muchas o pocas frutas?
2. ¿Quién compra muchas frutas: Carmen, Mercedes o Luis?
3. ¿Cuánto cuesta el pan?

192

Ofertas del día
Arroz
95 ptas.
Pan
50 ptas.
Leche - 100 ptas.

Middle School Classroom Management

Planning Ahead Add **Etapa 2** vocabulary to your vocabulary picture file. Cut out pictures of house interiors and exteriors, and pictures of people engaged in household and yard chores. If possible, have ready pictures of Antonio Gaudí's architecture and some background information about him (for p. 200). Students might contribute pictures to the file.

Time Saver Assign the **¿Qué ves?** questions the night before you want to discuss them in class.

Cross Cultural Connections

Ask students what similarities and differences they notice between the store in this picture and those in the U.S. Also have them notice Mercedes' shopping basket. Would they see this kind of basket in the U.S.?

Culture Highlights

● **BARCELONA** Legend says that Barcelona was founded as Barcina about 230 B.C. by General Hamilcar Barca, a Carthaginian. In the third century B.C., it became part of the Roman Empire. It was conquered by the Moors in 713, and then captured by Charlemagne in 801.

The modern center of Barcelona, known as **El Ensanche** (meaning "extension"), was built between 1870 and 1936. Some famous landmarks located here are **Sagrada Familia,** the University of Barcelona, and the **Plaza de Toros.**

Supplementary Vocabulary

la banana, el plátano	banana
la naranja	orange
la sandía	watermelon
el tomate	tomato
la canasta	basket

193

Teaching Middle School Students

Extra Help Make true/false statements about the picture. If the statement is false, have students correct it. For example: **Hay dos muchachas en la foto. (Cierto) El muchacho se llama Álvaro. (Falso. Se llama Luis.)**

Native Speakers Have native speakers write three additional questions about the photo. Students can answer each other's questions.

Multiple Intelligences

Logical/Mathematical With a partner, have students read the **Etapa** objectives and think what English words would fall under or meet each objective. Have students make a list of the words in their notebooks. Later, they can compare their lists to the Spanish vocabulary presented on pp. 194–195.

Block Schedule

Extension In small groups, have students write and perform skits dealing with Luis, Mercedes, and Carmen in the store. The skits should include discussions about what to buy. (For additional activities, see **Block Scheduling Copymasters.**)

Teaching Resource Options

Print

Unit 5 Resource Book
  Video Activities, pp. 74–75
  Videoscript, p. 77
  Audioscript, p. 80
  Audioscript *Para hispanohablantes,*
    p. 80

Audiovisual

OHT 151, 152, 153, 153A, 154, 154A,
157 (Quick Start)
Audio Program Cassette 14A / CD 14
Audio *Para hispanohablantes*
  Cassette 14A / CD 14
Video Program Videotape 5 /
  Videodisc 3A

Search Chapter 4, Play to 5
U5E2 • En contexto (Vocabulary)

Technology

Intrigas y aventuras CD-ROM, Disc 1

Quick Start Review

♻ Activities

Use OHT 157 or write on the board:
List at least 3 activities for each place:

1. en casa
2. en la escuela
3. al aire libre (outside)

Answers
Answers will vary. Answers could include:
  1. dormir, ver la televisión, comer
  2. estudiar, hablar, escuchar
  3. practicar deportes, ir de compras, sacar
     fotos

Language Note

Point out that the suffix **-ón** is used to
imply that something is large. **Un sillón**
is a large **silla.**

En contexto

VOCABULARIO

Luis and Carmen have a lot of chores to do!
See what they do to clean up their house.

A Luis **barre el suelo** de la cocina.

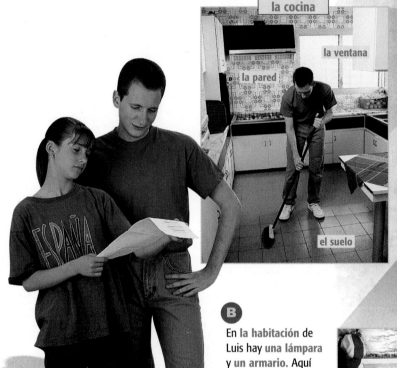

la cocina
la ventana
la pared
el suelo
el baño

B En **la habitación** de
Luis hay **una lámpara**
y **un armario.** Aquí
todo ya está limpio.

la habitación
la lámpara
el armario

194   ciento noventa y cuatro
Unidad 5

Middle School Classroom Community

TPR Walk around the classroom, repeatedly touching
different furniture and parts of the classroom (**la silla,
la pared, la ventana, el suelo, la puerta, la mesa, el
armario,** and so forth). As you touch each one, say a
Spanish word. Say correct and incorrect terms for the
items you touch. Students should raise their hands
when you say a correct response and shake their heads
no when you say an incorrect term.

Game Divide the class into 2 teams. Have students
from Team A pantomime a chore or action, such as
closing the door, sweeping the floor, and opening the
window. Team A gets 1 point and Team B gets $\frac{1}{2}$ point
for each action Team B guesses within 1 minute.

el jardín

el comedor

la mesa

la silla

quitar el polvo

D Luis **quita el polvo** de **la mesa** del **comedor**. También tiene que quitar el polvo de **las sillas**.

la puerta

la llave

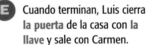
la aspiradora

E Cuando terminan, Luis cierra **la puerta** de la casa con la **llave** y sale con Carmen.

la sala

los muebles

el sillón

el sofá

C

En **la sala** Carmen **pasa la aspiradora**. Aquí hay **unos muebles**, como **el sofá** y **el sillón**. También hay **un televisor**.

Preguntas personales

1. ¿Tienes jardín?
2. ¿Prefieres barrer el suelo o pasar la aspiradora?
3. ¿Quitas el polvo en la sala o en tu habitación?
4. ¿Dónde hay una mesa en tu casa?
5. ¿Qué muebles hay en tu habitación?

ciento noventa y cinco **195**
Etapa 2

Teaching Suggestions
Introducing Vocabulary

• Have students look at pages 194–195. Use OHT 151 and 152 and Audio Cassette 14A / CD 14 to present the vocabulary.
• Ask the Comprehension Questions in order of yes/no (questions 1–3), either/or (questions 4–6), and simple word or phrase (questions 7–10). Expand by adding similar questions.
• Use the TPR activity to reinforce the meaning of individual words.
• Use the video vocabulary presentation for review and reinforcement.

Comprehension Questions

1. ¿Barre Luis el suelo de la cocina? (Sí.)
2. ¿Quita Luis el polvo de la pared? (No.)
3. ¿Tiene que quitar el polvo de las sillas? (Sí.)
4. ¿Tiene Luis un armario o dos armarios? (un armario)
5. ¿Ahora está sucia o limpia la habitación de Luis? (limpia)
6. ¿Tiene la casa jardín o no tiene jardín? (tiene jardín)
7. ¿Qué hace Carmen en la sala? (pasa la aspiradora)
8. ¿Qué hay en la sala? (un televisor, un sofá y un sillón)
9. ¿Qué usa Luis para cerrar la puerta de la casa? (una llave)
10. ¿Con quién sale Luis? (con Carmen)

Block Schedule

Categorize Have students work in pairs and make a complete list of chores (things to do in the house and outside). Then have them categorize the chores into those that need doing every day, twice a week, and once a week. Students could also then make a schedule and divide up the chores equally among the group members.

Teaching Middle School Students

Extra Help Use pictures of home interiors and exteriors from your vocabulary picture file. Ask **sí/no** questions about the pictures: ¿**Te gusta este comedor?** ¿**Es moderna esta sala?** ¿**Te gusta el sofá?** ¿**Es bonita esta habitación?**

Native Speakers Have students choose a room in their home and describe it in detail.

Multiple Intelligences

Interpersonal Have students bring to class a photo of their home. Pairs describe the exterior and interior of their homes to each other. (**En mi casa, hay tres habitaciones y un baño. El color de la cocina es amarilla,** etc.)

Teaching Resource Options

Print

Más práctica Workbook PE,
pp. 33–36
Para hispanohablantes Workbook PE,
pp. 33–34
Block Scheduling Copymasters
Unit 5 Resource Book
Más práctica Workbook TE, pp. 52–55
Para hispanohablantes Workbook
TE, pp. 60–61
Video Activities, p. 76
Videoscript, p. 78
Audioscript, p. 80
Audioscript *Para hispanohablantes*,
p. 80

Audiovisual

OHT 155, 156, 157 (Quick Start)
Audio Program Cassette 14A / CD 14
Audio *Para hispanohablantes*
Cassette 14A / CD 14
Video Program Videotape 5 /
Videodisc 3A

Search Chapter 5, Play to 6
U5E2 • En vivo (Dialog)

Technology

Intrigas y aventuras CD-ROM, Disc 1

🔔 Quick Start Review

♻️ Household chores
Use OHT 157 or write on the board:
List at least 5 household chores.

Answers
Answers will vary. Answers could include:
barrer el suelo, pasar la aspiradora, quitar el
polvo, hacer la cama, quitar la mesa, lavar los
platos, limpiar el cuarto

Gestures

Imitate some of the gestures used by the
characters in the dialog. Have students
identify the person and the scene number.
For example: Carmen standing with her
arms crossed in scene 2.

En vivo

 DIÁLOGO

¡A limpiar la casa!

Luis   Carmen   Mercedes

PARA ESCUCHAR • STRATEGY: LISTENING

Note and compare Jot down what you do to help around the house.
Then listen and note what Luis, Carmen, and Mercedes are doing.
How are your lists similar? How are they different? Who does
more? What do you think of Carmen's approach to her chores?

Yo	Luis, Carmen y Mercedes

1 ▶ Luis: Carmen, Mercedes, ¿me
ayudáis con los quehaceres?
Carmen: ¿Por qué te debo ayudar?
Luis: A ver. ¿Porque eres una
hermana muy maja?

5 ▶ Luis: En vez de sacar fotos, debes
ayudarme. Si no me ayudas,
vamos a llegar tarde a casa de
Álvaro.
Mercedes: Está bien, Luis. Ahora
te estoy ayudando.

6 ▶ Luis: Carmen, ¿qué estás haciendo? ¿Por
qué no estás pasando la aspiradora?
Carmen: Sí, sí, mira, estoy pasándola.

7 ▶ Luis: Pero, Carmen, debes pasarla
cuidadosamente. Mira, hazlo como
lo estoy haciendo yo, lentamente.
Carmen: ¡Ay, pero Luis! Quiero
terminar rápidamente.

196 ciento noventa y seis
Unidad 5

Middle School Classroom Community

TPR Have each student choose a chore from
pp. 194–195. Have them stand up when they hear
their chore mentioned in the video.

Storytelling Choose a video still and have groups
of students create a story about what happens before,
during, and after the picture. Have them tell their
stories to the class.

Group Activity Turn the sound off and replay the
video. Have groups of 3 students take turns dramatizing
and reading aloud the dialog.

2▶ **Luis:** Porque si limpias la sala, te llevo al cine mañana.
Carmen: ¿Eso es todo?
Luis: Te doy un regalo.

3▶ **Carmen:** ¿Qué me vas a dar? ¡Dámelo ahora!
Luis: No, no, después. Primero quita el polvo de la mesa.
Carmen: Ya, ya, estoy quitándolo.

4▶ **Luis:** ¿Todavía estás sacando fotos?
Mercedes: Sí, estoy sacándolas para algo muy importante.
Luis: Estoy barriendo el suelo.
Mercedes: Claro, veo que estás barriéndolo. Pero necesito las fotos.

8▶ **Luis:** Todavía hay que lavar los platos y sacar la basura.
Mercedes: Tú debes sacar la basura. Yo ayudo a Carmen a lavar los platos. ¿Está bien, Carmen?

9▶ **Carmen:** ¡Sí, perfecto!
Luis: Bueno. Y después vamos a la tienda.

10▶ **Luis:** Pero, ¿qué hacéis? ¿Y los platos?
Mercedes: Estamos lavándolos, ¿no ves?

ciento noventa y siete
Etapa 2 **197**

Teaching Middle School Students

Extra Help Before students become engaged with the video, you might have them look at the stills and identify the room and the activity that is taking place in each picture.

Challenge Have students rewrite Luis's part so that he doesn't seem so picky.

Multiple Intelligences

Intrapersonal Have students write about, draw, or dramatize their feelings about doing chores around the house.

Teaching Suggestions
Presenting the Dialog

• Prepare students for listening by focusing on the dialog context using yes/no or either/or questions. Reintroduce the characters and the setting: **¿Dónde están los muchachos? ¿Cómo se llama el muchacho? ¿Cómo se llama la muchacha que saca fotos: Carmen o Mercedes? ¿Son hermanas Carmen y Mercedes?**

• Use the video, audio cassette, or CD to present the dialog. The expanded dialog on video offers additional listening practice opportunities.

Video Synopsis

• Luis, his little sister Carmen, and his friend Mercedes complete a list of chores. For a complete transcript of the video dialog, see p. 191B.

Comprehension Questions

1. ¿Quiere Carmen ayudar a Luis con los quehaceres? (No.)
2. ¿Dice Luis que Carmen es una hermana muy mala? (No.)
3. Si Carmen limpia la sala, ¿va a ir al cine? (Sí.)
4. ¿Quién ayuda a Carmen y a Luis: Mercedes o Álvaro? (Mercedes)
5. ¿Va a recibir Carmen dinero o un regalo para limpiar la sala? (un regalo)
6. ¿Está Mercedes sacando fotos de Carmen o de Luis? (de Luis)
7. ¿Qué hace Luis cuando Mercedes saca fotos? (barre el suelo)
8. ¿Cómo pasa Carmen la aspiradora? (rápidamente)
9. ¿Quién va a sacar la basura? (Luis)
10. ¿Adónde van después de lavar los platos y sacar la basura? (a la tienda)

Block Schedule

Change of Pace Before beginning the grammar presentations, have students begin work on some bulletin boards or posters from **Ampliación,** TE p. 165A. (For additional activities, see **Block Scheduling Copymasters.**)

Teaching Resource Options

Print
Unit 5 Resource Book
  Videoscript, p. 76
  Audioscript, p. 80
  Audioscript *Para hispanohablantes*,
    p. 80

Audiovisual
OHT 158 (Quick Start)
Audio Program Cassette 14A / CD 14
Audio *Para hispanohablantes*
  Cassette 14A / CD 14
Video Program Videotape 5 /
  Videodisc 3A

Quick Start Review
♻ Dialog review
Use OHT 158 or write on the board:
Unscramble the words to make sentences
from the dialog.

1. quita / polvo / Primero / de /
   mesa / la / el
2. sacar / la / Tú / basura / debes
3. maja? / hermana / eres / muy /
   una / ¿Porque
4. barriendo / suelo / el / Estoy

Answers *See p. 191B.*

Teaching Suggestions
Comprehension Check

Use **Actividades 1** and **2** to assess
retention after the dialog. Have students
close their books. Act out some of the
chores in **Actividad 1** and see if
students can comprehend and answer
correctly.

Objective: Controlled practice
Listening comprehension/vocabulary

Answers (See script, p. 191B.)
Students point to 1, 3, 4, 6, and 8.

En acción
VOCABULARIO Y GRAMÁTICA

ACTIVIDAD 1

Los quehaceres

Escuchar Según el diálogo, señala los quehaceres que
hacen Luis, Carmen y Mercedes. *(Hint: Point to the chores that
Luis, Carmen, and Mercedes do.)*

OBJECTIVES

- Say what people are
  doing
- Persuade others
- Describe a house
- Negotiate
  responsibilities
- *Use pronouns with the
  present progressive*
- *Use the verb* ***deber***
- *Use adverbs that end
  in* ***-mente***

1.
2.
3.
4.
5.
6.
7.
8.

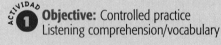

198
ciento noventa y ocho
Unidad 5

Streamlining To rapidly go over the answers to
Actividad 6, have all students who answered "X" raise
their hands.

Time Saver Create and duplicate the data sheet for
Actividad 6 ahead of time. This will allow students to
focus just on the process of the activity, not the chart-
building aspect. You might model a three-person mini-
version of the activity before students begin.

ACTIVIDAD 2

¡A limpiar!

Escuchar Completa las oraciones que describen el diálogo. *(Hint: Complete the sentences.)*

1. Luis tiene ____.
   a. muchos quehaceres
   b. muchas hermanas
   c. muchas fotos

2. Si Carmen limpia la sala, puede ____.
   a. quitar el polvo
   b. comprar regalos
   c. ir al cine

3. Mercedes está ____.
   a. pasando la aspiradora
   b. hablando por teléfono
   c. sacando fotos

4. Luis y Mercedes van ____ esta tarde.
   a. al cine
   b. a la casa de Álvaro
   c. a comprar una aspiradora nueva

5. Mercedes y ____ lavan los platos.
   a. Luis
   b. Carmen
   c. Álvaro

También se dice

There are different ways to describe a really wonderful person in Spanish. Luis uses one of them: **una hermana muy maja**.

Es muy maja: Spain

Es muy buena onda: Mexico

Es muy buena gente: many countries

ACTIVIDAD 3

El plano de la casa

Hablar/Escribir Imagínate que ésta es tu casa ideal. Indícales a unos amigos cada cuarto o lugar en el plano de esta casa imaginaria. *(Hint: Describe the ideal house.)*

modelo

Aquí está la sala. La sala tiene una puerta y tres ventanas.

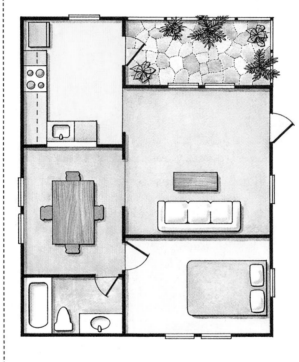

ciento noventa y nueve
Etapa 2 **199**

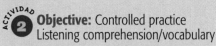

ACTIVIDAD 2

Objective: Controlled practice
Listening comprehension/vocabulary

Answers (See script, p. 191B.)
1. a   4. b
2. c   5. b
3. c

ACTIVIDAD 3

Objective: Transitional practice
Comprehension/vocabulary

Answers will vary.

Interdisciplinary Connection

Architecture The ideal Spanish house is arranged as typical Mediterranean homes were at the time of the Romans. It is organized around a plant-filled interior courtyard with a fountain. It usually has 2 stories. **La planta baja** has overhanging arched **subportales** and no windows, to keep it cool in summer. **El primer piso** has windows, letting in more light and heat in the winter.

Teaching Middle School Students

Extra Help For additional vocabulary practice, have pairs ask each other if they like to do the chores in **Actividad 1**: ¿Te gusta barrer el suelo? Sí, me gusta barrer. / No, no me gusta barrer.

Challenge Display the descriptions of ideal houses created for **Actividad 3**. Have students guess to whom each house belongs and explain the reasoning for their choices.

Native Speakers Ask native speakers to furnish additional words for the **También se dice.**

Multiple Intelligences

Naturalist Have students write or tell why their ideal house reflects their love of nature.

Block Schedule

Variety First have each student draw a house floor plan and include the household items in the wrong rooms. Then have students exchange drawings with a partner. Each student tells the other how to rearrange the house. For example: **Pon la cama en la habitación.**

Teaching Resource Options

Print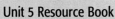

Unit 5 Resource Book
  Videoscript, p. 76
  Audioscript, p. 80
  Audioscript *Para hispanohablantes,*
    p. 80

Audiovisual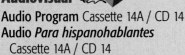

Audio Program Cassette 14A / CD 14
Audio *Para hispanohablantes*
  Cassette 14A / CD 14
Video Program Videotape 5 /
  Videodisc 3A

 4 **Objective:** Transitional practice
Vocabulary

Answers

Answers will vary but could include the following verbs.
1. estudio, duermo
2. leo, veo
3. juego, planto
4. preparo, lavo
5. como, hablo

 5 **Objective:** Transitional practice
Vocabulary

♻ **Daily chores**

Answers

Answers will vary but must contain the following.
1. barres / barro
2. quitas / quito
3. haces / hago
4. lavas / lavo
5. limpias / limpio
6. quitas / quito

Para hacer

Answers will vary.

ACTIVIDAD 4

En mi casa

Hablar/Escribir En general, ¿qué haces en cada cuarto o lugar de tu casa? *(Hint: Tell what you usually do in each room of your home.)*

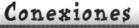
modelo

el baño: cantar, ducharse, ¿?
Me ducho en **el baño.**

1. tu habitación: estudiar, dormir, ¿?
2. la sala: leer, ver la televisión, ¿?
3. el jardín: jugar, plantar flores, ¿?
4. la cocina: preparar la comida, lavar los platos, ¿?
5. el comedor: comer, hablar, ¿?

ACTIVIDAD 5

♻ ¿Dónde?

Hablar Tu amigo(a) te pregunta dónde haces algún quehacer. Tú dices todos los cuartos en dónde se hace este quehacer. Cambien de papel. *(Hint: Tell in which rooms you do a chore.)*

modelo

pasar la aspiradora

Estudiante A: *¿Dónde **pasas la aspiradora?***
Estudiante B: ***Paso la aspiradora** en la sala, y en las habitaciones.*

el baño   la cocina   el comedor
  la habitación   la sala

1. barrer el suelo   4. lavar los platos
2. quitar el polvo   5. limpiar las ventanas
3. hacer la cama   6. quitar la mesa

Conexiones

El arte There are many fascinating buildings and sculptures in many sections of Barcelona. What do you think of this artwork? How does it make you feel?

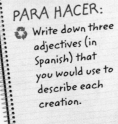
PARA HACER:
♻ Write down three adjectives (in Spanish) that you would use to describe each creation.

Casa Batlló

"A" by J. Brossa

200 doscientos
Unidad 5

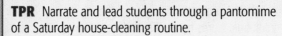
Middle School Classroom Community

TPR Narrate and lead students through a pantomime of a Saturday house-cleaning routine.

Storytelling Have small groups of students choose a picture of a home and tell each other stories about it and its occupants. A member from each group may share the group's favorite story with the class.

¿Quién lo hace?

Hablar/Escribir Trabaja en un grupo de tres personas. *(Hint: Work in a group of three.)*

1 En una hoja de papel, haz una tabla como ésta. Usa éstos y otros quehaceres en tu tabla. *(Hint: Make a table like this. Add other chores.)*

	todos los días	a veces	nunca
barrer el suelo			
hacer la cama			
lavar los platos			

2 Pregúntales a tus amigos con qué frecuencia tienen que hacer los quehaceres. Marca las respuestas con una X. *(Hint: Ask your classmates how often they have to do these chores. Record their answers with an X.)*

3 ¿Cuáles son los quehaceres más comunes? Habla con todos los grupos de la clase. *(Hint: Look at all groups' charts to determine the most common chores.)*

NOTA CULTURAL

In Spain and in most other Spanish-speaking countries, the first floor of a building is called **la planta baja**. The next floor is called **el primer piso**.

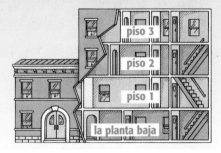

piso 3
piso 2
piso 1
la planta baja

---

7 Si tú pones la mesa...

PARA CONVERSAR
STRATEGY: SPEAKING

Negotiate Choose the chore you'd rather do. Then talk with your partner, who will express a preference. Decide who will do each.

Hablar Con otro(a) estudiante habla sobre los quehaceres. Escoge entre dos. *(Hint: Talk with a classmate about chores. Choose between two of them.)*

modelo

poner la mesa / preparar la cena

Estudiante A: *Si tú **pones la mesa**, yo **preparo la cena**.*

Estudiante B: *Prefiero **preparar la cena**.*

Estudiante A: *Está bien. Yo pongo la mesa y tú **preparas la cena**.*

Nota

Use **si** (with no accent!) to say *if*.

Si tú pones la mesa, yo preparo la cena.
If you set the table, I'll make dinner.

---

1. quitar la mesa / lavar los platos
2. hacer las camas / preparar el almuerzo
3. pasar la aspiradora / barrer el suelo
4. lavar la ropa / quitar el polvo
5. cuidar al hermano / ir al supermercado

doscientos uno
Etapa 2

201

---

6 Objective: Open-ended practice
Vocabulary

Answers will vary.

7 Objective: Open-ended practice
Vocabulary

Answers will vary.

Supplementary Vocabulary

Students may be prompted by the **Nota cultural** to ask about the ordinal numbers.

primero(a)	first
segundo(a)	second
tercero(a)	third
cuarto(a)	fourth
quinto(a)	fifth
sexto(a)	sixth
séptimo(a)	seventh
octavo(a)	eighth
noveno(a)	ninth
décimo(a)	tenth

Project

Suggest that interested students survey local charitable organizations to see if there are any **quehaceres** they might volunteer for. They could compile their results in a chart that's available for all students looking for an opportunity to help out in the community.

Teaching Middle School Students

Extra Help Work with students to make up a mnemonic device for remembering the difference between **si** and **sí**.

Native Speakers Have students describe in detail their feelings and opinions about the photos on p. 200.

Multiple Intelligences

Logical/Mathematical Have students graph the results of **Actividad 6**.

Intrapersonal Have students rank the chores in **Actividad 6** in order of least favorite to favorite (1 = least favorite).

Block Schedule

Retention Have students practice ordinal numbers and building descriptions by drawing a schematic of your school, labeling floors as well as rooms on each floor.

Teaching Resource Options

Print 📖

Más práctica Workbook PE,
  pp. 37–38
Para hispanohablantes Workbook PE,
  pp. 35–36
Block Scheduling Copymasters
Unit 5 Resource Book
  Más práctica Workbook TE,
    pp. 56–57
  Para hispanohablantes Workbook
    TE, pp. 62–63
  Audioscript, p. 81
  Audioscript *Para hispanohablantes*,
    p. 82

Audiovisual 🎧

OHT 158 (Quick Start)
Audio Program Cassettes 14A, 14B /
  CD 14
Audio *Para hispanohablantes*
  Cassette 14A / CD 14

Technology 💻 CD-ROM

Intrigas y aventuras CD-ROM, Disc 1

Quick Start Review

♻ Household chores

Use OHT 158 or write on the board:
Fill in the missing letters to review
vocabulary for household chores.

1. _ _ r _ _ _ el _ _ e _ _
2. _ _ c _ _ la _ _ s _ _ _
3. _ _ _ t _ _ el _ _ l _ _
4. _ a _ _ _ la c _ m _
5. _ _ s _ _ la _ s _ _ _ _ d _ _ _

Answers *See p. 191B.*

Teaching Suggestions
Presenting Using Pronouns with the Present Progressive

Tell students to return to the **Diálogo**
on pp. 196–197 and find examples of
the present progressive with pronouns.

GRAMÁTICA

Using Pronouns with the Present Progressive

♻ **¿RECUERDAS?** *1A, p. 262* Remember how you use the **present progressive** to describe actions in progress?

estoy **esperando**	estamos **esperando**
estás **esperando**	estáis **esperando**
está **esperando**	están **esperando**

When you use **pronouns** with the **present progressive**, you can put them in one of two places.

* Put pronouns **before** the conjugated form of estar...
* or **attach** them to the end of the **present participle** .

Mercedes says: ← *attached*

—**Estoy sacándolas** para
algo muy importante.
*I'm taking them (the pictures)
for something very important.*

You need to
add an **accent** when
you attach a pronoun.
barriéndolo

She could have said:

before ↘

—**Las** estoy **sacando** para algo muy importante.

····························

Some verbs you know have
irregular present participle forms.

* When the **stem** of an **-er** or **-ir**
verb ends in a vowel, change the
-iendo to **-yendo** to form the
present participle.

* **e → i** stem-changing verbs
have a vowel change in the stem.

* Some other verbs also have a
vowel change in the stem.

Verb	Irregular Present Participle
le er	le**y**endo
o ír	o**y**endo
tra er	tra**y**endo
pe dir	pidiendo
servir	sirviendo
de cir	diciendo
dormir	durmiendo
venir	viniendo

Middle School Classroom Community

Cooperative Learning Distribute a set of index
cards to each group of 5 as they work on **Actividad 8.**
Card 1 has subjects; Card 2 has pronouns; Card 3,
forms of **estar**; Card 4, **comprando** and **comprándo.**
Assign these roles: Student 1 asks the questions and
records; Student 2 is responsible for the subject;
Student 3, the pronoun; Student 4, the form of **estar**;
and Student 5, the present participle. Students work
together to form full-sentence answers with the cards.

Learning Scenario Create a class café and ask
groups of 5 or 6 to interact in character as they would
in situations you assign (ordering, arguing about the
bill, being out of an ordered item). Roles can include
waiter and customers.

ACTIVIDAD 8 Gramática

¿Quién lo compra?

Hablar Trabaja con otro(a) estudiante. Pregunten quién está comprando qué comida. *(Hint: Ask and answer questions about who is buying the food.)*

modelo

el arroz (Carmen)

Estudiante A: ¿Quién está comprando **el arroz?**

Estudiante B: *Carmen* lo está comprando.

　　　　　　o: Carmen está comprándolo.

1. los calamares (Luz y Rocío)
2. el chorizo (Ana y yo)
3. el jamón (Enrique y Pedro)
4. la tortilla española (Marta)
5. la lechuga (vosotros)
6. las aceitunas (María)

MÁS PRÁCTICA *cuaderno* pp. 37–38

PARA HISPANOHABLANTES *cuaderno* pp. 35–36

Vocabulario

Las tapas

las aceitunas *olives*

los calamares *squid*

el chorizo *sausage*

el jamón *ham*

la tortilla española *potato omelet*

Las tapas son porciones pequeñas de comida. ¿Cuáles te gustan?

ACTIVIDAD 9

¿Qué está pasando?

Hablar/Escribir El mesero de un restaurante quiere saber lo que ocurre en el restaurante esta noche. Con otro(a) estudiante, haz preguntas.

(Hint: Take turns asking what's going on in the restaurant.)

modelo

Estudiante A: ¿Está leyendo el menú?

Estudiante B: *Sí, está leyéndolo.*

　　　　　　o: Sí, lo está leyendo.

él

1. ellos　　　　　　2. él

3. vosotros　　　　　　4. ellos

doscientos tres
Etapa 2　**203**

Teaching Middle School Students

Extra Help Write a list of nouns on the board. Have the class name a pronoun for each noun. Write these next to each noun. Then, to practice position of pronoun and present progressive, organize a chain drill using **Estoy + sacando +** *pronoun* and *Pronoun* **+ estoy sacando: Estoy sacándolo; Lo estoy sacando.**

Multiple Intelligences

Musical/Rhythmic Suggest to students that they clap out the rhythm of sentences with the pronoun attached to the present participle.

Kinesthetic Slowly read the list of foods on p. 203. Have students use a thumbs-up gesture to indicate that they like the food or a thumbs-down gesture if they don't.

Teaching Suggestions
Presenting Vocabulary
Personalize the vocabulary by asking who has eaten each **tapa** or anything similar. Find out who likes **aceitunas** and who likes **calamares.**

ACTIVIDAD 8

Objective: Controlled practice
Present progressive/direct object pronouns

Answers

1. ¿Quién está comprando los calamares? Luz y Rocío los están comprando (están comprándolos).
2. ¿Quién está comprando el chorizo? Ana y yo lo estamos comprando (estamos comprándolo).
3. ¿Quién está comprando el jamón? Enrique y Pedro lo están comprando (están comprándolo).
4. ¿Quién está comprando la tortilla española? Marta la está comprando (está comprándola).
5. ¿Quién está comprando la lechuga? Vosotros la estáis comprando (estáis comprándola).
6. ¿Quién está comprando las aceitunas? María las está comprando (está comprándolas).

Quick Wrap-up

Ask a volunteer to give commands to individuals. **(Irene, come las aceitunas que están en tu escritorio.)** As the respondent pantomimes the action, the student who gave the command reports on what is being done. **(Irene está comiendo las aceitunas. Está comiéndolas muy despacio.)**

ACTIVIDAD 9

Objective: Transitional practice
Present progressive/direct object pronouns/vocabulary

Answers

Answers may vary but might be similar to the following.

1. ¿Están pidiendo la comida? Sí, están pidiéndola (la están pidiendo).
2. ¿Está diciendo "Adiós"? Sí, está diciéndolo (lo está diciendo).
3. ¿Estáis recibiendo las tapas? Sí, estamos recibiéndolas (las estamos recibiendo).
4. ¿Están sirviendo la comida? Sí, están sirviéndola (la están sirviendo).

Block Schedule

Variety Have groups of students write and perform a short comedy sketch about a restaurant interaction.

Teaching Resource Options

Print
Block Scheduling Copymasters
Unit 5 Resource Book
  Information Gap Activities, p. 68

Technology
Intrigas y aventuras CD-ROM, Disc 1

Objective: Transitional practice
Present progressive/reflexive
verbs/vocabulary

♻ **Reflexive verbs**

Answers
1. ¿Me puedes ayudar a lavar los platos?
   No puedo. Estoy lavándome los dientes
   (Me estoy lavando los dientes).
2. ¿Me puedes ayudar a preparar la comida?
   No puedo. Estoy lavándome la cabeza (Me
   estoy lavando la cabeza).
3. ¿Me puedes ayudar a poner la mesa?
   No puedo. Estoy maquillándome (Me estoy
   maquillando).
4. ¿Me puedes ayudar a hacer la cama?
   No puedo. Estoy afeitándome (Me estoy
   afeitando).

Objective: Transitional practice
Listening comprehension/present
progressive/vocabulary

Answers (See script, p. 191B.)
1. Está limpiando la casa.
2. Marta está quitando el polvo. Lucía está
   pasando la aspiradora.
3. Están barriendo el suelo.
4. Está diciéndoles a sus hermanos qué hacer.

♻ ¿Puedes ayudar?

Hablar Tienes muchos quehaceres. Pides ayuda, pero todos están
ocupados. *(Hint: You ask for help doing chores, but everyone is busy.)*

modelo

barrer el suelo

Estudiante A: *¿Me puedes ayudar a **barrer
el suelo?***

Estudiante B: *No puedo. Estoy **poniéndome
la ropa.***

*o: No puedo. Me estoy **poniendo
la ropa.***

Nota

When using the present progressive, place reflexive pronouns as you would place
direct and indirect object pronouns.

1. lavar los platos

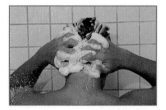

2. preparar la comida

3. poner la mesa

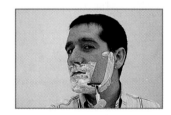

4. hacer la cama

¡Qué inteligente!

Escuchar Álvaro llama a una
amiga para invitarla a salir.
Escucha su conversación.
Luego, explica lo que están
haciendo las personas. *(Hint:
Álvaro is calling a friend to invite her to go
out. Listen and then explain what people
are doing.)*

1. la madre de Ana
2. sus hermanas
3. sus hermanos
4. Ana

NOTA CULTURAL

Paella and the **tortilla española**
are two important Spanish
dishes. **Paella** originated in the
Mediterranean city of Valencia
but is popular throughout the
country. It is a dish of rice and
vegetables laced with the rare
spice called saffron. It typically
contains all sorts of seafood—
shrimp, lobster, clams, mussels,
and squid—in addition to chicken
and **chorizo.**

---

204   doscientos cuatro
Unidad 5

Middle School Classroom Community

TPR Ask each student to choose one of the
quehaceres in **Actividad 12.** Choose one student
to mime his or her chore. All other students who
chose that chore stand and join the mime as they
recognize it.

Paired Activity Have pairs practice the present
progressive with reflexive verbs. Provide a handout of
reflexive verbs: **acostarse, bañarse, peinarse, lavarse
la cara, despertarse, ponerse la ropa.** Student A asks:
¿Me puedes ayudar? Student B responds: **No puedo.
Estoy acostándome,** etc. Have students swap roles.

¡Lo está haciendo ahora!

Hablar Álvaro y unos amigos están limpiando su casa. Su madre le pregunta si van a hacer algunos quehaceres. *(Hint: Say who's doing what.)*

modelo

vosotros

Su madre: ¿*Vosotros vais a **limpiar el cuarto**?*

Álvaro: *Lo estamos limpiando ahora.*   **o:** *Estamos limpiándolo ahora.*

■ **MÁS COMUNICACIÓN** p. R5

Vocabulario

Más quehaceres

mover (o → ue) los muebles
to move the furniture

ordenar (las flores, los libros)
to arrange (the flowers, books)

planchar (la ropa) *to iron
(the clothes)*

sacar la basura *to take out
the trash*

¿Quién hace estos quehaceres
en tu casa?

doscientos cinco
Etapa 2   **205**

Teaching Suggestions
Presenting Vocabulary

After presenting the new chores, have students recall those already learned. Call on volunteers to act out the various chores, while the rest of the class guesses.

Objective: Open-ended practice
Present progressive/vocabulary

Answers
1. ¿Isabel y Rocío van a hacer la cama?
   La están haciendo ahora. (Están haciéndola ahora.)
2. ¿Bárbara va a planchar la ropa?
   La está planchando ahora. (Está planchándola ahora.)
3. ¿Leticia va a ordenar las flores?
   Las está ordenando ahora. (Está ordenándolas ahora.)
4. ¿Andrés va a barrer el suelo?
   Lo está barriendo ahora. (Está barriéndolo ahora.)
5. ¿Jorge va a sacar la basura?
   La está sacando ahora. (Está sacándola ahora.)
6. ¿Linda va a pasar la aspiradora?
   La está pasando ahora. (Está pasándola ahora.)
7. ¿Paco va a quitar el polvo?
   Lo está quitando ahora. (Está quitándolo ahora.)
8. ¿Samuel y Pedro van a mover los muebles?
   Los están moviendo ahora. (Están moviéndolos ahora.)

Teaching Middle School Students

Extra Help Before students begin **Actividad 11**, model a sample explanation: ¿Qué está haciendo Ana? Ana está barriendo el suelo.

Native Speakers Have students report in detail about what the people are doing in the visual on p. 205. They can also include the day of week, time, and the activities that will happen next.

Multiple Intelligences
Verbal Have students make up sentences using the new vocabulary words. Then put them in groups of 4 to work their sentences into a short story.

Block Schedule

Variety Have students make a list of class chores and then produce a schedule for the rest of the month.

Teaching Resource Options

Print 📖

Más práctica Workbook PE, p. 39
Para hispanohablantes Workbook PE, p. 37
Block Scheduling Copymasters
Unit 5 Resource Book
  Más práctica Workbook TE, pp. 58–59
  Para hispanohablantes Workbook TE, pp. 64–65
  Audioscript, p. 81
  Audioscript *Para hispanohablantes*, p. 82

Audiovisual 🎧

OHT 159 (Quick Start)
Audio Program Cassettes 14A, 14B / CD 14
Audio *Para hispanohablantes* Cassette 14A / CD 14

Technology 💻

Intrigas y aventuras CD-ROM, Disc 1

🔔 Quick Start Review

♻️ **Pronouns with the present progressive**

Use OHT 159 or write on the board: Respond to these requests by saying that you are doing them.
Modelo: Limpia la cocina, por favor.
You write: Estoy limpiándola. *o:*
   La estoy limpiando.
1. Prepara la cena, por favor.
2. Pon la mesa, por favor.
3. Cuida a los niños, por favor.
4. Lava los platos, por favor.
5. Barre el suelo, por favor.

Answers
1. Estoy preparándola. *o:* La estoy preparando.
2. Estoy poniéndola. *o:* La estoy poniendo.
3. Estoy cuidándolos. *o:* Los estoy cuidando.
4. Estoy lavándolos. *o:* Los estoy lavando.
5. Estoy barriéndolo. *o:* Lo estoy barriendo.

Teaching Suggestions
Presenting Using the Verb deber

Point out that the use of **deber** + infinitive is a gentler alternative to a direct command. Ask students in what contexts they would use a direct command and when they would prefer to use **Debes** + infinitive.

GRAMÁTICA
Using the Verb deber

▶ The verb *deber* means *should* or *ought to.* To say what people should do, use a *conjugated form of deber* with the **infinitive** of another verb.

deber *should, ought to*

debo	debemos
debes	debéis
debe	deben

Debo **barrer** el suelo.
I should sweep the floor.

Debes **limpiar** la cocina.
You should clean the kitchen.

Debe **sacar** la basura.
He should take out the trash.

Remember you can put a **pronoun** in front of a conjugated verb or attach it to an infinitive.

Carmen asks Luis:
—¿Por qué **te** *debo* **ayudar**? *before*
Why should I help you?

Luis tells Mercedes:
—En vez de sacar fotos, *debes* **ayudarme**. *attached*
Instead of taking pictures, you should help me.

206
doscientos seis
Unidad 5

¡Organicemos una fiesta!

Escribir ¿Qué deben hacer estas personas para una fiesta? *(Hint: What should these people do to plan for a party?)*

modelo

Luis / comprar la comida
Luis debe **comprar la comida.**

1. yo / preparar una tortilla española
2. los amigos / limpiar la casa
3. tú y yo / escribir las invitaciones
4. tú / mandar las invitaciones
5. vosotros / hacer el pastel

Vocabulario

La fiesta

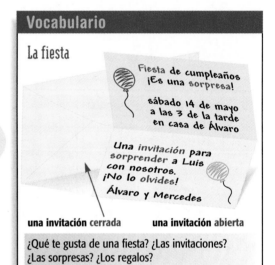

Fiesta de cumpleaños
¡Es una sorpresa!
sábado 14 de mayo
a las 3 de la tarde
en casa de Álvaro

Una invitación para sorprender a Luis con nosotros.
¡No lo olvides!
Álvaro y Mercedes

una invitación **cerrada**   una invitación **abierta**

¿Qué te gusta de una fiesta? ¿Las invitaciones? ¿Las sorpresas? ¿Los regalos?

Middle School Classroom Community

Group Activity Divide the class in half and have each group play "Simón dice…" with **deber**: Debes tocar la nariz. / No debes tocar la nariz. If a student accidentally performs the action when the leader says, "No debes…," he or she is out.

Portfolio Have students create an invitation for a party. They should decorate the invitation and provide a list of things guests should bring.

Rubric

Criteria	Scale
Creativity	1 2 3 4 5
Logical organization	1 2 3 4 5
Vocabulary use/spelling	1 2 3 4 5

A = 13–15 pts.
B = 10–12 pts.
C = 7–9 pts.
D = 4–6 pts.
F = < 4 pts.

ACTIVIDAD 14 Gramática

♻ ¿Me ayudas?

Hablar Estás organizando una cena y necesitas la ayuda de unos amigos. Los llamas por teléfono. ¿Qué dicen? *(Hint: You call your friends to help you organize a dinner. What do you say to each other?)*

modelo

Carmen: salir para comprar el postre

Carmen: ¿Debo **salir para comprar el postre?**

Tú: Sí, **sal para comprar el postre,** por favor.

1. Ana: ir a la tienda para comprar pan
2. Raúl: decirle a Pepe cómo llegar a la casa
3. Elena: hacer las tapas
4. Diego: venir temprano para ayudar
5. Ramón: salir para comprar refrescos
6. Carlos: ser simpático con todos

■ **MÁS PRÁCTICA** *cuaderno* p. 39

■ **PARA HISPANOHABLANTES** *cuaderno* p. 37

ACTIVIDAD 15

◆ ¡Hazlo!

Hablar Otro(a) estudiante te pregunta si debe hacer algo o no. Contéstale. *(Hint: Your classmate asks you if he or she should do certain things.)*

modelo

por la mañana

Estudiante A: ¿Debo hacer la cama **por la mañana**?

Estudiante B: Sí, debes hacerla.

1. después de comer

2. para andar en bicicleta

3. para sacar buenas notas

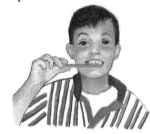

4. después de comer

5. antes de comer

6. tarde

doscientos siete **207**
Etapa 2

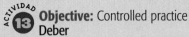

 ACTIVIDAD 13 Objective: Controlled practice Deber

Answers
1. Yo debo preparar una tortilla española.
2. Los amigos deben limpiar la casa.
3. Tú y yo debemos escribir las invitaciones.
4. Tú debes mandar las invitaciones.
5. Vosotros debéis hacer el pastel.

ACTIVIDAD 14 Objective: Controlled practice Deber

♻ Affirmative **tú** commands

Answers
1. ¿Debo ir a la tienda para comprar pan? Sí, ve a la tienda para comprar pan, por favor.
2. ¿Debo decirle a Pepe cómo llegar a la casa? Sí, dile a Pepe cómo llegar a la casa.
3. ¿Debo hacer las tapas? Sí, hazlas.
4. ¿Debo venir temprano para ayudar? Sí, ven temprano para ayudar.
5. ¿Debo salir para comprar refrescos? Sí, sal para comprarlos.
6. ¿Debo ser simpático con todos? Sí, sé simpático con todos.

🔔 Quick Wrap-up

Ask students to imagine they're having a class party. Have a volunteer give commands (**Marcos, debes ayudar a Marta a decorar la sala…**) As students act out these commands, review the present progressive by asking questions.

 ACTIVIDAD 15 Objective: Transitional practice **Deber**/vocabulary/direct object and reflexive pronouns

Answers
1. ¿Debo nadar después de comer? No, no debes nadar.
2. ¿Debo llevar un casco para andar en bicicleta? Sí, debes llevarlo.
3. ¿Debo hacer la tarea para sacar buenas notas? Sí, debes hacerla.
4. ¿Debo lavarme los dientes después de comer? Sí, debes lavarte los dientes.
5. ¿Debo lavarme las manos antes de comer? Sí, debes lavarte las manos.
6. ¿Debo acostarme tarde? No, no debes acostarte tarde.

■ Block Schedule

FunBreak Have students create drawings in which someone should do something (**Beto debe peinarse**). Display them and ask the class what should happen for each one. (For additional activities, see **Block Scheduling Copymasters**.)

Teaching Middle School Students

Challenge Have students write 4 more tasks for **Actividad 15** (some can be silly, others reasonable). Pairs work together to ask about the new sets of tasks.

Native Speakers Have students write a short paragraph (100 words) about a party they recently attended.

Multiple Intelligences

Musical/Rhythmic Have students develop chants or songs with **deber** + infinitive.

Teaching Resource Options

Print

Block Scheduling Copymasters
Unit 5 Resource Book
Más práctica Workbook TE, pp. 58–59
Para hispanohablantes Workbook
  TE, pp. 64–65
Audioscript, p. 81
Audioscript *Para hispanohablantes*,
  p. 82

Audiovisual

OHT 159 (Quick Start)
Audio Program Cassettes 14A, 14B /
  CD 14
Audio *Para hispanohablantes*
  Cassette 14A / CD 14

Technology

Intrigas y aventuras CD-ROM, Disc 1

16 Objective: Transitional practice
Listening comprehension/**deber**/
vocabulary

Answers (See script, p. 191B.)
The order is b, d, c, a.

17 Objective: Open-ended practice
Deber/vocabulary

Answers will vary.

Para hacer

Answers

1. b   4. d
2. a   5. e
3. c

¿En qué orden?

Escuchar Liliana y su familia
preparan una fiesta para su
abuelo. Escucha lo que dice.
Luego, indica el orden en que
deben hacer las actividades.
(Hint: In what order should they do things?)

a. preparar la comida
b. mandar las invitaciones
c. hacer la tarta
d. comprar el regalo

¡Todos ayudan!

Hablar/Escribir Trabaja en un grupo de tres personas. ¿Qué deben
hacer para organizar una buena fiesta? ¿Qué grupo tiene las
mejores ideas? *(Hint: What should you do to throw a great party? Which group has
the best ideas?)*

música   baile   ¿?

comida   bebidas

modelo

Para hacer una buena fiesta…
1. Debemos invitar a muchos amigos.
2. Debemos servir comida rica. Por ejemplo…
3. Debemos poner música de artistas como…

Conexiones

Los estudios sociales If you
travel to a Spanish-speaking country, it
will be important to know how to get
around. To do so, you will need to
understand certain
abbreviations.

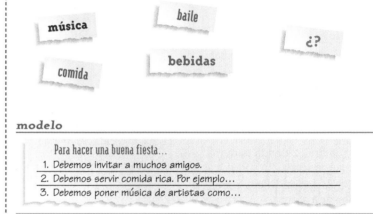

PARA HACER:
Match the abbreviations
with the full words.
1. 1er piso
2. C/
3. Avda. o Av.
4. dcha.
5. izqda.

a. calle
b. primer piso
c. avenida
d. a la derecha
e. a la izquierda

208 doscientos ocho
Unidad 5

GRAMÁTICA

Using Adverbs That End in -mente

To describe how something is done, use **adverbs.** Many adverbs in Spanish are made by changing an existing **adjective.**

- When an adjective ends in **e, l,** or **z,** simply add **-mente** to the end.

Adjective	Adverb
reciente *recent*	**reciente**mente *recently, lately*
frecuente *frequent*	**frecuente**mente *frequently, often*
fácil *easy*	**fácil**mente *easily*
normal *normal*	**normal**mente *normally*
especial *special*	**especial**mente *specially, especially*
feliz *happy*	**feliz**mente *happily*

- For adjectives with **-o** or **-a** endings, add **-mente** to the **feminine** form.

Adjective	Adverb
cuidadoso(a) *careful*	**cuidadosa**mente *carefully*
rápido(a) *fast, quick*	**rápida**mente *quickly*
lento(a) *slow*	**lenta**mente *slowly*
tranquilo(a) *calm*	**tranquila**mente *calmly*

Luis says:

—Pero, Carmen, debes pasarla **cuidadosa**mente.
*But Carmen, you should vacuum **carefully.***

Notice that you must keep an **accent** when an adjective is changed to an adverb.

    rápido ➡ **rápida**mente
    fácil ➡ **fácil**mente

When you use two adverbs, **drop** the **-mente** from the **first** one.

    lenta y **tranquila**mente

doscientos nueve
Etapa 2 | **209**

Teaching Middle School Students

Native Speakers Have students make a party etiquette list. (**Debes llegar un poco tarde. No debes llevar a un amigo sin pedir permiso.**)

Multiple Intelligences
Interpersonal Have students take turns making up sentences about an action and helping each other choose an appropriate adverb or adjective.

Visual Have students write adverbs in their notebooks using different colored markers to highlight **-mente** and any accent marks.

Quick Start Review
🔄 Vocabulary review
Use OHT 159 or write on the board: Write the word that does *not* belong with the other two words:

1. jamón   llave   aceitunas
2. reciente   suelo   pared
3. silla   mesa   tapas
4. planchar   deber   ordenar
5. baño   fiesta   sorpresa

Answers *See p. 191B.*

Teaching Suggestions
Reinforcing Using Adverbs That End in -mente
Point out to students that using adverbs will add vitality to their sentences when they speak and write. Have them give examples of sentences with and without adverbs.

Block Schedule
Variety Find some articles from Spanish magazines and distribute them to students. Have students look for adverbs that end in **-mente** and underline them. Then have students tell what adjectives they think the adverbs came from. Variation: Have students underline the adjectives in the articles and change them to adverbs. (For additional activities, see **Block Scheduling Copymasters.**)

Teaching Resource Options

Print

Block Scheduling Copymasters
Unit 5 Resource Book
  Information Gap Activities, pp. 69–70
  Audioscript, p. 81
  Audioscript *Para hispanohablantes*,
    p. 82

Audiovisual

Audio Program Cassette 14A / CD 14
Audio *Para hispanohablantes*
  Cassette 14A / CD 14

Technology

Intrigas y aventuras CD-ROM, Disc 1

18 Objective: Controlled practice
Adverbs

Answers
1. frecuentemente
2. especialmente
3. rápidamente
4. finalmente
5. tranquilamente

Quick Wrap-up

Give affirmative **tú** commands telling
the manner in which to do things.
(**Marcos, patina lentamente.**) Have
students mime the activity. After each
command, ask a follow-up question.
(**¿Cómo patina Marcos?**)

19 Objective: Transitional practice
Adverbs/vocabulary

Answers

Answers will vary.
1. Beto y Marta caminan tranquilamente.
2. Enrique pasa la aspiradora cuidadosamente.
3. Pedro come lentamente.
4. Todos bailan rápidamente.
5. *Answers will vary.*

18 Gramática

Mmm... ¡qué rico!

Leer/Escribir Luis habla de un
restaurante. Completa el
párrafo con adverbios de los
adjetivos entre paréntesis. *(Hint:
Complete the paragraph with adverbs.)*

modelo

Fui **recientemente** *(reciente)*
con mi familia a Casa Paco, un
restaurante buenísimo.

Comemos allí **1** *(frecuente)*
porque está cerca de mi casa y
¡la comida es riquísima! A mí me
gustan **2** *(especial)* los
calamares y el chorizo. Voy a
Casa Paco hoy con mis amigos.
Caminamos **3** *(rápido)*
porque tenemos mucha hambre.
¡Ah! ¡ **4** *(final)* llegamos!
En el restaurante, nadie tiene
prisa. Todos comemos **5**
(tranquilo). Cuando terminamos,
pedimos la cuenta y dejamos una
buena propina.

■ **MÁS PRÁCTICA** *cuaderno* p. 40
■ **PARA HISPANOHABLANTES**
cuaderno p. 38

19

¿Cómo hacen las actividades?

Hablar/Escribir Describe cómo hacen las cosas estas personas.
(Hint: Say how everyone does each activity.)

tranquilo   frecuente   cuidadoso
feliz   rápido   lento

modelo

Luis

Luis barre el suelo **rápidamente**.

1. Beto y Marta   2. Enrique

3. Pedro   4. todos   5. vosotros

También se dice

Many words are used to mean *bedroom*. Almost all are used in all countries.
A few are used a bit more often in specific countries.

- **la alcoba:** many countries
- **el dormitorio:** many countries
- **la pieza:** Argentina, Chile
- **el cuarto:** many countries
- **la habitación:** Spain
- **la recámara:** Mexico

Middle School Classroom Community

TPR Organize a narrated class TPR routine around
**Actividad 19: Baila lentamente; Come rápidamente;
Camina felizmente;** etc.

Group Activity Have each group brainstorm a list
of verbs and a list of adverbs that end in **-mente**.
Groups swap lists and write sentences with the lists,
starting each sentence in the third person.

ACTIVIDAD 20

♻ ¡La buena limpieza!

Leer/Escribir Imagínate que recibes este anuncio de la compañía Buena Limpieza. Lee el anuncio y después contesta las preguntas.
(Hint: Read the advertisement and answer the questions.)

Buena Limpieza

¡Con diez años de experiencia, limpiamos fácilmente todo tipo de hogar!

Llegamos rápidamente a su hogar para ofrecerle un servicio completo de limpieza.

➤ Quitar completamente el polvo
➤ Pasar lentamente la aspiradora
➤ Limpiar cuidadosamente todos los cuartos, especialmente los baños y la cocina

¡Llámenos hoy al 86-25-54 para tener una casa bien limpia mañana!

1. ¿Cómo limpia el servicio?
2. ¿Cómo llegan a la casa?
3. ¿Qué servicios ofrecen?
4. ¿Cómo pasan la aspiradora?
5. ¿Qué cuartos limpian especialmente bien?

ACTIVIDAD 21

Mi casa ideal

Hablar/Escribir Haz un plano de tu casa ideal. Después, muéstrale el plano a otro(a) estudiante y descríbele la casa.
(Hint: Design and describe your dream house.)

modelo

Mi casa ideal es grande y bonita. Tiene un jardín con muchas flores y plantas. También tiene una piscina y una cancha de tenis. Hay una sala donde vemos la televisión. Hay una cocina muy grande donde comemos todos los días. La casa también tiene…

■ **MÁS COMUNICACIÓN** p. R5

Pronunciación

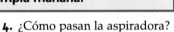

Trabalenguas

Pronunciación de la *c*, la *p* y la *t* When a **c** is followed by an **a**, **o**, or **u**, it sounds like the *c* in the English word *cat*. The letter combination **qu**, when followed by **e** or **i**, also makes this sound. This **c** sound and the letters **p** and **t** are pronounced similarly in Spanish and English. However, when you say them in English, a puff of air comes out of your mouth. In Spanish there is no puff of air. Try saying the following tongue twisters to practice these sounds.

Quince quiteños comen papas picantes.

No son tantas las tontas ni tantos los tontos muchachos.

doscientos once
Etapa 2
211

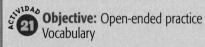

ACTIVIDAD 20 Objective: Transitional practice
Adverbs
♻ Interrogative words

Answers
1. Limpia fácilmente.
2. Llegan rápidamente.
3. Quitan el polvo, pasan la aspiradora y limpian todos los cuartos.
4. La pasan lentamente.
5. Limpian especialmente bien los baños y la cocina.

ACTIVIDAD 21 Objective: Open-ended practice
Vocabulary

Answers will vary.

🔔 Quick Wrap-up

Toss a soft ball to a student as you say an adjective. The student says the corresponding adverb. If you say **Sí**, he/she tosses the ball back to you. If you say **No**, he/she tosses the ball to another student who attempts the adverb.

Dictation

After students have read the tongue twisters in the **Pronunciación**, have them close their books. Dictate the tongue twisters in segments while students write them.

Teaching Middle School Students

Extra Help Have students first look at the visual in **Actividad 20** and read the words in bold type. Next have them locate all the adverbs that end in **-mente**.

Multiple Intelligences

Naturalist Encourage students to connect certain adverbs to images of nature: **Las estaciones cambian lentamente; El perro corre rápidamente.**

■ Block Schedule

Variety Have students work alone or in pairs to create their own advertisement for a household appliance (**aparato electrodoméstico**). Remind them that most ads use many adverbs.

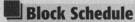

Teaching Resource Options

Print 📖

Unit 5 Resource Book
  Audioscript, p. 81
  Audioscript *Para hispanohablantes*,
    p. 82

Audiovisual

Audio Program Cassette 14A / CD 14
Audio *Para hispanohablantes*
  Cassette 14A / CD 14
OHT 159 (Quick Start)
Canciones Cassette / CD

🔔 Quick Start Review

♻ En el restaurante

Use OHT 159 or write on the board:
Write 5 things you should or should
not do in a nice restaurant. Begin your
sentences with **Debes...** or **No debes...**

Answers
Answers will vary. Answers could include:
Debes llevar ropa limpia.
No debes peinarte en la mesa.
Debes lavarte las manos antes de comer.
No debes cantar.
No debes jugar con la comida.

Teaching Suggestions
Presenting Cultura y comparaciones

• Begin by asking students to look at
  the pictures and tell if they have
  eaten anything like the foods
  pictured. Which dishes appeal to
  them? Do they like to try new foods?
• Have students complete the Strategy
  task. Then have them predict how
  Luis or Mercedes might feel about
  their favorite fast food restaurant.

Reading Strategy

Scan for crucial details Have
students scan the reading to pick up
certain details. Have them find answers
to the following questions: **¿Qué es una
tapa? ¿Cuáles son unos ingredientes?
¿Cuál es la especialidad de la casa?**

En colores

CULTURA Y COMPARACIONES

PARA CONOCERNOS

STRATEGY: CONNECTING CULTURES

Predict reactions about restaurants Fast food chains
are a U.S. invention being exported to other
countries. Think about a favorite one and
write down your answers to the questions in
the chart.

	comida rápida	tapas
¿Qué comida sirven?		
¿Por qué vamos?		
¿Con quién vamos?		

As you read, answer the same questions
about a place that serves **tapas**. Compare
the two eating experiences. How do you
think Luis or Mercedes would feel on their
first trip to your favorite fast food restaurant?

Las tapas

¿**T**e gustarían unas tapas? Son muy típicas de España. ¿Sabes
qué son? Una tapa es una porción pequeña de comida que la
gente normalmente come con una bebida antes de la cena.
¡Vamos a probar[1] unas!

En el café ponen todas las tapas en el
mostrador[2]. Hay tantas tapas diferentes.
Mucha gente está buscando mesa, pero
no hay. No es un problema porque es
muy común comer las tapas de pie.
Pagas un precio más barato si comes así[3].

---

[1]to try   [2]counter   [3]in this way

doscientos doce
Unidad 5

212

una experiencia muy española

Unos chicos están comiendo aceitunas, jamón y queso. Otros comen chorizo con pan. Las aceitunas, el jamón, el queso y el chorizo son tapas naturales[4]. También hay tapas cocidas[5], como la tortilla española y los calamares. La tortilla española es muy popular y es uno de los platos más famosos. Pero la especialidad de la casa es un plato típico de Barcelona y de toda Cataluña, el cocido catalán[6]. ¡Está riquísimo!

Comer tapas es una buena actividad para la familia o los amigos. A muchas personas les gusta conversar mientras comen las deliciosas tapas.

---

[4] served unheated   [5] cooked   [6] Catalonian stew

¿Comprendiste?

1. ¿Qué sirven en este café?
2. ¿Por qué no hay problema si todas las mesas están ocupadas?
3. ¿Qué son las tapas naturales?
4. ¿Qué tapa cocida piden muchas personas? ¿Qué otras tapas cocidas hay?
5. ¿Cómo se llama la especialidad de la casa?

¿Qué piensas?

En España comer tapas es una actividad social. ¿Hay una actividad similar en Estados Unidos? Descríbela.

Hazlo tú

Eres camarero(a) en un café español. Dos personas llegan y piden tapas. ¿Qué dicen? ¿Qué les sirves?

doscientos trece
Etapa 2   **213**

Teaching Resource Options

Print

Para hispanohablantes Workbook PE,
pp. 15–16

Block Scheduling Copymasters

Unit 5 Resource Book
Para hispanohablantes Workbook
 TE, pp. 66–67
 Information Gap Activities,
 p. 71
 Family Involvement, pp. 72–73
 Multiple Choice Test Questions,
 pp. 170–178

Audiovisual

OHT 160 (Quick Start)
Audio Program Testing Cassette T2 /
CD T2

Technology

**Electronic Teacher Tools/Test
 Generator**
Intrigas y aventuras CD-ROM, Disc 1

🔔 Quick Start Review
♻ Deber

Use OHT 160 or write on the board:
You have been granted 5 wishes. Using
the verb **deber,** tell your genie 5 things
that he/she should do for you.

Modelo: Debes limpiar mi habitación.

Answers will vary.

✔ Teaching Suggestions
What Have Students Learned?

• Have students look at the "Now you
 can…" notes listed on the left side of
 pages 214–215. Tell students to think
 about which areas they might not be
 sure of. For those areas, they should
 consult the "To review" notes.
• Use the video to review vocabulary
 and structures.

ETAPA **2**

En uso

REPASO Y MÁS COMUNICACIÓN

Now you can...
• say what people
 are doing.

To review
• pronouns with the
 present progressive,
 see p. 202.

ACTIVIDAD 1 🧑🏽 ¡A limpiar!

Luis habla con su madre por teléfono.
¿Qué le dice sobre los quehaceres?
*(Hint: Luis is talking on the telephone with his mother.
What does he tell her about the chores?)*

modelo

¿quitar el polvo de la mesa? (yo)
Mamá: ¿Quién está **quitando el polvo de la mesa**?
Luis: **Yo** estoy quitándolo. **o: Yo** lo estoy quitando.

1. ¿barrer el suelo? (yo)
2. ¿pasar la aspiradora? (Carmen)
3. ¿lavar los platos?
 (Mercedes y Carmen)
4. ¿sacar la basura? (yo)

5. ¿poner la mesa? (Carmen)
6. ¿limpiar los baños? (Mercedes y yo)
7. ¿hacer las camas? (yo)
8. ¿preparar las tapas? (nosotros)

ACTIVIDAD 2 ¡Una fiesta!

Tú y tus amigos van a hacer una fiesta en tu casa en una hora.
¿Qué deben o no deben hacer todos? *(Hint: You and your friends are having a
party. What should or shouldn't people do?)*

Now you can...
• persuade others.

To review
• the verb **deber,** see
 p. 206.
• adverbs that end in
 -mente, see p. 209.

modelo

yo: poner la mesa (lento)
*No debo **poner la mesa lentamente.***

1. ustedes: ordenar la casa
 (cuidadoso)
2. tú: hablar por teléfono (frecuente)
3. mis amigos y yo: preparar las
 tapas (rápido)

4. yo: ducharme (lento)
5. nosotros: hacer los quehaceres
 (tranquilo)
6. mis amigos: ayudarme (rápido)

214 doscientos catorce
Unidad 5

Middle School Classroom Community

TPR For **Actividad 3,** play "Simón dice…" using the
items in the house visual. (**Simón dice toca la cama.
Toca el televisor,** etc.)

Game As an extension to **Actividad 3,** have pairs
play the following game. Students first list all the rooms
of a house, including several bedrooms and the yard.
Student A describes the contents of a room/yard.
Student B guesses the room. Student A gets a point
and Student B gets $\frac{1}{2}$ point if Student B guesses
correctly.

Now you can...
• describe a house.

To review
• house and furniture vocabulary, see pp. 194–195.

ACTIVIDAD
3 ¡Una nueva casa!

Imagínate que tú y tu familia acaban de llegar a esta nueva casa. Describe lo que hay en estos cuartos. (Hint: Imagine you and your family just arrived at a new house. Describe what's in the rooms.)

modelo

En el baño hay una ventana y un armario.

Now you can...
• negotiate responsibilities.

To review
• **si** clauses with the present tense, see p. 201.

ACTIVIDAD
4 Si tú limpias...

Luis está hablando con Carmen sobre los quehaceres. ¿Qué le dice? (Hint: What does Luis say to Carmen about the chores?)

modelo

quitar la mesa / lavar los platos
Si tú **quitas la mesa,** yo **lavo los platos.**

1. lavar la ropa / planchar la ropa
2. barrer el suelo / sacar la basura
3. quitar el polvo / pasar la aspiradora
4. limpiar la sala / limpiar la cocina
5. poner la mesa / hacer las camas
6. limpiar las ventanas / ordenar los muebles

doscientos quince
Etapa 2 215

ACTIVIDAD
1 Answers

Mamá: ¿Quién está...?
1. Yo estoy barriéndolo. o: Yo lo estoy barriendo.
2. Carmen está pasándola. o: Carmen la está pasando.
3. Mercedes y Carmen están lavándolos. o: Mercedes y Carmen los están lavando.
4. Yo estoy sacándola. o: Yo la estoy sacando.
5. Carmen está poniéndola. o: Carmen la está poniendo.
6. Mercedes y yo estamos limpiándolos. o: Mercedes y yo los estamos limpiando.
7. Yo estoy haciéndolas. o: Yo las estoy haciendo.
8. Nosotros estamos preparándolas. o: Nosotros las estamos preparando.

ACTIVIDAD
2 Answers

1. Ustedes deben ordenar la casa cuidadosamente.
2. Tú no debes hablar por teléfono frecuentemente.
3. Mis amigos y yo debemos preparar las tapas rápidamente.
4. Yo no debo ducharme lentamente.
5. Nosotros debemos hacer los quehaceres tranquilamente.
6. Mis amigos deben ayudarme rápidamente.

ACTIVIDAD
3 Answers

En la sala hay dos ventanas, un sofá, un sillón, un televisor y una lámpara.
En el comedor hay una mesa, cuatro sillas y una ventana.
En mi habitación hay un armario, una ventana y una cama.
En la habitación de mis padres hay dos ventanas, dos armarios, una cama, dos mesas y dos lámparas.

ACTIVIDAD
4 Answers

1. Si tú lavas la ropa, yo plancho la ropa.
2. Si tú barres el suelo, yo saco la basura.
3. Si tú quitas el polvo, yo paso la aspiradora.
4. Si tú limpias la sala, yo limpio la cocina.
5. Si tú pones la mesa, yo hago las camas.
6. Si tú limpias las ventanas, yo ordeno los muebles.

Teaching Middle School Students

Extra Help To reinforce the placement of accent marks, suggest that students give answers to **Actividad 1** with the object pronoun attached to the participle. Students can swap papers and correct each other's work, paying close attention to the accent marks.

Multiple Intelligences
Kinesthetic For **Actividad 3,** as students tell what is in each room, have them touch each item.

Block Schedule

Authentic Materials Prepare ahead: Bring in real estate brochures with floor plans. Do a variation of **Actividad 3,** where students describe what is in each house. (For additional activities, see **Block Scheduling Copymasters.**)

Teaching Resource Options

Print

Unit 5 Resource Book
Cooperative Quizzes, pp. 84–85
Etapa Exam, Forms A and B,
  pp. 86–95
Para hispanohablantes **Etapa Exam,**
  pp. 96–100
Portfolio Assessment, pp. 101–102
Multiple Choice Test Questions,
  pp. 170–178

Audiovisual

OHT 160 (Quick Start)
Audio Program Testing Cassette T2 /
CD T2

Technology

**Electronic Teacher Tools/Test
  Generator**

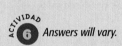 www.mcdougallittell.com

ACTIVIDAD 5

Rubric: Speaking

Criteria	Scale	
Sentence structure	1 2 3 4 5	A = 17–20 pts.
Vocabulary use	1 2 3 4 5	B = 13–16 pts.
Originality	1 2 3 4 5	C = 9–12 pts.
Fluency	1 2 3 4 5	D = 5–8 pts.
		F = < 5 pts.

ACTIVIDAD 6 *Answers will vary.*

ACTIVIDAD 7
En tu propia voz

Rubric: Writing

Criteria	Scale	
Vocabulary use	1 2 3 4 5	A = 13–15 pts.
		B = 10–12 pts.
Accuracy	1 2 3 4 5	C = 7–9 pts.
Creativity, appearance	1 2 3 4 5	D = 4–6 pts.
		F = < 4 pts.

Teaching Note: En tu propia voz

Suggest that students brainstorm a list of
descriptive words appropriate for a **fiesta**
in order to implement the writing strategy
"Use different kinds of descriptive words"
in the paragraph they will write.

ACTIVIDAD 5 Mi casa es así

PARA CONVERSAR

STRATEGY: SPEAKING
Detect misunderstandings Ask your partner
questions about what he or she said to make
sure you understand. To find out if you
understand each other, you can restate what
was said, do what was said, or draw what
was said. Draw what is described, then
compare your drawings. Together, identify
where any misunderstandings occurred.

Dibuja un cuarto. Descríbeselo a otro(a)
estudiante. Él o ella tiene que dibujar el
cuarto que tú describes y decir qué cuarto
es. *(Hint: Draw and describe a room.)*

modelo

Estudiante A: *Hay una ventana grande a la derecha de la
puerta. Cerca de la ventana hay un sofá y
dos sillones. Hay una mesa entre los
sillones…*

Estudiante B: *Es la sala.*

ACTIVIDAD 6 ¡Límpialo tú!

Tú y tus amigos tienen que preparar la casa
para una fiesta esta noche. Hagan una lista de
los quehaceres y después decidan quiénes van
a hacerlos. *(Hint: List chores and decide who does what.)*

modelo

Tú: *Si ustedes limpian el baño, yo paso la aspiradora.*

Estudiante A: *¡No! Tú debes limpiar el baño. Yo prefiero
pasar la aspiradora.*

Estudiante B: *Yo puedo limpiar el baño rápidamente si tú
me ayudas.*

Tú: *Bueno. Yo te ayudo a limpiar el baño.*

ACTIVIDAD 7 *En tu propia voz*

ESCRITURA Imagínate que estás en una fiesta
del Club de Español. Escribe una descripción
de lo que están haciendo todos. *(Hint: Describe what
people are doing.)*

modelo

*La fiesta es muy alegre. Gregorio está tocando la guitarra
y todos estamos cantando. La profesora está en la cocina.
Está preparando las tapas cuidadosamente…*

En la comunidad

Noemi is a high school student in New Jersey.
A native Spanish speaker, she helps out Spanish-
speaking customers in the clothing store where
she works. She also speaks Spanish with family
and friends. With whom do you speak Spanish?

216 doscientos dieciséis
Unidad 5

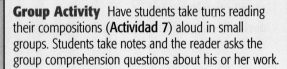

Middle School Classroom Community

Group Activity Have students take turns reading
their compositions (**Actividad 7**) aloud in small
groups. Students take notes and the reader asks the
group comprehension questions about his or her work.

Game: ¿Qué soy yo? Have students describe an item
from the **Vocabulario** while others try to guess what it
is. (**Abro la puerta. ¿Qué soy yo? [la llave]**)

En resumen

REPASO DE VOCABULARIO

PERSUADING OTHERS

cuidadosamente	carefully
cuidadoso(a)	careful
deber	should, ought to
especial	special
especialmente	specially, especially
fácilmente	easily
felizmente	happily
frecuente	frequent
frecuentemente	often, frequently
lentamente	slowly
lento(a)	slow
normal	normal
normalmente	normally
rápidamente	quickly
rápido(a)	fast, quick
reciente	recent
recientemente	lately, recently
tranquilamente	calmly

DESCRIBING A HOUSE

The House

el baño	bathroom
la cocina	kitchen
el comedor	dining room
la habitación	bedroom
el jardín	garden
la pared	wall
la puerta	door
la sala	living room
el suelo	floor
la ventana	window

Furniture

el armario	closet
la lámpara	lamp
la mesa	table
los muebles	furniture
la silla	chair
el sillón	armchair
el sofá	sofa, couch
el televisor	television set

WHAT PEOPLE ARE DOING

barrer el suelo	to sweep the floor
mover los muebles	to move the furniture
ordenar (las flores, los libros)	to arrange (the flowers, books)
pasar la aspiradora	to vacuum
planchar (la ropa)	to iron (the clothes)
quitar el polvo	to dust
sacar la basura	to take out the trash

OTHER WORDS AND PHRASES

abierto(a)	open
cerrado(a)	closed
la llave	key
olvidar	to forget
si	if

Food

las aceitunas	olives
los calamares	squid
el chorizo	sausage
el jamón	ham
las tapas	appetizers
la tortilla española	potato omelet

Invitations

la fiesta	party
la invitación	invitation
sorprender	to surprise
la sorpresa	surprise

Juego

¿En qué cuarto están?

1. Sofía come.

2. Felipe ve la televisión.

3. Cristina lava los platos.

doscientos diecisiete
Etapa 2   **217**

Community Connections

Have students brainstorm a list of people they might possibly speak Spanish with in your area. They could contact the local Chamber of Commerce to see if any local businesses are owned by Spanish speakers or employ Spanish speakers. Students might visit these businesses and practice their Spanish.

Quick Start Review

Etapa vocabulary

Use OHT 160 or write on the board: Write complete sentences describing what someone is doing in each room.

Modelo: la cocina
You write: **Mi padre está preparando la cena.**

1. el baño   4. la cocina
2. el comedor   5. la sala
3. la habitación

Answers
Answers will vary. Answers could include:
1. Mi hermano está lavándose los dientes.
2. Mi madre está quitando la mesa.
3. Yo estoy estudiando.
4. Mi abuela está ordenando las flores.
5. Mi hermana está pasando la aspiradora.

Teaching Suggestions
Vocabulary Review

Have students make flash cards of the vocabulary words. Put the cards in a box. Have 3 students at a time choose 2 words from the box and write a sentence using the words on the board.

Juego

Answers
1. Sofía está en el comedor.
2. Felipe está en la sala.
3. Cristina está en la cocina.

Block Schedule

Variety Have students write up **Actividad 7** as a school newspaper article. Students introduce the article by explaining that they are providing a minute-by-minute account of the great party for those students who were unable to be there. Students may change the **Club de Español** to another focus.

Teaching Middle School Students

Extra Help Before students begin **Actividad 5**, have them generate a list of helpful descriptive words, such as prepositions of location and adjectives.

Challenge Have students create conversations between inanimate objects from the **Vocabulario**. Students read conversations aloud while the class guesses the objects.

Multiple Intelligences
Verbal Have students review the words from the **Vocabulario** by combining items to create as long a sentence as possible.

Planning Guide CLASSROOM MANAGEMENT

OBJECTIVES

Communication
- Plan a party *pp. 220–221, 222–223*
- Describe past activities *pp. 222–223, 240–241*
- Express extremes *pp. 222–223*
- Purchase foods *pp. 222–223*

Grammar
- Use superlatives *pp. 228–229*
- Use regular preterite **-ar** verbs *pp. 230–232*
- Use preterite of **-car**, **-gar**, and **-zar** verbs *pp. 233–236*

Pronunciation
- Linking words *p. 237*
- Dictation *TE, p. 237*

Culture
- Regional vocabulary *p. 224*
- The **tortilla española** *p. 225*
- The Spanish **peseta** *p. 227*
- Barcelona's architecture *pp. 240–241*

♻ Recycling
- Adverbs of frequency *p. 226*
- Direct object pronouns *p. 226*
- Grooming vocabulary *p. 229*
- Reflexive verbs *p. 231*
- Daily chores *p. 232*

STRATEGIES

Listening Strategies
- Listen and take notes *p. 222*

Speaking Strategies
- Say what is the best and worst *p. 230*
- Maintain conversational flow *p. 244*

Reading Strategies
- Noting details *p. 238*

Writing Strategies
- Tell who, what, where, when, why, and how *TE p. 244*

Connecting Cultures Strategies
- Recognize variations in vocabulary *p. 224*
- Spanish cooking and ingredients *p. 225*
- Make a historical time line *p. 240*
- Connect and compare what you know about architecture in your community to help you learn about architecture in a new community *pp. 240–241*

PROGRAM RESOURCES

 Print

- *Más práctica* Workbook PE *pp. 41–48*
- Block Scheduling Copymasters *pp. 121–128*
- Unit 5 Resource Book
  Más práctica Workbook TE *pp. 103–110*
  Information Gap Activities *pp. 119–122*
- Family Involvement *pp. 123–124*
- Video Activities *pp. 125–127*
- Videoscript *pp. 128–130*
- Audioscript *pp. 131–134*
- Assessment Program, Unit 5 Etapa 3 *pp. 135–178*
- Answer Keys *pp. 179–200*

 Audiovisual

- Audio Program Cassettes 15A, 15B / CD 15
- *Canciones* Cassette / CD
- Video Program Videotape 5 / Videodisc 3A
- Overhead Transparencies M1–M5; GO1–GO5; 140, 161–170

 Technology

- Electronic Teacher Tools/Test Generator
- *Intrigas y aventuras* CD-ROM, Disc 1
- www.mcdougallittell.com

 Assessment Program Options

- **Cooperative Quizzes** (Unit 5 Resource Book)
- **Etapa Exam** Forms A and B (Unit 5 Resource Book)
- *Para hispanohablantes* Etapa Exam (Unit 5 Resource Book)
- **Portfolio Assessment** (Unit 5 Resource Book)
- **Unit 5 Comprehensive Test** (Unit 5 Resource Book)
- *Para hispanohablantes* Unit 5 Comprehensive Test (Unit 5 Resource Book)
- **Multiple Choice Test Questions** (Unit 5 Resource Book)
- **Audio Program** Testing Cassette T2 / CD T2
- **Electronic Teacher Tools/Test Generator**

Native Speakers
- *Para hispanohablantes* Workbook PE, *pp. 41–48*
- *Para hispanohablantes* Workbook TE (Unit 5 Resource Book)
- *Para hispanohablantes* Etapa Exam (Unit 5 Resource Book)
- *Para hispanohablantes* Unit 5 Comprehensive Test (Unit 5 Resource Book)
- Audio *Para hispanohablantes* Cassettes 15A, 15B, T2 / CD 15, T2
- Audioscript *Para hispanohablantes* (Unit 5 Resource Book)

| Álvaro | Marta | Iván | Beto |

Student Text Listening Activity Scripts

 Videoscript: Diálogo *pages 222–223*

• Videotape 5 • Videodisc 3A

Search Chapter 7, Play to 8
U5E3 • En vivo (Dialog)

• Use the videoscript with **Actividades 1, 2** *pages 224–225*

Luis: No lo puedo creer. Limpié la cocina, saqué la basura y tú, Carmen, pasaste la aspiradora...

Mercedes: ¿Y qué, Luis? ¿Qué es lo que no puedes creer?

Luis: Bueno, que es mi cumpleaños.

Mercedes: Sí, lo sé.

Luis: ¡El día empezó con demasiados quehaceres! ¿Por qué?

Mercedes: No lo sé, Luis.

Carmen: ¡Yo te ayudé, Luis!

Luis: Sí, Carmen, tú me ayudaste y Mercedes también me ayudó. Muchas gracias a vosotras. Lo más increíble es que son las dos y ¡todavía no terminamos!

Mercedes: No te preocupes, Luis. ¿Por qué no llamas a Álvaro?

Luis: Buena idea. Os veo en la tienda. Hola, Álvaro, soy Luis.

Álvaro: ¡Chht! ¡Es Luis! ¡Hola, Luis! ¿Dónde estás?

Luis: Estoy en la Plaza de San José. Voy a la tienda con Mercedes y Carmen.

Álvaro: ¿Qué haces allí?

Luis: Pues, no lo vas a creer pero tengo que hacer unas compras para mamá.

Álvaro: ¿Ahora? Hombre, te estoy esperando.

Luis: Ya lo sé, ya lo sé. Es una larga historia. Trabajé en casa toda la mañana. Tengo que hacer compras. Y ¡también tengo que cuidar a Carmen!

Álvaro: ¡Qué mala suerte! Pero, hombre, no te preocupes. Ven a casa con Mercedes. Y trae a Carmen también. Ella puede jugar con mis videojuegos.

Luis: Gracias, Álvaro. Nos vemos pronto.

Álvaro: ¡Adiós! Luis no tiene ni idea.

Marta: ¡La tarta está lista, Álvaro! ¡Mírala! Quedó perfecta.

Álvaro: ¡Quedó deliciosa! ¡Es la más deliciosa de Barcelona!

Marta: ¡Álvaro!

Álvaro: ¡Iván! ¡Gran Cocinero! ¿Está lista la carne de res?

Iván: Sí, claro.

Álvaro: Mmmm. ¡Excelente, como siempre! ¡Beto! ¿Qué haces?

Beto: Estoy preparando un plato de verduras. ¡Ay, Álvaro! ¡No te comas las zanahorias! ¿No ves que hay pocas? Oye, Álvaro... una pregunta. Marta preparó la tarta. Iván cocinó la carne. Y yo preparé las patatas y las verduras. ¿Qué cocinaste tú?

Álvaro: ¿Yo? ¡Yo no sé cocinar!

Beto: Entonces ¡tú vas a lavar los platos!

Todos: ¡Eso!

Luis: Hablé con Álvaro. Ahora él lo sabe todo.

Mercedes: Qué bien. Ahora, ¿qué tienes que comprar?

Luis: A ver. Buenas tardes. Necesito comprar leche, zumo, huevos y mantequilla.

Carmen: ¡Y el helado! ¡No olvides el helado! ¡El helado es lo más rico del mundo!

Mercedes: Y unas galletas.

Luis: ¿Cuánto es?

Carmen: ¿Cómo pagaste, Luis?

Luis: Pagué con el dinero de papá. Haces muchas preguntas, Carmen. Primero tenemos que llevar estas cosas a casa. Vamos, pronto.

Álvaro: Luis está a punto de llegar.

Beto: ¡Ssshhhh! ¡Cállate, Álvaro! ¡Silencio! ¡Callaos todos! ¡Ahí viene Luis!

Luis: Álvaro, ¿dónde estás?

Todos: ¡Feliz cumpleaños, Luis!

Luis: ¿Cómo puede ser? ¡Mercedes! ¡Álvaro!

Álvaro: Sí, amigo. Lo planeamos todo.

Luis: Pues, por fin, dime, Mercedes, ¿para qué son esas fotos?

Mercedes: Son para un concurso para la revista *Onda Internacional.* ¡Y tú eres la estrella de mi proyecto! Y el título de mi proyecto es "Un día especial en la vida de un joven español".

Luis: ¡Te voy a decir definitivamente que este día es muy especial!

ACTIVIDAD **11** 🎧 **¿Por qué no me invitaste?** *page 231*

Juana: ¡Qué bien lo pasamos en mi casa el viernes pasado! ¡La mejor fiesta sorpresa del año!

Miguel: ¿Qué celebraron?

Juana: Celebramos el cumpleaños de Yolanda.

Miguel: ¿Y por qué no me invitaste?

Juana: Porque invité sólo a chicas.

Miguel: ¿A cuántas chicas invitaste?

Juana: A diez.

Miguel: ¿Y a qué hora empezó la fiesta?

Juana: Bueno, todas llegaron entre las siete y media y las ocho. Yolanda llegó a las ocho y media. ¡Qué sorpresa para ella!

Miguel: ¿Cómo pasaron la noche?

Juana: Escuchamos música, cantamos, miramos fotos y... ¡hablamos!

ACTIVIDAD **17** 🎧 **¿Cuánto pagaron?** *page 235*

1. Elena compró una pulsera por 3.000 pesetas.
2. Yo compré aretes de oro por 8.600 pesetas.
3. Marta compó un collar por 5.500 pesetas.
4. Ana compró una cartera por 1.300 pesetas.
5. Linda compró un libro por 800 pesetas.

Sample Lesson Plan - 45 Minute Schedule

DAY 1

Etapa Opener
- Quick Start Review (TE, p. 218) 5 MIN.
- Anticipate/Activate prior knowledge: Discuss the *Etapa* Opener. 5 MIN.
- Answer the *¿Qué ves?* questions, p. 218. 5 MIN.

En contexto: Vocabulario
- Quick Start Review (TE, p. 220) 5 MIN.
- Have students use context and pictures to learn *Etapa* vocabulary. 10 MIN.
- Present Supplementary Vocabulary (TE, p. 221). 5 MIN.
- Have students work in pairs to answer the *Preguntas personales,* p. 221. 5 MIN.
- Ask pairs to share each other's answers to the *Preguntas personales,* p. 221. 5 MIN.

DAY 2

En vivo: Diálogo
- Quick Start Review (TE, p. 222) 5 MIN.
- Review the Listening Strategy, p. 222. 5 MIN.
- Play audio or show video for the dialog, pp. 222–223, as students take notes. 10 MIN.
- Check students' notes on the menu. 5 MIN.
- Replay as needed. 5 MIN.
- Read the dialog aloud, having students take the roles of characters. 5 MIN.
- Use the Situational OHTs for additional vocabulary practice. 10 MIN.

Homework Option:
- Video Activities, Unit 5 Resource Book, pp. 125–127.

DAY 3

En acción: Vocabulario y gramática
- Check homework. 5 MIN.
- Quick Start Review (TE, p. 224) 5 MIN.
- Use OHTs to review *En contexto* vocabulary. Ask students for a summary of the dialog to check recall. 5 MIN.
- Play the video/audio; have students do *Actividades* 1 and 2 orally. 10 MIN.
- Read and discuss the *También se dice,* p. 224. 5 MIN.
- Discuss the *Nota cultural,* p. 225. 5 MIN.
- Work orally with the class to complete *Actividad* 3. 10 MIN.

DAY 4

En acción (cont.)
- Quick Start Review (TE, p. 228) 5 MIN.
- Present the *Vocabulario,* p. 226. 5 MIN.
- Have students work in pairs on *Actividad* 4. 5 MIN.
- Ask selected pairs to model their conversations from *Actividad* 4. 5 MIN.
- Assign *Actividad* 5. 5 MIN.
- Ask selected students to share their responses to *Actividad* 5. 5 MIN.
- Read and discuss the *Conexiones,* p. 227. 5 MIN.
- Present *Gramática:* Talking About Extremes: Superlatives, p. 228. 10 MIN.

Homework Option:
- Have students do the *Para hacer,* p. 227.

DAY 5

En acción (cont.)
- Check homework. 5 MIN.
- Assign *Actividad* 6. 5 MIN.
- Ask volunteers to share their answers to *Actividad* 6. 5 MIN.
- Quick Wrap-up (TE, p. 229) 5 MIN.
- Discuss *Actividad* 7. 5 MIN.
- Have students write their responses to *Actividad* 7. 5 MIN.
- Present the Speaking Strategy, p. 230. 5 MIN.
- Have students work in pairs to do *Actividad* 8. 5 MIN.
- Ask pairs to share their conversations from *Actividad* 8. 5 MIN.

Homework Option:
- *Más práctica* Workbook, p. 45. *Para hispanohablantes* Workbook, p. 43.

DAY 6

En acción (cont.)
- Check homework. 5 MIN.
- Quick Start Review (TE, p. 230) 5 MIN.
- Present *Gramática:* Talking About the Past: The Preterite of Regular *-ar* Verbs, p. 230. 10 MIN.
- Assign *Actividad* 9. 5 MIN.
- Call on students to read their work from *Actividad* 9 to the class. 5 MIN.
- Assign *Actividad* 10. 5 MIN.
- Ask students to read their work from *Actividad* 10. 5 MIN.
- Present the *Vocabulario,* p. 231. 5 MIN.

Homework Option:
- *Más práctica* Workbook, pp. 46–47. *Para hispanohablantes* Workbook, pp. 44–45.

DAY 7

En acción (cont.)
- Check homework. 5 MIN.
- Play the audio and assign *Actividad* 11. 10 MIN.
- Discuss *Actividad* 12. 5 MIN.
- Have students write their responses to *Actividad* 12. 5 MIN.
- Have students work in groups to complete *Actividad* 13. 5 MIN.
- Ask groups to report their findings from *Actividad* 13 to the class. 5 MIN.
- Read and discuss *Apoyo para estudiar,* p. 232. 5 MIN.
- Read and discuss the *Nota cultural,* p. 232. 5 MIN.

DAY 8

En acción (cont.)
- Quick Start Review (TE, p. 233) 5 MIN.
- Present *Gramática:* Preterite of Verbs Ending in *-car, -gar,* and *-zar,* p. 233. 10 MIN.
- Have students write their responses to *Actividad* 14. 5 MIN.
- Ask volunteers to read their paragraph for *Actividad* 14. 5 MIN.
- Ask students to write their responses to *Actividad* 15. 5 MIN.
- Call on students to read their sentences from *Actividad* 15. 5 MIN.
- Present the *Vocabulario,* p. 234. 5 MIN.
- Assign *Actividad* 16. 5 MIN.

Homework Option:
- *Más práctica* Workbook, p. 48. *Para hispanohablantes* Workbook, p. 46.

DAY 9

En acción (cont.)
- Check homework. 5 MIN.
- Play the audio and assign *Actividad* 17. 5 MIN.
- Ask volunteers to share their answers to *Actividad* 17. 5 MIN.
- Read and discuss the *Conexiones,* p. 235. 5 MIN.
- Assign *Actividad* 18. 5 MIN.
- Ask volunteers to read their answers for *Actividad* 18. 5 MIN.
- Present the *Vocabulario,* p. 236. 5 MIN.
- Discuss *Actividad* 19. 5 MIN.
- Have students work in pairs on *Actividad* 19. 5 MIN.

DAY 10

En acción (cont.)
- Discuss *Actividad* 20. 5 MIN.
- Have students write their answers to *Actividad* 20. 5 MIN.
- Have students write their answers to *Actividad* 21. 10 MIN.
- Ask students to read their paragraphs from *Actividad* 21. 5 MIN.
- Use Information Gap Activities, Unit 5 Resource Book, pp. 120–121. 5 MIN.
- *Más comunicación,* p. R6. 5 MIN.
- Play the audio and have students practice the *Refranes,* p. 237. 10 MIN.

DAY 11

En voces: Lectura
- Quick Start Review (TE, p. 238) 5 MIN.
- Present the Reading Strategy, p. 238. 5 MIN.
- Have volunteers read the selection aloud as students note details in a web. 10 MIN.
- Discuss students' webs. 5 MIN.
- Work orally with students on the *¿Comprendiste?* questions (Answers, TE, p. 239). 5 MIN.
- Have students write answers to the *¿Comprendiste?* questions. 5 MIN.
- Discuss the *¿Qué piensas?* questions, p. 239. 10 MIN.

Homework Option:
- Have students write their answers to the *¿Qué piensas?* questions, p. 239.

DAY 12

En colores: Cultura y comparaciones
- Check homework. 5 MIN.
- Quick Start Review (TE, p. 240) 5 MIN.
- Discuss the Connecting Cultures Strategy, p. 240. 5 MIN.
- Make a frame for the time line suggested in the Connecting Cultures Strategy, p. 240. 5 MIN.
- Have volunteers read the selection aloud as students fill in their time lines. 10 MIN.
- Review students' time lines. 5 MIN.
- Work orally with students to answer the *¿Comprendiste?* questions (Answers, TE, p. 241). 5 MIN.
- Discuss the *¿Qué piensas?* question, p. 241. 5 MIN.

DAY 13

En uso: Repaso y más comunicación
- Quick Start Review (TE, p. 242) 5 MIN.
- Assign *Actividad* 1. 5 MIN.
- Work orally with students to complete *Actividades* 2–3. 10 MIN.
- Have students read and think about *Actividades* 4–5. 5 MIN.
- Call on students to give oral responses to *Actividad* 4. 5 MIN.
- Present the Speaking Strategy, p. 244. 5 MIN.
- Have students work in pairs on *Actividad* 5. 5 MIN.
- Have pairs share their work on *Actividad* 5. 5 MIN.

Homework Option:
- Have students review all of the *Gramática* boxes in *Etapa* 3.

DAY 14

En uso (cont.)
- Quick Start Review (TE, p. 245) 5 MIN.
- Review grammar questions as needed. 10 MIN.
- Have students work in groups on *Actividad* 6. 5 MIN.
- Ask groups to share their work from *Actividad* 6. 5 MIN.

En tu propia voz: Escritura
- Have students work independently to complete the writing activity, *Actividad* 7. 5 MIN.
- Ask volunteers to read their work from *Actividad* 7. 5 MIN.

En resumen: Repaso de vocabulario
- Review *Etapa* 3 vocabulary. 10 MIN.

Homework Option:
- Have students study for the *Etapa* exam.

DAY 15

En resumen: Repaso de vocabulario
- Answer questions related to *Etapa* 3 content. 10 MIN.
- Complete *Etapa* exam. 25 MIN.

Conexiones
- Have students read the *Conexiones,* pp. 246–247, as they complete the exam.

Classroom Management Tip

Vary classroom activities
Give students opportunities to get information from a variety of sources and combine it into interesting reports or displays.

Have students compile **El guía de flamenco,** including information about **castañuelas, palmadas, cantaores, tablao, taconeo, guitarra española,** and famous flamenco musicians. Culminate the research with reports highlighted with dancing and music.

Etapa Theme

Planning a party and talking about past activities

Grammar Objectives

• Using superlatives
• Using regular preterite **-ar** verbs
• Using preterite of **-car, -gar, -zar** verbs

Teaching Resource Options

Print

Block Scheduling Copymasters

Audiovisual

OHT 140, 167 (Quick Start)

🔔 Quick Start Review

♻ Commands/chores

Use OHT 167 or write on the board:
You and your friend Isabel are preparing for a party. Tell her 4 things she can do to help.

Modelo: Prepara la comida.

Answers
Answers will vary. Answers could include:
1. Escribe las invitaciones.
2. Ve de compras.
3. Haz las tapas.
4. Barre el suelo.
5. Compra un disco compacto.

Teaching Suggestions
Previewing the Etapa

• Ask students to study the picture on pp. 218–219 (1 min.).
• Close books; ask students to share at least 3 things they remember.
• Reopen books and look at the picture again. Have students describe the people and the setting.
• Use the **¿Qué ves?** questions to focus the discussion.

UNIDAD 5
ETAPA 3

¡Qué buena celebración!

• Plan a party

• Describe past activities

• Express extremes

• Purchase food

¿Qué ves?

Mira la foto de la fiesta para Luis.
1. ¿Está contento Luis?
2. ¿Qué hay en la mesa?
3. ¿Cuántas personas están en la fiesta?
4. ¿En qué cuarto de la casa están?

218

Middle School Classroom Management

Time Saver Have items such as empty milk, butter, and egg cartons, etc., ready for hands-on practice with the cooking vocabulary in the **En contexto** section.

Planning Ahead Gather posters and other visuals for the history and archaeological sequences at the end of the unit.

219

Cross Cultural Connections

Ask students to compare the photo of the party here with birthday celebrations they have been to. Have students talk about birthday traditions in the U.S.

Culture Highlights

● **LA COCINA** The cuisine of Barcelona includes a variety of cakes and tarts made with fruits. Some examples are **tarta de frutas** (fruit tart), **torta de manzanas** (apple cake), **torta de naranjas** (orange cake), and **pan de banana** (banana bread).

● **EL TURRÓN** Turrón is a delicious gourmet sweet that is very popular in Spain. It consists of peeled toasted almonds mixed with wild honey, sugar, and glucose. It has a chewy consistency.

Supplementary Vocabulary

los adornos	decorations
los globos	balloons
la bandera	banner
el papel de envolver	wrapping paper
la cinta	ribbon

Following are the words to "Happy Birthday":
Cumpleaños feliz
Te deseamos a ti.
Cumpleaños feliz
Te deseamos a ti.

▨ Block Schedule

Streamlining Assign one of the ¿Qué ves? questions to each student. They will be responsible for not only answering the question, but expanding on it. For example: for question #1, students should also talk about how the other people feel. (For additional activities, see **Block Scheduling Copymasters**.)

Teaching Middle School Students

Extra Help Display the names of the characters shown in the picture of the party. Have students identify the ones they already know, and then tell them to guess who the others may be.

Native Speakers Ask native speakers to discuss with other students regional differences in party vocabulary.

Multiple Intelligences

Interpersonal Ask students to make a list of things they usually do at parties. Have them work in pairs and note similarities and differences in their lists. Call time and have students volunteer party activities to make a class list. After reading about Luis's party, they could compare their parties with his.

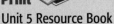

Teaching Resource Options

Print 📖

Unit 5 Resource Book
  Video Activities, pp. 125–126
  Videoscript, p. 128
  Audioscript, p. 131
  Audioscript *Para hispanohablantes*,
    p. 131

Audiovisual

OHT 161, 162, 163, 163A, 164, 164A,
167 (Quick Start)
Audio Program Cassette 15A / CD 15
Audio *Para hispanohablantes*
  Cassette 15A / CD 15
Video Program Videotape 5 /
  Videodisc 3A

Search Chapter 6, Play to 7
U5E3 • En contexto (Vocabulary)

Technology 💻🎧

Intrigas y aventuras **CD-ROM**, Disc 1

🔔 Quick Start Review

♻ Food vocabulary

Use OHT 167 or write on the board:
Write 5 food items you have eaten
recently.

Answers
Answers will vary. Answers could include:
una hamburguesa, unas papas fritas,
una torta, unos tacos, un sándwich,
unas tortillas, un bistec, una ensalada,
una enchilada, un pastel

Language Notes

• In Spain, the word **tarta** is often used
for *cake*. In earlier **Etapas**, students
learned the words **pastel** (Mexico)
and **torta** (Latin America).

• **Patatas alioli** is a dish that is similar to
potato salad. Two ingredients are garlic
and olive oil, from which it derives its
name. In **catalán**, **ali** is *garlic* and **oli**
is *oil*.

En contexto

🎧💿 VOCABULARIO

Luis's friends are finishing their preparations for his
surprise birthday party. Look at all of the food!

A Hay mucha comida para la fiesta. En
el frigorífico hay **una lata de zumo** y
crema. ¿Y en **el congelador?** ¡**Helado!**

el congelador

el helado

el frigorífico

el horno

la crema

Crema

la lata de zumo

B Para hacer la tarta, Marta usa
harina, huevos, mantequilla y
leche. Acaba de hacer **galletas.**

los huevos

la leche

las galletas

la mantequilla

la harina

las verduras

las salchichas

los tomates

las zanahorias

C Hay **verduras, tomates** y **zanahorias.**
También hay **salchichas.**

220 doscientos veinte
Unidad 5

Middle School Classroom Community

TPR Display visuals of kitchen appliances in various
parts of the room. Tell a student that he or she needs
something in the kitchen. **(Necesitas mantequilla y
leche.)** The student must go to the appropriate visual
(refrigerator).

Game Have students play a guessing game with the
food items. Display real items or visuals of food on a
table. Choose a student from Team A to look at the
table and to then turn his or her back. Have a student
from Team B come up and remove an item. Then, the
student from Team A turns around and has 30 seconds
to name the missing item.

cocinar

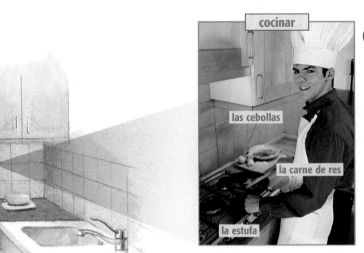

D

Iván **cocina** en la **estufa**.
Cocina **carne de res** con
cebollas.

las cebollas

la carne de res

la estufa

las patatas

la botella de aceite

el microondas

el lavaplatos

la pimienta   la sal

E Para **las patatas** alioli, Beto usa patatas, un
poco de **aceite**, **sal** y **pimienta**. También
usa mayonesa y otros ingredientes.

¡Cállate!

apagar la luz

F Cuando Luis llega, Marta **apaga la luz**.
Beto le dice a Marta «**¡Cállate!**».
¡Quieren silencio para darle la sorpresa a Luis!

Preguntas personales

1. ¿Te gusta cocinar?
2. ¿Qué postre prefieres, helado o galletas?
3. ¿Cuál usas más, la estufa o el microondas?
4. ¿Qué preparas?
5. ¿Qué hay en tu frigorífico?

doscientos veintiuno
Etapa 3

221

Teaching Resource Options

Print 📖

Más práctica Workbook PE, pp. 41–44
Para hispanohablantes Workbook PE, pp. 41–42
Block Scheduling Copymasters
Unit 5 Resource Book
  Más práctica Workbook TE, pp. 103–106
  Para hispanohablantes Workbook TE, pp. 111–112
  Video Activities, pp. 125–126
  Videoscript, p. 129
  Audioscript, p. 131
  Audioscript *Para hispanohablantes*, p. 131

Audiovisual 📼

OHT 165, 166, 167 (Quick Start)
Audio Program Cassette 15A / CD 15
Audio *Para hispanohablantes*
  Cassette 15A / CD 15
Video Program Videotape 5 / Videodisc 3A

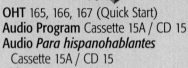

Search Chapter 7, Play to 8
U5E3 • En vivo (Dialog)

Technology 💻

Intrigas y aventuras CD-ROM, Disc 1

🔔 Quick Start Review

 Kitchen/cooking vocabulary
Use OHT 167 or write on the board:
Complete the following sentences logically.
1. Voy a hacer galletas. Necesito ___ , ___ y ___ .
2. Mis verduras favoritas son ___ y ___ .
3. En mi cocina no hay lavaplatos, pero sí hay ___ y ___ .
4. En nuestro congelador, siempre tenemos ___ .

Answers *See p. 217B.*

Gestures

In scene 4, Álvaro says, **Hombre…**
Although the stress is usually on the next-to-last syllable, an exasperated Spaniard will stress the last syllable and throw up his/her hands at the same time: **¡Hom<u>bre</u>!**

En vivo

🎧📺 **DIÁLOGO**

Álvaro

Marta

Iván

Beto

¡De compras!

PARA ESCUCHAR • STRATEGY: LISTENING

Listen and take notes There are many different ways to celebrate a birthday. Luis's friends have prepared a meal for him. Listen and write down the menu. Were all categories mentioned?

Bebidas	Carne	Verduras	Postre

1▶ Luis: No lo puedo creer. Limpié la cocina, saqué la basura y tú, Carmen, pasaste la aspiradora.
Mercedes: ¿Y qué, Luis? ¿Qué es lo que no puedes creer?
Luis: Que es mi cumpleaños.

5▶ Luis: Trabajé en casa toda la mañana. Y ¡también tengo que cuidar a Carmen!
Álvaro: Ven a casa con Mercedes. Y trae a Carmen también.
Luis: Gracias. Nos vemos pronto.

6▶ Marta: ¡La tarta está lista, Álvaro! ¡Mírala!
Álvaro: ¡Quedó deliciosa! ¡Es la más deliciosa de Barcelona!
Marta: ¡Álvaro!
Álvaro: ¡Iván! ¿Está lista la carne de res?
Iván: Sí, claro.

7▶ Álvaro: ¡Beto! ¿Qué haces?
Beto: Estoy preparando un plato de verduras. ¡No te comas las zanahorias! ¿No ves que hay pocas?

222   doscientos veintidós
Unidad 5

Middle School Classroom Community

TPR Ask each student to choose one of the menu categories from the Listening Strategy. Replay the video and have students raise their hands as items in their category are mentioned.

Storytelling Have students imagine that the party is over. Ask them to take turns telling what the characters do then. Each contribution should complement the previous one so that a cohesive story is created.

Paired Activity Have students work in pairs to write a short dialog about a person who is going to be given a surprise birthday party. Have the partners act it out for the class.

2▶ **Luis:** ¡El día empezó con demasiados quehaceres!
Carmen: ¡Yo te ayudé, Luis!
Luis: Sí, Carmen, tú me ayudaste y Mercedes también me ayudó.

3▶ **Luis:** Lo más increíble es que son las dos y ¡todavía no terminamos!
Mercedes: No te preocupes, Luis. ¿Por qué no llamas a Álvaro?
Luis: Buena idea. Os veo en la tienda.

4▶ **Luis:** Hola, Álvaro, soy Luis.
Álvaro: ¡Hola, Luis! ¿Dónde estás?
Luis: Voy a la tienda con Mercedes y Carmen. Tengo que hacer unas compras.
Álvaro: ¿Ahora? Hombre, te estoy esperando.

8▶ **Luis:** Necesito comprar leche, zumo, huevos y mantequilla.
Carmen: ¡No olvides el helado! ¡Es lo más rico del mundo!
Luis: Tenemos que llevar estas cosas a casa. Vamos, pronto.

9▶ **Todos:** ¡Feliz cumpleaños, Luis!
Luis: ¿Cómo puede ser? ¡Mercedes! ¡Álvaro!
Álvaro: Sí, amigo. Lo planeamos todo.
Luis: Pues, por fin, dime, Mercedes, ¿para qué son esas fotos?

10▶ **Mercedes:** Son para un concurso. ¡Y tú eres la estrella de mi proyecto! Y el título de mi proyecto es «Un día especial en la vida de un joven español».
Luis: ¡Te voy a decir definitivamente que este día es muy especial!

doscientos veintitrés
Etapa 3

223

Teaching Middle School Students

Extra Help Review the names of Luis's friends and what they prepared for the party before watching the video and reading **En vivo**.

Multiple Intelligences
Musical/Rhythmic Have students find and share recordings of Spanish or Latin music that might be played at a party. The music could be traditional or popular.

Teaching Suggestions
Presenting the Dialog
• Prepare students for listening by focusing on the dialog context using yes/no or either/or questions. Reintroduce the characters and setting: **¿Es Luis el hermano de Carmen? ¿Es hoy el cumpleaños de Mercedes o de Luis? ¿Hace Álvaro los quehaceres con sus amigos?**
• Use the video, audio cassette, or CD to present the dialog. The expanded dialog on video offers additional listening practice opportunities.

Video Synopsis
• Luis, Carmen, and Mercedes have more errands to run while Álvaro and other friends get ready for Luis's birthday party. For a complete transcript of the video dialog, see p. 217B.

Comprehension Questions
1. ¿Están de paseo Luis, Carmen y Mercedes? (No.)
2. ¿Sacó Luis la basura? (Sí.)
3. ¿Empezó el día con muchos quehaceres? (Sí.)
4. En la foto 3, ¿son las dos o son las dos y media? (son las dos)
5. ¿Quién va a llamar a Álvaro, Mercedes o Luis? (Luis)
6. ¿Está preparando la tarta Marta o Álvaro? (Marta)
7. ¿Qué está preparando Beto? (un plato de verduras)
8. ¿Qué quiere Carmen en la tienda? (helado)
9. ¿Cuál es la sorpresa para Luis? (una fiesta de cumpleaños)
10. ¿Por qué sacó Mercedes tantas fotos de Luis? (para el concurso)

Block Schedule
Previewing Point out to students that in this **Etapa** they will learn how to talk about events that have already happened. Tell them that there are several verbs in the dialog in the past tense. Have students try to identify them using context. (For additional activities, see **Block Scheduling Copymasters**.)

Teaching Resource Options

Print 📖

Unit 5 Resource Book
Video Activities, p. 127
Videoscript, p. 130
Audioscript, p. 131
Audioscript *Para hispanohablantes*,
p. 131

Audiovisual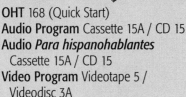

OHT 168 (Quick Start)
Audio Program Cassette 15A / CD 15
Audio *Para hispanohablantes*
Cassette 15A / CD 15
Video Program Videotape 5 /
Videodisc 3A

🔔 Quick Start Review

♻ Dialog review

Use OHT 168 or write on the board:
Complete the following sentences from
the dialog.

1. El día empezó con demasiados
   ___ .

2. ¡Iván! ¿Está lista la ___ ?

3. Necesito comprar leche, zumo,
   ___ y mantequilla.

4. Estoy preparando un plato de
   ___ .

5. ¡Y tú eres la estrella de mi ___ !

Answers
1. quehaceres   4. verduras
2. carne de res 5. proyecto
3. huevos

Teaching Suggestions
Comprehension Check

Use **Actividades 1** and **2** to assess
retention after the dialog. Have students
close their books. For **Actividad 2,** read
the items and see if students can
respond. Have them add 3 items
to **Actividad 2.**

 Objective: Controlled practice
Listening comprehension/vocabulary

Answers (See script, p. 217B.)
1. b   3. a
2. c   4. d

En acción
VOCABULARIO Y GRAMÁTICA

OBJECTIVES

- Plan a party
- Describe past activities
- Express extremes
- Purchase food
- *Use superlatives*
- *Use regular preterite -ar verbs*
- *Use preterite of -car, -gar, and -zar verbs*

En otras palabras

Escuchar Según el diálogo, escoge la oración
que mejor describe lo que pasa en cada foto.
(Hint: Match the sentences with the photos.)

a. Luis está hablando por teléfono.

b. Los amigos preparan la comida.

c. Luis y su hermana van de compras.

d. Los amigos de Luis le dicen «¡Feliz
   cumpleaños!»

También se dice

Sometimes **el frigorífico** is used in Spain to talk about the
refrigerator. Other words are also used for this appliance.

- **la nevera:** Ecuador, Puerto Rico,   Also, Spaniards say
  parts of Spain   **zumo** for *juice.*
- **la heladera:** Argentina   Latin Americans use
- **el refrigerador:** Mexico   **jugo.**

Middle School Classroom Management

Time Saver Make students aware of the use of the
past tense in the **En vivo.** Have them watch the video
again and listen for the new verb usage. This will make
the formal introduction on p. 230 go more smoothly.

Peer Review In small groups, students should
practice or review something in the lesson. Then have
each group member write a quiz question based on
the practice. Each member asks his or her question
and the other students write the answer. Have the
students check their work and report the results.

ACTIVIDAD 2 **Objective:** Transitional practice
Listening comprehension/vocabulary

Answers (See script, p. 217B.)
1. falso; No le gusta hacer los quehaceres.
2. cierto
3. cierto
4. falso; Quiere comprar helado.
5. falso; Son para el concurso.

ACTIVIDAD 3 **Objective:** Controlled practice
Vocabulary

Answers
1. Necesito sal.
2. Necesito patatas.
3. Necesito aceite.
4. Necesito huevos.

ACTIVIDAD 2

¿Cierto o falso?

Escuchar ¿Son ciertas o falsas las oraciones que describen el diálogo? Si las oraciones son falsas, di la frase cierta. *(Hint: Tell whether the sentences are true or false. If they are false, correct them.)*

1. A Luis le gusta hacer los quehaceres.
2. Luis tiene que hacer unas compras.
3. Iván prepara la carne de res.
4. Carmen quiere comprar una tarta.
5. Las fotos son para los abuelos de Luis.

NOTA CULTURAL

You may have tasted a Mexican tortilla, but have you ever tasted a **tortilla española**? In Spain it's a popular dish made with potatoes, eggs, olive oil, salt, and pepper.

tortilla española

The Mexican tortilla, on the other hand, is made from a corn or wheat flour dough. The dough is patted into flat cakes and baked in an oven. People fill them with meat, vegetables, cheese, or beans. The **tortilla española** is more like a potato omelet that is cooked on the stove. While most people like to eat their Mexican tortillas warm, the **tortilla española** can be enjoyed hot or cold!

tortillas

ACTIVIDAD 3

La tortilla española

Hablar ¿Qué necesitas para hacer una tortilla española? *(Hint: Say what you need.)*

modelo

*Necesito **pimienta**.*

1.

2.

3.

4.

doscientos veinticinco
Etapa 3

225

Project

Give this out-of-sequence recipe for **tortilla española** to pairs of students. Provide a dictionary, and encourage students to use context cues to decipher unfamiliar vocabulary. Ask them to place the steps in a logical order. If possible, have them try the recipe at home or in the cooking room at school.

Ingredientes: 4 patatas, 1/2 taza de aceite de oliva, 1 cebolla, 1 cucharadita de sal, 8 huevos.

Como hacerlo:
(1) Pelar las patatas y la cebolla cortar en pedazos pequeños
(10) Servir caliente o fría con pan francés
(4) Quitarlas el aceite
(7) Cocer a fuego lento
(9) Poner la tortilla en un plato
(2) Calentar el aceite y echar las patatas a freír
(3) Cuidado con aceite caliente
(5) Batir los huevos y echarlos la sal
(6) Mezclar las patatas con los huevos
(8) Dar la vuelta a la tortilla

Teaching Middle School Students

Extra Help Have students work in small groups to review the foods introduced on these pages. Tell them to sort all the food words they know into categories (**postres, carne,** etc.).

Native Speakers Ask native speakers which words in the **También se dice** are used in their countries.

Multiple Intelligences

Interpersonal Ask students to list the new foods under the headings **Me gusta mucho, Me gusta un poco, No me gusta**. Have students share this information with their partners. Then, partners share with the class the responses they have in common. (**Nos gusta mucho la pasta,** etc.).

Block Schedule

Expansion Expand **Actividad 3** into an activity using real recipes. Have students bring in their favorite recipes and tell the class what is needed. For additional vocabulary, they may consult dictionaries or native speakers in the classroom.

Teaching Resource Options

Print 📖

Unit 5 Resource Book
Video Activities, p. 127
Videoscript, p. 130
Audioscript, p. 131
Audioscript *Para hispanohablantes*,
   p. 131

Audiovisual 🎧

OHT 168 (Quick Start)
Audio Program Cassette 15A / CD 15
Audio *Para hispanohablantes*
   Cassette 15A / CD 15
Video Program Videotape 5 /
   Videodisc 3A

Teaching Suggestions
Presenting Vocabulary

Present the food vocabulary on p. 226
and review the food vocabulary on
pp. 220–221 and 136–137. Then have
students sort and classify the foods
as **Carne/Pescado, Producto lácteo,
Grano, Fruta/Verdura,** or **Dulce.**

 ACTIVIDAD 4 Objective: Open-ended practice
Vocabulary

♻ Adverbs of frequency,
   direct object pronouns

Answers

*Answers will vary but must contain the following
questions and direct object pronouns.*
1. ¿Comes pasta? / la
2. ¿Comes pescado? / lo
3. ¿Comes yogur? / lo
4. ¿Comes helado? / lo
5. ¿Comes zanahorias? / las
6. ¿Comes cereal? / lo
7. ¿Comes cebollas? / las
8. ¿Comes galletas? / las

♻ **¿Qué comes?**

Hablar Trabaja con otro(a) estudiante. Indica con qué frecuencia
comes esta comida, usando estas frases: **a veces, todos los días,
nunca.** *(Hint: Tell how often you eat the following foods.)*

modelo

Estudiante A: ¿Comes **tomates**?

Estudiante B: *Sí, a veces los como.*

   o: Sí, los como todos los días.

   o: ¡Nunca los como! No me gustan.

1. 2. 3. 4. 5. 6. 7. 8.

Vocabulario

La comida

la pasta

el pescado

el cereal

el puerco

el yogur

¿Qué te gusta comer?

Middle School Classroom Community

Learning Scenario Set up a context in which pairs
of students "prepare" a dish for a cooking contest. Give
students time to organize and practice their presentation.
Pairs should describe what they are doing as they move
logically through the preparation. Have the class vote
for the best presentation.

Portfolio Ask students to plan and present menus
for one day.

Rubric

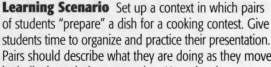

Criteria	Scale	
Creativity	1 2 3 4 5	A = 13–15 pts.
Logical organization	1 2 3 4 5	B = 10–12 pts.
Vocabulary use/spelling	1 2 3 4 5	C = 7–9 pts.

D = 4–6 pts.
F = < 4 pts.

ACTIVIDAD 5

¡La fiesta!

Leer/Hablar Todos están muy ocupados con los preparativos para la fiesta de Luis. Explica lo que hacen. *(Hint: Explain what they do.)*

1. Marta saca la leche _____ .
   a. de la estufa
   b. del frigorífico
   c. del lavaplatos

2. Álvaro pone el helado en _____ .
   a. el congelador
   b. la mantequilla
   c. la harina

3. Iván cocina _____ .
   a. la pimienta
   b. el zumo
   c. la carne de res

4. Beto saca _____ para el café.
   a. el azúcar
   b. la sal
   c. el aceite

5. Mercedes pone los platos sucios en _____ .
   a. el lavaplatos
   b. el microondas
   c. la estufa

Conexiones

Las matemáticas When shopping in Spain, take along many **pesetas**. The **peseta** is the national currency, and you will need a lot of them when you shop! Sometimes you will see the word **pesetas** abbreviated as **ptas**.

una camiseta
1.800 ptas.

unos jeans
5.250 ptas.

una entrada al cine
900 ptas.

PARA HACER:
To find out the current exchange rate with the U.S. dollar, check the financial section of a newspaper. How many dollars would you need to exchange to buy these three items?

227

ACTIVIDAD 5

Objective: Controlled practice
Vocabulary

Answers
1. b
2. a
3. c
4. a
5. a

Para hacer

Answers will vary, depending on the current exchange rate.

Teaching Middle School Students

Native Speakers Have native speakers talk to students about different kinds of meat, fish, vegetables, etc., eaten in their countries, and what they are called. The vocabulary may be different from that in the textbook.

Multiple Intelligences

Logical/Mathematical Provide students with one or two Spanish cookbooks and a customary-metric conversion chart. Have them prepare a presentation on how to convert the measurements so that English-only students could use the recipes. Then have them convert U.S. recipe measurements to metric for use by Spanish-speaking people.

Block Schedule

Variety Have the class visit the food storage area of the school cafeteria. Ask them to take notes in Spanish so that when they return to class they can create a shopping checklist for the food service buyer. Encourage students to use the dictionary for items for which they don't have vocabulary.

Teaching Resource Options

Print

Más práctica Workbook PE, p. 45
Para hispanohablantes Workbook PE, p. 43
Block Scheduling Copymasters
Unit 5 Resource Book
  Más práctica Workbook TE, p. 107
  Para hispanohablantes Workbook TE, p. 113
  Information Gap Activities, p. 119

Audiovisual

OHT 168 (Quick Start)

Technology

Intrigas y aventuras CD-ROM, Disc 1

Quick Start Review

♻ Comparisons

Use OHT 168 or write on the board: Complete the following comparison sentences with a logical adjective.

1. Mi mejor amiga es más ___ que yo.
2. El béisbol es más ___ que el tenis.
3. Carmen estudia todo el tiempo. Es más ___ que Anita.
4. Las botas cuestan mucho. Son más ___ que los zapatos.

Answers
Answers will vary. Answers could include:
1. alta
2. divertido
3. trabajadora
4. caras

Teaching Suggestions
Teaching Talking About Extremes: Superlatives

Show 3 of the same article (**tres libros**). First make comparisons with them. (**El libro de español es más nuevo que el libro de historia. El libro de historia es más nuevo que el libro de matemáticas.**) Then state the superlative. (**El libro de español es el más nuevo.**)

GRAMÁTICA

Talking About Extremes: Superlatives

♻ **¿RECUERDAS?** *1A, p. 234* Remember how you make comparisons? These phrases say that one item has **more** or **less** of a certain quality than another item has.

más… que

menos… que

When you want to say that something has the **most** or the **least** of a certain quality, use a **superlative**.

el más…	el menos…
los más…	los menos…
la más…	la menos…
las más…	las menos…

Luis es **el** más **alto**. Carmen es **la** más **pequeña**. Mercedes es **la** menos **cansada**.
*Luis is **the tallest**. Carmen is **the smallest**. Mercedes is **the least tired**.*

To use a **noun** with the superlative form, put it **after** the article.

matches

Luis es **el chico** más **alto**. Mercedes es **la chica** menos **cansada**.
*Luis is **the tallest boy**. Mercedes is **the least tired girl**.*

matches

Iván prepara **las comidas** más **sabrosas**.
*Iván makes **the tastiest meals**.*

> Be sure the adjective matches the noun in both gender and number.

When you refer to an idea or concept, which has no gender, use the neuter article **lo**.

Luis says: —**Lo** más **increíble** es que son las dos…
The most incredible (thing) is that it's two o'clock…

Remember to use these **irregular** forms you learned with comparatives when referring to the *best, worst, oldest,* and *youngest*.

el mejor   **el peor**   **el mayor**   **el menor**

Luis es **el mayor**. Carmen es **la menor**.
*Luis is **the oldest**. Carmen is **the youngest**.*

> **Mayor** and **menor** are used only when describing people.

Middle School Classroom Community

Paired Activity Have students look at the pictures of Luis's party on pp. 222–223. Ask them to write five sentences about the characters and/or the food, using the superlative (**La tarta es la mejor comida**). Call time, and ask several students to write one of their sentences on the board. Compare and discuss.

Game Start by making a superlative statement about something in the room. Have students guess what you are describing. (**Es el __ más grande.**) Have them respond using the whole sentence in order to get the "feel" of the superlative word order.

ACTIVIDAD 6 · Gramática

¿Qué decides?

Leer/Hablar ¿Qué decides después de comparar? Lee y compara la información. Luego contesta las preguntas. *(Hint: Read and compare the information. Then answer the questions.)*

modelo

Tina: diez cuartos

Emilio: ocho cuartos

Carlos: seis cuartos

¿Quién tiene la casa más pequeña?

Carlos tiene la casa más pequeña.

1. cebollas: 90 pesetas
   patatas: 120 pesetas
   tomates: 140 pesetas
   ¿Qué es lo menos caro?

2. Eva: 12 años
   Celia: 14 años
   Juana: 15 años
   ¿Quién es la menor?

3. la doctora: 1,7 m
   el profesor: 1,8 m
   el policía: 1,9 m
   ¿Quién es el más alto?

4. Pablo: A en música
   Ramón: B en música
   Tomás: C en música
   ¿Quién es el mejor estudiante?

MÁS PRÁCTICA *cuaderno* p. 45

PARA HISPANOHABLANTES *cuaderno* p. 43

ACTIVIDAD 7

♻ Cosas del baño

Hablar/Escribir Estas cosas se encuentran en el baño de Luis. Compáralas. *(Hint: Compare the items.)*

modelo

corto / largo

*El peine azul es el más **corto**.*

*El peine negro es el más **largo**.*

1. sucio / limpio

2. barato / caro

3. grande / pequeño

4. nuevo / viejo

ACTIVIDAD 6 Objective: Controlled practice Superlatives

Answers
1. Las cebollas son lo menos caro.
2. Eva es la menor.
3. El policía es el más alto.
4. Pablo es el mejor estudiante.

🔔 Quick Wrap-up

Write categories such as the following on the board and ask students to name the best in each case: **los cantantes, las cantantes, los actores, las actrices, los atletas, las atletas, los conjuntos (grupos).**

ACTIVIDAD 7 Objective: Transitional practice Superlatives/vocabulary

♻ Grooming vocabulary

Answers
1. La toalla verde es la más sucia. La toalla blanca es la más limpia.
2. El champú blanco es el más barato. El champú verde es el más caro.
3. El espejo blanco es el más grande. El espejo azul es el más pequeño.
4. El jabón marrón es el más nuevo. El jabón amarillo es el más viejo.

Teaching Middle School Students

Multiple Intelligences

Visual Have students work in small groups with pictures representing vocabulary. Tell them to take turns laying out pictures of at least two similar items. The other group members must use superlatives to make a sentence about the items. (**La casa roja es la más grande; La casa blanca es la menos bonita;** etc.).

Intrapersonal Ask students to think about 4 family members and/or friends. Tell them to write sentences about who is the tallest, the most interesting, etc. Students may share with a partner or the class, if appropriate.

Block Schedule

Retention Have students bring in bottles of shampoo and soap in as many sizes as they can find. Put all of the bottles in a center at the back of the room and give students time to make, sort by size, and describe collections of these bottles.

Teaching Resource Options

Print 📖

Más práctica Workbook PE, pp. 46–47
Para hispanohablantes Workbook PE, pp. 44–45
Block Scheduling Copymasters
Unit 5 Resource Book
  Más práctica Workbook TE, pp. 108–109
  Para hispanohablantes Workbook TE, pp. 114–115
  Audioscript, p. 132
  Audioscript *Para hispanohablantes*, p. 132

Audiovisual 💻

OHT 168 (Quick Start)
Audio Program Cassettes 15A, 15B / CD 15
Audio *Para hispanohablantes* Cassette 15A / CD 15

Technology 💻

Intrigas y aventuras CD-ROM, Disc 1

8 Objective: Open-ended practice
Superlatives/vocabulary

Answers will vary.

🔔 Quick Start Review

♻ Superlatives

Use OHT 168 or write on the board:
Write a superlative statement based on the following information.

1. Carlos, 5 ft. 7 in. / Ana, 5 ft. 3 in. / Sofía, 5 ft. 8 in.
2. Roberto, D (nota) / Jaime, A / Miguel, C
3. el sofá, $375 / el sillón, $60 / la mesa, $200
4. Sr. Ruíz, 75 años / Sr. Ricardo, 80 años / Sr. Fernández, 60 años

Answers *See p. 217B.*

Teaching Suggestions
Presenting The Preterite of Regular -ar Verbs
Present the vocabulary words in sample sentences using a calendar. Mark an X for today. Then point to each appropriate day, week, month, year as you give each sentence.

ACTIVIDAD 8

En mi opinión...

PARA CONVERSAR
STRATEGY: SPEAKING
Saying what is the best and worst After Activity 8, decide which is the best **(el mejor)** or the worst **(el peor)** of these categories: **equipo de baloncesto, grupo musical, película del año.**

Hablar Todos tienen opiniones. Da tu opinión sobre las siguientes cosas. *(Hint: Give your opinion on the following topics.)*

modelo

la comida más rica

Estudiante A: ¿Cuál es **la comida más rica** para ti?
Estudiante B: El bistec es **la comida más rica.**

1. la música más popular
2. el deporte menos divertido
3. la clase menos difícil
4. el peor quehacer
5. el lugar más bonito
6. la película menos interesante
7. el actor más guapo
8. la actriz más bonita
9. la clase más difícil
10. el libro más cómico

■ **MÁS COMUNICACIÓN** p. R6

GRAMÁTICA
Talking About the Past: The Preterite of Regular -ar Verbs

When you want to talk about actions completed in the past, use the **preterite tense**. To form the preterite of a regular **-ar** verb, add the appropriate preterite **ending** to the verb's **stem**.

limpiar *to clean*

Notice that the first and third person singular forms have an **accent** over the final vowel.

limpi**é**	limpi**amos**
limpi**aste**	limpi**asteis**
limpi**ó**	limpi**aron**

The **nosotros(as)** form is the same in the **preterite** as in the **present** tense.

Luis says:

—**Limpié** la cocina…
—Sí, Carmen, tú me **ayudaste** y Mercedes también me **ayudó**.

I cleaned the kitchen…
Yes, Carmen, you helped me and Mercedes helped me also.

Middle School Classroom Community

TPR Display pictures, objects, etc., around the room. Use a superlative to tell a student to go to something in the room (**Ve a la comida más deliciosa,** etc.). For wider participation, have students do this activity in pairs.

Storytelling Have students work in groups to make up a story about their school (**la mejor escuela**) or a favorite restaurant (**el mejor restaurante de la ciudad**). Everything they say must be in the superlative. Have the groups share their stories with the class, and have them vote for the best one.

ACTIVIDAD 9 Gramática

Las compras

Leer/Escribir Álvaro le explica a Beto qué compraron para la fiesta. Completa lo que dice con la forma correcta de **comprar**. *(Hint: Use correct forms of the preterite tense of **comprar**.)*

Nosotros __1__ cosas riquísimas para la fiesta de Luis, ¿verdad? Marta __2__ los huevos, la harina, la mantequilla y la leche para hacer la tarta. Iván __3__ la carne de res y las cebollas para hacer su plato riquísimo. Tú __4__ las patatas y el aceite para hacer las patatas alioli. Bárbara y Luisa __5__ los refrescos. ¿Y yo? Pues, yo __6__ lo más rico de todo, ¡el helado!

ACTIVIDAD 10 Gramática

Esta mañana

Escribir Estas personas hicieron varias cosas esta mañana. Usa la forma correcta del verbo para escribir lo que hicieron. *(Hint: Use the correct preterite verb form to describe what these people did this morning.)*

modelo

Luis / levantarse temprano

*Esta mañana **Luis se levantó temprano**.*

1. mis hermanas / bañarse
2. yo / ducharse
3. mi padre / afeitarse
4. nosotros /lavarse los dientes
5. tú / lavarse la cara
6. vosotros /peinarse

MÁS PRÁCTICA *cuaderno* pp. 46–47

PARA HISPANOHABLANTES *cuaderno* pp. 44–45

ACTIVIDAD 11

¿Por qué no me invitaste?

Escuchar Juana y su amigo Miguel hablan de una fiesta. Escucha su conversación. Luego, contesta las preguntas. *(Hint: Listen to the conversation between Juana and Miguel and answer the questions.)*

1. ¿Qué celebraron las chicas?
2. ¿Cuándo celebraron?
3. ¿Por qué Juana no invitó a Miguel?
4. ¿A cuántas chicas invitó?
5. ¿Cómo pasaron la noche?

Vocabulario

El pasado

anoche *last night*
anteayer *the day before yesterday*
el año pasado *last year*
ayer *yesterday*
el mes pasado *last month*
la semana pasada *last week*

¿Cuándo patinaste (nadaste, cocinaste)?

Teaching Middle School Students

Extra Help Brainstorm **-ar** verbs that are regular in the preterite. (Students will learn the preterite of verbs ending in **-car**, **-gar**, and **-zar** next; **dar**, **estar**, and **andar** are irregular in the preterite.) Also, list some past markers such as **ayer**, **la semana pasada**, etc. Call on students to say something they did (**Ayer estudié**). Ask the class to write what the person did (**Ayer Antonio estudió**). Correct orally and in writing.

Multiple Intelligences

Verbal Ask students to write five things they did yesterday. Have them take turns telling their partners what they did. Group them with another pair and have the first pair tell the second pair what their partners did. Ask them to discover all the activities they have in common.

ACTIVIDAD 9 **Objective:** Controlled practice
Preterite of **-ar** verbs

Answers
1. compramos
2. compró
3. compró
4. compraste
5. compraron
6. compré

ACTIVIDAD 10 **Objective:** Controlled practice
Preterite of **-ar** verbs

Daily routine vocabulary

Answers
1. Mis hermanas se bañaron.
2. Yo me duché.
3. Mi padre se afeitó.
4. Nosotros nos lavamos los dientes.
5. Tú te lavaste la cara.
6. Vosotros os peinasteis.

Quick Wrap-up

Write on the board activities students are likely to have done recently. Ask questions about who has participated in these activities. As students answer in full sentences, keep a tally of their responses. Then ask volunteers to summarize.

ACTIVIDAD 11 **Objective:** Transitional practice
Listening comprehension/preterite of **-ar** verbs/vocabulary

Answers (See script, p. 217B.)
1. Celebraron el cumpleaños de Yolanda.
2. Celebraron el viernes pasado.
3. Invitó sólo a chicas.
4. Invitó a diez chicas.
5. Escucharon la música, cantaron, miraron fotos y hablaron.

Block Schedule

Interviews Have students write a series of interview questions to ask a partner. Suggest a common theme, such as "what you studied last year" or "what you cooked last week." Have students take notes and report findings to the class. (For additional activities, see **Block Scheduling Copymasters**.)

Teaching Resource Options

Print

Más práctica Workbook PE, p. 48
Para hispanohablantes Workbook PE,
p. 46
Unit 5 Resource Book
  Más práctica Workbook TE, p. 110
  Para hispanohablantes Workbook
  TE, p. 116

Audiovisual

OHT 169 (Quick Start)

Technology

Intrigas y aventuras CD-ROM, Disc 1

 Objective: Transitional practice
Preterite of **-ar** verbs

♻ Daily chores

Answers
1. Álvaro pasó la aspiradora ayer.
2. Ana y Marta lavaron los platos anoche.
3. Mercedes y yo limpiamos la sala la semana
   pasada.
4. Tú cocinaste en la estufa anteayer.
5. Yo quité el polvo el domingo pasado.
6. Ellos prepararon las tapas ayer por la tarde.

 Objective: Open-ended practice
Preterite of **-ar** verbs

Answers
Answers will vary but must contain the following.
lavaste, lavé, lavó
estudiaste, estudié, estudió
pasaste, pasé, pasó
limpiaste, limpié, limpió
usaste, usé, usó
celebraste, celebré, celebró

♻ ¿Cuándo lo terminaron?

Hablar/Escribir Luis habla de los quehaceres
que él y sus amigos terminaron. ¿Cuándo los
terminaron? *(Hint: Say when Luis and his friends finished
various chores.)*

modelo

Luis / quitar la mesa / anoche
Luis quitó la mesa anoche.

1. Álvaro / pasar la aspiradora / ayer
2. Ana y Marta / lavar los platos / anoche
3. Mercedes y yo / limpiar la sala / la semana
   pasada
4. tú / cocinar en la estufa / anteayer
5. yo / quitar el polvo / el domingo pasado
6. ellos / preparar las tapas / ayer por la tarde

Another of Barcelona's intriguing sights
is a lizard-shaped fountain located in
the arcade of the **Parque Güell.**
Designed by Barcelona's beloved Gaudí,
the park, originally intended as a housing
complex, is known for its unusual
architecture.

¿Y ustedes?

Hablar/Escribir Pregúntales a cuatro estudiantes
cuándo hicieron varias actividades. Después,
infórmale a la clase. *(Hint: Ask four classmates when they
did various things and report back to the class.)*

modelo

quitar la mesa
Estudiante A: *¿Cuándo quitaste la mesa?*
Estudiante B: *Quité la mesa anoche.*
Estudiante A (a la clase): *Irene quitó la mesa anoche.*

¿Qué?	¿Cuándo?
lavar los platos	anteayer
estudiar para un examen	ayer
pasar la aspiradora	el mes pasado
limpiar tu habitación	el año pasado
usar la computadora	la semana pasada
celebrar tu cumpleaños	anoche
¿?	¿?

APOYO PARA
ESTUDIAR

Preterite Tense

Since the **nosotros** form of a regular -ar verb is the
same in both the preterite and the present tenses,
how can you determine the tense? Use context clues
to help you. Look for time indicators, like those in the
vocabulary box, and the tense of other verbs.

Middle School Classroom Community

Paired Activity List the time markers and a
selection of people on the board. Have students write
sentences imagining what 5 of the people listed did
and when they did each activity. Have students take
turns reading their sentences to their partners and
making corrections when needed.

Portfolio Ask students to write about a busy
week that they had similar to Mercedes's week in
Actividad 14.

Rubric

Criteria	Scale	
Vocabulary use/spelling	1 2 3 4 5	A = 17–20 pts.
Correct sentence structure/grammar	1 2 3 4 5	B = 13–16 pts.
Logical organization	1 2 3 4 5	C = 9–12 pts.
Creativity	1 2 3 4 5	D = 5–8 pts.
		F = <5 pts.

Preterite of Verbs Ending in -car, -gar, and -zar

Regular verbs that end in **-car**, **-gar**, or **-zar** have a spelling change in the **yo form** of the preterite.

becomes

sa**c**ar	**c**	**qu**	(yo) sa**qu**é
pa**g**ar	**g**	**gu**	(yo) pa**gu**é
empe**z**ar	**z**	**c**	(yo) empe**c**é

Luis says: —…sa**qu**é la basura…

…**I took out** the trash…

ACTIVIDAD 14 Gramática

¡Una semana llena!

Leer Mercedes habla de sus actividades de la semana pasada. ¿Qué dice? Completa sus oraciones con el pretérito de cada verbo. *(Hint: Complete what Mercedes says.)*

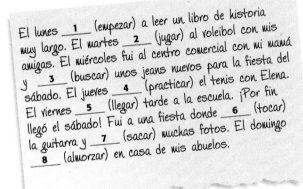

El lunes __1__ (empezar) a leer un libro de historia muy largo. El martes __2__ (jugar) al voleibol con mis amigas. El miércoles fui al centro comercial con mi mamá y __3__ (buscar) unos jeans nuevos para la fiesta del sábado. El jueves __4__ (practicar) el tenis con Elena. El viernes __5__ (llegar) tarde a la escuela. ¡Por fin llegó el sábado! Fui a una fiesta donde __6__ (tocar) la guitarra y __7__ (sacar) muchas fotos. El domingo __8__ (almorzar) en casa de mis abuelos.

■ **MÁS PRÁCTICA** *cuaderno* p. 48

■ **PARA HISPANOHABLANTES** *cuaderno* p. 46

ACTIVIDAD 15

Un sábado ocupado

Escribir Carmen tuvo un sábado ocupado. Completa las oraciones con el pretérito del verbo correcto. *(Hint: Complete the sentences to describe Carmen's Saturday.)*

empezar
llegar
almorzar
tocar
sacar
jugar

1. En la mañana, ella _____ la ropa del armario.
2. Luego _____ a desayunar.
3. A las diez _____ el piano.
4. Luego _____ en un restaurante.
5. _____ el béisbol en la tarde.
6. Por fin _____ a casa.

🔔 Quick Start Review

♻ Preterite of **-ar** verbs

Use OHT 169 or write on the board: Complete the following sentences with the appropriate preterite forms.

1. Ayer Tomás ____ la aspiradora en casa. (pasar)
2. Anoche Susana y Sylvia ____ todas sus camisas. (planchar)
3. El mes pasado Eduardo y yo ____ la casa de nuestra abuela. (limpiar)
4. Esta mañana tú ____ la basura, ¿no? (sacar)
5. Anteayer, yo ____ mi libro de español en casa. (olvidar)

Answers *See p. 217B.*

Teaching Suggestions
Teaching Preterite of Verbs Ending in -car, -gar, and -zar

• Emphasize that these spelling changes take place only in the **yo** form. Have students write out the entire conjugations.
• Dictate short sentences using some of these verbs and have students underline them.

ACTIVIDAD 14 **Objective:** Controlled practice
Preterite of **-ar** verbs with spelling changes

Answers

1. empecé	5. llegué
2. jugué	6. toqué
3. busqué	7. saqué
4. practiqué	8. almorcé

ACTIVIDAD 15 **Objective:** Transitional practice
Preterite of **-ar** verbs with spelling changes

Answers

1. sacó	4. almorzó
2. empezó	5. Jugó
3. tocó	6. llegó

■ Block Schedule

Variety Organize a spelling bee focused on preterite tense **-ar** verbs. Divide the class into teams. As you announce a word, a member of each team runs to the board. The person who writes the correct spelling of the word first wins a point for his or her team.

Teaching Middle School Students

Challenge Ask students to write what they did in the morning, in the afternoon, and at night on a certain day in the recent past (¿Ayer? ¿El sábado pasado? ¿El día de tu cumpleaños?).

Multiple Intelligences

Kinesthetic Have students work in groups. Have them each write a household chore that is an **-ar** verb on an index card and then shuffle and stack the cards facedown. A student draws a card and pantomimes the chore. The other group members tell the student what he or she did (**Limpiaste la sala**). When all the cards have been drawn, have students summarize by saying what each one did (**José limpió la sala, Marta lavó los platos,** etc.).

Teaching Resource Options

Print

Unit 5 Resource Book
Más práctica Workbook TE, p. 110
Para hispanohablantes Workbook
TE, p. 116

Audiovisual

OHT 169 (Quick Start)

Technology

Intrigas y aventuras CD-ROM, Disc 1

Teaching Suggestions
Presenting Vocabulary

- Have students practice numbers by counting by 10s, 20s, 50s, etc. Have them count backwards from 1000 to 100 by 100s, 50s, etc.
- Dictate 4-digit numbers and have students write the numerals on the board.

16 Objective: Open-ended practice Numbers

Answers

1. quinientos cuarenta y nueve
2. 242
3. doce mil setecientas veinticinco
4. cuatrocientos mil
5. 379
6. seis mil ochocientas

Culture Highlights

● **LAS PESETAS** Looking at **peseta** coins can help determine when they were minted. Old coins display a likeness of Franco; newer ones show King Juan Carlos. **Peseta** bills have the king on one side and pictures of famous Spaniards on the other.

ACTIVIDAD 16

Palabras y números

Escribir ¿Cómo escribes los números? Si la oración tiene números, escríbela con palabras. Si la oración tiene palabras, escríbela con números. *(Hint: If the sentence has words, use numbers. If the sentence has numbers, use words.)*

modelo

Hay un millón de personas en esta ciudad.

Hay 1.000.000 de personas en esta ciudad.

1. La estufa cuesta 549 dólares.
2. Esta noche el restaurante sirve a doscientas cuarenta y dos personas.
3. Carmen pagó la cuenta de 12.725 pesetas.
4. La casa cuesta más de 400.000 dólares.
5. Quiero comprar la videograbadora que cuesta trescientos setenta y nueve dólares.
6. La mujer tiene 6.800 pesetas en su bolsa.

Vocabulario

Los números de 200 a 1.000.000

doscientos(as) 200	
trescientos(as) 300	
cuatrocientos(as) 400	
quinientos(as) 500	
seiscientos(as) 600	
setecientos(as) 700	
ochocientos(as) 800	
novecientos(as) 900	
mil 1.000	
un millón 1.000.000	

Periods are used instead of commas for thousands and millions. The word **y** is used as you previously learned. It is *not* used after hundreds, thousands, or millions.

148 = ciento cuarenta **y** ocho   1.968 = mil novecientos sesenta **y** ocho

250 = doscientos cincuenta   1.000.562 = un millón quinientos sesenta **y** dos

The word **ciento** is used instead of **cien** before numbers greater than 100.

La bicicleta costó **cien** dólares.   El radio costó **ciento cincuenta** dólares.

Numbers ending in 200–900 agree in gender and number with nouns.

Costó doscient**os dólares**.   Pagué doscient**as pesetas**.

Un millón is followed by **de** before nouns.

un millón **de** dólares

¿Qué cuesta más de cien dólares?

234 doscientos treinta y cuatro
Unidad 5

Middle School Classroom Community

Cooperative Learning The task is to work in groups to convert numerals in newspaper ads to spoken and written numbers. All students share in the actual conversion, but they also take other roles as group members. The roles are as follows:

- Student 1 distributes ads.
- Student 2 reviews the numbers.
- Student 3 checks the papers to see that all prices have been written.
- Student 4 leads the group through the oral checking process.

¿Cuánto pagaron?

Escuchar Alicia, una amiga de Luis, habla de las cosas que ella y sus amigas compraron. Escucha lo que dice. ¿Cuánto pagaron por cada cosa?

(Hint: Listen to what Alicia says about things that she and her friends bought. How much did they pay for each item?)

1.

2.

3.

4.

5.

Conexiones

Las matemáticas Spain and Spanish-speaking countries (as well as most non-English-speaking countries in the world), use the metric system of measurement. Liquids, such as milk and olive oil, are sold in **litros (l)**; certain items of food are sold in **kilogramos (or kilos)**; and smaller food items, such as beans, grains, and nuts, are sold in **gramos (g)**. Also recall that distances are measured not in miles but in **kilómetros (km)**.

PARA HACER:
Give the U.S. equivalents for the following.
1/2 litro de leche
1 kilo de naranjas
500 gramos de pasta

1 l = 1.06 cuartos de galón (quarts)
1 kilo = 2.2 libras (pounds)
1 g = .002 libras

doscientos treinta y cinco
Etapa 3
235

Objective: Transitional practice Listening comprehension/numbers/vocabulary

Answers (See script, p. 217B.)
1. tres mil pesetas
2. ocho mil seiscientas pesetas
3. cinco mil quinientas pesetas
4. mil trescientas pesetas
5. ochocientas pesetas

Para hacer

Answers
1/2 litro = .53 quart
1 kilo = 2.2 pounds
500 gramos = 1 pound

Interdisciplinary Connection

History Bring in examples of **peseta** coins and bills. Make a list of people pictured on them. Have students research these people and why they are important.

Teaching Middle School Students

Native Speakers Ask native speakers to talk about metric measures vs. the English measures we use. They may have opinions as to which is more efficient, or they may have had problems adjusting to the differences between the systems.

Multiple Intelligences

Logical/Mathematical Have students research the Spanish **peseta**. If possible, obtain various **peseta** notes from a local bank to display in class.

Block Schedule

Process Time Have students use as many of the **-car, -gar,** and **-zar** verbs in the **yo** form of the preterite as possible. For example, **Saqué la basura. Empecé la tarea.** Limit their time to 3–5 minutes. Have volunteers read some of their sentences to the class.

Teaching Resource Options

Print

Block Scheduling Copymasters
Unit 5 Resource Book
  Information Gap Activities, pp. 120–121
  Audioscript, p. 132
  Audioscript *Para hispanohablantes*,
  p. 132

Audiovisual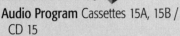

Audio Program Cassettes 15A, 15B /
CD 15
Audio *Para hispanohablantes*
  Cassette 15A / CD 15

Technology

Intrigas y aventuras CD-ROM, Disc 1

Teaching Suggestions
Presenting Vocabulary

Present the words for quantities in familiar contexts. For example: **una docena de huevos, un litro de leche, un paquete de azúcar.** Have students add more examples.

18 Objective: Transitional practice Preterite of **pagar**/numbers/vocabulary

Answers
1. Mercedes pagó mil doscientas pesetas por la camisa.
2. Iván y Beto pagaron dos mil quinientas pesetas por el videojuego.
3. Los padres de Luis pagaron quince mil pesetas por el radiocasete.
4. Yo pagué setecientas cincuenta pesetas por la cartera.

19 Objective: Open-ended practice Numbers/vocabulary

Answers will vary.

Los regalos

Hablar/Escribir Todos le compraron a Luis un regalo de cumpleaños. ¿Cuánto pagaron?
(Hint: How much did they pay for Luis's birthday presents?)

Álvaro

modelo

Álvaro pagó ochocientas pesetas por el disco compacto.

1. Mercedes   **2.** Iván y Beto

3. los padres de Luis   **4.** yo

Vocabulario

Las cantidades

la docena *dozen*	**el paquete** *package*
el gramo *gram*	**el pedazo** *piece*
el kilo *kilogram*	**cuarto(a)** *quarter*
el litro *liter*	**medio(a)** *half*

Use the definite article when talking about the price of a specific quantity of food.

  Los huevos cuestan 200 pesetas **la** docena.

  El pescado cuesta 1.500 pesetas **el** kilo.

¿Cuándo usas estas cantidades?

Compras para la fiesta

Hablar/Leer Imagínate que estás en España. Tú y un(a) amigo(a) van a hacer una fiesta. Tienen 7.500 pesetas para comprar comida y refrescos. Lee el anuncio. ¿Qué van a comprar? *(Hint: You have 7,500 pesetas to buy food and drinks for a party. Read the advertisement and decide what you will buy.)*

modelo

Estudiante A: ¿Compramos salchicha?
Estudiante B: ¿A cuánto está?
Estudiante A: Está a setecientas cincuenta pesetas el kilo.
Estudiante B: Bueno, vamos a comprar dos kilos.

Nota

¿A cuánto está(n)…? is an expression used to ask how much something costs. It is often used with food items that may increase or decrease in price given a good or bad harvest. It may also indicate changing prices during a sale.

¡SuperEspeciales!

210 ptas/ 2 botellas	500 ptas

Supermercado BuenPrecio

750 ptas/ kilo	550 ptas/ kilo
285 ptas/ kilo	250 ptas/ kilo
125 ptas/ kilo	550 ptas/ 6 botellas
400 ptas/ 3 latas	¡Especiales de la semana!

Middle School Classroom Community

TPR Display objects or visuals around the room with prices attached to them. Tell students that they have a certain number of **pesetas** and that they must go around the room until they find an item with the right price.

Learning Scenario Tell students that they are in a **supermercado**. Designate some as customers, others as employees, etc. Customers might make shopping lists; employees might choose to run registers, bag, put up stock, etc. You are the store manager and can circulate to keep things moving, help with dialog, etc.

¡Qué suerte!

Hablar/Escribir Ganaste un concurso y ahora estás pasando dos semanas en España con tu familia y un(a) amigo(a). ¿Qué van a comprar tú y estas personas con todo el dinero que tienen? *(Hint: What is everyone going to buy?)*

modelo

mi amigo(a) / 1.500 ptas.

*Va a comprar tres libros con **mil quinientas pesetas**.*

1. yo / 3.000 ptas.
2. mi hermano(a) / 2.500 ptas.
3. mi madre / 7.000 ptas.
4. mis tíos / 80.000 ptas.
5. mis padres / 25.000 ptas.
6. mis primos / 10.000 ptas.

Una fiesta fantástica

Escribir Contesta las preguntas para describir una fiesta real o imaginaria. *(Hint: Describe a real or imaginary party, answering the questions.)*

- ¿Por qué organizaron la fiesta?
- ¿Cuándo organizaron la fiesta?
- ¿Dónde organizaron la fiesta?
- ¿Cómo ayudó la familia?

modelo

El mes pasado celebramos el cumpleaños de mi tío Carlos con una fiesta en mi casa. Toda la familia ayudó. Mis hermanos limpiaron la casa. Mi papá cocinó la carne de res y mi mamá preparó las verduras y el arroz. Yo preparé un postre riquísimo. Cuando mi tío llegó…

■ **MÁS COMUNICACIÓN** p. R6

Pronunciación

Refranes

Linking words Native speakers may seem to speak quickly when they link their words together in breath groups. Instead of pronouncing each word separately, they run some words together. This is common in all languages. Practice linking words in the following sentences.

El que algo quiere, algo le cuesta.

Aceite de oliva, todo el mal quita.

La larga experiencia, más que los libros enseña.

doscientos treinta y siete
Etapa 3
237

Teaching Middle School Students

Native Speakers Ask native speakers to talk about stores, markets, and supermarkets in their countries. Find out whether there are differences in vocabulary regarding what stores and typical store furnishings are called.

Multiple Intelligences

Verbal Have students work in pairs to expand the theme of winning a contest (**Actividad 20**). Tell them to take turns talking about what they and various other people want to buy with their **pesetas**. Finish by having a number of pairs tell about what one person bought and how much the item cost.

 Objective: Open-ended practice
Numbers/vocabulary

Answers

Answers will vary but must contain the following.
1. Yo voy a comprar… con tres mil pesetas.
2. Mi hermano(a) va a… con dos mil quinientas…
3. Mi madre va a… con siete mil…
4. Mis tíos van a… con ochenta mil…
5. Mis padres van a… con veinticinco mil…
6. Mis primos van a… con diez mil…

Objective: Open-ended practice
Preterite of **-ar** verbs/vocabulary

Answers will vary.

Dictation

After presenting the **Pronunciación,** have students close their books. Dictate the **refranes** in segments while students write them.

Block Schedule

FunBreak Pass out self-stick slips of paper to half the class. These students will label their clothing, jewelry, books, etc., and add prices. They will also cut out pictures of expensive items from magazines, label these, and display them. Pass out several thousand dollars in play money to the other half of the class. These students will walk around the room and practice the art of **el regateo.** When a sale is made, the buyer counts out the money to the seller and collects the price tag. At the end of "market day," find out who spent the most, sold the most, sold the least, etc. (For additional activities, see **Block Scheduling Copymasters.**)

Teaching Resource Options

Print
Block Scheduling Copymasters
Unit 5 Resource Book
  Audioscript, p. 133
  Audioscript *Para hispanohablantes*,
    p. 133

Audiovisual
OHT 169 (Quick Start)
Audio Program Cassette
Audio *Para hispanohablantes*
  Cassette 15A / CD 15
Canciones Cassette / CD

Quick Start Review

♻ Quantities

Use OHT 169 or write on the board:
Complete the sentences with an
appropriate quantity.

1. Los huevos cuestan 200 pesetas
   ____ .
2. Ayer compré ____ de galletas.
3. Este pescado cuesta 1.500
  pesetas ____ .
4. ¿Cuántos ____ de pimienta quiere
  usted?
5. Diego, cómprame ____ de
  limonada.

Answers
1. la docena   4. gramos
2. un paquete   5. un litro
3. el kilo

Teaching Suggestions

- **Prereading** Ask students to recall
La Tomatina, from **Etapa 1**.
- **Strategy: Noting details** Have
students start a web to help them
keep track of details while they read
the **Lectura**.
- **Reading** As students read, have
them point to the illustrations that
depict or suggest the following
words: **correo electrónico, gigantes,
dragón, fuego**, *castells* (torres
humanas).
- **Post-reading** Ask students to
imagine that they are in Barcelona
participating in this festival. How
would they like to join in?

En voces

LECTURA

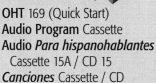

PARA LEER
STRATEGY: READING
Noting details The e-mail below
describes **festes**, cultural
celebrations that take place in
Cataluña. As you read, use
a web to note details about the
celebrations.

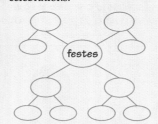

festes

Correo electrónico[1] desde Barcelona

Aquí tienes un mensaje que escribió un grupo de
estudiantes norteamericanos que viajaron a España con su
maestra de español.

 jeff carter   11:52:31 AM

To: Rogers Middle School
From: Colegio San Marco
Subject: Barcelona festival

Queridos amigos:

El clima es muy bonito en Barcelona y la gente es muy alegre.
Hay fiestas (o **festes** como dicen en catalán) todo el tiempo.
Pero no son como las fiestas de nosotros. Algunas de las
costumbres empezaron ¡hace casi 800 años!

Anoche caminamos al centro de la ciudad y enfrente de nosotros
pasaron los gigantes. Son unas figuras grandes de madera[2] y
papier-mâché. Después marcharon los dragones que echaron
fuego[3] ¡por las narices!

Luego, al final, los músicos tocaron una música especial. La gente
empezó a formar los **castells** (torres[4] humanas). Un grupo de
personas formó la base y otro grupo subió encima del[5] primero.
Luego otro grupo subió encima del segundo[6] grupo, etc., etc.
Entonces, el niño más chico subió hasta lo más alto. Ahora
nosotros queremos aprender a hacer los **castells** al regresar
a Estados Unidos la semana próxima.

Con el cariño de siempre,

Jeff, Susan, Amy, Emily, Josh, Frank

[1] e-mail   [3] fire   [5] *subió encima del* climbed on top of
[2] wood   [4] towers   [6] second

238   doscientos treinta y ocho
Unidad 5

Middle School Classroom Community

Storytelling Divide the class into groups. Ask them
to create a story about a parade or festival they
attended—real or imaginary. When they are happy with
their story, have them write and illustrate it to share
with the class.

Portfolio Have students write a letter about a place
they visited or an event they attended.

Rubric

Criteria	Scale	
Vocabulary use/spelling	1 2 3 4 5	A = 17–20 pts.
Correct sentence structure/grammar	1 2 3 4 5	B = 13–16 pts.
Logical organization	1 2 3 4 5	C = 9–12 pts.
Creativity	1 2 3 4 5	D = 5–8 pts.
		F = < 5 pts.

You may wish to inform students of the various opportunities for study in Spain and other Spanish-speaking countries. Each issue of the *Foreign Language Annals,* published by the American Council on the Teaching of Foreign Languages, advertises several programs. The American Field Service, located in New York City, is also a good source.

Critical Thinking

Ask students to discuss, then write about, which festival they would attend—Barcelona's or Buñol's (**La Tomatina,** pp. 186–187)—if they had to choose.

¿Comprendiste?

Answers
1. Un grupo de estudiantes norteamericanos que están en Barcelona lo mandaron.
2. Barcelona tiene un clima muy bonito y la gente es muy alegre.
3. Hay gigantes, dragones, *castells* y música.
4. Les gustaron más los *castells.*

¿Comprendiste?

1. ¿Quiénes mandaron el mensaje?
2. ¿Cómo es Barcelona?
3. ¿Qué hay en las fiestas de Barcelona?
4. ¿Qué les gustó más de todo a los muchachos?

¿Que piensas?

1. ¿Cómo son diferentes o similares las fiestas de Barcelona a otras fiestas que conoces?
2. ¿Qué celebran las fiestas culturales?

doscientos treinta y nueve
Etapa 3   **239**

Teaching Middle School Students

Extra Help Before reading the letter, have students relate the vocabulary to the illustrations and alert them to the **catalán** words in the text.

Multiple Intelligences

Visual Be a tour guide in Barcelona and lead the students through the city. If possible, display posters and other visuals around the room. Invite individuals to tell the group what they see on the tour.

Block Schedule

Variety Have students write an e-mail similar to the one in the **Lectura** to a pen pal in Spain. Have them discuss a local celebration in your area.

Teaching Resource Options

Print ✎

Unit 5 Resource Book
  Audioscript, p. 133
  Audioscript *Para hispanohablantes*,
    p. 133

Audiovisual 🎧📼

Audio Program Cassette 15A / CD 15
Audio *Para hispanohablantes*
  Cassette 15A / CD 15
OHT 169 (Quick Start)
Video Program Videotape 5 /
  Videodisc 3A

Search Chapter 8, Play to 9
U5E3 • En colores (Culture)

Quick Start Review

🔔 Places in a city

Use OHT 169 or write on the board:
List at least 10 places/buildings you
would find in a typical city.

Answers
Answers will vary. Answers could include:
un centro, una plaza, un museo, un parque,
una iglesia, un restaurante, un café, un banco,
una farmacia, una tienda, un correo, una
biblioteca, un cine, un teatro, una calle, una
avenida, un hotel, un aeropuerto

Teaching Suggestions
Presenting Cultura y comparaciones

• Have students read the Connecting
  Cultures Strategy and discuss how
  students will create their time lines.

• Have students look at the buildings
  in the photos. Ask them to suggest
  adjectives that describe them. Write
  their suggestions on the board.

• Show students a street map of
  Barcelona and point out where these
  buildings are. Have students count
  the number of blocks between them.
  Do they recommend walking or
  taking a bus?

• Expand the cultural information by
  showing the video culture presentation.

En colores

CULTURA Y COMPARACIONES

Casa Amatller

PARA CONOCERNOS

STRATEGY: CONNECTING CULTURES

Make a historical time line Place Barcelona's
rich architectural history on a time line from
ancient times to the present. First label each
period with a word or two to identify it.
Next add a word or pictorial symbol of
an important detail from that time.
Finally, use your time line to
summarize for a classmate the
main points of «Barcelona:
Joya de arquitectura».

Barcelona
Joya de arquitectura

*Escena típica del
Barrio Gótico*

Barcelona es una ciudad de muchos barrios[1] y de
una gran variedad de estilos de arquitectura. Los
romanos fueron los primeros en construir una
ciudad aquí en el año 15 a.C.[2] Hoy no hay casi
nada de la ciudad romana. Hay sólo unas ruinas y
murallas[3] en el Barrio Gótico[4].

El Barrio Gótico de Barcelona es la ciudad
vieja, un barrio de calles estrechas[5] y plazas
pequeñas. Tiene muchos edificios[6] y monumentos
impresionantes de los siglos XIII, XIV y XV, época[7]
de la arquitectura gótica. Si caminas por la calle
Montcada puedes ver las casas y los palacios de las

N O T A CULTURAL

Barcelona's Gothic Quarter was built when the
Spanish Empire was at its height. The profits from
Spain's colonies funded the construction of
palaces, churches, and public buildings.

---

[1] districts   [3] walls   [5] narrow   [7] period
[2] B.C.   [4] Gothic Quarter   [6] buildings

240 doscientos cuarenta
Unidad 5

Middle School Classroom Community

Paired Activity Post pictures of Barcelona around
the room. Have students work in pairs. They will take
turns telling their partners to visit someplace in
Barcelona. If students do not know where the place is,
tell them to ask other students until they find it. Then
tell them to come back to their partner and say that
they visited the place.

Group Activity Have students work in groups
using the library, Internet, travel agencies, etc., to find
out more about Barcelona's historic buildings. Have
each group work on a different period, and ask them
to find pictures to share with the class.

Casa Battló

Casa Viçens

La Pedrera—apartamentos

Parque Güell

Reading Strategy

Ask students to use the Reading Strategy they learned on p. 238: **Noting details.** Have them use a web to organize the information about architecture in Barcelona. They should list what buildings are found in Barcelona from each of the 3 **épocas** (romana, medieval, moderna).

Culture Highlights

● **EL BARRIO GÓTICO DE BARCELONA**
At the heart of the **Barrio Gótico** is the **Plaza de San Jaume,** which dates back to the time of the Roman occupation of Spain. This plaza used to be a Roman forum. Other points of interest in the **Barrio Gótico** are the **Plaza del Rei,** the **Palacio Real Mayor,** and the **Iglesia de Santa Agata.**

familias principales de Barcelona de la época medieval. Hoy estas casas están convertidas en museos y galerías de arte.

La ciudad moderna tiene grandes avenidas, como Las Ramblas. El arquitecto catalán Antonio Gaudí (1852–1926) construyó⁸ edificios originales de estilo modernista. Trabajó con formas y estructuras experimentales. Gaudí trabajó primero en el Parque de la Ciudadela, donde actualmente⁹ está el Museo de Arte Moderno. Años más tarde diseñó el Parque Güell, ciudad y parque dentro de Barcelona. Gaudí también diseñó casas privadas, cada una con un diseño único. Su obra maestra¹⁰, nunca terminada, es una iglesia, La Sagrada Familia¹¹.

---

⁸built ⁹nowadays ¹⁰masterpiece ¹¹The Holy Family

¿Comprendiste?

1. ¿Queda algo de la ciudad romana en Barcelona? Explica.
2. ¿Cómo se llama la ciudad vieja de Barcelona? ¿Por qué?
3. ¿Qué lugares de interés puedes ver en el Barrio Gótico?
4. ¿Cómo es la ciudad moderna?
5. ¿Qué importancia tiene Gaudí?

¿Qué piensas?

¿Es cierto que la historia de Barcelona empieza en la época medieval? Explica tus razones.

Hazlo tú

Eres un(a) guía y tienes que hablar de Barcelona. ¿Qué dices?

Quick Wrap-up

Have students identify the following:
1. Antonio Gaudí
2. el Barrio Gótico
3. Las Ramblas
4. el Parque Güell

¿Comprendiste?

Answers
1. Hoy no hay casi nada de la ciudad romana. Hay sólo unas ruinas y murallas en el Barrio Gótico.
2. Se llama el Barrio Gótico porque tiene edificios y monumentos de la época de la arquitectura gótica.
3. Puedes ver las casas y los palacios de las familias principales de Barcelona de la época medieval.
4. Tiene grandes avenidas.
5. Gaudí construyó edificios originales de estilo modernista. Su obra maestra es La Sagrada Familia.

Teaching Middle School Students

Native Speakers Ask native speakers to talk about the history and architecture of their hometowns. Find out about different ways of saying things that students are learning.

Multiple Intelligences

Visual Have students work in pairs. They will take turns describing a building or a place in Barcelona. Their partners guess what they are describing before changing roles.

Block Schedule

Research Have students select another city in Spain to research and/or create a travel brochure. They should include a map, an **Almanaque,** some historical facts, some well-known people, some important sites, etc.

Teaching Resource Options

Print

Block Scheduling Copymasters
Unit 5 Resource Book
  Para hispanohablantes Workbook
    TE, pp. 117–118
  Information Gap Activities, p. 122
  Family Involvement, pp. 123–124
  Multiple Choice Test Questions,
    pp. 170–178

Audiovisual

OHT 170 (Quick Start)
Audio Program Testing Cassette T2 /
  CD T2

Technology

Electronic Teacher Tools/Test
  Generator
Intrigas y aventuras CD-ROM, Disc 1

Quick Start Review

♻ **Preterite of regular -ar verbs**

Use OHT 170 or write on the board:
First, match the verbs in column A with
the objects in column B. Then use the
pairs to write sentences with the **yo**
preterite form of the verbs.

A	B
1. ___ escuchar	a. el piano
2. ___ lavar	b. el pescado
3. ___ tocar	c. los platos
4. ___ cocinar	d. música
5. ___ sacar	e. la luz
6. ___ apagar	f. fotos

Answers
1. d. Escuché música.
2. c. Lavé los platos.
3. a. Toqué el piano.
4. b. Cociné el pescado.
5. f. Saqué fotos.
6. e. Apagué la luz.

✔ Teaching Suggestions
What Have Students Learned?

Have students look at the "Now you
can…" notes listed on the left side
of pages 242–243. Remind them to
review the material in the "To review"
notes before doing the activities or
taking the test.

ETAPA 3

Now you can...
- plan a party.

To review
- regular preterite **-ar** verbs, see p. 230.

Now you can...
- describe past activities.

To review
- preterite of **-car, -gar, -zar** verbs, see p. 233.

En uso

REPASO Y MÁS COMUNICACIÓN

OBJECTIVES
- Plan a party
- Describe past activities
- Express extremes
- Purchase food

ACTIVIDAD 1 ¡A preparar!

Explica quiénes ayudaron y quiénes no ayudaron
a preparar la fiesta en la casa de Álvaro.
(Hint: Tell who helped and who didn't help prepare for the party.)

modelo

Luis: cuidar a Carmen

Luis no ayudó. **Cuidó a Carmen.**

tú: lavar los platos

Tú ayudaste. **Lavaste los platos.**

1. Álvaro: limpiar la casa
2. yo: nadar en la piscina
3. Iván: cocinar la carne de res
4. Elena y Arturo: escuchar música
5. tú: patinar en el parque
6. Beto: preparar las patatas y verduras
7. nosotros: hablar por teléfono
8. Marta: preparar la tarta

ACTIVIDAD 2 ¡Una fiesta terrible!

Carmen habla con Luis sobre una fiesta muy mala que celebraron
en su casa el mes pasado. ¿Qué dice? *(Hint: Tell what Carmen says about a
terrible party.)*

modelo

yo (buscar) los vasos y no los (encontrar)
Yo busqué los vasos y no los encontré.

1. nadie (sacar) la basura antes de la fiesta
2. yo (pagar) todas las compras con mi dinero
3. pocas personas (llegar)
4. yo (tocar) el piano muy mal
5. yo no (almorzar) nada el día de la fiesta
6. nosotros (jugar) con unos videojuegos aburridos
7. yo (sacar) unas fotos terribles
8. tú (apagar) la luz durante la fiesta

Middle School Classroom Community

TPR Place pictures, real items, etc., around the room
and tell the class that they are in a supermarket in
Spain, and they have to find the food items that their
partner asks for. Students take turns asking their
partners to find an item and point out its location.

Group Activity Tell the class to imagine that they
are students in Spain, and that they are going to
prepare a meal for their parents and friends. Have
them work in groups to discuss what they are going
to serve and how much the food will cost in **pesetas**
(refer to **Actividad 4**). Have each group tell the class
what their dinner will be and how much it will cost.

Now you can...
• express extremes.

To review
• superlatives, see
p. 228.

ACTIVIDAD 3 Opiniones

Luis expresa sus opiniones sobre las siguientes cosas. ¿Qué dice?
(Hint: Give Luis's opinions.)

modelo

Carmen: más / joven (de mi familia)
Carmen *es la* **menor.**

1. Mercedes: más / bonito (de mis amigas)
2. helado: más / bueno (de los postres)
3. papá: más / viejo (de mi familia)
4. zanahorias: menos / delicioso (de las verduras)
5. tarta: más / sabroso (de los postres)
6. tenis: más / malo (de los deportes)
7. limonada: más / dulce (de las bebidas)
8. calamares: menos / rico (de las tapas)

ACTIVIDAD 4 ¡Buenos precios!

Imagínate que estás comprando comida en España. ¿Cuáles son
los precios de hoy? *(Hint: Imagine you are buying food in Spain. Tell today's prices.)*

modelo

Las zanahorias están a doscientas veinticinco pesetas el kilo.

Now you can...
• purchase food.

To review
• numbers, see
p. 234.

doscientos cuarenta y tres
Etapa 3
243

ACTIVIDAD 1 Answers

1. Álvaro ayudó. Limpió la casa.
2. Yo no ayudé. Nadé en la piscina.
3. Iván ayudó. Cocinó la carne de res.
4. Elena y Arturo no ayudaron. Escucharon música.
5. Tú no ayudaste. Patinaste en el parque.
6. Beto ayudó. Preparó las patatas y verduras.
7. Nosotros no ayudamos. Hablamos por teléfono.
8. Marta ayudó. Preparó la tarta.

ACTIVIDAD 2 Answers

1. Nadie sacó la basura antes de la fiesta.
2. Yo pagué todas las compras con mi dinero.
3. Pocas personas llegaron.
4. Yo toqué el piano muy mal.
5. Yo no almorcé nada el día de la fiesta.
6. Nosotros jugamos con unos videojuegos aburridos.
7. Yo saqué unas fotos terribles.
8. Tú apagaste la luz durante la fiesta.

ACTIVIDAD 3 Answers

1. Mercedes es la más bonita.
2. El helado es el mejor.
3. Papá es el mayor.
4. Las zanahorias son las menos deliciosas.
5. La tarta es la más sabrosa.
6. El tenis es el peor.
7. La limonada es la más dulce.
8. Los calamares son los menos ricos.

ACTIVIDAD 4 Answers

1. Las patatas están a ciento treinta y cinco pesetas el kilo.
2. La salchicha está a setecientas cuarenta pesetas el kilo.
3. El zumo está a ciento setenta y cinco pesetas la lata.
4. El aceite está a quinientas pesetas la botella.
5. Las galletas están a cuatrocientas diez pesetas el paquete.
6. Las cebollas están a trescientas pesetas el kilo.
7. La carne de res está a novecientas cinco pesetas el kilo.
8. Los huevos están a doscientas quince pesetas la docena.

Teaching Middle School Students

Extra Help Have students brainstorm **-ar** verbs that
are regular in the preterite and write them on the
board. Tell them to write 4 things they did yesterday,
using the verbs on the list. Call on students to answer
orally or to write on the board. Use these as a
springboard for practicing second- and third-person
plural forms.

Multiple Intelligences

Naturalist Ask students to research types of plants
native to or crops grown in Catalonia. Have them
report their findings to the class.

Block Schedule

Change of Pace Have students write
and present some Top Five lists; for
example, best classes in school, best
athletes, best actresses, best musical
groups, etc. Students should use
comparatives and superlatives in their
presentations. (For additional activities,
see **Block Scheduling Copymasters**.)

Teaching Resource Options

Print

Unit 5 Resource Book
  Cooperative Quizzes, pp. 135–136
  Etapa Exam, Forms A and B,
    pp. 137–146
  Para hispanohablantes Etapa Exam,
    pp. 147–151
  Portfolio Assessment, pp. 152–153
  Unit 5 Comprehensive Test,
    pp. 154–161
  Para hispanohablantes Unit 5
    Comprehensive Test, pp. 162–169
  Multiple Choice Test Questions,
    pp. 170–178

Audiovisual

OHT 170 (Quick Start)
Audio Program Testing Cassette T2 /
  CD T2

Technology

Electronic Teacher Tools/Test
  Generator

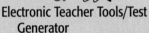 www.mcdougallittell.com

ACTIVIDAD 5

Rubric: Speaking

Criteria	Scale	
Vocabulary use	1 2 3 4 5	A = 13–15 pts.
Sentence structure	1 2 3 4 5	B = 10–12 pts. C = 7–9 pts.
Ease, fluency	1 2 3 4 5	D = 4–6 pts. F = < 4 pts.

ACTIVIDAD 6 *Answers will vary.*

ACTIVIDAD 7 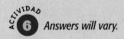 **En tu propia voz**

Rubric: Writing

Criteria	Scale	
Vocabulary use	1 2 3 4 5	A = 13–15 pts.
Accuracy	1 2 3 4 5	B = 10–12 pts. C = 7–9 pts.
Creativity, appearance	1 2 3 4 5	D = 4–6 pts. F = < 4 pts.

Teaching Note: En tu propia voz

Remind students to review the writing strategy "Tell who, what, where, when, why, and how" before beginning the description of the party. A well-written paragraph uses many details to communicate information.

ACTIVIDAD 5

El fin de semana pasado

PARA CONVERSAR

STRATEGY: SPEAKING

Maintain conversational flow To keep continuity in a conversation, acknowledge what was said, then add your own ideas. The model shows how this is done. You can build interest by withholding information: **Compré algo bonito. ¿Sabes qué es?**

Usando las actividades de la lista, habla con otro(a) estudiante sobre sus actividades del fin de semana pasado. *(Hint: Talk about what you did last weekend.)*

> almorzar en un restaurante
> limpiar la casa
> comprar algo interesante
> alquilar un video
> tocar algún instrumento
> practicar algún deporte
> trabajar

modelo

Estudiante A: *Compré algo interesante.*

Estudiante B: *¿Qué compraste?*

Estudiante A: *Compré…*

ACTIVIDAD 6  **En el supermercado**

Imagínate que tú y un(a) amigo(a) están comprando comida en España. Hay tres papeles: un(a) comprador(a) optimista, un(a) comprador(a) pesimista y una persona que trabaja en el supermercado. Cambien de papel. *(Hint: Shop in the supermarket. One person is an optimist, another is a pessimist, and the third works at the supermarket. Change roles.)*

modelo

Optimista: *¿A cuánto están los tomates?*

Trabajador(a): *Nuestros tomates son los más sabrosos de la comunidad. Hoy están a…*

Optimista: *¡Qué bien! Los compro.*

Pesimista: *¡No los compres! Los tomates de aquí son…*

ACTIVIDAD 7 ✐ *En tu propia voz*

Escritura Imagínate que tú y tus amigos celebraron una fiesta el sábado pasado. ¿Cómo participaron todos? *(Hint: Describe how everyone participated in a class party last Saturday.)*

modelo

Antes de la fiesta, todos limpiamos la casa. Sara pasó la aspiradora y yo lavé los platos. Durante la fiesta, Marcos tocó la guitarra y…

Conexiones

La salud What kind of food do you like the most? Which ethnic foods do you prefer? Is there a special dish from your region? Survey ten people at your school to find out their favorite food. Then create a menu featuring the foods chosen. Add prices and indicate the dishes that are good for your health.

Persona	La comida favorita

Middle School Classroom Community

Game Give the first person in each row a paper with past indicators printed on the left. Tell students that they are going to write **una historia de Enrique.** Have the first student write a verb in the preterite next to the first past indicator and then pass the paper to the next student. When everyone in the row has written a sentence, have each row read their story. Repeat the game with other subjects.

Paired Activity Have students take turns reviewing numbers for each other. Have them write several combinations and dictate them to each other for comprehension. They may also practice spelling the numbers for each other.

En resumen

REPASO DE VOCABULARIO

PLANNING A PARTY

apagar la luz	to turn off the light
¡Cállate!	Be quiet!

PURCHASING FOOD

¿A cuánto está(n)…?	How much is (are)…?

Food

el aceite	oil
la carne de res	beef
la cebolla	onion
el cereal	cereal
la crema	cream
la galleta	cookie, cracker
la harina	flour
el helado	ice cream
el huevo	egg
la leche	milk
la mantequilla	butter
la pasta	pasta
la patata	potato
el pescado	fish
la pimienta	pepper
el puerco	pork
la sal	salt
la salchicha	sausage
el tomate	tomato
la verdura	vegetable
el yogur	yogurt
la zanahoria	carrot
el zumo	juice

Packaging

la botella	bottle
la lata	can
el paquete	package

REQUESTING QUANTITIES

cuarto(a)	quarter
la docena	dozen
el gramo	gram
el kilo	kilogram
el litro	liter
medio(a)	half
el pedazo	piece
doscientos(as)	two hundred
trescientos(as)	three hundred
cuatrocientos(as)	four hundred
quinientos(as)	five hundred
seiscientos(as)	six hundred
setecientos(as)	seven hundred
ochocientos(as)	eight hundred
novecientos(as)	nine hundred
mil	one thousand
un millón	one million

DESCRIBING PAST ACTIVITIES

anoche	last night
anteayer	the day before yesterday
el año pasado	last year
ayer	yesterday
el mes pasado	last month
la semana pasada	last week

OTHER WORDS AND PHRASES

la estrella	star
sabroso(a)	tasty

In the Kitchen

cocinar	to cook
el congelador	freezer
la estufa	stove
el frigorífico	refrigerator
el horno	oven
el lavaplatos	dishwasher
el microondas	microwave

Juego

¿Qué son estas cosas? ¿Dónde las pones?

1. laheod
2. suplacitosos
3. elhce
4. neredecasr

Interdisciplinary Connections

Health Have students research the average caloric content of several of the foods learned in this and other **Etapas**. Have them make a chart with pictures of the foods and the number of calories in an average serving. Variation: Have students research the latest nutritional guidelines and prepare posters showing a balanced breakfast, lunch, and dinner with pictures and labels in Spanish.

Quick Start Review

♻ **Etapa** vocabulary

Use OHT 170 or write on the board: Write 3 complete sentences. Each sentence must contain one word from each of the following categories: Purchasing Food, Requesting Quantities, Describing Past Activities.

Answers will vary.

Teaching Suggestions
Vocabulary Review

Have students make flash cards of the vocabulary. Put students in groups of 3. Deal 5 cards per group. In 3 minutes, see how many sentences they can make using 2 cards per sentence.

Juego

Answers
1. helado: en el congelador
2. platos sucios: en el lavaplatos
3. leche: en el frigorífico
4. carne de res: en la estufa

Teaching Middle School Students

Challenge Have students make a sketch of a food, kitchen appliance, or type of food packaging. Divide the class into two teams and have students take turns showing their drawings to their team. The team must guess correctly the first time to win a point.

Multiple Intelligences
Musical/Rhythmic Have students use the tune to *Old MacDonald* to write a song about items in a store.

Block Schedule

Time Saver Assign **Actividad 7** for immediately after the **Etapa** exam. This way, students who finish first have something to work on while other students complete the test. The assignment can then be finished at home.

Teaching Resource Options

Print
Block Scheduling Copymasters

Audiovisual
OHT GO1–GO5; 170 (Quick Start)

Technology
Intrigas y aventuras CD-ROM, Disc 1

www.mcdougallittell.com

Quick Start Review

Reflexive verbs/commands
Use OHT 170 or write on the board:
Write the affirmative **tú** command and
the negative **tú** command for each of
the following:

1. acostarse   4. lavarse
2. levantarse   5. dormirse
3. bañarse

Answers

1. acuéstate   no te acuestes
2. levántate   no te levantes
3. báñate   no te bañes
4. lávate   no te laves
5. duérmete   no te duermas

Teaching Suggestions
La historia

- Direct students to a map of the Iberian Peninsula and North Africa. Have them locate the Strait of Gibraltar and surmise why the Moors were able to invade Spain so easily.

- In addition to the palace of the Alhambra (the last stronghold of the Moors prior to the Christian reconquest) in Granada, the Mosque (**mezquita**) in Córdoba is another wonderful example of Moorish architecture. If you show illustrations of these edifices, you may wish to point out the absence of human figures, which was prohibited by Islamic law.

- One of the most practical of Moorish achievements was their advanced knowledge of irrigation systems. The Spaniards learned these techniques, and, in turn, put them into practice in their colonization of the Americas.

Conexiones

OTRAS DISCIPLINAS Y PROYECTOS

La historia

A stunning example of Moorish influence, the Alhambra still stands in Granada, Spain.

In the summer of 711 when the Moors crossed the Strait of Gibraltar from northern Africa into Spain, they brought much more with them than their language and their religion. Many things you know and use every day were introduced to Europe by the North Africans. Until the Moorish influence, Europeans ate their meals with knives and their fingers—the Moors brought forks. Europeans hung tapestries in their castles to protect against cold drafts—the Moors brought carpets and pillows. In addition to these conveniences, the Moors also brought advanced medical techniques, new styles of architecture, astronomy, algebra, the concept of zero, and the game of chess!

Look through your Spanish dictionary and list nouns that begin with the letters **al**. *Most of these words are adaptations of Arabic words brought by the North Africans.*

The Garden of Daraxa in the Alhambra includes this fountain of spouting lions.

Las ciencias

The Arabic people who lived in southern Spain (in the region called **Al-Andalus** then, and **Andalucía** now) were proficient astronomers. They invented instruments to observe the night skies and paved the way for later scientists like Copernicus and Galileo. By the twelfth century, many people were traveling to Spain to learn the new science of astronomy.

The following stars were named by Arabic astronomers. Look at this star map and find each one. What are the names of the constellations these stars appear in?

1. *Betelgueze*
2. *Aldebarán*
3. *Rigel*

246   doscientos cuarenta y seis
Unidad 5

Middle School Classroom Community

Learning Scenario   Have students research early Moorish influence in Europe. Then have them imagine that they are living in Spain during the time of the Moors. Ask some to be Moors and some to be Europeans. Have them create a dialog in which the Moors teach the Europeans about new and better ways to do things, such as use forks.

Portfolio   Have students write a short report about Moorish inventions and discoveries.

Rubric

Criteria	Scale	
Accuracy of information	1 2 3 4 5	A = 13–15 pts.
Logical organization	1 2 3 4 5	B = 10–12 pts.
		C = 7–9 pts.
Vocabulary use	1 2 3 4 5	D = 4–6 pts.
		F = < 4 pts.

Proyecto cultural

There are several regions in Spain where residents speak another language in addition to Spanish. In Barcelona, tourists can expect to hear people speaking **catalán** as well as Spanish.

Create a bilingual travel reference for visitors to Barcelona.

1. Decide what to include in your bilingual travel guide. Do you want to focus on conversations or places?

español	catalán
aeropuerto	aeroport
banco	banca
iglesia	església
jardín	jardí
hotel	hotel
biblioteca	biblioteca
parque	parc
gente	gent
calle	carrer
tren	tren
chico	xicot

2. Use the Internet or reference books to find pictures of Barcelona. Write labels in **español** and **catalán,** using your research and the vocabulary given here. Plan where all the words and pictures will appear.

3. Present your travel guide to the class in Spanish. Then, have a class discussion about the differences and similarities each group notices between **catalán** and **español**.

Many signs in Barcelona are in catalán and Spanish.

español	catalán
hola	hola
adiós	adéu
¿Qué tal?	Que tal?
Bien, gracias.	Be, gracies.
Buenos días.	Bon dia.
Buenas noches.	Bona nit.

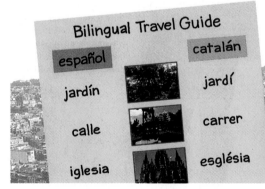

Bilingual Travel Guide

español	catalán
jardín	jardí
calle	carrer
iglesia	església

doscientos cuarenta y siete
Unidad 5   247

Teaching Suggestions
Las ciencias

During a great part of the Middle Ages, while the rest of Europe was experiencing a cultural eclipse, Spain was thriving, thanks to the contributions of the Arabs and the large Jewish population. Toledo was the governmental and cultural center of the peninsula. It was also home to an important school of translation; scientific information was constantly being translated from Greek and Latin into Arabic, Hebrew, and **castellano** (*Castilian,* the variety of Spanish spoken in the region at the time).

Teaching Middle School Students

Native Speakers Ask native speakers to prepare reports about the influence of other cultures on the art, architecture, music, and language of their home countries.

Multiple Intelligences

Musical/Rhythmic Have students find recordings of Spanish music that has Arabic influence. Have them look for videos of performances of Spanish music and/or dancing.

Block Schedule

Variety Have students research typical Moorish design elements. Encourage them to use these techniques to create interesting tiling patterns of their own. They should then write short paragraphs naming and describing their patterns.

Unit Theme
Comparing life in the city (Quito, Ecuador) and in the country (Otavalo, Ecuador)

Communication
- Talking about the past
- Describing city buildings
- Talking about professions
- Pointing out people and things and where they are located
- Discussing the present and future
- Giving instructions

Cultures
- Learning about Quito, Ecuador, and its buildings
- Learning about the people of Otavalo, Ecuador
- Learning about other interesting places to visit in Ecuador
- Learning about international foods

Connections
- Connecting to Science: Finding out about animals
- Connecting to Health: Preparing a typical meal from a Spanish-speaking country

Comparisons
- Comparing place names in Ecuador and in the U.S.
- Comparing cultural groups in Ecuador and in the U.S.
- Comparing foods and what your family eats

Communities
- Using Spanish in the workplace
- Using Spanish to help others

Teaching Resource Options

Print
Block Scheduling Copymasters

Audiovisual
OHT M4; 171, 172
Canciones Audiocassette/CD
Video Program Videotape 6 / Videodisc 3B

Search Chapter 1, Play to 2
U6 Cultural Introduction

UNIDAD 6

QUITO
ECUADOR

LA CIUDAD Y EL CAMPO

OBJECTIVES

ETAPA 1 La vida de la ciudad
- Tell what happened
- Make suggestions to a group
- Describe city buildings
- Talk about professions

ETAPA 2 A conocer el campo
- Point out specific people and things
- Tell where things are located
- Talk about the past

ETAPA 3 ¡A ganar el concurso!
- Talk about the present and future
- Give instructions to someone
- Discuss the past

248

LA CASA DE SUCRE was once the home of independence leader Mariscal Antonio José de Sucre. It houses items from Quito's colonial and independence periods. What historic museums have you visited?

ISLAS GALÁPAGOS

OCÉANO PACÍFICO

PAPAS, a staple of the Ecuadorian diet, have been cultivated in the Andes since before the time of the Incas. This New World food was introduced by Spain to the European diet. What dishes made with potatoes do you eat?

Middle School Classroom Community

Paired Activity Ask students to work in pairs to invent a conversation between the two teens pictured here.

Game Ask students to form a circle to play **Papa caliente.** Put on some Andean music, and ask students to pass a potato around until the music stops. The student holding the potato when the music stops must say a sentence in Spanish.

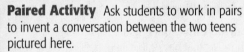

ALMANAQUE

Población: 1.500.000
Altura: 2.700 metros (8.775 pies)
Clima: 21° C (70° F) de día, 12° C (54° F) de noche
Comida típica: llapingachos, locros, fritada, humitas
Gente famosa de Quito: Oswaldo Guayasamín (pintor), Jorge Icaza (escritor), Carlota Jaramillo (cantante)

¿Vas a Quito? Quito es la capital de Ecuador. Su nombre viene de los indígenas quituas, un grupo muy antiguo.

 For more information about Quito, access www.mcdougallittell.com

VENEZUELA

Ecuador

LA MITAD DEL MUNDO is a monument built where the equator was measured. Ecuador's name comes from the fact that the equator (**el ecuador**) runs through it. What other countries of the world lie along the equator?

TAPICES are woven wall hangings and rugs made from the wool of sheep or alpaca. You will find these multicolored wall hangings in stores and outdoor markets. Where have you seen weavings?

OTAVALO

★ **QUITO**

COLOMBIA

ECUADOR

GUAYAQUIL

CUENCA

ATAHUALPA (1500–1533), son of the Incan king Huanya-Capac and grandson of Duchicela, king of Quito, is considered the first great Ecuadorian. He was heir to the kingdom of Quito and became leader of the Incan empire. Can you think of other Native American leaders?

PERÚ

UN RONDADOR is a wind instrument that has been used for more than 2000 years. It is made of cane or bamboo pieces of different widths and lengths. Each produces a distinct musical note. What other wind instruments do you know?

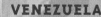

BRASIL

249

Teaching Middle School Students

Challenge Interested students may want to research Ecuadoran folk art and report back to the class.

Native Speakers Ask students to talk about a famous historical figure in their home countries. What did the person do? How is the person remembered?

Multiple Intelligences

Visual Ask students to make a detailed map of Ecuador showing the Andes and the principal cities.

Musical/Rhythmic Ask students to research Andean folk music and bring in recordings to share with the class.

Teaching Suggestions
Previewing the Unit

Tell students that this unit centers on the city and the country in Ecuador. Ask students to scan these two pages for 15 seconds, then close their books. Then ask them to tell you what they remember. You may wish to use the introduction to the video to preview the unit.

Culture Highlights

● **ANTONIO JOSÉ DE SUCRE** General Sucre led the revolutionary forces of Ecuador in a battle that took place on the slopes of Mt. Pichincha in 1822. The anniversary of this battle is May 24, a national holiday. Plaza Santo Domingo in Quito has a statue of General Sucre. The figure points to the site of this battle.

● **PAPAS** When the New World explorers introduced the potato to Europe, the Europeans refused to eat it because they thought it was ugly. They were unaccustomed to eating something that came from a tuber rather than a seed.

● **LA MITAD DEL MUNDO** This monument is located a half hour north of Quito, in San Antonio de Pichincha.

● **ATAHUALPA** Atahualpa was the last Inca ruler. He was taken prisoner and executed by the Spanish explorer Francisco Pizarro.

● **TAPICES** The art of weaving is practiced throughout the Americas. The use of cloaks covered by feathers of rare birds woven into them was not unusual among the Aztecs and the Incas.

● **EL RONDADOR** El rondador is a single-row panpipe. Other traditional instruments are the **antara** and **siku** (single- and double-row panpipes) and the **quena** (vertical end-notched flute).

Block Schedule

Sort and Organize After looking at the Unit 6 Cultural Opener, have students look back at the Cultural Openers for Units 4–5 and compare what they see. Have them compile a list of categories, then sort and organize the informational paragraphs. (For additional activities, see **Block Scheduling Copymasters**.)

Ampliación

These activities may be used at various points in the Unit 6 sequence.

■ For Block Schedule, you may find that these projects will provide a welcome change of pace while reviewing and reinforcing the material presented in the unit. See the **Block Scheduling Copymasters.**

● PROJECTS

Create a nature travel guide of Ecuador. Divide the class into 4 groups and assign one of the following regions of Ecuador to each:

- the highlands
- the coast
- the rain forests
- the Galápagos Islands

Each group should research and collect information about the flora and fauna of their region. Within each group, students may be assigned specific animals or plants. Using drawings or photos, have each group write a travel guide entry of their region. Collect and bind the 4 reports to share with other classes.

> PACING SUGGESTION: Upon completion of Etapa 2.

Interview Have students work in groups of 5 to role-play people of different professions, including 1 journalist. The journalist will tape interviews (video or audio) with each person, asking questions about what they did to prepare for the profession, why they chose it, etc.

> PACING SUGGESTION: Upon completion of Etapa 2.

OTAVALO
•
★
QUITO

● STORYTELLING

Cinquain poems After reviewing vocabulary for professions, model a cinquain (5-line) poem for students. Write guidelines on the board for students to follow as you read:

GUIDELINES	CINQUAIN
noun (subject of poem)	Maestro(a)
2 adjectives or 1 noun and 1 adjective	Inteligente, exigente
3-word sentence or 3 infinitives	Preguntar, responder, calificar
4-word sentence expressing an emotion	Quiere a los alumnos
noun or adjective restating the subject	Confidente

ECUADOR

Have each student write a cinquain poem about 3 different professions. Variation: Have students all write about the same 3 professions to contrast ideas.

Otros temas Have students write 2 cinquain poems about contrasting subjects; for example, city vs. country, horse vs. car, etc.

> PACING SUGGESTION: Upon completion of Etapa 3.

PERÚ

● BULLETIN BOARD/POSTERS

Bulletin Board Have students create maps of Ecuador. Each map should depict a different aspect of the country: topography, rainfall, agriculture, animals, crafts, landmarks, etc. Students can decorate their maps with drawings, photos, or small objects.

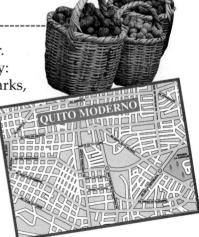

QUITO MODERNO

Posters Have students create •**Advertisement** posters for the market and crafts in Otavalo •**Job fair** fliers announcing booths for different professions •**Travel posters** for the main attractions in Ecuador (the equator, the Galápagos Islands, etc.)

GAMES

La pregunta es...

Prepare ahead: Create Jeopardy!™-style clues and questions for several categories: **profesiones, el campo, la ciudad, los animales,** etc. For example: clue = **Escribe artículos para el periódico.** Question = **¿Quién es un periodista?** To play, divide the class into 3 or 4 teams. Choose a category. After reading a clue from that category, call on the first student who raises his/her hand. The student must provide an appropriate question. If the student answers correctly, the team gets one point and the student chooses the next category. If the student answers incorrectly, the first student from another team to raise his/her hand may try to provide the correct question. The team with the most points at the end of a predetermined time limit wins.

PACING SUGGESTION: Upon completion of Etapa 2.

En la ciudad

Prepare ahead: Make 5 gameboard maps of a city with specific locations numbered, and a corresponding set of numbered cards. Divide the class into 5 groups. Each group receives a map and the corresponding set of numbers. Students pick numbers, then take turns giving directions to a particular building or location. The group completing all directions in the shortest time wins.

PACING SUGGESTION: Upon completion of Etapa 3.

MUSIC

Andean music has gained in popularity throughout the world. Many contemporary groups have recorded traditional songs and new compositions that are a fusion of Andean music and other rhythms. Play recordings by groups such as Inti Illimani, Viento de los Andes, and Ecuador Manta. Have students describe the sounds. Refer them to p. 249 and also show them photos of instruments such as the **quena** (vertical end-notched flute) and the **siku** (double-row pan pipe). More music samples are available on your *Canciones* Cassette or CD.

OMBIA

HANDS-ON CRAFTS

Display the flag of Ecuador. Point out that the coat of arms includes palm and laurel branches (symbolizing victory), the condor with outstretched wings (symbolizing shelter and protection), and an image of Chimborazo (the highest mountain in the Andes) and the Guayas River (representing unity between the coast and mountains). The yellow band symbolizes abundance and fertility of crops and land; the blue symbolizes sea and sky; and the red symbolizes bloodshed during independence battles. Have students design flags on posterboards. The flags can represent their school, city, state, etc. Have students present their flags and explain them.

RECIPE

Quimbolitos are sweet biscuits made with corn flour, wrapped in leaves, and steamed. The traditional recipe calls for achira leaves. However, since these leaves are not exported to the U.S., plantain leaves have been substituted. You can also use bamboo leaves, cornhusks, or even wax paper.

BRASIL

Receta

Quimbolitos

2 tazas de harina de maíz tostado	1 taza de leche
1 cucharadita de polvo de hornear	2 huevos
1 taza de mantequilla	1 taza de azúcar
1 taza de jugo de naranja	1 taza de uvas pasas
1 cucharadita de esencia de vainilla	12 hojas de plátano

Mezcle la harina con el polvo de hornear, la mantequilla, el jugo de naranja, la esencia de vainilla y la leche. Separe los huevos. Bata las claras a punto de nieve. Agregue el azúcar y las yemas. Mezcle las dos preparaciones anteriores hasta formar una masa suave y homogénea. Lave las hojas de plátano y coloque la masa en el centro de cada una. Luego añada las uvas pasas. Cierre las hojas. Cocine los quimbolitos al vapor por 20 minutos.

Planning Guide CLASSROOM MANAGEMENT

OBJECTIVES

Communication
- Tell what happened *pp. 254–255*
- Make suggestions to a group *pp. 254–255*
- Describe city buildings *pp. 252–253*
- Talk about professions *pp. 252–253, 254–255*

Grammar
- Use preterite of regular **-er** and **-ir** verbs *pp. 260–261*
- Use preterite of verbs with a **y** spelling change *pp. 262–263*
- Use preterite of **hacer, ir, ser** *pp. 264–267*

Pronunciation
- Pronunciation of **d** *p. 269*
- Dictation *TE p. 269*

Culture
- History and culture of Quito, Ecuador *pp. 248–249, 259, 263, 264*
- Volcanoes in Ecuador *p. 265*
- Regional vocabulary *p. 266*
- Currency *p. 268*
- **Soroche** *p. 269*

♻ Recycling
- Superlatives *p. 259*
- Places *p. 266*

STRATEGIES

Listening Strategies
- Distinguish between what is said and not said *p. 254*

Speaking Strategies
- Exaggerate and react to exaggerations *p. 259*
- Relate details *p. 274*

Reading Strategies
- Follow the sequence *p. 270*

Writing Strategies
- Use different kinds of descriptive words *TE p. 274*

Connecting Cultures Strategies
- Learn about Quito, Ecuador *pp. 248–249, 259, 263, 264*
- Recognize regional vocabulary *p. 266*

PROGRAM RESOURCES

 Print

- *Más práctica* Workbook PE, *pp. 49–56*
- Block Scheduling Copymasters, *pp. 129–136*
- Unit 6 Resource Book
  Más práctica Workbook TE, *pp. 1–8*
  Information Gap Activities *pp. 17–20*

- Family Involvement *pp. 21–22*
- Video Activities *pp. 23–25*
- Videoscript *pp. 26–28*
- Audioscript *pp. 29–32*
- Assessment Program, Unit 6 Etapa 1 *pp. 33–51; 170–178*
- Answer Keys *pp. 187–202*

 Audiovisual

- Audio Program Cassettes 16A, 16B / CD 16
- *Canciones* Cassette / CD
- Video Program Videotape 6 / Videodisc 3B
- Overhead Transparencies M1–M5; 171, 174–184

 **Technology**

- Electronic Teacher Tools/Test Generator
- *Intrigas y aventuras* CD-ROM, Disc 1

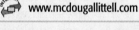 www.mcdougallittell.com

 Assessment Program Options

- Cooperative Quizzes (Unit 6 Resource Book)
- Etapa Exam Forms A and B (Unit 6 Resource Book)
- *Para hispanohablantes* Etapa Exam (Unit 6 Resource Book)
- Portfolio Assessment (Unit 6 Resource Book)
- Multiple Choice Test Questions (Unit 6 Resource Book)
- Audio Program Testing Cassette T2 / CD T2
- Electronic Teacher Tools/Test Generator

Native Speakers

- *Para hispanohablantes* Workbook PE, *pp. 49–56*
- *Para hispanohablantes* Workbook TE (Unit 6 Resource Book)
- *Para hispanohablantes* Etapa Exam (Unit 6 Resource Book)
- Audio *Para hispanohablantes* Cassettes 16A, 16B, T2 / CD 16, T2
- Audioscript *Para hispanohablantes* (Unit 6 Resource Book)

Patricia | Miguel | Sra. Martínez | Sr. González

Student Text
Listening Activity Scripts

 Videoscript: Diálogo *pages 254–255*

• Videotape 6 • Videodisc 3B

Search Chapter 3, Play to 4
U6E1 • En vivo (Dialog)

• Use the videoscript with **Actividades 1, 2** *pages 256–257*

Patricia: Decidí participar en el concurso porque leí que los ganadores van a viajar a otros países y van a trabajar como periodistas para la revista *Onda Internacional.*

Miguel: ¿Y por qué necesitas mi ayuda?

Patricia: Pues, quiero hacer entrevistas con personas que viven en la ciudad y personas que viven en el campo. Tú tienes familia en el campo, ¿no?

Miguel: Sí. Mi tío, y también la prima de mi madre. ¿Los llamo para ver si puedes hablar con ellos?

Patricia: ¡Sí, muchas gracias, Miguel! Oye, vamos a pedir algo, ¿no? En un rato tengo que entrevistar a unas personas y no quiero llegar tarde.

Patricia: Buenos días, señora.

Sra. Martínez: Buenos días.

Patricia: ¿Puede darme algunos minutos de su tiempo? Me llamo Patricia López Carrera. Estoy preparando un artículo para un concurso de la revista *Onda Internacional.*

Sra. Martínez: Claro que sí.

Patricia: Muchas gracias. A ver, ¿dónde empezamos? Muy bien, ¿cómo se llama y cuál es su profesión?

Sra. Martínez: Me llamo Ana Martínez. Soy una mujer de negocios. Trabajo en un banco aquí, en Quito.

Patricia: ¿Le gusta vivir en la ciudad?

Sra. Martínez: Sí, mucho. Pero también tiene sus problemas.

Patricia: ¿Cómo qué?

Sra. Martínez: La contaminación del aire, el tráfico, como en todas las ciudades grandes.

Patricia: Me puede decir, ¿cómo se preparó para ser una mujer de negocios?

Sra. Martínez: Bueno, hice todo lo necesario. Primero, fui a la universidad. Después me ofrecieron un trabajo en la oficina del banco. Y después de muchos años, llegué a ser gerente.

Patricia: ¿Y siempre vivió en Quito?

Sra. Martínez: Sí. Mis padres abrieron una panadería aquí.

Sr. González: Pase, por favor.

Patricia: Buenas tardes, arquitecto González.

Sr. González: Buenas tardes, señorita López Carrera. Tome asiento, por favor.

Patricia: Gracias por su tiempo.

Sr. González: Es un placer. ¿Para qué es la entrevista?

Patricia: Estoy participando en un concurso. Voy a escribir sobre el contraste entre la vida en la ciudad y en el campo.

Sr. González: Ah, sí. ¿Qué quiere saber?

Patricia: ¿Le gusta vivir en la ciudad?

Sr. González: La ciudad es interesante, y nunca aburrida. Sí, me gusta. Pero sabe, la vida en el campo es mucho más tranquila.

Patricia: ¿Vivió usted alguna vez en el campo?

Sr. González: De niño viví en el campo, en la casa de mis abuelos en la Argentina. Pero ahora, por mi trabajo, tengo que vivir en Quito, es decir en la ciudad.

Patricia: ¿Y cuándo decidió venir a la ciudad?

Sr. González: Cuando entré a la universidad. Luego, cuando recibí mi título de arquitecto, vi que en la ciudad hay más oportunidades profesionales que en el campo.

Miguel: ¿Aló?

Patricia: ¿Miguel? Soy Patricia.

Miguel: ¡Hola, Patricia! ¿Cómo fueron las entrevistas?

Patricia: Excelente. Ya hice dos. ¿Llamaste a tu familia?

Miguel: Sí. Todo está listo para el sábado. El autobús sale a las ocho. ¿Nos vemos en la estación?

Patricia: Perfecto. ¡Hasta el sábado entonces!

Miguel: ¡Adiós!

 **4 ¿Cómo son?** *page 258*

Esta ciudad tiene muchos estilos de arquitectura. Los edificios altos son los más modernos de Quito. Las oficinas de muchas compañías internacionales están allí. A la derecha hay un banco con un estilo de arquitectura tradicional en un edificio bajo. Mis edificios favoritos son los antiguos como la iglesia colonial al lado de la farmacia. Es bonita, ¿no? De vez en cuando la ciudad tiene que destruir unos edificios viejos, como el edificio grande y feo al final de la calle.

18 Un sábado especial *page 266*

Patricia: Hola, Andrea, ¿qué hiciste el sábado?

Andrea: Por la mañana, le escribí una carta a mi amigo Raúl. Después, fui a un partido de fútbol donde vi a muchos amigos.

Patricia: Y tú, Marta, ¿hiciste algo interesante?

Marta: Sí. Por la tarde, fui de compras con Lucía. Luego, salí con Pedro.

Andrea: ¿Adónde fueron?

Marta: Fuimos a Casa Linda. Comimos una comida riquísima.

Andrea: Y tú, Patricia, ¿qué hiciste?

Patricia: Por la mañana corrí en el parque con algunos amigos. Por la noche, salí para el cine con Antonio.

Andrea: ¿Qué vieron?

Patricia: Vimos una película de acción buenísima.

Andrea: ¡Creo que fue un sábado interesante para todas!

▲ **Quick Start Review Answers**

p. 254 Professions
1. un(a) taxista
2. un(a) arquitecto(a)
3. un hombre/una mujer de negocios
4. un(a) periodista
5. un(a) cartero(a)
6. un(a) fotógrafo(a)

p. 262 Preterite of **-er** and **-ir** verbs
Answers will vary. Answers could include:
1. Yo aprendí a cocinar.
2. Tú escribiste una carta a tu abuela.

3. Tomás corrió 5 kilómetros.
4. Mis amigos me ofrecieron una merienda.
5. Nosotros decidimos comer a las ocho.

p. 272 Preterite
Answers will vary. Answers could include:
1. fui en autobús
2. llegaron tarde
3. salieron a las seis
4. fuiste al parque
5. no me hizo ninguno

Sample Lesson Plan - 45 Minute Schedule

DAY 1

Unit Opener
- Anticipate/Activate prior knowledge: Present the *Almanaque* and the cultural notes. Use Map OHTs as needed. 10 MIN.

Etapa Opener
- Quick Start Review (TE, p. 250) 5 MIN.
- Have students look at the *Etapa* Opener and answer the *¿Qué ves?* questions, p. 250. 10 MIN.

En contexto: Vocabulario
- Quick Start Review (TE, p. 252) 5 MIN.
- Have students use context and pictures to learn *Etapa* vocabulary. 10 MIN.
- Have students answer the *Preguntas personales*, p. 253. 5 MIN.

DAY 2

En vivo: Diálogo
- Quick Start Review (TE, p. 254) 5 MIN.
- Review the Listening Strategy, p. 254. 5 MIN.
- Play audio or show video for the dialog, pp. 254–255. 5 MIN.
- Discuss students' Listening Strategy checklist results. 5 MIN.
- Replay the audio or video, then have students take the roles of the characters. 10 MIN.

En acción: Vocabulario y gramática
- Quick Start Review (TE, p. 256) 5 MIN.
- Have students open to *En contexto*, pp. 252–253, for reference. Use OHTs to review vocabulary. 10 MIN.

Homework Option:
- Video Activities, Unit 6 Resource Book, pp. 23–25.

DAY 3

En acción (cont.)
- Check homework. 5 MIN.
- Play the video/audio. 5 MIN.
- Have students do *Actividad* 1 orally. 5 MIN.
- Do *Actividad* 2 orally. 5 MIN.
- Have students work independently on *Actividad* 3. 5 MIN.
- Ask volunteers to share their responses to *Actividad* 3. 5 MIN.
- Present the *Vocabulario,* p. 258. 5 MIN.
- Play the audio while students think about the order of pictures in *Actividad* 4. 5 MIN.
- Have students share their responses to *Actividad* 4. 5 MIN.

DAY 4

En acción (cont.)
- Have students work in pairs to do *Actividad* 5. 5 MIN.
- Ask pairs to model their descriptions for *Actividad* 5. 5 MIN.
- Assign *Actividad* 6. 10 MIN.
- Ask volunteers to read their postcards from *Actividad* 6. 5 MIN.
- Present the Speaking Strategy, p. 259. 5 MIN.
- Have students work in pairs on *Actividad* 7. 5 MIN.
- Call on pairs to share their work on *Actividad* 7. 5 MIN.
- Discuss the Project (TE, p. 259). 5 MIN.

Homework Option:
- Have students start work on the postcard-stamp project.

DAY 5

En acción (cont.)
- Quick Start Review (TE, p. 260) 5 MIN.
- Present *Gramática:* Talking About the Past: The Preterite of *-er* and *-ir* Verbs, and the *Vocabulario,* p. 260. 10 MIN.
- Work orally with students on *Actividad* 8. 5 MIN.
- Have students write their answers to *Actividad* 8. 5 MIN.
- Have students work in groups on *Actividad* 9. 5 MIN.
- Ask each group to share its results from *Actividad* 9. 5 MIN.
- Have pairs do *Actividad* 10. 5 MIN.
- Ask volunteers to share their work on *Actividad* 10. 5 MIN.

Homework Option:
- *Más práctica* Workbook, pp. 53–54. *Para hispanohablantes* Workbook, pp. 51–52.

DAY 6

En acción (cont.)
- Check homework. 5 MIN.
- Quick Start Review (TE, p. 262) 5 MIN.
- Present *Gramática:* Talking About the Past: Verbs with a *y* Spelling Change, p. 262. 10 MIN.
- Work orally with the class on *Actividad* 11. 5 MIN.
- Have students write their responses to *Actividad* 11. 5 MIN.
- Work on *Actividad* 12 orally. 5 MIN.
- Have students write their responses to *Actividad* 12. 5 MIN.
- Read and discuss the *Nota cultural,* p. 263. 5 MIN.

Homework Option:
- *Más práctica* Workbook, p. 55. *Para hispanohablantes* Workbook, p. 53.

DAY 7

En acción (cont.)
- Check homework. 5 MIN.
- Quick Start Review (TE, p. 264) 5 MIN.
- Have students work in pairs on *Actividad* 13. 5 MIN.
- Call on selected pairs to share their work on *Actividad* 13. 5 MIN.
- Work orally with the class on *Actividad* 14. 5 MIN.
- Have students write their responses to *Actividad* 14. 5 MIN.
- Present *Gramática:* Using Irregular Verbs in the Preterite: *hacer, ir, ser,* p. 264. 10 MIN.
- Read and discuss the *Nota cultural,* p. 264. 5 MIN.

DAY 8

En acción (cont.)
- Work orally with the class on *Actividad* 15. 5 MIN.
- Have students write their answers to *Actividad* 15. 5 MIN.
- Present the *Vocabulario,* p. 265. 5 MIN.
- Assign *Actividad* 16. 5 MIN.
- Ask volunteers to read their responses to *Actividad* 16. 5 MIN.
- Read and discuss the *Conexiones,* p. 265. 5 MIN.
- Have pairs do *Actividad* 17. 5 MIN.
- Play the audio as students do *Actividad* 18. 5 MIN.
- Ask volunteers to share their responses to *Actividad* 18. 5 MIN.

Homework Option:
- *Más práctica* Workbook, p. 56. *Para hispanohablantes* Workbook, p. 54.

DAY 9

En acción (cont.)
- Check homework. 5 MIN.
- Read and discuss the *También se dice,* p. 266. 5 MIN.
- Work orally with the class on *Actividad* 19. 5 MIN.
- Have students write their responses to *Actividad* 19. 5 MIN.
- Read and discuss the *Apoyo para estudiar,* p. 267. 5 MIN.
- Have students work in pairs to do *Actividad* 20. 5 MIN.
- Ask volunteers to give their responses to *Actividad* 20. 5 MIN.
- Have students work in pairs to do *Actividad* 21. 5 MIN.
- Ask volunteers to share their calendars from *Actividad* 21. 5 MIN.

DAY 10

En acción (cont.)
- Work orally with the class on *Actividad* 22. 5 MIN.
- Have students write individual responses to *Actividad* 22. 5 MIN.
- Model some responses to *Actividad* 23. 5 MIN.
- Assign *Actividad* 23 as a written activity. 5 MIN.
- Use Information Gap Activities, Unit 6 Resource Book, pp. 18–19. 5 MIN.
- Read and discuss the *Conexiones,* p. 269. 5 MIN.
- *Más comunicación,* p. R7. 5 MIN.
- Play the audio. 5 MIN.
- Discuss and demonstrate the *Pronunciación,* p. 269. 5 MIN.

Homework Option:
- Have students write 3 sentences for the *Para hacer,* p. 269.

DAY 11

En voces: Lectura
- Check homework. 5 MIN.
- Quick Start Review (TE, p. 270) 5 MIN.
- Review the Reading Strategy, p. 270. 5 MIN.
- Ask students to scan the reading and find the sequencing words. 5 MIN.
- Have students read the *Lectura,* pp. 270–271, silently. 5 MIN.
- Ask volunteers to read the story orally. 10 MIN.
- Have students answer the *¿Comprendiste?* questions for the *Lectura* (Answers, TE, p. 271). 5 MIN.
- Work orally with students to answer the *¿Qué piensas?* questions for the *Lectura,* p. 271. 5 MIN.

DAY 12

En uso: Repaso y más comunicación
- Quick Start Review (TE, p. 272) 5 MIN.
- Present the *Repaso y más comunicación* using the Teaching Suggestions (TE, p. 272). 10 MIN.
- Do the TPR activitiy (TE, p. 272). 5 MIN.
- Have students write their responses to *Actividad* 1. 5 MIN.
- Check answers for *Actividad* 1 with the whole class. 5 MIN.
- Work with students to do *Actividad* 2 orally. 5 MIN.
- Assign *Actividad* 3. 5 MIN.
- Ask volunteers to share their answers to *Actividad* 3. 5 MIN.

DAY 13

En uso (cont.)
- Have students read and prepare to answer *Actividad* 4. 5 MIN.
- Ask volunteers to read their answers to *Actividad* 4. 5 MIN.
- Present the Speaking Strategy, p. 274. 5 MIN.
- Have pairs do *Actividad* 5. 5 MIN.
- Have volunteer pairs model their work for *Actividad* 5. 5 MIN.
- Have students work in groups to do *Actividad* 6. 10 MIN.
- Ask groups to volunteer to share their work from *Actividad* 6. 5 MIN.
- Read and discuss *En la comunidad,* p. 274. 5 MIN.

Homework Option:
- Have students review all the *Gramática* boxes in *Etapa* 1 to prepare for *En uso.*

DAY 14

En tu propia voz: Escritura
- Quick Start Review (TE, p. 275) 5 MIN.
- Check homework. 5 MIN.
- Have students do the writing activity, *Actividad* 7, independently. 10 MIN.
- Call on selected students to read their work from *Actividad* 7. 5 MIN.

En resumen: Repaso de vocabulario
- Follow the Teaching Suggestions (TE, p. 275). 10 MIN.
- Review grammar questions, etc., as necessary. 5 MIN.
- Have students solve the *Juego* (Answers, TE, p. 275). 5 MIN.

Homework Option:
- Have students study for *Etapa* exam.

DAY 15

En resumen: Repaso de vocabulario
- Answer questions related to *Etapa* 1 content. 10 MIN.
- Complete *Etapa* exam. 25 MIN.

Ampliación
- Use a suggested project, game, or activity (TE, pp. 249A–249B) as students complete the exam.

Classroom Management Tip

Vary classroom activities For students to truly enjoy and see the benefits of learning Spanish, their use of it must get beyond what's in the book. Help them make connections with the real world by doing research on topics related to the contexts used in *¡En Español!*

One way to make the connection is to research banana production and trade. You could also grow a dwarf banana tree in class. These trees grow rapidly and need little care.

Etapa Theme

Describing a city and talking about professions

Grammar Objectives
- Using preterite of regular **-er** and **-ir** verbs
- Using preterite of verbs with a **y** spelling change
- Using preterite of **hacer, ir, ser**

Teaching Resource Options

Print

Block Scheduling Copymasters

Audiovisual

OHT 172, 181 (Quick Start)

Quick Start Review

♻ Preterite of **-ar** verbs

Use OHT 181 or write on board: Write 1 thing that happened at each of these times, using an **-ar** verb in the preterite.

1. ayer   3. el mes pasado
2. anoche   4. el año pasado

Answers

Answers will vary. Answers could include:
1. Empecé a leer una novela.
2. Mi hermano preparó la comida.
3. Celebré mi cumpleaños.
4. Mis padres compraron una videograbadora.

Teaching Suggestions
Previewing the Etapa
- Ask students to study the photo on pp. 250–251 (1 min.).
- Close books; ask students to share at least 3 things that they noticed.
- Reopen books and look at the picture again. Give students the beginning of statements for them to finish; for example: **La mujer...**
- Use the **¿Qué ves?** questions to focus the discussion.

Supplementary Vocabulary

el edificio	building
el edificio de	apartment
departamentos	building

UNIDAD 6

ETAPA 1

La vida de la ciudad

- **Tell what happened**
- **Make suggestions to a group**
- **Describe city buildings**
- **Talk about professions**

¿Qué ves?

Mira la foto de un parque de Quito.

1. ¿Las montañas están cerca o lejos del parque?
2. ¿Qué hacen los dos jóvenes?
3. ¿Qué joyas lleva la señora?
4. ¿Cuántos parques hay en el mapa?

250

QUITO MODERNO

Middle School Classroom Management

Planning Ahead You may want to get a supply of brown paper lunch bags for use as puppets in an activity on p. 264.

Cooperative Learning Ask students to work in groups of 4 to research Quito. Students should brainstorm questions they would like answered, use the Internet and library resources to find information, make a map of the city, and then report back to the class. Students should decide which person will be responsible for each activity. There should be a researcher, recorder, mapmaker, and presenter.

251

Cross Cultural Connections

Have students talk about local or national parks they have been to and how they compare to this one. Ask if they prefer trips to the country or city and why.

Culture Highlights

● **QUITO** Quito, the capital of Ecuador and the Pichincha Province, is located in a valley on the lower slopes of the Pichincha volcano of the Andes Mountains. It is the oldest South American capital.

The architecture of most of Quito's buildings is in the Spanish Baroque style. The most well-known buildings are the Cathedral and the churches of San Francisco, San Agustín, La Compañía, and Santo Domingo.

There are many parks and flower gardens in Quito. The one shown in this photo is the **Parque Sueco,** a small park in **el Quito Moderno.** Two others are **La Carolina** and **El Ejido.**

● **EL TIEMPO EN QUITO** The weather in Quito is changeable. It can go from sunny to rainy to foggy in the course of one day. The temperature can drop 15 degrees on a sunny day when clouds pass overhead.

● **LAS DIRECCIONES EN QUITO** In Quito, all streets that run from east to west are called **calles.** Those that go north to south are **carreras.** If the address you are looking for is **Calle 108-20,** this means the building is on 10th Street, 20 meters from the intersection with **Carrera 8.**

Teaching Middle School Students

Extra Help Help students to make lists of words describing the photo. Use these categories: **personas, ropa, números, acciones, naturaleza.**

Native Speakers Have native speakers interview a Spanish-speaking relative or friend about his or her job.

Multiple Intelligences

Verbal Ask students to invent a dialog between the two people seated on the bench in the photo and then to perform it for the class.

Naturalist Ask students to research and report on how vegetation might be different in a city at a high elevation along the equator. Have them do the same for a city at sea level.

Block Schedule

Change of Pace Set up a park scene similar to the one in the photo. Have roaming "news reporters" move from one person to the next, describing the scene and asking the people questions. (For additional activities, see **Block Scheduling Copymasters.**)

Teaching Resource Options

Print

Unit 6 Resource Book
Video Activities, pp. 23–24
Videoscript, p. 26
Audioscript, p. 29
Audioscript *Para hispanohablantes,*
p. 29

Audiovisual

OHT 175, 176, 177, 177A, 178, 178A, 181 (Quick Start)
Audio Program Cassette 16A / CD 16
Audio *Para hispanohablantes*
Cassette 16A / CD 16
Video Program Videotape 6 / Videodisc 3B

Search Chapter 2, Play to 3
U6E1 • En contexto (Vocabulary)

Technology

Intrigas y aventuras CD-ROM, Disc 1

Quick Start Review

♻ Present progressive

Use OHT 181 or write on the board:
Tell what the following people are
doing right now in the locations
indicated.

Modelo: Eva / la cocina
You write: **Eva está lavando los platos.**

1. los estudiantes / la cafetería
2. los maestros / el departamento
   de español
3. Miguel / la biblioteca
4. la Sra. Ruiz / el supermercado
5. Susana / su habitación

Answers

Answers will vary. Answers could include:
1. Los estudiantes están comiendo.
2. Los maestros están hablando español.
3. Miguel está leyendo una novela.
4. La Sra. Ruiz está comprando la comida.
5. Susana está durmiendo.

En contexto

VOCABULARIO

Patricia is interviewing different people in Quito about their
jobs. As she walks through old and new Quito, she describes
different professions.

A **¡Hola!** Me llamo Patricia y voy a explicarles
cómo son las profesiones de varias personas. Ahora
estoy hablando con **un bombero.** Quiero saber algo de
su trabajo. Con mi **grabadora** le hago **una entrevista.**

el edificio moderno

el edificio antiguo y tradicional

la cámara

la grabadora

el bombero

la fotógrafa

B Ella es **fotógrafa.** Saca fotos
con **una cámara.** Está sacando
una foto de **un edificio** muy
antiguo y tradicional.

el cartero

el taxista

C El **cartero** lleva cartas a
todos los edificios. A veces
trabaja en el correo.

D Él es **taxista.** En su taxi lleva
a la gente por toda la ciudad.

252 doscientos cincuenta y dos
Unidad 6

Middle School Classroom Community

TPR Begin by telling the class that many people
change jobs often. Say that you are going to name a
profession, and they will act out doing that job until
you name another one. Also use the **Vocabulario
adicional** on pp. R12–R13 (**Más profesiones**).

Game Ask students to gather old magazines,
newspapers, or catalogs. Have them cut out small
pictures representing professions and glue them to
index cards. Then each pair or small group places its
cards in a facedown pile, taking turns turning them
over and saying what the profession is. The player who
can identify the profession keeps the card. The player
with more cards when the pile is gone wins.

E Mujer de negocios:
Me gusta vender y
comprar productos.
Ser una mujer de
negocios es el trabajo
perfecto para mí.

el hombre de negocios

la mujer de negocios

Hombre de negocios:
Siempre leo todas las
revistas de economía.
Para ser un hombre
de negocios hay que
saber mucho.

F Él trabaja para un periódico. Le gusta
escribir y hacer entrevistas. Por eso
es **periodista**.

el periodista

el arquitecto

G Él es **arquitecto**. Hace planos
de construcción. El edificio que
planea aquí es el más grande
de Quito. ¡Su oficina está en un
edificio **enorme** y muy **moderno**!

Preguntas personales

1. ¿Te gusta hacer entrevistas?
2. ¿Prefieres edificios tradicionales o modernos?
3. ¿Tienes una cámara o una grabadora?
4. ¿Quién te lleva cartas?
5. ¿Cuál de estos trabajos te gustaría hacer?

doscientos cincuenta y tres
Etapa 1 **253**

Teaching Suggestions
Introducing Vocabulary

• Have students look at pages 252–253.
Use OHT 175 and 176 and Audio
Cassette 16A / CD 16 to present the
vocabulary.
• Ask the Comprehension Questions in
order of yes/no (questions 1–3),
either/or (questions 4–6), and simple
word or phrase (questions 7–10).
Expand by adding similar questions.
• Use the TPR activity to reinforce the
meaning of individual words.
• Use the video vocabulary presentation
for review and reinforcement.

Comprehension Questions

1. ¿Está Patricia hablando con un policía?
(No.)
2. ¿Saca fotos la fotógrafa de un edificio
antiguo? (Sí.)
3. ¿Trabaja el cartero en el correo a
veces? (Sí.)
4. ¿Pasa el taxista el día caminando o
manejando? (manejando)
5. ¿Le gusta a la mujer de negocios
vender o hacer productos? (vender)
6. ¿Qué lee siempre el hombre de
negocios: novelas o revistas de
economía? (revistas de economía)
7. ¿Qué hace el periodista? (Escribe y
hace entrevistas.)
8. ¿Quién hace planos de construcción?
(el arquitecto)
9. ¿Cómo es el edificio que planea el
arquitecto en Quito? (Es el más
grande de Quito.)
10. ¿En qué tipo de edificio está la oficina
del arquitecto? (Es un edificio enorme y
muy moderno.)

Block Schedule

Change of Pace Have each student
choose 1 profession from pp. 252–253,
or a profession listed in the **Vocabulario
adicional** on pp. R12–R13 (**Más
profesiones**). They should write down 2
questions they might ask a person in
this profession. You then play the roles
of these professionals and students ask
you their questions.

Teaching Middle School Students

Extra Help Have students choose a profession and
then memorize the description. Every so often during
the lesson, ask one student to name and describe his
or her profession.

Challenge Ask students to write about a day in the
life of a professional of interest to them.

Multiple Intelligences

Intrapersonal Ask students to write down two
or three professions they would like to have and
to explain their reasoning.

Interpersonal Ask students to work in pairs, telling
each other what profession(s) they would like to have
or what their parents' professions/occupations are.

Print 📖

Más práctica Workbook PE,
   pp. 49–52

Para hispanohablantes Workbook PE,
   pp. 49–50

Block Scheduling Copymasters

Unit 6 Resource Book

Más práctica Workbook TE, pp. 1–4

Para hispanohablantes Workbook
   TE, pp. 9–10

Video Activities, pp. 23–24

Videoscript, p. 27

Audioscript, p. 29

Audioscript *Para hispanohablantes*,
   p. 29

Audiovisual 🎞️

OHT 179, 180, 181 (Quick Start)

Audio Program Cassette 16A / CD 16

Audio *Para hispanohablantes*
   Cassette 16A / CD 16

Video Program Videotape 6 / Videodisc
   3B

Search Chapter 3, Play to 4
U6E1 • En vivo (Dialog)

Technology 💻 CD-ROM

Intrigas y aventuras CD-ROM, Disc 1

🔔 Quick Start Review

♻️ **Professions**

Use OHT 181 or write on the board:
Write the profession associated with
each of the following activities:

1. manejar un taxi
2. hacer planos de construcción
3. estudiar economía
4. escribir y hacer entrevistas
5. llevar cartas
6. sacar fotos

Answers *See p. 249D.*

Gestures

Point out the eye contact and open-hand
gestures in scenes 2, 4, 5, 8, 9. These, and
the handshake in 7, are nonverbal ways of
affirming connection between speakers.
What does it mean when speakers don't
look at each other or make any gestures?

En vivo

🎧 💿 **DIÁLOGO**

Patricia   Miguel   Sra. Martínez   Sr. González

PARA ESCUCHAR • STRATEGY: LISTENING

Distinguish between what is said and not said Being a good listener
means being careful and accurate. Which of these are mentioned
in Patricia's interviews about city life? Which are not?

los trabajos	sí	mucha gente	
la calidad del aire		muchos vehículos	
el crimen		la vida aburrida	

En la ciudad

1 ▶ Patricia: Decidí participar en el
concurso porque leí que los
ganadores van a viajar. Quiero
hacer entrevistas con personas en
la ciudad y personas en el campo.
Tú tienes familia en el campo, ¿no?

5 ▶ Sra. Martínez: Sí, pero
también tiene sus problemas.
La contaminación del aire,
el tráfico…

Patricia: ¿Cómo se preparó para
ser una mujer de negocios?

6 ▶ Sra. Martínez: Hice todo lo necesario. Fui
a la universidad. Después me ofrecieron
trabajo en el banco. Y llegué a ser gerente.

Patricia: ¿Y siempre vivió en Quito?

Sra. Martínez: Sí. Mis padres abrieron una
panadería aquí.

7 ▶ Patricia: Buenas tardes, arquitecto
González. Voy a escribir sobre el
contraste entre la vida en la ciudad
y en el campo.

Sr. González: ¿Qué quiere saber?

Patricia: ¿Le gusta vivir en la ciudad?

254 doscientos cincuenta y cuatro
Unidad 6

Middle School Classroom Community

TPR Ask each student to choose one item from the
Listening Strategy. As you play the video, students stand
if/when their item is discussed.

Group Activity Ask students to practice portions of
the dialog together and then take turns acting it out for
the class.

Portfolio Ask students to write a newspaper
recruiting ad for a profession they find interesting.

Rubric

Criteria	Scale	
Vocabulary use/spelling	1 2 3 4 5	A = 17–20 pts.
Correct sentence structure/grammar	1 2 3 4 5	B = 13–16 pts.
Logical organization	1 2 3 4 5	C = 9–12 pts.
Creativity	1 2 3 4 5	D = 5–8 pts.
		F = < 5 pts.

2 ▶ **Miguel:** Sí. ¿Los llamo?
Patricia: ¡Sí, muchas gracias, Miguel! Oye, vamos a pedir algo, ¿no? En un rato tengo que entrevistar a unas personas y no quiero llegar tarde.

3 ▶ **Patricia:** Buenos días. ¿Puede darme algunos minutos de su tiempo? Estoy preparando un artículo para un concurso.
Sra. Martínez: Claro que sí.
Patricia: Muy bien. ¿Cómo se llama y cuál es su profesión?

4 ▶ **Sra. Martínez:** Me llamo Ana Martínez. Soy una mujer de negocios. Trabajo en un banco aquí, en Quito.
Patricia: ¿Le gusta vivir en la ciudad?

8 ▶ **Sr. González:** La ciudad es interesante. Pero la vida en el campo es mucho más tranquila.
Patricia: ¿Vivió en el campo?
Sr. González: De niño viví en el campo, en casa de mis abuelos.

9 ▶ **Patricia:** ¿Y cuándo decidió venir a la ciudad?
Sr. González: Cuando entré a la universidad. Cuando recibí mi título de arquitecto, vi que en la ciudad hay más oportunidades que en el campo.

10 ▶ **Patricia:** ¿Miguel? Soy Patricia.
Miguel: ¿Cómo fueron las entrevistas?
Patricia: Excelente. Ya hice dos. ¿Llamaste a tu familia?
Miguel: Sí. Todo está listo para el sábado.

doscientos cincuenta y cinco
Etapa 1

255

Teaching Suggestions
Presenting the Dialog

• Prepare students for listening by reintroducing the characters using simple questions: **¿Cómo se llama la chica? ¿Cuál es la profesión de la Sra. Martínez? ¿Cómo se llama el arquitecto?**
• Use the video, audio cassette, or CD to present the dialog. The expanded dialog on video offers additional listening practice opportunities.

Video Synopsis

• Patricia tells her friend Miguel about her project for the contest. She is going to interview people in the city and in the country. For a complete transcript of the video dialog, see p. 249D.

Comprehension Questions

1. ¿Van a viajar los ganadores del concurso? (Sí.)
2. ¿Tiene Miguel familia en el campo? (Sí.)
3. ¿Tiene Patricia mucho tiempo antes de su próxima entrevista? (No.)
4. ¿Trabaja la Sra. Martínez en el campo o en la ciudad? (en la ciudad)
5. ¿Abrieron sus padres una panadería o un banco? (una panadería)
6. ¿Escribe Patricia sobre las profesiones o sobre el contraste entre la vida en la ciudad y el campo? (sobre el contraste entre la vida en la ciudad y el campo)
7. ¿Qué adjetivo usa el Sr. González para describir la vida en la ciudad? (interesante)
8. ¿Qué adjetivo usa el Sr. González para describir la vida en el campo? (tranquila)
9. ¿Cuándo vivió en el campo? (de niño)
10. ¿Por qué es mejor buscar trabajo en la ciudad? (Hay más oportunidades.)

▪ Block Schedule

Variety Working in pairs, have students make 2 lists of words: those associated with the city and those with the country. They should include professions, clothing, landscape, buildings, etc. Then have them share their lists with another pair and see if the new pair can guess "city" or "country" based on the words in the list. (For additional activities, see **Block Scheduling Copymasters**.)

Teaching Middle School Students

Extra Help Have students write out Patricia's schedule for the day, including enough information in each entry for another reader to follow.

Multiple Intelligences

Verbal Ask students to work in pairs to write a skit about a job interview and then perform it for the class.

Intrapersonal Ask students to write about where they would like to live and why.

Naturalist Ask students to make a poster about the benefits of living in the city.

Quick Start Review

♻ Dialog review

Use OHT 182 or write on the board:
Identify the speaker of each quote.

1. Trabajo en un banco aquí, en
   Quito.
2. Quiero hacer entrevistas con
   personas en la ciudad y personas
   en el campo.
3. Todo está listo para el sábado.
4. De niño viví en el campo...
5. ¿Llamaste a tu familia?

Answers

1. Sra. Martínez   4. Sr. González
2. Patricia   5. Patricia
3. Miguel

Teaching Suggestions
Comprehension Check

Use **Actividades 1** and **2** to assess
retention after the dialog. After
completing the activities, have students
write out **Actividad 1** in paragraph form
and insert at least 2 more events.

Objective: Controlled practice
Listening comprehension/vocabulary

Answers (See script, p. 249D.)

1. a
2. a
3. b
4. a

En acción

VOCABULARIO Y GRAMÁTICA

OBJECTIVES

- Tell what happened
- Make suggestions to
  a group
- Describe city buildings
- Talk about professions
- *Use preterite of*
  regular **-er** *and*
  -ir *verbs*
- *Use preterite of*
  verbs with a
  y *spelling change*
- *Use preterite of*
  hacer, ir, ser

ACTIVIDAD **1**

Un día en la ciudad

Escuchar Según el diálogo, señala la foto que
mejor completa cada oración. *(Hint: Point to the
photo that best completes each statement.)*

1. _____ quiere hacer entrevistas con personas.

2. Patricia habla con _____ sobre su familia.

3. _____ es una mujer de negocios.

4. _____ dice que la ciudad es interesante.

256   doscientos cincuenta y seis
Unidad 6

Objective: Transitional practice
Listening comprehension/vocabulary

Las entrevistas

Escuchar ¿Son ciertas o falsas las oraciones? Si las oraciones son falsas, di la oración cierta. *(Hint: Tell whether the sentences are true or false. If they are false, correct them.)*

1. Patricia decidió participar en el concurso porque los ganadores van a viajar.

2. Patricia llegó tarde para entrevistar a la señora Martínez.

3. Patricia habla con la señora Martínez porque quiere ser una mujer de negocios.

4. La señora Martínez trabajó en una panadería.

5. El arquitecto dice que hay más oportunidades en la ciudad.

6. La señora Martínez vive en la ciudad.

7. El señor González piensa que la vida en la ciudad es tranquila.

8. Miguel llamó a su familia en el campo.

¿Quién soy yo?

Leer ¿Qué comentario va con cada dibujo? *(Hint: Match the remarks with the drawings of the persons who could make them.)*

1. Me gusta sacar fotos.

2. Hago planos de construcción.

3. Uso un vehículo rojo y grande.

4. Llevo a la gente por toda la ciudad.

5. Llevo cartas a los edificios.

6. Me gusta hacer entrevistas y escribir.

7. Leo revistas y periódicos de la economía.

Objective: Transitional practice
Listening comprehension/vocabulary

Answers (See script, p. 249D.)
1. cierto
2. falso (Llegó temprano.)
3. falso (Prepara un artículo.)
4. falso (Sus padres trabajan allí.)
5. cierto
6. cierto
7. falso (Piensa que es interesante.)
8. cierto

Objective: Transitional practice
Vocabulary

Answers
1. a
2. e
3. c
4. d
5. g
6. b
7. f

Teaching Middle School Students

Extra Help Describe each photo from **Actividad 1** in random order. Ask students to point to the photo you are describing.

Multiple Intelligences

Visual Ask students to make up a collage of magazine pictures about themselves and then explain it to the class. They can include where they live, what they want to do, etc.

Verbal Following the example of **Actividad 2**, ask students to make up several true or false statements about the class, for example: **La clase de español es muy pequeña.** Ask the rest of the class to decide whether the statement is **cierto** or **falso** and to correct false statements.

Block Schedule

Research Have students research a Latin American city of their choosing. Have them sketch a map of the city and write a description of it. They should also plan a walking tour, using directions and names of buildings, monuments, parks, etc. Have them present their work.

Teaching Resource Options

Teaching Resource Options

Print

Unit 6 Resource Book
Video Activities, p. 25
Videoscript, p. 28
Audioscript, pp. 29–30
Audioscript *Para hispanohablantes,*
pp. 29–30

Audiovisual

Audio Program Cassettes 16A, 16B / CD 16

Audio *Para hispanohablantes*
Cassette 16A / CD 16

Video Program Videotape 6 / Videodisc 3B

4 Objective: Transitional practice
Listening comprehension/vocabulary

Answers (See script, p. 249D.)
a. 4
b. 3
c. 2
d. 1

5 Objective: Open-ended practice
Vocabulary

Answers will vary.

Teaching Suggestions
Reinforcing Vocabulary

Have various students name buildings or streets in your town or city. The other students describe these places using an adjective from the **Vocabulario**.

¿Cómo son?

Escuchar Imagínate que haces una excursión por Quito. El guía describe los edificios. Indica el orden en que describe los edificios. *(Hint: Give the order.)*

a.

b.

c.

d.

Vocabulario

La ciudad

ancho(a) *wide*	**formal** *formal*	**lujoso(a)** *luxurious*
estrecho(a) *narrow*	**informal** *informal*	**ordinario(a)** *ordinary*
		sencillo(a) *simple, plain*

¿Cómo son los edificios y las calles donde tú vives?

En tu comunidad

Hablar/Escribir Con otro(a) estudiante, describe tres de los siguientes lugares de tu comunidad. *(Hint: Describe three of these places.)*

modelo

los supermercados

Estudiante A: *Los supermercados son grandes y modernos...*

Estudiante B: *Hay uno que es muy lujoso...*

a. la avenida principal
b. un hotel/motel
c. la escuela
d. una iglesia/un templo
e. las casas, en general
f. ¿?

Middle School Classroom Community

Paired Activity Ask students to work in pairs to describe their houses, their streets, and their neighborhoods.

Portfolio Ask students to design and describe either a favorite house or an ideal house. They may want to illustrate this project with cutouts or original drawings.

Rubric

Criteria	Scale	
Creativity	1 2 3 4 5	A = 13–15 pts.
Logical organization	1 2 3 4 5	B = 10–12 pts.
Vocabulary use/spelling	1 2 3 4 5	C = 7–9 pts.
		D = 4–6 pts.
		F = < 4 pts.

ACTIVIDAD 6

Una tarjeta postal

Escribir Haz una tarjeta postal de tu ciudad en español. *(Hint: Make a postcard.)*

❶ Usa un papel de 6" x 8". *(Hint: Use 6" x 8" paper.)*

❷ Pon una foto de un edificio o dibuja un edificio en el papel. *(Hint: Use a picture of a building.)*

❸ Al revés, escribe tres o cuatro oraciones sobre el edificio y tu comunidad. *(Hint: On the other side, write some sentences about the building.)*

Querido John:
La Compañía es una iglesia muy antigua. Está en la Plaza Santo Domingo. Tiene pilares de piedra y mucho ornamento.
Tu amiga,
Carlota

John Vivas
4231 Avenue M
Galveston, TX 77550
E.E.U.U.

Saludos de Quito

ACTIVIDAD 7

♻ ¿Cuál es tu opinión?

PARA CONVERSAR
STRATEGY: SPEAKING

Exaggerate and react to exaggerations As you discuss your opinions, you can be truthful or you can exaggerate. If you question the truth of what you hear, you can use these ways of expressing disbelief: **¿de veras?, ¿verdad?, ¡increíble!, ¡no me digas!, ¡no lo creo!** Use them when necessary.

Hablar Pregúntale a otro(a) estudiante cuál es su opinión. *(Hint: Give your opinion.)*

modelo

los edificios más interesantes

Estudiante A: *Los edificios más interesantes* son modernos. ¿Estás de acuerdo?

Estudiante B: No estoy de acuerdo. Para mí *los edificios más interesantes* son antiguos.

Nota

Estar de acuerdo means *to agree.*
To say *I agree,* say **estoy de acuerdo.**

1. el edificio más bonito
2. la profesión más peligrosa
3. el actor más popular
4. el deporte menos aburrido
5. el mejor lugar para vivir
6. la profesión más interesante
7. el edificio más feo
8. la comida más rica
9. la peor estación del año

doscientos cincuenta y nueve
Etapa 1

259

ACTIVIDAD 6
Objective: Open-ended practice
Vocabulary

Answers will vary.

ACTIVIDAD 7
Objective: Open-ended practice
Vocabulary

♻ **Superlatives**

Answers will vary.

Project

After completing **Actividad 6**, have students design a stamp for the postcard illustrated on p. 259. Stamps should commemorate some aspect of Ecuador: history, geography, indigenous groups, music, arts and crafts, flora and fauna, culture, etc. Have students present their creations in class with an explanation of what the stamp contains and why they chose it to highlight. You may wish to have students vote on the one that most captures what Ecuador is like, is the most well-executed, is most like a real stamp, etc.

■ Block Schedule

Variety Have students study, discuss, and even try out this popular Ecuadoran recipe.

Moje de plátanos y frijoles
2 chorizos (pelados, picados y cocinados)
1 cebolla
2 dientes de ajo aplastados
2 chiles poblanos sin semillas
1/2 taza de salsa de tomate
2 tazas de judías con algo de su jugo
4 plátanos maduros

Teaching Middle School Students

Extra Help Encourage students to write postcards to each other in Spanish to practice describing people and places.

Native Speakers Ask students to share postcards from friends or relatives in Spanish-speaking countries.

Multiple Intelligences

Visual Place an assortment of postcards on the chalkboard, and ask a student to choose and describe one without letting others know which. Ask students to guess which postcard it is.

Teaching Resource Options

Print

Más práctica Workbook PE,
  pp. 53–54
Para hispanohablantes Workbook PE,
  pp. 51–52
Block Scheduling Copymasters
Unit 6 Resource Book
  Más práctica Workbook TE, pp. 5–6
  Para hispanohablantes Workbook
  TE, pp. 11–12

Audiovisual

OHT 182 (Quick Start)

Technology

Intrigas y aventuras CD-ROM, Disc 1

Quick Start Review

♻ Preterite of **-ar** verbs

Use OHT 182 or write on the board:
Use the following verbs to tell 5 things
that happened in the past week.

1. estudiar   4. sacar
2. limpiar   5. empezar
3. levantarse

Answers
Answers will vary. Answers could include:
1. Tú estudiaste para el examen de inglés.
2. Mi madre limpió mi habitación.
3. Hoy me levanté a las siete.
4. Ayer mi hermano sacó la basura.
5. Anoche el concierto empezó a las ocho.

Teaching Suggestions
**Teaching the Preterite of
-er and -ir Verbs**

Explain to students that by learning the
preterite of regular **-er** and **-ir** verbs,
they will be able to more fully use the
past tense and therefore be able to
communicate better in Spanish.

Objective: Controlled practice
Preterite forms

Answers
1. Enrique y Anita movieron la mesa.
2. Yo abrí la ventana.
3. Patricia y yo salimos para el supermercado.
4. Tú devolviste las sillas al comedor.
5. Miguel y Enrique barrieron todos los suelos.
6. Anita ordenó la sala.
7. Nosotros limpiamos el baño.
8. Usted escribió la lista de quehaceres.

GRAMÁTICA

Talking About the Past: The Preterite of -er and -ir Verbs

♻ **¿RECUERDAS?** *p. 230* You've already
learned to talk about completed past
actions using regular **-ar** verbs.

▶ Regular **-er** and **-ir** verbs follow a similar pattern.
Notice that in the preterite, **-er** and **-ir** verb
endings **match** each other.

*The **yo** forms
and the **usted, él,
ella** forms take
accents.*

Patricia asks: —¿**Viv**ió en el campo?
***Did you live** in the country?*

limpiar *to clean*

limpié	**limpi**amos
limpiaste	**limpi**asteis
limpió	**limpi**aron

ofrecer *to offer*

ofrecí	**ofrec**imos
ofreciste	**ofrec**isteis
ofreció	**ofrec**ieron

decidir *to decide*

decidí	**decid**imos
decidiste	**decid**isteis
decidió	**decid**ieron

ACTIVIDAD 8 Gramática

¡Qué desorden!

Hablar/Escribir Después de la fiesta, Patricia y sus
amigos limpiaron la casa otra vez. Decide qué
hicieron. *(Hint: Tell what Patricia and her friends did to clean up.)*

1. Enrique y Anita / mover la mesa
2. yo / abrir la ventana
3. Patricia y yo / salir para el supermercado
4. tú / devolver las sillas al comedor
5. Miguel y Enrique / barrer todos los suelos
6. Anita / ordenar la sala
7. nosotros / limpiar el baño
8. usted / escribir la lista de quehaceres

▨ **MÁS PRÁCTICA** *cuaderno* pp. 53–54
▨ **PARA HISPANOHABLANTES** *cuaderno* pp. 51–52

Vocabulario

These verbs you know are
regular in the preterite tense:

-er verbs

aprender	**devolver**
barrer	**entender**
beber	**mover**
comer	**perder**
comprender	**vender**
correr	**volver**

-ir verbs

abrir	**recibir**
compartir	**salir**
escribir	**vivir**

Middle School Classroom Community

Paired Activity Ask students to work in pairs telling
each other 5 activities that each completed yesterday.

Learning Scenario Have students work in groups.
Tell them they are the volunteer cleanup crew after a
school dance. Have them organize themselves and
make sure everything gets done. When they're ready,
ask them to demonstrate their planning and their actual
activities for the class.

¿Qué comiste?

Hablar Pregúntales a cinco estudiantes qué comieron y bebieron ayer. Preséntale a la clase un resumen de las respuestas. *(Hint: Ask five students what they ate and drank yesterday.)*

modelo

Estudiante A: *¿Qué comiste y bebiste para el desayuno?*

Estudiante B: *Comí cereal y bebí jugo.*

Resumen: *Para el desayuno, tres personas comieron cereal y dos comieron yogur. Cuatro personas bebieron jugo y una bebió leche.*

La comida	Estudiante B	Estudiante C
el desayuno	cereal, jugo	
el almuerzo		
la merienda		
la cena		

Una visita

Hablar/Escribir Con otro(a) estudiante, cuenta lo que pasó cuando Martina, la estudiante ecuatoriana, fue a Ecuador con su amiga Nancy a visitar a sus abuelos. *(Hint: Tell what happened in each frame using verbs from the list.)*

Nota

The verb **ver** is regular in the preterite but does not have accents in any of its forms.

comprar   vender   ofrecer **ver** visitar

recibir   **comer** salir **¿?**

doscientos sesenta y uno **261**
Etapa 1

Language Note

Point out that the verb **ofrecer** has an irregular **yo** form in the present: **ofrezco**.

ACTIVIDAD 9 Objective: Transitional practice Preterite forms/vocabulary

Answers will vary.

ACTIVIDAD 10 Objective: Open-ended practice Preterite forms/vocabulary

Answers

Answers may resemble the following.

1. Martina y Nancy salieron para Quito a las ocho menos cuarto.
2. Vieron muchos lugares históricos.
3. Comieron en un restaurante con los abuelos. Martina pidió pescado.
4. Visitaron un mercado. Un vendedor ecuatoriano le ofreció una artesanía a una de las chicas. La chica la compró.

Critical Thinking

Have students form groups of 3 and, on one card, write 3 **-ar**, **-er**, or **-ir** verbs that are regular in the preterite; the names of 3 characters from this book; a theme involving decision-making or opinion; and the word *past*, *present*, or *future*. The cards are collected and redistributed among the groups. Give each group 10 minutes to write a dialog using the information it received. Give the groups time to practice, and then ask them to perform their work.

Teaching Middle School Students

Extra Help Have students add to their vocabulary flash cards the preterite forms of regular **-er** and **ir** verbs. They should use their flash cards often, both alone and with a partner.

Multiple Intelligences

Interpersonal Ask students to work together in pairs asking and answering five questions about what they did yesterday. For example, **¿Qué estudiaste ayer?**, **¿Qué comiste ayer?**, etc.

Block Schedule

Change of Pace Have students write a "children's book" about **una semana excelente** or **una semana horrible**, using the preterite tense. They should also illustrate the book. (For additional activities, see **Block Scheduling Copymasters**.)

Teaching Resource Options

Print

Más práctica Workbook PE, p. 55
Para hispanohablantes Workbook PE, p. 53
Block Scheduling Copymasters
Unit 6 Resource Book
  Más práctica Workbook TE, p. 7
  Para hispanohablantes Workbook TE, p. 13
  Information Gap Activities, p. 17

Audiovisual
OHT 182 (Quick Start)

Technology
Intrigas y aventuras CD-ROM, Disc 1

🔔 Quick Start Review

♻ Preterite of **-er** and **-ir** verbs

Use OHT 182 or write on the board:
Write complete past tense sentences using the following words:

1. yo / aprender
2. tú / escribir
3. Tomás / correr
4. mis amigos / ofrecer
5. nosotros / decidir

Answers *See p. 249D.*

Teaching Suggestions
Teaching Verbs with a y Spelling Change

After teaching the preterite forms with a **y** spelling change, tell students about yourself using **oír, leer,** and **creer.**

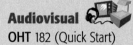 **Objective:** Controlled practice
Preterite forms with spelling changes

Answers
1. leyó   5. leímos
2. oyeron   6. creyeron
3. oí   7. leí
4. creíste   8. oímos

 Objective: Transitional practice
Preterite of **leer**

Answers
Answers will vary but must contain the following.
1. leí   5. leímos
2. leyó   6. leyeron
3. leyeron   7. leyó
4. leyó   8. leyó

262 **Vocabulary/Grammar • UNIDAD 6 Etapa 1**

Talking About the Past: Verbs with a y Spelling Change

To write the third person **preterite** forms of **-er** and **-ir** verbs with stems that end in a vowel, change the **i** to **y**. Notice that all of these preterite forms require an accent, except the **ustedes, ellos(as)** forms.

o**ír** *to hear*	
o**í**	o**ímos**
o**íste**	o**ísteis**
o**yó**	o**yeron**

le**er** *to read*	
le**í**	le**ímos**
le**íste**	le**ísteis**
le**yó**	le**yeron**

cre**er** *to believe*	
cre**í**	cre**ímos**
cre**íste**	cre**ísteis**
cre**yó**	cre**yeron**

Patricia le**yó** algo del concurso.

Patricia read something about the contest.

11 **Gramática**

¿Oyó, leyó o creyó?

Hablar/Escribir Completa las oraciones con la forma correcta del pretérito de **oír, leer** o **creer**.
(Hint: Complete the sentences with the preterite.)

modelo

Arturo __oyó__ el carro.

1. Marta _____ una carta de su amiga.
2. Susana y Marcos _____ los perros.
3. Yo _____ el disco compacto de mi hermano.
4. ¿Tú _____ en Santa Claus alguna vez?
5. Mi amigo y yo _____ muchas novelas.
6. Mis padres _____ en la buena vida.
7. Yo _____ el periódico ayer.
8. Nosotros _____ la música de una guitarra.

■ **MÁS PRÁCTICA** *cuaderno* p. 55
■ **PARA HISPANOHABLANTES** *cuaderno* p. 53

12

¡A leer!

Hablar/Escribir ¿Qué leyeron estas personas?
(Hint: What did they read?)

la revista el poema
el menú el periódico
la novela
la tarea el libro

modelo

mi madre
Mi madre *leyó la revista.*

1. yo   5. mi amigo(a) y yo
2. mi amigo(a)   6. mis amigos
3. mis padres   7. mi hermano(a)
4. mi padre   8. mi maestro(a)

262 doscientos sesenta y dos
Unidad 6

Middle School Classroom Community

Paired Activity Ask students to interview each other about which books they have read or what music they have listened to recently.

Group Activity Ask students to form several small circles. Have one student begin, saying **Leí...** If another in the circle has read the book, ask him or her to add **Yo también leí...** and ask about another book.

Portfolio Ask students to write an annotated list of the books they have read or music they have listened to in the last month or so.

Rubric

Criteria	Scale	
Accuracy of information	1 2 3 4 5	A = 13–15 pts.
Logical organization	1 2 3 4 5	B = 10–12 pts.
Vocabulary use	1 2 3 4 5	C = 7–9 pts.
		D = 4–6 pts.
		F = < 4 pts.

ACTIVIDAD 13

¿Verdad?

Hablar Los estudiantes oyeron muchas cosas en la cafetería ayer. Pregúntale a otro(a) estudiante lo que oyeron estas personas. *(Hint: Ask another student what these people heard yesterday.)*

modelo

tu hermano

Estudiante A: *¿Qué oyó **tu hermano**?*

Estudiante B: *Oyó que Paula va a la biblioteca.*

1. tu amigo(a)
2. tus amigos(as)
3. tú
4. tú y tu amigo(a)
5. tu maestro(a)
6. un(a) estudiante

NOTA CULTURAL

Quito is the second highest capital city in the world after La Paz, Bolivia. It is surrounded by mountains and volcanoes. The old city has colonial buildings with whitewashed walls and red-tiled roofs. The new city has many modern buildings.

ACTIVIDAD 14

¿Qué leyeron o...?

Hablar/Escribir ¿Qué leyeron o oyeron estas personas de niños? Si no sabes, usa tu imaginación. *(Hint: What did these people read or hear when they were children?)*

Heidi

los discos de canciones para niños

los discos de los Chipmunks

¿?

los misterios de los muchachos Hardy

los misterios de Nancy Drew

los casetes de música de Disney

modelo

mi padre

Mi padre *leyó los libros de deportes.*

1. mi madre
2. mis abuelos
3. mi amigo(a)
4. yo
5. mis amigos y yo
6. mis tíos

■ **MÁS COMUNICACIÓN** p. R7

doscientos sesenta y tres
Etapa 1 **263**

Teaching Middle School Students

Challenge Ask students to work together in small groups to make a **Las grandes ciudades del mundo** poster. They should do research on the world's big cities to find the biggest, smallest, highest, lowest, most beautiful, etc., and illustrate their posters with drawings or photos.

Multiple Intelligences

Kinesthetic Ask the class to chant the conjugations in the **Gramática** box, clapping each time they say a **y**-change form.

Logical/Mathematical Have students write the name of a favorite piece of childhood literature on a card. Then organize the cards into a chart titled **Leímos,** with the categories: **libro, revista, poema, novela.**

 ACTIVIDAD 13 **Objective:** Transitional practice
Preterite of **oír**

Answers

Answers will vary but must contain the following.

1. oyó
2. oyeron
3. oí (oíste)
4. oímos (oyeron)
5. oyó
6. oyó

ACTIVIDAD 14 **Objective:** Open-ended practice
Preterite in verbs with spelling changes

Answers will vary.

Interdisciplinary Connection

Science Ecuador and the **Islas Galápagos** are peppered with volcanoes and have experienced destructive seismic events: **Otavalo** (1868), **Ambato** (1949), **Volcán La Cumbre** (1988), etc. Have student pairs gather information on these events: where and why they occur, warning signs, protection from them, etc. *National Geographic* magazine is an invaluable source.

■ Block Schedule

Variety Ask students to help you temporarily expand your classroom library by sharing books and CDs of their own. Set up a library role-play where some students are librarians and others are library patrons looking for something. This can be a recurring activity in a corner of the room.

Teaching Resource Options

Print

Más práctica Workbook PE, p. 56
Para hispanohablantes Workbook PE, p. 54
Block Scheduling Copymasters
Unit 6 Resource Book
  Más práctica Workbook TE, p. 8
  Para hispanohablantes Workbook TE, p. 14

Audiovisual

OHT 183 (Quick Start)

Technology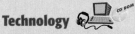

Intrigas y aventuras CD-ROM, Disc 1

Quick Start Review

 Oír, leer, creer

Use OHT 183 or write on the board:
Answer the following questions:

1. ¿Oíste algo interesante ayer?
2. ¿Qué revista leíste recientemente? ¿Le gustó?
3. De niño(a), ¿creíste en Santa Claus? ¿Hasta qué año?

Answers will vary.

Teaching Suggestions
Teaching Irregular Verbs in the Preterite: hacer, ir, ser

Point out that **hacer** in a question is usually replaced by another verb in the answer: **¿Qué hiciste ayer? / Fui al cine.** Have students ask and answer original questions using these 3 verbs.

ACTIVIDAD 15 Objective: Controlled practice
Preterite of **hacer**

Answers
1. hizo
2. hicieron
3. hice
4. hicimos
5. hizo
6. hicimos
7. hiciste
8. hicieron

 GRAMÁTICA

Using Irregular Verbs in the Preterite: hacer, ir, ser

♻ **¿RECUERDAS?** *p. 143* Remember how to say *I went* and *you went* in Spanish?

fui	fuiste

▶ The verb **ir** is irregular in the **preterite**. Its preterite forms are exactly the **same** as the preterite forms of **ser. Hacer** also has irregular **preterite** forms. These verbs don't have any accents in the preterite.

ir/ser *to go/to be*

fui	fuimos
fuiste	fuisteis
fue	fueron

hacer *to make, to do*

hice	hicimos
hiciste	hicisteis
hizo	hicieron

Notice that the **c** becomes **z** before **o.**

The businesswoman says:

—**Hice** todo lo necesario. **Fui** a la universidad…
*I **did** everything necessary. I **went** to the university…*

ACTIVIDAD 15 Gramática

El sábado en casa

Hablar/Escribir Todos trabajaron en casa el sábado pasado. Completa las oraciones con el pretérito del verbo **hacer.**
(Hint: Tell what people did at home last Saturday.)

1. Mamá _____ un vestido para mi hermana.
2. Papá y abuelito _____ los sándwiches para el almuerzo.
3. Yo _____ toda la tarea para el lunes.
4. Abuelita y yo _____ un pastel.
5. Mi hermana _____ una entrevista para su clase de historia.
6. Mis amigos y yo _____ ejercicio con un video.
7. Tú ____ las camas.
8. Mamá y abuelita _____ la cena.

NOTA CULTURAL

One of Quito's most historic sights is the **Plaza de la Independencia,** also called the **Plaza Grande.** In this square you will find the sculpture of Liberty, a bronze and marble statue portraying Ecuador's struggle for independence from Spain.

---

264 doscientos sesenta y cuatro
Unidad 6

Middle School Classroom Community

Storytelling Ask students to form a circle. The first student will begin a story with a sentence in the past tense, which will be continued by the next student, and so on.

Group Activity Have students decorate brown paper lunch bags to make puppets. Students will then have the puppets make statements about what they did yesterday.

Portfolio Ask students to choose a memorable day in the past and write what they did on that day.

Rubric

Criteria	Scale
Creativity	1 2 3 4 5
Logical organization	1 2 3 4 5
Vocabulary use/spelling	1 2 3 4 5

A = 13–15 pts.
B = 10–12 pts.
C = 7–9 pts.
D = 4–6 pts.
F = < 4 pts.

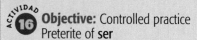

ACTIVIDAD 16 Gramática

Recuerdos del pasado

Leer/Escribir Varias personas hablan de sus viejas profesiones. Di qué ocupación tuvo cada persona. *(Hint: Tell each person's occupation.)*

modelo

Enseñó muchas clases de español. (escritor / maestro)

Fue maestro.

1. El señor Cano sacó muchas fotos de personas importantes. (receptionista / fotógrafo)
2. Ellos hicieron muchas entrevistas. (periodista / bombero)
3. Alfredo llevó muchísimas cartas. (cartero / escritor)
4. Hiciste planos de casas modernas. (operador / arquitecto)
5. Contestamos el teléfono en la oficina. (operador / editor)
6. Llevaron a muchas personas al aeropuerto. (bombero / taxista)
7. Escribí más de mil cartas para mi jefa. (secretario / gerente)
8. La señora Flores leyó los manuscritos de muchos escritores. (jefa / editora)

■ **MÁS PRÁCTICA** *cuaderno* p. 56

■ **PARA HISPANOHABLANTES** *cuaderno* p. 54

Vocabulario

Las profesiones

la arquitectura *architecture*	**el (la) gerente** *manager*
la compañía *company*	**el (la) jefe(a)** *boss*
el (la) contador(a) *accountant*	**el (la) operador(a)** *operator*
el (la) editor(a) *editor*	**el (la) recepcionista** *receptionist*
el (la) escritor(a) *writer*	**el (la) secretario(a)** *secretary*

¿Cuándo visitas a estas personas?

Conexiones

La geografía Ecuador has several volcanoes, including the overactive **Tungurahua**, located south of Quito. **Tungurahua** has erupted at least seventeen times, most recently in 1944. The tallest volcano is **Chimborazo** (shown below) at 6310 m (20,697 ft) in altitude. Closer to Quito are the Iliniza sisters, **Iliniza Norte** at 5116 m (16,882 ft) and **Iliniza Sur** at 5263 m (17,367 ft), volcanic peaks that were originally one and were broken apart in a magma explosion.

PARA HACER:
The Spanish word for "volcano" is *volcán*. Use the altitudes given to write descriptive comparisons of these volcanoes.

ACTIVIDAD 16 Objective: Controlled practice
Preterite of **ser**

Answers
1. Fue fotógrafo.
2. Fueron periodistas.
3. Fue cartero.
4. Fuiste arquitecto(a).
5. Fuimos operadores.
6. Fueron taxistas.
7. Fui secretario(a).
8. Fue editora.

Para hacer

Answers

Answers may vary.
El volcán más alto es Chimborazo, de 6310 metros. El volcán Iliniza Sur, de 5263 metros, es más alto que Iliniza Norte, de 5116 metros.

Teaching Suggestions
Teaching Vocabulary

Have each student select a profession from this **Vocabulario** or from pp. 252–253 and write down 3 nouns or verbs associated with it. Call on students to read their lists. Have the class try to guess the profession.

Quick Wrap-up

Write action verbs on index cards. Distribute the cards to various individuals who will perform the actions indicated. As each one does so, ask the class, **¿Qué hizo?** The class responds. To practice other forms of **hacer**, distribute one card to 2 students and ask, **¿Qué hicieron?** Or, directly ask the doer of an action, **¿Qué hiciste?**

Block Schedule

Project Tell students to contact 2–3 friends and family members of different professions. For each person, they should report on the profession, where the person studied, previous employment, current job, and how much the person enjoys working in that profession. (For additional activities, see **Block Scheduling Copymasters**.)

Teaching Middle School Students

Extra Help Ask students to tell which vocabulary words are cognates.

Native Speakers Ask students to share stories about volcanoes in their home countries.

Multiple Intelligences

Kinesthetic Have students work in pairs. They choose one exercise from **Actividad 16** and prepare a mime of it. Call on random pairs to perform their mimes. As other students recognize the profession, they write it on a piece of paper and hold it up.

Teaching Resource Options

Print

Block Scheduling Copymasters
Unit 6 Resource Book
  Information Gap Activities, pp. 18–19
  Audioscript, p. 30
  Audioscript *Para hispanohablantes*,
  p. 30

Audiovisual

Audio Program Cassettes 16A, 16B /
CD 16
Audio *Para hispanohablantes*
Cassette 16A / CD 16

Technology

Intrigas y aventuras CD-ROM, Disc 1

Objective: Transitional practice
Preterite of **ir**

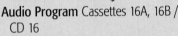 Places

Answers

1. ¿Adónde fue tu hermano? Fue al correo.
2. ¿Adónde fueron ustedes? Fuimos a la zapatería.
3. ¿Adónde fueron tus abuelos? Fueron a la panadería.
4. ¿Adónde fueron tus amigos y tú? Fuimos a la joyería.
5. ¿Adónde fuiste tú? Fui a la papelería.
6. ¿Adónde fue tu hermana? Fue a la tienda de música y videos.

Objective: Transitional practice
Listening comprehension/preterite
forms

Answers (See script, p. 249D.)

1. Patricia
2. Patricia
3. Andrea
4. Marta
5. Andrea
6. Marta

Language Note

The words **chompa** and **saco** may be used in slightly different ways than the English words *jacket* and *sweater*. A **chompa** is any jacket-like outerwear that opens in the front. Woven woolen outerwear with buttons or a zipper up the front would be called a **chompa**. All leather and cloth jackets would also be called **chompas**. Sweaters that pull on over the head are called **sacos**.

♻ Fuimos a...

Hablar Pregúntale a otro(a) estudiante adónde fueron estas personas ayer. *(Hint: Take turns with your partner asking and telling where these people went yesterday.)*

modelo

tu mamá

Estudiante A: *¿Adónde fue tu mamá?*

Estudiante B: *Fue al banco.*

1. tu hermano

2. ustedes

3. tus abuelos

4. tus amigos y tú

5. tú

6. tu hermana

Un sábado especial

Escuchar Lee lo que hicieron Patricia, Marta y Andrea. Luego escucha la conversación y explica quién hizo cada actividad. *(Hint: Listen to the conversation and explain who did each activity.)*

1. Vio una película de acción.
2. Corrió en el parque.
3. Escribió una carta.
4. Comió en el restaurante Casa Linda.
5. Fue a un partido de fútbol.
6. Fue de compras.

También se dice

Ecuador has its own regionalisms for many of the items you already know in Spanish.

- **chompa:** chaqueta
- **departamento:** apartamento
- **esfero:** pluma, bolígrafo
- **saco:** suéter

Middle School Classroom Community

Cooperative Learning Ask students to work in threes to write and present a skit with a newspaper interviewer, a customer, and a professional (such as **panadero** or **zapatero**) about what happened yesterday when the customer entered the shop. They can write their own roles and then critique each other's work as they integrate the roles into a logically organized skit.

Portfolio Ask students to list and describe the places they went during a recent weekend or school vacation.

Rubric

Criteria	Scale	
Creativity	1 2 3 4 5	A = 13–15 pts.
Logical organization	1 2 3 4 5	B = 10–12 pts. C = 7–9 pts.
Vocabulary use/spelling	1 2 3 4 5	D = 4–6 pts. F = < 4 pts.

ACTIVIDAD 19

¿Adónde fueron?

Hablar/Escribir Todos salieron ayer. Di adónde fue cada persona y cómo fue el día. *(Hint: Tell where each person went, and give their opinion of the day.)*

modelo

Patricia: interesante

Patricia fue a la oficina del arquitecto. Fue **interesante**.

1. Miguel: divertido

2. tú: aburrido

3. Miguel y yo: ¿?

4. ustedes: ¿?

5. yo: ¿?

6. mi familia: ¿?

ACTIVIDAD 20

¿Adónde fue...?

Hablar Pregúntale a otro(a) estudiante adónde fueron las personas y qué hicieron el fin de semana pasado. *(Hint: Ask where the people went and what they did.)*

modelo

tus hermanos

Estudiante A: *¿Adónde fueron y qué hicieron* **tus hermanos** *el fin de semana pasado?*

Estudiante B: *Fueron al campo. Vieron un partido de fútbol.*

1. tu mejor amigo(a)

2. tus amigos

3. tú

4. tú y tu amigo(a)

5. tus padres

6. tu hermano(a)

APOYO PARA ESTUDIAR

Preterite of *ir* and *ser*

Since these verbs are the same in the preterite, how can you tell which is meant? Look at the context. If you see words that say where, *ir* is intended; if you see a description, **ser** is intended.

—¿Adónde **fuiste** anoche?

—**Fui** al cine. Ví una película de Antonio Banderas.

—¿**Fue** interesante?

—Sí, y también **fue** muy divertida.

doscientos sesenta y siete
Etapa 1
267

Teaching Middle School Students

Extra Help Duplicate a mixed-up list of verb forms in the present and in the preterite. Help students annotate all of the preterite forms with their infinitive form and person.

Multiple Intelligences

Logical/Mathematical Ask students to create mazes for others, the final destination being a shop. In order to get through the maze, students must answer simple questions in the past.

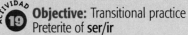
ACTIVIDAD 19
Objective: Transitional practice
Preterite of **ser/ir**

Answers
1. Miguel fue al campo de fútbol. Fue divertido.
2. Tú fuiste al centro comercial. Fue aburrido.
3. Miguel y yo fuimos al cine. Fue…
4. Ustedes fueron a la fiesta. Fue…
5. Yo fui al gimnasio. Fue…
6. Mi familia fue al restaurante. Fue…

ACTIVIDAD 20
Objective: Open-ended practice
Preterite forms

Answers will vary.

Critical Thinking

After reviewing the **Apoyo para estudiar**, ask students to write 5 sentences using **ir** in the preterite and 5 sentences using **ser** in the preterite. Each sentence should be on a separate slip of paper. Collect the slips of paper and scramble them. Then read the sentences aloud without the verb. Have the whole class indicate when **ir** or when **ser** is used.

Block Schedule

Variety Have pairs of students interview each other for a "Who's Who in Our School" column in the Spanish Club newsletter. Students must ask for biographical information, past events, a special activity, a hobby, or an interest. (For additional activities, see **Block Scheduling Copymasters**.)

Teaching Resource Options

Print

Block Scheduling Copymasters
Unit 6 Resource Book
Information Gap Activities, pp. 18–19
Audioscript, p. 30
Audioscript *Para hispanohablantes*, p. 30

Audiovisual

Audio Program Cassettes 16A, 16B / CD 16
Audio *Para hispanohablantes*
Cassette 16A / CD 16

Technology

Intrigas y aventuras CD-ROM, Disc 1

---

21 Objective: Open-ended practice
Preterite forms

Answers will vary.

22 Objective: Transitional practice
Vamos a + infinitive/vocabulary

Answers
1. ¡Vamos a hacer ejercicio!
   (¡Vamos a jugar al baloncesto!)
2. ¡Vamos a nadar!
3. ¡Vamos a ir de compras!
4. ¡Vamos a jugar al fútbol!

Game

Have each student bring in a picture of a place. On the back, he or she writes a fictional sentence about what happened to whom there. (**patio → Mi familia celebró el cumpleaños de mi abuela en el patio el verano pasado.**) Collect the pictures, select one, and in row order have students ask the student who brought the picture questions about the image. The goal is to learn the details described on the back. A positive response allows him or her to continue questioning. A negative response means it's the next questioner's turn. The row that identifies complete details of the most pictures wins the game.

21

Tu calendario

Hablar/Escribir Haz un calendario imaginario o real de lo que hiciste la semana pasada. Habla con otro(a) estudiante sobre lo que hicieron. *(Hint: Make a calendar of your activities last week.)*

modelo

Estudiante A: ¿Qué hiciste el lunes?
Estudiante B: *Aprendí un poema.*

> lunes - aprendí un poema
> martes -
> miércoles -
> jueves -
> viernes -
> sábado -
> domingo -

> ### NOTA CULTURAL
>
> The currency of Ecuador is the **sucre**. Where does its name come from? Check p. 248.

22

Vamos a...

Hablar/Escribir Ana siempre quiere hacer algo con sus amigos. ¿Cómo los invita? *(Hint: What does Ana say when she invites her friends to do something with her?)*

modelo

¡Vamos a comer!

Nota

When you want to say *Let's…!* use **Vamos a** + an infinitive.

1.

2.

3.

4.

Middle School Classroom Community

TPR Have students raise their hands each time they hear the hard **d** sound as you read the tongue twister.

Paired Activity Ask students to work in pairs to make suggestions about what to do and where to go after class using **Vamos a…** For example, **Vamos a comer pizza.**

Storytelling Ask students to sit in a circle to tell a continuing story. The first student will suggest a place to go, such as **Vamos a la playa.** The next student must suggest an activity appropriate to the place, such as **Vamos a nadar.** Each student in the circle adds another element to the story.

ACTIVIDAD
23

El año pasado

Hablar/Escribir ¿Qué hicieron tú, tu familia y tus amigos el año pasado? Describe una actividad que hiciste con tu familia o con tus amigos.
(Hint: Describe a fun activity you did with your family or friends last year.)

modelo

El año pasado fui a la cuidad con mi familia. Mi mamá y yo visitamos un museo de arte. Mi padre y mi hermana fueron a un partido de béisbol. Nosotros vimos muchos lugares interesantes. Finalmente cenamos en un restaurante. Comimos una cena deliciosa.

■ **MÁS COMUNICACIÓN** p. R7

Conexiones

Las ciencias If you visit the Andean region of Ecuador, you might become ill from **soroche**, an illness suffered by people who are not used to living at high altitudes. Some of the symptoms are dizziness, fatigue, headache, and nausea. The body usually adapts to the high altitude after a day or two.

PARA HACER:
Pretend you are hiking in the Andes. Use the words here to write three sentences describing what it feels like to suffer from *soroche*.
- fatiga
- náusea
- vértigo
- dolor de cabeza

Pronunciación

Trabalenguas

Pronunciación de la *d* When **d** begins a word or follows the letters **n** or **l**, it is pronounced with a hard sound, as it is in English. When **d** is between two vowels or at the end of a word, it is pronounced like the *th* in the English word *they*. To practice the **d**, try the following tongue twister.

Dos alcaldes, David Machado y Daniela Amador, danzan el fandango el sábado.

Alcalde Machado   Alcalde Amador

ACTIVIDAD
23 **Objective:** Open-ended practice
Preterite forms/vocabulary

Answers will vary.

🔔 Quick Wrap-up

Have students complete the following:
Quiero ser ____ (profesión) porque me gusta ____ (infinitivo).

Para hacer

Answers

Answers may vary.
1. Una persona tiene vértigo.
2. Siente náuseas.
3. Tiene un dolor de cabeza.

Dictation

After students have read the **trabalenguas** in the **Pronunciación,** have them close their books. Dictate the **trabalenguas** in two segments while students write it.

Teaching Middle School Students

Native Speaker Ask students to tell about the location and geography of their home cities or villages.

Multiple Intelligences

Musical/Rhythmic Ask students to research Andean folk music and report back to the class.

Naturalist Ask students to make a map of the Andes. What other countries do these mountains go through? What other cities might be so high as to provoke altitude sickness?

■ Block Schedule

Variety Have students write fanciful diaries about one week's activities for an Ecuadoran teenager. This should involve some research as well as a peer-editing process so that the final products do reflect both Ecuadoran life and sound Spanish grammar and vocabulary.

Teaching Resource Options

Print

Activity and Assessment Book
  Audioscript, pp. 54–58

Audiovisual

Audio Program Cassette 16A / CD 16
Audio *Para hispanohablantes*
  Cassette 16A / CD 16
OHT 183 (Quick Start)
Canciones Cassette / CD

🔔 Quick Start Review

♻️ **Los edificios**

Use OHT 183 or write on the board:
Use these adjectives to write sentences
about famous buildings you have
visited or read about.

1. antiguo(a)   4. lujoso(a)
2. enorme   5. moderno(a)
3. formal   6. tradicional

Answers will vary.

Teaching Suggestions

- **Prereading** Tell students they are
  about to read an Ecuadoran fable in
  which animals are the main characters.
- **Strategy: Follow the sequence**
  Have students scan quickly for
  sequencing words and phrases.
  Start a list of these words.
- **Reading** Use the sequencing words
  as mileposts to keep track of the
  action in the story.
- **Post-reading** After reading the
  story, ask students to retell the story
  from memory, using the list of
  sequencing words as an aid.

En voces
LECTURA

PARA LEER
STRATEGY: READING
Follow the sequence It is important to
recognize the order of events in a
story. The selection you are about to
read has three repetitive segments.
Scan the reading to try to identify
what they are. Look for sequencing
words in Spanish such as **un día,
una vez más**, and **por última vez**
to help you follow the story.

> Sequencing Words
> un día

Un cuento ecuatoriano
El tigre y el conejo

Un día Tío Tigre pasó por el bosque en camino a su
casa. Tenía[1] una canasta[2] de comida muy rica. El amigo
conejo lo vio y pensó: «¡Yo tengo hambre. Quiero esa
comida!» y saltó[3] por el bosque y se adelantó[4] a Tío
Tigre. Se echó como muerto[5]. Cuando llegó Tío Tigre,
vio al conejo pero siguió el camino[6].

---

[1] He had   [4] got ahead
[2] basket   [5] *Se echó...muerto.* He pretended to be dead.
[3] hopped   [6] *siguió...camino* he continued on his way

270   doscientos setenta
              Unidad 6

Middle School Classroom Community

TPR Read the story to the class. Ask them to touch
their heads each time they hear a sequencing word
or phrase.

Group Activity Ask students to work in threes,
choosing one member to narrate a shortened version
of the story, and the other two to act it out.

El amigo conejo pensó y dijo: «Pues, voy a tratar[7] una vez más» y saltó y se adelantó otra vez a Tío Tigre. Otra vez se echó como muerto. Y una veza más pasó Tío Tigre, vio al conejo y siguió su camino.

El amigo conejo pensó: «Bueno, voy a tratar por última vez» y saltó camino adelante y otra vez se echó como muerto. Esta vez se paró[8] Tío Tigre. Decidió que tres conejos muertos en el camino era demasiado bueno para perder. Dejó la canasta y regresó por los otros dos conejos.

Y así el amigo conejo agarró[9] la canasta y le robó al tigre su comida.

---

[7] to try
[8] stopped
[9] grabbed

¿Comprendiste?

1. ¿Por dónde pasó el tigre?
2. ¿Qué tenía en la canasta?
3. ¿Qué pensó el conejo cuando vio la canasta?
4. ¿Qué hizo el conejo?
5. ¿Cómo terminó todo?

¿Qué piensas?

1. ¿Cuál de los dos animales es más fuerte? ¿Cuál es más inteligente? ¿Por qué?
2. En tu opinión, ¿qué nos dice este cuento?

doscientos setenta y uno
Etapa 1
271

Critical Thinking

Have students brainstorm animal stories and fables they read as children. Who were the main characters? Who outsmarted whom?

Game

Write a key action phrase from the story on a card or a piece of paper. Scramble the cards and place them randomly on the chalkboard tray. Have students reorder them as quickly as possible. Once the cards are in chronological order, have volunteers offer one additional piece of information related to each action.

¿Comprendiste?

Answers
1. Pasó por el bosque.
2. Tenía comida.
3. Pensó: "Tengo hambre".
4. Se adelantó al tigre y se echó como muerto.
5. La última vez que el conejo se echó como muerto, el tigre dejó la canasta y volvió por los "otros conejos muertos".

Teaching Middle School Students

Challenge Have students write their own fable. Remind them that the action must carry a message of some sort.

Native Speakers Ask native speakers to share fables or other animal stories they have heard.

Multiple Intelligences

Interpersonal Ask students to share with each other ideas for a different ending to the story.

■ Block Schedule

Change of Pace Have students begin work on a Project, Bulletin Board/Poster, or Hands-On Craft from the **Ampliación** on TE pp. 249A–249B.

Teaching Resource Options

Print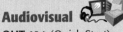

Unit 6 Resource Book
Para hispanohablantes Workbook
TE, pp. 15–16
Information Gap Activities, p. 20
Family Involvement, pp. 21–22
Multiple Choice Test Questions,
pp. 170–178

Audiovisual

OHT 184 (Quick Start)
Audio Program Testing Cassette T2 /
CD T2

Technology

Electronic Teacher Tools/Test
Generator
Intrigas y aventuras CD-ROM, Disc 1

Quick Start Review

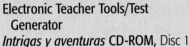 Preterite

Use OHT 184 or write on the board:
Complete the following sentences with
a logical verb in the preterite and any
other necessary words.

1. Normalmente, voy a pie a la
   escuela, pero ayer _____ .
2. Mis amigos siempre llegan a
   tiempo a clase, pero esta
   mañana, _____ .
3. Mis padres casi siempre salen
   de la oficina a las cinco, pero
   anoche _____ .
4. Frecuentemente, te gusta ir a
   la biblioteca después de clases,
   pero ayer tú _____ .
5. En general, mi madre me hace
   un sándwich, pero hoy _____ .

Answers *See p. 249D.*

Teaching Suggestions
What Have Students Learned?

Have students look at the "Now you
can…" notes and give examples of
each category. Have them spend extra
time reviewing categories they feel they
are weak in by consulting the "To
review" notes.

ETAPA 1

Now you can...

• tell what happened.

To review

• preterite of regular
-er and **-ir** verbs,
see p. 260.

Now you can...

• tell what happened.

To review

• preterite of verbs
with a **y** spelling
change, see p. 262.

En uso

REPASO Y
MÁS COMUNICACIÓN

OBJECTIVES

• Tell what happened
• Make suggestions to
  a group
• Describe city buildings
• Talk about professions

ACTIVIDAD 1 ¡Muy ocupados!

Todos participaron en un festival internacional el domingo
pasado. ¿Qué hicieron? *(Hint: Tell what everyone did at the international
festival last Sunday.)*

modelo

usted: barrer el suelo después del festival
Usted barrió el suelo después del festival.

1. tú: recibir un regalo
2. mis amigos y yo: aprender algunos bailes
   mexicanos
3. mi madre: vender unas tapas
4. los periodistas: escribir muchos artículos sobre el festival
5. yo: compartir un postre enorme con mis hermanos
6. nosotros: beber mucha limonada
7. los niños: correr por todas partes
8. el fotógrafo: decidir sacar fotos de todas las actividades
9. tú: comer muchos tacos
10. yo: ver artesanías muy interesantes

ACTIVIDAD 2 ¿Lo creíste tú?

Imagínate que Patricia ganó el concurso, pero nadie lo creyó.
¿Dónde oyeron o leyeron el anuncio? *(Hint: Nobody believed that Patricia
won the contest. Tell where they heard or read about the winner.)*

modelo

Miguel: por teléfono	*el arquitecto: en el periódico*
Miguel lo oyó **por teléfono,** pero no lo creyó.	**El arquitecto** lo leyó **en el periódico,** pero no lo creyó.

1. Patricia: en una carta
2. tú: en la televisión
3. la mujer de negocios: en la radio
4. los tíos de Miguel: por teléfono
5. yo: en la revista
6. nosotros: en el periódico

---

272 doscientos setenta y dos
Unidad 6

Middle School Classroom Community

TPR Write action verbs on cards or slips of paper.
Have each student choose a card. During regular
lesson activities, students raise their cards whenever
their words are used.

Game Split the class into 2 teams. Two students from
Team A come to the front of the class and consult with
you to choose a profession. Then the rest of Team A
asks 5 yes/no and either/or questions. If they guess the
profession, they get a point. After 5 questions, play
goes to Team B.

Now you can...

• describe city buildings.

• tell what happened.

• talk about professions.

To review

• preterite of **hacer, ir, ser,** see p. 264.

 3 ¿Qué fuiste tú?

Todos hablan de sus antiguas profesiones. ¿Qué dicen?
(Hint: Talk about people's former jobs.)

modelo

ella / gerente de un restaurante lujoso: ¿trabajar en un edificio formal o informal?
Ella fue gerente de un restaurante lujoso. Trabajó en un edificio formal.

1. ellos / hombres de negocios: ¿hacer contratos o ejercicio?
2. nosotros / bomberos: ¿ir a muchos conciertos o edificios?
3. tú / recepcionista de una compañía grande: ¿trabajar en un edificio pequeño o enorme?
4. tú y yo / periodistas: ¿hacer muchas tareas o entrevistas?
5. él / taxista: ¿ir a muchos o pocos lugares diferentes?
6. yo / escritor(a): ¿escribir cartas o novelas?
7. tú / cartero(a): ¿ir a muchos parques o muchas casas?
8. usted / arquitecto(a): ¿hacer planos o preguntas?

4 ¡Vamos a divertirnos!

Tu amigo(a) te invita a participar en varias actividades hoy. ¿Qué dice? *(Hint: Suggest activities for you and your friend to do today.)*

modelo

nadar

*¡Vamos a **nadar**!*

1. levantar pesas
2. ir al cine
3. escuchar música
4. comer en un restaurante lujoso
5. jugar al tenis
6. ver la televisión
7. escribirle una carta al editor del periódico
8. pasear en el parque

Now you can...

• make suggestions to a group.

To review

• **vamos a** + infinitive, see p. 268.

1 Answers
1. Tú recibiste un regalo.
2. Mis amigos y yo aprendimos algunos bailes mexicanos.
3. Mi madre vendió unas tapas.
4. Los periodistas escribieron muchos artículos sobre el festival.
5. Yo compartí un postre enorme con mis hermanos.
6. Nosotros bebimos mucha limonada.
7. Los niños corrieron por todas partes.
8. El fotógrafo decidió sacar fotos de todas las actividades.
9. Tú comiste muchos tacos.
10. Yo vi artesanías muy interesantes.

2 Answers
1. Patricia lo leyó en una carta, pero no lo creyó.
2. Tú lo oíste en la televisión, pero no lo creíste.
3. La mujer de negocios lo oyó en la radio, pero no lo creyó.
4. Los tíos de Miguel lo oyeron por teléfono, pero no lo creyeron.
5. Yo lo leí en la revista, pero no lo creí.
6. Nosotros lo leímos en el periódico, pero no lo creímos.

3 Answers
1. Ellos fueron hombres de negocios. Hicieron contratos.
2. Nosotros fuimos bomberos. Fuimos a muchos edificios.
3. Tú fuiste recepcionista de una compañía grande. Trabajaste en un edificio enorme.
4. Tú y yo fuimos periodistas. Hicimos muchas entrevistas.
5. Él fue taxista. Fue a muchos lugares diferentes.
6. Yo fui escritor(a). Escribí novelas.
7. Tú fuiste cartero(a). Fuiste a muchas casas.
8. Usted fue arquitecto(a). Hizo planos.

4 Answers
1. ¡Vamos a levantar pesas!
2. ¡Vamos a ir al cine!
3. ¡Vamos a escuchar música!
4. ¡Vamos a comer en un restaurante lujoso!
5. ¡Vamos a jugar al tenis!
6. ¡Vamos a ver la televisión!
7. ¡Vamos a escribirle una carta al editor del periódico!
8. ¡Vamos a pasear en el parque!

Teaching Middle School Students

Extra Help Prepare ahead: 10–12 sets of 10 subject noun/pronoun cards and 10 verb infinitive cards. Give a set of cards to pairs or small groups of students. Have each student pick one subject card and one verb card from each set and make up a sentence using the words.

Challenge Have students extend **Actividad 1** with more items.

Multiple Intelligences

Interpersonal Have students work with a partner and expand **Actividad 4**. One student proposes the activity to the other who accepts or declines, stating a reason in either case.

Block Schedule

FunBreak Have students work in small groups to create sets of cards of the various professions (4 for each of 13 professions). Then have them play **Peces** (Go Fish!) with their cards.

Teaching Resource Options

Print

Unit 6 Resource Book
Cooperative Quizzes, pp. 33–34
Etapa Exam, Forms A and B,
   pp. 35–44
Para hispanohablantes Etapa Exam,
   pp. 45–49
Portfolio Assessment, pp. 50–51
Multiple Choice Test Questions,
   pp. 170–178

Audiovisual

OHT 184 (Quick Start)
Audio Program Testing Cassette T2 /
CD T2

Technology

**Electronic Teacher Tools/Test
Generator**

www.mcdougallittell.com

Rubric: Speaking

Criteria	Scale	
Sentence structure	1 2 3 4 5	A = 17–20 pts.
Vocabulary use	1 2 3 4 5	B = 13–16 pts.
Originality	1 2 3 4 5	C = 9–12 pts.
Ease, fluency	1 2 3 4 5	D = 5–8 pts.
		F = < 5 pts.

 6 Answers will vary.

Variation: Have students take turns going around the room instead of having the person who guesses correctly invent a profession.

 7 En tu propia voz

Rubric: Writing

Criteria	Scale	
Vocabulary use	1 2 3 4 5	A = 13–15 pts.
Accuracy	1 2 3 4 5	B = 10–12 pts.
Creativity, appearance	1 2 3 4 5	C = 7–9 pts.
		D = 4–6 pts.
		F = < 4 pts.

Teaching Note: En tu propia voz

Suggest that students brainstorm a list of appropriate descriptive words (basic details, points of interest, descriptive adjectives) in order to implement the writing strategy "Use different kinds of descriptive words" in their descriptions.

ACTIVIDAD 5 ¿Qué hiciste ayer?

PARA CONVERSAR

STRATEGY: SPEAKING

Relate details When retelling a past event, tell more than what you did (**¿qué hiciste?**). People like to know details, such as where (**¿dónde?**), with whom (**¿con quién?**), and how it was (**¿cómo fue?**). If your partner doesn't tell you all of the details, ask for them by using these questions.

Quieres saber lo que hizo otro(a) estudiante ayer. Usando los verbos de la lista, hazle preguntas. *(Hint: Use the verbs from the list to ask what another student did yesterday.)*

modelo

Estudiante A: *¿Hiciste ejercicio ayer?*

Estudiante B: *Sí, hice ejercicio en el parque. Caminé con mi perro. ¿Y tú?*

Estudiante A: *Yo jugué al tenis.*

Estudiante B: *¿Qué comiste anoche?*

Estudiante A: *Comí…*

ACTIVIDAD 6 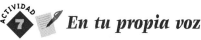 Profesiones interesantes

Eres una persona profesional que ya no trabaja. Ahora estás visitando la clase de español. Los estudiantes te hacen preguntas para identificar tu profesión. La persona que identifica la profesión correcta es el (la) nuevo(a) profesional. *(Hint: Ask questions to determine what people did for a living.)*

modelo

Estudiante A: *¿Sacó usted fotos en su trabajo?*

Profesional: *No, no saqué fotos.*

Estudiante B: *¿Trabajó usted en una oficina?*

Profesional: *Sí. Trabajé en una oficina muy lujosa.*

Estudiante B: *¿Fue usted jefe(a)?*

Profesional: *Sí. Fui jefe(a) de una compañía enorme.*

ACTIVIDAD 7 *En tu propia voz*

Escritura ¿Cómo es la ciudad ideal para ti? Dibújala y descríbela con un mínimo de seis oraciones. *(Hint: Draw and describe the ideal city.)*

modelo

En la ciudad ideal…

En la comunidad

Maynor, a native speaker of Spanish, is a high school student in California. He sometimes interprets for Spanish-speaking people who don't speak English when he's at his part-time job with a construction company. He also uses Spanish at his volunteer job at a Boy Scout camp. This helps boys who are more comfortable speaking in their native language. Additionally, he helps his friends who are learning Spanish to practice speaking the language. When do you use Spanish?

274 doscientos setenta y cuatro
Unidad 6

Middle School Classroom Community

Paired Activity Ask students to work together to conduct an interview. One student will be the interviewer; the other will be the professional. The questions should be about work.

Portfolio Ask students to imagine that yesterday was an ideal day and to write down what they did.

Rubric

Criteria	Scale	
Creativity	1 2 3 4 5	A = 13–15 pts.
Logical organization	1 2 3 4 5	B = 10–12 pts.
Vocabulary use/spelling	1 2 3 4 5	C = 7–9 pts.
		D = 4–6 pts.
		F = < 4 pts.

En resumen
REPASO DE VOCABULARIO

DESCRIBING CITY BUILDINGS

ancho(a)	wide
antiguo(a)	old, ancient
el edificio	building
enorme	huge, enormous
estrecho(a)	narrow
formal	formal
informal	informal
lujoso(a)	luxurious
moderno(a)	modern
ordinario(a)	ordinary
sencillo(a)	simple, plain
tradicional	traditional

TELLING WHAT HAPPENED

la cámara	camera
la entrevista	interview
la grabadora	tape recorder

TALKING ABOUT PROFESSIONS

el (la) arquitecto(a)	architect
la arquitectura	architecture
el bombero	firefighter
el (la) cartero(a)	mail carrier
la compañía	company
el (la) contador(a)	accountant
el (la) editor(a)	editor
el (la) escritor(a)	writer
el (la) fotógrafo(a)	photographer
el (la) gerente	manager
el hombre de negocios	businessman
el (la) jefe(a)	boss
la mujer de negocios	businesswoman
el (la) operador(a)	operator
el (la) periodista	journalist
la profesión	profession
el (la) recepcionista	receptionist
el (la) secretario(a)	secretary
el (la) taxista	taxi driver

MAKING SUGGESTIONS TO A GROUP

Vamos a…	Let's…

OTHER WORDS AND PHRASES

la contaminación del aire	air pollution
decidir	to decide
estar de acuerdo	to agree
el (la) ganador(a)	winner
ofrecer	to offer
el tráfico	traffic

Juego

¿Qué hacen sus padres?

El padre de Susana usa una cámara.
El Sr. Rodríguez tiene un trabajo
peligroso. Al papá de Adriana le
gusta trabajar con los números.

1. ¿Quién es contador?
2. ¿Quién es fotógrafo?
3. ¿Quién es bombero?

Have students think of 3–5 professions in
which knowing Spanish would be helpful,
and have them list several ways in which
the language might be useful. Then have
them contact and interview some people
in these professions. Were their ideas
right?

Quick Start Review
🔄 Preterite review
Use OHT 184 or write on the board:
Answer the following questions:
1. ¿Qué hiciste ayer?
2. ¿Qué comiste?
3. ¿Adónde fuiste?
4. ¿Qué escribiste?
5. ¿Con quién hablaste?

Answers will vary.

Teaching Suggestions
Vocabulary Review
- Provide words associated with each
profession and have students name
the profession.
- Name local or well-known buildings.
Have students give adjectives to
describe them.

Juego
Answers
1. el papá de Adriana
2. el padre de Susana
3. el Sr. Rodríguez

Teaching Middle School Students

Extra Help Help students to make lists that group
the vocabulary in ways that help them to remember it,
for example: Cognates, Words That Start the Same Way
As Their English Counterparts, Words I Already Know,
and Tough Ones. Each student will have a different
Tough Ones list, so they can help each other on those.

Multiple Intelligences

Kinesthetic Ask students to choose a profession from
the vocabulary list and pantomime it for the rest of the
class.

Musical/Rhythmic Have students write a song to the
tune of the alphabet song. Each pair or group writes a
verse about a profession from the **Etapa** vocabulary.

Block Schedule

Variety Have students work in small
groups to write and videotape skits,
using the **Diálogo** as a model. One
student plays an interviewer. The others
play interviewees who talk about their
professions.

Planning Guide CLASSROOM MANAGEMENT

OBJECTIVES

Communication
- Point out specific people and things *pp. 278–279, 296–297*
- Tell where things are located *pp. 278–279, 280–281, 296–297*
- Talk about the past *pp. 280–281*

Grammar
- Use location words *pp. 286–287*
- Use demonstratives *pp. 289–290*
- Use ordinal numbers *pp. 291–292*
- Use irregular verbs in the preterite *pp. 293–294*

Pronunciation
- Pronunciation of **l** *p. 295*
- Dictation *TE p. 295*

Culture
- An indigenous language *p. 283*
- Regional vocabulary *p. 290*
- **Los otavaleños** *pp. 296–297*

 Recycling
- Professions *p. 284*
- Places *p. 285*
- School and personal items *p. 287*
- Comparatives *p. 291*

STRATEGIES

Listening Strategies
- Listen for implied statements *p. 280*

Speaking Strategies
- Recall what you know *p. 287*
- Use words that direct others' attention *p. 300*

Reading Strategies
- Recognize place names *TE p. 296*

Writing Strategies
- Organize information chronologically and by category *TE p. 300*

Connecting Cultures Strategies
- Learn about an indigenous language in Ecuador *p. 283*
- Recognize variations in regional vocabulary *p. 290*
- Learn about the artisans of Otavalo *pp. 296–297*
- Connect and compare what you know about cultural groups in your community to help you learn about cultural groups in a new community *pp. 296–297*

PROGRAM RESOURCES

 Print

- *Más práctica* Workbook PE *pp. 57–64*
- Block Scheduling Copymasters *pp. 137–144*
- Unit 6 Resource Book
  Más práctica Workbook TE *pp. 52–59*
  Information Gap Activities *pp. 68–71*

- Family Involvement *pp. 72–73*
- Video Activities *pp. 74–76*
- Videoscript *pp. 77–79*
- Audioscript *pp. 80–83*
- Assessment Program, Unit 6 Etapa 2 *pp. 84–102, 170–178*
- Answer Keys *pp. 187–202*

 **Audiovisual**

- **Audio Program** Cassettes 17A, 17B / CD 17
- *Canciones* Cassette / CD
- **Video Program** Videotape 6 / Videodisc 3B
- **Overhead Transparencies** M1–M5; 173; 185–194

 Technology

- Electronic Teacher Tools/Test Generator
- *Intrigas y aventuras* CD-ROM, Disc 1
- www.mcdougallittell.com

Assessment Program Options

- Cooperative Quizzes (Unit 6 Resource Book)
- Etapa Exam Forms A and B (Unit 6 Resource Book)
- *Para hispanohablantes* Etapa Exam (Unit 6 Resource Book)
- Portfolio Assessment (Unit 6 Resource Book)
- Multiple Choice Test Questions (Unit 6 Resource Book)
- Audio Program Testing Cassette T2 / CD T2
- Electronic Teacher Tools/Test Generator

Native Speakers

- *Para hispanohablantes* Workbook PE, *pp. 57–64*
- *Para hispanohablantes* Workbook TE (Unit 6 Resource Book)
- *Para hispanohablantes* Etapa Exam (Unit 6 Resource Book)
- Audio *Para hispanohablantes* Cassettes 17A, 17B, T2 / CD 17, T2
- Audioscript *Para hispanohablantes* (Unit 6 Resource Book)

Patricia   Miguel   Bárbara   Julio

Student Text Listening Activity Scripts

 Videoscript: Diálogo *pages 280–281*

• Videotape 6   • Videodisc 3B

Search Chapter 5, Play to 6
U6E2 • En vivo (Dialog)

• Use the videoscript with **Actividades 1, 2** *pages 282–283*

Miguel:	¡Buenos días, tía Bárbara!
Bárbara:	¡Miguel! ¡Bienvenidos! ¿Y tú eres Patricia?
Patricia:	Sí. Es un placer, señora Olivera.
Bárbara:	Ay, hija, llámame Bárbara. ¿Te gusta mi taller?
Patricia:	Sí, mucho.
Bárbara:	Vengan, pasen. Siéntate.
Patricia:	Gracias. Tengo esta grabadora. ¿Me permite usarla?
Bárbara:	Cómo no, hija.
Patricia:	Muchas gracias. Bárbara, ¿cuándo vino usted a vivir aquí?
Bárbara:	Vine en el año 1990 con mi esposo y mi hijo.
Patricia:	¿Y le gusta vivir en el campo, en este pueblo pequeño?
Bárbara:	Sí, mucho. Es muy tranquilo aquí. A ver... ¿dónde están las tijeras? Ah, sí, allí están. Miguel, ¿me das las tijeras que están sobre la mesa?
Miguel:	Claro.
Patricia:	¿Cómo fueron sus primeros años aquí?
Bárbara:	Uy, tuvimos que trabajar muchísimo. Fue muy difícil hasta el tercer año.
Patricia:	¿Y venden los sacos y los gorros en los mercados?
Bárbara:	Sí, claro. El mejor mercado es el mercado de Otavalo. Estuvimos ahí el domingo pasado.
Miguel:	¡A mí me gusta mucho ese mercado! La última vez que estuve allí, compré una mochila fenomenal. Vamos hoy después de visitar a mi tío Julio.
Bárbara:	Ya lo sé. Julio nos llamó anoche y nos dijo. ¡Ay!, perdóname, Patricia. Viniste para hacerme preguntas.
Patricia:	No se preocupe. Sólo tengo una pregunta más. En su opinión, ¿cuál es la diferencia más grande entre la vida en la ciudad y la vida en el campo?
Bárbara:	Creo que todo va más lento en el campo. No tenemos tanta prisa como la gente de la ciudad.
Patricia:	Muchas gracias, Bárbara. Me ayudó mucho.

Bárbara:	No hay de qué, hija. Miguel, ¿me bajas aquel saco? Está allí arriba. Te lo doy como recuerdo de tu visita.
Patricia:	¡Ay, Bárbara! ¡No es necesario!
Bárbara:	Claro que no es necesario. Miguel... busca un saco para ti también.
Miguel:	Gracias, tía Bárbara...
Julio:	Sí, soy de una familia de ganaderos. Esta granja fue de mi abuelo.
Patricia:	¿Sus hijos lo ayudan con el trabajo?
Julio:	Sí. Todos los días mi hijo les da de comer a las gallinas y a las vacas. Mi hija, la menor, cuida los cerdos y los caballos. Y hablando de caballos... Miguel, ¿recuerdas la primera vez que viniste a visitarnos?
Miguel:	Ay, tío Julio, por favor... Patricia no quiere oír esas viejas historias.
Patricia:	¡Sí, las quiero oír!
Julio:	Pues, fue al corral para ver al caballo. Abrió la cerca y el caballo se escapó. Lo buscamos por todas partes.
Miguel:	¡Tío Julio!
Julio:	Luego les dio de comer a las gallinas. ¡Les dio una bolsa de comida! Fue suficiente comida para toda una semana...
Miguel:	Tío Julio, por favor...
Julio:	Está bien, está bien. Sabes, Patricia, hay gente que debe vivir en la ciudad y gente que debe vivir en el campo. ¡Miguel debe vivir en la ciudad!
Patricia:	¿Qué piensa Ud. de la ciudad?
Julio:	Vamos a Quito todos los meses para visitar a mi hija mayor y su familia. Es muy interesante y hay mucho trabajo. Pero vivimos aquí y estamos felices.
Patricia:	Gracias, Julio.
Julio:	Dice Miguel que ustedes van a Otavalo esta tarde.
Patricia:	Sí.
Julio:	¿Te contó Miguel de la segunda vez que él nos acompañó a Otavalo?
Miguel:	¡Tío Julio!

¿Qué son? *page 284*

1. Soy artesana. Trabajo en un taller haciendo sacos.
2. Soy pastor. Cuido las llamas y otros animales.
3. Soy secretario. Escribo muchas cartas.
4. Soy arquitecta. Hago los planos de las casas nuevas.

Un día bonito *page 295*

El domingo pasado, Luisa y su amiga Amalia hicieron un viaje a la granja de los abuelos de Luisa. Cuando llegaron allí, fueron primero al establo para ver los caballos. A Luisa le gustan mucho los caballos. Después, Luisa les dio de comer a las gallinas. Y Amalia les dio de comer a los cerdos. ¡Cuánto comieron los cerdos! Al mediodía las amigas almorzaron con los abuelos. ¡Qué simpáticos! ¡Y qué rica fue la comida! Después del almuerzo, fueron al mercado. Amalia compró un saco bonito. Luisa no compró nada porque no tuvo dinero. Las amigas volvieron a la ciudad a las siete de la noche. En el autobús, las amigas dijeron al mismo tiempo: «¡Qué día bonito tuvimos en el campo!».

Quick Start Review Answers

p. 282 Dialog review
1. ganaderos
2. sobre
3. este
4. viniste

p. 289 Location words
1. Las gallinas están dentro del corral.
2. Los animales que están lejos son llamas.
3. El gallo está encima de la cerca.
4. Patricia quiere un gorro de abajo.
5. Los cerdos están fuera del corral.

p. 291 Vocabulary review
1. arriba
2. saco
3. esto
4. caballo
5. lana

Sample Lesson Plan - 45 Minute Schedule

DAY 1

Etapa Opener
- Quick Start Review (TE, p. 276) 5 MIN.
- Anticipate/Activate prior knowledge: Discuss the *Etapa* Opener. 5 MIN.
- Answer the *¿Qué ves?* questions, p. 276. 5 MIN.

En contexto: Vocabulario
- Quick Start Review (TE, p. 278) 5 MIN.
- Read and discuss the Culture Highlights (TE, p. 279). 5 MIN.
- Have students use context and pictures to learn *Etapa* vocabulary. 5 MIN.
- Ask the Comprehension Questions (TE, p. 279). 5 MIN.
- Use the Situational OHTs for additional practice. 5 MIN.
- Have students work in pairs to answer the *Preguntas personales*, p. 279. 5 MIN.

DAY 2

En vivo: Diálogo
- Quick Start Review (TE, p. 280) 5 MIN.
- Review the Listening Strategy, p. 280. 5 MIN.
- Play audio or show video for the dialog, pp. 280–281. 10 MIN.
- Work orally with the class to decide which of the Listening Strategy statements are true, p. 280. 5 MIN.
- Discuss the Language Note (TE, p. 280). 5 MIN.
- Replay the audio/video as needed. 5 MIN.
- Read the dialog aloud, having students take the roles of characters. 10 MIN.

Homework Option:
- Video Activities, Unit 6 Resource Book, pp. 74–76.

DAY 3

En acción: Vocabulario y gramática
- Check homework. 5 MIN.
- Quick Start Review (TE, p. 282) 5 MIN.
- Use OHTs to review *En contexto* vocabulary. Ask students for a summary of the dialog to check recall. 10 MIN.
- Play the video/audio; do *Actividad* 1 orally with the class. 5 MIN.
- Do *Actividad* 2 orally. 5 MIN.
- Have students work in pairs to do *Actividad* 3. 5 MIN.
- Have volunteers share their responses to *Actividad* 3. 5 MIN.
- Read and discuss the *Nota cultural*, p. 283. 5 MIN.

DAY 4

En acción (cont.)
- Discuss *Actividad* 4. 5 MIN.
- Have students write their responses to *Actividad* 4. 5 MIN.
- Play the audio as students work on *Actividad* 5. 5 MIN.
- Call on selected students to tell which picture they chose for *Actividad* 5. 5 MIN.
- Do the Critical Thinking activity (TE, p. 285). 5 MIN.
- Have students work in pairs to plan and prepare their debate for *Actividad* 6. 10 MIN.
- Ask pairs to perform their debates from *Actividad* 6. 10 MIN.

DAY 5

En acción (cont.)
- Quick Start Review (TE, p. 286) 5 MIN.
- Work orally with the class on *Actividad* 7. 5 MIN.
- Present *Gramática:* Saying Where Things Are Located, p. 286. 10 MIN.
- Assign *Actividad* 8. 5 MIN.
- Present the Speaking Strategy, p. 287. 5 MIN.
- Have students work in pairs to complete *Actividad* 9. 5 MIN.
- Call on pairs to share their responses to *Actividad* 9 with the class. 5 MIN.
- Have students work in pairs to do *Actividad* 10. 5 MIN.

Homework Option:
- *Más práctica* Workbook, p. 61. *Para hispanohablantes* Workbook, p. 59.

DAY 6

En acción (cont.)
- Check homework. 5 MIN.
- Quick Start Review (TE, p. 289) 5 MIN.
- Read and discuss the *Conexiones*, p. 288. 5 MIN.
- Present *Gramática:* Pointing Out Specific Things Using Demonstratives, p. 289. 10 MIN.
- Share the mnemonic device in the Teaching Note (TE, p. 289). 5 MIN.
- Assign *Actividad* 11. 5 MIN.
- Call on selected students to read their full-sentence responses to *Actividad* 11. 5 MIN.
- Quick Wrap-up (TE, p. 290) 5 MIN.

Homework Option:
- *Más práctica* Workbook, p. 62. *Para hispanohablantes* Workbook, p. 60.

DAY 7

En acción (cont.)
- Check homework. 5 MIN.
- Quick Start Review (TE, p. 291) 5 MIN.
- Assign *Actividad* 12. 5 MIN.
- Ask volunteers to share their work on *Actividad* 12. 5 MIN.
- Read and discuss the *También se dice*, p. 290. 5 MIN.
- Have students work in groups to complete *Actividad* 13. 5 MIN.
- Ask volunteer groups to share their work on *Actividad* 13. 5 MIN.
- Present *Gramática:* Ordinal Numbers, p. 291. 10 MIN.

DAY 8

En acción (cont.)
- Read and discuss the *Conexiones*, p. 291. 5 MIN.
- Have students draw the map for the *Para hacer*, p. 291. 10 MIN.
- Assign *Actividad* 14. 5 MIN.
- Call on selected students to give their responses to *Actividad* 14. 5 MIN.
- Assign *Actividad* 15. 5 MIN.
- Call on volunteers to read their answers to *Actividad* 15. 5 MIN.
- Assign *Actividad* 16. 5 MIN.
- Ask volunteers to share their lists from *Actividad* 16. 5 MIN.

Homework Option:
- *Más práctica* Workbook, p. 63. *Para hispanohablantes* Workbook, p. 61.

DAY 9

En acción (cont.)
- Check homework. 5 MIN.
- Quick Start Review (TE, p. 293) 5 MIN.
- Present *Gramática:* Irregular Preterite Verbs, p. 293. 10 MIN.
- Assign *Actividad* 17. 5 MIN.
- Call volunteers to share their answers to *Actividad* 17. 5 MIN.
- Have students work in pairs to do *Actividad* 18. 5 MIN.
- Call on selected pairs to model their conversations for *Actividad* 18. 5 MIN.
- Assign *Actividad* 19. 5 MIN.

Homework Option:
- *Más práctica* Workbook, p. 64. *Para hispanohablantes* Workbook, p. 62.

DAY 10

En acción (cont.)
- Check homework. 5 MIN.
- Quick Start Review (TE, p. 296) 5 MIN.
- Play the audio as students do *Actividad* 20. 5 MIN.
- Call on students to share their sequencing for the photos in *Actividad* 20. 5 MIN.
- Assign *Actividad* 21. 5 MIN.
- Call on selected students to write their answers for *Actividad* 21 on the board. 5 MIN.
- Play the audio. Discuss the *Pronunciación,* p. 295. 5 MIN.

En colores: Cultura y comparaciones
- Discuss the Connecting Cultures Strategy, p. 296. 5 MIN.
- Have volunteers read *Los otavaleños,* pp. 296–297, aloud. 5 MIN.

DAY 11

En colores (cont.)
- Quick Start Review (TE, p. 298) 5 MIN.
- Discuss the *¿Comprendiste?* and *¿Qué piensas?* questions, p. 297. 10 MIN.
- Have students work in groups to complete the *Hazlo tú,* p. 297. 5 MIN.
- Discuss the Culture Highlights (TE, p. 297). 5 MIN.

En uso: Repaso y más comunicación
- Assign *Actividad* 1. 5 MIN.
- Call on students to share their work from *Actividad* 1. 5 MIN.
- Have students write their answers to *Actividad* 2 independently. 5 MIN.
- Call on volunteers to write their answers to *Actividad* 2 on the board. 5 MIN.

DAY 12

En uso (cont.)
- Work orally with the class on *Actividad* 3. 5 MIN.
- Have students write out answers to *Actividad* 3. 5 MIN.
- Assign *Actividad* 4. 5 MIN.
- Call on students to read each sentence in *Actividad* 4. 5 MIN.
- Present the Speaking Strategy, p. 300. 5 MIN.
- Have students work in pairs on *Actividad* 5. 10 MIN.
- Call on selected pairs to model their conversations from *Actividad* 5 for the class. 5 MIN.
- Read and discuss the *Conexiones,* p. 300. 5 MIN.

DAY 13

En uso (cont.)
- Have students work in groups on *Actividad* 6. 10 MIN.
- Call on selected groups to model their work from *Actividad* 6. 5 MIN.

En tu propia voz: Escritura
- Discuss the *modelo* for *Actividad* 7. 5 MIN.
- Have students make a list of months in this school year and brainstorm things that happened in each month. 5 MIN.
- Have students work independently on the writing activity in *Actividad* 7. 10 MIN.
- Ask volunteers to read their work from *Actividad* 7 to the class. 10 MIN.

Homework Option:
- Have students review all the *Gramática* boxes in *Etapa* 2 as preparation for the exam.

DAY 14

En resumen: Repaso de vocabulario
- Review grammar questions as necessary. 5 MIN.
- Quick Start Review (TE, p. 301) 5 MIN.
- Follow the Teaching Suggestions (TE, p. 301). 5 MIN.
- Call on students to read their vocabulary sentences aloud. 10 MIN.
- Discuss the Interdisciplinary Connection (TE, p. 301). 5 MIN.
- Ask students to solve the *Juego,* p. 301. 10 MIN.
- Answer the *Juego* orally (Answers, TE, p. 301). 5 MIN.

Homework Option:
- Have students study for *Etapa* exam.

DAY 15

En resumen (cont.)
- Answer questions related to *Etapa* 2 content. 10 MIN.
- Complete *Etapa* exam. 25 MIN.

Ampliación
- Use a suggested project, game, or activity (TE, pp. 249A–249B) as students complete the exam.

Classroom Management Tip

Involve movement Encourage students to make research projects come to life by doing something, not just writing about it. One good project to use would be about Ecuadoran crafts.

Ecuador produces wonderful crafts that students might enjoy researching, studying, and trying. For example, at Otavalo's Saturday market, Otavalo weavers in traditional dress sell ponchos, sweaters, sashes, bags, weavings, etc. Have students research patterns and methods for creating a weaving using authentic designs. An excellent project would include a sample weaving.

Etapa Theme
Visiting the country, pointing things out, and talking about the past

Grammar Objectives
- Using location words
- Using demonstratives
- Using ordinal numbers
- Using irregular verbs in the preterite

Teaching Resource Options

Print
Block Scheduling Copymasters

Audiovisual
OHT 173, 191 (Quick Start)

Quick Start Review
♻ Preterite review

Use OHT 191 or write on the board: Answer the following questions, using complete sentences in the preterite.

1. ¿Qué hiciste ayer antes de la escuela?
2. ¿Qué hiciste ayer en la escuela?
3. ¿Qué hiciste ayer después de la escuela?
4. ¿Qué hiciste anoche?

Answers
Answers will vary. Answers could include:
1. Me lavé los dientes.
2. Aprendí mucho en la clase de matemáticas.
3. Fui al parque con mis amigos.
4. Vi la televisión.

Teaching Suggestions
Previewing the Etapa
- Ask students to study the picture on pp. 276–277 (1 min.).
- Have them close their books and share at least 3 items that they noticed.
- Have students open their books and look at the **Etapa** title. Ask what they think the relationship is between the title and the photo.
- Use the **¿Qué ves?** questions to focus the discussion.

UNIDAD 6

A conocer el campo

- Point out specific people and things

- Tell where things are located

- Talk about the past

¿Qué ves?
Mira la foto de un taller en el campo de Ecuador.

1. ¿Las personas de la foto están contentas o tristes?
2. ¿Hay muchos o pocos sacos?
3. ¿De qué colores son los sacos?
4. ¿Cuál es el teléfono del taller?

CENTRO ARTESANAL

Juan León Mera 804   Fax 502-301
Telf. 548-235

276

Middle School Classroom Management

Planning Ahead If possible, try to locate an Ecuadoran wool sweater to bring to class for a Show and Tell. You might also collect pictures of farm animals, farm buildings, and plastic toy animals to bring to class for students to use during vocabulary activities.

Time Saver Have students say aloud together the answers to the **¿Qué ves?** section.

Cross Cultural Connections

Ask students to notice the labels in their clothing. Point out that often they will see **Hecho en...** Have them look at their clothing labels at home to see if any were made in a Spanish-speaking country. Also have them look for cleaning instructions in Spanish and copy them down to read in class.

Culture Highlights

● **LOS QUECHUA** The Quechua people are the native people of the South American Andes. Quechua was the official language of the Inca Empire and is currently spoken by more than 10 million people. The Quechua language and culture are found in the countryside and in some towns of the Andean highlands, especially in Otavalo. In Ecuador, the language is usually referred to as "Quichua," but it is derived from the same language base. Quechua people built bridges and roads throughout the Andes, and many routes are still in use today. The Quechua artisans produce high-quality textiles and pottery.

● **OTAVALO** The most famous place in Otavalo is its market. On Saturdays, people begin trading animals and crafts early in the morning before dawn. There are other interesting places to visit, such as the **Instituto Otavaleño de Antropología** and the **Museo Arqueológico.**

Supplementary Vocabulary

el telar	loom
tejer	to weave
trabajar/tejer a punto de aguja	to knit
tejer con aguja de gancho	to crochet

Block Schedule

Bulletin Board Display a map of South America on the bulletin board. Have each student research an interesting fact, animal, place, person, etc., from one area of South America. Then have each student make a visual for that information, display it near the map, and stretch a piece of colored yarn from the visual to the country. (For additional activities, see **Block Scheduling Copymasters.**)

Teaching Middle School Students

Extra Help To introduce or review vocabulary, ask: ¿Cuántos sacos son del color verde? ¿Marrón?

Native Speakers Have students create an ad for this **taller** that includes the shop's name, catchy descriptions of what is sold there, its address, the phone number, etc.

Multiple Intelligences

Naturalist Have students examine the photo to identify textures, colors, patterns, geometric shapes, etc. How many are alike? How many are different? What are the sweaters made of? What do the colors and designs of the sweaters tell about the climate of the region?

277

Teaching Resource Options

Print ✎
Unit 6 Resource Book
  Video Activities, pp. 74–75
  Videoscript, p. 77
  Audioscript, p. 80
  Audioscript *Para hispanohablantes*,
    p. 80

Audiovisual
OHT 185, 186, 187, 187A, 188, 188A,
191 (Quick Start)
Audio Program Cassette 17A / CD 17
Audio *Para hispanohablantes*
  Cassette 17A / CD 17
Video Program Videotape 6 /
  Videodisc 3B

Search Chapter 4, Play to 5
U6E2 • En contexto (Vocabulary)

Technology
Intrigas y aventuras CD-ROM, Disc 1

♻ Quick Start Review

Descriptions, colors

Use OHT 191 or write on the board:
Describe 5 people or items, including
a color in your description.

Modelos: Jeff lleva una camiseta azul.
        Tengo tres lápices amarillos.

Answers will vary.

Teaching Suggestions
Introducing Vocabulary

• Have students look at pages 278–279.
Use OHT 185 and 186 and Audio
Cassette 17A / CD 17 to present the
vocabulary.
• Ask the Comprehension Questions in
order of yes/no (questions 1–3),
either/or (questions 4–6), and simple
word or phrase (questions 7–10).
Expand by adding similar questions.
• Use the TPR activity to reinforce the
meaning of individual words.
• Use the video vocabulary presentation
for review and reinforcement.

En contexto

VOCABULARIO

Patricia has left the city and is visiting the country. Look at
the sights she sees and the people she meets.

A Aquí, en **el taller**, **la artesana** hace mucha ropa. Usa
lana de muchos colores. La lana azul está **encima de**
la mesa. La lana roja está **debajo de** la mesa.

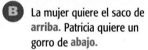

B La mujer quiere el saco de
arriba. Patricia quiere un
gorro de **abajo**.

C En la granja hay varios animales. **El ganadero** cuida
estas vacas que están aquí muy cerca. Ese animal,
que está al otro lado de **la cerca**, es un **toro**.

278   doscientos setenta y ocho
            Unidad 6

Middle School Classroom Community

TPR Put pictures of farm animals and structures on
the chalk ledge. Direct students to touch the pictures
in the following ways: **Toca la granja. Pásale el cerdo
a (nombre de estudiante). Pon el gallo en tu
escritorio. Pon el ganadero al lado del corral.**

Game Play **Yo veo...** (Twenty Questions) with the
items pictured: **Yo veo algo marrón. ¿Es un animal?
¿Es el caballo?**, etc.

las llamas

el pastor

E **Aquellas** animales, que están lejos, son **llamas**. **El pastor** cuida las llamas.

la granja

los cerdos

F Aquí hay unos **cerdos**. El ganadero también tiene **un caballo**.

el corral

las gallinas

el gallo

D Aquí hay **unas gallinas** y **un gallo**. Las gallinas están **dentro del corral**. El gallo está **fuera**.

el caballo

Preguntas personales

1. ¿Te gustan los caballos?
2. ¿Vives en el campo o en la ciudad?
3. ¿Te gustaría trabajar en una granja o en un taller?
4. ¿Qué hay encima de tu escritorio? ¿Debajo de tu escritorio?
5. ¿Qué ropa de lana tienes?

doscientos setenta y nueve
Etapa 2

279

Culture Highlights

● **ANIMALES** The Quechua people use the llama and the alpaca to supply them with meat, wool, grease, fertilizer, fuel, and leather. Some of the wild animals found in Ecuador are bears, jaguars, and wildcats. The ocelot is an endangered cat that lives in the tropics and subtropics of the Americas. It has been hunted mercilessly for the beauty of its fur.

Comprehension Questions

1. ¿Está la artesana en el taller? (Sí.)
2. ¿Usa la artesana lana de sólo un color? (No.)
3. ¿Está la lana roja encima de la mesa? (No.)
4. ¿Quiere la mujer el saco de abajo o de arriba? (de arriba)
5. ¿Quién quiere el gorro de abajo, Patricia o la artesana? (Patricia)
6. ¿Están la gallinas dentro o fuera del corral? (dentro)
7. ¿Qué hace el pastor? (Cuida las llamas.)
8. ¿Quién trabaja en la granja y qué hace? (El ganadero trabaja en la granja. Cuida los animales.)
9. ¿Dónde está el toro? (al otro lado de la cerca)
10. ¿Cuántos caballos tiene el ganadero? (un caballo)

Teaching Note

You may want to expand on questions 1 and 3 of the **Preguntas personales** with a follow-up question, such as **¿Dónde ves caballos?**

Block Schedule

Categorize Have students make flash cards of the vocabulary for animals on pp. 278–279 and the **Vocabulario adicional** on p. R12. Then have them determine categories for them (mammals/birds, domestic/wild, single color/multicolor, etc.) and sort the cards according to the categories.

Teaching Middle School Students

Extra Help Before students look at the visual, have them generate a list of animals and buildings they would expect to see on a farm. Once you go over the vocabulary, have them check off the items on their lists.

Multiple Intelligences

Logical/Mathematical Have students count all the animals pictured and make a chart with these headings: **Número de patas** (legs) and **Número de orejas**.

Musical/Rhythmic Have students make silly rhymes with the animals: **La llama está en la cama; El toro es de oro; El gallo cantó en mayo; La vaca se llama Paca;** etc.

Teaching Resource Options

Print

Más práctica Workbook PE,
  pp. 57–60
Para hispanohablantes Workbook PE,
  pp. 57–58
Block Scheduling Copymasters
Unit 6 Resource Book
  Más práctica Workbook TE, pp. 52–55
  Para hispanohablantes Workbook
    TE, pp. 60–61
  Video Activities, p. 76
  Videoscript, p. 78
  Audioscript, p. 80
  Audioscript *Para hispanohablantes*,
    p. 80

Audiovisual

OHT 189, 190, 191 (Quick Start)
Audio Program Cassette 17A / CD 17
Audio *Para hispanohablantes*
  Cassette 17A / CD 17
Video Program Videotape 6 /
  Videodisc 3B

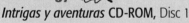

Search Chapter 5, Play to 6
U6E2 • En vivo (Dialog)

Technology

Intrigas y aventuras CD-ROM, Disc 1

Quick Start Review

♻ Vocabulary review
Use OHT 191 or write on the board:
List at least 3 items you find in each
place:

• el taller de artículos de lana
• la granja

Answers
Answers will vary. Answers could include:
• un saco, un gorro, una manta, unos guantes
• una vaca, un caballo, un cerdo, unas gallinas

Language Note

Point out that Patricia addresses Bárbara in
the **usted** form as a sign of respect for
Miguel's older relative. Bárbara, however,
addresses Patricia as **tú** because Patricia is
much younger.

En vivo

🎧💿 DIÁLOGO

Patricia

Miguel

Bárbara

Julio

PARA ESCUCHAR • STRATEGY: LISTENING

Listen for implied statements Some things are said directly; others are
suggested, but not stated. They are implied. Listen and decide
which of the following are implied:
1. A slow, quiet life is boring.
2. Farm life requires hard work.
3. Life in both the city and the country is interesting.
What did you hear that influenced your decision?

En el campo

1 ▶ Miguel: ¡Buenos días, tía Bárbara!
Bárbara: ¡Miguel! ¡Bienvenidos! ¿Y
tú eres Patricia?
Patricia: Sí. Es un placer.
Bárbara: ¿Te gusta mi taller?
Patricia: Sí, mucho.

5 ▶ Bárbara: Sí, ya lo sé. Miguel, ¿me
bajas aquel saco? Está allí arriba.
Patricia: ¡Ay! No es necesario.
Bárbara: Miguel, busca un saco
para ti también.
Miguel: Gracias, tía Bárbara.

6 ▶ Julio: Soy de una familia de ganaderos.
Esta granja fue de mi abuelo. Todos los
días mi hijo les da de comer a las gallinas
y a las vacas. Mi hija menor cuida los
cerdos y los caballos. Y hablando de
caballos…

7 ▶ Julio: Miguel, ¿recuerdas la primera
vez que viniste a visitarnos?
Miguel: Patricia no quiere oír esas
viejas historias.
Julio: Pues, fue al corral, abrió la
cerca y el caballo se escapó.

280 doscientos ochenta
Unidad 6

Middle School Classroom Community

TPR Have students make a quick sketch of one of the
farm animals. Collect the sketches and pass them out
to groups of students. Organize a TPR routine such as
the following: **Pon el gallo al lado del caballo. Pon la
llama delante de la vaca, etc.**

Group Activity Have student volunteers act out
different sections of the video.

2 ▶ Patricia: ¿Cuándo vino usted a vivir aquí?
Bárbara: Vine en el año 1990.
Patricia: ¿Y le gusta vivir en el campo, en este pueblo pequeño?
Bárbara: Sí, es muy tranquilo.

3 ▶ Bárbara: A ver… ¿dónde están las tijeras? Ah, sí, allí están. Miguel, ¿me das las tijeras que están sobre la mesa?
Patricia: ¿Cómo fueron sus primeros años aquí?
Bárbara: Tuvimos que trabajar muchísimo.

4 ▶ Patricia: ¿Y venden los sacos y los gorros?
Bárbara: Sí, el mejor mercado es el mercado de Otavalo. Estuvimos ahí el domingo pasado.
Miguel: ¡A mí me gusta mucho ese mercado! ¡Vamos hoy!

8 ▶ Julio: Luego les dio de comer a las gallinas. ¡Les dio una bolsa de comida!
Miguel: ¡Tío Julio, por favor!
Julio: ¿Sabes, Patricia? ¡Miguel debe vivir en la ciudad!

9 ▶ Patricia: ¿Qué piensa usted de la ciudad?
Julio: Vamos a Quito todos los meses para visitar a mi hija mayor y su familia. Es muy interesante y hay mucho trabajo, pero vivimos aquí y estamos felices.
Patricia: Gracias, Julio.

10 ▶ Julio: Dice Miguel que ustedes van a Otavalo esta tarde.
Patricia: Sí.
Julio: ¿Te contó Miguel de la segunda vez que él nos acompañó a Otavalo?
Miguel: ¡Tío Julio!

Teaching Middle School Students

Native Speakers Ask students to give a verbal summary of the video.

Challenge Have students pretend to be Patricia, the interviewer, and write 3 more questions to ask the artisan and the farmer. Have volunteers role-play these people.

Multiple Intelligences

Visual As students move through the **Etapa**, have them create a picture dictionary of the nouns, verbs, and phrases that are introduced.

Teaching Suggestions
Presenting the Dialog

• Prepare students for listening by focusing on the dialog context and the characters. Ask who Patricia and Miguel are and why they have come to Bárbara's workshop.

• Use the video, audio cassette, or CD to present the dialog. The expanded dialog on video offers additional listening practice opportunities.

Video Synopsis

• Patricia interviews Miguel's relatives about life in the country. For a complete transcript of the video dialog, see p. 275B.

Comprehension Questions

1. ¿Es Bárbara la tía de Patricia? (No.)
2. ¿Quiere Patricia hacerle una entrevista a Bárbara? (Sí.)
3. ¿Fueron fáciles los primeros años de Bárbara en el campo? (No.)
4. ¿Participó Bárbara en el mercado de Otavalo el domingo pasado o el sábado pasado? (el domingo pasado)
5. ¿Qué les da Bárbara a Patricia y a Miguel, unos gorros o unos sacos? (unos sacos)
6. ¿Quién es Julio, el tío o el abuelo de Miguel? (el tío)
7. ¿Qué trabajo hace el hijo de Julio? (Les da de comer a las gallinas y a las vacas.)
8. ¿Qué trabajo hace la hija menor de Julio? (Cuida los cerdos y los caballos.)
9. ¿Qué pasó cuando Miguel fue al corral y abrió la cerca? (El caballo se escapó.)
10. ¿Por qué va Julio a Quito todos los meses? (Va para visitar a su hija mayor y su familia.)

▪ Block Schedule

FunBreak Have students work in groups of 4. Tape the name of an animal on each student's back. Students then ask the other group members questions in order to determine what animal they are. At the end of 5 minutes, group members tell who they think they are and why. (For additional activities, see **Block Scheduling Copymasters**.)

Teaching Resource Options

Print

Unit 6 Resource Book
  Videoscript, p. 76
  Audioscript, pp. 80–81
  Audioscript *Para hispanohablantes,*
    pp. 80–81

Audiovisual

OHT 192 (Quick Start)
Audio Program Cassettes 17A, 17B /
  CD 17
Audio *Para hispanohablantes*
  Cassette 17A / CD 17
Video Program Videotape 6 / Videodisc
  3B

Quick Start Review

♻ Dialog review

Use OHT 192 or write on the board:
Complete the sentences from the dialog:

1. Soy de una familia de ___.
2. Miguel, ¿me das las tijeras que
   están ___ la mesa?
3. ¿Y le gusta vivir en el campo, en
   ___ pueblo pequeño?
4. Miguel, ¿recuerdas la primera vez
   que ___ a visitarnos?

Answers *See p. 275B.*

Teaching Suggestions
Comprehension Check

Use **Actividades 1** and **2** to assess
retention after the dialog. Have students
close their books. Read sentences in
Actividad 2, replacing the proper
nouns with pronouns. Have students
identify the proper nouns.

 Objective: Controlled practice
Listening comprehension/vocabulary

Answers (See script, p. 275B.)
  1. c
  2. d
  3. b
  4. a

En acción
VOCABULARIO Y GRAMÁTICA

OBJECTIVES

- Point out specific
  people and things
- Tell where things are
  located
- Talk about the past
- *Use location words*
- *Use demonstratives*
- *Use ordinal numbers*
- *Use irregular verbs in
  the preterite*

ACTIVIDAD 1

Un día en el campo

Escuchar Según el diálogo, indica quién es cada
persona. *(Hint: Match each photo to its description.)*

1. Vende sacos y gorros en
   su taller.
2. Tiene una granja; es de
   una familia de ganaderos.
3. Julio es su tío.
4. Le hace entrevistas a la
   gente del campo.

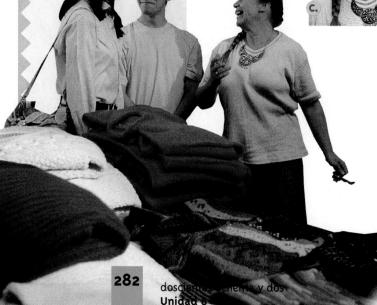

282 doscientos ochenta y dos
Unidad 6

Middle School Classroom Management

Peer Review Have pairs swap papers and correct
each other's work for **Actividades 1–2**.

Cooperative Learning You can use cooperative
learning groups to check homework and to clarify
any concepts students don't understand. In each
group there should be an explainer and an accuracy
checker. The group goal is to make sure everyone
has completed the homework and understands how
to do it.

Las entrevistas

Escuchar Combina las frases para hacer oraciones basadas en el diálogo. *(Hint: Make sentences based on the dialog.)*

1. A Bárbara le gusta vivir en el campo...
2. Bárbara vende ropa...
3. La granja de Julio fue...
4. Los hijos de Julio...
5. Después de visitar a Julio, Patricia y Miguel...

a. de su abuelo.
b. lo ayudan con el trabajo.
c. van a Otavalo.
d. porque es muy tranquilo.
e. en el mercado de Otavalo.

Miau, miau...

Hablar Con otro(a) estudiante, haz preguntas para identificar los animales. *(Hint: With your partner, ask questions to identify the animals.)*

modelo

Estudiante A: *Es un caballo, ¿verdad?*

Estudiante B: *¡Claro que no! Es un toro.*

1.

2.

3.

4.

5.

6.

doscientos ochenta y tres
283
Etapa 2

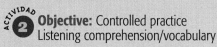
Answers (See script, p. 275B.)
1. d
2. e
3. a
4. b
5. c

3 **Objective:** Transitional practice
Vocabulary

Answers
Questions will vary.
1. Es un caballo.
2. Es un gallo.
3. Son unas gallinas.
4. Es una llama.
5. Es una vaca.
6. Es un cerdo.

Language Note

Point out how animals "talk" in Spanish. Have students give the English equivalents.

el perro	guau guau
el gato	miau
la vaca	mu
el pollito	pío pío
el gallo	quiquiriquí

Block Schedule

Change of Pace Have students write 3-stanza poemas. Stanza 1 describes city life; stanza 2 describes country life; stanza 3 says which type the student prefers. Have volunteers read their poems. Discuss the reasons for preferring one type of life over the other. (For additional activities, see **Block Scheduling Copymasters.**)

Teaching Middle School Students

Extra Help You might provide a mini two-column model for **Actividad 2** before students begin: **El mejor mercado está… en Otavalo.**

Multiple Intelligences

Musical/Rhythmic Reinforce the names of the animals in Spanish by singing with the class **"El señor MacDonald tenía una granja"** to the tune of "Old MacDonald Had a Farm."

Teaching Resource Options

Print

Unit 6 Resource Book
  Videoscript, p. 76
  Audioscript, pp. 80–81
  Audioscript *Para hispanohablantes*,
    pp. 80–81

Audiovisual

Audio Program Cassettes 17A, 17B /
CD 17
Audio *Para hispanohablantes*
Cassette 17A / CD 17
Video Program Videotape 6 / Videodisc
3B

4 Objective: Transitional practice
Vocabulary

Answers
1. Un ganadero los compra.
2. Vende alimento para animales.
3. Veo una vaca, un cerdo, un gallo y un caballo.
4. Está abierta de lunes a sábado, desde las siete de la mañana hasta las seis.
5. La tienda está en la avenida Chimborazo de Otavalo, Ecuador.

5 Objective: Transitional practice
Listening comprehension/vocabulary

♻ Professions

Answers (See script, p. 275B.)
a. 2
b. 4
c. 1
d. 3

ACTIVIDAD 4

Animales felices

Leer/Hablar Patricia y Miguel ven este anuncio en el camino al campo. Lee el anuncio y contesta las preguntas. *(Hint: Answer the questions.)*

Tienda Villagómez

Vendemos alimento para todos los animales.

¡Alimento bueno, animales felices!

Avenida Chimborazo 138
Otavalo, Ecuador
Días: lunes a sábado
Horas: 7:00 a 6:00
tel: 23-83-69

1. ¿Quién compra artículos de esta tienda?
2. ¿Qué vende la tienda?
3. ¿Qué animales ves en el anuncio?
4. ¿Qué días y horas está abierta la tienda?
5. ¿Dónde queda la tienda?

ACTIVIDAD 5

♻ ¿Qué son?

Escuchar Todos hablan de su profesión. Escucha lo que dice cada persona e indica qué es, escogiendo la foto apropiada. *(Hint: Choose the correct picture.)*

a.

b.

c.

d.

Middle School Classroom Community

Cooperative Learning Have groups create a mural of life on a farm or life in the city. Students must discuss what to include in the mural, decide who will draw what, and write a story about it. Assigned roles might be labeler of drawings, person who asks teacher questions, writer, editor, group story narrator.

Learning Scenario Have students role-play a vendor and a customer at the Tienda Villagómez. You might hand out these role cards: Farmer wants to buy feed for an animal. Customer calls to find out hours and directions. Customer returns an item. Customer wants something that the store is out of. Tourist enters store and asks about the area.

¡Debate!

Hablar/Escribir ¿Cuál es mejor, vivir en el campo o en la ciudad? Trabaja con otro(a) estudiante para convencer a los otros compañeros que su opinión es la mejor. *(Hint: Is the country or the city a better place to live? Convince your classmates.)*

❶ Decidan ustedes si prefieren el campo o la ciudad. *(Hint: Do you prefer the country or the city?)*

❷ Piensen ustedes en todas las palabras que puedan asociarse con el campo y la ciudad. *(Hint: What words do you associate with the country and the city?)*

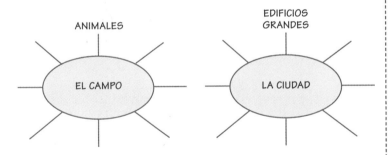

ANIMALES

EL CAMPO

EDIFICIOS GRANDES

LA CIUDAD

❸ Organicen y escriban estas palabras en dos gráficas: una para la ciudad; otra para el campo. *(Hint: Write the words in word webs.)*

❹ Escriban una lista de ideas que pueden usar en el debate. *(Hint: Make a list of ideas you can use in the debate.)*

 ¿Dónde?

Hablar Son las nueve de la mañana. Adivina dónde están estas personas. *(Hint: Guess where these people most likely are.)*

modelo

el cartero

El cartero está en el correo.

1. yo
2. mi mejor amigo(a)
3. mi maestro(a) de...
4. la artesana
5. el ganadero
6. el pastor
7. la arquitecta
8. el equipo de fútbol
9. la mesera
10. el taxista

doscientos ochenta y cinco **285**
Etapa 2

 Objective: Open-ended practice
Vocabulary

Answers will vary.

 Objective: Open-ended practice
Vocabulary

♻ **Places**

Answers

Answers will vary.
1. Yo estoy en la clase de...
2. Mi mejor amigo(a) está...
3. Mi maestro(a) de...
4. La artesana está en el taller.
5. El ganadero está en la granja.
6. El pastor está en el campo.
7. La arquitecta está en la oficina.
8. El equipo de fútbol está en el campo de fútbol.
9. La mesera está en el restaurante.
10. El taxista está en el taxi.

Critical Thinking

Ask students what they think farm animals need to be healthy. How does this compare to what household pets need? What about animals in the wild or animals in a zoo? Which needs are common to all animals and which are special to one group? Have the class make Venn diagrams to reflect their thinking.

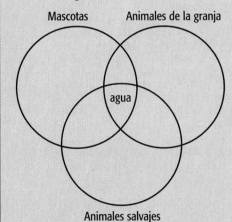

Mascotas

Animales de la granja

agua

Animales salvajes

Teaching Middle School Students

Extra Help Before starting **Actividad 7**, have students brainstorm names of places where people work.

Multiple Intelligences

Logical/Mathematical Students might take a poll of how many prefer the country to the city and then graph the results.

Verbal Make two mixed-up lists. One has animals: **el perro, el gato, la vaca, el pollito,** and **el gallo**. The other has animal voices: **guau guau, miau, mu, pío pío,** and **quiquiriquí.** Have students match the lists and talk about why these sounds might differ from their English counterparts.

Block Schedule

Retention Expand on the debate in **Actividad 6** by having groups of students write position papers on the merits of living in the country or the city. These papers should be peer edited and should go through several revision cycles before being submitted for evaluation.

Teaching Resource Options

Print

Más práctica Workbook PE, p. 61
Para hispanohablantes Workbook PE, p. 59
Block Scheduling Copymasters
Unit 6 Resource Book
  Más práctica Workbook TE, p. 56
  Para hispanohablantes Workbook TE, p. 62

Audiovisual

OHT 192 (Quick Start)

Technology

Intrigas y aventuras CD-ROM, Disc 1

Quick Start Review

♻ Prepositions of location

Use OHT 192 or write on the board:
Complete the sentences to make true statements about your classroom.

1. _____ está cerca _____ .
2. _____ y _____ están detrás _____ .
3. _____ y yo estamos lejos de _____ .
4. _____ está al lado de la profesora/del profesor.
5. _____ está delante de la computadora.

Answers

Answers will vary. Answers could include:
1. La puerta está cerca del pizarrón.
2. Rosa y Beto están detrás de Juan.
3. Yolanda y yo estamos lejos de la computadora.
4. La videograbadora está al lado de la profesora/del profesor.
5. El teclado está delante de la computadora.

Teaching Suggestions
Presenting Saying Where Things Are Located

• Review recycled prepositions of location and teach the new ones using manipulatives.
• Call on students by their relative positions rather than by names. Have them stand up to show understanding.

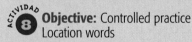

Objective: Controlled practice Location words

Answers
1. encima   4. arriba
2. fuera   5. debajo
3. dentro

GRAMÁTICA

Saying Where Things Are Located

♻ **¿RECUERDAS?** *p. 95* Remember prepositions of location?

You can also talk about the location of things using these words that you learned in **En contexto:**

cerca (de)	entre
a la derecha (de)	a la izquierda (de)
detrás (de)	al lado (de)
enfrente (de)	lejos (de)

The words **arriba** and **abajo** are never followed by *de.*

| abajo | debajo (de) | encima (de) |
| arriba | dentro (de) | fuera (de) |

Use *de* only when a **specific location** follows the expression.

Están *dentro del* taller.
*They are **inside** the workshop.*

—Miguel, ¿me bajas aquel saco? Está allí **arriba.**
*Miguel, (will you) get down that sweater for me? It's **up** there.*

8 Gramática

¿Dónde están?

Escribir Explica dónde están las personas y los animales, según los dibujos. *(Hint: Complete each sentence to tell where the people and animals are.)*

1. El gato está _____ de la cerca.

2. El artesano está _____ de su taller.

3. El cerdo está _____ del corral.

4. La periodista está _____ .

5. El perro está _____ de la mesa.

■ **MÁS PRÁCTICA** *cuaderno p. 61*   ■ **PARA HISPANOHABLANTES** *cuaderno p. 59*

286   doscientos ochenta y seis
Unidad 6

Middle School Classroom Community

Game: ¿Dónde está? Two students leave the classroom. The remaining students hide something in the room. The students return and try to guess where the object is located by asking questions with prepositions of location: ¿Está detrás del escritorio del maestro?

Paired Activity Have pairs sit back to back. Using prepositions of location, Student A tells Student B how to draw a letter. Student A checks Student B's work, and then they swap roles.

ACTIVIDAD 9 Para el viaje

PARA CONVERSAR • STRATEGY: SPEAKING

Recall what you know When describing where items are located, remember to use phrases that you learned earlier, such as **al lado de** and **a la derecha de,** as well as those you just learned.

♻️ **Hablar** Mira las cosas que Patricia va a llevar en su viaje al campo. Trabaja con otro(a) estudiante para preguntar dónde está cada cosa, según el dibujo. *(Hint: Work with a partner to ask and answer questions about where each thing is.)*

modelo

1. la grabadora

Estudiante A: *¿Dónde está **la grabadora**?*

Estudiante B: *Está encima del escritorio.*

doscientos ochenta y siete
Etapa 2 **287**

Teaching Resource Options

Print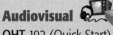
Block Scheduling Copymasters
Unit 6 Resource Book
  Information Gap Activities, p. 68
  Más práctica Workbook TE, p. 57
  Para hispanohablantes Workbook
  TE, p. 63

Audiovisual
OHT 192 (Quick Start)

Technology
Intrigas y aventuras CD-ROM, Disc 1

Objective: Open-ended practice
Vocabulary/location words

Answers will vary.

Para hacer

Answers
Animales de las Américas:
la alpaca, el búfalo, la llama.
Animales del resto del mundo:
el hámster, el gato, el caballo.

¿Limpia o sucia?

Hablar ¿Cómo está tu
habitación? ¿Está limpia o
sucia? ¿Qué cosas hay allí?
¿Dónde están? Haz un dibujo
de tu habitación (o de una
habitación imaginaria) y
dáselo a otro(a) estudiante.
El (la) otro(a) estudiante tiene
que describirlo. *(Hint: Draw a
picture of your bedroom or of an imaginary
one. Your partner will describe it to you.)*

modelo

*La habitación está muy limpia. Toda la
ropa está en el armario. Los zapatos
están en el suelo del armario. En el
escritorio hay papel y lápices…*

Conexiones

Las ciencias When the Spanish came
to the Americas at the end of the fifteenth
century, they found animals that were
unknown in Europe. Why? Look at a map of
the world. The Americas are separated from
the other continents by the Atlantic and Pacific
Oceans. It makes sense
that animals would
develop
differently in
Europe than in
the Americas.

PARA HACER:
Sort the animals shown
here into two groups:
*Animales de las
Américas* and *Animales
del resto del mundo.*

la alpaca

el hámster

el caballo

el búfalo

la llama

el gato

Middle School Classroom Community

TPR As you call out items in the classroom, have
students point to them: **Miren estos lápices. Miren
esos libros. Miren aquellos borradores,** etc.

Storytelling Have students tell a story modeled
after a children's story about the life of one of the
animals on page 288.

Group Activity Fold a set of six 3" x 5" cards in
half. Write a demonstrative on each one. Stand cards
at stations around the room. Have teams of students
work at one station at a time. Set a time limit of 5
minutes. Students describe the relative location of items
in the room using the demonstrative at that station.
After time is up, teams move to the next station.

GRAMÁTICA

Pointing Out Specific Things Using Demonstratives

When you point out specific things, you use **demonstrative** adjectives and **pronouns**. In **En contexto** you saw how demonstrative adjectives are used. A **demonstrative** adjective describes the location of a **noun** in relation to a person.

Masculine		Feminine	
Singular	**Plural**	**Singular**	**Plural**
este **cerdo**	estos **cerdos**	esta **mesa**	estas **mesas**
this pig	*these pigs*	*this table*	*these tables*
ese **cerdo**	esos **cerdos**	esa **mesa**	esas **mesas**
that pig	*those pigs*	*that table*	*those tables*
aquel **cerdo**	aquellos **cerdos**	aquella **mesa**	aquellas **mesas**
that pig (over there)	*those pigs (over there)*	*that table (over there)*	*those tables (over there)*

Bárbara says:

—Miguel, ¿me bajas aquel **saco**?
*Miguel, (will you) get down **that sweater** for me?*

> *Adjective **relates location** of the **noun** to a person.*

Demonstrative **pronouns** are used in place of the **adjective** and the **noun.** They are the same as the demonstrative adjectives except that they have an accent.

Masculine		Feminine	
Singular	**Plural**	**Singular**	**Plural**
éste *this one*	éstos *these*	ésta *this one*	éstas *these*
ése *that one*	ésos *those*	ésa *that one*	ésas *those*
aquél *that one (over there)*	aquéllos *those (over there)*	aquélla *that one (over there)*	aquéllas *those (over there)*

Bárbara might have said: —Miguel, ¿me bajas aquél que está arriba?
*Miguel, would you get down **that one** up there for me?*

There are also **demonstrative pronouns** that refer to ideas or unidentified things that do not have a specific gender.

Esto es importante.   ¿Qué es **eso**?   ¿Qué es **aquello**?
***This** is important.*   *What's **that**?*   *What's **that over there**?*

doscientos ochenta y nueve
Etapa 2
289

Teaching Middle School Students

Extra Help Use toy pigs or other classroom objects to illustrate the demonstrative adjectives in the grammar presentation. (Place a pig close to you, then farther from you, and then far away from you.)

Native Speakers Write sentences with demonstrative adjectives and pronouns without accent marks. Have students add the accent marks.

Multiple Intelligences

Verbal Write sentences with demonstrative adjectives and sentences with demonstrative pronouns on the board or on a handout. Have students identify the different types of demonstratives.

Vocabulary/Grammar

Quick Start Review

♻ Prepositions of location

Use OHT 192 or write on the board: Unscramble the following words to make logical sentences:

1. dentro / las / del / gallinas / corral / están
2. lejos / animales / los / llamas / que / están / son
3. cerca / está / gallo / encima / el / de / la
4. un / Patricia / gorro / abajo / de / quiere
5. corral / están / cerdos / los / del / fuera

Answers *See p. 275B.*

Teaching Suggestions
Presenting Pointing Out Specific Things Using Demonstratives

- Point out that demonstrative adjectives "demonstrate" which items you are talking about.
- Use gestures and demonstrative adjectives as you pick up items around the room and tell to whom they belong.
- Find 2 objects of the same category and use a demonstrative adjective to describe the first one, and a demonstrative pronoun for the second.

Teaching Note

You may want to teach students this mnemonic device for remembering the difference between **este** and **ese**: *"This* and *these* have the *t's."*

Block Schedule

Change of Pace Have pairs of students plan and present skits in which one person wants certain articles and the other person keeps giving the wrong ones. For example, a little child asking his/her mother for something, a customer asking for articles in a store, or a couch potato asking a friend to get everything he or she wants. (For additional activities, see **Block Scheduling Copymasters**.)

Teaching Resource Options

Print

Más práctica Workbook PE, p. 62
Para hispanohablantes Workbook
  PE, p. 60

Block Scheduling Copymasters
Unit 6 Resource Book
  Information Gap Activities, p. 68
  Más práctica Workbook TE, p. 57
  Para hispanohablantes Workbook
    TE, p. 63

Audiovisual

OHT 193 (Quick Start)

Technology

Intrigas y aventuras CD-ROM, Disc 1

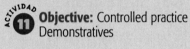**Objective:** Controlled practice
Demonstratives

Answers

1. esta
2. esa
3. este
4. aquel
5. esa
6. aquella

Quick Wrap-up

Display pairs of objects (or pictures of pairs of objects), placing one closer to the students than the other. Have students identify the objects then express a preference for one of them using a demonstrative. Example: **Son dos canastas. Me gusta esa canasta más que ésta.**

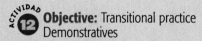**Objective:** Transitional practice
Demonstratives

Answers will vary.

En el mercado

Leer Patricia y Miguel están en el mercado. Completa sus oraciones con un adjetivo demostrativo. *(Hint: Complete what they say.)*

Patricia: ¿Te gusta __1__ bufanda amarilla?

Miguel: Prefiero __2__ bufanda blanca.

Patricia: ¿Y __3__ saco marrón?

Miguel: No es mi color favorito. Prefiero __4__ saco verde.

Patricia: Bueno, si te gusta el color verde, ¿por qué no compras __5__ mochila verde?

Miguel: La verdad es que prefiero __6__ mochila marrón.

Patricia: Ay, Miguel, ¡no te entiendo!

■ **MÁS PRÁCTICA** *cuaderno* p. 62
■ **PARA HISPANOHABLANTES** *cuaderno* p. 60

En la granja

Escribir Estás en una granja con unos amigos. Todos hablan de varios animales. Completa sus comentarios con un adjetivo demostrativo y una distancia apropiada. Usa las distancias **muy cerca, cerca** y **lejos**. *(Hint: Talk about the animals. Use a demonstrative adjective to tell whether they are very close, nearby, or far.)*

modelo

_____ cerdos son muy grandes.

Esos **cerdos son muy grandes.** *Están cerca.*

1. _____ gallinas comen mucho.
2. ¡Mira _____ llamas tan cómicas!
3. No me gusta _____ toro.
4. _____ caballos corren muy rápidamente.
5. _____ vaca es mi favorita. Se llama Verónica.
6. _____ gallo me despierta todas las mañanas ¡a las cinco!

También se dice

There are several words for *farm*.

• **la chacra:** many countries
• **la finca:** Colombia, Puerto Rico
• **la granja:** Argentina, Ecuador, Spain
• **la hacienda:** many countries
• **el rancho:** Mexico

---

290 doscientos noventa
Unidad 6

Middle School Classroom Community

Paired Activity Have students compare answers to **Actividades 11–12** before going over them with the class.

Portfolio Ask students: "If you could be an animal, which would you choose to be?" Once students decide, they should look up the word in a Spanish dictionary and then choose a way to express the idea: draw and label themselves; write about themselves as the animal; or even pantomime the animal.

Rubric

Criteria	Scale	
Creativity	1 2 3 4 5	A = 13–15 pts.
Logical organization	1 2 3 4 5	B = 10–12 pts.
Vocabulary use/spelling	1 2 3 4 5	C = 7–9 pts.
		D = 4–6 pts.
		F = < 4 pts.

Conexiones

Los estudios sociales One of farming's most important technologies emerged from the Incan civilization in Ecuador, a civilization of expert farmers. Most of the productive soil was in the steep Andes, so their crops were often devastated by mudslides during the rainy seasons. In order to reduce this devastation, they developed a system of farming on terraces (**los andenes**).

PARA HACER:
Draw a map of a terraced field using the crops given here. Label each terrace with an ordinal number.
- maíz
- batata
- papa
- calabaza
- mandioca

ACTIVIDAD 13

♻ Nuestras cosas

Hablar En grupos de tres personas, comparen las cosas que tiene cada persona. Usen estas palabras. *(Hint: Compare your things.)*

modelo

cuaderno(s)

*Esos **cuadernos** son más nuevos que éstos.*

sillas	libros	
		escritorios
plumas	borradores	
¿? mochilas		ropa

■ **MÁS COMUNICACIÓN** p. R8

GRAMÁTICA

Ordinal Numbers

▶ When you talk about the order of items, use ordinal numbers. At the right are the first ten ordinal numbers.

- When used with nouns, they must agree in number and gender.
- Ordinals are placed before **nouns**.
- Primer⊙ and tercer⊙ drop the ⊙ before a **masculine singular** noun.

primera segunda tercera cuarta quinta sexta séptima octava novena décima

Patricia asks: *before the noun*
—¿Cómo fueron sus primeros **años** aquí?
*How were your **first** years here?*

Bárbara might say: *drops the ⊙*
—Fue muy difícil hasta el tercer año.
*It was very difficult until the **third** year.*

▶ To say *last*, use último(a). La última vez que Miguel fue a Otavalo...
*The **last** time Miguel went to Otavalo...*

Teaching Middle School Students

Native Speakers Have students research former civilizations from their family's country of origin and be prepared to share their findings with the class.

Multiple Intelligences
Visual Suggest that students make a drawing or a diagram of the farm, showing the location of each kind of animal. They can use this as a visual aid for doing **Actividad 12**.

ACTIVIDAD 13
Objective: Open-ended practice Vocabulary/demonstratives

♻ **Comparatives**
Answers will vary.

Para hacer
Answers will vary, but check students' drawings for proper use of ordinal numbers.

🔔 Quick Start Review

♻ **Vocabulary review**
Use OHT 193 or write on the board: Write the word that does *not* belong with the other two words:

1. aquella   arriba   aquel
2. llama   cerdo   saco
3. fuera de   abajo   esto
4. caballo   taller   artesana
5. ésta   lana   aquélla

Answers *See p. 275B.*

Teaching Suggestions
Teaching Ordinal Numbers

Ask students what they know about adjectives. Write their responses and examples on the board. Point out that ordinal numbers are also adjectives and follow the same rules.

Block Schedule

Variety Divide the class into 3 or 4 groups. Assign each student in each group an ordinal number from 1–10. Then have groups come to the front of the class and, by talking among themselves, determine how to line up in order. Then have each student state his or her position. (For additional activities, see **Block Scheduling Copymasters**.)

Teaching Resource Options

Print

Más práctica Workbook PE, p. 63
Para hispanohablantes Workbook PE, p. 61
Block Scheduling Copymasters
Unit 6 Resource Book
  Más práctica Workbook TE, p. 58
  Para hispanohablantes Workbook TE, p. 64

Audiovisual
OHT 193 (Quick Start)

Technology
Intrigas y aventuras CD-ROM, Disc 1

 Objective: Controlled practice Ordinals

Answers
1. Felipe es el sexto.
2. Miguel es el primero.
3. Carlos es el quinto.
4. Antonio es el tercero.
5. Marta es la octava.
6. Ramona es la séptima.
7. Diego es el noveno.
8. Ana es la décima.
9. Linda es la cuarta.

 Objective: Transitional practice Ordinals

Answers
1. Elena fue la séptima chica en llegar.
2. Antonio fue el primer chico en llegar.
3. Ramón fue el tercer chico en llegar.
4. Linda fue la octava chica en llegar.
5. Carlos fue el décimo chico en llegar.
6. Miguel fue el cuarto chico en llegar.
7. Marta fue la sexta chica en llegar.
8. Alfredo fue el noveno chico en llegar.
9. Diego fue el quinto chico en llegar.

 Objective: Open-ended practice Ordinals/preterite

Answers will vary.

Quick Wrap-up

Write 10 activities that your students commonly do. Be sure there is a blend of fun and not-so-fun items (**jugar al béisbol, hacer la tarea, nadar,** etc.). As you point to each one, have students show their interest or lack of interest in it by a show of hands. Write the number of hands raised after each activity. Finally, have students order from **primero** to **décimo** the popularity of each activity.

 **Gramática**

El orden

Hablar Patricia está con un grupo de amigos. Hacen cola para ver una película. Tú le preguntas a tu amigo(a) quiénes son. *(Hint: Ask who they are.)*

modelo

Patricia

Tú: *¿Quién es **Patricia**?*

Tu amigo(a): *Ella es la segunda.*

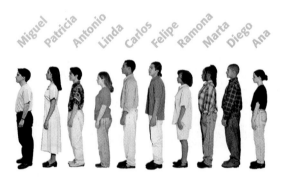

1. Felipe
2. Miguel
3. Carlos
4. Antonio
5. Marta
6. Ramona
7. Diego
8. Ana
9. Linda

■ **MÁS PRÁCTICA** *cuaderno* p. 63
■ **PARA HISPANOHABLANTES** *cuaderno* p. 61

 15

¿Quién llegó primero?

Hablar/Escribir Patricia y sus amigos participaron en una carrera. ¿En qué orden llegaron? *(Hint: Give their order in the race.)*

modelo

Patricia: 2   ***Patricia** fue la **segunda** chica en llegar.*

1. Elena: 7
2. Antonio: 1
3. Ramón: 3
4. Linda: 8
5. Carlos: 10
6. Miguel: 4
7. Marta: 6
8. Alfredo: 9
9. Diego: 5

 16

Las vacaciones

Escribir Piensa en unas vacaciones memorables. Explica en qué día hiciste las cosas. *(Hint: What did you do on each day of your vacation?)*

modelo

El primer día mis tíos y yo llegamos en avión a Quito...
El segundo día fui a un museo.

1. primero(a)
2. segundo(a)
3. tercero(a)
4. cuarto(a)
5. quinto(a)
6. último(a)

ir al campo

visitar a los amigos

nadar en la piscina

pescar en el lago

cenar en el restaurante

ir de compras

descansar

Middle School Classroom Community

TPR Divide the class into large groups and have students quickly line up in order of height. Call out ordinal numbers and ask students in those positions to move to a new position in line.

Group Activity Have small groups work together to write questions with the preterite of all the verbs mentioned on page 293. Groups then swap questions with other groups to answer.

GRAMÁTICA

Irregular Preterite Verbs

You've learned that **hacer, ir,** and **ser** are irregular in the preterite. Here are some other irregular preterite verbs. Notice that the forms for **dar** are similar to **ver. Decir** and **venir** have their own special forms.

dar *to give*

di	dimos
diste	disteis
dio	dieron

decir *to say, to tell*

dije	dijimos
dijiste	dijisteis
dijo	dijeron

venir *to come*

vine	vinimos
viniste	vinisteis
vino	vinieron

Although the verbs **tener** and **estar** have irregular endings in the preterite, their forms follow similar patterns.

tener *to have*

tuve	tuvimos
tuviste	tuvisteis
tuvo	tuvieron

estar *to be*

estuve	estuvimos
estuviste	estuvisteis
estuvo	estuvieron

Bárbara says:

—**Vine** en el año 1990.
I came in 1990.

—**Tuvimos** que trabajar muchísimo.
We had to work a whole lot.

—**Estuvimos** ahí el domingo pasado.
We were there last Sunday.

Estar is never used in the preterite to express feelings.

Todos ayudaron en la granja

Escribir Hay muchos animales en la granja del tío Julio. Muchas personas lo ayudaron con el trabajo. ¿A qué animales les dieron de comer cada persona? *(Hint: Which animals did they feed?)*

modelo

Patricia: los cerdos

Patricia les dio de comer a los cerdos.

Nota

The expression **darle(s) de comer** means *to feed.*

Les di de comer a mis gatos.
I fed my cats.

---

1. yo: el toro
2. ustedes: los gatos
3. Miguel: las llamas
4. tú: el gallo
5. mi hija: los caballos
6. mis hijos y yo: las vacas

MÁS PRÁCTICA *cuaderno* p. 64

PARA HISPANOHABLANTES
cuaderno p. 62

Objective: Transitional practice
Preterite of **venir, tener**

Answers
1. ¿Por qué vinieron Juan y Jorge?
   Juan y Jorge vinieron porque tuvieron que estudiar.
2. ¿Por qué viniste tú?
   Vine porque tuve que usar la computadora.
3. ¿Por qué vino Felipe?
   Felipe vino porque tuvo que hacer su tarea.
4. ¿Por qué vinieron tu hermana y tú?
   Vinimos porque tuvimos que buscar un libro sobre los indios quechua.
5. ¿Por qué vino Enrique?
   Enrique vino porque tuvo que leer el periódico.
6. ¿Por qué vinieron Carlos y Alicia?
   Carlos y Alicia vinieron porque tuvieron que alquilar unos videos.
7. ¿Por qué vinimos Elena y yo?
   Elena y tú vinieron porque tuvieron que devolver un libro.
8. ¿Por qué vino el señor Martínez?
   El señor Martínez vino porque tuvo que trabajar por la tarde.

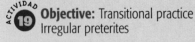 **Objective:** Transitional practice
Irregular preterites

Answers will vary.

En la biblioteca

Hablar Muchos amigos están en la biblioteca hoy. Con otro(a) estudiante, háganse preguntas. *(Hint: Ask why everybody came to the library today.)*

modelo

Ana (leer un libro)

Estudiante A: *¿Por qué vino **Ana**?*

Estudiante B: ***Ana** vino porque tuvo que **leer un libro**.*

1. Juan y Jorge (estudiar)
2. tú (usar la computadora)
3. Felipe (hacer su tarea)
4. tu hermana y tú (buscar un libro sobre los indios quechua)
5. Enrique (leer el periódico)
6. Carlos y Alicia (alquilar unos videos)
7. Elena y yo (devolver un libro)
8. el señor Martínez (trabajar por la tarde)

294 | doscientos noventa y cuatro
Unidad 6

Un día ocupado

Escribir Ayer fue un día ocupado. Describe lo que hicieron estas personas. *(Hint: Describe what these people did yesterday.)*

darle de comer a un cerdo   ir de compras

ir a una fiesta de cumpleaños

decir algo importante

estar en una tienda de ropa

tener un buen día

sacar la basura

empezar a leer un libro

hacer un viaje al campo

ver una película cómica

estar en la oficina de la contadora

modelo

Miguel

***Miguel** tuvo un buen día.*

1. mis padres
2. tú
3. Ana y yo
4. ustedes
5. Julio
6. yo
7. nosotros
8. Amelia
9. mi padre
10. la mujer de negocios

ACTIVIDAD 20

Un día bonito

Escuchar Escucha el párrafo sobre el viaje que hizo Luisa. Luego ordena las fotos según lo que escuchaste. *(Hint: Listen to the paragraph. Then put the photographs in order.)*

a.

b.

c.

d.

ACTIVIDAD 21

¡Qué bien lo pasé!

Escribir Escribe un párrafo sobre un viaje real o imaginario que hiciste. Usa las preguntas como ayuda. *(Hint: Write a paragraph about a trip you once took.)*

- ¿Adónde fuiste?
- ¿Qué hiciste?
- ¿Oíste música? ¿Qué tipo? ¿Te gustó?
- ¿Con quiénes fuiste?
- ¿Qué viste?
- ¿Cuánto tiempo estuviste allí?
- ¿Qué les dijiste a tus amigos cuando los viste?

■ **MÁS COMUNICACIÓN** p. R8

Pronunciación

Trabalenguas

Pronunciación de la *l* The letter *l* is pronounced like the *l* in the English word *lucky.* Practice its sound by saying this tongue twister.

Lana, Lena, Lina y Lulú
van y ven al león con el balón.
Al león con el balón ven
Lana, Lena, Lina y Lulú.

doscientos noventa y cinco
Etapa 2 **295**

Teaching Middle School Students

Extra Help Assign 2 "pet" verbs per night. Students master the forms and write samples for each. This will make the effort required when dealing with the irregular preterites seem less daunting.

Multiple Intelligences

Interpersonal Have students turn to a partner and tell 3 things they had to do yesterday.

Intrapersonal Have students write what they did yesterday in chronological order. Ask them to begin with the time they woke up and include lots of detail.

ACTIVIDAD 20

Objective: Transitional practice
Listening comprehension/vocabulary/preterite tense

Answers (See script, p. 275B.)
1. d
2. a
3. c
4. b

ACTIVIDAD 21

Objective: Open-ended practice
Vocabulary/preterite tense

Answers will vary.

Dictation

After students have read the tongue twister in the **Pronunciación,** have them close their books. Dictate the tongue twister in segments while students write it.

■ Block Schedule

FunBreak Prepare ahead: sets of 12–15 cards with a variety of past actions, using the **yo** form of the verb, written on them. (Be sure to use known preterite forms.) Students work in teams of 5–6. Give each team a set of cards. One team member selects a card and has 1 minute to draw the activity on the board while the team guesses, using the **tú** form of the verb. (For additional activities, see **Block Scheduling Copymasters.**)

Teaching Resource Options

Print

Unit 6 Resource Book
  Audioscript, p. 81
  Audioscript *Para hispanohablantes,*
  p. 82

Audiovisual

Audio Program Cassette 17A / CD 17
Audio *Para hispanohablantes*
Cassette 17A / CD 17
OHT 193 (Quick Start)
Video Program Videotape 6 /
Videodisc 3B

Search Chapter 6, Play to 7
U6E2 • En colores (Culture)

Quick Start Review

♻ **El mercado**

Use OHT 193 or write on the board:
Write at least 5 words or expressions
that you associate with **el mercado.**

Answers
Answers will vary. Answers could include:
la artesanía, regatear, el (la) vendedor(a),
el precio, ¿Cuánto cuesta(n)...?, ¡Es muy
caro!, Le puede ofrecer...

Teaching Suggestions
**Presenting Cultura y
comparaciones**

• Begin by asking students to compare
  the photos on pp. 296–297 and
  make 2 observations for each.
• Have students complete the Strategy
  task. Have several students present
  their questions.
• Expand the cultural information by
  showing the video culture presentation.

Reading Strategy

Recognize place names Have students
identify the following place names by
looking for words nearby that explain what
they are: **Imbabura y Cotacachi, Otavalo,
Peguche, Carabuela.**

En colores
CULTURA Y
COMPARACIONES

LOS OTAVALEÑOS

PARA CONOCERNOS
**STRATEGY:
CONNECTING CULTURES**

Research cultural groups The term
indigenous people is used to refer
to the original or native
inhabitants of a region. Who
were or are the indigenous
people where you live? When
researching, make sure to ask
the five W questions: who?,
what?, when?, where?, and
why? Make up five research
questions about the original
people of your area, using
these words as prompts.

¿Quién?	
¿Qué?	
¿Cuándo?	
¿Dónde?	
¿Por qué?	

Use these questions to gather
information as you read
«Los otavaleños».

Si sales de Quito por la Carretera Panamericana[1] hacia el norte
del país, vas a ver un paisaje[2] impresionante. Hay espléndidas
vistas de montañas, volcanes y lagos. Entre Quito y la frontera[3]
con Colombia hay un valle entre las montañas Imbabura y
Cotacachi. Allí queda el pueblo de Otavalo.

Aquí viven los otavaleños. Este grupo indígena se conoce[4]
por su artesanía, su éxito[5] económico y la preservación de sus
costumbres folclóricas. Los sábados, los otavaleños organizan un
mercado tradicional. Hay frutas y verduras, animales y lo más
interesante para los turistas: tejidos[6] y artesanías. En este mercado

---

[1] Pan-American Highway   [3] border   [5] success
[2] landscape   [4] is known   [6] textiles

296 doscientos noventa y seis
Unidad 6

Middle School Classroom Community

Paired Activity Before reading the essay, have
pairs discuss what they already know about markets
in Spanish-speaking countries.

Cooperative Learning Divide the class into 4
groups. Each group is responsible for telling the class
about one of the paragraphs. Groups become experts
and then ask other groups content questions about
their paragraphs.

puedes comprar ponchos, chompas y tapices de lana hechos[7] por los otavaleños. Los otavaleños también venden sombreros hechos a medida[8]. Como en todo mercado, ¡es importante regatear!

Hacer tejidos es una tradición de los indígenas de Otavalo. En 1917 empezaron a imitar los casimires[9] ingleses y así nació[10] la industria textil. Las personas que hacen los tejidos son de Otavalo y los pueblos cercanos, como Peguche, Ilumán, Carabuela y Quinchuqui.

Si visitas Otavalo, debes conocer la Plaza Bolívar, donde está la estatua del general inca Rumiñahui. También puedes aprender un poco de la historia y la arqueología de esta región en el Instituto Otavaleño de Antropología.

[7] made
[8] custom-made
[9] tweeds
[10] was born

Ropa tradicional otavaleña

¿Comprendiste?

1. ¿Dónde queda Otavalo? ¿Cómo llegas?
2. ¿Qué importancia tiene Otavalo?
3. ¿Qué cosas venden en el mercado de Otavalo?
4. ¿Cómo y cuándo empezó la industria textil?
5. ¿Qué lugares puedes conocer en Otavalo?

¿Qué piensas?

1. ¿Por qué debes regatear si visitas Otavalo?
2. ¿Qué puedes hacer para aprender más de la vida de los otavaleños de hoy?

Hazlo tú

¿Hay artesanos en tu comunidad? Explica qué hacen. Si no hay, investiga alguna artesanía de Estados Unidos y haz un reportaje sobre esto.

doscientos noventa y siete
Etapa 2
297

Culture Highlights

● **LA RUTA DE LOS VOLCANES** The Cordillera de los Andes passes across Ecuador. This mountain chain has the most concentrated area of active volcanoes in the world. It includes 2 parallel mountain chains, 1 eastern and 1 western. The valleys formed between them have fertile soil.

Cross Cultural Connections

Ask students to compare the market in Otavalo with shopping places in the U.S.: outdoor markets, supermarkets, shopping malls. How do they compare in terms of physical layout and what goes on at each one?

Interdisciplinary Connections

Economics Have students choose one traditional craft and try to name and calculate the costs involved in it: for example, equipment, supplies, packaging, etc.

¿Comprendiste?

Answers

1. Queda entre Quito y la frontera con Colombia, en un valle entre las montañas Imbabura y Cotacachi. Llegas por la Carretera Panamericana.
2. Otavalo se conoce por su artesanía, su éxito económico y la preservación de sus costumbres folclóricas. Tiene un mercado tradicional.
3. Venden frutas y verduras, animales, tejidos y artesanías.
4. Empezó en 1917 cuando los indígenas de Otavalo empezaron a imitar los casimires ingleses.
5. Puedes conocer la Plaza Bolívar y el Instituto Otavaleño de Antropología.

■ Block Schedule

Research Have students visit local stores or on-line stores that sell international crafts. Have them list all the items from Spanish-speaking countries, the countries of origin, and the prices. Compile a list of items in class. Is there any one kind of item that is more prevalent than others?

Teaching Resource Options

Print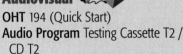

Para hispanohablantes Workbook
PE, pp. 95–96
Block Scheduling Copymasters
Unit 6 Resource Book
Para hispanohablantes Workbook
TE, pp. 66–67
Information Gap Activities,
p. 71
Family Involvement, pp. 72–73
Multiple Choice Test Questions,
pp. 170–178

Audiovisual

OHT 194 (Quick Start)
Audio Program Testing Cassette T2 /
CD T2

Technology
Electronic Teacher Tools/Test
Generator
Intrigas y aventuras CD-ROM, Disc 1

Quick Start Review

♻ **Vocabulary and preterite review**

Use OHT 194 or write on the board:
Write 3 sentences saying what Miguel's
Uncle Julio did this morning.

Answers
Answers will vary. Answers could include:
Cuidó las vacas.
Les dio de comer a las gallinas.
Visitó a Bárbara en su taller.
Habló con el pastor.
Le dio de comer al caballo.

Teaching Suggestions
What Have Students Learned?

• Have students look at the "Now you can…" notes listed on the left side of pages 298–299. Tell students to think about which areas they might not be sure of. For those areas, they should consult the "To review" notes.
• Use the video to review vocabulary and structures.

ETAPA **2**

En uso

REPASO Y MÁS COMUNICACIÓN

Now you can…
• tell where things are located.

To review
• location words, see p. 286.

ACTIVIDAD 1 En el campo

Imagínate que estás en el campo. ¿Qué ves? *(Hint: Tell what you see in the country.)*

modelo

dentro del corral, con los cerdos
*El ganadero está **dentro del corral, con los cerdos.***

1. debajo del árbol
2. arriba, con las llamas
3. encima de la cerca
4. abajo
5. fuera de su casa
6. dentro del corral, con el ganadero

ACTIVIDAD 2 ¿En qué carro?

Estas personas participaron en una carrera. ¿En qué carro manejó cada uno? *(Hint: Say who drove what car in the race.)*

modelo

Campos: 4
***Campos** manejó el cuarto carro.*

1. Molina: 2
2. Anaya: 7
3. Valencia: 9
4. Ibarra: 1
5. Quintana: 5
6. Blanco: 10
7. Rojas: 8
8. Espinoza: 3
9. Santana: 6

Now you can…
• point out specific people and things.

To review
• ordinal numbers, see p. 291.

Middle School Classroom Community

Paired Activity For further practice with location words, hand out instruction cards to pairs of students **(La gallina está encima del taller).** Students take turns selecting a card and instructing their partners to draw the picture described on the card. Students check each other's work.

Storytelling Bring or have students bring pictures of farm scenes to class. Groups tell stories about the scenes to the class.

¿Quiénes son?

Hay una fiesta de disfraces hoy. ¿Quiénes son estas personas?
(Hint: Identify the people at the costume party.)

modelo
_____
maestra   Esa mujer es **maestra**.

1. policías   4. periodista   7. mujeres de negocios
2. fotógrafa   5. cartero   8. doctor
3. bomberos   6. taxista

Un día especial

Patricia se encuentra con una amiga en Otavalo. Completa lo
que dice con la forma correcta de los verbos **dar, decir, estar,
tener** o **venir.** *(Hint: Complete Patricia's story of her day in Otavalo with the correct form of the verb.)*

Hoy Miguel y yo __1__ en el campo toda la mañana. Yo __2__
tiempo de hacer algunas entrevistas para mi proyecto. Los
parientes de Miguel me __3__ muchas cosas interesantes sobre
la vida en el campo. El tío Julio también me __4__ algunas cosas
cómicas sobre Miguel. Al final de la entrevista con Bárbara, ella
me __5__ un regalo: este saco bonito. Después de la segunda
entrevista, el tío Julio y su esposa nos __6__ de comer. Luego
nosotros __7__ aquí a Otavalo.

doscientos noventa y nueve
Etapa 2
299

Now you can...
• point out specific
  people and things.

To review
• demonstratives, see
  p. 289.

Now you can...
• talk about the past.

To review
• irregular preterite
  verbs, see p. 293.

Answers

1. Las gallinas están debajo del árbol.
2. El pastor está arriba, con las llamas.
3. El gallo está encima de la cerca.
4. Las vacas están abajo.
5. El perro está fuera de su casa.
6. Los cerdos están dentro del corral, con el ganadero.

Answers

1. Molina manejó el segundo carro.
2. Anaya manejó el séptimo carro.
3. Valencia manejó el noveno carro.
4. Ibarra manejó el primer carro.
5. Quintana manejó el quinto carro.
6. Blanco manejó el décimo carro.
7. Rojas manejó el octavo carro.
8. Espinoza manejó el tercer carro.
9. Santana manejó el sexto carro.

Answers

1. Estas mujeres son policías.
2. Aquella mujer es fotógrafa.
3. Esos hombres son bomberos.
4. Este hombre es periodista.
5. Aquel hombre es cartero.
6. Este hombre es taxista.
7. Aquellas mujeres son mujeres de negocios.
8. Ese hombre es doctor.

Answers

1. estuvimos
2. tuve
3. dijeron
4. dijo
5. dio
6. dieron
7. vinimos

Teaching Middle School Students

Challenge Have ready, or ask students to bring to
class, pictures that show people doing things in the
foreground and background. Students write or tell five
things about the people pictured, using demonstrative
adjectives. Students must come up with descriptions in
a given time limit.

Multiple Intelligences

Interpersonal Have pairs work together with flash
cards to practice conjugating the irregular preterite
verbs **dar**, **decir**, **estar**, **tener**, and **venir**.

■ Block Schedule

Change of Pace Have students act out
the general scene in **Actividad 3** in
groups of 8–9. One student plays a TV
commentator, introduces the various
professionals, and asks each one a few
questions. You may wish to videotape
the activity. (For additional activities, see
Block Scheduling Copymasters.)

Teaching Resource Options

Print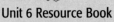

Unit 6 Resource Book
Cooperative Quizzes, pp. 84–85
Etapa Exam, Forms A and B,
  pp. 86–95
Para hispanohablantes Etapa Exam,
  pp. 96–100
Portfolio Assessment, pp. 101–102
Multiple Choice Test Questions,
  pp. 170–178

Audiovisual

OHT 194 (Quick Start)
Audio Program Testing Cassette T2 /
CD T2

Technology

Electronic Teacher Tools/Test
Generator

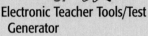 www.mcdougallittell.com

Rubric: Speaking

Criteria	Scale	
Sentence structure	1 2 3 4 5	A = 17–20 pts.
Vocabulary use	1 2 3 4 5	B = 13–16 pts.
Originality	1 2 3 4 5	C = 9–12 pts.
Fluency	1 2 3 4 5	D = 5–8 pts.
		F = < 5 pts.

 Answers will vary.

 En tu propia voz

Rubric: Writing

Criteria	Scale	
Vocabulary use	1 2 3 4 5	A = 13–15 pts.
Accuracy	1 2 3 4 5	B = 10–12 pts.
Creativity, appearance	1 2 3 4 5	C = 7–9 pts.
		D = 4–6 pts.
		F = < 4 pts.

Teaching Note: En tu propia voz

Suggest that students first brainstorm a list
of events, then make a list of the months
of the year. This way they can implement
the writing strategy "Organize information
chronologically and by category" by
putting each event next to the appropriate
month.

 **¿Y aquel caballo?**

> **PARA CONVERSAR**
> **STRATEGY: SPEAKING**
> **Use words that direct others' attention** You now
> have many ways to indicate one person,
> animal, or object among several. Remember
> to use them all.
> • Indicate location (**al lado de,** etc.).
> • Indicate order (**el segundo, el último**).
> • Indicate distance (**este, ese, aquel**).

Imagínate que tienes dos mil dólares para
comprar animales de la granja de un(a)
ganadero(a). Regatea para recibir el mejor
precio. *(Hint: You have $2000 to buy farm animals. Bargain
for the best prices.)*

modelo

Tú: *¿Cuánto cuesta aquella vaca?*

Ganadero(a): *Aquélla es muy buena. Da mucha leche.
Cuesta mil dólares.*

Tú: *¡Es demasiado! Le puedo ofrecer ochocientos.*

Ganadero(a): *No puedo vender aquélla por menos de
novecientos, pero le dejo esta vaca más
pequeña en setecientos.*

Tú: *Está bien. ¿Y ese cerdo que está en el corral?…*

 **¿Dónde está?**

Tus amigos buscan algo en la clase. Sólo
tú sabes qué es y dónde está. Contesta sus
preguntas. *(Hint: Your friends are looking for something
in the classroom. Only you know what and where it is. Answer
their questions.)*

modelo

Estudiante A: *¿Está encima del escritorio de la maestra?*

Tú: *No, no está encima del escritorio de la maestra.*

Estudiante B: *¿Está dentro de tu mochila?*

Tú: *Sí, está dentro de mi mochila.*

Estudiante C: *¿Es tu libro de inglés?*

Tú: *Sí, es mi libro de inglés.*

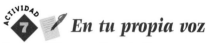 **En tu propia voz**

Escritura Haz una lista de diez cosas que
pasaron en la escuela este año. Pon los sucesos
en orden cronológico y escribe oraciones
explicando cada uno. *(Hint: List in chronological order
and explain ten things that happened at school this year.)*

modelo

*Primero, las clases comenzaron en agosto y todos los
estudiantes vinieron a la escuela. Segundo, tuvimos que
aprender los nombres de los estudiantes en español
durante la primera semana de clases. Tercero, en octubre…*

Conexiones

Las ciencias Choose an animal whose name
you've learned, such as the **llama,** or find out the
Spanish name for another animal that is found in Ecuador.
(**Vicuñas** and **alpacas** are close relatives of the **llama.**)
Do some research on the animal. Draw a picture of it
and write a short paragraph that answers the questions
in the chart.

¿Cómo es el animal?
¿De qué color(es) es?
¿Dónde vive?
¿Qué come?
¿Es útil para la gente? ¿Para qué?

300 trescientos
Unidad 6

Middle School Classroom Community

TPR Have students position their bodies according to
commands with location words: **Pon el pie encima del
escritorio. Ve al lado de la puerta. Ve a la derecha
del pizarrón. Pon las manas debajo del escritorio.**

Storytelling Have students tell a continuing story
that links the animals in the **Conexiones** together.

Game Play Hangman with the **Etapa** vocabulary.

En resumen

REPASO DE VOCABULARIO

POINTING OUT SPECIFIC PEOPLE AND THINGS

Indicating Which One

aquel(la)	*that (over there)*
aquél(la)	*that one (over there)*
aquello	*that (over there)*
ese(a)	*that*
ése(a)	*that one*
eso	*that*
este(a)	*this*
éste(a)	*this one*
esto	*this*

Ordinal Numbers

primero(a)	*first*
segundo(a)	*second*
tercero(a)	*third*
cuarto(a)	*fourth*
quinto(a)	*fifth*
sexto(a)	*sixth*
séptimo(a)	*seventh*
octavo(a)	*eighth*
noveno(a)	*ninth*
décimo(a)	*tenth*

People

el (la) artesano(a)	*artisan*
el (la) ganadero(a)	*farmer*
el (la) pastor(a)	*shepherd(ess)*

At the Farm

el caballo	*horse*
la cerca	*fence*
el cerdo	*pig*
el corral	*corral, pen*
la gallina	*hen*
el gallo	*rooster*
la granja	*farm*
la llama	*llama*
el toro	*bull*
la vaca	*cow*

TELLING WHERE THINGS ARE LOCATED

abajo	*down*
arriba	*up*
debajo (de)	*underneath, under*
dentro (de)	*inside (of)*
encima (de)	*on top (of)*
fuera (de)	*outside (of)*

OTHER WORDS AND PHRASES

el campo	*countryside, country*
darle(s) de comer	*to feed*
la lana	*wool*
el taller	*workshop*
las tijeras	*scissors*
último(a)	*last*

Juego

¿En qué orden terminaron la carrera?

trescientos uno
Etapa 2 **301**

Teaching Middle School Students

Extra Help Quiz students on vocabulary. For "Ordinal Numbers," hold up some fingers and point to one, asking for its order. For "People" and "At the Farm," show pictures of toys. For "Telling Where Things Are Located," point to things in the classroom.

Multiple Intelligences

Kinesthetic You might set up a station where students can mold farm animals and farm scenes out of clay, while reviewing **Etapa** vocabulary.

Naturalist Have students research and report on the many exotic animals found off the coast of Ecuador on the Galápagos Islands.

Interdisciplinary Connection

Science Have students do research on the potato, a staple of the Ecuadoran diet. They should first write appropriate variations of the 5 questions in the **Conexiones.** The research should provide answers to these questions, as well as the nutritional value of the potato.

Quick Start Review

♻ **Etapa** vocabulary

Use OHT 194 or write on the board: Choose 5 new vocabulary words from this **Etapa** and write a short paragraph using the words.

Answers will vary.

Teaching Suggestions
Vocabulary Review
Divide the class into groups of 3–4. See how many sentences students can make using 3 vocabulary words per sentence.

Juego

Answers
1. El cerdo fue primero.
2. La llama fue segunda.
3. La vaca fue tercera.

Block Schedule

Variety **Prepare ahead:** Cut out pictures from magazines, trying to find several with farm animals in them. You should have enough pictures so that each group in class has 5 pictures. Divide the class into groups of 4. Give each group 5 pictures. Students must try to tie all the pictures together in a story. They should paste the pictures on a posterboard and present the visual and the story to the class.

Planning Guide CLASSROOM MANAGEMENT

OBJECTIVES

Communication
- Talk about the present and future *pp. 304–305*
- Give instructions to someone *pp. 305, 306–307*
- Discuss the past *pp. 305, 306–307, 324–325*

Grammar
- Review: Present progressive and **ir a...** *pp. 312–313*
- Review: Affirmative **tú** commands *pp. 314–315*
- Review: Preterite tense *pp. 315–319*

Pronunciation
- Pronunciation of **x** *p. 321*
- Dictation *TE p. 321*

Culture
- Regional vocabulary *p. 309*
- The Pan-American Highway *p. 311*
- **Maracas** and **claves** *p. 317*
- The habitats of Ecuador *p. 320*

♻ **Recycling**
- Text vocabulary *p. 309*
- Clothing vocabulary *p. 310*
- Activities *p. 310*
- Family, daily routine, preferences *p. 311*

STRATEGIES

Listening Strategies
- Listen and take notes *p. 306*

Speaking Strategies
- Use storytelling techniques *p. 313*
- Rely on the basics *p. 328*

Reading Strategies
- Use pictures *p. 322*
- Combine strategies *TE p. 325*

Writing Strategies
- Tell who, what, where, when, why, and how *TE p. 328*

Connecting Cultures Strategies
- Recognize variations in vocabulary *p. 309*
- Get to know Ecuador *p. 320*
- Connect and compare what you know about foods that are regularly part of your diet to help you learn about foods from other countries *pp. 324–325, 328*

PROGRAM RESOURCES

 Print
- *Más práctica* Workbook PE *pp. 65–72*
- Block Scheduling Copymasters *pp. 145–152*
- Unit 6 Resource Book
  Más práctica Workbook TE *pp. 103–110*
  Information Gap Activities *pp. 119–122*
- Family Involvement *pp. 123–124*
- Video Activities *pp. 125–127*
- Videoscript *pp. 128–130*
- Audioscript *pp. 131–134*
- Assessment Program, Unit 6 Etapa 3 *pp. 135–186*
- Answer Keys *pp. 187–202*

 Audiovisual
- **Audio Program** Cassettes 18A, 18B / CD 18
- *Canciones* Cassette / CD
- **Video Program** Videotape 6 / Videodisc 3B
- **Overhead Transparencies** M1–M5; GO1–GO5; 174, 195–204

 Technology
- Electronic Teacher Tools/Test Generator
- *Intrigas y aventuras* CD-ROM, Disc 1
- www.mcdougallittell.com

 Assessment Program Options
- **Cooperative Quizzes** (Unit 6 Resource Book)
- **Etapa Exam** Forms A and B (Unit 6 Resource Book)
- *Para hispanohablantes* **Etapa Exam** (Unit 6 Resource Book)
- **Portfolio Assessment** (Unit 6 Resource Book)
- **Unit 6 Comprehensive Test** (Unit 6 Resource Book)
- *Para hispanohablantes* **Unit 6 Comprehensive Test** (Unit 6 Resource Book)
- **Final Test** (Unit 6 Resource Book)
- **Multiple Choice Test Questions** (Unit 6 Resource Book)
- **Audio Program** Testing Cassette T2 / CD T2
- **Electronic Teacher Tools/Test Generator**

Native Speakers
- *Para hispanohablantes* Workbook PE, *pp. 65–72*
- *Para hispanohablantes* Workbook TE (Unit 6 Resource Book)
- *Para hispanohablantes* Etapa Exam (Unit 6 Resource Book)
- *Para hispanohablantes* Unit 6 Comprehensive Test (Unit 6 Resource Book)
- Audio *Para hispanohablantes* Cassettes 18A, 18B, T2 / CD 18, T2
- Audioscript *Para hispanohablantes* (Unit 6 Resource Book)

Patricia

Miguel

Student Text
Listening Activity Scripts

 Videoscript: Diálogo *pages 306–307*

• Videotape 6 • Videodisc 3B

Search Chapter 8, Play to 9
U6E3 • En vivo (Dialog)

• Use the videoscript with **Actividades 1, 2** *pages 308–309*

Miguel: ¿Y estás feliz con tus entrevistas?
Patricia: Sí, estoy muy feliz. Hice entrevistas con un arquitecto, la gerente de un banco, un hombre de negocios, un taxista y también con tu tío Julio y Bárbara.
Miguel: ¿Cuál fue la mejor entrevista?
Patricia: No sé... Creo que fue la entrevista con tu tío Julio.
Miguel: ¿Y por qué? ¿Porque te habló de la vida en una granja?
Patricia: No, porque me dijo qué hiciste tú la primera vez que estuviste en la granja.
Miguel: ¡Patricia!... ¿Y aprendiste algo de tus entrevistas?
Patricia: Sí, mucho. Sobre todo aprendí que la gente que vive en el campo no es tan diferente de la gente que vive en la ciudad. Es sólo el estilo de vida que es diferente. ¡A cada pájaro le gusta su nido! Pero aprendí algo mucho más importante también...
Miguel: ¿Sí? Dime.
Patricia: Aprendí que no tienes ni idea de lo que hay que hacer en una granja. ¡Abriste la cerca del corral! ¡Mira, Miguel! ¡Es un mercado fenomenal! Voy a comprarle un regalo a mi hermana. Su cumpleaños es el veintidós de este mes.
Miguel: Cómprale una bolsa o un artículo de cuero. La artesanía de Otavalo es excelente.
Patricia: No sé si tengo suficiente dinero... a ver... tengo 40 mil sucres en efectivo. ¿Crees que puedo regatear aquí?
Miguel: ¡Claro que sí! Es un mercado, ¿no? ¡Ven! ¿Cuándo mandas tu proyecto a la revista?
Patricia: Después del fin de semana. Todavía tengo que escribir mucho.
Miguel: Hazme un favor... ¿Puedo leerlo antes?
Patricia: ¿Por qué?
Miguel: ¿Por qué? ¡Porque creo que va a salir muy bien y lo quiero ver!
Patricia: ¿Crees que va a salir bien? Gracias, Miguel. Eres un buen amigo.
Miguel: Y también...
Patricia: ¿Sí?
Miguel: ¡Quiero ver si escribiste algo de mi experiencia con la cerca y el caballo!
Patricia: Hice todo lo posible. Trabajé mucho. Espero tener buena suerte.

 Videoscript: Epílogo *page 302 (optional, p. 321)*

• Videotape 6 • Videodisc 3B

Search Chapter 9, Play to 10
Epilogue

¡Por fin! Recibí mi copia de *Onda Internacional.* Vamos a ver quiénes ganaron el concurso... a ver... aquí. Ah, yo no gané. Qué lástima. ¿Pero quieren saber ustedes quiénes ganaron? ¡Hay dos ganadores! Un muchacho... y una muchacha. El muchacho se llama Francisco García Flores... y ¡es de Miami, Florida! Francisco va a viajar a Puerto Rico y a Costa Rica. La muchacha se llama Isabel Palacios... ¡y es de la Ciudad de México! Isabel va a viajar a España y a Ecuador. ¡Felicidades, Francisco e Isabel!

 **ACTIVIDAD 5** **Las actividades** *page 310*

1. Alma escribe.
2. Ricardo juega al baloncesto.
3. Isabel lee una revista.
4. Iván cocina algo riquísimo.
5. Diana e Ignacio alquilan un video.
6. Patricia hace una entrevista.
7. Luis se peina.
8. Ignacio y Diana van de compras.
9. Rosa, Sofía y Carlos piden la comida.
10. Luis y Carmen limpian la casa.

ACTIVIDAD 19 **Un buen fin de semana** *page 318*

María: ¡Hola, Rosa! ¿Qué hiciste el fin de semana?
Rosa: Fui al campo para visitar a mis abuelos.
María: ¿Cómo fue?
Rosa: Pues, fenomenal. Me gusta mucho ir al campo.
María: ¿Qué hiciste?
Rosa: Pues, llegué a la granja el viernes a las ocho y media. Cenamos a las nueve.
María: ¿Y el sábado?
Rosa: El sábado me levanté a las siete. Después de desayunar, ayudé a mi abuelo a darles de comer a las gallinas. ¡Qué cómicas fueron las gallinas y qué ruido hicieron!
María: Y por la tarde, ¿qué hiciste?
Rosa: Fui al mercado con mi prima.
María: ¿Viste cosas interesantes?
Rosa: Sí, vi un saco que me gustó mucho.
María: ¿Lo compraste?
Rosa: No. Me encontré con una amiga y salimos a tomar un refresco.
María: ¡Qué divertido! ¿Y qué hicieron esa noche?
Rosa: No hicimos nada especial. Vi la televisión, leí una revista y me acosté temprano. Fue un fin de semana muy tranquilo.
María: ¿Cuándo vas a volver?
Rosa: Mi madre dijo que vamos a volver en dos semanas.
María: ¿Puedo ir con ustedes?
Rosa: ¡Claro que sí!

 **Quick Start Review Answers**

p. 326 Hacer, ir
Answers will vary.
Answers could include:
hacer
1. Ayer hizo muchos quehaceres.
2. Patricia hace entrevistas.
3. Vamos a hacer un viaje en Ecuador.

ir
1. Anoche fui al cine.
2. Voy a la biblioteca a las cuatro.
3. Vamos a poner la mesa.

UNIDAD 6 ETAPA 3 Pacing Guide

Sample Lesson Plan - 45 Minute Schedule

DAY 1

Etapa Opener
- Quick Start Review (TE, p. 302) **5 MIN.**
- Anticipate/Activate prior knowledge: Discuss the *Etapa* Opener. **5 MIN.**
- Present the Supplementary Vocabulary (TE, p. 303). **5 MIN.**
- Answer the *¿Qué ves?* questions, p. 302. **5 MIN.**

En contexto: Vocabulario
- Quick Start Review (TE, p. 304) **5 MIN.**
- Have students use context and pictures to review vocabulary. **10 MIN.**
- Present the Supplementary Vocabulary (TE, p. 305). **5 MIN.**
- Have students work in pairs to answer the *Preguntas personales*, p. 305. **5 MIN.**

DAY 2

En vivo: Diálogo
- Quick Start Review (TE, p. 306) **5 MIN.**
- Review the Listening Strategy, p. 306. **5 MIN.**
- Play audio or show video for the dialog, pp. 306–307, as students take notes. **10 MIN.**
- Check students' notes on Patricia's project. **5 MIN.**
- Read the dialog aloud, having students take the roles of characters. **5 MIN.**
- Do the Gestures activity (TE, p. 306). **5 MIN.**
- Use the Situational OHTs for additional vocabulary practice. **10 MIN.**

Homework Option:
- Video Activities, Unit 6 Resource Book, pp. 125–127.

DAY 3

En acción: Vocabulario y gramática
- Check homework. **5 MIN.**
- Quick Start Review (TE, p. 308) **5 MIN.**
- Use OHTs to review *En contexto* vocabulary. Ask students for a summary of the dialog to check recall. **5 MIN.**
- Play the video/audio; have students do *Actividades* 1 and 2 orally. **10 MIN.**
- Read and discuss the *También se dice*, p. 309. **5 MIN.**
- Work orally with the class to complete *Actividad* 3. **5 MIN.**
- Have students work in groups to complete *Actividad* 4. **5 MIN.**
- Ask groups to share the results of *Actividad* 4. **5 MIN.**

DAY 4

En acción (cont.)
- Quick Start Review (TE, p. 312) **5 MIN.**
- Play the audio as students work on *Actividad* 5. **5 MIN.**
- Ask selected students to share their responses to *Actividad* 5. **5 MIN.**
- Have students work in pairs on *Actividad* 6. **10 MIN.**
- Ask selected pairs to model their interviews for *Actividad* 6. **5 MIN.**
- Read and discuss the *Conexiones*, p. 311. **5 MIN.**
- Present *Repaso:* Review: Present Progressive and *ir a* + infinitive, p. 312. **10 MIN.**

Homework Option:
- Have students do the *Para hacer*, p. 311.

DAY 5

En acción (cont.)
- Check homework. **5 MIN.**
- Work orally with the class on *Actividad* 7. **5 MIN.**
- Have students write their responses to *Actividad* 7. **5 MIN.**
- Assign *Actividad* 8. **5 MIN.**
- Call on volunteers to say their answers to *Actividad* 8. **5 MIN.**
- Quick Wrap-up (TE, p. 313) **5 MIN.**
- Have students work in groups on *Actividad* 9. **5 MIN.**
- Call on selected groups to share their work on *Actividad* 9. **5 MIN.**
- Present the Speaking Strategy, p. 313. **5 MIN.**

Homework Option:
- *Más práctica* Workbook, p. 69. *Para hispanohablantes* Workbook, p. 67.

DAY 6

En acción (cont.)
- Check homework. **5 MIN.**
- Quick Start Review (TE, p. 314) **5 MIN.**
- Have students work in pairs to do *Actividad* 10. **5 MIN.**
- Ask pairs to share their work from *Actividad* 10. **5 MIN.**
- Assign *Actividad* 11. **5 MIN.**
- Ask volunteers to read their letters from *Actividad* 11. **5 MIN.**
- Present *Repaso:* Review: Affirmative *tú* Commands, p. 314. **10 MIN.**
- Assign *Actividad* 12. **5 MIN.**

Homework Option:
- *Más práctica* Workbook, p. 70. *Para hispanohablantes* Workbook, p. 68.

DAY 7

En acción (cont.)
- Check homework. **5 MIN.**
- Quick Start Review (TE, p. 315) **5 MIN.**
- Have students work in pairs to complete *Actividad* 13. **5 MIN.**
- Ask pairs to share their work on *Actividad* 13 with the class. **5 MIN.**
- Assign *Actividad* 14. **5 MIN.**
- Ask volunteers to read their lists from *Actividad* 14. **5 MIN.**
- Present *Repaso:* Review: Regular Preterite, p. 315. **10 MIN.**
- Assign the *Juego* (Answer, TE, p. 316). **5 MIN.**

DAY 8

En acción (cont.)
- Have students write their responses to *Actividad* 15. **5 MIN.**
- Ask volunteers to read their paragraph for *Actividad* 15. **5 MIN.**
- Quick Wrap-up (TE, p. 316) **5 MIN.**
- Ask students to write their responses to *Actividad* 16. **5 MIN.**
- Call on students to read their sentences from *Actividad* 16. **5 MIN.**
- Assign *Actividad* 17. **5 MIN.**
- Call on selected students to read their sentences from *Actividad* 17. **5 MIN.**
- Read and discuss the *Conexiones*, p. 317. **5 MIN.**
- Assign the *Para hacer*, p. 317. **5 MIN.**

Homework Option:
- *Más práctica* Workbook, p. 71. *Para hispanohablantes* Workbook, p. 69.

DAY 9

En acción (cont.)
- Check homework. **5 MIN.**
- Quick Start Review (TE, p. 318) **5 MIN.**
- Assign *Actividad* 18. **5 MIN.**
- Ask volunteers to read their lists from *Actividad* 18. **5 MIN.**
- Present *Repaso:* Review: Irregular Preterite, p. 318. **5 MIN.**
- Play the audio and assign *Actividad* 19. **5 MIN.**
- Ask volunteers to share their answers to *Actividad* 19. **5 MIN.**
- Assign *Actividad* 20. **5 MIN.**
- Ask volunteers to read their answers to *Actividad* 20. **5 MIN.**

Homework Option:
- *Más práctica* Workbook, p. 72. *Para hispanohablantes* Workbook, p. 70.

DAY 10

En acción (cont.)
- Check homework. **5 MIN.**
- Have students work in groups to complete *Actividad* 21. **5 MIN.**
- Ask students to read their summaries from *Actividad* 21 to the class. **5 MIN.**
- Assign *Actividad* 22. **5 MIN.**
- Have students work in pairs to complete *Actividad* 23. **5 MIN.**
- Ask volunteers to share their questions and answers from *Actividad* 23. **5 MIN.**
- Assign *Actividades* 24 and 25. **5 MIN.**
- Have students share their work on *Actividad* 24. **5 MIN.**
- Play the audio and have students practice the *Refrán*, p. 321. **5 MIN.**

DAY 11

En voces: Lectura
- Quick Start Review (TE, p. 322) **5 MIN.**
- Present the Reading Strategy, p. 322. **5 MIN.**
- Ask students to skim the *Lectura* and to look at the pictures to remember what a *murciélago* is. **5 MIN.**
- Have volunteers read the selection aloud. **10 MIN.**
- Work orally with students on the *¿Comprendiste?* questions (Answers, TE, p. 323). **5 MIN.**
- Have students write answers to the *¿Comprendiste?* questions. **5 MIN.**
- Discuss the *¿Qué piensas?* questions, p. 323. **10 MIN.**

Homework Option:
- Have students write their answers to the *¿Qué piensas?* questions, p. 323.

DAY 12

En colores: Cultura y comparaciones
- Check homework. **5 MIN.**
- Quick Start Review (TE, p. 324) **5 MIN.**
- Discuss the Connecting Cultures Strategy, p. 324. **5 MIN.**
- Have students brainstorm a list of dishes made with potatoes, tomatoes, and corn. **5 MIN.**
- Discuss the Culture Highlights (TE, p. 325). **5 MIN.**
- Have volunteers read the selection aloud. **10 MIN.**
- Work orally with students to answer the *¿Comprendiste?* questions (Answers, TE, p. 325). **5 MIN.**
- Discuss the *¿Qué piensas?* questions, p. 325. **5 MIN.**

Homework Option:
- Have students work on the assignment in the Connecting Cultures Strategy, p. 324.

DAY 13

En uso: Repaso y más comunicación
- Check homework. **5 MIN.**
- Quick Start Review (TE, p. 326) **5 MIN.**
- Assign *Actividad* 1. **5 MIN.**
- Work orally with students to complete *Actividades* 2 and 3. **5 MIN.**
- Have students read and think about *Actividad* 4. **5 MIN.**
- Call on students to give oral responses to *Actividad* 4. **5 MIN.**
- Present the Speaking Strategy, p. 328. **5 MIN.**
- Have pairs work on *Actividad* 5. **5 MIN.**
- Have pairs share their work on *Actividad* 5. **5 MIN.**

Homework Option:
- Have students review all the *Gramática* boxes in *Etapa* 3.

DAY 14

En uso (cont.)
- Quick Start Review (TE, p. 329) **5 MIN.**
- Review grammar questions as needed. **5 MIN.**
- Have students work in groups on *Actividad* 6. **5 MIN.**
- Ask groups to share their work from *Actividad* 6. **5 MIN.**

En tu propia voz: Escritura
- Have students work independently to complete the writing activity, *Actividad* 7. **10 MIN.**
- Ask volunteers to read their work from *Actividad* 7. **5 MIN.**

En resumen: Repaso de vocabulario
- Go over *En resumen* with the class. **10 MIN.**

Homework Option:
- Have students study for *Etapa* exam.

DAY 15

En resumen (cont.)
- Quick Start Review (TE, p. 330) **5 MIN.**
- Answer questions related to *Etapa* 3 content. **5 MIN.**
- Complete *Etapa* exam. **25 MIN.**

Conexiones
- Have students read the *Conexiones*, pp. 330–331, as they complete the exam. **10 MIN.**

Classroom Management Tip

Use technology A good way to extend your classroom library is to make use of the Internet. You should prescreen sites or search words you ask students to use.

Use the search word *Galapagos* in your web browser to find some wonderful sites for students to use to do research. Divide the class into groups to gather information on the islands' geological features, flora and fauna, and so forth. Have students find graphics they can use to present the information to the class.

Etapa Theme
Remembering what you have learned and summing up the magazine contest

Grammar Objectives
- Reviewing the present progressive and **ir a...**
- Reviewing affirmative **tú** commands
- Reviewing the preterite tense

Teaching Resource Options
Print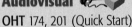

Block Scheduling Copymasters

Audiovisual

OHT 174, 201 (Quick Start)

Quick Start Review
♻ **Otavalo**

Use OHT 201 or write on the board:
Write at least 3 things you know about Otavalo, Ecuador.

Answers
Answers will vary. Answers could include:
Queda en Ecuador, entre Quito y la frontera con Colombia.
La gente se llama los otavaleños.
Los sábados hay un mercado tradicional.
Puedes visitar el Instituto Otavaleño de Antropología.
En la Plaza Bolívar hay una estatua del general inca Rumiñahui.

Teaching Suggestions
Previewing the Etapa
- Ask students to study the picture on pp. 302–303 (1 min.).
- Close books; ask students to share at least 3 things they remember.
- Reopen books and look at the picture again. Have students describe the people and the setting.
- Use the **¿Qué ves?** questions to focus the discussion.

UNIDAD 6

ETAPA 3

¡A ganar el concurso!

- **Talk about the present and future**
- **Give instructions to someone**
- **Discuss the past**

¿Qué ves?
Mira la foto del mercado de Otavalo.

1. ¿Las vendedoras sólo venden ropa?
2. ¿Hace mucho calor o no? ¿Cómo lo sabes?
3. ¿De qué color es la blusa tradicional de las mujeres de Otavalo?
4. ¿Para qué es la carta que Patricia escribió?

Patricia López Carrera
Calle Oriente 253 y P. Fermín Cevallos
Quito

Revista Onda Internacional
Concurso latino
Apartado 1216
Quito

302

Middle School Classroom Management

Planning Ahead Take advantage of the fact that the grammar in this lesson is review. Take stock of your class and note areas of weakness. Plan to make remedial use of the activities in this **Etapa** and add other activities as needed.

Peer Teaching Declare a **día loco** and rearrange your class so that students with a weakness are working with students who are strong in that area. Set up Round Robin groups, each one practicing different areas of the lesson. Have students change groups every 5 minutes.

303

Teaching Middle School Students

Extra Help Have students brainstorm all the things they see in the illustration. Help them with unknown vocabulary. Use the picture to review descriptions.

Native Speakers Ask native speakers to talk about craft markets in the area where they lived. Ask them to tell students what some of the more popular or "typical" items are and what they are called.

Multiple Intelligences

Interpersonal Ask students to write down 3 things in the market that they like and 3 that they don't like. Have them respond in class and give reasons for their opinions.

Cross Cultural Connections

Ask students to compare the address, the stamps, and the handwriting on Patricia's envelope to one they would see in the United States

Culture Highlights

● **LOS TEJIDOS DE OTAVALO** Otavalo is renowned for its textiles. The market in Otavalo, where this photo was taken, is filled with beautiful weavings by the skilled people from Otavalo.

● **EL SOMBRERO DE PAJA TOQUILLA** Otavalo is also known for other craft specialties, including woodcarving, leatherworking, and the so-called "Panama" hats. The name comes from the fact that workers on the Panama Canal wore them. A Panama hat is a natural-colored, hand-woven straw hat made from the fibers of the jipijapa plant (named after Jipijapa, a city in western Ecuador). Panama hats were once Ecuador's biggest export item and have maintained their reputation as a fashion item throughout the years.

Supplementary Vocabulary

un sello	stamp
un sobre	envelope
una muñeca	doll
los tejidos	textiles
un tapiz	tapestry
un tapete	rug
un poncho	poncho

Block Schedule

Expansion Have students count off from 1 to 4. Their number represents the **¿Qué ves?** question that they are responsible for. They must answer the question and expand on it for 3–4 sentences more by adding more description or explanation. They can also add a personal comment. (For additional activities, see **Block Scheduling Copymasters**.)

Teaching Resource Options

Print

Unit 6 Resource Book
Video Activities, pp. 125–126
Videoscript, p. 128
Audioscript, p. 131
Audioscript *Para hispanohablantes*,
   p. 131

Audiovisual

OHT M1–M5; 195, 196, 197, 197A, 198,
198A, 201 (Quick Start)
Audio Program Cassette 18A / CD 18
Audio *Para hispanohablantes*
   Cassette 18A / CD 18
Video Program Videotape 6 /
   Videodisc 3B

Search Chapter 7, Play to 8
U6E3 • En contexto (Vocabulary)

Canciones Cassette / CD

Technology

Intrigas y aventuras CD-ROM, Disc 1

Quick Start Review

🔄 Character descriptions

Use OHT 201 or write on the board:
Write 1 true statement about 5 of the
main characters in this book:

Alma, Francisco, Isabel, Ricardo,
Diana, Ignacio, Roberto, Carlos, Rosa,
Sofía, Luis, Mercedes, Miguel, Patricia
Answers will vary.

Teaching Suggestions
Reviewing Vocabulary

• Have students look at pages 304–305.
  Use OHT 195 and 196 and Audio
  Cassette 18A / CD 18 to review the
  vocabulary.
• Ask the Comprehension Questions in
  order of yes/no (questions 1–3),
  either/or (questions 4–6), and simple
  word or phrase (questions 7–10).
  Expand by adding similar questions.
• Use the TPR activity to reinforce the
  meaning of individual words.
• Use the video vocabulary presentation
  for review and reinforcement.

En contexto

 VOCABULARIO 🔄

Do you remember all that you have learned this year? You have learned to talk
about the present, the future, and the past, and to give instructions. Take a look
at these people and places for a quick review of what you have learned.

¡Hola! Aprendiste mucho este año.
¿Recuerdas todo lo que ves aquí?

MIAMI

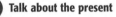 **Talk about the present**

Alma: Arturo, te **presento** a
Francisco García. Él **es** mi vecino.

Arturo: Francisco, **es** un placer.

Francisco: Igualmente, Arturo.

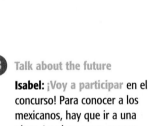

CIUDAD DE MÉXICO

B **Talk about the future**

Isabel: **¡Voy a participar** en el
concurso! Para conocer a los
mexicanos, hay que ir a una
plaza. La plaza es un poema.

304   trescientos cuatro
Unidad 6

Middle School Classroom Community

TPR Tell students that you are going to talk about the
places and people you've studied during the year.
Whenever you use the present tense, they raise their
hands. Whenever you use the preterite, they touch
their heads. When you talk about the future, they touch
their noses.

Group Activity Assign students the role of one of
the main characters in the units. Designate areas of the
room to be Miami, Quito, etc. Tell students to go
"home," and when they get to their "city," have them
interact, in character, with other students.

PUERTO RICO

OAXACA

C Say what is happening

Ignacio: ¡Está lloviendo!
¡Y no tengo paraguas!

Roberto: Te estamos
esperando, hombre.

D Give instructions

Carlos: Vas a llegar a un
parque. **Cruza** el parque.
Enfrente de la estatua está
la calle Morelos.

Rosa: Muchas gracias…

E Discuss the past

Luis: ¡El día empezó con
demasiados quehaceres!

Carmen: ¡Yo te ayudé, Luis!

Luis: Sí, Carmen, tú me
ayudaste y Mercedes
también me ayudó.

BARCELONA

QUITO

F Discuss the past

Miguel: ¿Cómo fueron las entrevistas?

Patricia: Excelente. Ya hice dos.

Preguntas personales

1. ¿Quién es tu mejor amigo? ¿amiga?
2. ¿Qué vas a hacer este fin de semana?
3. ¿Qué está pasando en tu clase?
4. Explica cómo llegar a tu casa.
5. ¿Qué hiciste este año?

trescientos cinco
Etapa 3 **305**

Comprehension Questions

1. ¿Son hermanos Alma y Francisco? (No.)
2. ¿Está Isabel en la plaza? (Sí.)
3. ¿Va a participar Isabel en el concurso? (Sí.)
4. En la foto C, ¿necesita Ignacio unas gafas de sol o un paraguas? (un paraguas)
5. ¿Está la calle Morelos enfrente de o detrás de la estatua? (enfrente)
6. ¿Quién ayudó a Luis con los quehaceres, Rosa o Carmen? (Carmen)
7. ¿Quién es Francisco? (el vecino de Alma)
8. En la foto C, ¿qué tiempo hace? (Está lloviendo.)
9. ¿Cómo empezó el día de Luis? (Empezó con demasiados quehaceres.)
10. ¿Cómo fueron las entrevistas de Patricia? (excelente)

Critical Thinking

Have students decide what should be included in a first-year English textbook used by students in Latin America or Spain.

Supplementary Vocabulary

el globo	globe
el atlas	atlas
la longitud	longitude
la latitud	latitude
un continente	continent

Teaching Middle School Students

Challenge Have students write a summarizing paragraph about each of the 6 units.

Native Speakers Ask native speakers to tell you how their Spanish language skills have improved and how they intend to use and improve their skills in the future.

Multiple Intelligences

Intrapersonal Ask students to think about the characters and their locations. Have them write down the characters and locations they liked the best and the least, and tell why. Have students share their opinions with their partners and compare responses. If appropriate, have students share with the class.

Block Schedule

Change of Pace Ask students to choose a commercial from TV and prepare a similar one in Spanish. Have them present their commercials to the class. Videotape the commercials and have students critique their performances on the basis of language accuracy, pronunciation, acting, and creativity.

Quick Start Review

♻ **Miguel and Patricia**

Use OHT 201 or write on the board:
Write 3 true statements about Miguel
and 3 true statements about Patricia:

Answers

Answers will vary. Answers could include:
Miguel vive en Quito, Ecuador.
Miguel tiene familia en el campo.
La primera vez que Miguel visitó a su tío Julio,
  fue al corral, abrió la cerca y el caballo se
  escapó.
Patricia decidió participar en el concurso.
Patricia les hizo entrevistas a una mujer de
  negocios y a un arquitecto.
Patricia visitó a Bárbara en su taller.

Gestures

Have volunteers mime the various scenes
in the **Diálogo,** trying to imitate the body
language of Miguel and Patricia. Ask them
to compare this body language to what
they might do in a similar situation.

En vivo

 ## DIÁLOGO

¡Vamos a Otavalo!

Patricia   Miguel

PARA ESCUCHAR • STRATEGY: LISTENING

Listen and take notes This conversation sums up Patricia's work
on her project. What does she think about her work? As you jot
down her ideas, listen for answers to *who? what? when? where?*
and *why?* Use your notes to make a summary statement about
Patricia's project.

1▶ Miguel: ¿Estás feliz con tus
entrevistas?
Patricia: Sí, estoy muy feliz. Hice
entrevistas con un arquitecto, la
gerente de un banco, y también
con tu tío Julio y Bárbara.

5▶ Patricia: Pero aprendí algo mucho
más importante también.
Miguel: ¿Sí? Dime.
Patricia: Aprendí que no tienes ni
idea de lo que hay que hacer en
una granja. ¡Abriste la cerca!

6▶ Patricia: ¡Mira, Miguel! ¡Es un mercado
fenomenal! Voy a comprarle un regalo a
mi hermana. Su cumpleaños es este mes.
Miguel: Cómprale una bolsa o un artículo
de cuero. La artesanía de Otavalo es
excelente.

7▶ Patricia: No sé si tengo suficiente
dinero… a ver… tengo 40 mil
sucres en efectivo. ¿Crees que
puedo regatear aquí?
Miguel: ¡Claro que sí! Es un
mercado, ¿no? ¡Ven!

306 trescientos seis
Unidad 6

Middle School Classroom Community

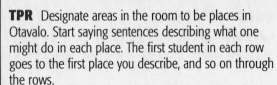

TPR Designate areas in the room to be places in
Otavalo. Start saying sentences describing what one
might do in each place. The first student in each row
goes to the first place you describe, and so on through
the rows.

Learning Scenario Tell students that they are in
a large farmers' market. Some students should be
vendors, and some should be shoppers. Ask them to
interact in character, buying and selling or sitting down
for a snack and talking about their experiences at the
market.

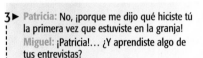

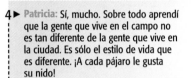

2 ▶ Miguel: ¿Cuál fue la mejor entrevista?
Patricia: No sé… Creo que fue la entrevista con tu tío Julio.
Miguel: ¿Y por qué? ¿Porque te habló de la vida en una granja?

3 ▶ Patricia: No, ¡porque me dijo qué hiciste tú la primera vez que estuviste en la granja!
Miguel: ¡Patricia!… ¿Y aprendiste algo de tus entrevistas?

4 ▶ Patricia: Sí, mucho. Sobre todo aprendí que la gente que vive en el campo no es tan diferente de la gente que vive en la ciudad. Es sólo el estilo de vida que es diferente. ¡A cada pájaro le gusta su nido!

8 ▶ Miguel: ¿Cuándo mandas tu proyecto a la revista?
Patricia: Después del fin de semana. Todavía tengo que escribir mucho.

9 ▶ Miguel: Hazme un favor… ¿Puedo leerlo antes? ¡Creo que va a salir muy bien y lo quiero ver! Y también…
Patricia: ¿Sí?
Miguel: ¡Quiero ver si escribiste algo de mi experiencia con la cerca y el caballo!

10 ▶ Patricia: Hice todo lo posible. Trabajé mucho. Espero tener buena suerte.

trescientos siete
Etapa 3
307

Teaching Suggestions
Presenting the Dialog
- Prepare students for listening by focusing on the dialog context. Have them tell you who the characters are, where they are coming from, where they are going, and why.
- Use the video, audio cassette, or CD to present the dialog. The expanded dialog on video offers additional listening practice opportunities.

Video Synopsis
- Patricia talks to Miguel about what she has learned while interviewing people in the city and the country. For a complete transcript of the video dialog, see p. 301B.

Comprehension Questions
1. ¿Está Patricia feliz con sus entrevistas? (Sí.)
2. ¿Hizo Patricia cuatro entrevistas? (Sí.)
3. ¿Fue la mejor entrevista con el arquitecto? (No.)
4. ¿Aprendió Patricia mucho o poco de sus entrevistas? (mucho)
5. ¿Hay gran diferencia o poca diferencia entre la gente del campo y la gente de la ciudad? (poca diferencia)
6. ¿Cuál es la diferencia entre la vida del campo y la vida de la ciudad, la gente o el estilo de vida? (el estilo de vida)
7. ¿Por qué dice Patricia que Miguel no sabe nada de vivir en una granja? (Porque Miguel abrió la cerca y el caballo se escapó.)
8. ¿Por qué quiere Patricia comprarle un regalo a su hermana? (Porque su cumpleaños es este mes.)
9. ¿Por qué está Patricia preocupada? (Porque no sabe si tiene suficiente dinero.)
10. ¿Cuándo va Patricia a mandar su proyecto a la revista? (después del fin de semana)

Block Schedule
Variety Have 2 students play the roles of Miguel and Patricia, who have come to spend a week at your school. Have the class ask them questions. (For additional activities, see **Block Scheduling Copymasters**.)

Teaching Middle School Students

Multiple Intelligences

Verbal Have students read the **En vivo** dialog with their partner. Tell them to practice until they are very fluent and are using good expression. Have them tape (audio or video) their performance and critique their own presentations.

Kinesthetic Have students work in pairs to pantomime interviewing, bargaining for an item, opening the gate at the farm, and other scenes from the lesson as their partners moderate the performance.

Teaching Resource Options

Print

Unit 6 Resource Book
Video Activities, p. 127
Videoscript, p. 130
Audioscript, pp. 131–132
Audioscript *Para hispanohablantes,*
pp. 131–132

Audiovisual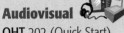

OHT 202 (Quick Start)
Audio Program Cassettes 18A, 18B /
CD 18
Audio *Para hispanohablantes*
Cassette 18A / CD 18
Video Program Videotape 6 / Videodisc
3B

Quick Start Review

♻ Dialog review

Use OHT 202 or write on the board:
Complete the following sentences from
the dialog.

1. Pero ____ algo mucho más
   importante también.
2. ¿Estás feliz con tus ____ ?
3. ¡Creo que va a ____ muy bien y lo
   quiero ver!
4. Espero tener buena ____ .
5. ____ tengo que escribir mucho.
6. Es ____ el estilo de vida que es
   diferente.

Answers

1. aprendí	4. suerte
2. entrevistas	5. Todavía
3. salir	6. sólo

Teaching Suggestions
Comprehension Check

Use **Actividades 1** and **2** to assess
retention after the dialog. Have students
close their books. Read the items and
see if students can respond. Have
students add 2 items to **Actividad 2.**

 Objective: Controlled practice
Listening comprehension/vocabulary

Answers (See script, p. 301B.)

1. Patricia	4. Patricia
2. Patricia	5. Miguel
3. Miguel	6. Patricia

En acción
VOCABULARIO Y GRAMÁTICA

OBJECTIVES

- Talk about the present and future
- Give instructions to someone
- Discuss the past
- *Review present progressive and* ir a*...*
- *Review affirmative* tú *commands*
- *Review the preterite tense*

 ACTIVIDAD **1**

¿Patricia o Miguel?

Escuchar Según el diálogo, ¿a quién se refiere
cada pregunta: a Patricia o a Miguel? *(Hint: Say
who is being described.)*

Patricia   Miguel

1. ¿Quién está feliz?
2. ¿Quién hizo entrevistas?
3. ¿Quién abrió la cerca en la granja?
4. ¿Quién va a comprar un regalo?
5. ¿Quién quiere leer el proyecto?
6. ¿Quién trabajó mucho?

308 trescientos ocho
Unidad 6

Middle School Classroom Management

Planning Ahead Help students summarize verb
tenses by letting them make a picture chart of one
regular **-ar, -er,** and **-ir** verb in the present, present
progressive, preterite, and affirmative **tú** command
forms. Let students choose one verb or several,
write the various tenses, and illustrate each one with
drawings, magazine cutouts, computer graphics, etc.

Time Saver Have materials (flash cards, worksheets,
etc.) for review and practice in permanent locations
so that students can have access to them without
interrupting you or wasting time.

ACTIVIDAD 2

La conversación

Escuchar Escoge la mejor respuesta para cada frase. A veces tienes que escribir la respuesta. *(Hint: Choose or write the phrase that completes each sentence.)*

1. ¿Patricia está hablando con…
   a. Julio.
   b. Miguel.
   c. ¿?

2. Los amigos hablan…
   a. del proyecto de Patricia.
   b. de varias profesiones.
   c. ¿?

3. Patricia y Miguel van…
   a. a la granja.
   b. al banco.
   c. ¿?

4. Van a comprar…
   a. un gorro o un artículo de lana.
   b. una bolsa de plástico.
   c. ¿?

5. Patricia está feliz porque…
   a. trabajó mucho y terminó su proyecto.
   b. va a trabajar para una revista.
   c. ¿?

ACTIVIDAD 3

♻ Juego de palabras

Hablar Patricia y Miguel juegan a este juego de palabras. Tú también puedes jugar. Di qué palabra no debe estar en cada grupo y por qué. *(Hint: Why doesn't one word belong?)*

modelo

| abrigo | bufanda | gorro | revista |

Una revista no es ropa.

1. cerdo	jefe	vaca	gallo
2. raqueta	bola	patines	cansado
3. anillo	arete	casete	collar
4. casco	cuchara	cuchillo	tenedor
5. plato	bota	olla	jarra
6. cancha	contento	campo	estadio
7. hombre	chico	mujer	suelo
8. café	té	cuenta	limonada
9. espejos	orejas	piernas	brazos
10. cepillo	jabón	jamón	champú

También se dice

There are many ways to say "To each his own," or in other words, "Each person has his or her own taste."

• «A cada pájaro le gusta su nido.» *Every bird likes its nest.*

• «Zapatero, a tus zapatos.» *Shoemaker, (attend) to your shoes!*

• «A cada cual lo suyo.» *To each his own.*

• «Cada oveja con su pareja.» *Every sheep has its mate.*

trescientos nueve
Etapa 3 **309**

Teaching Middle School Students

Extra Help Reinforce present progressive and **ir a** constructions. Use the **En vivo** stills or the video (or other appropriate materials) to have students describe (orally, in writing, or both) what the characters are doing, and then what they are going to do in the next sequence.

Native Speakers Ask students how they say "To each his own" in their countries of origin. Ask them to share other commonly used expressions or proverbs.

Multiple Intelligences

Verbal Have students work in pairs to write their own **Juego de palabras** (or **El intruso**). Have students trade with other pairs to solve.

UNIDAD 6 Etapa 3
Vocabulary/Grammar

ACTIVIDAD 2

Objective: Transitional practice
Listening comprehension/vocabulary

Answers (See script, p. 301B.)
1. b
2. a
3. c (al mercado)
4. c (una bolsa o un artículo de cuero)
5. a

ACTIVIDAD 3

Objective: Transitional practice
Vocabulary

 Text vocabulary

Answers

Answers will resemble the following.
1. Un jefe no es un animal.
2. Cansado no es equipo deportivo.
3. Un casete no es joyas.
4. Un casco no es un utensilio.
5. Una bota no es cerámica.
6. Contento no es un lugar para jugar a un deporte.
7. Un suelo no es una persona.
8. Una cuenta no es una bebida.
9. Espejos no son partes del cuerpo.
10. Jamón no es algo del baño.

Project

Crear un crucigrama Supply students with graph paper and pencils with erasers. Have each small group make a crossword puzzle whose words conform to a theme. They should present their puzzle to the class in ready-to-solve form, with the squares numbered, unused squares colored in, the definitions listed in horizontal and vertical order, and illustrations to make things interesting.

Block Schedule

FunBreak Have students work on expressive speech by creating a neutral sentence or two and taping it using several tones of voice. They should write down the effect they intended and then survey classmates about the effect they heard on the tape. Students should then edit their tapes before submitting them as finished product for evaluation.

Vocabulary/Grammar • UNIDAD 6 Etapa 3 **309**

Teaching Resource Options

Print

Unit 6 Resource Book
  Video Activities, p. 127
  Videoscript, p. 130
  Audioscript, pp. 131–132
  Audioscript *Para hispanohablantes,*
    pp. 131–132

Audiovisual

Audio Program Cassettes 18A, 18B /
  CD 18
Audio *Para hispanohablantes*
  Cassette 18A / CD 18
Video Program Videotape 6 / Videodisc
  3B

Objective: Open-ended practice
Vocabulary

 Clothing vocabulary

Answers will vary.

Objective: Transitional practice
Listening comprehension/vocabulary

Activities

Answers (See script, p. 301B.)

1. d	6. j
2. a	7. b
3. f	8. c
4. e	9. h
5. g	10. i

¿Quién lo tiene?

Hablar ¿Quién en la clase tiene estas cosas? *(Hint: Find out who in the class has the items on your list.)*

1 En una hoja de papel, escribe seis cosas de la lista. *(Hint: List six items.)*

2 Pregúntales a los otros estudiantes si tienen las cosas. *(Hint: Ask classmates if they have the items.)*

3 Cuando una persona contesta que sí, él o ella debe escribir su nombre al lado del nombre de la cosa. ¿Cuántas firmas *(signatures)* consigues en cinco minutos? *(Hint: If they have an item, they sign their name. How many signatures can you get in five minutes?)*

- un vestido azul
- un suéter blanco
- una chaqueta negra
- unos zapatos marrones
- un gorro rojo
- una camiseta amarilla
- una blusa verde
- una falda negra
- los calcetines blancos
- ¿?

Las actividades

Escuchar Todas estas personas están ocupadas. ¿Qué oración describe lo que hace cada una? *(Hint: Describe each picture.)*

310 | trescientos diez
Unidad 6

Middle School Classroom Community

TPR Tell students to find another student who has or is wearing certain things (**un lápiz rojo, una camiseta azul,** etc.). Have the student bring that person back to you and point out the item.

Portfolio Have students write their interview for **Actividad 6,** including questions, answers, and the summarizing paragraph.

Rubric

Criteria	Scale	
Accuracy of information	1 2 3 4 5	A = 13–15 pts.
Logical organization	1 2 3 4 5	B = 10–12 pts.
Vocabulary use	1 2 3 4 5	C = 7–9 pts.
		D = 4–6 pts.
		F = < 4 pts.

La entrevista

Hablar/Escribir ¿Conoces bien a los otros estudiantes? Haz una entrevista con otro(a) estudiante. *(Hint: Interview a classmate.)*

❶ Escoge seis preguntas de las siguientes tres categorías. Cópialas en una hoja de papel. *(Hint: Write six questions.)*

❷ Habla con otro(a) estudiante. Escribe sus respuestas al lado de las preguntas. *(Hint: Write down your friend's answers.)*

❸ Ahora, organiza las respuestas y escribe un párrafo sobre él o ella. *(Hint: Write a paragraph.)*

❹ Lee el párrafo y busca errores. *(Hint: Correct errors.)*

❺ Comparte tu entrevista con la clase sin anunciar el nombre de otro(a) estudiante. ¿Puede la clase identificar quién es? *(Hint: Share the interview. Can the class guess who it is?)*

La vida familiar

* ¿Cuántas personas hay en tu familia? ¿Cómo se llaman? ¿Cuántos años tienen?
* ¿Quiénes hacen los quehaceres en tu casa? ¿Cuáles son estos quehaceres?
* ¿Cuál es la fecha de tu cumpleaños? ¿Cuál es tu manera *(way)* favorita de celebrarlo?

La vida diaria

* ¿A qué hora te levantas? ¿Qué haces después de levantarte?
* ¿A qué hora te acuestas normalmente?
* ¿Cuál es tu clase favorita? ¿Por qué?

Los intereses

* ¿Qué te gusta hacer después de las clases?
* ¿Qué te gusta comer y beber?
* ¿Cuál es tu deporte favorito? ¿Por qué?

Conexiones

La geografía You can drive from the U.S. border with Mexico to the southern tip of Chile on the Pan-American Highway. Part of this highway follows the **Camino Inca**, which was laid out by the Incas hundreds of years ago.

PARA HACER:
How many countries does the Pan-American Highway pass through? Make a list of these countries.

trescientos once
Etapa 3 | **311**

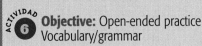

Objective: Open-ended practice Vocabulary/grammar

♻ Family, daily routine, preferences

Answers will vary.

Para hacer

Answers
The Pan-American Highway passes through 17 countries: Mexico, Guatemala, El Salvador, Honduras, Nicaragua, Costa Rica, Panama, Colombia, Venezuela, Bolivia, Paraguay, Uruguay, Argentina, Brazil, Ecuador, Peru, and Chile.

Critical Thinking

In colonial times, every Spanish city was laid out according to the same plan. There was always a central plaza, a church, an **ayuntamiento,** and a military headquarters. Old Quito represents Spanish colonial architecture at its best. In 1978, it was declared a world treasure by UNESCO. Have students find pictures of it and compare and contrast them with pictures of other Latin American and U.S. colonial cities.

Teaching Middle School Students

Multiple Intelligences

Logical/Mathematical Have students figure the distance covered by the Pan-American Highway in miles and kilometers. Have them show the countries with the longest and shortest stretches, those with the flattest and most mountainous terrains, etc.

Visual Have students work in groups to cut out magazine pictures that can be used for review. They should browse through **Etapa** vocabulary pages to get ideas. When they have a varied collection, have them use their cutouts to create scenes that they can describe and discuss.

Block Schedule

Change of Pace Have students work in small groups. Using the photos in **Actividad 5,** they should write a dialog or monolog that might be heard at each place. Have them choose their favorite to perform for the class.

Teaching Resource Options

Print

Más práctica Workbook PE, p. 69
Para hispanohablantes Workbook PE, p. 67
Block Scheduling Copymasters
Unit 6 Resource Book
 Más práctica Workbook TE, p. 107
 Para hispanohablantes Workbook TE, p. 113

Audiovisual

OHT 174, 202 (Quick Start)

Technology

Intrigas y aventuras CD-ROM, Disc 1

Quick Start Review

 Present tense

Use OHT 202 or write on the board:
Write the appropriate present tense form for each subject pronoun.

1. ir: yo ____
2. decir: tú ____
3. tener: él ____
4. ser: nosotros ____
5. hacer: yo ____
6. estar: ustedes ____

Answers
1. voy
2. dices
3. tiene
4. somos
5. hago
6. están

Teaching Suggestions
Reviewing the Present Progressive

Remind students that Spanish does not use the present progressive as often as English. In Spanish, the simple present is used to describe routine actions. The present progressive is for something happening right at this very moment.

ACTIVIDAD 7

Objective: Controlled practice
Present progressive/vocabulary

Answers

Answers will vary.
1. Patricia y Miguel están hablando con Bárbara.
2. Patricia está regateando. (Está comprando algo.)
3. Patricia está mandando su proyecto.
4. Miguel está leyendo las notas de Patricia. Patricia está escribiendo en su cuaderno.

 REPASO

Review: Present Progressive and *ir a* + infinitive

You have learned to use verbs in the present tense three different ways:
• **simple present** tense
• **present progressive** tense
• **ir a** + *infinitive*

 ¿RECUERDAS? *pp. A262, 202* Remember the **present progressive?** The **present progressive** is used only to talk about actions that are **happening**. It is never used to refer to the future.

¿RECUERDAS? *p. A170* To talk about what you are going to do, use **ir a** + *infinitive*. Although this is a present tense, you are talking about something that is going to happen in the **future**.

estoy **habl**ando	estamos **habl**ando	voy a **hablar**	vamos a **hablar**
estás **com**iendo	estáis **com**iendo	vas a **comer**	vais a **comer**
está **escrib**iendo	están **escrib**iendo	va a **escribir**	van a **escribir**

Miguel y Patricia **están camin**ando y **habl**ando.
*Miguel and Patricia **are walking** and **talking**.*

Patricia says:
—**Voy a comprar**le un regalo a mi hermana.
*I'm **going to buy** a gift for my sister.*

Remember to change **-iendo** to **-yendo** when the **stem** of an **-er** or an **-ir** verb ends in a **vowel**.

creer → cre**yendo**   **l**eer → le**yendo**   **o**ír → o**yendo**

ACTIVIDAD 7 Gramática

¿Qué están haciendo?

Hablar/Escribir Patricia y Miguel hacen muchas cosas. ¿Qué están haciendo en estas fotos?
(Hint: What are they doing?)

modelo

Patricia y Miguel están caminando.

Middle School Classroom Community

TPR Have pairs describe an activity the other partner should do. For example, **estás cantando** or **estás leyendo**. The partner acts out the activity.

Storytelling Have students work in groups to tell a story about a character who is doing something (present progressive) and then is going to do something else (**ir a**). You may have the characters speak or have them pantomime the action and let a narrator describe the actions.

ACTIVIDAD 8 Gramática Ir a...

Hablar/Escribir ¿Qué van a hacer estas personas? Escribe la forma correcta del verbo. *(Hint: Write the correct form of the verb to tell what these people are going to do.)*

modelo

Arturo (comprar) un disco compacto nuevo.

Arturo va a comprar **un disco compacto nuevo.**

1. Yo (leer) una revista interesante.
2. Tú (trabajar) en el jardín toda la mañana.
3. Antonio y José (comer) una merienda.
4. Mi mamá y yo (hacer ejercicio) en el gimnasio.
5. Elena (jugar) al voleibol con sus amigas.
6. Ustedes (sacar) fotos de la ciudad.
7. Nosotros (estudiar) para el examen de matemáticas.

■ **MÁS PRÁCTICA** *cuaderno* p. 69
■ **PARA HISPANOHABLANTES** *cuaderno* p. 67

ACTIVIDAD 9  En clase

Hablar/Escribir Describe lo que ustedes están haciendo en clase. *(Hint: Describe what you and your classmates are doing in class.)*

leer	escuchar	hacer	hablar	¿?
preparar	escribir	jugar	mirar	

modelo

mi compañero y yo   **Mi compañero y yo** *estamos haciendo la tarea.*

1. todos los estudiantes
2. el (la) maestro(a)
3. los estudiantes y yo
4. mi amigo(a)
5. yo
6. un chico
7. una chica
8. ¿?

ACTIVIDAD 10

Un sábado loco

PARA CONVERSAR

STRATEGY: SPEAKING
Use storytelling techniques Unexpected contrasts add interest to stories. Imagine an upside-down Saturday in which everyone decides to do spur-of-the-moment things. Example: **Mis padres no van a limpiar la casa. Van a buscar una nueva casa.**

Hablar Todos tienen planes para el sábado. Pero hay una diferencia —es un sábado loco. Trabaja con tu compañero(a) para inventar actividades locas. *(Hint: Take turns with a classmate to tell what the people are going to do on a crazy Saturday.)*

modelo

mi hermana

Mi hermana *no va a hacer la tarea. Va a bailar en la mesa y cantar en francés.*

1. mis padres
2. yo
3. mi maestro(a)
4. mi hermano(a)
5. mis amigos y yo
6. ¿?

trescientos trece
Etapa 3
313

Answers
1. Voy a leer una revista interesante.
2. Tú vas a trabajar en el jardín toda la mañana.
3. Antonio y José van a comer una merienda.
4. Mi mamá y yo vamos a hacer ejercicio en el gimnasio.
5. Elena va a jugar al voleibol con sus amigas.
6. Ustedes van a sacar fotos de la ciudad.
7. Vamos a estudiar para el examen de matemáticas.

Quick Wrap-up

Call out infinitives. One student gives the present progressive form. Another student uses it in a sentence. Do the same for **ir a** + infinitive.

9 Objective: Transitional practice
Present progressive

Answers will vary.

 10 Objective: Open-ended practice
Ir a + infinitive/vocabulary

Answers will vary.

Block Schedule

Change of Pace First, have students brainstorm a list of locations. Next, have them brainstorm a list of people (names, professions, etc.). Finally, have students write 10 sentences, matching up people and locations and saying what the people are doing, using the present progressive. (For additional activities, see **Block Scheduling Copymasters**.)

Teaching Middle School Students

Multiple Intelligences

Intrapersonal Have students think about and write down what they and several other people (**yo, mi hermano, mi amigo y yo, el maestro**, etc.) are doing on **un lunes lluvioso**. Have them share with their partners, and with the class, if appropriate.

Kinesthetic Tell students to imagine they are walking through the town of Otavalo and to describe what they are doing there. Have everyone stand up, and ask various students to call out an activity (**caminar**). Have students do the activity while saying what they are doing (**Estoy caminando**).

Teaching Resource Options

Print

Más práctica Workbook PE, p. 70
Para hispanohablantes Workbook
 PE, p. 68
Block Scheduling Copymasters
Unit 6 Resource Book
 Más práctica Workbook TE, p. 108
 Para hispanohablantes Workbook
  TE, p. 114
 Information Gap Activities, p. 119

Audiovisual

OHT 202, 203 (Quick Start)

Technology

Intrigas y aventuras CD-ROM, Disc 1

 Objective: Open-ended practice
Ir a + infinitive/present progressive/
vocabulary

Answers will vary.

Quick Start Review

♻ Affirmative **tú** commands

Use OHT 202 or write on the board:
Write 5 commands your Spanish
teacher might give you.

Answers
Answers will vary. Answers could include:
Mira la foto.
Trabaja con (Claudia).
Contesta las preguntas.
Lee el diálogo.
Levanta la mano.

Teaching Suggestions
Reviewing Affirmative tú
Commands

Have the first student in each row turn
and give a command to the second
student. That student acts out the
command then turns to the third
student and gives another command,
and so on. The last student in each row
gives a command to the first student.

Una carta

Escribir Estás de vacaciones
en un lugar divertido.
Escríbele una carta a un(a)
amigo(a) describiendo tus
actividades (reales o
imaginarias). *(Hint: Write a letter
telling about your activities on vacation,
real or imaginary.)*

- ¿Dónde estás?
- ¿Cómo es?
- ¿Qué están haciendo tu
  familia y tú?
- ¿Qué van a hacer mañana?

modelo

Querido Carlos:

*Estamos en el campo. ¡Qué
tranquilo es! Mis padres están
tomando un refresco…*

*Mañana mis hermanos y yo
vamos a…*

 REPASO

Review: Affirmative **tú** Commands

♻ **¿RECUERDAS?** *pp. 97, 177* Remember that **tú commands** are
used to give instructions to a friend or family member. The
affirmative tú command form of a regular verb is the same as
the **third person singular** of the simple present tense.

hablar → Habla.   **comer** → Come.   **escribir** → Escribe.

▸ Remember to attach **direct object**, **indirect object**, and **reflexive
pronouns** to **affirmative commands**. When you do, you usually need
to add an accent.

Háblame.   **Cómelo.**   **Escríbeles.**
Speak to me.   *Eat it.*   *Write to them.*

Miguel says: —**Cómprale** una bolsa…
Buy her *a handbag…*

▸ You also learned eight irregular **affirmative tú commands.**

decir → di	**ir** → ve	**salir** → sal	**tener** → ten
hacer → haz	**poner** → pon	**ser** → sé	**venir** → ven

 **12** Gramática **¡Haz lo que te digo!**

Hablar/Escribir Estás cuidando a tu primito. Dile lo que debe
hacer. *(Hint: You're baby-sitting a six-year-old. Tell him what to do.)*

modelo

lavar los platos   *Lava los platos.*

1. comer tus verduras
2. tener cuidado con el gato
3. salir temprano para la escuela
4. decir «por favor» y «gracias»
5. ir a tu habitación
6. compartir tus cosas
7. venir conmigo al jardín
8. ser bueno con tu hermana

■ **MÁS PRÁCTICA** *cuaderno p. 70*

■ **PARA HISPANOHABLANTES**
cuaderno p. 68

---

314 trescientos catorce
Unidad 6

Middle School Classroom Community

TPR Have students work in pairs to take turns sending
each other to various parts of the room to do chores.
(**Ve a la puerta y barre el suelo.**) You might also have
them report what they did when they return (**Fui a la
puerta y barrí el suelo**) and whether they liked it or
not (**No me gustó nada. Me encantó**).

Group Activity Ask students to think of five things
they did yesterday. Then have them work in groups
to make a list telling who did what (**Clara limpió su
habitación; Inés y Jaime leyeron un libro;** etc.). Have
groups share their lists with the class.

ACTIVIDAD 13

¡Hazlo ahora!

Hablar Tu amigo(a) quiere ayudarte. Dile lo que debe hacer. *(Hint: Tell your friend what to do to help you.)*

cerrar   apagar   **lavar**   hacer

preparar   sacar   **pasar**   contestar

poner   **tener**

1. ¡ _____ los platos!
2. ¡ _____ el teléfono!
3. ¡ _____ la luz!
4. ¡ _____ el almuerzo!
5. ¡ _____ las camas!
6. ¡ _____ la aspiradora!
7. ¡ _____ la puerta!
8. ¡ _____ cuidado!
9. ¡ _____ la basura!
10. ¡ _____ la mesa!

ACTIVIDAD 14

¡Ay, hermanito!

Escribir Tu hermanito(a) no está haciendo sus quehaceres. Haz una lista de los quehaceres que necesita hacer después de las clases. *(Hint: Make a list of chores for your little brother or sister to do after school.)*

> Lava los platos.
> Barre el suelo.

■ **MÁS COMUNICACIÓN** *p. R9*

REPASO

Review: Regular Preterite

♻ **¿RECUERDAS?** *pp. 230, 233, 260, 262* To talk about completed actions in the past, use the **preterite** tense.

-ar verbs		-er verbs		-ir verbs	
habl**é**	habl**amos**	com**í**	com**imos**	escrib**í**	escrib**imos**
habl**aste**	habl**asteis**	com**iste**	com**isteis**	escrib**iste**	escrib**isteis**
habl**ó**	habl**aron**	com**ió**	com**ieron**	escrib**ió**	escrib**ieron**

- Remember that the verb **ver** is regular in the **preterite** but has no accents.

- Remember that verbs ending in **-car, -gar,** and **-zar** have a spelling change in the **yo** form of the **preterite**.

  marcar → marqué   llegar → llegué   cruzar → crucé

- Third person forms of **-er** and **-ir** verbs with **stems** that end in a **vowel** require a **y** in the **preterite**.

l**e**í	l**e**ímos
l**e**íste	l**e**ísteis
l**ey**ó	l**ey**eron

Miguel says: —¿Y **aprendiste** algo de tus entrevistas?
*And **did you learn** something from your interviews?*

trescientos quince
Etapa 3

315

Teaching Middle School Students

Extra Help Work together on **Actividad 14** with students who need extra help. Talk through possible responses before asking them to write.

Multiple Intelligences

Musical/Rhythmic Have students write a short chant describing a typical baby-sitting scenario.

Intrapersonal Have students review the explanations of affirmative **tú** commands on pp. 97 and 177. Have them redo some of the related activities.

ACTIVIDAD 12

Objective: Controlled practice
Affirmative **tú** commands

Answers
1. Come tus verduras.
2. Ten cuidado con el gato.
3. Sal temprano para la escuela.
4. Di «por favor» y «gracias».
5. Ve a tu habitación.
6. Comparte tus cosas.
7. Ven conmigo al jardín.
8. Sé bueno con tu hermana.

ACTIVIDAD 13

Objective: Transitional practice
Affirmative **tú** commands

Answers
1. Lava	6. Pasa
2. Contesta	7. Cierra
3. Apaga	8. Ten
4. Prepara	9. Saca
5. Haz	10. Pon

ACTIVIDAD 14

Objective: Open-ended practice
Affirmative **tú** commands

Answers will vary.

🔔 **Quick Start Review**

♻ **Preterite**

Use OHT 203 or write on the board:
¿Qué hiciste ayer? Escribe 3 oraciones.

Answers
Answers will vary. Answers could include:
Visité a mis abuelos.
Leí una novela.
Preparé la tarea de español.

Teaching Suggestions
Reviewing Regular Preterite

Say a verb infinitive and a subject pronoun. Toss a soft ball to a student who gives the form. If correct, the student tosses the ball back to you. If incorrect, he/she tosses it to another student. Continue with more verbs.

■ **Block Schedule**

Retention Check students' retention of the preterite by distributing a worksheet of preterite forms of verbs minus the accent marks. Give students a time limit and have them add the accent marks. (For additional activities, see **Block Scheduling Copymasters**.)

Teaching Resource Options

Print

Más práctica Workbook PE, p. 71
Para hispanohablantes Workbook PE, p. 69
Unit 6 Resource Book
  Más práctica Workbook TE, p. 109
  Para hispanohablantes Workbook TE, p. 115

Technology

Intrigas y aventuras CD-ROM, Disc 1

ACTIVIDAD 15 Objective: Controlled practice
Preterite

Answers

1. A las seis y media patinó en la cocina.
2. A las siete jugó con la tarántula.
3. A las siete y trece jugó con la computadora de su papá.
4. A las siete y media se acostó en el sofá con zapatos sucios.
5. A las ocho menos veintidós lavó el gato con detergente.
6. A las ocho menos cuarto comió chicharrones antes de la cena.

Quick Wrap-up

Extend **Actividad 15** to practice **yo** forms of the preterite. Ask students if, when they were younger, they did any of the activities mentioned. For example: **¿Patinaste en la cocina (en la casa) alguna vez?** You may also wish to vary sentences as appropriate and add more of your own. Students may wish to brainstorm additional **travesuras**.

ACTIVIDAD 16 Objective: Controlled practice
Preterite

Answers

1. Ellos se lavaron los dientes.
2. Nosotros desayunamos.
3. Usted se quedó en la cama.
4. Luisa limpió la casa.

Juego

Answer: a

ACTIVIDAD 15 Gramática

¡No lo hagas!

Escribir Cuidaste a un niño de seis años que se portó muy mal. Anotaste todas sus travesuras *(pranks)*. Haz un resumen de todo lo que hizo esta noche. (*Hint:* You baby-sat a misbehaving child. Write down the things he did.)

modelo

6:00 / Está escribiendo en las paredes.
A las seis escribió en las paredes.

1. 6:30 / Está patinando en la cocina.
2. 7:00 / Está jugando con la tarántula.
3. 7:13 / Está jugando con la computadora de su papá.
4. 7:30 / Está acostándose en el sofá con zapatos sucios.
5. 7:38 / Está lavando el gato con detergente.
6. 7:45 / Está comiendo chicharrones antes de la cena.

▪ **MÁS PRÁCTICA** *cuaderno* p. 71
▪ **PARA HISPANOHABLANTES** *cuaderno* p. 69

ACTIVIDAD 16

¡Tanta actividad!

Escribir ¿Qué hicieron estas personas ayer por la mañana? (*Hint:* What did these people do yesterday morning?)

modelo

el señor Ruiz / afeitarse
El señor Ruiz se afeitó *ayer.*

1. ellos / lavarse los dientes

2. nosotros / desayunar

3. usted / quedarse en la cama

4. Luisa / limpiar la casa

Juego

Si tu mamá te dice «¡Sal para la escuela!», ¿qué vas a necesitar?

a.   b.

Middle School Classroom Community

Storytelling Have students create a story about someone's very unusual day (**un día loco**) in which the daily routines were upset. (**Un día Roberto se lavó los dientes antes de levantarse; Tomó la cena por la mañana y el desayuno por la noche**; etc.)

Game Have students divide into groups. Give each member a piece of paper, and ask them to write an infinitive on it. Put all the papers facedown and have each student draw one. One student makes a short sentence with the verb and passes it to the next student, who must make another sentence with a different subject. Award points for each correct sentence.

ACTIVIDAD 17

¿Qué hicieron?

Hablar/Escribir Describe qué hicieron todos. *(Hint: Describe what everyone did.)*

modelo

Patricia visitó una granja el sábado pasado.

Patricia y Miguel yo mi hermano(a) mis padres mi mejor amigo(a) mis amigos y yo ¿?	almorzar comer compartir escribir jugar leer ver visitar	¿?	ayer el sábado pasado anoche anteayer el año pasado el verano pasado la semana pasada

ACTIVIDAD 18

El domingo pasado

Escribir Imagínate qué hicieron varias personas y animales el domingo pasado. Escribe una lista de sus actividades. *(Hint: Write what various people and animals did last Sunday.)*

modelo

mis abuelos

Mis abuelos *salieron a comer a un restaurante elegante.*

1. el (la) maestro(a) de…
2. los bomberos
3. los caballos
4. el (la) cartero(a)
5. mis amigos y yo
6. el cerdo
7. los padres de mis amigos
8. los ganaderos

Conexiones

La música Latin American music is often characterized by lively percussion. Many percussion instruments are handmade and carefully constructed in order to produce the desired sound. Some instruments are filled with beans so that they rattle; others have jingling bells. **Maracas** come from Latin America, as do **claves**, a set of sticks that are hit together to produce a hollow, melodic sound.

PARA HACER:
Guess what these percussion instruments are, and draw a picture of each. You can check your guess in a dictionary or an encyclopedia.
• triángulo
• címbalos
• tímpano

trescientos diecisiete
Etapa 3
317

ACTIVIDAD 17
Objective: Transitional practice
Preterite

Answers will vary.

ACTIVIDAD 18
Objective: Open-ended practice
Preterite/vocabulary

Answers will vary.

Para hacer

Answers
triángulo = triangle
címbalos = cymbals
tímpano = timpani (kettledrum)

Block Schedule

FunBreak Have students write their own "mad libs." Each student writes 1–2 paragraphs relating an event that took place in the past. They then rewrite the paragraph(s) and replace various words with blanks. Under the blanks they put the part of speech that is required. Working with a partner, the student asks for words of the appropriate part of speech and writes them in the blanks. Finally, the student rereads the paragraph(s) with the inserted words.

Teaching Middle School Students

Native Speakers Ask students to talk about musical instruments in their home countries.

Multiple Intelligences

Musical/Rhythmic Have students look for recordings and/or videos of Latin American music with percussion instruments similar to the ones discussed in the **Conexiones**. Ask them to make a presentation for the class.

Teaching Resource Options

Print

Más práctica Workbook PE, p. 72
Para hispanohablantes Workbook PE, p. 70
Unit 6 Resource Book
  Más práctica Workbook TE, p. 109
  Para hispanohablantes Workbook TE, p. 115

Audiovisual

OHT 203 (Quick Start)

Technology

Intrigas y aventuras CD-ROM, Disc 1

Quick Start Review

 Preterite of regular verbs

Use OHT 203 or write on the board: Write 3 past tense sentences using some of the following verbs:

almorzar / sacar / empezar / leer / comer / escribir / buscar / poner

Answers

Answers will vary. Answers could include:
Anoche leí una revista.
La semana pasada mi hermano sacó la basura.
Ayer, la familia comió a las siete.

Teaching Suggestions
Reviewing Irregular Preterites

Call out present tense forms of the verbs with irregular preterites. Students must give the equivalent preterite form. For example: **hago / hice.**

19 Objective: Transitional practice Listening comprehension/preterite/vocabulary

Answers (See script, p. 301B.)

1. El fin de semana pasado, Rosa fue al campo a visitar a sus abuelos.
2. Las gallinas fueron muy cómicas e hicieron mucho ruido.
3. Por la tarde, Rosa fue al mercado con su prima.
4. Rosa no compró el saco porque se encontró con una amiga y salió a tomar un refresco.
5. El sábado por la noche, Rosa no hizo nada especial.

 REPASO

 ## Review: Irregular Preterite

♻ **¿RECUERDAS?** *pp. 264, 293* These are the irregular preterite verbs that you have learned.

dar *to give*	
di	dimos
diste	disteis
dio	dieron

decir *to say, to tell*	
dije	dijimos
dijiste	dijisteis
dijo	dijeron

estar *to be*	
estuve	estuvimos
estuviste	estuvisteis
estuvo	estuvieron

hacer *to make, to do*	
hice	hicimos
hiciste	hicisteis
hizo	hicieron

ir *to go* / ser *to be*	
fui	fuimos
fuiste	fuisteis
fue	fueron

tener *to have*	
tuve	tuvimos
tuviste	tuvisteis
tuvo	tuvieron

venir *to come*	
vine	vinimos
viniste	vinisteis
vino	vinieron

Patricia might say:

—La entrevista con tu tío Julio **fue** la mejor porque él me **dijo** lo que **hiciste** tú la primera vez que **estuviste** en la granja.

*The interview with your Uncle Julio **was** the best because he **told** me what you **did** the first time you **were** on the farm.*

 **19 Gramática** 🎧

Un buen fin de semana

Escuchar Escucha la conversación entre María y Rosa y completa las oraciones. *(Hint: Complete the sentences.)*

1. El fin de semana pasado, Rosa…
2. Las gallinas…
3. Por la tarde, Rosa…
4. Rosa no compró el saco porque…
5. El sábado por la noche, Rosa…

Middle School Classroom Community

Cooperative Learning The task is to work in groups to write sentences using irregular preterite verbs. The roles are (1) a student to lead the group in a review of **dar, hacer,** and **venir**; (2) a student to lead the group in a review of **decir, ir/ser, estar,** and **tener**; (3) a student to assign each member a subject and a verb; (4) a student to make sure that all have accurately written sentences. Students pass the papers around and check the work and then repeat the activity with different verbs.

20 Gramática

¡Excusas, excusas y más excusas!

Escribir La maestra no está contenta. Muchos estudiantes no hicieron la tarea. Explica por qué. *(Hint: Write why the students did not do their homework.)*

modelo

Ana y Horacio / hacer…

Ana y Horacio hicieron *un viaje con su familia.*

1. yo / ir…
2. mis amigos(as) y yo / tener…
3. mi abuelo(a) / venir…
4. mi familia y yo / estar…
5. mis amigos(as) / decir…
6. mis padres / dar…

■ **MÁS PRÁCTICA** *cuaderno* p. 72
■ **PARA HISPANOHABLANTES** *cuaderno* p. 70

21

¿Y tus excusas?

Hablar/Escribir Imagínate que varias personas no vinieron a tu fiesta. ¿Qué excusas te dieron? Habla con cuatro estudiantes para oír sus excusas. Escribe un resumen. *(Hint: Ask four students about their excuses for not attending your party. Then write a summary.)*

modelo

Estudiante A: *¿Por qué no viniste a mi fiesta anoche?*

Estudiante B: *No vine porque fui a un concierto.*

Resumen: *Julio no vino porque fue a un concierto. Clara no vino porque sus padres le dijeron que no. Martín no vino porque tuvo un partido de béisbol. Alicia no vino porque tuvo que ayudar en casa.*

Conexiones

El arte The painting shown here, *Ésta es fiesta de Reyes Magos,* was painted by Hugo Licta, an Ecuadorian painter, and shows a village scene in the Andes. It is an example of the naïf folk style of art. Painters using this style are known for creating simple images and for capturing the feel of a way of life.

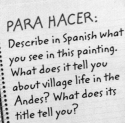

PARA HACER: Describe in Spanish what you see in this painting. What does it tell you about village life in the Andes? What does its title tell you?

trescientos diecinueve
Etapa 3
319

Answers

Answers will vary.
1. Yo fui…
2. Mis amigos(as) y yo tuvimos…
3. Mi abuelo(a) vino…
4. Mi familia y yo estuvimos…
5. Mis amigos(as) dijeron…
6. Mis padres dieron…

21 **Objective:** Open-ended practice Preterite/vocabulary

Answers will vary.

Teaching Middle School Students

Native Speakers Ask students to talk about art and artists in their home countries. This might be a good way for students to choose artists for research.

Multiple Intelligences

Visual Ask students to research other Latin American artists or artisans. Have them consult various sources and choose several artists and their works to present to the class.

Block Schedule

FunBreak Expand on **Actividades 20** and **21** by making a master class list of silly excuses for not doing something. Turn this into a poster for display in the classroom.

Teaching Resource Options

Print

Block Scheduling Copymasters
Unit 6 Resource Book
  Information Gap Activities, pp. 120–121
  Audioscript, p. 132
  Audioscript *Para hispanohablantes,*
    p. 132

Audiovisual

Audio Program Cassettes 18A, 18B /
CD 18
Audio *Para hispanohablantes*
  Cassette 18A / CD 18

Technology

Intrigas y aventuras **CD-ROM,** Disc 1

---

22 Objective: Open-ended practice
Preterite/vocabulary

Answers will vary.

23 Objective: Open-ended practice
Preterite/vocabulary

Answers will vary.

Project

Distinct regions—mountains, jungle, coast, plus the Galápagos Islands—make Ecuador an ecotourist's paradise. Assign a region to each of 4 groups. Each group plans the itinerary for an ecotourism trip. They should present this itinerary, along with their reasons for choosing their destinations, to the class in the form of a travelogue.

Animales de la granja

Hablar/Escribir Piensa en las actividades de estos animales. Imagínate qué hicieron ayer. *(Hint: What did the animals do yesterday?)*

> **modelo**
>
> *los cerdos*
>
> *Los cerdos* comieron todas las verduras.

comer	ver
correr	ir
beber	estar
compartir	venir

1. los caballos
2. el gallo
3. la llama
4. el toro
5. las gallinas
6. las vacas

¡Qué noticias!

Leer/Hablar Estás leyendo un artículo sobre algo que pasó en Quito, y un(a) amigo(a) te pregunta sobre lo que leíste. Contesta sus preguntas. *(Hint: Read the article and answer your classmate's questions.)*

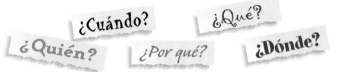

¿Cuándo? ¿Qué? ¿Quién? ¿Por qué? ¿Dónde?

Un turista contentísimo

Redacción Puyó

Quito— Ayer, en el centro de Quito, un turista mexicano pasó un día interesante. El turista perdió una bolsa con su pasaporte, su dinero, su tarjeta de crédito… y algo más.
«No sé cómo la perdí», dijo el turista, «pero hablé con un policía y me ayudó de una manera interesante».
El policía mandó al turista a un departamento especial. ¡Allí el turista encontró un perro con su bolsa! Otro policía le explicó todo:
«Salí con mi perro Nacho para hacer nuestra rutina diaria y, al llegar a la esquina, Nacho vio a otro perro con la bolsa. Cuando el perro sacó un sándwich de la bolsa, llegó Nacho y la tomó.
Afortunadamente Nacho sabe hacer bien su trabajo. ¡No hay ningún robo, solamente mucha hambre!»

NOTA CULTURAL

Ecuador is made up of three widely diverse regions: the Pacific coast, the Andes mountains, and the jungles of the Amazon. The variety of habitats makes Ecuador a popular ecotourism destination.

la Amazonia

Middle School Classroom Community

Learning Scenario Have students in groups imagine that someone in the group lost something valuable in a strange place. They act out the loss, its discovery, and attempts to recover it. When they're comfortable with their roles, have them perform for the class.

Portfolio Have students use **Actividad 25** as a portfolio opportunity. Have them make corrections and write a final draft before adding it to their portfolios.

Rubric

Criteria	Scale	
Vocabulary use/spelling	1 2 3 4 5	A = 17–20 pts.
Correct sentence structure/grammar	1 2 3 4 5	B = 13–16 pts.
Logical organization	1 2 3 4 5	C = 9–12 pts.
Creativity	1 2 3 4 5	D = 5–8 pts.
		F = < 5 pts.

ACTIVIDAD 24

Y el ganador es...

Hablar/Escribir Piensa en las personas de los diálogos. ¿Quién va a ganar el concurso? Escoge a una persona y explica por qué esta persona debe ganar. *(Hint: Choose a contest winner and explain why that person should win.)*

Francisco

Isabel

Ignacio

Carlos

Mercedes

Patricia

modelo

Pienso que Patricia debe ganar el concurso. Ella hizo… Trabajó mucho…

ACTIVIDAD 25

¿Cómo pasaste ayer?

Hablar/Escribir Describe cómo pasaste ayer. Preséntale tu historia a la clase. *(Hint: Describe what you did yesterday.)*

modelo

Me desperté a las seis y media, pero no me levanté hasta las siete. Desayuné y fui a la escuela. Aprendí mucho en la clase de matemáticas porque el maestro me dio...

■ **MÁS COMUNICACIÓN** p. R9

Pronunciación 🎧

Refrán

Pronunciación de la x The letter **x** is pronounced several different ways. Before a vowel, before the letters **ce** or **ci**, or at the end of a word, it sounds like the English *x* in the word *taxi*. At the beginning of a word or before a consonant, the **x** is pronounced like the *s* in *same*. To practice these sounds, pronounce the following.

¡Es un examen excepcional!   **Xochimilco y Taxco son lugares bonitos.**

In Mexico and Central America, the letter **x** also has the following sounds in words that come from other languages.

j as in **jarra:**   **México, Oaxaca, Xalapa**

sh as in *shoe:*   **Ixtepec, Uxmal**

Now try the **refrán** about the taxi.

El taxi gratis no existe.

Teaching Middle School Students

Extra Help Have sentences in the preterite on the board or an overhead. Ask the students to tell you who, when, why, etc., about the sentences. Then have them make sentences of their own as you tell them the elements they are to have in the sentences (who, what, where, etc.).

Multiple Intelligences

Naturalist Have students research areas in Ecuador of ecotouristic interest. A number of the areas, such as the Galápagos Islands, have web sites.

ACTIVIDAD 24
Objective: Open-ended practice
Ir a + infinitive/preterite/vocabulary

Answers will vary.

ACTIVIDAD 25
Objective: Open-ended practice
Preterite/vocabulary

Answers will vary.

🔔 Quick Wrap-up

Call on students at random to name 1 thing that happened last year in class or in school.

Teaching Note

You may wish to show the Video Epilogue segment here. See script, TE p. 301B. The Epilogue may also be shown during review (see TE p. 326).

Dictation

After presenting the **Pronunciación,** have students close their books. Dictate the **refrán** in segments while students write it.

📖 Block Schedule

Research Have students work in pairs to find out more about the 3 diverse regions of Ecuador. One student will be responsible for finding information in books and magazines, while the other researches on the Internet. Have them pool their information and submit a short written report, supported by illustrations. Have pairs present their work to the class. (For additional activities, see **Block Scheduling Copymasters**.)

Teaching Resource Options

Print

Block Scheduling Copymasters
Unit 6 Resource Book
  Audioscript, p. 133
  Audioscript *Para hispanohablantes*,
  p. 133

Audiovisual

OHT 203 (Quick Start)
Audio Program Cassette 18A / CD 18
Audio *Para hispanohablantes*
  Cassette 18A / CD 18
Canciones Cassette / CD

🔔 Quick Start Review

♻ **Ecuador**

Use OHT 203 or write on the board:
Write 5 statements about Ecuador that
you learned in this unit.

Answers
Answers will vary. Answers could include:
Ecuador queda en América del Sur.
La capital de Ecuador es Quito.
El dinero de Ecuador se llama el sucre.
Unas personas hablan quichua.
El ecuador pasa por Ecuador.

Teaching Suggestions

- **Prereading** Have students
  brainstorm all they know about bats
  and their habits.

- **Strategy: Use pictures** Have
  students skim the story and study the
  pictures for clues about the content
  of the story.

- **Reading** Have students scan the
  reading for direct quotes. Ask them
  how quotes in Spanish differ from
  those in English (the use of
  guillemets or dashes, not quotation
  marks).

- **Post-reading** Ask students to
  describe each illustration for the
  Lectura and to tie it to the story.

En voces
LECTURA

PARA LEER
STRATEGY: READING
Use pictures In this legend,
the **murciélago** is the main
character of the narrative.
Skim the reading and look at
the pictures to remember
what a **murciélago** is. What
other characters are part of
this reading?

El murciélago cobarde

Un día, los animales del bosque y los pájaros del cielo[1]
decidieron luchar[2]. Los animales llamaron al murciélago
y le dijeron: «Ven y pelea[3] con nosotros contra los pájaros.»
Pero el murciélago contestó: «¿No ven ustedes que soy
pájaro? ¿No ven que tengo alas[4]?»

Entonces, fueron los pájaros al murciélago y le dijeron:
«Ven y pelea con nosotros contra los animales.» Pero
el murciélago les dijo: «¿No ven que soy animal?
Tengo dientes y no tengo plumas.»

---

[1] sky   [3] fight
[2] to fight   [4] wings

322 trescientos veintidós
Unidad 6

Middle School Classroom Community

Group Activity Have students dramatize **El
murciélago cobarde**. Have the class work together to
write the script. Let them choose the students to play
the characters, others to design costumes and set, etc.

Paired Activity After students find out what the
unfamiliar animals in the illustrations are called, let
them work in pairs to make drawings, computer
pictures, etc., of the **Lectura** animals. Have students
label their creations and make a display for the class.

Empezó la lucha y, viendo que ganaban[5] los animales, el murciélago fue con ellos. Pero los animales lo rechazaron[6]. Luego vio que los pájaros ganaban y fue con ellos, pero los pájaros también lo rechazaron.

Por fin, fatigados por la lucha, los dos campos pusieron fin[7] al conflicto. Hicieron una fiesta para todos. El murciélago trató de[8] entrar a la fiesta. Cuando todos lo vieron, se pusieron[9] furiosos y lo expulsaron de la fiesta. Le gritaron: «¡De aquí en adelante vas a vivir en una cueva[10] y sólo vas a salir de noche porque eres un cobarde[11]!»

Y así, pues, el murciélago tiene miedo de los animales y los pájaros y por eso no quiere salir de día.

[5] were winning	[7] *pusieron fin* put an end	[10] cave
[6] rejected	[8] *trató de* tried to	[11] coward
	[9] became	

¿Comprendiste?

1. ¿Qué pasó entre los animales y los pájaros?
2. ¿Qué hicieron los animales después de la lucha?
3. ¿Qué hizo el murciélago después de la lucha?
4. ¿Qué le dijeron los animales y los pájaros al murciélago?

¿Qué piensas?

1. ¿Crees que es un cobarde el murciélago? ¿Por qué o por qué no?
2. ¿Qué es el murciélago, pájaro o mamífero *(mammal)*? ¿Cómo lo sabes?
3. ¿Qué otros cuentos explican cómo son los animales?

323

Interdisciplinary Connections

Science Have students point to the animals on these pages that are **pájaros**. Then announce the names of the following land animals pictured on the pages. (These are cognates.) As you say the names, have students point to each one: jaguar, marsupial, iguana. Students may also be interested in learning the names of the other animals: anteater (**oso hormiguero**), deer (**ciervo/venado**) and monkey (**mono**).

Language Note

Ask students to think of English words related to the following Spanish words (via Latin)—line 1: **cielo** (*celestial, ceiling*); line 9: **dientes** (*dentist, dental, denture, indent*); **pluma** (*plume, plumage*). Finally, students may be interested to learn that the Spanish word for *bat* is made of two words: *mouse* ("mus" in Latin) and *sky* (**cielo**, in Spanish).

¿Comprendiste?

Answers

1. Empezó una lucha.
2. Hicieron una fiesta para todos.
3. Trató de entrar a la fiesta.
4. Le dijeron que tiene que vivir en una cueva y salir sólo de noche porque es un cobarde.

Teaching Resource Options

Print

Unit 6 Resource Book
Audioscript, p. 133
Audioscript *Para hispanohablantes,*
p. 133

Audiovisual

Audio Program Cassette 18A / CD 18
Audio *Para hispanohablantes*
Cassette 18A / CD 18
OHT 204 (Quick Start)

Quick Start Review

♻ Foods

Use OHT 204 or write on the board:
List at least 2 foods for each of the
following:

• desayuno
• almuerzo
• merienda
• cena

Answers
Answers will vary. Answers could include:
• desayuno: los huevos, el jamón
• almuerzo: la hamburguesa, la sopa
• merienda: las papas fritas, las tapas
• cena: el pescado, el arroz

Teaching Suggestions
Presenting Cultura y comparaciones

• Have students read the Connecting
Cultures Strategy and write their
grocery lists. Tell them to talk with a
grocer some time over the next week
to find out where the products come
from and when they are out of season
in the U.S.
• Have students brainstorm a list of
dishes made with potatoes, tomatoes,
and corn. Ask if any of the dishes
have any particular cultural
association (such as spaghetti or
tortillas).
• Ask if any students have worked on a
farm that grows fruits or vegetables
or if they have a vegetable garden.
What does it take for the farm or
garden to be successful?

En colores

CULTURA Y COMPARACIONES

Cómo las Américas cambiaron la comida europea

PARA CONOCERNOS

STRATEGY:
CONNECTING CULTURES

Identify international foods Make
a grocery list of fresh fruits
and vegetables (4 or 5 items)
that are regularly part of your
family's diet. When is their
growing season in the U.S.?
Where do they come from
when out-of-season? Check
with the produce manager
of your grocery store. Then
decide which foods that your
family eats come from other
countries.

Comida	Estación
naranja	marzo-abril

¿**P**uedes imaginarte tu dieta sin papas? Pues, en Europa
no había[1] papas hasta que los conquistadores llegaron a las
Américas. Los europeos comieron la papa por primera vez
en América. La papa, planta nativa de Perú, era[2] la comida
principal de los incas, indígenas de esa zona. La palabra
papa es de origen quechua, la lengua de los incas.

Los españoles empezaron a llevar papas a España.
Comida barata para los marineros[3], así llegó la papa a
Europa. Hoy la papa es una de las comidas principales
de Irlanda, Alemania, Rusia y Polonia.

---
[1] there were no   [2] was   [3] sailors

324 trescientos veinticuatro
Unidad 6

Middle School Classroom Community

Paired Activity Have students take turns with their
partners naming a meal or a food that includes one of
the three vegetables. Call time and have the class make
contributions to a class list of foods.

those vegetables and how those meals would taste
without them.

Rubric

Portfolio Have students write 2 or 3 paragraphs
about the importance of potatoes, tomatoes, and corn
in their diet. Tell them to think of meals that include

Criteria	Scale	
Vocabulary use/spelling	1 2 3 4 5	A = 17–20 pts.
Correct sentence structure/grammar	1 2 3 4 5	B = 13–16 pts.
Logical organization	1 2 3 4 5	C = 9–12 pts.
Creativity	1 2 3 4 5	D = 5–8 pts.
		F = < 5 pts.

El maíz[4] también es de las Américas. El cultivo de maíz empezó en México alrededor del año 3500 a.C.[5] Llegó a Perú alrededor de 3200 a.C., pero no fue tan importante en la dieta de los peruanos como en la dieta de los mexicanos. En México se hicieron las tortillas del maíz.

Otro producto americano que cambió la comida europea es el tomate. No sabemos exactamente cómo y cuándo el tomate llegó a Europa, pero su cultivo era fácil en los países mediterráneos.

Entonces, las papas fritas y la salsa de tomate para los espaguetis son de origen europeo, pero sus ingredientes principales llegaron a Europa de América. ¿Ves? Los viajes de Colón cambiaron muchas cosas, ¡entre ellas la comida europea!

---

4 corn   5 B.C.

¿Comprendiste?

1. ¿De dónde vino la papa?
2. ¿Cómo llegó la papa a Europa?
3. ¿De dónde vino el maíz?
4. El maíz tuvo más importancia en la dieta de qué país, ¿Perú o México?
5. ¿Cómo llegó el tomate a Europa?

¿Qué piensas?

1. En tu opinión, ¿cómo sería la comida europea sin la papa y el tomate? ¿Y la comida norteamericana? ¿Por qué?
2. ¿Cómo crees que llegó la papa de España a otras partes de Europa?

Hazlo tú

Busca una receta con papas, tomates o maíz. Escribe la receta en español. Prepárala y comparte la comida con la clase. ¿Es una receta europea o americana? Explica su origen.

trescientos veinticinco
Etapa 3

Teaching Resource Options

Print

Para hispanohablantes Workbook
PE, pp. 47–48
Block Scheduling Copymasters
Unit 6 Resource Book
Para hispanohablantes Workbook
TE, pp. 117–118
Videoscript, p. 128
Information Gap Activities, p. 122
Family Involvement, pp. 123–124
Multiple Choice Test Questions,
pp. 170–178

Audiovisual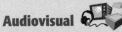

OHT 204 (Quick Start)
Audio Program Testing Cassette T2 /
CD T2
Video Program Videotape 6 /
Videodisc 3B

Search Chapter 9, Play to 10
Epilogue

Technology

Electronic Teacher Tools/Test
Generator
Intrigas y aventuras CD-ROM, Disc 1

Teaching Note

You may choose to show the Video Epilogue
segment, which reveals the contest winners.

Quick Start Review

Hacer, ir

Use OHT 204 or write on the board:
Write 3 sentences each for the verbs
hacer and **ir**. Sentence 1 must use the
preterite, sentence 2 the present, and
sentence 3 **ir a**...

Answers *See p. 301B.*

Teaching Suggestions
What Have Students Learned?

Have students look at the "Now you
can..." notes listed on the left side
of pages 326–327. Remind them to
review the material in the "To review"
notes before doing the activities or
taking the test.

Now you can...

• talk about the
present and future.

To review

• present progressive
and **ir a** + infinitive,
see p. 312.

Now you can...

• give instructions to
someone.

To review

• affirmative **tú**
commands, see
p. 314.

En uso

REPASO Y
MÁS COMUNICACIÓN

OBJECTIVES

• Talk about the present and
future
• Give instructions to someone
• Discuss the past

ACTIVIDAD 1 ¡Muy ocupados!

Miguel y sus amigos hablan por teléfono de sus actividades.
¿Qué dicen? *(Hint: Tell present and future activities.)*

modelo

yo: estudiar matemáticas / ir al campo
*Ahora **yo** estoy estudiando **matemáticas**, pero más tarde voy a **ir al campo**.*

1. Patricia: escribir cartas / hacer unas entrevistas
2. tú: hacer la tarea / alquilar un video
3. mis padres: limpiar la casa / caminar con el perro
4. yo: leer una novela / ir al cine
5. nosotros: ver la televisión / hacer ejercicio en el gimnasio
6. mi hermana: maquillarse / salir con Bernardo
7. ustedes: comer chicharrones / cenar en un restaurante elegante
8. tú: abrir unas cartas / andar en bicicleta

ACTIVIDAD 2 Una cena importante

El arquitecto que Patricia entrevistó viene a cenar
con ella y su familia esta noche. La madre de
Patricia necesita su ayuda. ¿Qué le dice? *(Hint: Say
what Patricia's mother tells her to do to prepare for a dinner guest.)*

modelo

limpiar el baño
Limpia el baño.

1. lavar los platos
2. barrer el suelo
3. poner la mesa
4. hacer los quehaceres
   cuidadosamente
5. tener cuidado
6. ir al supermercado a comprar
   más refrescos
7. ponerte un vestido
8. servir las bebidas
9. ser simpática durante la cena
10. pasar la aspiradora

326 trescientos veintiséis
Unidad 6

Middle School Classroom Community

Group Activity Tell the class to imagine that they
visited a farm last weekend. Have them tell what they
saw (preterite tense), what they liked and disliked, etc.

Game Start the game by telling the students on Team
A where they are going. Have them take turns telling
what they are going to do there. (**Vamos al gimnasio:
Voy a hacer ejercicio; Carlos va a jugar al baloncesto;
Tú vas a ver un partido;** etc.) Award one point for
each logical activity. Take turns with other destinations
and activities.

Now you can...
· discuss the past.

To review
· regular preterite verbs, see p. 315.

ACTIVIDAD 3 ¿Qué hiciste?

Patricia habla con una amiga sobre el fin de semana pasado. ¿Qué dice? *(Hint: Tell what happened last weekend.)*

modelo
yo: tomar el autobús al campo · *Yo tomé el autobús al campo.*

1. yo: visitar una granja en el campo
2. Miguel: decidir acompañarme
3. Miguel y yo: ver muchos animales
4. yo: sacar muchas fotos
5. mi madre: escribir cartas
6. mi padre: leer unas revistas
7. mis hermanos: correr en el parque
8. yo: ver a Ana en el mercado de Otavalo
9. ella: comprar algunas artesanías a muy buen precio
10. yo: llegar a casa muy tarde

Now you can...
· discuss the past.

To review
· irregular preterite verbs, see p. 318.

ACTIVIDAD 4 Un día especial

Patricia habla con su madre. Completa lo que dicen con el pretérito de los verbos. *(Hint: Complete what Patricia and her mother are saying about what happened yesterday.)*

Mamá: Patricia, tú __1__ (venir) a casa muy tarde ayer.

Patricia: Sí, mamá. Miguel y yo __2__ (ir) al campo.

Mamá: ¿Y qué __3__ (hacer) ustedes allí?

Patricia: Yo __4__ (hacer) entrevistas con el tío Julio y Bárbara.

Mamá: ¿Ellos te __5__ (decir) algo interesante?

Patricia: Sí. El tío Julio me __6__ (decir) mucho sobre la vida en una granja. La entrevista con Bárbara, la artesana, también __7__ (ser) interesante, y ella me __8__ (dar) este saco.

Mamá: ¡Qué bonito! ¿Ustedes __9__ (ir) a Otavalo por la tarde?

Patricia: Sí, mamá. Nosotros __10__ (estar) en el mercado por tres horas. Allí yo __11__ (tener) la oportunidad de entrevistar a un vendedor. Por eso, yo __12__ (venir) a casa tan tarde. Lo siento.

ACTIVIDAD 1 Answers

1. Ahora Patricia está escribiendo cartas, pero más tarde va a hacer unas entrevistas.
2. Ahora tú estás haciendo la tarea, pero más tarde vas a alquilar un video.
3. Ahora mis padres están limpiando la casa, pero más tarde van a caminar con el perro.
4. Ahora yo estoy leyendo una novela, pero más tarde voy a ir al cine.
5. Ahora nosotros estamos viendo la televisión, pero más tarde vamos a hacer ejercicio en el gimnasio.
6. Ahora mi hermana está maquillándose (se está maquillando), pero más tarde va a salir con Bernardo.
7. Ahora ustedes están comiendo chicharrones, pero más tarde van a cenar en un restaurante elegante.
8. Ahora tú estás abriendo unas cartas, pero más tarde vas a andar en bicicleta.

ACTIVIDAD 2 Answers

1. Lava los platos.
2. Barre el suelo.
3. Pon la mesa.
4. Haz los quehaceres cuidadosamente.
5. Ten cuidado.
6. Ve al supermercado a comprar más refrescos.
7. Ponte un vestido.
8. Sirve las bebidas.
9. Sé simpática durante la cena.
10. Pasa la aspiradora.

ACTIVIDAD 3 Answers

1. Yo visité una granja en el campo.
2. Miguel decidió acompañarme.
3. Miguel y yo vimos muchos animales.
4. Yo saqué muchas fotos.
5. Mi madre escribió cartas.
6. Mi padre leyó unas revistas.
7. Mis hermanos corrieron en el parque.
8. Yo vi a Ana en el mercado de Otavalo.
9. Ella compró algunas artesanías a muy buen precio.
10. Yo llegué a casa muy tarde.

ACTIVIDAD 4 Answers

1. viniste	5. dijeron	9. fueron
2. fuimos	6. dijo	10. estuvimos
3. hicieron	7. fue	11. tuve
4. hice	8. dio	12. vine

Teaching Middle School Students

Extra Help To help students sort out the tenses, draw a chart on the board. Headings are **ahora**, **más tarde**, and **ayer**. Generate a verb phrase, and ask them to write one phrase for each category. Example: **lavar los platos: Más tarde voy a lavar los platos; Ahora estoy lavando los platos; Ayer lavé los platos.**

Multiple Intelligences

Kinesthetic Have students take turns telling their partners what to do. The partners respond to the commands first by pantomiming the action and then by describing the action using the present progressive.

Block Schedule

Change of Pace Have students create time lines that mark off at least 6 important dates. Next to each date they write what happened or what they did on that date. (For additional activities, see **Block Scheduling Copymasters**.)

Teaching Resource Options

Print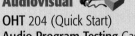

Unit 6 Resource Book
Cooperative Quizzes, pp. 135–136
Etapa Exam, Forms A and B,
  pp. 137–146
Para hispanohablantes Etapa Exam,
  pp. 147–151
Portfolio Assessment, pp. 152–153
Unit 6 Comprehensive Test,
  pp. 154–161
Para hispanohablantes Unit 6
  Comprehensive Test, pp. 162–169
Final Test, pp. 179–186
Multiple Choice Test Questions,
  pp. 170–178

Audiovisual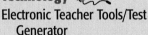

OHT 204 (Quick Start)
Audio Program Testing Cassette T2 /
  CD T2

Technology

Electronic Teacher Tools/Test
  Generator

 www.mcdougallittell.com

ACTIVIDAD 5

Rubric: Speaking

Criteria	Scale	
Vocabulary use	1 2 3 4 5	**A** = 13–15 pts.
Sentence structure	1 2 3 4 5	**B** = 10–12 pts.
Ease, fluency	1 2 3 4 5	**C** = 7–9 pts.
		D = 4–6 pts.
		F = < 4 pts.

ACTIVIDAD 6 *Answers will vary.*

ACTIVIDAD 7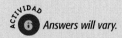
En tu propia voz

Rubric: Writing

Criteria	Scale	
Vocabulary use	1 2 3 4 5	**A** = 13–15 pts.
Accuracy	1 2 3 4 5	**B** = 10–12 pts.
Creativity, appearance	1 2 3 4 5	**C** = 7–9 pts.
		D = 4–6 pts.
		F = < 4 pts.

Teaching Note: En tu propia voz

Remind students to review the writing strategy ""Tell who, what, where, when, why, and how" before beginning their vacation paragraphs. A well-written paragraph uses many details to communicate information.

ACTIVIDAD 5 ¿Quién soy yo?

PARA CONVERSAR
STRATEGY: SPEAKING
Rely on the basics You have practiced many speaking strategies for different contexts. These work in all situations. Keep them in mind as you speak.

1. Don't be afraid to make mistakes.
2. Encourage yourself; think positively.
3. Take your time.
4. Take risks; improvise.
5. Say more, rather than less.

And enjoy speaking… now that you have plenty you can say!

Imagínate que eres una de las personas de este libro. Dile a otro(a) estudiante qué hiciste ayer, qué estás haciendo ahora y qué vas a hacer mañana. Él o ella tiene que adivinar quién eres. *(Hint: Play the role of a character. Your partner must guess who you are.)*

Francisco **Ignacio** Mercedes Diana
Alma Ricardo **Patricia** Luis **Miguel**
Isabel Carlos Sofía

ACTIVIDAD 6 ¿Qué hago?

Vas a uno de estos lugares por primera vez. Los otros estudiantes van a decirte qué debes hacer allí. *(Hint: Select a place; classmates will tell you what to do there.)*

la playa   **el campo**   **un bosque tropical**
una granja   **una ciudad grande**   **¿?**
un mercado mexicano   **las montañas**

modelo

Estudiante A: *Voy a una ciudad grande por primera vez. ¿Qué hago?*

Estudiante B: *Ve a un concierto.*

ACTIVIDAD 7 *En tu propia voz*

Escritura Estás pensando en las vacaciones de verano. Escribe un párrafo sobre lo que hiciste el verano pasado y otro párrafo sobre lo que vas a hacer este verano. *(Hint: Write a paragraph about what you did last summer and another paragraph about what you are going to do this summer.)*

Conexiones

La salud You have just read how New World foods changed European cuisine. Select a Spanish-speaking country and write a brief report about what people in that country typically eat. Prepare the food you would most like to taste. Was it difficult or easy to prepare? Is it nutritious?

¿Qué desayunan? ¿Almuerzan? ¿Cenan?
¿A qué hora almuerzan? ¿Cenan?
¿Qué meriendas hay?
¿Qué hay de postre?
¿Cuál es el plato más famoso de este país?

Middle School Classroom Community

Group Activity Before doing **Actividad 7**, have students use **tú** commands to write suggestions for activities to do during summer vacation (**Ve a la playa; Visita a tus abuelos;** etc.). Tell each group to compile the suggestions and share them with the class.

Portfolio Have students put a copy of the final draft of their paragraphs about last summer and next summer (**Actividad 7**) in their portfolios.

Rubric

Criteria	Scale	
Vocabulary use	1 2 3 4 5	**A** = 13–15 pts.
Accuracy	1 2 3 4 5	**B** = 10–12 pts.
Creativity Appearance	1 2 3 4 5	**C** = 7–9 pts.
		D = 4–6 pts.
		F = < 4 pts.

En resumen

♻ YA SABES

TALKING ABOUT THE PRESENT AND FUTURE

Simple Present

Estoy muy feliz.	I am very happy.
¡Es un mercado fenomenal!	It's a phenomenal market!
La artesanía de Otavalo es excelente.	The handicrafts from Otavalo are excellent.

Present Progressive

Miguel y Patricia están caminando y hablando.	Miguel and Patricia are walking and talking.

Ir a + *infinitive*

Voy a comprarle un regalo a mi hermana.	I am going to buy a present for my sister.
¡Creo que va a salir muy bien y lo quiero ver!	I think that it is going to come out very well and I want to see it!

DISCUSSING THE PAST

Regular Preterite

¿Porque te habló de la vida en una granja?	Because he talked to you about life on a farm?
¿Y aprendiste algo de tus entrevistas?	And did you learn something from your interviews?
Pero aprendí algo mucho más importante también.	But I learned something much more important too.
¡Abriste la cerca!	You opened the fence!
Trabajé mucho.	I worked a lot.

Irregular Preterite

¿Cuál fue la mejor entrevista?	Which was the best interview?
No, ¡porque me dijo qué hiciste tú la primera vez que estuviste en la granja!	No, because he told me what you did the first time that you were at the farm!
Hice todo lo posible.	I did everything possible.

GIVING INSTRUCTIONS TO SOMEONE

Dime.	Tell me.
¡Mira, Miguel!	Look, Miguel!
Cómprale una bolsa o un artículo de cuero.	Buy her a handbag or leather goods.
¡Ven!	Come on!
Hazme un favor.	Do me a favor.

Juego

1. ¿Qué pasa ahora?   3. ¿Qué va a pasar?

2. ¿Qué pasó antes?

¡El caballo se va a escapar del corral!

La llama está jugando con Rocío.

El ganadero buscó su merienda.

trescientos veintinueve
Etapa 3 **329**

Interdisciplinary Connections

Health Have students research the nutritional value of foods that are typical of or originated in Latin America, such as potatoes, corn, tomatoes, bananas, etc. They should find out the vitamin content, the fat content, and the caloric content of a typical serving.

🔔 Quick Start Review

♻ Verb tense review

Use OHT 204 or write on the board: For each sentence, write Past, Present, or Future.

1. Hablaron francés en la fiesta.
2. ¿Qué estás comiendo?
3. ¿Quién abrió la puerta?
4. ¿A qué hora van a salir?
5. La clase empieza a las nueve.
6. Fui a Puerto Rico.
7. Voy a trabajar mucho.
8. ¿Qué estás haciendo ahora?

Answers

1. Past	5. Present
2. Present	6. Past
3. Past	7. Future
4. Future	8. Present

Teaching Suggestions
Verb Tense Review

Have students sketch a scene showing some kind of action. Then have them exchange papers with a partner. Students must write a past tense sentence, a present tense sentence, and a sentence with **ir a...** that describe their partner's action scene.

Juego

Answers
1. La llama está jugando con Rocío.
2. El ganadero buscó su merienda.
3. ¡El caballo se va a escapar del corral!

Teaching Middle School Students

Multiple Intelligences

Interpersonal Have students make a list of 6 people (students in the class, family members, students and teachers in other classes, etc.). Have them alternate with partners to say what those people are probably doing right now. Have them share answers with the class.

Intrapersonal Ask students to make 2 lists of what they are going to do during the summer. Label one list **Me gusta…** and the other **No me gusta…** Have them share the information with their partners. (**Voy a trabajar para mi abuelo. Me gusta.**)

▉ Block Schedule

FunBreak Have students play one of the games in the **Ampliación** on TE p. 249A.

Teaching Resource Options

Print
Block Scheduling Copymasters

Audiovisual
OHT GO1–GO5; 204 (Quick Start)

Technology
Intrigas y aventuras CD-ROM, Disc 1

www.mcdougallittell.com

Quick Start Review

♻ Academic skills

Use OHT 204 or write on the board:
¿Qué hace un buen estudiante?
Escribe 5 oraciones.

Answers
Answers will vary. Answers could include:
Hace todas las tareas.
Estudia mucho para los exámenes.
Siempre trae el libro y el cuaderno a clase.
Escucha al (a la) profesor(a).
Trabaja bien con los otros estudiantes.
Levanta la mano cuando quiere hablar.

Teaching Suggestions
Los estudios sociales
Direct students to a topographical map of the western hemisphere (North, Central, and South America). Ask them what parts of the U.S. have great regional contrasts (western states, due to the influence of ocean currents, deserts, and mountainous areas).

Conexiones
OTRAS DISCIPLINAS Y PROYECTOS

Los estudios sociales

Although Ecuador is one of the smallest countries in South America, it has an extraordinary geography. The Andes mountains divide it down the middle. Cotopaxi, at 5,897 meters, is among the three highest active volcanoes in the world. The Pacific Ocean lies to the west. The Amazon jungle is to the east.

In addition to coastal plains (**la llanura litoral**), jungles (**selvas**), and mountains (**montañas**), Ecuador has the rain forest (**el bosque tropical**), the cloud forest (**el bosque nuboso**), and the astonishing **Islas Galápagos**—13 volcanic islands. These islands have animals found nowhere else on earth. Visitors from all over the world visit the Galápagos each year.

1. *Look at a Spanish-language topographical map of Ecuador. Locate each of the geographical regions mentioned.*

2. *Calculate the height of Cotopaxi in feet and miles. These formulas will help.*

   un metro = 3,28 pies
   un milla = 5.280 pies

This now-calm bay in the Galápagos Islands was once a steamy sea of lava and ash.

La historia

The powerful Inca civilization began near Lake Titicaca, between Bolivia and Peru, in the twelfth century. Eventually, the Inca empire included territory from Colombia to Chile. The Incas developed sophisticated systems of government, architecture, agriculture, transportation, communications, and science.

Tierras de los incas, siglo XVI

Since they lived in a region prone to earthquakes (**temblores de tierra**), the Incas became very adept at building earthquake-resistant structures. Today you can still see ancient buildings that were constructed with stones weighing many tons, interconnecting like jigsaw puzzle pieces. The stones fit together so tightly that not even a knife blade can pass between them.

Draw or trace a map of South America. Color in and label the countries where the Inca empire once existed.

Ingapirca was built by the Incas in the 15th century. These are its ruins.

330 trescientos treinta
Unidad 6

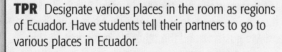

Middle School Classroom Community

TPR Designate various places in the room as regions of Ecuador. Have students tell their partners to go to various places in Ecuador.

Group Activity Divide the class into groups. Have the groups discuss the problems caused by earthquakes and then research the issue of earthquake-safe construction. Ask them to make drawings or models to demonstrate what they have learned.

Proyecto cultural

Working in a group of three or four, prepare a presentation (in Spanish!) on one of Ecuador's diverse geographical areas.

1. Choose from among the following regions.

   - the Galápagos Islands
   - the Andes mountain range
   - the rain forest
   - the coast

2. Make a map of the area of your choice, carefully labeling distinctive landmarks.

3. Through the Internet or other resources available in your library, obtain copies of photos of your region.

4. Work together to prepare an informative report about your geographical area. Be sure to talk about both the human and animal populations inhabiting your region.

5. Share your work with the class.

The blue-footed booby is one of the many species found on the Galápagos Islands.

las islas Galápagos

ECUADOR

la costa

el bosque tropical

los Andes

trescientos treinta y uno
Unidad 6

331

Teaching Middle School Students

Native Speakers Ask native speakers to discuss regions in their home countries and the climate and geography associated with them.

Multiple Intelligences

Logical/Mathematical Have students research the height of other mountains and volcanoes in Ecuador. Also have them research the effect of the altitude on the climate, since Ecuador is literally on the equator.

Teaching Suggestions
La historia

- Show students or direct them to appropriate sources for photographs of buildings in Ecuador and Peru built by the Incas hundreds of years ago (Cuzco and Machu Picchu, Peru, are excellent sources) so they can see how expert the Incas were at building earthquake-resistant structures. Try to locate a photo of the characteristically Incan trapezoidal door.

- Discuss with students how vast the Inca empire was (direct students to the map on this page) and how nearly impassable the terrain was (the Andes soar to 23,000 feet). In spite of these obstacles, the entire region was linked by many roads (the Incas were also expert engineers). Information was transmitted from one area to another by the use of runners (similar to the U.S. pony express), who carried encoded messages (called **quipus**) from place to place.

Block Schedule

Variety Artistically oriented students may be interested in making a topographical map of Ecuador using papier-mâché. Have them indicate the various regions by painting each one an appropriate color (ocean–blue, coast–brown/green, mountains–brown/white, jungle–deep green).

RECURSOS

RECURSOS

1 ¿Qué es?

Unidad 4 Etapa 1 p. 251

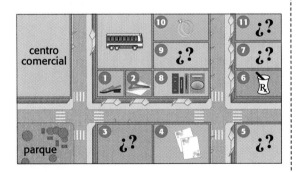

Estudiante A Tú no conoces el centro muy bien. Habla con tu amigo(a) para identificar todos los lugares. *(Hint: Identify the places.)*

modelo

Estudiante A: ¿Qué está enfrente del centro comercial?

Estudiante B: ...está enfrente del centro comercial.

Estudiante B Tú no conoces el centro muy bien. Habla con tu amigo(a) para identificar todos los lugares. *(Hint: Identify the places.)*

modelo

Estudiante A: ¿Qué está enfrente del centro comercial?

Estudiante B: La estación de autobuses está enfrente del centro comercial.

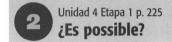

2 ¿Es possible?

Unidad 4 Etapa 1 p. 225

1. sacar una foto
2. jugar al baloncesto
3. comer pizza
4. andar en bicicleta
5. beber un refresco
6. escribir tu nombre en un papel

Estudiante A: Toca el piano.

Estudiante B: No es posible.

modelo

tocar el piano

Estudiante A Dile a tu amigo(a) qué hacer. Si tiene lo necesario, va a dramatizarla. Si no lo tiene, va a decirte que no es posible. Cambien de papel. *(Hint: Tell your partner what to do. If possible, your partner will act it out.)*

Estudiante B Tu amigo(a) te va a decir qué hacer. Si tienes el objeto necesario, dramatiza la actividad. Si no lo tienes, dile que no es posible. Cambien de papel. *(Hint: Your partner will say what to do. If possible, act it out. If not, say so.)*

modelo

tocar el piano

Estudiante A: Toca el piano.

Estudiante B: No es posible.

7. escribir en el pizarrón
8. usar la computadora
9. comer una hamburguesa
10. tocar la guitarra
11. correr en tu lugar
12. leer un libro

---

1 Answers

Answers will vary. Students should think of themselves as standing on the sidewalk and looking at the doors of the stores in order to orient themselves.

1. A: ¿Qué está al lado (o a la derecha) de la estación de autobuses?
   B: La zapatería está al lado (o a la derecha) de la estación de autobuses.
2. A: ¿Qué está al lado (o a la derecha) de la zapatería?
   B: La carnicería está al lado (o a la derecha) de la zapatería.
3. B: ¿Qué está enfrente de la zapatería y la carnicería?
   A: La pastelería está enfrente de la zapatería y la carnicería.
4. A: ¿Qué está al lado (o a la izquierda) de la pastelería?
   B: La papelería está al lado (o a la izquierda) de la pastelería.
5. B: ¿Qué está enfrente de la papelería?
   A: La tienda de música y videos está enfrente de la papelería.
6. A: ¿Qué está a la izquierda de la tienda de música y videos?
   B: La farmacia está a la izquierda de la tienda de música y videos.
7. B: ¿Qué está al lado (o a la izquierda) de la farmacia?
   A: El banco está al lado (o a la izquierda) de la farmacia.
8. A: ¿Qué está enfrente de la farmacia (o la papelería)?
   B: La librería está enfrente de la farmacia (o la papelería).
9. B: ¿Qué está al lado (o a la derecha) de la librería?
   A: El correo está al lado (o a la derecha) de la librería.
10. A: ¿Qué está al lado (o a la derecha) del correo?
    B: La joyería está al lado (o a la derecha) del correo.
11. A: ¿Qué está enfrente de la joyería?
    B: El café está enfrente de la joyería.

2 Answers

1. A: Saca una foto.
   B: [acts out taking a picture]
2. A: Juega al baloncesto.
   B: [acts out playing basketball]
3. A: Come pizza.
   B: No es posible.
4. A: Anda en bicicleta.
   B: No es posible.
5. A: Bebe un refresco.
   B: [acts out drinking a soft drink]
6. A: Escribe tu nombre en un papel.
   B: [acts out writing name on paper]
7. B: Escribe en el pizarrón.
   A: No es posible.
8. B: Usa la computadora.
   A: No es posible.
9. B: Come una hamburguesa.
   A: [acts out eating a hamburger]
10. B: Toca la guitarra.
    A: [acts out playing the guitar]
11. B: Corre en tu lugar.
    A: [acts out running in place]
12. B: Lee un libro.
    A: [acts out reading a book]

3 Answers

1. A: ¿Puede hacer ejercicio bien?
   B: Sí, puede hacer ejercicio bien.
2. A: ¿Puede hacer un proyecto sobre los pájaros bien?
   B: No, no puede hacer un proyecto sobre los pájaros bien.
3. A: ¿Puede trabajar con números bien?
   B: Sí, puede trabajar con números bien.
4. A: ¿Puede hablar español bien?
   B: Sí, puede hablar español bien.
5. A: ¿Puede comprender los mapas bien?
   B: No, no puede comprender los mapas bien.

4 Answers

A: ¿Qué le da a su madre?
B: Le da unos aretes a su madre. ¿Cuánto cuestan los aretes?
A: Cuestan treinta dólares.
B: ¿Qué les da a sus hermanos?
A: Les da unas carteras. ¿Cuánto cuestan las carteras?
B: Cuestan veinte dólares.
A: ¿Qué le da a su padre?
B: Le da un cinturón. ¿Cuánto cuesta el cinturón?
A: Cuesta veinticinco dólares.
B: ¿Qué les da a sus abuelos?
A: Les da una olla. ¿Cuánto cuesta la olla?
B: Cuesta dieciocho dólares.
B: ¿Qué le da a su prima?
A: Le da un casete. ¿Cuánto cuesta el casete?
B: Cuesta nueve dólares.
A: ¿Qué le da a su amiga?
B: Le da una pulsera. ¿Cuánto cuesta la pulsera?
A: Cuesta quince dólares.

3 Unidad 4 Etapa 2 p. 272
¿Puede hacerlo bien?

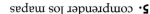

Estudiante A Tu amigo(a) tiene las notas de Emilia. Pregúntale si puede hacer las siguientes actividades bien. (Hint: Ask if Emilia does these well.)

modelo

Estudiante A: ¿Puede hacer ejercicio bien?

Estudiante B: …

1. hacer ejercicio
2. hacer un proyecto sobre los pájaros
3. trabajar con números
4. hablar español
5. comprender los mapas

Estudiante B Mira las notas de Emilia y contesta las preguntas de tu amigo(a). (Hint: Tell if Emilia does these well.)

modelo

Estudiante A: ¿Puede hacer ejercicio bien?

Estudiante B: Sí, puede hacer ejercicio bien.

Colegio Alta Vista

Emilia Villarreal			
	1	**2**	**3**
Español	A		
Matemáticas	B		
Ciencias	D		
Estudios sociales	C−		
Educación física	A+		

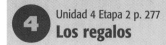

4 Unidad 4 Etapa 2 p. 277
Los regalos

mi madre	$30	
mis hermanos		carteras
mi padre	$25	
mis abuelos		olla
mi prima		casete
mi amiga	$15	

Estudiante A: ¿Qué le da a su madre?

Estudiante B: Le da… a su madre. ¿Cuánto cuesta(n)…?

Estudiante A: Cuesta(n) treinta dólares.

Estudiante A Chavela hace una tabla de los regalos que da para la Navidad. Con tu amigo(a), completa la tabla. (Hint: Complete the chart.)

modelo

Estudiante A: ¿Qué le da a su madre?

Estudiante B: Le da unos aretes a su madre. ¿Cuánto cuestan los aretes?

Estudiante A: Cuesta(n)…

Estudiante B Chavela hace una tabla de los regalos que da para la Navidad. Con tu amigo(a), completa la tabla. (Hint: Complete the chart.)

modelo

Estudiante A: ¿Qué le da a su madre?

Estudiante B: Le da unos aretes a su madre. ¿Cuánto cuestan los aretes?

Estudiante A: Cuesta(n)…

mi madre		aretes
mis hermanos	$20	
mi padre		cinturón
mis abuelos	$18	
mi prima	$9	
mi amiga		pulsera

5 ¿Riquísimo o no?

Unidad 4 Etapa 3 p. 293

Estudiante A Vas a un restaurante con Memo y tu amigo(a). ¿A ellos les gustan estas comidas y bebidas? *(Hint: Do Memo and your partner like these?)*

modelo

Estudiante A: ¿Te gusta el bistec? ¿A Memo le gusta?
Estudiante B: …

1. el bistec
2. la salsa
3. el flan
4. la limonada
5. los frijoles

	Memo	Mi amigo(a)
las enchiladas	sí	¿?
el té	no	¿?
los postres	sí	¿?
el arroz	sí	¿?
la ensalada	no	¿?

Estudiante B Vas a un restaurante con Memo y tu amigo(a). ¿A ellos les gustan estas comidas y bebidas? *(Hint: Do Memo and your partner like these?)*

modelo

Estudiante A: ¿Te gusta el bistec? ¿A Memo le gusta?
Estudiante B: A mí me gusta el bistec. A Memo no le gusta.

6. las enchiladas
7. el té
8. los postres
9. el arroz
10. la ensalada

	Memo	Mi amigo(a)
el bistec	no	¿?
la salsa	sí	¿?
el flan	sí	¿?
la limonada	no	¿?
los frijoles	sí	¿?

6 ¿Qué sirven?

Unidad 4 Etapa 3 p. 299

Estudiante A Roberto pide las siguientes comidas. ¿Las sirven en el café Veracruz? *(Hint: Say what Roberto is ordering.)*

modelo

Estudiante A: Pide papas fritas.
Estudiante B: …

1. ensalada	6. bistec
2. flan	5. pan
3. sopa	4. pollo
9. enchiladas	10. queso
8. pastel	11. pan dulce
7. hamburguesa	12. arroz

Estudiante B Dile a tu amigo(a) si sirven las comidas que pide Roberto en el café Veracruz.
(Hint: Tell your partner if these are served.)

modelo

papas fritas
Estudiante A: Pide papas fritas.
Estudiante B: Sí, sirven papas fritas.

5 Answers

1. A: ¿Te gusta el bistec? ¿A Memo le gusta?
   B: A mí (no) me gusta el bistec. A Memo no le gusta.
2. A: ¿Te gusta la salsa? ¿A Memo le gusta?
   B: A mí (no) me gusta la salsa. A Memo le gusta.
3. A: ¿Te gusta el flan? ¿A Memo le gusta?
   B: A mí (no) me gusta el flan. A Memo le gusta.
4. A: ¿Te gusta la limonada? ¿A Memo le gusta?
   B: A mí (no) me gusta la limonada. A Memo no le gusta.
5. A: ¿Te gustan los frijoles? ¿A Memo le gustan?
   B: A mí (no) me gustan los frijoles. A Memo le gustan.
6. B: ¿Te gustan las enchiladas? ¿A Memo le gustan?
   A: A mí (no) me gustan las enchiladas. A Memo le gustan.
7. B: ¿Te gusta el té? ¿A Memo le gusta?
   A: A mí (no) me gusta el té. A Memo no le gusta.
8. B: ¿Te gustan los postres? ¿A Memo le gustan?
   A: A mí (no) me gustan los postres. A Memo le gustan.
9. B: ¿Te gusta el arroz? ¿A Memo le gusta?
   A: A mí (no) me gusta el arroz. A Memo le gusta.
10. B: ¿Te gusta la ensalada? ¿A Memo le gusta?
    A: A mí (no) me gusta la ensalada. A Memo no le gusta.

6 Answers

1. A: Pide ensalada.
   B: Sí, sirven ensalada.
2. A: Pide flan.
   B: No, no sirven flan.
3. A: Pide sopa.
   B: Sí, sirven sopa.
4. A: Pide pollo.
   B: Sí, sirven pollo.
5. A: Pide pan.
   B: Sí, sirven pan.
6. A: Pide bistec.
   B: No, no sirven bistec.
7. A: Pide una hamburguesa.
   B: Sí, sirven hamburguesas.
8. A: Pide pastel.
   B: Sí, sirven pastel.
9. A: Pide enchiladas.
   B: No, no sirven enchiladas.
10. A: Pide queso.
    B: Sí, sirven queso.
11. A: Pide pan dulce.
    B: No, no sirven pan dulce.
12. A: Pide arroz.
    B: Sí, sirven arroz.

7 Answers

1. A: ¿Pongo la mesa hoy?
   B: Sí, pon la mesa.
2. A: ¿Toco el piano hoy?
   B: No, no está en tu calendario.
3. A: ¿Voy al mercado hoy?
   B: Sí, ve al mercado.
4. A: ¿Salgo a las siete y media hoy?
   B: Sí, sal a las siete y media.
5. A: ¿Escribo una carta hoy?
   B: No, no está en tu calendario.
6. A: ¿Hago la tarea hoy?
   B: Sí, haz la tarea.

8 Answers

1. A: Siempre estoy muy cansado(a).
   B: No te acuestes tan tarde.
2. A: Tengo mucho calor.
   B: Báñate en agua fresca.
3. A: Quiero ver un programa a las diez.
   B: No te duermas antes de las diez.
4. A: No llevo nada en los pies.
   B: Ponte los zapatos.
5. B: Siempre llego tarde a la escuela.
   A: No te despiertes tan tarde.
6. B: No me gusta la pasta de dientes.
   A: Lávate los dientes con otra pasta de dientes.
7. B: No me gusta el pelo hoy.
   A: Péinate.
8. B: Tengo frío.
   A: No te pongas shorts.

---

7 — Unidad 5, Etapa 1 p. 323
¿Qué hago?

Estudiante A No recuerdas qué hacer hoy y tu amigo(a) tiene tu calendario. Adivina las cuatro actividades de la lista. *(Hint: Guess the four activities.)*

modelo

hacer la cama

Estudiante A: ¿Hago la cama hoy?

Estudiante B: Sí, haz la cama.

   o: No, no está en tu calendario.

1. poner la mesa
2. tocar el piano
3. ir al mercado
4. salir a las 7:30
5. escribir una carta
6. hacer la tarea

Estudiante B Tu amigo(a) no recuerda qué hacer hoy y tú tienes su calendario. Cuando te pregunta, dile que hacer según su calendario. *(Hint: Tell your partner what to do.)*

modelo

hacer la cama

Estudiante A: ¿Hago la cama hoy?

Estudiante B: Sí, haz la cama.

   o: No, no está en tu calendario.

8 abril
poner la mesa
ir al mercado
salir a las 7:30
hacer la tarea

---

8 — Unidad 5 Etapa 1 p. 327
Problemas y soluciones

Estudiante A Tú le dices varios problemas a tu amigo(a) y te dice una solución. Cambien de papel. *(Hint: Tell your partner your problems.)*

modelo

Estudiante A: No tengo secador de pelo.

Estudiante B: ...

1. Siempre estoy muy cansado(a).
2. Tengo mucho calor.
3. Quiero ver un programa a las diez.
4. No llevo nada en los pies.

no ponerse shorts

no despertarse tan tarde

lavarse los dientes con otra pasta de dientes

peinarse

Estudiante B Tu amigo(a) te dice problemas. Dile una solución con las expresiones de la lista. Cambien de papel. *(Hint: Suggest solutions to your partner.)*

ponerse los zapatos

bañarse en agua fresca

no acostarse tan tarde

secarse el pelo con una toalla

no dormirse antes de las diez

modelo

Estudiante A: No tengo secador de pelo.

Estudiante B: Sécate el pelo con una toalla.

5. Siempre llego tarde a la escuela.
6. No me gusta la pasta de dientes.
7. No me gusta el pelo hoy.
8. Tengo frío.

9 ¿Dónde?
Unidad 5 Etapa 2 p. 344

10 ¿Cómo?
Unidad 5 Etapa 2 p. 349

Activity 9 (Estudiante A — shown inverted)

4. quitar la mesa
3. planchar la ropa
2. pasar la aspiradora
1. barrer el suelo

Estudiante A: ¿Dónde están ordenando las flores?
Estudiante B: Están ordenándolas en...

modelo
ordenar las flores

Estudiante A Diana y su familia preparan una fiesta. Pregúntale a tu amigo(a) dónde están haciendo los siguientes quehaceres. *(Hint: Ask where they do each chore.)*

Activity 10 (Estudiante A — shown inverted)

6. manejar
5. hacer la cama
4. hacer la tarea
3. barrer el suelo
2. sacar la basura
1. pasar la aspiradora

Estudiante A: ¿Cómo debe quitar el polvo?
Estudiante B: Debe quitarlo...

modelo
quitar el polvo

Estudiante A ¿Cómo debe hacer Pedro las siguientes actividades? *(Hint: How should Pedro do these?)*

Estudiante B (Activity 9)

Estudiante B Diana y su familia preparan una fiesta. Dile a tu amigo(a) dónde están haciendo los siguientes quehaceres. *(Hint: Tell where they do each chore.)*

modelo

ordenar las flores

Estudiante A: ¿Dónde están ordenando las flores?
Estudiante B: Están ordenándolas en la cocina.

Estudiante B (Activity 10)

Estudiante B ¿Cómo debe hacer Pedro las siguientes actividades? *(Hint: How should Pedro do these?)*

modelo

quitar el polvo: cuidadoso

Estudiante A: ¿Cómo debe quitar el polvo?
Estudiante B: Debe quitarlo cuidadosamente.

a. sacar la basura: rápido
b. hacer la tarea: paciente
c. manejar: tranquilo
d. pasar la aspiradora: lento
e. hacer la cama: fácil
f. barrer el suelo: frecuente

9 Answers

1. A: ¿Dónde están barriendo el suelo?
   B: Están barriéndolo en el baño.
2. A: ¿Dónde están pasando la aspiradora?
   B: Están pasándola en la sala.
3. A: ¿Dónde están planchando la ropa?
   B: Están planchándola en la habitación.
4. A: ¿Dónde están quitando la mesa?
   B: Están quitándola en la cocina.

10 Answers

1. A: ¿Cómo debe pasar la aspiradora?
   B: Debe pasarla lentamente.
2. A: ¿Cómo debe sacar la basura?
   B: Debe sacarla rápidamente.
3. A: ¿Cómo debe barrer el suelo?
   B: Debe barrerlo frecuentemente.
4. A: ¿Cómo debe hacer la tarea?
   B: Debe hacerla pacientemente.
5. A: ¿Cómo debe hacer la cama?
   B: Debe hacerla fácilmente.
6. A: ¿Cómo debe manejar?
   B: Debe manejar tranquilamente.

11 Answers

1. A: ¿Quién es la menor?
   B: Inés es la menor.
2. A: ¿Quién tiene el pelo más largo?
   B: Olivia tiene el pelo más largo.
3. A: ¿Quién es la más contenta?
   B: Lina es la más contenta.
4. A: ¿Quién es la menos alta?
   B: Lina es la menos alta.
5. A: ¿Quién tiene el pelo más corto?
   B: Inés tiene el pelo más corto.
6. A: ¿Quién es la mayor?
   B: Lina es la mayor.
7. A: ¿Quién es la más cansada?
   B: Olivia es la más cansada.

12 Answers

1. A: ¿Qué compraron ustedes por mil doscientas veinticinco pesetas?
   B: Compramos cuatro botellas de zumo.
2. A: ¿Qué compró la señora García por trescientas quince pesetas?
   B: Compró dos litros de leche.
3. A: ¿Qué compraste tú por ciento cuarenta pesetas?
   B: Compré una docena de huevos.
4. A: ¿Qué compraron Alejandra y Cristóbal por mil cuatrocientas veinticinco pesetas?
   B: Compraron un kilo de jamón.
5. B: ¿Qué compró la señora Martínez por mil trescientas ochenta pesetas?
   A: Compró cuatro paquetes de galletas.
6. B: ¿Qué compraste tú por quinientas setenta y cinco pesetas?
   A: Compré dos paquetes de helado.
7. B: ¿Qué compró tu amigo por doscientas cincuenta pesetas?
   A: Compró dos kilos de patatas.
8. B: ¿Qué compró el señor Aguilera por novecientas sesenta y cinco pesetas?
   A: Compró dos latas de aceite.

---

11 ¿Quién es?

Unidad 5 Etapa 3 p. 365

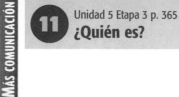

Estudiante A Pregúntale a tu amigo(a) sobre tres nuevas estudiantes. *(Hint: Ask about three students.)*

modelo

más alta

Estudiante A: ¿Quién es la más alta?
Estudiante B: ... es la más alta.

1. menor
2. pelo más largo
3. más contenta
4. menos alta
5. pelo más corto
6. mayor
7. más cansada

Estudiante B Contesta las preguntas de tu amigo(a) sobre las tres nuevas estudiantes.
(Hint: Answer questions about three students.)

modelo

Estudiante A: ¿Quién es la más alta?

Estudiante B: Olivia es la más alta.

Lina -17 años   Olivia -16 años   Inés - 15 años

---

12 En el supermercado

Unidad 5 Etapa 3 p. 371

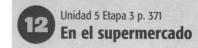

965 ptas 2/

1.380 ptas 4/

250 ptas 2 kilos/

575 ptas 2/

4. Alejandra y Cristóbal / 1.425 pesetas
3. tú / 140 pesetas
2. la señora García / 315 pesetas
1. ustedes / 1.225 pesetas

Estudiante B: Compró...

Estudiante A: ¿Qué compró el señor Matute por ochocientas cuarenta pesetas?

modelo

el señor Matute / 840 pesetas

Estudiante A Pregúntale a tu amigo(a) qué compraron las siguientes personas. Cambien de papel. *(Hint: Ask what they bought.)*

Estudiante B Dile a tu amigo(a) qué compraron. Cambien de papel. *(Hint: Say what they bought.)*

modelo

Estudiante A: ¿Qué compró el señor Matute por ochocientas cuarenta pesetas?

Estudiante B: Compró medio kilo de salchichas.

5. la señora Martínez / 1.380 pesetas
6. tú / 575 pesetas
7. tu amigo / 250 pesetas
8. el señor Aguilera / 965 pesetas

2 litros/ 315 ptas   4/ 1.225 ptas   1 kilo/ 1.425 ptas   12/ 140 ptas   1/2 kilo/ 840 ptas

13 Unidad 6 Etapa 1 p. 395
Una noche larga

Estudiante A ¿Qué leyeron u oyeron estas personas en sus camas? Completa la tabla con tu amigo(a). *(Hint: Complete the chart.)*

modelo

Estudiante A: ¿Ángela oyó o leyó algo?

Estudiante B: Ángela...

Tavo	una revista
Alfredo y Paco	los aviones
Gloria	
Quique y Alex	
María y Elena	una novela
Ángela	

Estudiante B ¿Qué leyeron u oyeron estas personas en sus camas? Completa la tabla con tu amigo(a). *(Hint: Complete the chart.)*

modelo

Estudiante A: ¿Ángela oyó o leyó algo?

Estudiante B: Ángela oyó los pájaros.

Ángela	los pájaros
María y Elena	
Quique y Alex	el periódico
Gloria	el tren
Alfredo y Paco	
Tavo	

14 Unidad 6 Etapa 1 p. 399
Vamos a...

Estudiante A Le sugieres a tu amigo(a) a hacer algo. Tu amigo(a) te dice la última vez que lo hizo. Cambien de papel. *(Hint: Suggest you an activity.)*

la semana pasada
anteayer
anoche   el... pasado   ayer

modelo

Estudiante A: Vamos a estudiar.

Estudiante B: Estudié ayer.

estudiar

1. jugar al baloncesto
2. ver la televisión
3. ¿?
4. ¿?
5. leer revistas
6. ir a una fiesta
7. ¿?
8. ¿?

Estudiante B Tu amigo(a) te sugiere hacer algo. Dile la última vez que lo hiciste. Cambien de papel. *(Hint: Say the last time you did an activity after you hear the suggestion.)*

la semana pasada   anteayer
anoche   el... pasado   ayer

modelo

Estudiante A: Vamos a estudiar.

Estudiante B: Estudié ayer.

1. ¿?
2. ¿?
3. ir al cine
4. correr
5. ¿?
6. ¿?
7. comer helado
8. escuchar música

13 Answers

A: ¿Ángela oyó o leyó algo?
B: Ángela oyó los pájaros.
B: ¿María y Elena oyeron o leyeron algo?
A: María y Elena leyeron una novela.
A: ¿Quique y Alex oyeron o leyeron algo?
B: Quique y Alex leyeron el periódico.
A: ¿Gloria oyó o leyó algo?
B: Gloria oyó el tren.
B: ¿Alfredo y Paco oyeron o leyeron algo?
A: Alfredo y Paco oyeron los aviones.
B: ¿Tavo oyó o leyó algo?
A: Tavo leyó una revista.

14 Answers

Answers will vary.
1. A: Vamos a jugar al baloncesto.
   B: Jugué al baloncesto [el año pasado].
2. A: Vamos a ver la televisión.
   B: Vi la televisión [anoche].
3. B: Vamos a ir al cine.
   A: Fui al cine [la semana pasada].
4. B: Vamos a correr.
   A: Corrí [anteayer].
5. A: Vamos a leer revistas.
   B: Leí revistas [el mes pasado].
6. A: Vamos a ir a una fiesta.
   B: Fui a una fiesta [el sábado pasado].
7. B: Vamos a comer helado.
   A: Comí helado [el verano pasado].
8. B: Vamos a escuchar música.
   A: Escuché música [ayer].

15 Answers

Answers will vary.

A: Hay un corral en el centro. El ganadero está dentro del corral con dos cerdos. Está entre los dos cerdos. El ganadero lleva un sombrero. Tiene una bolsa de comida para los cerdos. Les da de comer. Los cerdos son rosados y negros. Un gallo y una gallina están enfrente del corral. El gallo está a la izquierda de la gallina. Hay una cerca detrás del corral. Un caballo marrón está detrás de la cerca. Cuatro pájaros negros están encima de la cerca. Otro pájaro viene.

B: Hay un corral en el centro. Un toro y una vaca están dentro del corral. Son marrones y blancos. Dos gallinas marrones están debajo de la cerca del corral. Hay un caballo blanco detrás del corral. El ganadero está encima del caballo. El ganadero lleva jeans, una camisa roja y un sombrero. Arriba hay un pastor con cuatro llamas.

16 Answers

A: ¿Quién es la primera?
B: La primera es número cincuenta.
B: ¿Quién es el segundo?
A: El segundo es número noventa y ocho.
A: ¿Quién es el tercero?
B: El tercero es número veinticuatro.
A: ¿Quién es la cuarta?
B: La cuarta es número setenta y seis.
B: ¿Quién es el quinto?
A: El quinto es número sesenta y tres.
B: ¿Quién es la sexta?
A: La sexta es número diez.
A: ¿Quién es el séptimo?
B: El séptimo es número cuarenta y dos.
B: ¿Quién es el octavo?
A: El octavo es número ochenta y siete.
A: ¿Quién es la novena?
B: La novena es número treinta y nueve.
B: ¿Quién es la décima?
A: La décima es número setenta y cinco.

---

15 Unidad 6 Etapa 2 p. 417
¿Dónde están?

modelo

Estudiante A: *Hay un corral en el centro…*

Estudiante A Descríbele la granja a tu amigo(a). Él (Ella) la va a dibujar. Cambien de papel. *(Hint: Describe the farm.)*

Estudiante B Tu amigo(a) te describe una granja. Dibuja lo que oyes. Cambien de papel. *(Hint: Draw the farm described.)*

modelo

Estudiante A: *Hay un corral en el centro…*

---

16 Unidad 6 Etapa 2 p. 421
La carrera

modelo

Estudiante A: *¿Quién es la primera?*
Estudiante B: *La primera es número…*

Estudiante A Hay una carrera y no puedes ver bien. Trabaja con tu amigo(a) para identificar a todos los participantes. *(Hint: Identify all the racers.)*

Estudiante B Hay una carrera y no puedes ver bien. Trabaja con tu amigo(a) para identificar a todos los participantes. *(Hint: Identify all the racers.)*

modelo

Estudiante A: *¿Quién es la primera?*
Estudiante B: *La primera es número cincuenta.*

---

17 Unidad 6 Etapa 3 p. 439
¿Lo hago?

6. estar en casa a las 8:30
5. ir al cine
4. mandar una carta
3. sacar la basura
2. estudiar en la biblioteca
1. almorzar con Angélica

Estudiante B: *Sí, barre el suelo hoy.* **o:** *Hoy no.*

Estudiante A: *¿Barro el suelo hoy?*

barrer el suelo

modelo

(Hint: Ask what you'll do today.)

Estudiante A No recuerdas qué hacer hoy y tu amigo(a) tiene tu calendario. Pregúntale qué haces hoy.

Estudiante B Tu amigo(a) no recuerda qué hacer hoy y tú tienes su calendario. Cuando te pregunta, dile qué hacer según su calendario.
(Hint: Tell your partner what to do according to the calendar.)

modelo

barrer el suelo

Estudiante A: *¿Barro el suelo hoy?*

Estudiante B: *Sí, barre el suelo hoy.* **o:** *Hoy no.*

26 junio

almorzar con Angélica
sacar la basura
ir al cine
estar en casa a las 8:30

---

18 Unidad 6 Etapa 3 p. 443
Parte de la historia

Estudiante B: *Un hombre se levantó a las seis de la mañana.*

modelo

happened.)

Tu amigo(a) empieza. *(Hint: Take turns telling what*

Estudiante A Viste algo en la televisión, pero solamente sabes parte de la historia. Con tu amigo(a), cuenta lo que pasó según los dibujos.

Estudiante B Viste algo en la televisión, pero solamente sabes parte de la historia. Con tu amigo(a), cuenta lo que pasó según los dibujos. Tú empiezas. *(Hint: Take turns telling what happened.)*

modelo

Estudiante B: *Un hombre se levantó a las seis de la mañana.*

1.   3.   5.

---

17 Answers

1. A: ¿Almuerzo con Angélica hoy?
   B: Sí, almuerza con Angélica hoy.
2. A: ¿Estudio en la biblioteca hoy?
   B: Hoy no.
3. A: ¿Saco la basura hoy?
   B: Sí, saca la basura.
4. A: ¿Mando una carta hoy?
   B: Hoy no.
5. A: ¿Voy al cine hoy?
   B: Sí, ve al cine.
6. A: ¿Estoy en casa a las ocho y media hoy?
   B: Sí, está en casa a las ocho y media.

18 Answers

Answers will vary.
1. B: El hombre se lavó la cara.
2. A: El hombre habló por teléfono.
3. B: El hombre manejó a la ciudad.
4. A: El hombre compró flores.
5. B: El hombre entró en un edificio con las flores.
6. A: El hombre le dio las flores a una mujer.

Juegos—respuestas

UNIDAD 4

Etapa 1 **En uso,** p. 107: Adriana va al aeropuerto. Andrés va a la farmacia. Arturo va al banco.

Etapa 2 **En acción,** p. 122: Lola quiere darle la lila a Lidia.; **En uso,** p. 133: Compras un plato barato por pocos pesos.

Etapa 3 **En uso,** p. 161: Pablo le sirve sopa a Marco, ensalada a Martina y azúcar a Marisol.

UNIDAD 5

Etapa 1 **En acción,** p. 177: Necesita peinarse.; **En uso,** p. 191: 1. un despertador, 2. un secador de pelo, 3. un peine, 4. un espejo

Etapa 2 **En uso,** p. 217: 1. Sofía está en el comedor. 2. Felipe está en la sala. 3. Cristina está en la cocina.

Etapa 3 **En uso,** p. 245: 1. helado: el congelador, 2. platos sucios: el lavaplatos, 3. leche: el frigorífico, 4. carne de res: la estufa

UNIDAD 6

Etapa 1 **En uso,** p. 275: 1. El papá de Adriana es contador. 2. El padre de Susana es fotógrafo. 3. El Sr. Rodríguez es bombero.

Etapa 2 **En uso,** p. 301: El cerdo llegó primero, la llama llegó segunda y la vaca llegó tercera.

Etapa 3 **En acción,** p. 316: a; **En uso,** p. 329: 1. La llama está jugando con Rocío. 2. El ganadero buscó su merienda. 3. ¡El caballo se va a escapar del corral!

Vocabulario adicional

Here are lists of additional vocabulary to supplement the words you know. They include musical instruments, animals, professions, classes, sports, and foods.

Los instrumentos

el acordeón	accordion
la armónica	harmonica
el arpa (fem.)	harp
el bajo	bass
el bajón	bassoon
el banjo	banjo
la batería	drum set
el clarinete	clarinet
el corno francés	French horn
el corno inglés	English horn
la flauta	flute
la flauta dulce	recorder
el flautín	piccolo
la mandolina	mandolin
el oboe	oboe
el órgano	organ
la pandereta	tambourine
el saxofón	saxophone
el sintetizador	synthesizer
el tambor	drum
el trombón	trombone
la trompeta	trumpet
la tuba	tuba
la viola	viola
el violín	violin
el violonchelo	cello
el xilófono	xylophone

Más animales

la abeja	bee	el león	lion
el águila (fem.)	eagle	el leopardo	leopard
el alce	moose	el lobo	wolf
la araña	spider	el loro	parrot
la ardilla	squirrel	el mono	monkey
la ballena	whale	el mapache	raccoon
el buey	ox	la mariposa	butterfly
el búho	owl	la mosca	fly
el burro	donkey	el mosquito	mosquito
la cabra	goat	el (la) oso(a)	bear
el cangrejo	crab	la oveja	sheep
el chapulín	grasshopper	la paloma	pigeon, dove
el cisne	swan	la pantera	panther
el conejillo de Indias	guinea pig	el pato	duck
el conejo	rabbit	el pavo	turkey
el coyote	coyote	el pavo real	peacock
el delfín	dolphin	el pingüino	penguin
el elefante	elephant	la rana	frog
el ganso	goose	la rata	rat
el gerbo	gerbil	el ratón	mouse
el grillo	cricket	el sapo	toad
el hámster	hamster	la serpiente	snake
la hormiga	ant	el tiburón	shark
el hurón	ferret	el tigre	tiger
el jaguar	jaguar	la tortuga	turtle
la jirafa	giraffe	el venado	deer
la lagartija	small lizard	el zorro	fox

Más profesiones

el (la) abogado(a)	lawyer
el actor	actor
la actriz	actress
el (la) agente de bolsa	stockbroker
el (la) agente de viajes	travel agent
el (la) alcalde	mayor
el (la) artista	artist
el (la) asistente social	social worker
el (la) atleta	athlete
el (la) auxiliar de vuelo	flight attendant
el (la) cantante	singer
el (la) carnicero(a)	butcher
el (la) carpintero(a)	carpenter
el (la) científico(a)	scientist
el (la) dentista	dentist
el (la) director(a)	principal, director
el (la) empleado(a) de banco	bank clerk
el (la) enfermero(a)	nurse
el (la) farmacéutico(a)	pharmacist
el (la) funcionario(a)	civil servant
el (la) guía	guide
el (la) ingeniero(a)	engineer
el (la) jardinero(a)	gardener
el (la) joyero(a)	jeweler
el (la) mecánico(a)	mechanic
el militar	soldier
el (la) modelo	model
el (la) músico(a)	musician
el (la) panadero(a)	baker
el (la) peluquero(a)	hairstylist
el (la) pescador(a)	fisher
el (la) piloto(a)	pilot
el (la) plomero(a)	plumber
el (la) profesor(a)	teacher, professor
el (la) sastre	tailor
el (la) vendedor(a)	salesperson
el (la) veterinario(a)	veterinarian
el (la) zapatero(a)	shoemaker

Las clases

el alemán	German
la álgebra	algebra
la biología	biology
el cálculo	calculus
la composición	writing
la contabilidad	accounting
la física	physics
el francés	French
la geografía	geography
la geología	geology
la geometría	geometry
el italiano	Italian
el japonés	Japanese
el latín	Latin
la química	chemistry
el ruso	Russian
la salud	health
la trigonometría	trigonometry

Los deportes

el árbitro	referee, umpire
el arquero	goalie
el (la) bateador(a)	batter
el boxeo	boxing
el (la) campeón(ona)	champion
el campeonato	championship
la carrera	race
el cesto	basket
el (la) entrenador(a)	trainer, coach
el esquí	ski
la gimnasia	gymnastics
el golf	golf
los juegos olímpicos	Olympics
el (la) lanzador(a)	pitcher
el marcador	scoreboard
el palo	stick, club
el (la) parador(a)	catcher
la pista	racetrack
la red	net
la tabla hawaiana	surfboard
el trofeo	trophy
el uniforme	uniform

Las frutas y las verduras

el aguacate	avocado
la alcachofa	artichoke
el apio	celery
el arándano	blueberry
la banana	banana
la berenjena	eggplant
el bróculi	broccoli
el calabacín	zucchini
la calabaza	squash
la cereza	cherry
la ciruela	plum
el coco	coconut
la col	cabbage
la coliflor	cauliflower
el dátil	date
el espárrago	asparagus
la espinaca	spinach
la frambuesa	raspberry
la fresa	strawberry
la guayaba	guava
el kiwi	kiwi
el lima	lime
el limón	lemon
el mango	mango
la manzana	apple
el melocotón	peach
el melón	melon
la mora	blackberry
la naranja	orange
la papaya	papaya
el pepino	cucumber
la pera	pear
el plátano	banana, plantain
la sandía	watermelon
la toronja	grapefruit

Gramática—resumen

Grammar Terms

Adjective (1A, pp. 63, 65): a word that describes a noun

Adverb (1A, p. 121; 1B, p. 209): a word that describes a verb, an adjective, or another adverb

Article (1A, pp. 60, 62): a word that identifies the class of a noun (masculine or feminine, singular or plural); English articles are *a, an,* or *the*

Command (1B, p. 97): a verb form used to tell someone to do something

Comparative (1A, p. 234): a phrase that compares two things

Conjugation (1A, p. 118; 1B, p. 230): a verb form that uses the stem of an infinitive and adds endings that reflect subject and tense

Direct Object (1A, p. 259): the noun, pronoun, or phrase that receives the action of the main verb in a sentence

Gender (1A, p. 63): a property that divides adjectives, nouns, pronouns, and articles into masculine and feminine groups

Indirect Object (1B, p. 121): a noun, pronoun, or phrase that tells to whom/what or for whom/what an action is done

Infinitive (1A, p. 41): the basic form of a verb; it names the action without giving tense, person, or number

Interrogative (1A, p. 150): a word that asks a question

Noun (1A, p. 60): a word that names a thing, person, animal, place, feeling, or situation

Number (1A, p. 65): a property that divides adjectives, nouns, pronouns, articles, and verbs into singular and plural groups

Preposition (1A, p. 88): a word that shows the relationship between its object and another word in the sentence

Pronoun (1A, p. 36): a word that can be used in place of a noun

Reflexive Verb (1B, p. 175): a verb for which the subject and the direct object are the same participant

Subject (1A, p. 36): the noun, pronoun, or phrase in a sentence that performs the action, is the focus of attention

Superlative (1B, p. 228): a phrase that describes which item has the most or least of a quality

Tense (1A, p. 118; 1B, p. 230): when the action of a verb takes place

Nouns, Articles, and Pronouns

Nouns

Nouns identify things, people, animals, places, feelings, or situations. Spanish nouns are either masculine or feminine. They are also either **singular** or **plural**. **Masculine nouns** usually end in **-o** and **feminine nouns** usually end in **-a.**

To make a noun **plural**, add **-s** to a word ending in a vowel and **-es** to a word ending in a consonant.

Singular Nouns	
Masculine	**Feminine**
amigo	amiga
chico	chica
hombre	mujer
suéter	blusa
zapato	falda

Plural Nouns	
Masculine	**Feminine**
amigo**s**	amiga**s**
chico**s**	chica**s**
hombre**s**	mujer**es**
suéter**es**	blusa**s**
zapato**s**	falda**s**

Articles

Articles identify the class of a noun: masculine or feminine, singular or plural. **Definite articles** are the equivalent of the English word *the*. **Indefinite articles** are the equivalent of *a, an,* or *some.*

Definite Articles	Masculine	Feminine
Singular	**el** amigo	**la** amiga
Plural	**los** amigos	**las** amigas

Indefinite Articles	Masculine	Feminine
Singular	**un** amigo	**una** amiga
Plural	**unos** amigos	**unas** amigas

Pronouns

A **pronoun** can take the place of a noun. The pronoun used is determined by its function or purpose in the sentence.

Subject Pronouns	
yo	nosotros(as)
tú	vosotros(as)
usted	ustedes
él, ella	ellos(as)

Pronouns Used After Prepositions	
de **mí**	de **nosotros(as)**
de **ti**	de **vosotros(as)**
de **usted**	de **ustedes**
de **él, ella**	de **ellos(as)**

Direct Object Pronouns	
me	nos
te	os
lo, la	los, las

Indirect Object Pronouns	
me	nos
te	os
le	les

Reflexive Pronouns	
me	nos
te	os
se	se

Demonstrative Pronouns	
éste(a), esto	éstos(as)
ése(a), eso	ésos(as)
aquél(la), aquello	aquéllos(as)

Adjectives

Adjectives describe nouns. In Spanish, adjectives must match the **number** and **gender** of the nouns they describe. When an adjective describes a group with both genders, the masculine form is used. To make an adjective plural, apply the same rules that are used for making a noun plural. Most adjectives are placed after the noun.

Adjectives	Masculine	Feminine
Singular	el chico **guapo**	la chica **guapa**
	el chico **paciente**	la chica **paciente**
	el chico **fenomenal**	la chica **fenomenal**
	el chico **trabajador**	la chica **trabajadora**
Plural	los chicos guapo**s**	las chicas guapa**s**
	los chicos paciente**s**	las chicas paciente**s**
	los chicos fenomenal**es**	las chicas fenomenal**es**
	los chicos trabajador**es**	las chicas trabajadora**s**

Adjectives cont.

Sometimes adjectives are placed before the noun and **shortened**. **Grande** is shortened before any singular noun. Several others are shortened before a masculine singular noun.

Shortened Forms			
alguno	**algún** chico	primero	**primer** chico
bueno	**buen** chico	tercero	**tercer** chico
malo	**mal** chico		
ninguno	**ningún** chico	grande	**gran** chico(a)

Possessive adjectives identify to whom something belongs. They agree in gender and number with the possessed item, not with the person who possesses it.

Possessive Adjectives				
	Masculine		**Feminine**	
Singular	**mi** amigo	**nuestro** amigo	**mi** amiga	**nuestra** amiga
	tu amigo	**vuestro** amigo	**tu** amiga	**vuestra** amiga
	su amigo	**su** amigo	**su** amiga	**su** amiga
Plural	**mis** amigos	**nuestros** amigos	**mis** amigas	**nuestras** amigas
	tus amigos	**vuestros** amigos	**tus** amigas	**vuestras** amigas
	sus amigos	**sus** amigos	**sus** amigas	**sus** amigas

Demonstrative adjectives point out which noun is being referred to. Their English equivalents are *this*, *that*, *these*, and *those*.

Demonstrative Adjectives		
	Masculine	**Feminine**
Singular	**este** amigo	**esta** amiga
	ese amigo	**esa** amiga
	aquel amigo	**aquella** amiga
Plural	**estos** amigos	**estas** amigas
	esos amigos	**esas** amigas
	aquellos amigos	**aquellas** amigas

Interrogatives

Interrogative words are used to ask questions.

Interrogatives		
¿Adónde?	¿Cuándo?	¿Por qué?
¿Cómo?	¿Cuánto(a)? ¿Cuántos(as)?	¿Qué?
¿Cuál(es)?	¿Dónde?	¿Quién(es)?

Comparatives and Superlatives

Comparatives

Comparatives are used when comparing two different things.

Comparatives		
más (+) **más** interesante **que…** Me gusta correr **más que** nadar.	menos (−) **menos** interesante **que…** Me gusta nadar **menos que** correr.	tan(to) (=) **tan** interesante **como…** Me gusta leer **tanto como** escribir.

There are a few irregular comparatives. When talking about the age of people, use **mayor** and **menor**.

Age	Quality
mayor menor	mejor peor

When talking about numbers, **de** is used instead of **que**.

> **más (menos) de** cien…

Superlatives

Superlatives are used to distinguish one item from a group. They describe which item has the most or least of a quality.

The ending **-ísimo(a)** can be added to an adjective to form a superlative.

Superlatives		
	Masculine	**Feminine**
Singular	**el** chico **más** alto **el** chico **menos** alto	**la** chica **más** alta **la** chica **menos** alta
Plural	**los** chicos **más** altos **los** chicos **menos** altos	**las** chicas **más** altas **las** chicas **menos** altas
Singular	mole buen**ísimo**	pasta buen**ísima**
Plural	frijoles buen**ísimos**	enchiladas buen**ísimas**

Affirmative and Negative Words

Affirmative words are used to talk about something or someone, or to say that an event also or always happens. **Negative** words are used to refer to no one or nothing, or to say that events do not happen.

Affirmative	Negative
algo	nada
alguien	nadie
algún (alguna)	ningún (ninguna)
alguno(a)	ninguno(a)
siempre	nunca
también	tampoco

Adverbs

Adverbs modify a verb, an adjective, or another adverb. Many adverbs in Spanish are made by changing an existing adjective.

Adjective	→	Adverb
reciente	→	reciente**mente**
frecuente	→	frecuente**mente**
fácil	→	fácil**mente**
normal	→	normal**mente**
especial	→	especial**mente**
feliz	→	feliz**mente**
cuidadoso(a)	→	cuidadosa**mente**
rápido(a)	→	rápida**mente**
lento(a)	→	lenta**mente**
tranquilo(a)	→	tranquila**mente**

Verbs: Present Tense

Regular Verbs

Regular verbs ending in **-ar,** **-er,** or **-ir** always have regular endings in the present.

-ar Verbs		-er Verbs		-ir Verbs	
hablo	hablamos	como	comemos	vivo	vivimos
hablas	habláis	comes	coméis	vives	vivís
habla	hablan	come	comen	vive	viven

Verbs with Irregular yo Forms

Some verbs have regular forms in the present except for their **yo** forms.

Infinitive	→	Yo form
conocer	→	conozco
dar	→	doy
hacer	→	hago
ofrecer	→	ofrezco
poner	→	pongo
saber	→	sé
salir	→	salgo
traer	→	traigo
ver	→	veo

Stem-Changing Verbs

u → ue	
juego	jugamos
juegas	jugáis
juega	juegan

Jugar is the only verb with a **u → ue** stem change.

e → ie	
cierro	cerramos
cierras	cerráis
cierra	cierran

Other **e → ie** verbs: **empezar, entender, merendar, nevar, pensar, perder, preferir, querer.** Reflexive: **despertarse.**

o → ue	
vuelvo	volvemos
vuelves	volvéis
vuelve	vuelven

Other **o → ue** verbs: **almorzar, contar, costar, devolver, dormir, encontrar, llover, mover, poder, recordar.** Reflexive: **acostarse.**

e → i	
pido	pedimos
pides	pedís
pide	piden

Other **e → i** verbs: **repetir, seguir, servir.**

Irregular Verbs

decir	
digo	decimos
dices	decís
dice	dicen

esquiar	
esquío	esquiamos
esquías	esquiáis
esquía	esquían

estar	
estoy	estamos
estás	estáis
está	están

ir	
voy	vamos
vas	vais
va	van

oír	
oigo	oímos
oyes	oís
oye	oyen

ser	
soy	somos
eres	sois
es	son

tener	
tengo	tenemos
tienes	tenéis
tiene	tienen

venir	
vengo	venimos
vienes	venís
viene	vienen

Verbs: Present Participles

Present participles are used to talk about something that is in the process of happening.

Regular Participles		
-ar Verbs	**-er Verbs**	**-ir Verbs**
hablando	comiendo	compartiendo
tocando	haciendo	saliendo
usando	perdiendo	viviendo

y Spelling Change		
creer	→	creyendo
leer	→	leyendo
oír	→	oyendo
traer	→	trayendo

Stem Changes		
decir	→	diciendo
dormir	→	durmiendo
pedir	→	pidiendo
servir	→	sirviendo
venir	→	viniendo

Verbs: tú Commands

Affirmative tú Commands

Affirmative tú commands are used to tell a friend or family member to do something. Regular **tú** commands are the same as the third person singular form of the present tense.

Regular Commands		
-ar Verbs	**-er Verbs**	**-ir Verbs**
habla	come	vive
piensa	entiende	pide
almuerza	vuelve	sirve

Irregular Commands	
Infinitive → Tú Command	
decir	→ di
hacer	→ haz
ir	→ ve
poner	→ pon
salir	→ sal
ser	→ sé
tener	→ ten
venir	→ ven

Negative tú Commands

Negative tú commands are used to tell a friend or family member **not** to do something.

Regular Commands		
-ar Verbs	**-er Verbs**	**-ir Verbs**
no hables	no comas	no vivas
no mires	no hagas	no oigas
no entres	no vuelvas	no vengas

Commands with Spelling Changes		
-car Verbs	**-gar Verbs**	**-zar Verbs**
no busques	no juegues	no almuerces
no practiques	no llegues	no cruces
no toques	no pagues	no empieces

Irregular Commands	
Infinitive → Tú Command	
dar	→ no des
estar	→ no estés
ir	→ no vayas
ser	→ no seas

Verbs: Preterite Tense

Regular Verbs

Regular preterite verbs ending in **-ar, -er,** or **-ir** have regular endings.

-ar Verbs		-er Verbs		-ir Verbs	
bailé	bailamos	corrí	corrimos	abrí	abrimos
bailaste	bailasteis	corriste	corristeis	abriste	abristeis
bailó	bailaron	corrió	corrieron	abrió	abrieron

Verbs with Spelling Changes

-car Verbs		-gar Verbs		-zar Verbs	
c → qu		g → gu		z → c	
practiqué	practicamos	pagué	pagamos	crucé	cruzamos
practicaste	practicasteis	pagaste	pagasteis	cruzaste	cruzasteis
practicó	practicaron	pagó	pagaron	cruzó	cruzaron

creer		leer		oír	
i → y		i → y		i → y	
creí	creímos	leí	leímos	oí	oímos
creíste	creísteis	leíste	leísteis	oíste	oísteis
creyó	creyeron	leyó	leyeron	oyó	oyeron

Irregular Verbs

dar		decir		estar		hacer	
di	dimos	dije	dijimos	estuve	estuvimos	hice	hicimos
diste	disteis	dijiste	dijisteis	estuviste	estuvisteis	hiciste	hicisteis
dio	dieron	dijo	dijeron	estuvo	estuvieron	hizo	hicieron

ir		ser		tener		venir	
fui	fuimos	fui	fuimos	tuve	tuvimos	vine	vinimos
fuiste	fuisteis	fuiste	fuisteis	tuviste	tuvisteis	viniste	vinisteis
fue	fueron	fue	fueron	tuvo	tuvieron	vino	vinieron

GLOSARIO
español-inglés

This Spanish-English glossary contains all of the active vocabulary words that appear in the text as well as passive vocabulary from readings, culture sections, and extra vocabulary lists. Most inactive cognates have been omitted. The active words are accompanied by the number of the unit and **etapa** in which they are presented. For example, **a pie** can be found in **4.1** (*Unidad* 4, *Etapa* 1). **EP** refers to the *Etapa preliminar*. Stem-changing verbs are indicated by the change inside the parentheses—**poder (ue)**, as are irregular **yo** forms.

a to, at
  A la(s)... At.... o'clock. **2.2**
  a la derecha (de)
    to the right (of) **4.1**
  a la izquierda (de)
    to the left (of) **4.1**
  a pie on foot **4.1**
  ¿A qué hora es...?
    (At) What time is...? **2.2**
  a veces sometimes **2.1**
abajo down **6.2**
abierto(a) open **5.2**
el abogado lawyer
el abrigo coat **3.3**
abril April **1.3**
abrir to open **2.3**
la abuela grandmother **1.3**
el abuelo grandfather **1.3**
los abuelos grandparents **1.3**
aburrido(a) boring **1.2**
acá here **4.1**
acabar de... to have just... **3.1**
el aceite oil **5.3**
las aceitunas olives **5.2**
acostarse (ue) to go to bed **5.1**
actualmente nowadays
Adiós. Good-bye. **EP**
adónde (to) where **2.2**
la aduana customs
el aeropuerto airport **4.1**
afeitarse to shave oneself **5.1**

agosto August **1.3**
el agua (fem.) water **2.2**
el águila eagle
ahora now **1.3**
¡Ahora mismo! Right now! **2.1**
al to the **2.2**
  al aire libre outdoors **3.2**
  al lado (de) beside, next to **4.1**
la ala wings
alegre happy **3.1**
algo something **4.3**
alguien someone **4.3**
  conocer a alguien to know, to
    be familiar with someone **2.3**
alguno(a) some **4.3**
allá there **4.1**
allí there **4.1**
almorzar (ue) to eat lunch **4.2**
el almuerzo lunch **2.2**
alquilar un video
  to rent a video **3.1**
alto(a) tall **1.2**
amarillo(a) yellow **1.2**
el (la) amigo(a) friend **1.1**
anaranjado(a) orange **1.2**
ancho(a) wide **6.1**
andar
  andar en bicicleta
    to ride a bike **2.3**
  andar en patineta
    to skateboard **3.2**
el anillo ring **4.2**
el animal animal **2.3**
anoche last night **5.3**
anteayer day before yesterday **5.3**

antes (de) before **2.3**
antiguo(a) old, ancient **6.1**
el año year **1.3**
  el año pasado last year **5.3**
  ¿Cuántos años tiene...?
    How old is...? **1.3**
  Tiene... años.
    He/She is... years old. **1.3**
apagar la luz
  to turn off the light **5.3**
el apartamento apartment **1.1**
aparte separate
  Es aparte. Separate checks. **4.3**
el apellido last name, surname **EP**
aprender to learn **2.3**
aquel(la) that (over there) **6.2**
aquél(la) that one (over there) **6.2**
aquello that (over there) **6.2**
aquí here **4.1**
el árbol tree **3.3**
el arete earring **4.2**
el armario closet **5.2**
el (la) arquitecto(a) architect **6.1**
la arquitectura architecture **6.1**
arriba up **6.2**
el arroz rice **4.3**
el arte art **2.1**
la artesanía handicraft **4.2**
el (la) artesano(a) artisan **6.2**
los artículos de cuero
  leather goods **4.2**
asado(a) roasted
el auditorio auditorium **2.2**
el autobús bus **4.1**
la avenida avenue **4.1**

el **avión** airplane **4.1**
ayer yesterday **5.3**
ayudar (a) to help **2.1**
    ¿Me ayuda a pedir? Could
        you help me order? **4.3**
el **azúcar** sugar **4.3**
azul blue **1.2**

bailar to dance **1.1**
bajo(a) short (height) **1.2**
el **baloncesto** basketball **3.2**
el **banco** bank **4.1**
bañarse to take a bath **5.1**
el **baño** bathroom **5.2**
barato(a) cheap, inexpensive **4.2**
el **barco** ship **4.1**
barrer el suelo to sweep the
    floor **5.2**
el **barrio** district
el **bate** bat **3.2**
beber to drink **2.3**
    ¿Quieres beber…?
        Do you want to drink…? **2.2**
    Quiero beber…
        I want to drink… **2.2**
la **bebida** beverage, drink **4.3**
el **béisbol** baseball **3.2**
la **biblioteca** library **2.2**
bien well **1.1**
    (No muy) Bien, ¿y tú/usted?
        (Not very) Well, and you? **1.1**
bienvenido(a) welcome **1.1**
el **bistec** steak **4.3**
blanco(a) white **1.2**
la **blusa** blouse **1.2**
la **boca** mouth **5.1**
el **bohique** storyteller
la **bola** ball **3.2**
la **bolsa** bag **1.2**; handbag **4.2**
el **bombero** firefighter **6.1**
bonito(a) pretty **1.2**
el **borrador** eraser **2.1**
el **bosque** forest **3.3**
las **botas** boots **4.2**
la **botella** bottle **5.3**
el **brazo** arm **5.1**
el **bronceador** suntan lotion **3.3**

bueno(a) good **1.2**
    Buenas noches.
        Good evening. **EP**
    Buenas tardes.
        Good afternoon. **EP**
    Buenos días. Good morning. **EP**
la **bufanda** scarf **3.3**
buscar to look for, to search **2.1**

el **caballo** horse **6.2**
la **cabeza** head **5.1**
    lavarse la cabeza
        to wash one's hair **5.1**
cada each, every **2.3**
el **café** café **4.1**; coffee **4.3**
la **cafetería** cafeteria,
    coffee shop **2.2**
los **calamares** squid **5.2**
el **calcetín** sock **1.2**
la **calculadora** calculator **2.1**
la **calidad** quality **4.2**
caliente hot, warm **4.3**
¡Cállate! Be quiet! **5.3**
la **calle** street **4.1**
calor
    Hace calor. It is hot. **3.3**
    tener calor to be hot **3.3**
la **cama** bed **5.1**
    hacer la cama
        to make the bed **5.1**
la **cámara** camera **6.1**
los **camarones** shrimp
cambiar to change, to exchange **4.2**
el **cambio** change,
    money exchange **4.2**
caminar con el perro
    to walk the dog **2.3**
el **camino** road **4.1**
el **camión** truck
la **camisa** shirt **1.2**
la **camiseta** T-shirt **1.2**
el **campo** field **3.2**;
    countryside, country **6.2**
la **canasta** basket
la **cancha** court **3.2**
la **canción** song
cansado(a) tired **3.1**
cantar to sing **1.1**
la **cara** face **5.1**

la **carne** meat **4.3**
la **carne de res** beef **5.3**
la **carnicería** butcher's shop **4.1**
caro(a) expensive **4.2**
    ¡Es muy caro(a)!
        It's very expensive! **4.2**
el **carro** car **4.1**
la **cartera** wallet **4.2**
el **(la) cartero(a)** mail carrier **6.1**
la **casa** house **1.1**
el **casco** helmet **3.2**
el **casete** cassette **4.2**
castaño(a) brown hair **1.2**
catorce fourteen **1.3**
la **cebolla** onion **5.3**
la **cena** supper, dinner **2.3**
cenar to have dinner, supper **2.3**
el **centro** center, downtown **4.1**
el **centro comercial**
    shopping center **4.1**
el **cepillo (de dientes)**
    brush (toothbrush) **5.1**
la **cerámica** ceramics **4.2**
la **cerca** fence **6.2**
cerca (de) near (to) **4.1**
el **cerdo** pig **6.2**
el **cereal** cereal **5.3**
cero zero **EP**
cerrado(a) closed **5.2**
cerrar (ie) to close **3.2**
el **champú** shampoo **5.1**
la **chaqueta** jacket **1.2**
chévere awesome
    ¡Qué chévere!
        How awesome! **1.3**
la **chica** girl **1.1**
los **chicharrones** pork rinds **2.3**
el **chico** boy **1.1**
el **chorizo** sausage **5.2**
cien one hundred **1.3**
las **ciencias** science **2.1**
cinco five **EP**
cincuenta fifty **1.3**
el **cinturón** belt **4.2**
la **cita** appointment **2.2**
la **ciudad** city **1.3**
¡Claro que sí! Of course! **3.1**
la **clase** class, classroom **2.1**
el **cobarde** coward
la **cocina** kitchen **5.2**
cocinar to cook **5.3**
la **cola** tail
el **collar** necklace **4.2**

el color color **1.2**
  ¿De qué color…?
    What color…? **1.2**
el comedor dining room **5.2**
comer to eat **1.1**
  darle(s) de comer to feed **6.2**
  ¿Quieres comer…?
    Do you want to eat…? **2.2**
  Quiero comer…
    I want to eat… **2.2**
cómico(a) funny, comical **1.2**
la comida food, a meal **2.3**
como like, as
cómo how **2.2**
  ¿Cómo es?
    What is he/she like? **1.2**
  ¿Cómo está usted?
    How are you? (formal) **1.1**
  ¿Cómo estás?
    How are you? (familiar) **1.1**
  ¡Cómo no! Of course! **4.1**
  ¿Cómo se llama?
    What is his/her name? **EP**
  ¿Cómo te llamas?
    What is your name? **EP**
  Perdona(e), ¿cómo llego a…?
    Pardon, how do I get to…? **4.1**
la compañía company **6.1**
compartir to share **2.3**
comprar to buy **2.2**
comprender to understand **2.3**
la computación
    computer science **2.1**
la computadora computer **2.1**
la comunidad community **1.1**
con with **1.3**
  con rayas striped **3.3**
  Con razón. That's why. **2.1**
el concierto concert **3.1**
el concurso contest **1.1**
el congelador freezer **5.3**
conmigo with me **3.1**
conocer (conozco) to know,
    to be familiar with **2.3**
  conocer a alguien to know, to
    be familiar with someone **2.3**
el (la) contador(a) accountant **6.1**
la contaminación del aire
    air pollution **6.1**
contar (ue) to count, to (re)tell **4.2**
contento(a) content, happy,
    pleased **3.1**
contestar to answer **2.1**

contigo with you **3.1**
el corazón heart **2.3**
el cordero sheep
corto(a) short (length) **1.2**
el corral corral, pen **6.2**
el correo post office **4.1**
  el correo electrónico e-mail
correr to run **1.1**
la cosa thing **4.1**
costar (ue) to cost **4.2**
  ¿Cuánto cuesta(n)…?
    How much is (are)…? **4.2**
la costumbre custom
creer to think, to believe **3.3**
  Creo que sí/no. I think so./
    I don't think so. **3.3**
la crema cream **5.3**
cruzar to cross **4.1**
el cuaderno notebook **2.1**
la cuadra city block **4.1**
cuál(es) which (ones), what **2.2**
  ¿Cuál es la fecha?
    What is the date? **1.3**
  ¿Cuál es tu teléfono? What is
    your phone number? **EP**
cuando when, whenever **3.1**
cuándo when **2.2**
cuánto how much **4.2**
  ¿A cuánto está(n)…?
    How much is (are)…? **5.3**
  ¿Cuánto cuesta(n)…?
    How much is (are)…? **4.2**
  ¿Cuánto es?
    How much is it? **4.3**
  ¿Cuánto le doy de propina?
    How much do I tip? **4.3**
cuántos(as) how many
  ¿Cuántos años tiene…?
    How old is…? **1.3**
cuarenta forty **1.3**
cuarto(a) quarter **5.3;** fourth **6.2**
cuatro four **EP**
cuatrocientos(as) four hundred **5.3**
la cuchara spoon **4.3**
el cuchillo knife **4.3**
la cuenta bill, check **4.3**
  La cuenta, por favor.
    The check, please. **4.3**
la cuerda string
el cuero leather
  los artículos de cuero
    leather goods **4.2**
el cuerpo body **5.1**

la cueva cave
cuidadosamente carefully **5.2**
cuidadoso(a) careful **5.2**
cuidar (a) to take care of **2.3**
el cumpleaños birthday **1.3**

dar (doy) to give **4.2**
  darle(s) de comer to feed **6.2**
de of, from **1.1**
  de cuadros plaid, checked **3.3**
  de la mañana in the morning **2.2**
  de la noche at night **2.2**
  de la tarde in the afternoon **2.2**
  De nada. You're welcome. **1.1**
  de vez en cuando
    once in a while **2.1**
debajo (de) underneath, under **6.2**
deber should, ought to **5.2**
decidir to decide **6.1**
décimo(a) tenth **6.2**
decir to say, to tell **4.1**
dejar to leave (behind)
  dejar un mensaje
    to leave a message **3.1**
  **Deje un mensaje después
    del tono.** Leave a message
    after the tone. **3.1**
  Le dejo… en…
    I'll give… to you for… **4.2**
  **Quiero dejar un mensaje
    para…** I want to leave a
    message for… **3.1**
del from the **3.1**
delgado(a) thin **1.2**
delicioso(a) delicious **4.3**
demasiado(a) too much **4.2**
dentro (de) inside (of) **6.2**
el deporte sport
  practicar deportes
    to play sports **3.1**
deprimido(a) depressed **3.1**
la derecha right
  a la derecha (de)
    to the right (of) **4.1**
derecho straight ahead **4.1**
desayunar to have breakfast **4.3**
el desayuno breakfast **4.3**
descansar to rest **2.2**
desde from **4.1**

el desierto desert **3.3**
el despertador alarm clock **5.1**
despertarse (ie) to wake up **5.1**
después (de) after, afterward **2.3**
detrás (de) behind **4.1**
devolver (ue) to return (item) **4.2**
el día day **EP**
 Buenos días. Good morning. **EP**
 ¿Qué día es hoy?
  What day is today? **EP**
 todos los días every day **2.1**
el diccionario dictionary **2.1**
diciembre December **1.3**
diecinueve nineteen **1.3**
dieciocho eighteen **1.3**
dieciséis sixteen **1.3**
diecisiete seventeen **1.3**
el diente tooth **5.1**
 lavarse los dientes
  to brush one's teeth **5.1**
diez ten **EP**
difícil difficult, hard **2.1**
el dinero money **4.2**
el diós god
la dirección address, direction **4.1**
el disco compacto
 compact disc **4.2**
divertido(a) enjoyable, fun **1.2**
doblar to turn **4.1**
doce twelve **1.3**
la docena dozen **5.3**
el (la) doctor(a) doctor **1.1**
el dólar dollar **4.2**
domingo Sunday **EP**
dónde where **2.2**
 ¿De dónde eres?
  Where are you from? **EP**
 ¿De dónde es?
  Where is he/she from? **EP**
dormir (ue) to sleep **4.2**
dormirse (ue) to fall asleep **5.1**
dos two **EP**
doscientos(as) two hundred **5.3**
ducharse to take a shower **5.1**
dulce sweet **4.3**
durante during **2.2**
duro(a) hard, tough **5.1**

la edad age **1.3**
el edificio building **6.1**
el (la) editor(a) editor **6.1**
la educación física
 physical education **2.1**
el efectivo cash **4.2**
él he **1.1**
ella she **1.1**
ellos(as) they **1.1**
emocionado(a) excited **3.1**
empezar (ie) to begin **3.2**
Encantado(a). Delighted/
 Pleased to meet you. **EP**
la enchilada enchilada **4.3**
en in **1.1**
 en vez de instead of
encima (de) on top (of) **6.2**
encontrar (ue) to find, to meet **4.2**
enero January **1.3**
enfermo(a) sick **3.1**
enfrente (de) in front (of) **4.1**
enojado(a) angry **3.1**
enorme huge, enormous **6.1**
la ensalada salad **4.3**
enseñar to teach **2.1**
entender (ie) to understand **3.2**
entonces then, so **2.3**
entrar (a, en) to enter **2.1**
entre between **4.1**
la entrevista interview **6.1**
la época period
el equipo team **3.2**
escribir to write **1.1**
el (la) escritor(a) writer **6.1**
el escritorio desk **2.1**
escuchar to listen (to) **2.1**
la escuela school **2.1**
ese(a) that **6.2**
ése(a) that one **6.2**
eso that **6.2**
el español Spanish **2.1**
especial special **5.2**
especialmente (e)specially, **5.2**
el espejo mirror **5.1**
esperar to wait for, to expect **2.1**
la esposa wife
el esposo husband
esquiar to ski **3.2**
la esquina corner **4.1**

la estación de autobuses
 bus station **4.1**
las estaciones seasons **3.3**
el estadio stadium **3.2**
estar to be **2.2**
 ¿Está incluido(a)…?
  Is… included? **4.3**
 estar de acuerdo to agree **6.1**
este(a) this **6.2**
éste(a) this one **6.2**
esto this **6.2**
el estómago stomach **5.1**
estrecho(a) narrow **6.1**
la estrella star **5.3**
el (la) estudiante student **1.1**
estudiar to study **2.1**
los estudios sociales
 social studies **2.1**
la estufa stove **5.3**
el examen test **2.1**
el éxito success

fácil easy **2.1**
fácilmente easily **5.2**
la falda skirt **1.2**
la familia family **1.1**
la farmacia pharmacy,
 drugstore **4.1**
favorito(a) favorite **3.2**
febrero February **1.3**
la fecha date **1.3**
 ¿Cuál es la fecha?
  What is the date? **1.3**
felicidades congratulations **1.3**
feliz happy **1.3**
felizmente happily **5.2**
feo(a) ugly **1.2**
la fiesta party **5.2**
el flan caramel custard dessert **4.3**
la flor flower **3.3**
el folleto brochure
formal formal **6.1**
la foto picture
 sacar fotos to take pictures **3.3**
el (la) fotógrafo(a) photographer **6.1**
frecuente frequent **5.2**
frecuentemente often, frequently **5.2**
el frigorífico refrigerator **5.3**

frío
    Hace frío. It is cold. **3.3**
    tener frío to be cold **3.3**
la frontera border
la fruta fruit **2.2**
el fuego fire
fuera (de) outside (of) **6.2**
fuerte strong **1.2**
el fútbol soccer **3.2**
el fútbol americano football **3.2**

las gafas de sol sunglasses **3.3**
la galleta cookie, cracker **5.3**
la gallina hen **6.2**
el gallo rooster **6.2**
el (la) ganadero(a) farmer **6.2**
el (la) ganador(a) winner **6.1**
ganar to win **3.2**
el (la) gato(a) cat **1.2**
la gente people **2.3**
el (la) gerente manager **6.1**
el gimnasio gymnasium **2.2**
el gobierno government
el gol goal **3.2**
gordo(a) fat **1.2**
la gorra baseball cap **3.2**
el gorro cap **3.3**
la grabadora tape recorder **6.1**
Gracias. Thank you. **1.1**
    Gracias, pero no puedo.
        Thanks, but I can't. **3.1**
el grado degree **3.3**
el gramo gram **5.3**
grande big, large **1.2**
la granja farm **6.2**
el guante glove **3.2**
guapo(a) good-looking **1.2**
la guerra war
el guerrero warrior
la guía telefónica phone book **3.1**
gustar to like
    Le gusta... He/She likes... **1.1**
    Me gusta... I like... **1.1**
    Me gustaría... I'd like... **3.1**
    Te gusta... You like... **1.1**
    ¿Te gustaría...?
        Would you like...? **3.1**

el gusto pleasure
    El gusto es mío.
        The pleasure is mine. **EP**
    Mucho gusto.
        Nice to meet you. **EP**

la habitación bedroom **5.2**
hablar to talk, to speak **2.1**
    ¿Puedo hablar con...?
        May I speak with...? **3.1**
hacer (hago) to make, to do **2.3**
    Hace buen tiempo.
        It is nice outside. **3.3**
    Hace calor. It is hot. **3.3**
    Hace fresco. It is cool. **3.3**
    Hace frío. It is cold. **3.3**
    Hace mal tiempo.
        It is bad outside. **3.3**
    Hace sol. It is sunny. **3.3**
    Hace viento. It is windy. **3.3**
    hacer ejercicio to exercise **2.3**
    hacer la cama
        to make the bed **5.1**
    ¿Qué tiempo hace?
        What is the weather like? **3.3**
la hamburguesa hamburger **2.2**
la harina flour **5.3**
hasta until, as far as **4.1**
    Hasta luego. See you later. **EP**
    Hasta mañana.
        See you tomorrow. **EP**
hay there is, there are **1.3**
    hay que one has to, must **2.1**
    Hay sol. It's sunny. **3.3**
    Hay viento. It's windy. **3.3**
el helado ice cream **5.3**
la hermana sister **1.3**
la hermanastra stepsister
el hermanastro stepbrother
el hermano brother **1.3**
los hermanos brother(s) and
    sister(s) **1.3**
la hija daughter **1.3**
el hijo son **1.3**
los hijos son(s) and daughter(s),
    children **1.3**
la historia history **2.1**
el hockey hockey **3.2**
Hola. Hello. **EP**

el hombre man **1.1**
el hombre de negocios
    businessman **6.1**
el horario schedule **2.2**
el horno oven **5.3**
el hotel hotel **4.1**
hoy today **EP**
    Hoy es... Today is... **EP**
    ¿Qué día es hoy?
        What day is today? **EP**
el huevo egg **5.3**

la iglesia church **4.1**
Igualmente. Same here. **EP**
el impermeable raincoat **3.3**
la impresora printer **2.1**
informal informal **6.1**
el inglés English **2.1**
inteligente intelligent **1.2**
interesante interesting **1.2**
el invierno winter **3.3**
la invitación invitation **5.2**
invitar to invite
    Te invito. I'll treat you.
        I invite you. **3.1**
ir to go **2.2**
    ir a... to be going to... **2.3**
    ir al cine
        to go to a movie theater **3.1**
    ir al supermercado to go
        to the supermarket **2.3**
    ir de compras
        to go shopping **3.1**
    Vamos a... Let's... **6.1**
irse to leave, to go away **5.1**
la isla island
la izquierda left
    a la izquierda (de)
        to the left (of) **4.1**

el jabón soap **5.1**
el jamón ham **5.2**
el jardín garden **5.2**
la jarra pitcher **4.2**
los jeans jeans **1.2**

el (la) jefe(a) boss **6.1**
joven young **1.3**
las joyas jewelry **4.2**
la joyería jewelry store **4.1**
jueves Thursday **EP**
el (la) jugador(a) player
jugar (ue) to play **3.2**
julio July **1.3**
junio June **1.3**
juntos together **4.2**

el kilo kilogram **5.3**

el lago lake **3.3**
la lámpara lamp **5.2**
la lana wool **6.2**
el lápiz pencil **2.1**
largo(a) long **1.2**
la lata can **5.3**
el lavaplatos dishwasher **5.3**
lavar los platos
    to wash the dishes **5.1**
lavarse to wash oneself **5.1**
    lavarse la cabeza
        to wash one's hair **5.1**
    lavarse los dientes
        to brush one's teeth **5.1**
la lección lesson **2.1**
la leche milk **5.3**
la lechuga lettuce **4.3**
leer to read **1.1**
lejos (de) far (from) **4.1**
    ¿Queda lejos? Is it far? **4.1**
la lengua language **4.3**
lentamente slowly **5.2**
lento(a) slow **5.2**
el letrero sign
levantar pesas
    to lift weights **3.2**
levantarse to get up **5.1**
la librería bookstore **4.1**
el libro book **2.1**
la limonada lemonade **4.3**
limpiar el cuarto
    to clean the room **5.1**

limpio(a) clean **5.1**
listo(a) ready **4.3**
la literatura literature **2.1**
el litro liter **5.3**
la llama llama **6.2**
la llamada call **3.1**
llamar to call **3.1**
    Dile/Dígale que me llame.
        Tell him or her to call me. **3.1**
la llave key **5.2**
llegar to arrive **2.1**
    llegar a ser to become
llevar to wear, to carry **2.1**;
    to take along **3.3**
llover (ue) to rain **3.3**
la lluvia rain **3.3**
Lo siento… I'm sorry… **4.1**
loco(a) crazy **3.2**
el loro parrot
luego later **2.3**
    Hasta luego. See you later. **EP**
el lugar place **1.1**
lujoso(a) luxurious **6.1**
lunes Monday **EP**
la madrastra stepmother
la madre mother **1.3**
el (la) maestro(a) teacher **1.1**

la madera wood
el maíz corn
malo(a) bad **1.2**
mandar una carta
    to send a letter **2.3**
manejar to drive **4.1**
la mano hand **5.1**
la manta blanket **5.1**
la mantequilla butter **5.3**
mañana tomorrow **EP**
    Hasta mañana.
        See you tomorrow. **EP**
    Mañana es… Tomorrow is… **EP**
la mañana morning **2.2**
    de la mañana
        in the morning **2.2**
    por la mañana
        during the morning **2.2**
el mapa map **4.1**
maquillarse to put on makeup **5.1**

la máquina contestadora
    answering machine **3.1**
el mar sea **3.3**
marcar to dial **3.1**
marrón brown **1.2**
martes Tuesday **EP**
marzo March **1.3**
más more **1.3**
    más de more than **3.2**
    más… que more… than **3.2**
las matemáticas mathematics **2.1**
la materia subject **2.1**
mayo May **1.3**
mayor older **1.3**
Me llamo… My name is… **EP**
la media hermana half-sister
la medianoche midnight **2.2**
medio(a) half **5.3**
el medio hermano half-brother
el mediodía noon **2.2**
mejor better **3.2**
menor younger **1.3**
menos to, before **2.2**; less **3.2**
    menos de less than **3.2**
    menos… que less… than **3.2**
el menú menu **4.3**
el mercado market **4.2**
merendar (ie) to have a snack **3.2**
la merienda snack **2.2**
el mes month **1.3**
    el mes pasado last month **5.3**
la mesa table **5.2**
    poner la mesa to set the table **4.3**
    quitar la mesa
        to clear the table **5.1**
el (la) mesero(a) waiter
    (waitress) **4.3**
el metro subway **4.1**
mi my **1.3**
el microondas microwave **5.3**
miércoles Wednesday **EP**
mil one thousand **5.3**
un millón one million **5.3**
mirar to watch, to look at **2.1**
mismo(a) same **2.1**
la mochila backpack **2.1**
moderno(a) modern **6.1**
el momento moment
    Un momento. One moment. **3.1**
la montaña mountain **3.3**
morado(a) purple **1.2**
moreno(a) dark hair and skin **1.2**

la **moto(cicleta)** motorcycle **4.1**
mover (ue) los muebles
   to move the furniture **5.2**
la **muchacha** girl **1.1**
el **muchacho** boy **1.1**
mucho often **2.1**
mucho(a) much, many **1.1**
los **muebles** furniture **5.2**
la **mujer** woman **1.1**
la **mujer de negocios**
   businesswoman **6.1**
el **mundo** world **1.1**
el **museo** museum **2.3**
la **música** music **2.1**
muy very **1.3**

nada nothing **4.3**
nadar to swim **1.1**
nadie no one **4.3**
la **nariz** nose **5.1**
necesitar to need **2.1**
negro(a) black **1.2**
nervioso(a) nervous **3.1**
nevar (ie) to snow **3.3**
la **nieta** granddaughter
el **nieto** grandson
los **nietos** grandchildren
la **nieve** snow **3.3**
ninguno(a) none, not any **4.3**
el **niño** boy
la **niña** girl
no no **EP**; not **1.1**
   ¡No digas eso! Don't say that! **1.2**
   ¡No te preocupes!
      Don't worry! **3.1**
la **noche** night, evening
   Buenas noches.
      Good evening. **EP**
   de la noche at night **2.2**
   por la noche
      during the evening **2.2**
el **nombre** name, first name **EP**
normal normal **5.2**
normalmente normally **5.2**
nosotros(as) we **1.1**
novecientos(as) nine hundred **5.3**
la **novela** novel **2.3**
noveno(a) ninth **6.2**
noventa ninety **1.3**

noviembre November **1.3**
nublado cloudy
   Está nublado. It is cloudy. **3.3**
nuestro(a) our **1.3**
nueve nine **EP**
nuevo(a) new **1.2**
nunca never **2.1**

o or **1.1**
la **obra** work
   la **obra maestra** masterpiece
ochenta eighty **1.3**
ocho eight **EP**
ochocientos(as) eight hundred **5.3**
octavo(a) eighth **6.2**
octubre October **1.3**
ocupado(a) busy **3.1**
la **oficina** office **2.2**
ofrecer (ofrezco) to offer **6.1**
   Le puedo ofrecer…
      I can offer you… **4.2**
oír to hear **2.3**
el **ojo** eye **1.2**
la **olla** pot **4.2**
olvidar to forget **5.2**
once eleven **1.3**
el **(la) operador(a)** operator **6.1**
ordenar to arrange **5.2**
ordinario(a) ordinary **6.1**
la **oreja** ear **5.1**
el **oro** gold **4.2**
el **otoño** fall **3.3**
otro(a) other, another **1.2**

paciente patient **1.2**
el **padrastro** stepfather
el **padre** father **1.3**
los **padres** parents **1.3**
pagar to pay **4.2**
el **país** country **1.1**
el **pájaro** bird **2.3**
el **pan** bread **4.3**
el **pan dulce** sweet roll **4.3**
la **panadería** bread bakery **4.1**
la **pantalla** screen **2.1**

los **pantalones** pants **1.2**
   los **pantalones cortos** shorts
la **papa** potato
las **papas fritas** french fries **2.2**
el **papel** paper **2.1**
la **papelería** stationery store **4.1**
el **paquete** package **5.3**
para for, in order to **4.2**
el **paraguas** umbrella **3.3**
la **pared** wall **5.2**
el **parque** park **2.3**
el **partido** game **3.2**
pasar to happen, to pass (by) **2.1**
   pasar la aspiradora
      to vacuum **5.2**
   pasar un rato con los amigos
      to spend time with friends **2.3**
pasear to go for a walk **2.3**
la **pasta** pasta **5.3**
la **pasta de dientes** toothpaste **5.1**
el **pastel** cake **4.3**
la **pastelería** pastry shop **4.1**
el **(la) pastor(a)** shepherd(ess) **6.2**
la **patata** potato **5.3**
patinar to skate **1.1**
los **patines** skates **3.2**
la **patineta** skateboard **3.2**
   andar en patineta
      to skateboard **3.2**
el **pedazo** piece **5.3**
pedir (i) to ask for, to order **4.3**
   ¿Me ayuda a pedir?
      Could you help me order? **4.3**
peinarse to comb one's hair **5.1**
el **peine** comb **5.1**
la **película** movie **3.1**
peligroso(a) dangerous **3.2**
pelirrojo(a) redhead **1.2**
el **pelo** hair **1.2**
la **pelota** baseball **3.2**
pensar (ie) to think, to plan **3.2**
peor worse **3.2**
pequeño(a) small **1.2**
perder (ie) to lose **3.2**
Perdona(e)… Pardon…
   Perdona(e), ¿cómo llego a…?
      Pardon, how do I get to…? **4.1**
perezoso(a) lazy **1.2**
perfecto(a) perfect **4.2**
el **periódico** newspaper **2.3**
el **(la) periodista** journalist **6.1**
pero but **1.1**

el (la) perro(a) dog **1.2**
  caminar con el perro
    to walk the dog **2.3**
el pescado fish **5.3**
el pez fish **2.3**
picante spicy **4.3**
el pie foot **5.1**
  a pie on foot **4.1**
la pierna leg **5.1**
la pimienta pepper **5.3**
pintar to paint **2.3**
la piña pineapple
la piscina swimming pool **3.2**
el pizarrón chalkboard **2.1**
el placer pleasure
  Es un placer. It's a pleasure. **EP**
planchar to iron **5.2**
la planta plant **3.3**
la plata silver **4.2**
el plato plate **4.2**
la playa beach **3.3**
la plaza town square **4.1**
la pluma pen **2.1**
poco a little **2.1**
poder (ue) to be able, can **4.2**
  Gracias, pero no puedo.
    Thanks, but I can't. **3.1**
  Le puedo ofrecer…
    I can offer you… **4.2**
  ¿Puedes (Puede usted) decirme
    dónde queda…? Could you
    tell me where… is? **4.1**
  ¿Puedo hablar con…?
    May I speak with…? **3.1**
el poema poem **2.3**
la poesía poetry **2.3**
el (la) policía police officer **1.1**
el pollo chicken **4.3**
poner (pongo) to put **4.3**
  poner la mesa to set the table **4.3**
ponerse (me pongo) to put on **5.1**
  ponerse la ropa to get dressed **5.1**
por for, by, around **4.1**
  por favor please **2.2**
  por fin finally **2.3**
  por la mañana
    during the morning **2.2**
  por la noche
    during the evening **2.2**
  por la tarde
    during the afternoon **2.2**
  por qué why **2.2**
porque because **3.1**

el postre dessert **4.3**
practicar deportes to play sports **3.1**
el precio price **4.2**
preferir (ie) to prefer **3.2**
preocupado(a) worried **3.1**
preparar to prepare **2.1**
presentar to introduce
  Te/Le presento a…
    Let me introduce you to… **1.1**
la primavera spring **3.3**
primero first **2.3**
el primero first of the month **1.3**
primero(a) first **6.2**
el (la) primo(a) cousin **1.3**
el problema problem **2.3**
la profesión profession **6.1**
el programa program
pronto soon **2.1**
la propina tip **4.3**
  ¿Cuánto le doy de propina?
    How much do I tip? **4.3**
la prueba quiz **2.1**
el pueblo town, village **4.3**
el puerco pork **5.3**
la puerta door **5.2**
pues well **1.2**
la pulsera bracelet **4.2**

qué what **2.2**
  ¿A qué hora es…? (At) What
    time is…? **2.2**
  ¡Qué (divertido)! How (fun)! **1.2**
  ¿Qué día es hoy? What day
    is today? **EP**
  ¿Qué hora es? What time is it? **2.2**
  ¡Qué lástima! What a shame! **3.1**
  ¿Qué lleva?
    What is he/she wearing? **1.2**
  ¿Qué tal? How is it going? **1.1**
  ¿Qué tiempo hace?
    What is the weather like? **3.3**
quedar (en) to stay, to be (in a
  specific place), to agree on **4.1**
  ¿Puedes (Puede usted) decirme
    dónde queda…? Could you
    tell me where… is? **4.1**
  ¿Queda lejos? Is it far? **4.1**
los quehaceres chores **5.1**

querer (ie) to want **3.2**
  ¿Quieres beber…?
    Do you want to drink…? **2.2**
  ¿Quieres comer…?
    Do you want to eat…? **2.2**
  Quiero beber…
    I want to drink… **2.2**
  Quiero comer…
    I want to eat… **2.2**
  Quiero dejar un mensaje
    para… I want to leave a
    message for… **3.1**
el queso cheese **4.3**
quién(es) who **2.2**
  ¿De quién es…? Whose is…? **1.3**
  ¿Quién es? Who is it? **1.3**
  ¿Quiénes son? Who are they? **1.3**
quince fifteen **1.3**
quinientos(as) five hundred **5.3**
quinto(a) fifth **6.2**
Quisiera… I would like… **4.3**
quitar
  quitar el polvo to dust **5.2**
  quitar la mesa
    to clear the table **5.1**

el radio radio **4.2**
el radiocasete radio-tape player **4.2**
rápidamente quickly **5.2**
rápido(a) fast, quick **5.2**
la raqueta racket **3.2**
rara vez rarely **2.1**
el ratón mouse **2.1**
la razón reason **2.1**
  Con razón. That's why. **2.1**
  tener razón to be right **3.3**
el (la) recepcionista receptionist **6.1**
el receso break **2.2**
recibir to receive **2.3**
reciente recent **5.2**
recientemente lately, recently **5.2**
recordar (ue) to remember **4.2**
el refresco soft drink **2.2**
el regalo gift **4.2**
regatear to bargain **4.2**
la regla rule
regresar to return
  Regresa más tarde.
    He/She will return later. **3.1**

ESPAÑOL—INGLÉS

Regular. So-so. **1.1**
el reloj clock, watch **2.2**
el restaurante restaurant **4.3**
el retrato portrait
la revista magazine **2.3**
rico(a) tasty **4.3**; rich
el río river **3.3**
riquísimo(a) very tasty **4.3**
rojo(a) red **1.2**
la ropa clothing **1.2**
   ponerse la ropa to get dressed **5.1**
rosado(a) pink **1.2**
rubio(a) blond **1.2**

sábado Saturday **EP**
saber (sé) to know **3.2**
sabroso(a) tasty **5.3**
sacar
   sacar fotos to take pictures **3.3**
   sacar la basura
      to take out the trash **5.2**
   sacar una buena nota
      to get a good grade **2.1**
la sal salt **5.3**
la sala living room **5.2**
   la sala de espera waiting room
la salchicha sausage **5.3**
salir (salgo) to go out, to leave **4.1**
la salsa salsa **4.3**
Se llama… His/Her name is… **EP**
el secador de pelo hair dryer **5.1**
secarse to dry oneself **5.1**
el (la) secretario(a) secretary **6.1**
segundo(a) second **6.2**
seis six **EP**
seiscientos(as) six hundred **5.3**
la semana week **EP**
   la semana pasada last week **5.3**
   el semestre semester **2.2**
sencillo(a) simple, plain **6.1**
la señal sign
el señor Mr. **1.1**
la señora Mrs. **1.1**
la señorita Miss **1.1**
septiembre September **1.3**
séptimo(a) seventh **6.2**

ser to be **1.1**
   Es la…/Son las…
      It is… o'clock. **2.2**
   ser de… to be from… **1.1**
serio(a) serious **1.2**
servir (i) to serve **4.3**
sesenta sixty **1.3**
setecientos(as) seven hundred **5.3**
setenta seventy **1.3**
sexto(a) sixth **6.2**
los shorts shorts **3.3**
si if **5.2**
sí yes **EP**
   Sí, me encantaría.
      Yes, I would love to. **3.1**
siempre always **2.1**
siete seven **EP**
el siglo century
la silla chair **5.2**
el sillón armchair **5.2**
simpático(a) nice **1.2**
sin without **4.3**
sobre on, about
   sobre hielo on ice **3.2**
el sofá sofa, couch **5.2**
el sol sun **3.3**
   las gafas de sol sunglasses **3.3**
   Hace sol. It is sunny. **3.3**
   Hay sol. It's sunny. **3.3**
   tomar el sol to sunbathe **3.3**
sólo only **1.3**
solo(a) alone **3.1**
el sombrero hat **1.2**
el sonido sound
la sopa soup **4.3**
sorprender to surprise **5.2**
sorpresa surprise **5.2**
su your *(formal)*, his, her, its,
   their **1.3**
sucio(a) dirty **5.1**
el suelo floor **5.2**
   barrer el suelo
      to sweep the floor **5.2**
el suéter sweater **1.2**
el surfing surfing **3.2**

Tal vez otro día.
   Maybe another day. **3.1**

el taller workshop **6.2**
también also, too **1.1**
el tambor drum
tampoco neither, either **4.3**
tan… como as… as **3.2**
tanto como as much as **3.2**
las tapas appetizers **5.2**
tarde late **2.1**
la tarde afternoon **2.2**
   Buenas tardes.
      Good afternoon. **EP**
   de la tarde in the afternoon **2.2**
   por la tarde
      during the afternoon **2.2**
la tarea homework **2.1**
la tarjeta de crédito credit card **4.2**
el taxi taxi, cab **4.1**
el (la) taxista taxi driver **6.1**
la taza cup **4.3**
el té tea **4.3**
el teatro theater **2.3**
la tecla key (of an instrument)
el teclado keyboard **2.1**
el tejido textile
el teléfono telephone **3.1**
   ¿Cuál es tu teléfono? What is
      your phone number? **EP**
el televisor television set **5.2**
la temperatura temperature **3.3**
temprano early **3.1**
el tenedor fork **4.3**
tener to have **1.3**
   ¿Cuántos años tiene…?
      How old is…? **1.3**
   tener calor to be hot **3.3**
   tener cuidado to be careful **3.3**
   tener frío to be cold **3.3**
   tener ganas de… to feel like… **3.3**
   tener hambre to be hungry **2.3**
   tener miedo to be afraid **3.3**
   tener prisa to be in a hurry **3.3**
   tener que to have to **2.1**
   tener razón to be right **3.3**
   tener sed to be thirsty **2.3**
   tener sueño to be sleepy **3.3**
   tener suerte to be lucky **3.3**
   Tiene… años.
      He/She is… years old. **1.3**
el tenis tennis **3.2**
tercero(a) third **6.2**
terminar to finish **2.2**
Terrible. Terrible./Awful. **1.1**
la tía aunt **1.3**

el tiempo time **3.1**; weather **3.3**
   Hace buen tiempo.
      It is nice outside. **3.3**
   Hace mal tiempo.
      It is bad outside. **3.3**
   ¿Qué tiempo hace?
      What is the weather like? **3.3**
   el tiempo libre free time **3.1**
la tienda store **2.3**
   la tienda de deportes
      sporting goods store **3.2**
   la tienda de música y videos
      music and video store **4.1**
la tierra land
las tijeras scissors **6.2**
el tío uncle **1.3**
los tíos uncle(s) and aunt(s) **1.3**
la tiza chalk **2.1**
el tlacuache possum
la toalla towel **5.1**
tocar to play (an instrument)
   tocar el piano
      to play the piano **2.3**
   tocar la guitarra
      to play the guitar **2.3**
todavía still, yet **4.3**
todo(a) all **1.3**
   todos los días every day **2.1**
tomar to take, to eat or drink **2.2**
   tomar el sol to sunbathe **3.3**
el tomate tomato **5.3**
la tormenta storm **3.3**
el toro bull **6.2**
la torta sandwich (sub) **2.2**
la tortilla española potato omelet **5.2**
trabajador(a) hard-working **1.2**
trabajar to work **1.1**
tradicional traditional **6.1**
traer (traigo) to bring **4.3**
   ¿Me trae…?
      Could you bring me…? **4.3**
el tráfico traffic **6.1**
el traje de baño bathing suit **3.3**
tranquilamente calmly **5.2**
tranquilo(a) calm **3.1**
trece thirteen **1.3**
treinta thirty **1.3**
el tren train **4.1**
tres three **EP**
trescientos(as) three hundred **5.3**
triste sad **3.1**
tu your (familiar) **1.3**
tú you (familiar singular) **1.1**

último(a) last **6.2**
uno one **EP**
usar to use **2.1**
usted you (formal singular) **1.1**
ustedes you (plural) **1.1**

la vaca cow **6.2**
el vaso glass
   el vaso de glass of **2.2**
el (la) vecino(a) neighbor
vegetariano(a) vegetarian **4.3**
veinte twenty **1.3**
vender to sell **2.3**
venir to come **3.1**
la ventana window **5.2**
ver (veo) to see **2.3**
   ¿Me deja ver…? May I see…? **4.2**
   Nos vemos. See you later. **EP**
   ver la televisión
      to watch television **2.3**
el verano summer **3.3**
la verdad truth **2.2**
   Es verdad. It's true. **1.2**
verde green **1.2**
la verdura vegetable **5.3**
el vestido dress **1.2**
viajar to travel **4.1**
el viaje trip **4.1**
la vida life **2.3**
el video video **4.2**
   alquilar un video
      to rent a video **3.1**
la videograbadora VCR **4.2**
el videojuego video game **4.2**
viejo(a) old **1.3**
el viento wind **3.3**
   Hace viento. It is windy. **3.3**
   Hay viento. It's windy. **3.3**
viernes Friday **EP**
visitar to visit **2.2**
vivir to live **2.3**
   Vive en… He/She lives in… **1.1**
   Vivo en… I live in… **1.1**
el voleibol volleyball **3.2**

volver (ue) to return,
   to come back **4.2**
vosotros(as) you (familiar plural) **1.1**
vuestro(a) your (familiar plural) **1.3**

y and **1.1**
   y cuarto quarter past **2.2**
   y media half past **2.2**
ya already, now
ya no no longer **3.1**
yo I **1.1**
el yogur yogurt **5.3**

la zanahoria carrot **5.3**
la zapatería shoe store **4.1**
el zapato shoe **1.2**
el zumo juice **5.3**

GLOSARIO
español-inglés

This English–Spanish glossary contains all of the active words that appear as well as passive ones from readings, culture sections, and extra vocabulary lists. Active words are indicated by the unit and **etapa** number when they appear.

about sobre
accountant el (la) contador(a) **6.1**
address la dirección **4.1**
to be afraid tener miedo **3.3**
after después (de) **2.3**
afternoon la tarde **2.2**
   during the afternoon
      por la tarde **2.2**
   Good afternoon
      Buenas tardes. **EP**
   in the afternoon de la tarde **2.2**
afterward después **2.3**
age la edad **1.3**
to agree (on) quedar (en) **4.1,**
   estar de acuerdo **6.1**
air pollution la contaminación
   del aire **6.1**
airplane el avión **4.1**
airport el aeropuerto **4.1**
alarm clock el despertador **5.1**
all todo(a) **1.3**
alone solo(a) **3.1**
already ya
also también **1.1**
always siempre **2.1**
ancient antiguo(a) **6.1**
and y **1.1**
angry enojado(a) **3.1**
animal el animal **2.3**
another otro(a) **1.2**
to answer contestar **2.1**
answering machine
   la máquina contestadora **3.1**
apartment el apartamento **1.1**
appetizers las tapas **5.2**

appointment la cita **2.2**
April abril **1.3**
architect el (la) arquitecto(a) **6.1**
architecture la arquitectura **6.1**
arm el brazo **5.1**
armchair el sillón **5.2**
around por **4.1**
to arrange ordenar **5.2**
to arrive llegar **2.1**
art el arte **2.1**
artisan el (la) artesano(a) **6.2**
as como
   as… as tan… como **3.2**
   as far as hasta **4.1**
   as much as tanto como **3.2**
to ask for pedir (i) **4.3**
at a
   At… o'clock. A la(s)… **2.2**
auditorium el auditorio **2.2**
August agosto **1.3**
aunt la tía **1.3**
avenue la avenida **4.1**
awesome: How awesome!
   ¡Qué chévere! **1.3**
awful terrible **1.1**

backpack la mochila **2.1**
bad malo(a) **1.2**
   It is bad outside.
      Hace mal tiempo. **3.3**
bag la bolsa **1.2**
bakery (bread) panadería **4.1,**
   (pastry) pastelería **4.1**
ball la bola **3.2**
bank el banco **4.1**
to bargain regatear **4.2**

baseball (sport) el béisbol **3.2;**
   (ball) la pelota **3.2**
baseball cap la gorra **3.2**
basket la canasta
basketball el baloncesto **3.2**
bat el bate **3.2**
bathing suit el traje de baño **3.3**
bathroom el baño **5.2**
to be ser **1.1;** estar **2.2**
   to be (in a specific place)
      quedar (en) **4.1**
   to be able poder (ue) **4.2**
   to be afraid tener miedo **3.3**
   to be careful tener cuidado **3.3**
   to be cold tener frío **3.3**
   to be familiar with conocer **2.3**
   to be from… ser de… **1.1**
   to be going to… ir a… **2.3**
   to be hot tener calor **3.3**
   to be hungry tener hambre **2.3**
   to be in a hurry tener prisa **3.3**
   to be lucky tener suerte **3.3**
   to be right tener razón **3.3**
   to be sleepy tener sueño **3.3**
   to be thirsty tener sed **2.3**
beach la playa **3.3**
because porque **3.1**
to become llegar a ser
bed la cama **5.1**
   to go to bed acostarse (ue) **5.1**
   to make the bed
      hacer la cama **5.1**
bedroom la habitación **5.2**
beef la carne de res **5.3**
before antes (de) **2.3**
to begin empezar (ie) **3.2**
behind detrás (de) **4.1**
to believe creer **3.3**
belt el cinturón **4.2**

beside al lado (de) **4.1**
better mejor **3.2**
between entre **4.1**
beverage la bebida **4.3**
big grande **1.2**
bike la bicicleta
   to ride a bike
     andar en bicicleta **2.3**
bill la cuenta **4.3**
bird el pájaro **2.3**
birthday el cumpleaños **1.3**
black negro(a) **1.2**
blanket la manta **5.1**
blond rubio(a) **1.2**
blouse la blusa **1.2**
blue azul **1.2**
body el cuerpo **5.1**
book el libro **2.1**
bookstore la librería **4.1**
boots las botas **4.2**
border la frontera
boring aburrido(a) **1.2**
boss el (la) jefe(a) **6.1**
bottle la botella **5.3**
boy el chico **1.1**, el muchacho **1.1**,
   el niño
bracelet la pulsera **4.2**
bread el pan **4.3**
break el receso **2.2**
breakfast el desayuno **4.3**
to bring traer **4.3**
   Could you bring me…?
     ¿Me trae…? **4.3**
brochure el folleto
brother el hermano **1.3**
brown marrón **1.2**
brown hair castaño(a) **1.2**
brush el cepillo **5.1**
to brush one's teeth
   lavarse los dientes **5.1**
building el edificio **6.1**
bull el toro **6.2**
bus el autobús **4.1**
bus station
   la estación de autobuses **4.1**
businessman
   el hombre de negocios **6.1**
businesswoman
   la mujer de negocios **6.1**
busy ocupado(a) **3.1**
but pero **1.1**
butcher's shop la carnicería **4.1**
   butter la mantequilla **5.3**

to buy comprar **2.2**
by por **4.1**

C

cab el taxi **4.1**
café el café **4.1**
cafeteria la cafetería **2.2**
cake el pastel **4.3**
calculator la calculadora **2.1**
call la llamada **3.1**
to call llamar **3.1**
calm tranquilo(a) **3.1**
calmly tranquilamente **5.2**
camera la cámara **6.1**
can la lata **5.3**
can (to be able) poder (ue) **4.2**
   I can offer you…
     Le puedo ofrecer… **4.2**
   Thanks, but I can't.
     Gracias, pero no puedo. **3.1**
cap (knit) el gorro **3.3**,
   (baseball) la gorra **3.2**
car el carro **4.1**
careful cuidadoso(a) **5.2**
   to be careful tener cuidado **3.3**
carefully cuidadosamente **5.2**
carrot la zanahoria **5.3**
to carry llevar **2.1**
cash el efectivo **4.2**
cassette el casete **4.2**
cat el (la) gato(a) **1.2**
cave la cueva
center el centro **4.1**
century el siglo
ceramics la cerámica **4.2**
cereal el cereal **5.3**
chair la silla **5.2**
chalk la tiza **2.1**
chalkboard el pizarrón **2.1**
change el cambio **4.2**
to change cambiar **4.2**
cheap barato(a) **4.2**
check la cuenta **4.3**
   Separate checks. Es aparte. **4.3**
   The check, please.
     La cuenta, por favor. **4.3**
checked de cuadros **3.3**
cheese el queso **4.3**
chicken el pollo **4.3**
chores los quehaceres **5.1**

church la iglesia **4.1**
city la ciudad **1.3**
   city block la cuadra **4.1**
class la clase **2.1**
classroom la clase **2.1**
to clean the room
   limpiar el cuarto **5.1**
clock el reloj **2.2**
to close cerrar (ie) **3.2**
closed cerrado(a) **5.2**
closet el armario **5.2**
clothing la ropa **1.2**
cloudy nublado
   It is cloudy. Está nublado. **3.3**
coat el abrigo **3.3**
coffee el café **4.3**
   coffee shop la cafetería **2.2**
cold
   to be cold tener frío **3.3**
   It is cold. Hace frío. **3.3**
color el color
   What color…?
     ¿De qué color…? **1.2**
comb el peine **5.1**
to comb one's hair peinarse **5.1**
to come venir **3.1**
   to come back volver(ue) **4.2**
comical cómico(a) **1.2**
community la comunidad **1.1**
compact disc
   el disco compacto **4.2**
company la compañía **6.1**
computer la computadora **2.1**
computer science
   la computación **2.1**
concert el concierto **3.1**
congratulations felicidades **1.3**
content contento(a) **3.1**
contest el concurso **1.1**
to cook cocinar **5.3**
cookie la galleta **5.3**
cool: It is cool. Hace fresco. **3.3**
corn el maíz
corner la esquina **4.1**
corral el corral **6.2**
to cost costar (ue) **4.2**
couch el sofá **5.2**
to count contar (ue) **4.2**
country el país **1.1**; el campo **6.2**
countryside el campo **6.2**
court la cancha **3.2**
cousin el (la) primo(a) **1.3**
coward el cobarde

cow la vaca **6.2**
cracker la galleta **5.3**
crazy loco(a) **3.2**
cream la crema **5.3**
credit card la tarjeta de crédito **4.2**
to cross cruzar **4.1**
cup la taza **4.3**
custom la costumbre
customs la aduana

to dance bailar **1.1**
dangerous peligroso(a) **3.2**
dark hair and skin moreno(a) **1.2**
date la fecha **1.3**
   What is the date?
      ¿Cuál es la fecha? **1.3**
daughter la hija **1.3**
day el día **EP**
   the day before yesterday
      anteayer **5.3**
   What day is today?
      ¿Qué día es hoy? **EP**
December diciembre **1.3**
to decide decidir **6.1**
degree el grado **3.3**
delicious delicioso(a) **4.3**
depressed deprimido(a) **3.1**
desert el desierto **3.3**
desk el escritorio **2.1**
dessert el postre **4.3**
to dial marcar **3.1**
dictionary el diccionario **2.1**
difficult difícil **2.1**
dining room el comedor **5.2**
dinner la cena **2.3**
direction la dirección **4.1**
dirty sucio(a) **5.1**
dishwasher el lavaplatos **5.3**
district el barrio
to do hacer **2.3**
doctor el (la) doctor(a) **1.1**
dog el (la) perro(a) **1.2**
   to walk the dog
      caminar con el perro **2.3**
dollar el dólar **4.2**
door la puerta **5.2**
down abajo **6.2**
downtown el centro **4.1**

dozen la docena **5.3**
dress el vestido **1.2**
drink la bebida **4.3**
to drink tomar **2.2**; beber **2.3**
   Do you want to drink…?
      ¿Quieres beber…? **2.2**
   I want to drink…
      Quiero beber… **2.2**
to drive manejar **4.1**
drugstore la farmacia **4.1**
drum el tambor
to dry oneself secarse **5.1**
during durante **2.2**
to dust quitar el polvo **5.2**

e-mail el correo electrónico
each cada **2.3**
eagle la águila
ear la oreja **5.1**
early temprano **3.1**
earring el arete **4.2**
easily fácilmente **5.2**
easy fácil **2.1**
to eat comer **1.1**, tomar **2.2**
   Do you want to eat…?
      ¿Quieres comer…? **2.2**
   to eat a snack merendar (ie) **3.2**
   to eat breakfast desayunar **4.3**
   to eat dinner cenar **2.3**
   to eat lunch almorzar (ue) **4.2**
   I want to eat…
      Quiero comer… **2.2**
editor el (la) editor(a) **6.1**
egg el huevo **5.3**
eight ocho **EP**
eight hundred ochocientos(as) **5.3**
eighteen dieciocho **1.3**
eighth octavo(a) **6.2**
eighty ochenta **1.3**
eleven once **1.3**
enchilada la enchilada **4.3**
English el inglés **2.1**
enjoyable divertido(a) **1.2**
enormous enorme **6.1**
to enter entrar (a, en) **2.1**
eraser el borrador **2.1**
especially especialmente **5.2**

evening la noche
   during the evening
      por la noche **2.2**
   Good evening.
      Buenas noches. **EP**
every cada **2.3**
   every day todos los días **2.1**
to exchange cambiar **4.2**
excited emocionado(a) **3.1**
to exercise hacer ejercicio **2.3**
to expect esperar **2.1**
expensive caro(a) **4.2**
   It's very expensive!
      ¡Es muy caro(a)! **4.2**
eye el ojo **1.2**

face la cara **5.1**
fall el otoño **3.3**
to fall asleep dormirse (ue) **5.1**
familiar: to be familiar with
   someone conocer a alguien **2.3**
family la familia **1.1**
far (from) lejos (de) **4.1**
   Is it far? ¿Queda lejos? **4.1**
farm la granja **6.2**
farmer el (la) ganadero(a) **6.2**
fast rápido(a) **5.2**
fat gordo(a) **1.2**
father el padre **1.3**
favorite favorito(a) **3.2**
February febrero **1.3**
to feed darle(s) de comer **6.2**
to feel like… tener ganas de… **3.3**
fence la cerca **6.2**
field el campo **3.2**
fifteen quince **1.3**
fifth quinto(a) **6.2**
fifty cincuenta **1.3**
finally por fin **2.3**
to find encontrar (ue) **4.2**
to finish terminar **2.2**
fire el fuego
firefighter el bombero **6.1**
first primero **2.3**; primero(a) **6.2**
first name el nombre **EP**
fish el pez **2.3**; el pescado **5.3**
five cinco **EP**
five hundred quinientos(as) **5.3**
floor el suelo **5.2**

flour la harina **5.3**
flower la flor **3.3**
food la comida **2.3**
foot el pie **5.1**
    on foot a pie **4.1**
football el fútbol americano **3.2**
for por **4.1;** para **4.2**
forest el bosque **3.3**
to forget olvidar **5.2**
fork el tenedor **4.3**
formal formal **6.1**
forty cuarenta **1.3**
four cuatro **EP**
four hundred cuatrocientos(as) **5.3**
fourteen catorce **1.3**
fourth cuarto(a) **6.2**
free time el tiempo libre **3.1**
freezer el congelador **5.3**
french fries las papas fritas **2.2**
frequent frecuente **5.2**
frequently frecuentemente **5.2**
Friday viernes **EP**
friend el (la) amigo(a) **1.1**
    to spend time with friends
        pasar un rato con los
        amigos **2.3**
from de **1.1;** desde **4.1**
fruit la fruta **2.2**
fun divertido(a) **1.2**
funny cómico(a) **1.2**
furniture los muebles **5.2**

game el partido **3.2**
garden el jardín **5.2**
to get dressed ponerse la ropa **5.1**
to get up levantarse **5.1**
gift el regalo **4.2**
girl la chica **1.1,** la muchacha **1.1,**
    la niña
to give dar **4.2**
    I'll give… to you for…
        Le dejo… en… **4.2**
glass el vaso **2.2**
glove el guante **3.2**
to go ir **2.2**
    to go away irse **5.1**
    to go for a walk pasear **2.3**
    to go out salir **4.1**
    to go to bed acostarse (ue) **5.1**

goal el gol **3.2**
god el diós
gold el oro **4.2**
good bueno(a) **1.2**
    Good afternoon.
        Buenas tardes. **EP**
    Good evening.
        Buenas noches. **EP**
    Good morning. Buenos días. **EP**
Good-bye. Adiós. **EP**
good-looking guapo(a) **1.2**
government el gobierno
grade la nota
    to get a good grade
        sacar una buena nota **2.1**
gram el gramo **5.3**
grandchildren los nietos
granddaughter la nieta
grandfather el abuelo **1.3**
grandmother la abuela **1.3**
grandparents los abuelos **1.3**
grandson el nieto
green verde **1.2**
guitar la guitarra **2.3**
gymnasium el gimnasio **2.2**

hair el pelo **1.2**
hair dryer el secador de pelo **5.1**
half medio(a) **5.3**
    half past y media **2.2**
half-brother el medio hermano
half-sister la media hermana
ham el jamón **5.2**
hamburger la hamburguesa **2.2**
hand la mano **5.1**
handbag la bolsa **4.2**
handicraft la artesanía **4.2**
to happen pasar **2.1**
happily felizmente **5.2**
happy feliz **1.3,** alegre **3.1,**
    contento(a) **3.1**
hard difícil **2.1;** duro(a) **5.1**
hard-working trabajador(a) **1.2**
hat el sombrero **1.2**
to have tener **1.3**
    to have just… acabar de… **3.1**
    to have to tener que **2.1**
    one has to hay que **2.1**
he él **1.1**

head la cabeza **5.1**
to hear oír **2.3**
heart el corazón **2.3**
Hello. Hola. **EP**
helmet el casco **3.2**
to help ayudar (a) **2.1**
    Could you help me order?
        ¿Me ayuda a pedir? **4.3**
hen la gallina **6.2**
her su **1.3**
here acá/aquí **4.1**
his su **1.3**
history la historia **2.1**
hockey el hockey **3.2**
homework la tarea **2.1**
horse el caballo **6.2**
hot caliente **4.3**
    to be hot tener calor **3.3**
    It is hot. Hace calor. **3.3**
hotel el hotel **4.1**
house la casa **1.1**
how cómo **2.2**
    How (fun)! ¡Qué (divertido)! **1.2**
    How are you?
        (familiar) ¿Cómo estás? **1.1**
        (formal) ¿Cómo está usted? **1.1**
    How is it going? ¿Qué tal? **1.1**
    How old is…?
        ¿Cuántos años tiene…? **1.3**
    Pardon, how do I get to…?
        Perdona(e), ¿cómo llego
        a…? **4.1**
how much cuánto
    How much do I tip? ¿Cuánto le
        doy de propina? **4.3**
    How much is (are)…?
        ¿Cuánto cuesta(n)…? **4.2;**
        ¿A cuánto está(n)…? **5.3**
    How much is it? ¿Cuánto es? **4.3**
huge enorme **6.1**
to be hungry tener hambre **2.3**
to be in a hurry tener prisa **3.3**
husband el esposo

I yo **1.1**
ice el hielo
    on ice sobre hielo **3.2**
ice cream el helado **5.3**
if si **5.2**

in en **1.1**
   in front (of) enfrente (de) **4.1**
   in order to para **4.2**
included incluido(a)
   Is… included?
     ¿Está incluido(a)…? **4.3**
inexpensive barato(a) **4.2**
informal informal **6.1**
inside (of) dentro (de) **6.2**
instead of en vez de
intelligent inteligente **1.2**
interesting interesante **1.2**
interview la entrevista **6.1**
introduce: Let me introduce you
   (familiar/formal) **to…**
   Te/Le presento a… **1.1**
invitation la invitación **5.2**
to invite invitar
   I invite you. Te invito. **3.1**
to iron planchar **5.2**
island la isla
its su **1.3**

jacket la chaqueta **1.2**
January enero **1.3**
jeans los jeans **1.2**
jewelry las joyas **4.2**
jewelry store la joyería **4.1**
journalist el (la) periodista **6.1**
juice el zumo **5.3**
July julio **1.3**
June junio **1.3**

key la llave **5.2**; la tecla
keyboard el teclado **2.1**
kilogram el kilo **5.3**
kitchen la cocina **5.2**
knife el cuchillo **4.3**
to know (a fact) saber **3.2**
   to know someone
     conocer a alguien **2.3**

lake el lago **3.3**
lamp la lámpara **5.2**
land la tierra
language la lengua **4.3**
large grande **1.2**
last último(a) **6.2**
   last month el mes pasado **5.3**
   last name el apellido **EP**
   last night anoche **5.3**
   last week la semana pasada **5.3**
   last year el año pasado **5.3**
late tarde **2.1**
lately recientemente **5.2**
later luego **2.3**
   See you later. Hasta luego. **EP,**
     Nos vemos. **EP**
lawyer el abogado
lazy perezoso(a) **1.2**
to learn aprender **2.3**
leather goods
   los artículos de cuero **4.2**
to leave salir **4.1**, irse **5.1**; **(behind)**
   dejar **3.1**
   I want to leave a message for…
     Quiero dejar un mensaje
     para… **3.1**
   to leave a message
     dejar un mensaje **3.1**
   Leave a message after the tone.
     Deje un mensaje después del
     tono. **3.1**
left la izquierda
   to the left (of) a la izquierda
     (de) **4.1**
leg la pierna **5.1**
lemonade la limonada **4.3**
less menos
   less than menos de **3.2**
   less… than menos… que **3.2**
lesson la lección **2.1**
Let's… Vamos a… **6.1**
letter la carta
   to send a letter mandar una
     carta **2.3**
lettuce la lechuga **4.3**
library la biblioteca **2.2**

life la vida **2.3**
to lift weights levantar pesas **3.2**
like (as) como
to like gustar
   He/She likes… Le gusta… **1.1**
   I like… Me gusta… **1.1**
   I would like…
     Me gustaría… **3.1**
   Would you like…?
     ¿Te gustaría…? **3.1**
   You like… Te gusta… **1.1**
to listen (to) escuchar **2.1**
liter el litro **5.3**
literature la literatura **2.1**
a little poco **2.1**
to live vivir **2.3**
living room la sala **5.2**
llama la llama **6.2**
long largo(a) **1.2**
to look at mirar **2.1**
to look for buscar **2.1**
to lose perder (ie) **3.2**
to be lucky tener suerte **3.3**
lunch el almuerzo **2.2**
   to eat lunch almorzar (ue) **4.2**
luxurious lujoso(a) **6.1**

magazine la revista **2.3**
mail carrier el (la) cartero(a) **6.1**
to make hacer **2.3**
   to make the bed
     hacer la cama **5.1**
man el hombre **1.1**
manager el (la) gerente **6.1**
many mucho(a) **1.1**
map el mapa **4.1**
March marzo **1.3**
market el mercado **4.2**
masterpiece la obra maestra
mathematics las matemáticas **2.1**
May mayo **1.3**
maybe tal vez
   Maybe another day.
     Tal vez otro día. **3.1**
meal la comida **2.3**
meat la carne **4.3**

to meet encontrar (ue) **4.2**
menu el menú **4.3**
message el mensaje
    I want to leave a message for…
        Quiero dejar un mensaje
        para… **3.1**
    to leave a message dejar un
        mensaje **3.1**
    Leave a message after the tone.
        Deje un mensaje después del
        tono. **3.1**
microwave el microondas **5.3**
midnight la medianoche **2.2**
milk la leche **5.3**
million un millón **5.3**
mirror el espejo **5.1**
Miss la señorita **1.1**
modern moderno(a) **6.1**
moment el momento
    One moment. Un momento. **3.1**
Monday lunes **EP**
money el dinero **4.2**
    money exchange el cambio **4.2**
month el mes **1.3**
more más **1.3**
    more than más de **3.2**
    more… than más… que **3.2**
morning la mañana **2.2**
    during the morning
        por la mañana **2.2**
    Good morning. Buenos días. **EP**
    in the morning de la mañana **2.2**
mother la madre **1.3**
motorcycle la moto(cicleta) **4.1**
mountain la montaña **3.3**
mouse el ratón **2.1**
mouth la boca **5.1**
to move (the furniture) mover
    (ue) (los muebles) **5.2**
movie la película **3.1**
    to go to a movie theater
        ir al cine **3.1**
Mr. el señor **1.1**
Mrs. la señora **1.1**
much mucho(a) **1.1**
    as much as tanto como **3.2**
museum el museo **2.3**
music la música **2.1**
    music and video store la tienda
        de música y videos **4.1**
must: one must hay que **2.1**
my mi **1.3**

name el nombre **EP**
    His/Her name is…
        Se llama… **EP**
    My name is… Me llamo… **EP**
    What is his/her name?
        ¿Cómo se llama? **EP**
    What is your name?
        ¿Cómo te llamas? **EP**
narrow estrecho(a) **6.1**
near (to) cerca (de) **4.1**
necklace el collar **4.2**
to need necesitar **2.1**
neighbor el (la) vecino(a)
neither tampoco **4.3**
nervous nervioso(a) **3.1**
never nunca **2.1**
new nuevo(a) **1.2**
newspaper el periódico **2.3**
next to al lado de **4.1**
nice simpático(a) **1.2**
    It is nice outside.
        Hace buen tiempo. **3.3**
    Nice to meet you.
        Mucho gusto. **EP**
night la noche **2.2**
    at night de la noche **2.2**
nine nueve **EP**
nine hundred novecientos(as) **5.3**
nineteen diecinueve **1.3**
ninety noventa **1.3**
ninth noveno(a) **6.2**
no no **EP**
no longer ya no **3.1**
no one nadie **4.3**
none ninguno(a) **4.3**
noon el mediodía **2.2**
normal normal **5.2**
normally normalmente **5.2**
nose la nariz **5.1**
not no **1.1**
notebook el cuaderno **2.1**
nothing nada **4.3**
novel la novela **2.3**
November noviembre **1.3**
now ahora **1.3**
    Right now! ¡Ahora mismo! **2.1**
nowadays actualmente

number el número
    What is your phone number?
        ¿Cuál es tu teléfono? **EP**

October octubre **1.3**
of de
    Of course! ¡Claro que sí! **3.1,**
        ¡Cómo no! **4.1**
to offer ofrecer **6.1**
    I can offer you…
        Le puedo ofrecer… **4.2**
office la oficina **2.2**
often mucho **2.1,**
    frecuentemente **5.2**
oil el aceite **5.3**
old viejo(a) **1.3;** antiguo(a) **6.1**
    How old is…?
        ¿Cuántos años tiene…? **1.3**
older mayor **1.3**
olives las aceitunas **5.2**
on en **1.1,** sobre
    on ice sobre hielo **3.2**
    on top (of) encima (de) **6.2**
once in a while
    de vez en cuando **2.1**
one uno **EP**
one hundred cien **1.3**
onion la cebolla **5.3**
only sólo **1.3**
open abierto(a) **5.2**
to open abrir **2.3**
operator el (la) operador(a) **6.1**
or o **1.1**
orange anaranjado(a) **1.2**
to order pedir (i) **4.3**
    Could you help me order?
        ¿Me ayuda a pedir? **4.3**
ordinary ordinario(a) **6.1**
other otro(a) **1.2**
ought to deber **5.2**
our nuestro(a) **1.3**
outdoors al aire libre **3.2**
outside (of) fuera (de) **6.2**
oven el horno **5.3**

P

package el paquete **5.3**
to paint pintar **2.3**
pants los pantalones **1.2**
paper el papel **2.1**
Pardon, how do I get to…?
Perdona(e), ¿cómo llego
a…? **4.1**
parents los padres **1.3**
park el parque **2.3**
parrot el loro
party la fiesta **5.2**
to pass (by) pasar **2.1**
pasta la pasta **5.3**
pastry shop la pastelería **4.1**
patient paciente **1.2**
to pay pagar **4.2**
pen (enclosure) el corral **6.2**,
(instrument) la pluma **2.1**
pencil el lápiz **2.1**
people la gente **2.3**
pepper la pimienta **5.3**
perfect perfecto(a) **4.2**
period la época
pharmacy la farmacia **4.1**
phone book la guía telefónica **3.1**
photographer
el (la) fotógrafo(a) **6.1**
physical education la educación
física **2.1**
piano el piano **2.3**
piece el pedazo **5.3**
picture la foto
to take pictures sacar fotos **3.3**
pig el cerdo **6.2**
pineapple la piña
pink rosado(a) **1.2**
pitcher la jarra **4.2**
place el lugar **1.1**
plaid de cuadros **3.3**
plain sencillo(a) **6.1**
to plan pensar (ie) **3.2**
plant la planta **3.3**
plate el plato **4.2**
to play tocar **2.3**; practicar **3.1**,
jugar (ue) **3.2**
to play sports
practicar deportes **3.1**
to play (the guitar, piano)
tocar (la guitarra, el piano) **2.3**

player el (la) jugador(a)
please por favor **2.2**
pleased contento(a) **3.1**
Pleased to meet you.
Encantado(a). **EP**
pleasure
It's a pleasure. Es un placer. **EP**
The pleasure is mine.
El gusto es mío. **EP**
poem el poema **2.3**
poetry la poesía **2.3**
police officer el (la) policía **1.1**
pork el puerco **5.3**
pork rinds los chicharrones **2.3**
portrait el retrato
post office el correo **4.1**
pot la olla **4.2**
potato la patata **5.3**, la papa
to practice practicar **3.1**
to prefer preferir (ie) **3.2**
to prepare preparar **2.1**
pretty bonito(a) **1.2**
price el precio **4.2**
printer la impresora **2.1**
problem el problema **2.3**
profession la profesión **6.1**
purple morado(a) **1.2**
to put poner **4.3**
to put on (clothes) ponerse **5.1**
to put on makeup maquillarse **5.1**

Q

quality la calidad **4.2**
quarter cuarto(a) **5.3**
quarter past y cuarto **2.2**
quick rápido(a) **5.2**
quickly rápidamente **5.2**
quiet: Be quiet! ¡Cállate! **5.3**
quiz la prueba **2.1**

R

racket la raqueta **3.2**
radio el radio **4.2**
radio-tape player
el radiocasete **4.2**
rain la lluvia **3.3**
to rain llover (ue) **3.3**

raincoat el impermeable **3.3**
rarely rara vez **2.1**
to read leer **1.1**
ready listo(a) **4.3**
reason la razón **2.1**
to receive recibir **2.3**
recent reciente **5.2**
recently recientemente **5.2**
receptionist
el (la) recepcionista **6.1**
red rojo(a) **1.2**
redhead pelirrojo(a) **1.2**
refrigerator el frigorífico **5.3**
to remember recordar (ue) **4.2**
to rent a video alquilar un video **3.1**
to rest descansar **2.2**
restaurant el restaurante **4.3**
to retell contar (ue) **4.2**
to return regresar **3.1**, volver (ue)
4.2; **(an item)** devolver (ue) **4.2**
He/She will return later.
Regresa más tarde. **3.1**
rice el arroz **4.3**
rich rico(a)
right
to be right tener razón **3.3**
to the right (of)
a la derecha (de) **4.1**
ring el anillo **4.2**
river el río **3.3**
road el camino **4.1**
roasted asado(a)
room el cuarto **5.1**
rooster el gallo **6.2**
rule la regla
to run correr **1.1**

S

sad triste **3.1**
salad la ensalada **4.3**
salsa la salsa **4.3**
salt la sal **5.3**
same mismo(a) **2.1**
sandwich (sub) la torta **2.2**
Saturday sábado **EP**
sausage el chorizo **5.2**,
la salchicha **5.3**
to say decir **4.1**
Don't say that!
¡No digas eso! **1.2**

INGLÉS–ESPAÑOL

scarf bufanda **3.3**
schedule el horario **2.2**
school la escuela **2.1**
science las ciencias **2.1**
scissors las tijeras **6.2**
screen la pantalla **2.1**
sea el mar **3.3**
to search buscar **2.1**
seasons las estaciones **3.3**
second segundo(a) **6.2**
secretary el (la) secretario(a) **6.1**
to see ver **2.3**
    May I see…?
        ¿Me deja ver…? **4.2**
to sell vender **2.3**
semester el semestre **2.2**
to send a letter
    mandar una carta **2.3**
September septiembre **1.3**
serious serio(a) **1.2**
to serve servir (i) **4.3**
to set the table poner la mesa **4.3**
seven siete **EP**
seven hundred setecientos(as) **5.3**
seventeen diecisiete **1.3**
seventh séptimo(a) **6.2**
seventy setenta **1.3**
shame: What a shame!
    ¡Qué lástima! **3.1**
shampoo el champú **5.1**
to share compartir **2.3**
to shave afeitarse **5.1**
she ella **1.1**
sheep el cordero
shepherd(ess) el (la) pastor(a) **6.2**
ship el barco **4.1**
shirt la camisa **1.2**
shoe el zapato **1.2**
    shoe store la zapatería **4.1**
shopping
    to go shopping ir de compras **3.1**
    shopping center
        el centro comercial **4.1**
short (height) bajo(a) **1.2;**
    (length) corto(a) **1.2**
shorts los shorts **3.3,**
    los pantalones cortos
should deber **5.2**
sick enfermo(a) **3.1**
sign el letrero, la señal
silver la plata **4.2**
simple sencillo(a) **6.1**

to sing cantar **1.1**
sister la hermana **1.3**
six seis **EP**
six hundred seiscientos(as) **5.3**
sixteen dieciséis **1.3**
sixth sexto(a) **6.2**
sixty sesenta **1.3**
to skate patinar **1.1**
skateboard la patineta **3.2**
to skateboard
    andar en patineta **3.2**
skates los patines **3.2**
to ski esquiar **3.2**
skirt la falda **1.2**
to sleep dormir (ue) **4.2**
to be sleepy tener sueño **3.3**
slow lento(a) **5.2**
slowly lentamente **5.2**
small pequeño(a) **1.2**
snack la merienda **2.2**
    to have a snack merendar (ie) **3.2**
snow la nieve **3.3**
to snow nevar (ie) **3.3**
so entonces **2.3**
So-so. Regular. **1.1**
soap el jabón **5.1**
soccer el fútbol **3.2**
social studies
    los estudios sociales **2.1**
sock el calcetín **1.2**
sofa el sofá **5.2**
soft drink el refresco **2.2**
some alguno(a) **4.3**
someone alguien **4.3**
    to know, to be familiar
        with someone
        conocer a alguien **2.3**
something algo **4.3**
sometimes a veces **2.1**
son el hijo **1.3**
song la canción
soon pronto **2.1**
sorry: I'm sorry… Lo siento… **4.1**
sound el sonido
soup la sopa **4.3**
Spanish el español **2.1**
to speak hablar **2.1**
    May I speak with…?
        ¿Puedo hablar con…? **3.1**
special especial **5.2**
specially especialmente **5.2**
spicy picante **4.3**
spoon la cuchara **4.3**

sport el deporte
    to play sports
        practicar deportes **3.1**
sporting goods store
    la tienda de deportes **3.2**
spring la primavera **3.3**
squid los calamares **5.2**
stadium el estadio **3.2**
star la estrella **5.3**
stationery store la papelería **4.1**
to stay quedar (en) **4.1**
steak el bistec **4.3**
stepbrother el hermanastro
stepfather el padrastro
stepmother la madrastra
stepsister la hermanastra
still todavía **4.3**
stomach el estómago **5.1**
store la tienda **2.3**
storm la tormenta **3.3**
storyteller el bohique
stove la estufa **5.3**
straight ahead derecho **4.1**
street la calle **4.1**
string la cuerda
striped con rayas **3.3**
strong fuerte **1.2**
student el (la) estudiante **1.1**
to study estudiar **2.1**
subject la materia **2.1**
subway el metro **4.1**
success el éxito
sugar el azúcar **4.3**
summer el verano **3.3**
sun el sol **3.3**
to sunbathe tomar el sol **3.3**
Sunday domingo **EP**
sunglasses las gafas de sol **3.3**
sunny: It is sunny. Hace sol. **3.3,**
    Hay sol. **3.3**
suntan lotion el bronceador **3.3**
supermarket el supermercado
    to go to the supermarket
        ir al supermercado **2.3**
supper la cena **2.3**
    to have supper cenar **2.3**
surfing el surfing **3.2**
surname el apellido **EP**
surprise la sorpresa **5.2**
to surprise sorprender **5.2**
sweater el suéter **1.2**
to sweep the floor
    barrer el suelo **5.2**

sweet dulce **4.3**
    sweet roll el pan dulce **4.3**
to swim nadar **1.1**
swimming pool la piscina **3.2**

T-shirt la camiseta **1.2**
table la mesa **5.2**
    to clear the table
        quitar la mesa **5.1**
    to set the table poner la mesa **4.3**
tail la cola
to take tomar **2.2**
    to take a bath bañarse **5.1**
    to take a shower ducharse **5.1**
    to take along llevar **3.3**
    to take care of cuidar (a) **2.3**
    to take out the trash
        sacar la basura **5.2**
    to take pictures sacar fotos **3.3**
to talk hablar **2.1**
tall alto(a) **1.2**
tape recorder la grabadora **6.1**
tasty rico(a) **4.3**, sabroso(a) **5.3**
taxi el taxi **4.1**
taxi driver el (la) taxista **6.1**
tea el té **4.3**
to teach enseñar **2.1**
teacher el (la) maestro(a) **1.1**
team el equipo **3.2**
telephone el teléfono **3.1**
television la televisión
    to watch television
        ver la televisión **2.3**
television set el televisor **5.2**
to tell decir **4.1**, contar (ue) **4.2**
    Tell *(familiar/formal)* **him or her**
        to call me. Dile/Dígale que
        me llame. **3.1**
temperature la temperatura **3.3**
ten diez **EP**
tennis el tenis **3.2**
tenth décimo(a) **6.2**
terrible terrible **1.1**
test el examen **2.1**
textile el tejido
Thank you. Gracias. **1.1**
Thanks, but I can't.
    Gracias, pero no puedo. **3.1**

that ese(a), eso **6.2**
    that (over there)
        aquel(la) **6.2;** aquello **6.2**
    that one ése(a) **6.2**
    that one (over there)
        aquél(la) **6.2**
theater el teatro **2.3**
their su **1.3**
then entonces **2.3**
there allá/allí **4.1**
there is, there are hay **1.3**
they ellos(as) **1.1**
thin delgado(a) **1.2**
thing la cosa **4.1**
to think pensar (ie) **3.2;** creer **3.3**
    I think so. / I don't think so.
        Creo que sí/no. **3.3**
third tercero(a) **6.2**
thirsty: to be thirsty tener sed **2.3**
thirteen trece **1.3**
thirty treinta **1.3**
this este(a) **6.2;** esto **6.2**
this one éste(a) **6.2**
thousand mil **5.3**
three tres **EP**
three hundred trescientos(as) **5.3**
Thursday jueves **EP**
time el tiempo
    free time el tiempo libre **3.1**
    (At) What time is…?
        ¿A qué hora es…? **2.2**
    What time is it?
        ¿Qué hora es? **2.2**
tip la propina **4.3**
    How much do I tip? ¿Cuánto
        le doy de propina? **4.3**
tired cansado(a) **3.1**
to a
    to the left (of)
        a la izquierda (de) **4.1**
    to the right (of)
        a la derecha (de) **4.1**
today hoy **EP**
    Today is… Hoy es… **EP**
    What day is today?
        ¿Qué día es hoy? **EP**
together juntos **4.2**
tomato el tomate **5.3**
tomorrow mañana **EP**
    See you tomorrow.
        Hasta mañana. **EP**
    Tomorrow is… Mañana es… **EP**

too también **1.1**
too much demasiado(a) **4.2**
tooth el diente **5.1**
toothbrush
    el cepillo de dientes **5.1**
toothpaste la pasta de dientes **5.1**
tough duro(a) **5.1**
towel la toalla **5.1**
town el pueblo **4.3**
town square la plaza **4.1**
traditional tradicional **6.1**
traffic el tráfico **6.1**
train el tren **4.1**
trash la basura **5.2**
to travel viajar **4.1**
to treat: I'll treat you. Te invito. **3.1**
tree el árbol **3.3**
trip el viaje **4.1**
true: It's true. Es verdad. **1.2**
truth la verdad **2.2**
Tuesday martes **EP**
to turn doblar **4.1**
to turn off the light
    apagar la luz **5.3**
twelve doce **1.3**
twenty veinte **1.3**
two dos **EP**
two hundred doscientos(as) **5.3**

ugly feo(a) **1.2**
umbrella el paraguas **3.3**
uncle el tío **1.3**
under debajo (de) **6.2**
to understand comprender **2.3,**
    entender (ie) **3.2**
until hasta **4.1**
up arriba **6.2**
to use usar **2.1**

to vacuum pasar la aspiradora **5.2**
vacuum cleaner la aspiradora **5.2**
VCR la videograbadora **4.2**
vegetable la verdura **5.3**
vegetarian vegetariano(a) **4.3**

very muy **1.3**
video el video **4.2**
    to rent a video
        alquilar un video **3.1**
    video game el videojuego **4.2**
village el pueblo **4.3**
to visit visitar **2.2**
volleyball el voleibol **3.2**

to wait for esperar **2.1**
waiter el mesero **4.3**
waiting room la sala de espera
waitress la mesera **4.3**
to wake up despertarse (ie) **5.1**
to walk caminar
    to walk the dog caminar con
        el perro **2.3**
wall la pared **5.2**
wallet la cartera **4.2**
to want querer (ie) **3.2**
war la guerra
warrior el gerrero
warm caliente **4.3**
to wash lavar
    to wash one's hair
        lavarse la cabeza **5.1**
    to wash oneself lavarse **5.1**
    to wash the dishes
        lavar los platos **5.1**
watch el reloj **2.2**
to watch mirar **2.1**
    to watch television
        ver la televisión **2.3**
water el agua (*fem.*) **2.2**
wave la ola
we nosotros(as) **1.1**
to wear llevar **2.1**
    What is he/she wearing?
        ¿Qué lleva? **1.2**
weather el tiempo **3.3**
    What is the weather like?
        ¿Qué tiempo hace? **3.3**
Wednesday miércoles **EP**
week la semana **EP**
weights: to lift weights
    levantar pesas **3.2**
welcome bienvenido(a) **1.1**
    You're welcome. De nada. **1.1**

well bien **1.1;** pues **1.2**
    (Not very) Well, and you
        (familiar/formal)? (No muy)
        Bien, ¿y tú/usted? **1.1**
what cuál(es) **2.2;** qué **2.2**
    What a shame!
        ¡Qué lástima! **3.1**
    What day is today?
        ¿Qué día es hoy? **EP**
    What is he/she like?
        ¿Cómo es? **1.2**
    What is your phone number?
        ¿Cuál es tu teléfono? **EP**
when cuándo **2.2;** cuando **3.1**
where dónde **2.2; (to) where**
    adónde **2.2**
    Could you tell me where… is?
        ¿Puedes (Puede usted)
        decirme dónde queda…? **4.1**
    Where are you from?
        ¿De dónde eres? **EP**
    Where is he/she from?
        ¿De dónde es? **EP**
which (ones) cuál(es) **2.2**
white blanco(a) **1.2**
who quién(es) **2.2**
    Who are they?
        ¿Quiénes son? **1.3**
    Who is it? ¿Quién es? **1.3**
Whose is…? ¿De quién es…? **1.3**
why por qué **2.2**
    That's why. Con razón. **2.1**
wide ancho(a) **6.1**
wife la esposa
to win ganar **3.2**
wind el viento **3.3**
wing la ala
window la ventana **5.2**
windy: It is windy.
    Hace viento. **3.3,** Hay viento. **3.3**
winner el (la) ganador(a) **6.1**
winter el invierno **3.3**
with con **1.3**
    with me conmigo **3.1**
    with you contigo **3.1**
without sin **4.3**
woman la mujer **1.1**
wood la madera
wool la lana **6.2**
to work trabajar **1.1**
workshop el taller **6.2**
world el mundo **1.1**

worried preocupado(a) **3.1**
to worry: Don't worry!
    ¡No te preocupes! **3.1**
worse peor **3.2**
to write escribir **1.1**
writer el (la) escritor(a) **6.1**

year el año **1.3**
    He/She is… years old.
        Tiene… años. **1.3**
yellow amarillo(a) **1.2**
yes sí **EP**
    Yes, I would love to.
        Sí, me encantaría. **3.1**
yesterday ayer **5.3**
yet todavía **4.3**
yogurt el yogur **5.3**
you tú *(familiar singular)* **1.1,**
    usted *(formal singular)* **1.1,**
    ustedes *(formal plural)* **1.1,**
    vosotros(as) *(familiar plural)* **1.1**
young joven **1.3**
younger menor **1.3**
your su *(formal)* **1.3,**
    tu *(familiar)* **1.3,**
    vuestro(a) *(plural familiar)* **1.3**

zero cero **EP**

Índice

Créditos

Photography

vi School Division, Houghton Mifflin Company (t); **vii** Robert Frerck/Odyssey Productions/Chicago (t); **viii** Tom Stack (t); **ix** School Division, Houghton Mifflin Company (t); **xi** RMIP/Richard Haynes (bl); **xii** RMIP/Richard Haynes (bl); **xiii** RMIP/Richard Haynes (bl); **xiv** School Division, Houghton Mifflin Company (t); **xxvi** Courtesy ¡Qué onda! Magazine (+1); **xxix** Larry Bussaca/Retna Ltd. (cr); **xxx** The Flower Seller by Diego Rivera, oil on masonite, 1942, Christie's Images/The Bridgeman Art Library (br); **1** Farrell Grehan/Photo Researchers, Inc. (bc); RMIP/Richard Haynes (bl); **2** RMIP/Richard Haynes (+); **4** Michael Newman/PhotoEdit (tc); **9** Alain Benainous/Liaison Agency, Inc. (mid cl); **13** School Division, Houghton Mifflin Company (bl); **28** RMIP/Richard Haynes (+); **54** RMIP/Richard Haynes (+); **63** School Division, Houghton Mifflin Company (bl); Steve Azzara/Liaison Agency, Inc. (br); **64** Chris Brown/Unicorn Stock Photography & Dick Young/Unicorn Stock Photography (montage br); **65** Dave Nagel/Liaison Agency, Inc. (bl); Scott Liles/Unicorn Stock Photo (br); **70** Randy Wells/Tony Stone Images, Inc./PNI (br); **71** Bob Daemmrich Photography (tr, br); David Simson/Stock Boston (cr); **72** K. Scott Harris (tc); Nik Wheeler (br); **77** School Division, Houghton Mifflin Company; **79** Bruno Maso/Photo Researchers, Inc.; **80** Patricia A. Eynon (bl); School Division, Houghton Mifflin Company (tr, br); **81** School Division, Houghton Mifflin Company (tl); The Granger Collection (tr); Women Reaching for the Moon by Rufino Tamayo, oil on canvas, 1946, the Cleveland Museum of Art, Gift of the Hanna Fund, 47.69 (br); **84** Patricia A. Eynon (tr); **85** David G. Houser (tc); **89** Patricia A. Eynon; **90** Patricia A. Eynon (cr); David G. Houser (br); **91** RMIP/Richard Haynes (br); **92** Dave G. Houser (c); Monkmeyer/Rogers (cr); **98** RMIP/Richard Haynes; **99** Pamela Harper/Harper Horticultural; **100** RMIP/Richard Haynes (br); **106** Galyn C. Hammond (bl); **115** RMIP/Richard Haynes (bl); **116** Robert Frerck/Odyssey/Chicago (tl); School Division, Houghton Mifflin Company (bl); **117** Norman Rothschild/International Stock Photo (tc); **120** School Division, Houghton Mifflin Company (br); **123** School Division, Houghton Mifflin Company (tl, b); RMIP/Richard Haynes (br); **127** RMIP/Richard Haynes (bl); **131** School Division, Houghton Mifflin Company; **133** School Division, Houghton Mifflin Company; **142** Ken O'Donoghue (r); **143** Ken O'Donoghue (b); **144** Tom Stack (cl); **146** RMIP/Richard Haynes (bl); School Division, Houghton Mifflin Company (cl); **151** School Division, Houghton Mifflin Company; **153** RMIP/Richard Haynes (br); **156** Joe Viesti/Viesti Associates, Inc. (cl); **160** James Schaffer/PhotoEdit (br); **162** School Division, Houghton Mifflin Company (tr); Otis Imboden/National Geographic Image Collection (bl); **163** RMIP/Richard Haynes (b); **164** P.G. Sclarandia/Black Star (bl); The Granger Collection (tr); Tor Eigeland (br); **165** Robert Frerck/Odyssey Productions/Chicago (tc); A.G.E. Fotostock (br); **175** Spencer Grant/PhotoEdit (tr); R. Blair/Monkmeyer Press (cl); **181** Tor Eigeland (bl); **183** Courtesy, Sony Music Entertainment (Spain) (tr); RMIP/Richard Haynes (br); **184** Self Portrait with Palette, Pablo Picasso/ARS/Spanish, Private Collection; **198** RMIP/Richard Haynes (bl); **200** Horta Cerca Del Velodromo, A de J. Brossa/A.G.E. Fotostock (br); **204** Spencer Grant/PhotoEdit (cr); **208** Tony Morrison/South American Pictures (bl); Joe Viesti/Viesti Associates, Inc. (br); **227** RMIP/Richard Haynes (br); **235** RMIP/Richard Haynes (br); **236** School Division, Houghton Mifflin Company; **237** RMIP/Richard Haynes (br); **246** Chuck Szymanski/International Stock Photo (tl); Michael J. Howell/Liaison Agency, Inc. (bc); **247** Joe Viesti/Viesti Associates, Inc. (tr); RMIP/Richard Haynes (br); **248** Inga Spence/DDB Stock Photo (br); **249** Robert Winslow/The Viesti Collection, Inc. (tl); **258** RMIP/Richard Haynes; **259** Robert Frerck/Odyssey Productions/Chicago (bl); **263** Joseph F. Viesti/The Viesti Collection, Inc.; **264** Tony Morrison/South American Pictures (br); **265** Ulrike Welsch (cr); RMIP/Richard Haynes (br); **266** School Division, Houghton Mifflin Company (br); **269** Wolfgang Kaehler; **273** Llewellyn/Uniphoto; **274** Tony Freeman/PhotoEdit (br); **275** Michele & Tom Grimm/Tony Stone Images, Inc. (cr); Sidney/Monkmeyer Press (br); **279** Robert Frerck/Odyssey Productions/Chicago; **279** Mary Altier; **283** Robert Frerck/Odyssey Productions/Chicago (t); **284** Bob Daemmrich/The Image Works (cr); Dorothy Littell Greco/Stock Boston (br); **285** Martha Cooper/Peter Arnold, Inc. (tl); **291** Klaus D. Francke/Peter Arnold, Inc.; **294** RMIP/Richard Haynes; **316** School Division, Houghton Mifflin Company (b); **317** RMIP/Richard Haynes (br); **319** Mireille Vautier/Woodfin Camp & Associates; **320** Robert Frerck/Odyssey Productions/Chicago; **325** Jan Butchofsky-Houser (background); Robert Pettit/Dembinsky Photo Association (b); Inga Spence/DDB Stock Photo (tr); Robert Frerck/Odyssey Productions/Chicago (cr); **327** Mary Altier; **330** Kimball Morrison/South American Pictures (tl); Superstock (bl); Suzanne Murphy-Larronde (inset, br); **331** John Giustina/FPG International (tr); RMIP/Richard Haynes (br); **R12** School Division, Houghton Mifflin Company (tr).

All other Photography: Martha Granger/EDGE Productions

Illustration

Gary Antonetti/Ortelius Design **xx-xxv**; Fian Arroyo **v, 10, 62, 142, 177, 182, 185, 186, 187, 210, 269, 295, 301, 316, 329**; Susan M. Blubaugh **52, 53, 91, 93, 226, 235**; Chris Costello **304, 311**; Ruben de Anda **102** (+); Jim Deigan **145, 201**; Eldon Doty **261**; Eduardo Espada **270, 271**; Susan Greenstein **115**; Brian Jenson **iv, 42, 66, 231, 288**; Catherine Leary **iii, 11, 27, 36, 68, 94, 203, 257, 321, R6, R8** (r); Jared D. Lee **101** (br) (+), **122, 125, 175**; John Lytle **12, 46, 107, 110**; Jim Nuttle **96, 198, 229**; Patrick O'Brien **38** (+), **84, 286, 324, R8** (l); Steve Patricia **84** (+), **287, 290**; Gail Piazza **173, 207**; Rick Powell **178, 179, 205, R9**; Matthew Pippin **4** (+), **20** (+), **30** (+), **56, 64, 252** (+); Donna Ruff **19, 298**; School Division, Houghton Mifflin Company **14, 15, 70, 105, 141, R1, R3, R5, R6** (r); Stacey Schuett **72** (+), **183**; Fabricio Vanden Broeck **128, 129, 154, 155, 180, 181**; Wood Ronsadille Harlin, Inc. **275** (+); Farida Zaman **136, 137**